# POLITICS AND SOCIETY

# POLITICS
# AND
# SOCIETY

STUDIES IN
*Comparative Political Sociology*

*Edited by*
ERIC A. NORDLINGER
*Brandeis University*

PRENTICE-HALL, INC., ENGLEWOOD CLIFFS, NEW JERSEY

PRENTICE-HALL INTERNATIONAL, INC., *London*
PRENTICE-HALL OF AUSTRALIA, PTY. LTD., *Sydney*
PRENTICE-HALL OF CANADA, LTD., *Toronto*
PRENTICE-HALL OF INDIA PRIVATE LIMITED, *New Delhi*
PRENTICE-HALL OF JAPAN, INC., *Tokyo*

FOR HARRY ECKSTEIN

# PREFACE

When I first thought about editing this book, I was enormously excited about the prospect of selecting and integrating a large number of readings that seemed to me to be invaluable in the teaching of political sociology and, more broadly, in the teaching of comparative politics. Fortunately, my excitement carried me through what turned out to be an especially difficult undertaking. For unlike such well defined subfields of political science as American governmental institutions, African politics, or international relations, the subfield of political sociology may be organized around a number of different foci, some of whose boundaries are exceptionally wide ranging. I have chosen to view political sociology in such an encompassing fashion; namely, the reliance upon certain social, economic, and cultural phenomena in trying to account for the emergence and contours of certain political phenomena with which political scientists have been most concerned, such as governmental institutions, the structure of political parties, political participation, voting behavior, political integration, and revolutions. But even after going through about a dozen different drafts of the subjects to be covered in the reader, I then went through the oftentimes agonizing process of selecting those readings that could best account for the political phenomena; I either had to make some extremely difficult choices from an overabundance of outstanding studies, or I ran up against a dearth of such studies. And even at this point I had to go through the unhappy process of reducing the manuscript size by a third, given the numerous social, economic, and cultural phenomena that have been used to account for the political ones. To those teachers and students of political sociology who might take exception to certain aspects of this book, I can at least say that I have diligently attempted to present an informative challenging, and coherent book of readings.

For their kindness in helping me to think through the nature of this enterprise and in offering comments on the suitability of various selections, I am grateful to Harry Eckstein, Donald Hindley, and Roy Macridis.

It is both personally and intellectually satisfying to be able to dedicate this book to the teacher who introduced me to the challenge and excitement of political sociology. Some academics are outstanding teachers, others are outstanding writers. The thoughtfulness, scholarship, and rigor that is found in Harry Eckstein's essay "On the Causes of Internal War," reprinted in this book, is equally evident in his teaching.

E. A. N.

*Cambridge, Massachusetts*
*May 1969*

# CONTENTS

*Introduction*

POLITICAL SOCIOLOGY: MARX AND WEBER    1
*Eric A. Nordlinger*


PART ONE: POLITY AND SOCIETY

*A.  The Polity*

PRIMITIVE STATES AND STATELESS SOCIETIES    23
*M. Fortes and E. E. Evans-Pritchard*

AUTHORITY AND LEGITIMACY    35
*Max Weber*

*B.  Social Stratification and Class Conflict*

SOCIAL STRATIFICATION:
CASTE, ESTATE AND CLASS    44
*T. H. Marshall*

POWER, PRIVILEGE AND PRESTIGE    48
*Gerhard Lenski*

THE NATURE OF CLASS CONFLICT    50
*T. H. Marshall*

# PART TWO: THE SOCIOLOGY
# OF WESTERN POLITICS

*A.   Governmental Decision-Makers: Bureaucrats and Legislators*

BUREAUCRATIC STRUCTURE AND
BUREAUCRATIC BEHAVIOR    59
*Robert K. Merton*

OCCUPATIONAL ROLE STRAINS:
THE AMERICAN LEGISLATOR    67
*William C. Mitchell*

*B. Political Parties*

ORGANIZATION AND DEMOCRACY WITHIN
POLITICAL PARTIES    80
*John D. May*

PARTY STRUCTURE AND SOCIO-ECONOMIC DUALISM:
THE ITALIAN COMMUNIST PARTY    97
*Sidney G. Tarrow*

*C.   Voting Behavior*

VOTING: THE EXPRESSION
OF THE DEMOCRATIC CLASS STRUGGLE    117
*Seymour Martin Lipset*

CLASS IDENTIFICATION AND VOTING:
THE WORKING-CLASS TORIES IN ENGLAND    131
*Eric A. Nordlinger*

*D.   Political Participation*

SOCIAL CLASS AND POLITICAL PARTICIPATION    142
*Robert E. Lane*

POVERTY, SUSPICIOUSNESS AND POLITICAL PASSIVITY:
A SOUTHERN ITALIAN TOWN    155
*Edward C. Banfield*

POLITICAL PARTICIPATION AND DEMOCRATIC STABILITY    164
*Gabriel A. Almond and Sidney Verba*

*E. Community Power*

COMMUNITY POWER STUDIES 176
*William Spinrad*


# PART THREE: THE SOCIOLOGY
# OF POLITICAL CHANGE

*A. Political Integration*

POLITICAL AND SOCIAL INTEGRATION:
FORMS AND STRATEGIES 197
*Myron Weiner*

PRIMORDIAL SENTIMENTS AND CIVIL POLITICS
IN THE NEW STATES 209
*Clifford Geertz*

ETHNICITY AND NATIONAL INTEGRATION
IN WEST AFRICA 218
*Immanuel Wallerstein*

THE RISE AND ROLE OF CHARISMATIC LEADERS 225
*Ann Ruth Willner and Dorothy Willner*

*B. Tradition and Change*

TRADITIONAL AND MODERN STYLES OF LEADERSHIP:
NORTHERN NIGERIA 235
*C. S. Whitaker, Jr.*

THE POLITICAL ROLE OF INDIA'S
CASTE ASSOCIATIONS 251
*Lloyd I. Rudolph and Susanne Hoeber Rudolph*

TRADITIONAL STRUCTURES AS OBSTACLES
TO REVOLUTIONARY CHANGE:
THE CASE OF SOVIET CENTRAL ASIA 266
*Gregory J. Massell*

*C. Political Instability: Revolution and Violence*

ON THE CAUSES OF INTERNAL WARS 287
*Harry Eckstein*

INEQUALITY AND INSTABILITY:
THE RELATION OF LAND TENURE
TO POLITICAL INSTABILITY   310
*Bruce M. Russett*

VIOLENCE AND SOCIAL
AND ECONOMIC MODERNIZATION   318
*Samuel P. Huntington*

D.   *Political Development*

POLITICAL DEVELOPMENT:
TIME SEQUENCES AND RATES OF CHANGE   329
*Eric A. Nordlinger*

*Suggested Readings*   348

# POLITICS AND SOCIETY

*Introduction*

# POLITICAL SOCIOLOGY:
# MARX AND WEBER

ERIC A. NORDLINGER

## I. *The Nature of Political Sociology*

Contemporary political science may be characterized broadly by two developments. A far greater emphasis has been placed on the "science" in political science; we have begun to formulate problems on the level of the general rather than the specific and unique, and in analyzing these problems we have relied on more or less objective and quantitative methods of comparison in attempting to devise explanatory hypotheses that are applicable across national boundaries. A second characteristic of recent political science is a utilization of sociology in the development of new methodological techniques, in the formulation of questions, and in directing our attention to certain social, economic, and cultural phenomena within which the answers to the questions can be found. The contemporary field of political sociology has emerged from a confluence of these two broad developments.

As students of political sociology it would seem desirable to have at our disposal a definition of the field. What is political sociology? Unfortunately, a satisfactory delimitation of the field is impossible, just as it is impossible to find a majority of political scientists agreeing on a definition of politics. Yet this gap is not a significant drawback for the study of political sociology. For just as there is no logical necessity for defining politics unless one is concerned with a general theory that purports to account for all of "politics," there is no real necessity for delimiting the field of political sociology unless we are attempting to formulate "the universal laws of political sociology." Fortunately little time has been wasted in this enterprise.

Nor does this leave us in a disoriented state, for we can arrive at a fairly accurate description (rather than a definition) of political sociology simply by looking at the kinds of analyses that political sociologists are concerned with in the writings of such leading figures as Seymour Martin Lipset, Rheinhard Bendix, Barrington Moore, William Kornhauser, Robert Lane, and in certain works of Karl Deutsch, Gabriel Almond, Sidney Verba, Harry Eckstein, and David Apter, among others. Despite their widely differing concerns and approaches, all of these writers have at least one thing in common: they are asking questions about the nature of political systems and political behavior whose answers have led them into the realms of society, culture, and economy. Used in this loose sense, a sizable minority of political scientists could be called political sociologists, which would suggest that the powerful uses of sociology have in one way or another made at least part-time sociologists out of many political scientists. Political sociology may then be characterized as a field of study that analyzes the interrelationships of political and societal phenomena. But while we speak of the interrelationships or reciprocal influences between the polity and society, the greatest efforts of contemporary political sociologists have been expended in showing how political phenomena are influenced by societal factors in the broad Marxist tradition of economic determinism. Consequently, most of the selections in this volume tend to view the political phenomena as the dependent variables whose contours are to be accounted for by the independent societal variables, even though it has never been demonstrated that this is the single or primary direction of the relationship, especially in light of the modern state's capabilities for social and economic change. Thus our focus upon those societal phenomena that help give rise to, and help shape the contours, of political phenomena should not be taken to mean that such relationships always exist, nor that societal variables are always better explanations of political variables than are other political ones, nor does this approach seek to deny that political phenomena sometimes help to account for certain societal variables. Rather, this collection of readings is based on a working assumption which must be shown to be valid in specific instances: it is hoped that these studies in political sociology will take us further along the path of learning how, when, where and why societal variables help pattern certain political ones.

Political sociology is thus about politics in its societal context, and as such, it constitutes a powerful approach. Presumably the works reproduced in this book of readings will heavily underscore its utility. However, the *necessity* of a sociological approach in accounting for certain political phenomena may also be demonstrated logically. A recent political phenomenon that has aroused the interest of political sociologists is the new student activism and radicalism on American campuses. Some observers have explained this phenomenon by relying upon other political phenomena, in particular the youthful appeal of President John F. Kennedy, his assassination, and the appearance of a militant civil rights movement among the blacks. The dual influences of President Kennedy and the militant blacks certainly help to account for the appearance of student radicalism in a particular country at a particular time. But since these political phenomena have been perceived by practically all American college students, we still have to explain why some students have reacted by becoming radicals and activists while others have remained indifferent. In short, a constant cannot explain variation. It would therefore seem appropriate to examine such nonpolitical variables as the students' differing class backgrounds, educational attainments, career aspirations, religious beliefs, relations with parents, and others, as these may help us understand why certain types of students became radicals and others had not.

The necessity of examining social factors also emerges from practically all of the recent voting studies. On the one hand, voting behavior may be explained by such political factors as the rational calculation of self-interest, the objective or dispassionate study of the relevant issues, and the perceptions of the candidates' personalities and abilities. On the other hand, it may be explained by such sociological factors as group pressures toward conformity, the socialization process within the family, class consciousness, and aspirations for social mobility. In attempting to underline the importance of the sociological explanations of voting behavior, we can first of all point out that the great majority of voters arrive at electoral decisions which correspond to (i.e., correlate with) at least one, and usually more than one, of these sociological factors. Secondly, if people do tend to vote according to the dictates of political and rational factors, then the group that we should focus upon are the so-called independent voters who claim to have made up their minds on the basis of a dispassionate analysis of the issues and candidates. If this were the case, then the independents should possess an above average amount of political information—they should readily be able to identify the issues and the positions that the parties and candidates have adopted on these issues. However, as it turns out, it is the independents who possess a remarkably low level of political awareness, interest, and information, without which they surely cannot make their electoral decisions in a rational, self-interested manner. In short, since it is highly improbable that independents who purportedly act on the basis of the political factors actually do so, it is even more unlikely that the voters who regularly support a party arrive at their electoral decisions primarily in such a fashion.

Thus Lewis Coser's analogy may be taken as a highly plausible statement with respect to the importance of political sociology: "Political science has tended to concentrate on the visible part of the political iceberg whereas political sociology has paid greater attention to the submerged portions."[1] And the submerged portion of an iceberg is, of course, many times larger than the portion above the water line. The question then arises of how the two parts of the "iceberg" are inter-related. Without entering into the much discussed methodological issues involved, we may say that a political or social phenomenon may be explained in two ways: by searching for the causes or conditions that account for its emergence and maintenance, or we may explain the phenomenon by analyzing the functions it performs in maintaining other political or social structures. A few illustrations should clarify this distinction.

Take for example the phenomenon of religion as analyzed by Marx. On the one hand, he stated that all political and social phenomena, including religion of course, are caused or conditioned by the economic substructure of society.

[1] Lewis A. Coser, ed., *Political Sociology* (New York: Harper and Row, Publishers, 1967), p. 5.

On the other hand, when Marx denounced religion as "the opiate of the people," he was also setting out a functional explanation. Religion is functional for maintaining the structure of capitalist society and the power of the ruling class because it alleviates and rechannels the suffering of the proletariat by offering them a future happiness in another world, consequently mitigating their antagonism towards the capitalist ruling class. A similar type of analysis is found in the writings of another towering figure among nineteenth century sociologists, Emile Durkheim. One of his primary concerns was the division of labor in nineteenth century Europe, and while he viewed its immediate cause in terms of a rapidly expanding technology, he also pointed out that the division of labor is the single most important factor in the maintenance of society's solidarity. "The economic services that [the division of labor] can render are picayune compared to the moral effect that it produces, and its true function is to create among two or more individuals a feeling of solidarity."[2] In the premodern period, according to Durkheim, societies were held together by a form of "mechanical solidarity" or consensus, in which individuals shared similar traditions and values. Modern societies are characterized by an "organic solidarity" based upon the division of labor in which the interests of individuals and groups are complementary, and this division of labor is then functional for the social and political integration of modern societies. Thus, while there is some overlap between function and cause, there are also important differences in the manner in which the two approaches analyze the interconnections between political and social phenomena.

## II. Political Sociology in the Nineteenth Century

This then is the nature of political sociology that serves as the framework for the selection and organization of the essays comprising this reader—essays that each in their own way relate political phenomena to their social context. The intention of this introductory essay to the volume is not to examine the generalizations that are found in the various selections; for given their wide range and diversity, the result would invariably be marked by an excessive artificiality and superficiality. Rather, it is thought that another set of purposes may be served in the introductory essay by discussing some outstanding figures of nineteenth century sociology—Tocqueville, Toennies, Simmel, Durkheim, Marx, and Weber—but focusing upon Marx and Weber in particular.

The questions that these sociologists asked are explicitly or implicitly the ones that we continue to grapple with today; these questions continue to provide political sociology's broadest framework and often its most penetrat-

---

[2] *The Division of Labor in Society*, trans. George Simpson (New York: Free Press, 1964) p. 56.

ing analyses. Robert Nisbet was only marginally overstating the case when he wrote that "we live, and should not forget it, in a late phase of the classical age of sociology. Strip from present-day sociology the perspectives and frameworks provided by men like Weber and Durkheim and little would be left but lifeless heaps of data and stray hypotheses."[3] In one way or another, Marx, Tocqueville, Durkheim, and Weber all dealt with such overarching and profound problems as the relationship between culture and institutions, between social stratification and the distribution and exercise of power, and between the social structure and the emergence and regulation of political conflicts. They classified, analyzed, and compared modern societies according to their patterns of economic relations, religion, alienation and anomie, industrialization, rationalization, bureaucratization, political egalitarianism, social stratification, and intermediary associations.

Thus nineteenth century European sociology tended to view societies as totalities, attempting to comprehend the many-faceted interrelationships of their parts rather than focusing upon the parts in isolation from each other. In contrast, American sociology has been far more concerned with particular institutions, such as the family, the factory, the school, and the peer group— a perspective which grew out of a policy-oriented concern for alleviating undesirable or deviant phenomena such as slums, juvenile delinquency, and prejudice. This is certainly not to belittle American sociology, but simply to suggest that if we are going to study the many-sided interrelationships between polity and society, it would be well to begin with a broadly gauged set of questions. So much of nineteenth century European sociology is relevant to political sociology today because no matter what sphere of society was being analyzed, the problems were sufficiently profound and encompassing to provide insights into their connections with the polity. Moreover, if one is going to delineate the relations between polity and society it would be advantageous to do so in terms of an historical and comparative perspective, providing vivid contrasts and striking similarities which would underscore the characteristic aspects of contemporary western societies. And this is just what Weber did in his comparative studies of ancient Asian and western societies, the "estates" of the Middle Ages, the absolutist monarchies of the eighteenth century, and the rationalized societies of the modern period. Durkheim contrasted primitive tribes, feudal society and the modern period. Toennies provided us with a multi-faceted contrast between earlier societies based upon *gemeinschaft* relations, in which individuals interacted in a face-to-face manner, engaging their diffuse selves, and societies based upon *gesellschaft* relations, in which interactions take place in an impersonal fashion, involving only a specific aspect of one's self. Marx was, of course, primarily concerned with the sharp differences between feudal, bourgeois, and communist societies, and the causes of the transformation from one to the other. Tocqueville delved into the striking contrasts between the inequality and hierarchy of the French

[3] Robert A. Nisbet, *The Sociological Tradition* (New York: Basic Books, 1966), p. 5.

*ancien régime,* and the relative social, economic, and political egalitarianism he found in the United States, concomitantly analyzing the impact of equality in one part of society upon another. Each of these sociologists was both personally and intellectually involved with his own society, yet each found it necessary to carry out broadly conceived comparative studies in order to illuminate, explain, and interpret his own society and project certain prominent trends into the future.

A number of reasons might account for the rise of a powerful comparative sociology in the second half of the nineteenth century. But among these reasons the most significant might very well be the appearance of two great watersheds in European history: the French Revolution and the Industrial Revolution. The two revolutions were seen as both the signal and the cause of widespread and fundamental changes in society and polity. The Industrial Revolution disrupted social and economic relationships based upon traditionally sanctified estates, hierarchically ordered status groups, and the land-owning aristocracy's legally sanctioned economic privileges; it transformed the meaning of life itself for those millions that were more or less gently ushered through the portals of the modern factory; and in general, the Industrial Revolution led to the replacement of communal, face-to-face relations, by large-scale impersonal organizations. The French Revolution helped transform both the form and legitimacy of monarchical government, simultaneously uprooting the traditional confluence of political authority and high social status, bringing into the political arena new strata with novel demands that were being pressed upon governments, and thus, in general, calling into question the form and substance according to which the polity had previously managed to carry out its dual functions of goal attainment and societal integration. It was these actual and foreboding changes that provided the sociologists with their problems—problems whose importance was multiplied many times over because of the clear recognition that their answers had vast normative and policy ramifications built into them. And it should be added that the kind of questions that inform political sociology could only be asked after the empirical and normative identification of state and society as two indistinguishable and mutually penetrating spheres had been shattered. Only then could their interrelations be studied by political sociologists.

For political sociologists, two of the most urgent and far reaching problems stemming from the French and Industrial Revolutions were the integration of societies and the protection of individual liberties. Once the traditional forms of political and social hierarchy began to crumble, what new forces would take their place in holding societies together and ordering them in a coherent manner? We have already referred to Durkheim's answer to this question in another connection. "Organic solidarity" with its mutual self-interest and social empathy stemming from the division of labor would actually insure a more stable and coherent form of societal integration than an earlier "mechanical solidarity" based on a value consensus. Georg Simmel, who continues to be our foremost guide in the study of social conflict, attempted an answer in a related vein by focusing upon the positive functions that conflicts may serve. In particular, he suggested that the breakup of traditional society into numerous conflicting interests would not necessarily lead to Hobbes' "war of all against all." Rather, the fact that these conflicting interests were cross-cutting, that individuals whose interests conflicted on one issue converged on other issues, would not only have the effect of mitigating the intensity of conflicts, but would also serve as a binding force making for societal integration. Weber did not address himself to the problem of social integration directly, perhaps because the shocks of the French and Industrial Revolutions had been softened by the time that he wrote in the early twentieth century, but much of his work provides a clear indication of his answer to the problem. A large number of individuals, even individuals sharing a common set of values, does not form an integrated society. Social integration, which Weber conceived of as the coordination of individual and group interests and activities, could only be achieved in a twofold manner. Individuals would have to form groups and associations in which their different interests were somehow compromised, and in which a large measure of authority accrued to the leaders of the associations in order to allow these associations to pursue those activities through which their interests could be realized.

Once monarchical and aristocratic rule had been replaced by democracy, how were individual liberties, that had previously been protected by traditions and corporate rights, to be preserved? Would not individual liberties be eradicated once Tocqueville's overbearing and tyrannous majority came to the fore, producing in its wake a centralized government whose activities would no longer be placed on a limited basis, as was true of monarchical governments? Tocqueville's answer was qualified. Individual liberties need not be threatened under these new conditions provided that the society contained a large number of voluntary associations; for these associations would group together like–minded individuals, provide them with the necessary political interests and resources that would mitigate the power of the central government—a solution to which Durkheim could only offer his heartiest assent when he wrote about the need for a strong economic corporatism to fill the newly created vacuum between the individual, on the one hand, and the state, on the other.[4] Weber provided an entirely different answer to the question. Despite his many fears regarding the unhappy consquences of an overly–developed bureaucracy, he nevertheless pointed to the civil servants as effective agents for the protection of liberties through the institutionalization of equality before the law.[5] Yet it should be noted that neither Tocqueville, Durkheim, nor Weber was especially sanguine about their "solutions" for the problem of liberty in an age of the powerful state and mass democracy.

---

[4] The political significance of voluntary associations are explored in the essays by Banfield, Wallerstein, and the Rudolphs.

[5] In the last section of his essay Merton offers some provoking thoughts on the relations between bureaucrats and their publics.

Thus, the reasons that these sociologists' generalizations and typologies contained such intellectual power and profundity stems not only from the vivid and deep-seated contrasts among societies that they highlighted, nor from their personal and intellectual confrontations with the Industrial and French Revolutions alone. Also relevant is the great overlap between the problems of classical sociology and the questions that informed the works of such classical political philosophers as Plato, Aristotle, Machiavelli, and Hobbes, centering about the dual problems of societal integration and the protection of individual liberties. Indeed, the answers of the political philosophers and the sociologists frequently overlapped, and, to a lesser extent, they even adhered to a common perspective that took in all of society, in which political and social phenomena were studied as inextricably linked phenomena.

## III. Karl Marx

To characterize political sociology as a century-long "dialogue" with Marx is not an overly exaggerated statement. Nor is it a particularly surprising statement since Marx did nothing less than to ask *the* question: How can we explain any society's major institutions—its governmental form, its educational patterns, its culture and religion, its lines of cleavage, indeed, its entire "superstructure." In answering that question, he offered what is easily the most powerful sociological theory ever delineated. Its powerfulness stems from a number of characteristics. The theory sought to account for the vast superstructure of society by relying upon a single explanatory factor; the theory purports to be applicable to all societies at all times; it explains major social, economic, and political change, amounting to a theory of historical change; the theory is securely anchored to the empirical world rather than residing in the rarefied atmosphere of abstract or philosophical reasoning; and finally, it contains a sharply focused, and to many, a most appealing political doctrine for both the present and the future. This then is the challenge of Marx, and it is a challenge that has been explicitly or implicitly picked up by generations of sociologists and political scientists.

In the most summary terms, we can say that all of Marxian theory is informed by the idea of dialectical materialism, although Marx himself did not coin the term. When this idea is given a specific empirical expression, it unfolds in the direction of the theory of class and class conflict, which then become the driving forces of history. Marx's twin assertions—that every society beyond the most primitive is divided into two or more classes (a ruling class and one or more subject classes) and that there is a perpetual conflict between these two—are well known. The theory only gains the proportions of a powerful and challenging statement in Marx's attempts to account for, or to underpin, these universal assertions.

The term "materialism" refers to any and all physical objects, but Marx's concern is obviously more specific. The starting point for the theory—the raw material that infuses the dialectic—is the tools that men use in keeping themselves alive. Men organize their lives in order to realize this, their primary goal. Everything else—culture, social structure, political institutions —takes its form in the light of the tools that men use and the ways in which they organize themselves in order to keep themselves alive. Marx makes an important distinction between the modes and relations of production. The modes of production refer to the tools, techniques, and equipment that are used in the production process, and the way in which men organize themselves in that process. The relations of production refer primarily to the relations of ownership and control of men and property. According to Marx, it is primarily the modes of production that pattern the relations of production and, in turn, the relations of production form the cleavage pattern of society (e.g., the class conflict based upon the ownership of property in capitalist society). It is these cleavages that are identical with the actual or future lines of political conflict.

It was, then, according to the relations of production that Marx characterized the four types of western society. The ancient Greek and Roman societies were based on slavery; medieval society was based on serfdom; the capitalist society was based on the propertyless wage-earner; and the future socialist society was to be founded upon the absence of any exploitative element in the relations of production. Marx devoted his empirical analysis largely to feudal society and its transition to capitalism, and to the contemporary capitalist society out of which socialist society was to emerge. In both cases the driving force that leads to the transition from one type of society to another was to be found in the contradictions and conflicts between the modes and relations of production. It was this encompassing historical transition from one type of society to another that primarily concerned Marx, out of which grew a powerful theory of conflict and change. This theory asserted that the modes of production have been steadily increasing in their productive efficiency, while the relations of production, since they are shaped by the former, take a longer time to change. Consequently, the ensuing contradictions and conflicts bring about a basic alteration in the relations of production and thus in the superstructure of society. Or, to put it somewhat differently, a new ruling class will emerge when the contradictions or conflicts between the modes and relations of production can no longer be contained within a particular societal structure.

In the case of feudalism, technological progress brought about a striking change in the tools of production, passing from the axe and the plow to the steam-powered machine. While feudal craftsmen, incorporated in professional guilds, owned and operated their own tools, at the most hiring a few assistants, the situation is of course quite different when steam-powered machines are used. Marx tells us that throughout the feudal period the modes and relations of production were in harmony; the handicraft technology and the guild form of economic organization were consistent. However, as the feudal period unfolded, technology began to run ahead of the relations of production, despite the efforts of the guilds to control the proliferation of the new technology, since it entailed the loss of their wealth and power in the growing towns and cities. Here then was the sharpest contradiction in feudalism that transformed most of western Europe into capitalist society. The invention of steam-powered machinery required the building of factories that could be owned by a single individual, but certainly could not be operated by one man. The new commercial and industrial bourgeoisie wanted to build the factories whose operation required a free labor market and a free buyers and sellers market. Yet the nascent bourgeoisie was hampered from all sides—by guild regulations, the absence of the freedom of contract, multitudinous local legal provisions, cumbersome tax systems, and the nobility's arrogantly exercised privileges. It was then the repercussions of heightened productivity and the desire for wealth that succeeded in bursting these restrictions, out of which developed nineteenth century capitalism. The bourgeoisie as a minority within feudal society organized the economy according to new relations of production, and because of its performance of socially dominant functions, this new class was able to topple the superstructure of feudal society.

Within the capitalist system, the factors which primarily dictate conflict between the modes and relations of production center about the effects of planning and organization. To put it most bluntly, the incompatibility between relations and modes is caused by the different ways that each is organized. On the one hand, the actual industrial or manufacturing process is highly organized, complex, and interdependent, within a given factory or industry. The intricacies of modern production demand a high degree of planning and coordination. On the other hand, the relations of production are organized according to the institutions of private property and the laissez-faire ideology. When the relations and modes are now seen side by side, the reason for their mutual antagonism becomes clear. The nature of industrial capitalism demands planning and cooperation between individual enterprises and industries if the frequent business cycles were not to become more recurrent and deeper. Yet the relations of production could not, and did not, allow for the required cooperation among capitalists. Each was out to secure for himself the most wealth in the shortest time. Laissez-faire ideology did not make it possible for the nineteenth century capitalists to see that their own ends could be best secured by controlling prices and production through interindustry cooperation. The totally individualistic relations of production obviated the extensive coordination and planning demanded by the modes of production.

Thus Marx did not maintain that the individual entrepreneur was acting irrationally; he distinguished between the irrationality of capitalism as an economic system and the rationality of the individual capitalists who were compelled to act as they did by the situation within which they operated,

Marx's distinction between the system on the one hand, and the individual entrepreneur's behavior on the other, allowed him to suggest that it was the system itself rather than the individuals comprising it that was exploitative. In short, unbridled competition as dictated by the rules of the capitalist game culminates in capitalism's downfall.

Two developments were to lead to Marx's predicted revolution: the law of the centralization of capital and the increasing misery of the proletariat. The starting point for both trends is found in the concept of surplus value. This is the difference between the amount paid the workers in wages and the amount the capitalist receives for his workers' labor through the sale of his product on the free market—the basic exploitation of the capitalist system. The capitalist is accumulating profits out of surplus value, yet competition with other capitalists forces him to add more and more machinery in order to cut costs even further and to expand production for bigger profits. But here he is causing his own downfall, for according to Marx (though later economists disagree), he is thereby decreasing his surplus value since machine production is necessarily less profitable than hand labor. According to Marxian theory the rapid installation of machines in a frantic race to catch up with the competition will lead to overproduction and thus to recurrent business cycles. And when these cycles hit their troughs, the bigger capitalists are in a position to buy out the marginal ones. This process is then repeated over and over again until only a few extremely wealthy capitalists remain.

The increasing misery of the proletarist—Marx's second law—is proceeding simultaneously. The purchase of more and more machines and the recurrent periods of overproduction lead to an increasing rate of unemployment along with lower wages. And as the proletariat is becoming increasingly immiserized, their plight becomes even more difficult to bear since it stands in stark contrast to the massive fortunes of the few. Out of this contrast will emerge the revolutionary consciousness of the workers; they will develop into a class in the fullest meaning of the term as they come to recognize the bonds that link together the workers in ties of overriding self-interest (class solidarity), as they recognize their interests to be diametrically opposed to those of the capitalists (class conflict), which was to culminate in concerted class war (the revolution). This predicted revolution was to have been the most thorough-going change experienced by any society. For in capitalist society, the lines of class cleavage are the most sharply drawn. Unlike feudal societies, the lines of economic conflict are not mitigated by any personal ties of respect, affection, or duty between members of different classes, while the internal contradictions of capitalism lead to the starkest distribution of wealth that is theoretically imaginable.[6]

This sketch of *one* crucial dimension of Marx's theory is just that—a sketch which does a great disservice to its complexities and sophistication. But rather

---

[6] Compare this analysis with T. H. Marshall's essay on class conflict.

than discussing other parts of Marxian theory, we will examine the work of the German sociologist Max Weber. For it was Weber who interpreted, modified, and added to Marxian theory as it comes down to us today. And it is just this "dialogue" or "debate" between Marx and Weber that forms much of the central core of contemporary political sociology. Thus, we will be coming back to Marx again and again in Weber.

## IV. Max Weber

### A. RATIONALIZATION AND AUTHORITY

We have already seen how the nineteenth century sociologists framed their analyses within a broadly gauged typology of societies, according to which they charted what was for each of them the fundamental characteristic of the transition from premodern to modern societies. Weber's work is similarly organized around a broadly conceived central idea—what he saw as the movement from "traditional" to "rational" societies. And as in the case of the other sociologists, Weber traced the process of rationalization in different institutional spheres, utilizing both the causal and functional approaches.

Weber's traditional and rational societies closely parallel Toennies' *gemeinschaft* and *gesellschaft* societies. For Weber, a traditional society is characterized by communal bonds, based upon a diffuse emotional identification and attachment among individuals, of which the family and the neighborhood group may serve as examples. In contrast, rational society is characterized by "associative" relationships, and these are based upon a rationally calculated mutual self-interest, of which the open buyers and sellers market is the prototypical example. This self-interested contractual relationship is not only found in the economic market-place; in a rationalized society, culture, religion, education, and politics are all infused with this type of social interaction. Thus Weber's interpretation of the West's historical development is one in which communal and traditional values and relationships have largely been replaced by impersonal and bureaucratized institutions. It is appropriate to view Weber as the sociologist of "the organizational revolution"—a process that Marx failed to recognize, as he had to fail, given his single-minded concern with the dominant role of private property. What Weber sets out to do is to show that foremost among the various changes of modern societies is the gradual replacement of proprietary by organizational incentives.

For political scientists, the most influential and well known of Weber's studies of rationalization is the typology and analysis of rational-legal authority exercised by a rationally organized bureaucracy. These studies are represented in this volume of readings,[7] and it is therefore not necessary to spell out Weber's accomplishments here in any detail. Thus, instead of delineating the

[7] See the selection by Weber.

characteristics of rational-legal authority and bureaucracy, it may be more useful to discuss their interrelations with other parts of the social structure, out of which emerges some suggestive lines of analysis for the study of social change. Indeed, one of Weber's major contributions is his analysis of the reciprocal influences between political institutions and the social structure, exploring these interrelationships through a powerful sociological foray into history. Someone once remarked that Weber's great achievement was due to the coming together of a Germanic sense of history with the French and positivist notion of scientific rigor.

The legitimacy of traditional authority rests upon respect for what actually, or allegedly, has always existed. There are time-honored beliefs and norms that are considered inviolable, which legitimize the authority of traditional rulers, simultaneously defining the rights, liberties, and duties of both rulers and ruled. Yet a distinct area of independent action is usually left to the traditional leader in which he may exercise his personal prerogative—economic activities in particular, since these are less óften "covered" by traditional norms. Indeed, Weber suggests that the usual effect of traditional authority is to weaken rational economic attitudes and activities. Given the ruler's prerogative to act as he pleases, the merchants will fear that he might preempt their property, limit their freedom of activity, or arbitrarily impose taxes on them, thereby hampering the development of an efficient economy featuring capital intensive production.

While Weber sees historical change as occurring through the gradual replacement of traditional authority by rational-legal authority, this general pattern is sometimes punctuated by the appearance of charismatic authority. During crisis periods, either traditional or rational-legal authority may disintegrate and a charismatic leader may arise whose legitimacy derives from beliefs in his extraordinary achievements or superhuman qualities.[8] Charismatic authority is, however, inherently unstable; for the regime's authority and its legitimacy are bound up in one and the same person. Or, to put it differently, the charismatic leader's authority can only be maintained if he can continue to convince his followers of his legitimacy—that he is truly a superhuman individual. Not only is this unlikely to continue throughout the leader's lifetime, but even when he does succeed, there is the commonly irreconcilable problem of passing on the charismatic mantle to a successor. Charismatic authority is thus always brittle, rarely becoming routinized, and consequently becoming transformed into traditional or rational-legal authority. And given the emotion-charged atmosphere of charisma, class structures and status pyramids may be destroyed in the wake of the powerful enthusiasm of the leader's followers.

Given the inherent instability of charismatic authority, Weber does not connect this type of authority to a specific form of economic organization; for the latter is viewed as a matter of settled routine, and the effect of

---

[8] See the essay by Willner and Willner.

charismatic authority is to upset whatever form of economic activity exists. This is not to say, however, that the charismatic leader is economically independent. Charismatic authority is based on either of two forms of economic supply: gifts or conquest for booty. An authority based on the latter is obviously unstable, for not every war is an economic success. In the case of the former, if the leader remains in power over time then these gifts will form a large estate for the ruler. Under such circumstances—a regular flow of income and the holding of property—it is likely that charismatic authority will be transformed into a more stable type, especially since the leader's followers want to see their income regularized and their positions secured. In short, the economic conditions are singularly instrumental in routinizing charisma in either a traditional or rational–legal direction, depending in part upon the specific economic and political circumstances.

Rational–legal authority is legitimized on the basis of its decision-making process, whose rational and legal characteristics are positively valued on just these nontraditional and nonemotional grounds. Legitimacy is derived from conformity to explicitly formulated rules. Thus the source of legitimacy does not reside with the occupant of the office, but with the office itself—a distinction that is not found in either traditional or charismatic authority. This rigid distinction between the occupant and the office is one of the three chief characteristics of bureaucracy. The second is a well–defined hierarchical distribution of authority, and the third, is the horizontal division of labor according to differentiated functions and technical skills.

The question then arises: what are the important interconnections between bureaucracy and its socioeconomic context? As has already been implied, a money economy is necessary to support a bureaucratic organization. Yet it is not monetary payment per se, it is rather the *regular* payment of the officials' salaries that makes bureaucracy possible, and in industrial society the most stable source of income is monetary taxation. Thus we can say with Weber that a monetary exchange system is a prerequisite for the bureaucratic organization of the state. Weber also makes the point that the complex arrangements of industrial society are increasingly in need of specialized experts. It is in this milieu that the technically capable bureaucrat comes into his own or, according to Weber, into an ascendant position. In turn, the need for well–trained experts (selected by special examinations) to staff the bureaucracy had its impact upon educational institutions, leading to a newfound emphasis on specialized training—a specialized training that is most sharply accentuated in the German law faculties which have been the chief source of that government's bureaucratic talent.

This alteration in the role of education may be viewed as part of a broader consequence of bureaucracy, namely, its socially leveling influence. Although bureaucracy is not an egalitarian institution—it has its own hierarchical prerogatives and authority—it necessarily places an emphasis on egalitarianism that is usually absent in a polity legitimized by traditional authority. To a large extent, achievement criteria have replaced inherited status in the selection and promotion of officials, while in their dealings with private citizens, the civil servants tend to treat members of different social classes as equals in the system of authority. Furthermore, the combination of social leveling in which former privileged statuses come to be irrelevant within the authority structure, and the appeal to rational-legal legitimation, have helped replace a well differentiated status-group (or estate) society with that of a socially less differentiated mass society. And it is just this type of society that is propitious for the rise of popular (sometimes charismatic) leaders, and the growth of political parties with their appeal to a mass electorate. Or to state the matter more generally, party competition in its democratic form feeds on the socially leveling consequences of rational-legal authority, and to take this proposition one step further, both democracy and bureaucracy are inextricably connected (as both cause and effect) with the demise of privileged political, economic, and status positions based on birth alone.[9]

Before leaving this discussion of the process of rationalization in Weber's work, it would be well to note that there are parallels between Weber's analysis of governmental bureaucratization and his analysis of capitalism as a rational economic system composed of increasingly bureaucratized organizations. For Weber, the central feature of modern capitalism is the "rational organization of free labor." And as in the case of governmental bureaucracy, "The 'objective' discharge of business primarily means a discharge of business according to *calculable rules* and 'without regard for persons.' "[10] Furthermore, both the free market mechanism and the efficiency of business bureaucracies tend to reduce inherited status in favor of the possession of achieved qualities and financial power. Unlike Marx, who did not conceive of the possible separation of ownership and management in business enterprises, Weber emphasized this now widely prevalent aspect of capitalism as a further manifestation of the rationalization process. The final stage of increasing rationalization—in the business organization as in any other organization— occurs when the operating goal is no longer the original *raison d'être* (i.e., the profit motive) but the maintenance of the organization *qua* organization.

## B. THE ROLE OF IDEAS IN SOCIAL AND POLITICAL CHANGE

The crucial aspect of the "dialogue" between Marx and Weber focuses on the role of ideas in influencing behavioral and institutional change. Along with the broad assertion that every society has a ruling class founded on the ownership of the means of production, Marx also put forward the hypothesis that the ruling class consolidates its hold over the society through the production and dissemination of ideas. The prevailing ideas are the ideas of the owning class. The nature of these ideas is dictated by the relations of production, legitimizing the ruling class's monopoly of economic wealth

---

[9] For a discussion of the replacement of a European estate society by a class society, see the first of Marshall's two essays. The relationships between organization and democracy are analyzed in May's essay.

[10] H. H. Gerth and C. Wright Mills, eds., *From Max Weber* (New York: Oxford University Press, 1958), p. 215.

and political power. In this sense, then, all ideas—in the realms of law, art, morality, religion, and even science—are basically "reflections" of the economic substructure, which are then put to use by the ruling class, i.e., there is a one-to-one relationship between economic interests and all manner of ideas. Weber would certainly not deny this thesis as a *possible* way in which polity and society are interrelated, but for him it is just one possibility among others, rather than a universal generalization. Both sociologists underscore the importance of ideas as instruments in the legitimation of economic and political power. However, Weber maintains that ideas need not always originate in the sphere of economic relations, that individuals sometimes subscribe to ideas that contradict their material interests, that there are sometimes conflicts between ideas and material interests, that in this conflict ideas may have a greater influence, and that consequently ideas have a power of their own rather than being "mere" reflections of economic relations. In fact, we have just noted a few instances in which the legitimizing ideas of political authority influence the structure of the polity, its relations with the society, and, indirectly, society itself. It should be emphasized that Weber was *not* attempting to stand Marx on his head; he was trying to round out Marx's overly narrow but powerful concentration upon economic forces by arguing that ideas have an independent influence of their own.

The divergences in the two approaches occur in their sharpest form in Marx and Weber's explanations for the rise of capitalism and their related treatment of religious ideas. We have already noted Marx's exclusively economic interpretation of the emergence of capitalism, focusing upon the changes in the modes and their consequent conflict with the relations of production, and we have also noted his view of religion as a set of beliefs that helps consolidate the control of the ruling class over the subject class. In Weber's monumental study, *The Protestant Ethic and the Spirit of Capitalism,* he readily accepts the broad argument that there are certain economic prerequisites that had to be fulfilled for capitalism to emerge, but the study is primarily devoted to the ideas or values that were equally important prerequisites—in particular, the ascetic Protestant ethic. This was the answer that Weber formulated in response to one of the "big" questions of historical sociology: How did sixteenth century Europe differ from earlier periods and other societies that could account for the fundamental fact that capitalism as we know it first developed there? According to Weber, the Protestant ethic accounts for the rise of capitalism in three important ways.

First, it did not allow for the spontaneous enjoyment of worldly goods, thereby restricting the consumption of luxuries, calling for thrift and abstinence instead. This factor was important in the emergence of capitalism because the vast savings of wealth which were accumulated were then invested in commerce and industry. Secondly, ascetic Protestantism made work into a religious calling, thereby legitimizing those commercial activities which the traditional Catholicism of feudal Europe did not sanction. Once work became an acceptable way of serving God, and once the religion approved of the rational accumulation and utilitarian use of wealth in the name of God, the manifest virtues of the Protestant elect—diligence, prudence, thrift, and sobriety—turned out to be exactly the same virtues that were crucial to the emergence of capitalism in Europe. Thirdly, Weber realized that the average Protestant would be exceptionally troubled not knowing whether or not he was a member of the elect who would enter the Kingdom of God; man needed a visible sign of his having achieved a state of grace. The minister could not help him since the Protestant layman could only derive knowledge of his future directly from God. Under these circumstances the accumulation of non-luxurious wealth became the visible sign for the individual himself, and for all those who knew him, that he had attained a state of grace. Business became a calling.

In order to provide a firm comparative support for his thesis, Weber would have to show that in other societies many of the requisites for the rise of capitalism were also present, but because the necessary value element was absent, capitalism did not in fact appear in these societies. In studying such disparate societies as India, China, and Judea at the relevant stages of their cultural development, Weber found that the material conditions were indeed propitious for the development of capitalism. In fact they compared favorably with the capitalistic potential of medieval and early modern Europe; for in these three nonwestern societies was found peace, a stable administration, freedom of movement, and the existence of large fortunes within the context of economic prosperity. Yet in each of these societies the economic ethic of the dominant religion was directly antagonistic to capitalistic enterprise. In China, for example, Confucianism took the form of a somewhat mystical religion that either disregarded or devalued the material aspects of life.

At the same time, however, Weber is not ignoring Marx's sociology, for he did point to the mandarin ruling strata as an additional hindrance to the emergence of capitalism in China. As a traditional ruling class, educated and socialized in the tradition of pure learning and devout religion, the mandarins did not think it in their interest to allow the capitalistic entrepreneurs to gain in power and wealth. Here Weber is following Marx: ideas are important in history, but only when they enjoy the support of economic interests and/or political elites. Thus Weber is not averse to handling the problem of the rise of capitalism in a Marxian fashion. In fact, at the end of *The Protestant Ethic and the Spirit of Capitalism* he writes that he is fully aware that he has handled the problem from one perspective alone; to get as close to historical reality as possible it is necessary to analyze the problem from other directions as well. It is simply that Weber has chosen—in large part as a reaction to Marx, attempting to develop a broader, more valid, and more sophisticated explanation—to deal with the impact of ideas rather than with the impact of material factors upon social and economic change. Weber does not posit a direct relationship between ideas and large scale change in an overly simplified manner. Rather, between ideas on the one hand and socio-economic and political change on the other, Weber has provided an insightful view of the subjective states of the individual actors. Specifically, he has shown how the ideas of ascetic Protestantism served the psychological needs, and thereby influenced the beliefs, values, and behaviors of individuals, which taken together led to the emergence of new economic institutions, and these in turn, had profound effects in reshaping political institutions.

## C. CLASS, STATUS, AND AUTHORITY

Marx's theory of class is remarkably simple, and thus immensely powerful. Not only does the ownership of property pattern membership in different classes, but class membership in turn also determines social status and political power. Just as the landed aristocracy in the eighteenth century occupied the topmost positions in all three of these stratification pyramids, in a capitalist society they are all occupied by the bourgeoisie. Marx's theory thus suggests that there is always a crystallization or congruence of high class, status, and authority positions, all predicated upon the relations of production. Within this theory there is no room for such phenomena as the simultaneous occupancy of high class and low status positions, or status anxieties and aspirations. It is much to Weber's credit that he recognized the great value of Marx's theory, underscoring its significance while modifying and adding to it. What Weber did was to disentangle and modify the way in which the three hierarchies of stratification—class, status, and authority— were conceptualized, followed by an analysis of their interrelationships.

For Weber, as for Marx before him, the basic determinant of "class" is the ownership or nonownership of property; Weber also goes a long way with Marx in asserting that the most important dividing line in industrial societies is the one that separates those who have property from those who do not; that economic power is closely connected with political power, the two reinforcing each other; and that the rise and cohesion of European working-class movements is due to the propertylessness, economic insecurity, and weak bargaining power of the workers. But after this point Weber begins to go his own way.

Weber significantly expanded the Marxian view of stratification when he added a second hierarchy or dimension of stratification to that of class, namely, the status hierarchy, which refers to the distribution of social "honor" or "prestige." According to Marx, status is inextricably connected to class, whereas for Weber this is true in some cases, but not in others. This point is related to the two sociologists' views of the relative influence of ideas and material factors on behavior. Weber conceives of status honor as stemming from the individual's "style of life." Although life styles are in great part dependent upon the ownership or nonownership of property, Weber suggested that subjective ideas of what constitutes a high-status life style have an independent force of their own; actual life styles are largely related to property, yet in different societies greater value is placed on certain life styles than on others. Consequently, the attachment to different values dictates that class and satus positions are not always identical, especially when high status is accorded to individuals on the basis of such values as religion, education, and "breeding" which are not completely determined by the economic factors of class. In fact, it is on the basis of just such noneconomic attributes that high status groups tend to reject or accept others in their "circle," thereby preventing at least the first generation of the newly rich from gaining high status positions. Moreover, class and status positions may diverge because economic conditions can change more rapidly than subjectively defined status positions; economic innovations and the fluctuations of the business cycle may suddenly alter the economic position of high status individuals, sometimes propelling low status individuals up the class hierarchy as well.

Weber's distinction between class and status has an important bearing upon both working-class and middle-class political behavior. Studies in various western countries have brought to light the fact that within the working class there is commonly found a sizeable minority who think of themselves as enjoying, or aspiring to, middle class status. These workers who claim or aspire to a status position that is higher than their class position are less likely to vote for the left party, and this happens even when their incomes are no higher than those manual workers who identify as such.[11] Marx's assumptions about the one-to-one relationship between class and status thus prevented him from seeing the relevance of this phenomenon as it detracts from the formation of a working class consciousness. Similarly, Marx's characterization of the white-collared office workers' "false consciousness" may be better understood when their relatively high status position are also taken into account, rather than exclusively stressing the point that these workers are in the same propertyless class position as the manual workers. This general point, that class and status positions are sometimes incongruent, may also be used to interpret the rise of radical political movements within the middle class stratum. The lower-middle-class individuals who constituted a disproportionate number of supporters of German Nazism, Poujadisme in France, and McCarthyism in the United States had at least one common characteristic: their dissatisfactions and anxieties were a product of a divergence between their deteriorating class positions and their relatively high status positions vis-à-vis the manual workers.

Weber never completed his seminal essay, "Class, Status, and Party," but there is enough content in the last part to clarify Weber's goal: to indicate that over and above the class and status hierarchies there is a third hierarchy of authority relations which is autonomous, yet interdependent with the other two hierarchies of stratification.[12] He was again attempting to refute and expand Marx's work by suggesting that individuals who enjoy high class and status positions do not necessarily hold similarly high positions of political power or authority, despite the interconnections among the three hierarchies. And while Marx suggests that there is an increasing congruence between the three hierarchies as capitalism begins to go through its death agonies, Weber suggests that the three hierarchies are being steadily separated because of

---

[11] See the selection by Nordlinger for an analysis of this phenomenon in England.
[12] Compare this statement with Lenski's essay.

the increasing rationalization of society. It is the bureaucrats, with their varied class and status backgrounds, that have largely inherited the authority that previously resided in individuals of high class and status positions. The power of the aristocracy gave way to the protoparties of high status notables, and in turn, these parties were transformed into mass parties frequently led by men with lower-class backgrounds. As society undergoes the process of rationalization, with achievement criteria replacing ascriptive ones of high status, and as education and technical training become increasingly important in government and business, it tends to follow that in any single generation, individuals will increasingly come to occupy class, status, and authority positions that do not coincide.

By distinguishing between the three hierarchies of class, status, and authority, and by stressing their relative divergence in modern rationalized societies, Weber's work implicitly directs our attention to the reasons why Marx's predicted class revolution has not occurred. It now becomes apparent that Marx's class cleavages are less sharp just because there is no longer an almost complete overlap among the three hierarchies: the upper strata of any of the three hierarchies are not as visible (or identifiable) to the workers, and there is less antagonism toward them since the people "at the top" do not invariably enjoy a monopoly of high class, status, and authority positions; there is also the influence of cross-pressures upon individuals in nonoverlapping positions, thereby lessening their ideological or emotional attachments to one particular political strata; there are separate conflicts in the class and authority pyramids, which means that their resolution is easier than if the two pyramids were congruent, allowing industrial conflicts, for example, to be settled within their own sphere without endangering political stability; and we are probably safe in thinking that upward mobility is easier and occurs more frequently when it is not necessary for an individual to be upwardly mobile in all three hierarchies simultaneously, the higher rates of mobility then detracting from the bitterness of economic and political conflicts. It is presumably factors such as these that take us a long way in accounting for the absence of a violent politics, and thus the democratic stability of numerous industrial-capitalist societies.

Lastly, it ought to be stressed that in reviewing the "dialogue" between Marx and Weber, the object was not to detract from Marx's theory. For while he was probably more often wrong than right, he not only provided brilliant insights that were to stimulate a later political sociology, but where he was wrong he was usually wrong in matters of degree. Or to put it differently, his generalizations invariably contained a good deal of validity, but they were too exclusively economic and too strongly deterministic to be valid as universal generalizations. It was Weber's great achievement to recognize the valid elements in Marxian theory, while at the same time modifying and adding to it in certain crucial respects. Although contemporary political sociology tends to see Weber as its most important guide and resource, the Marxian influence remains very much with us.

# PART ONE

# POLITY
# AND
# SOCIETY

*A. The Polity*

# PRIMITIVE STATES
# AND STATELESS SOCIETIES

M. FORTES AND E. E. EVANS-PRITCHARD

It will be noted that the political systems described here fall into two main categories. One group, which we refer to as Group A, consists of those African societies which have centralized authority, administrative machinery, and judicial institutions—in short, a government—and in which cleavages of wealth, privilege, and status correspond to the distribution of power and authority. This group comprises the Zulu, the Ngwato, the Bemba, the Banyankole, and the Kede. The other group, which we refer to as Group B, consists of those societies which lack centralized authority, administrative machinery, and constituted judicial institutions—in short which lack government—and in which there are no sharp divisions of rank, status, or wealth. This group comprises the Logoli, the Tallensi, and the Nuer. Those who consider that a state should be defined by the presence of governmental institutions will regard the first group as primitive states and the second group as stateless societies.

. . .

KINSHIP IN POLITICAL
ORGANIZATION

One of the outstanding differences between the two groups is the part played by the lineage system in political structure. We must here distinguish between the set of relationships linking the individual to other persons and to particular social units through the transient, bilateral family, which we shall call the kinship system, and the segmentary system of permanent, unilateral descent groups, which we call the lineage system. Only the latter establishes corporate units with political functions. In both groups of societies kinship and domestic ties have an important role in the lives of individuals, but their relation to the political system is of a secondary order. In the societies of Group A (the primitive states) it is the administrative organization, in societies of Group B (the stateless societies) the segmentary lineage system, which primarily regulates political relations between territorial segments.

This is clearest among the Ngwato, whose political system resembles the pattern with which we are familiar in the modern nation-state. The political unit is essentially a territorial grouping wherein the plexus of kinship ties serves merely to cement those already established by membership of the ward, district, and nation. In societies of this

Reprinted from M. Fortes and E. E. Evans-Pritchard, AFRICAN POLITICAL SYSTEMS (London: Oxford University Press for the International African Institute, 1940), pp. 5–23, by permission of Oxford University Press.

type the state is never the kinship system writ large, but is organized on totally different principles. In societies of Group B kinship ties appear to play a more prominent role in political organization, owing to the close association of territorial grouping with lineage grouping, but it is still only a secondary role.

It seems probable to us that three types of political system can be distinguished. Firstly, there are those very small societies, none of which are described in this book, in which even the largest political unit embraces a group of people all of whom are united to one another by ties of kinship, so that political relations are coterminous with kinship relations and the political structure and kinship organization are completely fused. Secondly, there are societies in which a lineage structure is the framework of the political system, there being a precise co-ordination between the two, so that they are consistent with each other, though each remains distinct and autonomous in its own sphere. Thirdly, there are societies in which an administrative organization is the framework of the political structure.

The numerical and territorial range of a political system would vary according to the type to which it belongs. A kinship system would seem to be incapable of uniting such large numbers of persons into a single organization for defence and the settlement of disputes by arbitration as a lineage system and a lineage system incapable of uniting such numbers as an administrative system.

.  .  .

## THE INFLUENCE OF MODE OF LIVELIHOOD

The density and distribution of population in an African society are clearly related to ecological conditions which also affect the whole mode of livelihood. It is obvious, however, that mere differences in modes of livelihood do not determine differences in political structure. The Tallensi and the Bemba are both agriculturalists, the Tallensi having fixed and the Bemba shifting cultivation, but they have very different political systems. The Nuer and Logoli of Group B and the Zulu and Ngwato of Group A alike practise mixed agriculture and cattle husbandry. In a general sense, modes of livelihood, together with environmental conditions, which always impose effective limits on modes of livelihood, determine the dominant values of the peoples and strongly influence their social organizations, including their political systems. This is evident in the political divisions of the Nuer, in the distribution of Kede settlements and the administrative organization embracing them, and in the class system of the Banyankole.

Most African societies belong to an economic order very different from ours. Theirs is mainly a subsistence economy with a rudimentary differentiation of productive labour and with no machinery for the accumulation of wealth in the form of commercial or industrial capital. If wealth is accumulated it takes the form of consumption goods and amenities or is used for the support of additional dependants. Hence it tends to be rapidly dissipated again and does not give rise to permanent class divisions. Distinctions of rank, status, or occupation operate independently of differences of wealth.

Economic privileges, such as rights to tax, tribute, and labour, are both the main reward of political power and an essential means of maintaining it in the political systems of Group A. But there are counterbalancing economic obligations no less strongly backed by institutionalized sanctions. It must not be forgotten, also, that those who derive maximum economic benefit from political office also have the maximum administrative, judicial, and religious responsibilities.

Compared with the societies of Group A, distinctions of rank and status are of minor significance in societies of Group B. Political office carries no economic privileges, though the possession of greater than average wealth may be a criterion of the qualities or status required for political leadership; for in these economically homogeneous, equalitarian, and segmentary societies the attainment of wealth depends either on exceptional personal qualities or accomplishments, or on superior status in the lineage system.

## COMPOSITE POLITICAL SYSTEMS AND THE CONQUEST THEORY

It might be held that societies like the Logoli, Tallensi, and Nuer, without central government or administrative machinery, develop into states like the Ngwato, Zulu, and Banyankole as a result of conquest. Such a development is suggested for the Zulu and Banyankole. But the history of all the peoples treated in this book is not well enough known to enable us to declare with any degree of certainty what course their political development has taken. The problem must therefore be stated in a different way. All the societies of Group A appear to be an amalgam of different peoples, each aware of its unique origin and history, and all except the Zulu and Bemba are still to-day culturally heterogeneous. Cultural diversity is most marked among the Banyankole and Kede, but it is also clear among the Ngwato. We may, therefore, ask to what extent cultural heterogeneity in a society is correlated with an administrative system and central authority. The evidence at our disposal in this book suggests that cultural and economic heterogeneity is associated with a state-like political structure. Centralized authority and an administrative organization seem to be necessary to accommodate culturally diverse groups within a single political system, especially if they have different modes of livelihood. A class or caste system may result if there are great cultural and, especially, great economic divergencies. But centralized forms of government are found also with peoples of homogeneous culture and little economic differentiation like the Zulu. It is possible that groups of diverse culture are the more easily welded into a unitary political system without the emergence of classes the closer they are to one another in culture. A centralized form of government is not necessary to enable different groups of closely related culture and pursuing the same mode of livelihood to amalgamate, nor does it necessarily arise out of the amalgamation. The Nuer have absorbed large numbers of conquered Dinka, who are a pastoral people like themselves with a very similar culture. They have incorporated them by adoption and other ways into their lineage system; but this has not resulted in a class or caste structure or in a centralized form of government. Marked divergencies in culture and economic pursuits are probably incompatible with a segmentary political system such as that of the Nuer or the Tallensi. We have not the data to check this. It is clear, however, that a conquest theory of the primitive state—assuming that the necessary historical evidence is available—must take into account not only the mode of conquest and the conditions of contact, but also the similarities or divergencies in culture and mode of livelihood of conquerors and conquered and the political institutions they bring with them into the new combination.

## THE TERRITORIAL ASPECT

The territorial aspect of early forms of political organization was justly emphasized by Maine in *Ancient Law* and other scholars have given much attention to it. In all the societies described in this book the political system has a territorial framework, but it has a different function in the two types of political organization. The difference is due to the dominance of an administrative and judicial apparatus in one type of system and its absence in the other. In the societies of Group A the administrative unit is a territorial unit; political rights and obligations are territorially delimited. A chief is the administrative and judicial head of a given territorial division, vested often with final economic and legal control over all the land within his boundaries. Everybody living within these boundaries is his subject, and the right to live in this area can be acquired only by accepting the obligations of a subject. The head of the state is a territorial ruler.

In the other group of societies there are no territorial units defined by an administrative system, but the territorial units are local communities the extent of which corresponds to the range of a particular set of lineage ties and the bonds of direct co-operation. Political office does not carry with it juridical rights over a particular, defined stretch of territory and its inhabitants. Membership of the local community, and the rights and duties that go with it, are acquired as a rule through genealogical ties, real or fictional. The lineage principle takes the place of political allegiance, and the interrelations of territorial segments are directly co-ordinated with the interrelations of lineage segments.

Political relations are not simply a reflexion of territorial relations. The political system, in its own right, incorporates territorial relations and invests them with the particular kind of political significance they have.

## THE BALANCE OF FORCES IN THE POLITICAL SYSTEM

A relatively stable political system in Africa presents a balance between conflicting tendencies and between divergent interests. In Group A it is a balance between different parts of the administrative organization. The forces that maintain the supremacy of the paramount ruler are opposed by the forces that act as a check on his powers. Institutions such as the regimental organization of the Zulu, the genealogical restriction of succession to kingship or chiefship, the appointment by the king of his kinsmen to regional chiefships, and the mystical sanctions of his office all reinforce the power of the central authority. But they are counterbalanced by other institutions, like the king's council, sacerdotal officials who have a decisive voice in the king's investiture, queen mothers' courts, and so forth, which work for the protection of law and custom and the control of centralized power. The regional devolution of powers and privileges, necessary on account of difficulties of communication and transport and of other cultural deficiencies, imposes severe restrictions on a king's authority. The balance between central authority and regional autonomy is a very important element in the political structure. If a king abuses his power, subordinate chiefs are liable to secede or to lead a revolt against him. If a subordinate chief seems to be getting too powerful and independent, the central authority will be supported by other subordinate chiefs in suppressing him. A king may try to buttress his authority by playing off rival subordinate chiefs against one another.

It would be a mistake to regard the scheme of constitutional checks and balances and the delegation of power and authority to regional chiefs as nothing more than an administrative device. A general principle of great importance is contained in these arrangements, which has the effect of giving every section and every major interest of the society direct or indirect representation in the conduct of government. Local chiefs represent the central authority in relation to their districts, but they also represent the people under them in relation to the central authority. Councillors and ritual functionaries represent the community's interest in the preservation of law and custom and in the observance of the ritual measures deemed necessary for its well-being. The voice of such functionaries and delegates is effective in the conduct of government on account of the general principle that power and authority are distributed. The king's power and authority are composite. Their various components are lodged in different offices. Without the co-operation of those who hold these offices it is extremely difficult, if not impossible, for the king to obtain his revenue, assert his judicial and legislative supremacy, or retain his secular and ritual prestige. Functionaries vested with essential subsidiary powers and privileges can often sabotage a ruler's acts if they disapprove them.

Looked at from another angle, the government of an African state consists in a balance between power and authority on the one side and obligation and responsibility on the other. Every one who holds political office has responsibilities for the public weal corresponding to his rights and privileges. The distribution of political authority provides a machinery by which the various agents of government can be held to their responsibilities. A chief or a king has the right to exact tax, tribute, and labour service from his subjects; he has the corresponding obligation to dispense

justice to them, to ensure their protection from enemies and to safeguard their general welfare by ritual acts and observances. The structure of an African state implies that kings and chiefs rule by consent. A ruler's subjects are as fully aware of the duties he owes to them as they are of the duties they owe to him, and are able to exert pressure to make him discharge these duties.

We should emphasize here, that we are talking of constitutional arrangements, not of how they work in practice. Africans recognize as clearly as we do that power corrupts and that men are liable to abuse it. In many ways the kind of constitution we find in societies of Group A is cumbrous and too loosely jointed to prevent abuse entirely. The native theory of government is often contradicted by their practice. Both rulers and subjects, actuated by their private interests, infringe the rules of the constitution. Though it usually has a form calculated to hold in check any tendency towards absolute despotism, no African constitution can prevent a ruler from sometimes becoming a tyrant. The history of Shaka is an extreme case, but in this and other instances where the contradiction between theory and practice is too glaring and the infringement of constitutional rules becomes too grave, popular disapproval is sure to follow and may even result in a movement of secession or revolt led by members of the royal family or subordinate chiefs. This is what happened to Shaka.

It should be remembered that in these states there is only one theory of government. In the event of rebellion, the aim, and result, is only to change the personnel of office and never to abolish it or to substitute for it some new form of government. When subordinate chiefs, who are often kinsmen of the king, rebel against him they do so in defence of the values violated by his malpractices. They have an interest greater than any other section of the people in maintaining the kingship. The ideal constitutional pattern remains the valid norm, in spite of breaches of its rules.

A different kind of balance is found in societies of Group B. It is an equilibrium between a number of segments, spatially juxtaposed and structurally equivalent, which are defined in local and lineage, and not in administrative terms. Every segment has the same interests as other segments of a like order. The set of intersegmentary relations that constitutes the political structure is a balance of opposed local loyalties and of divergent lineage and ritual ties. Conflict between the interests of administrative divisions is common in societies like those of Group A. Subordinate chiefs and other political functionaries, whose rivalries are often personal, or due to their relationship to the king or the ruling aristocracy, often exploit these divergent local loyalties for their own ends. But the administrative organization canalizes and provides checks on such inter-regional dissensions. In the societies without an administrative organization, divergence of interests between the component segments is intrinsic to the political structure. Conflicts between local segments necessarily mean conflicts between lineage segments, since the two are closely interlocked; and the stabilizing factor is not a superordinate juridical or military organization, but is simply the sum total of inter-segment relations.

THE INCIDENCE AND FUNCTION OF
ORGANIZED FORCE

In our judgement, the most significant characteristic distinguishing the centralized, pyramidal, state-like forms of government of the Ngwato, Bemba, &c., from the segmentary political systems of the Logoli, the Tallensi, and the Nuer

is the incidence and function of organized force in the system. In the former group of societies, the principal sanction of a ruler's rights and prerogatives, and of the authority exercised by his subordinate chiefs, is the command of organized force. This may enable an African king to rule oppressively for a time, if he is inclined to do so, but a good ruler uses the armed forces under his control in the public interest, as an accepted instrument of government— that is, for the defence of the society as a whole or of any section of it, for offence against a common enemy, and as a coercive sanction to enforce the law or respect for the constitution. The king and his delegates and advisers use organized force with the consent of their subjects to keep going a political system which the latter take for granted as the foundation of their social order.

In societies of Group B there is no association, class, or segment which has a dominant place in the political structure through the command of greater organized force than is at the disposal of any of its congeners. If force is resorted to in a dispute between segments it will be met with equal force. If one segment defeats another it does not attempt to establish political dominance over it; in the absence of an administrative machinery there is, in fact, no means by which it could do so. In the language of political philosophy, there is no individual or group in which sovereignty can be said to rest. In such a system, stability is maintained by an equilibrium at every line of cleavage and every point of divergent interests in the social structure. This balance is sustained by a distribution of the command of force corresponding to the distribution of like, but competitive, interests amongst the homologous segments of the society. Whereas a constituted judicial machinery is possible and is always found in societies of Group A, since it has the backing of organized force, the jural institutions of the Logoli, the Tallensi and the Nuer rest on the right of self-help.

## DIFFERENCES IN RESPONSE TO EUROPEAN RULE

The distinctions we have noted between the two categories into which these eight societies fall, especially in the kind of balance characteristic of each, are very marked in their adjustment to the rule of colonial governments. Most of these societies have been conquered or have submitted to European rule from fear of invasion. They would not acquiesce in it if the threat of force were withdrawn; and this fact determines the part now played in their political life by European administrations.

In the societies of Group A, the paramount ruler is prohibited, by the constraint of the colonial government, from using the organized force at his command on his own responsibility. This has everywhere resulted in diminishing his authority and generally in increasing the power and independence of his subordinates. He no longer rules in his own right, but as the agent of the colonial government. The pyramidal structure of the state is now maintained by the latter's taking his place as paramount. If he capitulates entirely, he may become a mere puppet of the colonial government. He loses the support of his people because the pattern of reciprocal rights and duties which bound him to them is destroyed. Alternatively, he may be able to safeguard his former status, to some extent, by openly or covertly leading the opposition which his people inevitably feel towards alien rule. Very often he is in the equivocal position of having to reconcile his contradictory roles as representative of his people against the colonial government and of the latter

against his people. He becomes the pivot on which the new system swings precariously. Indirect Rule may be regarded as a policy designed to stabilize the new political order, with the native paramount ruler in this dual role, but eliminating the friction it is liable to give rise to.

In the societies of Group B, European rule has had the opposite effect. The colonial government cannot administer through aggregates of individuals composing political segments, but has to employ administrative agents. For this purpose it makes use of any persons who can be assimilated to the stereotyped notion of an African chief. These agents for the first time have the backing of force behind their authority, now, moreover, extending into spheres for which there is no precedent. Direct resort to force in the form of self-help in defence of the rights of individuals or of groups is no longer permitted; for there is now, for the first time, a paramount authority exacting obedience in virtue of superior force which enables it to establish courts of justice to replace self-help. This tends to lead to the whole system of mutually balancing segments collapsing and a bureaucratic European system taking its place. An organization more like that of a centralized state comes into being.

## THE MYSTICAL VALUES ASSOCIATED WITH POLITICAL OFFICE

The sanction of force is not an innovation in African forms of government. We have stressed the fact that it is one of the main pillars of the indigenous type of state. But the sanction of force on which a European administration depends lies outside the native political system. It is not used to maintain the values inherent in that system. In both societies of Group A and those of Group B European governments can impose their authority; in neither are they able to establish moral ties with the subject people. For, as we have seen, in the original native system force is used by a ruler with the consent of his subjects in the interest of the social order.

An African ruler is not to his people merely a person who can enforce his will on them. He is the axis of their political relations, the symbol of their unity and exclusiveness, and the embodiment of their essential values. He is more than a secular ruler; in *that* capacity the European government can to a great extent replace him. His credentials are mystical and are derived from antiquity. Where there are no chiefs, the balanced segments which compose the political structure are vouched for by tradition and myth and their interrelations are guided by values expressed in mystical symbols. Into these sacred precincts the European rulers can never enter. They have no mythical or ritual warranty for their authority.

What is the meaning of this aspect of African political organization? African societies are not models of continuous internal harmony. Acts of violence, oppression, revolt, civil war, and so forth, chequer the history of every African state. In societies like the Logoli, Tallensi, and Nuer the segmentary nature of the social structure is often most strikingly brought to light by armed conflict between the segments. But if the social system has reached a sufficient degree of stability, these internal convulsions do not necessarily wreck it. In fact, they may be the means of reinforcing it, as we have seen, against the abuses and infringements of rulers actuated by their private interests. In the segmentary societies, war is not a matter of one segment enforcing its will on another, but is the way in which segments protect their particular interests within a field of common interests and values.

There are, in every African society,

innumerable ties which counteract the tendencies towards political fission arising out of the tensions and cleavages in the social structure. An administrative organization backed by coercive sanctions, clanship, lineage and age-set ties, the fine-spun web of kinship—all these unite people who have different or even opposed sectional and private interests. Often also there are common material interests such, as the need to share pastures or to trade in a common market-place, or complementary economic pursuits binding different sections to one another. Always there are common ritual values, the ideological superstructure of political organization.

Members of an African society feel their unity and perceive their common interests in symbols, and it is their attachment to these symbols which more than anything else gives their society cohesion and persistence. In the form of myths, fictions, dogmas, ritual, sacred places and persons, these symbols represent the unity and exclusiveness of the groups which respect them. They are regarded, however, not as mere symbols, but as final values in themselves.

To explain these symbols sociologically, they have to be translated into terms of social function and of the social structure which they serve to maintain. Africans have no objective knowledge of the forces determining their social organization and actuating their social behaviour. Yet they would be unable to carry on their collective life if they could not think and feel about the interests which actuate them, the institutions by means of which they organize collective action, and the structure of the groups into which they are organized. Myths, dogmas, ritual beliefs and activities make his social system intellectually tangible and coherent to an African and enable him to think and feel about it. Furthermore, these sacred symbols, which reflect the social system, endow it with mystical values which evoke acceptance of the social order that goes far beyond the obedience exacted by the secular sanction of force. The social system is, as it were, removed to a mystical plane, where it figures as a system of sacred values beyond criticism or revision. Hence people will overthrow a bad king, but the kingship is never questioned; hence the wars or feuds between segments of a society like the Nuer or the Tallensi are kept within bounds by mystical sanctions. These values are common to the whole society, to rulers and ruled alike and to all the segments and sections of a society.

The African does not see beyond the symbols; it might well be held that if he understood their objective meaning, they would lose the power they have over him. This power lies in their symbolic content, and in their association with the nodal institutions of the social structure, such as the kingship. Not every kind of ritual or any sort of mystical ideas can express the values that hold a society together and focus the loyalty and devotion of its members on their rulers. If we study the mystical values bound up with the kingship in any of the societies of Group A, we find that they refer to fertility, health, prosperity, peace, justice—to everything, in short, which gives life and happiness to a people. The African sees these ritual observances as the supreme safeguard of the basic needs of his existence and of the basic relations that make up his social order—land, cattle, rain, bodily health, the family, the clan, the state. The mystical values reflect the general import of the basic elements of existence: the land as the source of the whole people's livelihood, physical health as something universally desired, the family as the fundamental procreative unit, and so forth. These are the common interests of the whole society, as the native sees them. These are the

themes of taboos, observances and ceremonies in which, in societies of Group A, the whole people has a share through its representatives, and in societies of Group B all the segments participate, since they are matters of equal moment to all.

We have stressed the fact that the universal aspect of things like land or fertility are the subjects of common interest in an African society; for these matters also have another side to them, as the private interests of individuals and segments of a society. The productivity of his own land, the welfare and security of his own family or his own clan, such matters are of daily, practical concern to every member of an African society; and over such matters arise the conflicts between sections and factions of the society. Thus the basic needs of existence and the basic social relations are, in their pragmatic and utilitarian aspects, as sources of immediate satisfactions and strivings, the subjects of private interests; as common interests, they are non-utilitarian and nonpragmatic, matters of moral value and ideological significance. The common interests spring from those very private interests to which they stand in opposition.

To explain the ritual aspect of African political organization in terms of magical mentality is not enough; and it does not take us far to say that land, rain, fertility, &c., are 'sacralized' because they are the most vital needs of the community. Such arguments do not explain why the great ceremonies in which ritual for the common good is performed are usually on a public scale. They do not explain why the ritual functions we have been describing should be bound up, always, with pivotal political offices and should be part of the political theory of an organized society.

Again, it is not enough to dismiss these ritual functions of chiefship, kingship, &c., by calling them sanctions of political authority. Why, then, are they regarded as among the most stringent responsibilities of office? Why are they so often distributed amongst a number of independent functionaries who are thus enabled to exercise a balancing constraint on one another? It is clear that they serve, also, as a sanction against the abuse of political power and as a means of constraining political functionaries to perform their administrative obligations as well as their religious duties, lest the common good suffer injury.

When, finally, it is stated as an observable descriptive fact that we are dealing here with institutions that serve to affirm and promote political solidarity we must ask why they do so. Why is an all-embracing administrative machinery or a wide-flung lineage system insufficient by itself to achieve this?

We cannot attempt to deal at length with all these questions. We have already given overmuch space to them because we consider them to be of the utmost importance, both from the theoretical and the practical point of view. The 'supernatural' aspects of African government are always puzzling and often exasperating to the European administrator. But a great deal more of research is needed before we shall be able to understand them fully. The hypothesis we are making use of is, we feel, a stimulating starting-point for further research into these matters. That part of it which has already been stated is, perhaps, least controversial. But it is incomplete.

Any item of social behaviour, and therefore any political relation, has a utilitarian or pragmatic content. It means that material goods change hands, are disbursed or acquired, and that the direct purposes of individuals are achieved. Items of social behaviour and therefore political relations have also a

moral aspect; that is, they express rights and duties, privileges and obligations, political sentiments, social ties and cleavages. We see these two aspects clearly in such acts as paying tribute to a ruler or handing over blood-cattle in compensation for murder. In political relations, consequently, we find two types of interests working conjointly, material interests and moral interests, though they are not separated in this abstract way in native thought. Natives stress the material components of a political relation and generally state it in terms of its utilitarian and pragmatic functions.

A particular right or duty or political sentiment occurs as an item of behaviour of an individual or a small section of an African society and is enforceable by secular sanctions brought to bear on these individuals or small sections. But in a politically organized community a particular right, duty, or sentiment exists only as an element in a whole body of common, reciprocal, and mutually balancing rights, duties, and sentiments, the body of moral and legal norms. Upon the regularity and order with which this whole body of interwoven norms is maintained depends the stability and continuity of the structure of an African society. On the average, rights must be respected, duties performed, the sentiments binding the members together upheld or else the social order would be so insecure that the material needs of existence could no longer be satisfied. Productive labour would come to a standstill and the society disintegrate. This is the greatest common interest in any African society, and it is this interest which the political system, viewed in its entirety, subserves. This, too, is the ultimate and, we might say, axiomatic set of premises of the social order. If they were continually and arbitrarily violated, the social system would cease to work.

We can sum up this analysis by saying that the material interests that actuate individuals or groups in an African society operate in the frame of a body of interconnected moral and legal norms the order and stability of which is maintained by the political organization. Africans, as we have pointed out, do not analyse their social system; they live it. They think and feel about it in terms of values which reflect, in doctrine and symbol, but do not explain, the forces that really control their social behaviour. Outstanding among these values are the mystical values dramatized in the great public ceremonies and bound up with their key political institutions. These, we believe, stand for the greatest common interest of the widest political community to which a member of a particular African society belongs—that is, for the whole body of interconnected rights, duties, and sentiments; for this is what makes the society a single political community. That is why these mystical values are always associated with pivotal political offices and are expressed in both the privileges and the obligations of political office.

Their mystical form is due to the ultimate and axiomatic character of the body of moral and legal norms which could not be kept in being, as a body, by secular sanctions. Periodical ceremonies are necessary to affirm and consolidate these values because, in the ordinary course of events, people are preoccupied with sectional and private interests and are apt to lose sight of the common interest and of their political interdependence. Lastly, their symbolic content reflects the basic needs of existence and the basic social relations because these are the most concrete and tangible elements of all social and political relations. The visible test of how well a given body of rights, duties, and sentiments is being maintained and is working is to be found in the level of security and success with which the basic needs of existence are satisfied and the basic social relations sustained.

It is an interesting fact that under European rule African kings retain their 'ritual functions' long after most of the secular authority which these are said to sanction is lost. Nor are the mystical values of political office entirely obliterated by a change of religion to Christianity or Islam. As long as the kingship endures as the axis of a body of moral and legal norms holding a people together in a political community, it will, most probably, continue to be the focus of mystical values.

It is easy to see a connexion between kingship and the interests and solidarity of the whole community in a state with highly centralized authority. In societies lacking centralized government, social values cannot be symbolized by a single person, but are distributed at cardinal points of the social structure. Here we find myths, dogmas, ritual ceremonies, mystical powers, &c., associated with segments and defining and serving to maintain the relationship between them. Periodic ceremonies emphasizing the solidarity of segments, and between segments, as against sectional interests within these groups, are the rule among the Tallensi and Logoli no less than among the Bemba and Kede. Among the Nuer, the leopard-skin chief, a sacred personage associated with the fertility of the earth, is the medium through whom feuds are settled and, hence, inter-segment relations regulated. The difference between these societies of Group B and those of Group A lies in the fact that there is no person who represents the political unity of the people, such unity being lacking, and there may be no person who represents the unity of segments of the people. Ritual powers and responsibility are distributed in conformity with the highly segmentary structure of the society.

## THE PROBLEM OF THE LIMITS OF
## THE POLITICAL GROUP

We conclude by emphasizing two points of very great importance which are often overlooked. However one may define political units or groups, they cannot be treated in isolation, for they always form part of a larger social system. Thus, to take an extreme example, the localized lineages of the Tallensi overlap one another like a series of intersecting circles, so that it is impossible to state clearly where the lines of political cleavage run. These overlapping fields of political relations stretch almost indefinitely, so that there is a kind of interlocking even of neighbouring peoples, and while we can see that this people is distinct from that, it is not easy to say at what point, culturally or politically, one is justified in regarding them as distinct units. Among the Nuer, political demarcation is simpler, but even here there is, between segments of a political unit, the same kind of structural relationship as there is between this unit and another unit of the same order. Hence the designation of autonomous political groups is always to some extent an arbitrary matter. This is more noticeable among the societies of Group B, but among those of Group A also there is an interdependence between the political group described and neighbouring political groups and a certain overlapping between them. The Ngwato have a segmentary relationship to other Tswana tribes which in many respects is of the same order as that between divisions of the Ngwato themselves. The same is true of the other societies with centralized governments.

This overlapping and interlocking of societies is largely due to the fact that the point at which political relations, narrowly defined in terms of military action and legal sanctions, end is not the point at which all social relations cease. The social structure of a people stretches beyond their political system, so defined, for there are always social relations of one kind or another between peoples of different autonomous political groups. Clans, age-sets, ritual associations, relations of affinity and of trade, and social relations of other kinds unite people of different political units. Common language or closely related languages, similar customs and beliefs, and so on, also unite them. Hence a strong feeling of community may exist between groups which do not acknowledge a single ruler or unite for specific political purposes. Community of language and culture, as we have indicated, does not necessarily give rise to political unity, any more than linguistic and cultural dissimilarity prevents political unity.

Herein lies a problem of world importance: what is the relation of political structure to the whole social structure? Everywhere in Africa social ties of one kind or another tend to draw together peoples who are politically separated and political ties appear to be dominant whenever there is conflict between them and other social ties. The solution of this problem would seem to lie in a more detailed investigation of the nature of political values and of the symbols in which they are expressed. Bonds of utilitarian interest between individuals and between groups are not as strong as the bonds implied in common attachment to mystical symbols. It is precisely the greater solidarity, based on these bonds, which generally gives political groups their dominance over social groups of other kinds.

# AUTHORITY AND LEGITIMACY

MAX WEBER

'Imperative co-ordination' was defined [above] as the probability that certain specific commands (or all commands) from a given source will be obeyed by a given group of persons. It thus does not include every mode of exercising 'power' or 'influence' over other persons. The motives of obedience to commands in this sense can rest on considerations varying over a wide range from case to case; all the way from simple habituation to the most purely rational calculation of advantage. A criterion of every true relation of imperative control, however, is a certain minimum of voluntary submission; thus an interest (based on ulterior motives or genuine acceptance) in obedience.

Not every case of imperative co-ordination makes use of economic means; *still less* does it always have economic objectives. But normally (not always) the imperative co-ordination of the action of a considerable number of men requires control of a staff of persons. It is necessary, that is, that there should be a relatively high probability that the action of a definite, supposedly reliable group of persons will be primarily oriented to the execution of the supreme authority's general policy and specific commands.

The members of the administrative staff may be bound to obedience to their superior (or superiors) by custom, by affectual ties, by a purely material complex of interests, or by ideal (*wertrational*) motives. *Purely* material interests and calculations of advantage as the basis of solidarity between the chief and his administrative staff result, in this as in other connexions, in a relatively unstable situation. Normally other elements, affectual and ideal, supplement such interests. In certain exceptional, temporary cases the former may be alone decisive. In everyday routine life these relationships, like others, are governed by custom and in addition, material calculation of advantage. But these factors, custom and personal advantage, purely affectual or ideal motives of solidarity, do not, even taken together, form a sufficiently reliable basis for a system of imperative co-ordination. In addition there is normally a further element, the belief in legitimacy.

It is an induction from experience that no system of authority voluntarily limits itself to the appeal to material or affectual or ideal motives as a basis for guaranteeing its continuance. In addition every such system attempts to establish and to cultivate the belief in its 'legitimacy.' But according to the kind of legitimacy which is claimed, the type of obedience, the kind of administrative staff developed to guarantee it, and the mode of exercising authority, will all differ fundamentally. Equally fundamental is the variation in effect. Hence, it is useful to classify the types of authority according to the kind of claim to legitimacy typically made by each.

. . .

Reprinted from *Max Weber*, THE THEORY OF SOCIAL AND ECONOMIC ORGANIZATION *(New York: The Free Press, 1947), pp. 324–33, 341–45, 358–63, by permission of The Macmillan Co.*

*The Three Pure Types of
Legitimate Authority*

There are three pure types of legitimate authority. The validity of their claims to legitimacy may be based on:

1. Rational grounds—resting on a belief in the 'legality' of patterns of normative rules and the right of those elevated to authority under such rules to issue commands (legal authority).

2. Traditional grounds—resting on an established belief in the sanctity of immemorial traditions and the legitimacy of the status of those exercising authority under them (traditional authority); or finally,

3. Charismatic grounds—resting on devotion to the specific and exceptional sanctity, heroism or exemplary character of an individual person, and of the normative patterns or order revealed or ordained by him (charismatic authority).

In the case of legal authority, obedience is owed to the legally established impersonal order. It extends to the persons exercising the authority of office under it only by virtue of the formal legality of their commands and only within the scope of authority of the office. In the case of traditional authority, obedience is owed to the *person* of the chief who occupies the traditionally sanctioned position of authority and who is (within its sphere) bound by tradition. But here the obligation of obedience is not based on the impersonal order, but is a matter of personal loyalty within the area of accustomed obligations. In the case of charismatic authority, it is the charismatically qualified leader as such who is obeyed by virtue of personal trust in him and his revelation, his heroism or his exemplary qualities so far as they fall within the scope of the individual's belief in his charisma.

.  .  .

1. LEGAL AUTHORITY WITH A
BUREAUCRATIC ADMINISTRATIVE
STAFF

The effectiveness of legal authority rests on the acceptance of the validity of the following mutually inter-dependent ideas.

1. That any given legal norm may be established by agreement or by imposition, on grounds of expediency or rational values or both, with a claim to obedience at least on the part of the members of the corporate group. This is, however, usually extended to include all persons within the sphere of authority or of power in question—which in the case of territorial bodies is the territorial area—who stand in certain social relationships or carry out forms of social action which in the order governing the corporate group have been declared to be relevant.

2. That every body of law consists essentially in a consistent system of abstract rules which have normally been intentionally established. Furthermore, administration of law is held to consist in the application of these rules to particular cases; the administrative process in the rational pursuit of the interests which are specified in the order governing the corporate group within the limits laid down by legal precepts and following principles which are capable of generalized formulation and are approved in the order governing the group, or at least not disapproved in it.

3. That thus the typical person in authority occupies an 'office.' In the action associated with his status, including the commands he issues to others, he is subject to an impersonal order to which his actions are oriented. This is true not only for persons exercising legal authority who are in the usual sense 'officials,' but, for instance, for the elected president of a state.

4. That the person who obeys authority does so, as it is usually stated, only in his capacity as a 'member' of the corporate group and what he obeys is only 'the law.' He may in this connexion be the member of an association, of a territorial commune, of a church, or a citizen of a state.

5. In conformity with point 3, it is held that the members of the corporate group, in so far as they obey a person in authority, do not owe this obedience to him as an individual, but to the impersonal order. Hence, it follows that there is an obligation to obedience only within the sphere of the rationally delimited authority which, in terms of the order, has been conferred upon him.

The following may thus be said to be the fundamental categories of rational legal authority:—

(1) A continuous organization of official functions bound by rules.

(2) A specified sphere of competence. This involves (a) a sphere of obligations to perform functions which has been marked off as part of a systematic division of labour. (b) The provision of the incumbent with the necessary authority to carry out these functions. (c) That the necessary means of compulsion are clearly defined and their use is subject to definite conditions. A unit exercising authority which is organized in this way will be called an 'administrative organ.'

There are administrative organs in this sense in large-scale private organizations, in parties and armies, as well as in the state and the church. An elected president, a cabinet of ministers, or a body of elected representatives also in this sense constitute administrative organs. This is not, however, the place to discuss these concepts. Not every administrative organ is provided with compulsory powers. But this distinction is not important for present purposes.

(3) The organization of offices follows the principle of hierarchy; that is, each lower office is under the control and supervision of a higher one. There is a right of appeal and of statement of grievances from the lower to the higher. Hierarchies differ in respect to whether and in what cases complaints can lead to a ruling from an authority at various points higher in the scale, and as to whether changes are imposed from higher up or the responsibility for such changes is left to the lower office, the conduct of which was the subject of complaint.

(4) The rules which regulate the conduct of an office may be technical rules or norms. In both cases, if their application is to be fully rational, specialized training is necessary. It is thus normally true that only a person who has demonstrated an adequate technical training is qualified to be a member of the administrative staff of such an organized group, and hence only such persons are eligible for appointment to official positions. The administrative staff of a rational corporate group thus typically consists of 'officials,' whether the organization be devoted to political, religious, economic—in particular, capitalistic—or other ends.

(5) In the rational type it is a matter of principle that the members of the administrative staff should be completely separated from ownership of the means of production or administration. Officials, employees, and workers attached to the administrative staff do not themselves own the non-human means of production and administration. These are rather provided for their use in kind or in money, and the official is obligated to render an accounting of their use. There exists, furthermore, in principle complete separation of the property belonging to the organization, which is controlled within the sphere of office,

and the personal property of the official, which is available for his own private uses. There is a corresponding separation of the place in which official functions are carried out, the 'office' in the sense of premises, from living quarters.

(6) In the rational type case, there is also a complete absence of appropriation of his official position by the incumbent. Where 'rights' to an office exist, as in the case of judges, and recently of an increasing proportion of officials and even of workers, they do not normally serve the purpose of appropriation by the official, but of securing the purely objective and independent character of the conduct of the office so that it is oriented only to the relevant norms.

(7) Administrative acts, decisions, and rules are formulated and recorded in writing, even in cases where oral discussion is the rule or is even mandatory. This applies at least to preliminary discussions and proposals, to final decisions, and to all sorts of orders and rules. The combination of written documents and a continuous organization of official functions constitutes the 'office' which is the central focus of all types of modern corporate action.

(8) Bureaucratic administration means fundamentally the exercise of control on the basis of knowledge. This is the feature of it which makes it specifically rational. This consists on the one hand in technical knowledge which, by itself, is sufficient to ensure it a position of extraordinary power. But in addition to this, bureaucratic organizations, or the holders of power who make use of them, have the tendency to increase their power still further by the knowledge growing out of experience in the service. For they acquire through the conduct of office a special knowledge of facts and have available a store of documentary material peculiar to themselves. While not peculiar to bureaucratic organizations, the concept of 'official secrets' is certainly typical of them. It stands in relation to technical knowledge in somewhat the same position as commercial secrets do to technological training. It is a product of the striving for power.

Bureaucracy is superior in knowledge, including both technical knowledge and knowledge of the concrete fact within its own sphere of interest, which is usually confined to the interests of a private business—a capitalistic enterprise. The capitalistic entrepreneur is, in our society, the only type who has been able to maintain at least relative immunity from subjection to the control of rational bureaucratic knowledge. All the rest of the population have tended to be organized in large-scale corporate groups which are inevitably subject to bureaucratic control. This is as inevitable as the dominance of precision machinery in the mass production of goods.

## 2. TRADITIONAL AUTHORITY

A system of imperative co-ordination will be called 'traditional' if legitimacy is claimed for it and believed in on the basis of the sanctity of the order and the attendant powers of control as they have been handed down from the past, 'have always existed.' The person or persons exercising authority are designated according to traditionally transmitted rules. The object of obedience is the personal authority of the individual which he enjoys by virtue of his traditional status. The organized group exercising authority is, in the simplest case, primarily based on relations of personal loyalty, cultivated through a common process of education. The person exercising authority is not a 'superior,' but a personal 'chief.'

His administrative staff does not consist primarily of officials, but of personal retainers. Those subject to authority are not 'members' of an association, but are either his traditional 'comrades' or his 'subjects.' What determines the relations of the administrative staff to the chief is not the impersonal obligation of office, but personal loyalty to the chief.

Obedience is not owed to enacted rules, but to the person who occupies a position of authority by tradition or who has been chosen for such a position on a traditional basis. His commands are legitimized in one of two ways: (a) partly in terms of traditions which themselves directly determine the content of the command and the objects and extent of authority. In so far as this is true, to overstep the traditional limitations would endanger his traditional status by undermining acceptance of his legitimacy. (b) In part, it is a matter of the chief's free personal decision, in that tradition leaves a certain sphere open for this. This sphere of traditional prerogative rests primarily on the fact that the obligations of obedience on the basis of personal loyalty are essentially unlimited. There is thus a double sphere: on the one hand, of action which is bound to specific tradition; on the other hand, of that which is free of any specific rules.

In the latter sphere, the chief is free to confer 'grace' on the basis of his personal pleasure or displeasure, his personal likes and dislikes, quite arbitrarily, particularly in return for gifts which often become a source of regular income. So far as his action follows principles at all, these are principles of substantive ethical common sense, of justice, or of utilitarian expediency. They are not, however, as in the case of legal authority, formal principles. The exercise of authority is normally oriented to the question of what the chief and his administrative staff will normally permit, in view of the traditional obedience of the subjects and what will or will not arouse their resistance. When resistance occurs, it is

directed against the person of the chief or of a member of his staff. The accusation is that he has failed to observe the traditional limits of his authority. Opposition is not directed against the system as such.

It is impossible in the pure type of traditional authority for law or administrative rules to be deliberately created by legislation. What is actually new is thus claimed to have always been in force but only recently to have become known through the wisdom of the promulgator. The only documents which can play a part in the orientation of legal administration are the documents of tradition; namely, precedents.

A traditional chief exercises authority with or without an administrative staff. The typical administrative staff is recruited from one or more of the following sources:

(a) From persons who are already related to the chief by traditional ties of personal loyalty. This will be called 'patrimonial' recruitment. Such persons may be kinsmen, slaves, dependents who are officers of the household, clients, coloni, or freedmen.

(b) It may be recruited from other sources on an 'extra-patrimonial' basis. This category includes people in a relation of purely personal loyalty, such as all sorts of 'favourites,' people standing in a relation of fealty to their chief—'vassals'—and, finally, those who have of their own free will entered into a relation of personal loyalty as officials.

. . .

In the pure type of traditional authority, the following features of a bureaucratic administrative staff are absent: (a) a clearly defined sphere of competence subject to impersonal rules, (b) a rational ordering of relations of superiority and inferiority, (c) a regular system of appointment and promotion on the basis of free contract, (d) technical training as a regular requirement,

(e) fixed salaries, in the type case paid in money.

In place of a well-defined impersonal sphere of competence, there is a shifting series of tasks and powers commissioned and granted by a chief through his arbitrary decision of the moment. They then tend to become permanent and are often traditionally stereotyped. An important influence is exerted by competition for sources of income and advantage which are at the disposal of the persons acting on behalf of the chief or of the chief himself. It is often in the first instance through these interests that definite functional spheres are first marked off and, with them, genuine administrative organs.

In the first instance, those with permanent functions are household officials of the chief. Their functions outside the administration of the household itself are often in fields of activity which bear a relatively superficial analogy to their household function, or even which have originated in a completely arbitrary act of the chief, and have later become traditionally stereotyped. In addition to household officers, there have existed primarily only persons with *ad hoc* specific commissions.

The absence of clear spheres of competence is clearly evident from a perusal of the list of the titles of officials in any of the Ancient Oriental states. With rare exceptions, it is impossible to associate with these titles a set of functions rationally delimited in the modern Western sense which has remained stable over a considerable period.

The process of defining permanent functions in terms of competition among and compromise between interests seeking favours, income, and other forms of advantage is especially clearly evident in the Middle Ages. This phenomenon has had very important consequences. The interests in fees of the powerful Royal courts and of the powerful legal profession in England was largely responsible, partly for breaking the influence of Roman and Canon law, partly for limiting it. Existing irrational divisions of official functions have frequently in all periods been stereotyped by the existence of an established set of rights to fees and perquisites.

In contrast to the rational hierarchy of authority in the bureaucratic system, the question who shall decide a matter—which of his officials or the chief himself—or who shall deal with complaints, is, in a traditional regime, treated in one of two ways. (1) Traditionally, on the basis of the authority of particular received legal norms or precedents. (2) Entirely on the basis of the arbitrary decision of the chief. Whenever he intervenes personally, all others give way to him.

·  ·  ·

As opposed to the bureaucratic system of free appointment, household officials and favourites are very often recruited on a purely patrimonial basis from among the slaves or serfs of the chief. If, on the other hand, the recruitment has been extra-patrimonial, they have tended to be holders of benefices which he has granted as an act of grace without being bound by any formal rules. A fundamental change in this situation is first brought about by the rise of free vassals and the filling of offices by a contract of fealty. Since, however, such relations of fealty have been by no means primarily determined by considerations of objective function, this has not altered the situation with respect to definite spheres of competence or clearly determined hierarchical relationships. Except under certain circumstances when the administrative staff is organized on a basis of prebends, there is such a thing as 'promotion' only according to the arbitrary grace of the chief.

Rational technical training as a basic

qualification for office is scarcely to be found at all among household officials or the favourites of a chief. Where there is even a beginning of technical training for appointees, regardless of what it consists in, this fact everywhere makes for a fundamental change in the development of administrative practice.

For many offices a certain amount of empirical training has been necessary from very early times. This is particularly true of the 'art' of reading and writing which was originally truly an art with a high scarcity value. This has often, most strikingly in China, had a decisive influence on the whole development of culture through the mode of life of persons with a literary education. Among other things, it has eliminated the recruiting of officials from intrapatrimonial sources and has thus limited the power of the chief by making him dependent on a definite social group.

In place of regular salaries, household officials and favourites are usually supported and equipped in the household of the chief and from his personal stores. Generally, their exclusion from the lord's own table means the creation of benefices, at first usually benefices in kind. It is easy for these to become traditionally stereotyped in amount and kind. Along with the elements supported by benefices or in place of them, there are various agencies commissioned by the lord outside his own household, as well as various fees which are due him. The latter are often collected without any regular rate or scale, being agreed upon from case to case with those seeking favours.

· · ·

## 3. CHARISMATIC AUTHORITY

The term 'charisma' will be applied to a certain quality of an individual personality by virtue of which he is set apart from ordinary men and treated as endowed with supernatural, super-human, or at least specifically exceptional powers or qualities. These are such as are not accessible to the ordinary person, but are regarded as of divine origin or as exemplary, and on the basis of them the individual concerned is treated as a leader. In primitive circumstances this peculiar kind of deference is paid to prophets, to people with a reputation for therapeutic or legal wisdom, to leaders in the hunt, and heroes in war. It is very often thought of as resting on magical powers. How the quality in question would be ultimately judged from any ethical, aesthetic, or other such point of view is naturally entirely indifferent for purposes of definition. What is alone important is how the individual is actually regarded by those subject to charismatic authority, by his 'followers' or 'disciples.'

· · ·

1. It is recognition on the part of those subject to authority which is decisive for the validity of charisma. This is freely given and guaranteed by what is held to be a 'sign' or proof, originally always a miracle, and consists in devotion to the corresponding revelation, hero worship, or absolute trust in the leader. But where charisma is genuine, it is not this which is the basis of the claim to legitimacy. This basis lies rather in the conception that it is the *duty* of those who have been called to a charismatic mission to recognize its quality and to act accordingly. Psychologically this 'recognition' is a matter of complete personal devotion to the possessor of the quality, arising out of enthusiasm, or of despair and hope.

No prophet has ever regarded his quality as dependent on the attitudes of the masses toward him. No elective king or military leader has ever treated those who have resisted him or tried to ignore him otherwise than as delinquent in duty. Failure to take part in a military expedition under such leader, even though recruitment is formally voluntary, has universally been met with disdain.

2. If proof of his charismatic qualification fails him for long, the leader endowed with charisma tends to think his god or his magical or heroic powers have deserted him. If he is for long unsuccessful, above all if his leadership fails to benefit his followers, it is likely that his charismatic authority will disappear. This is the genuine charismatic meaning of the 'gift of grace.'

Even the old Germanic kings were sometimes rejected with scorn. Similar phenomena are very common among so-called 'primitive' peoples. In China the charismatic quality of the monarch, which was transmitted unchanged by heredity, was upheld so rigidly that any misfortune whatever, not only defeats in war, but drought, floods, or astronomical phenomena which were considered unlucky, forced him to do public penance and might even force his abdication. If such things occurred, it was a sign that he did not possess the requisite charismatic virtue, he was thus not a legitimate 'Son of Heaven.'

3. The corporate group which is subject to charismatic authority is based on an emotional form of communal relationship. The administrative staff of a charismatic leader does not consist of 'officials'; at least its members are not technically trained. It is not chosen on the basis of social privilege nor from the point of view of domestic or personal dependency. It is rather chosen in terms of the charismatic qualities of its members. The prophet has his disciples; the war lord his selected henchmen; the leader, generally, his followers. There is no such thing as 'appointment' or 'dismissal,' no career, no promotion. There is only a 'call' at the instance of the leader on the basis of the charismatic qualification of those he summons. There is no hierarchy; the leader merely

intervenes in general or in individual cases when he considers the members of his staff inadequate to a task with which they have been entrusted. There is no such thing as a definite sphere of authority and of competence, and no appropriation of official powers on the basis of social privileges. There may, however, be territorial or functional limits to charismatic powers and to the individual's 'mission.' There is no such thing as a salary or a benefice. Disciples or followers tend to live primarily in a communistic relationship with their leader on means which have been provided by voluntary gift. There are no established administrative organs. In their place are agents who have been provided with charismatic authority by their chief or who possess charisma of their own. There is no system of formal rules, of abstract legal principles, and hence no process of judicial decision oriented to them. But equally there is no legal wisdom oriented to judicial precedent. Formally concrete judgments are newly created from case to case and are originally regarded as divine judgments and revelations. From a substantive point of view, every charismatic authority would have to subscribe to the proposition, 'It is written..., but I say unto you...' The genuine prophet, like the genuine military leader and every true leader in this sense, preaches, creates, or demands *new* obligations. In the pure type of charisma, these are imposed on the authority of revelation by oracles, or of the leader's own will, and are recognized by the members of the religious, military, or party group, because they come from such a source. Recognition is a duty. When such an authority comes into conflict with the competing authority of another who also claims charismatic sanction, the only recourse is to some kind of a contest, by magical means or even an actual physical battle of the leaders. In principle, only one side can be in the right in such a conflict; the other must be guilty of a wrong which has to be expiated.

Charismatic authority is thus specifically outside the realm of everyday routine and the profane sphere. In this respect, it is sharply opposed both to rational, and particularly bureaucratic, authority, and to traditional authority, whether in its patriarchal, patrimonial, or any other form. Both rational and traditional authority are specifically forms of everyday routine control of action; while the charismatic type is the direct antithesis of this. Bureaucratic authority is specifically rational in the sense of being bound to intellectually analysable rules; while charismatic authority is specifically irrational in the sense of being foreign to all rules. Traditional authority is bound to the precedents handed down from the past and to this extent is also oriented to rules. Within the sphere of its claims, charismatic authority repudiates the past, and is in this sense a specifically revolutionary force. It recognizes no appropriation of positions of power by virtue of the possession of property, either on the part of a chief or of socially privileged groups. The only basis of legitimacy for it is personal charisma, so long as it is proved; that is, as long as it receives recognition and is able to satisfy the followers or disciples. But this lasts only so long as the belief in its charismatic inspiration remains.

The above is scarcely in need of further discussion. What has been said applies to the position of authority of such elected monarchs as Napoleon, with his use of the plebiscite. It applies to the 'rule of genius,' which has elevated people of humble origin to thrones and high military commands, just as much as it applies to religious prophets or war heroes.

4. Pure charisma is specifically foreign to economic considerations. Whenever it appears, it constitutes a 'call' in the most emphatic sense of the word, a 'mission' or a 'spiritual duty.' In the pure type, it disdains and repudiates economic exploitation of the gifts of grace as a source of income, though, to be sure, this often remains more an ideal than a fact. It is not that charisma always means the renunciation of property or even of acquisition, as under certain circumstances prophets and their disciples do. The heroic warrior and his followers actively seek 'booty'; the elective ruler or the charismatic party leader requires the material means of power. The former in addition requires a brilliant display of his authority to bolster his prestige. What is despised, so long as the genuinely charismatic type is adhered to, is traditional or rational everyday economizing, the attainment of a regular income by continuous economic activity devoted to this end. Support by gifts, sometimes on a grand scale involving foundations, even by bribery and grand-scale honoraria, or by begging, constitute the strictly voluntary type of support. On the other hand, 'booty,' or coercion, whether by force or by other means, is the other typical form of charismatic provision for needs. From the point of view of rational economic activity, charisma is a typical anti-economic force. It repudiates any sort of involvement in the everyday routine world. It can only tolerate, with an attitude of complete emotional indifference, irregular, unsystematic, acquisitive acts. In that it relieves the recipient of economic concerns, dependence on property income can be the economic basis of a charismatic mode of life for some groups; but that is not usually acceptable for the normal charismatic 'revolutionary.'

. . .

5. In traditionally stereotyped peri-

ods, charisma is the greatest revolutionary force. The equally revolutionary force of 'reason' works from without by altering the situations of action, and hence its problems, finally in this way changing men's attitudes toward them; or it intellectualizes the individual. Charisma, on the other hand, may involve a subjective or internal reorientation born out of suffering, conflicts, or enthusiasm. It may then result in a radical alteration of the central system of attitudes and directions of action with a completely new orientation of all attitudes toward the different problems and structures of the 'world.' In prerationalistic periods, tradition and charisma between them have almost exhausted the whole of the orientation of action.

## B. Social Stratification and Class Conflict

# SOCIAL STRATIFICATION: CASTE, ESTATE AND CLASS

T. H. MARSHALL

There are, and have been, many different kinds of stratification in human societies, and there is fairly general agreement among sociologists that they can usefully be classified into three main types: Caste, Estate, and Class.

The most perfect example of Caste is found in India—not in our present age, but at that point in the past when the caste system was at its height. Its principal characteristics can be briefly summarized. Marriage takes place between members of the same caste, and the children belong to the caste of their parents; these are the principles of endogamy and heredity. Membership is normally lifelong; there is, in other words, practically no social mobility.

Caste members are united by distinctive social customs and separated from other castes by rules limiting contact or enjoining avoidance. These include the restrictions on intermarriage, and also limitations on eating together, accepting food and drink from, and even (in some cases) coming into close proximity with members of other castes. These are the outward expressions of social distance. Castes form a hierarchy, being arranged in an order of superiority and inferiority, which is associated with ideas of purity and impurity. Each caste, also, is linked with a limited range of permitted occupations (in some cases with one only), and the classification of occupations also brings in the idea of purity and impurity, especially at the extremes of the scale. The prestige order of castes is not based on wealth.

Clearly this is a very rigid system. It is also one which penetrates deeply into the lives of the members of society. There is no room for any other principle of stratification or social ranking to exist side by side with it or to challenge its supremacy. If the caste system is in full vigour, caste membership is an indisputable and unalterable fact by which a man's position in the social structure is wholly determined. And, in addition to this, the system as a whole is not regarded as something freely invented and constructed by man, which may be changed by him or which can be made different by the spread of different ideas. The basic beliefs are upheld, not because they are traditional, but because they are true. As a modern authority says: 'The general Hindu feeling about the caste system is that it has been "established by divine ordinance" or at least with divine approval.'[1] It is rooted in the divine plan and in the nature of man and the universe. This is clearly seen in the doctrine of *Karma*, according to which 'a man's condition in this life is the result of his conduct in his last incarnation; his high or low caste is therefore the reward or punishment of his past behaviour', that is, of his behaviour in a previous life on earth.[2]

The Estate system, too, is marked by rigidity, but less complete and of a different kind. It is more difficult to find a perfect example of an estate system, but its principles can be recognized in the middle period of feudalism and the aristocratic societies of Europe in the seventeenth and eighteenth centuries. An estate may be defined as a group of people having the same status, in the sense in which that word is used by lawyers. A status in this sense is a position to which is attached a bundle of rights and duties, privileges and obligations, legal capacities or incapacities, which are publicly recognized and which can be defined and enforced by public

authority and in many cases by courts of law. The word is today so widely used by sociologists with a broader and less exact meaning[3] that, in order to avoid confusion, it is best to speak of 'legal status' when we refer to status in its original sense—the sense which has just been roughly defined above. We must add, also, that many legal statuses have little to do with stratification, for instance such statuses as those of minor, doctor, innkeeper or married woman. We are concerned here only with those which distinguish a social stratum or at least a substantial part of one.

The most important status distinction of this kind in medieval society was that between the free and the unfree. We may say that the serfs constituted an estate because their legal status was marked by a lack of rights, especially the right to personal liberty and the right to own property. We may also say that in England the greater barons who established their claim to be personally summoned to the King's Council, and who developed into the hereditary peerage sitting in the House of Lords, had a distinctive legal status. In pre-revolutionary France the nobility were distinguished, not only by the use of titles, but also by the enjoyment of certain legally recognized rights or privileges affecting in particular taxation and landholding, and by separate representation as an estate in the national assembly. We can also recognize the power of the estate system in Germany, where 'members of different estates could not intermarry at all, and later could at best enter into no marriage of full effect', and where 'military [knightly] life, civic industry and rustic field work were mutually exclusive occupations in the law of status.'[4]

Castes, as we saw, were endogamous and hereditary. Endogamy within estates

---

[1] J. H. Hutton: *Caste in India*, p. 164.
[2] *Ibid.*, p. 109.

[3] See below, pp. 196–97.
[4] R. Huebner: *A History of Germanic Private Law*, pp. 91–93.

was the normal practice but enforced more often by social custom (which could be defied) than by law. The French aristocrats, like the English, were not strictly endogamous; one of them cynically observed that 'to marry beneath oneself is merely taking dung to manure one's acres.'[5] Children inherited the position of their parents, except in so far as primogeniture restricted the full right of inheritance to the eldest son. But mobility was possible. It was, however, controlled. Status being legal and official in character, change of status must be by a legal or official act, as when a serf was liberated or a commoner ennobled. The sense of social distance was strongly marked, and each estate was linked with a limited range of permitted, or at least appropriate, occupations. Though at the lower levels this might operate as a disability, at the higher levels it represented a valuable monopoly. The estate system, then, reveals a precise and fairly rigid stratification, but in no case can it be said to give us the whole picture. Legal status rights did not permeate the whole of social life, and a description of stratification in terms of these rights alone is jejune and artificial. Our purpose here has been only to explain the nature of the principle.

The third type of stratification is Class, and its basis is economic. The concept has been widely used, notably by Karl Marx, and with various shades of meaning. It is not, in fact, and never can be, a very precise term, but it is an indispensable one. 'Classes', says Max Weber in one place, 'are groups of people who, from the standpoint of specific interests, have the same position in the economic system.'[6] The combination of the terms 'position' and 'interests' im-

plies that positions are to be regarded as the same if the lives of those occupying them are governed by the same forces and influenced in a similar way by the same circumstances—if they have, in Weber's phraseology, the same life chances within the economic system. A class system is a social structure in which stratification is dominated by this principle. And it is enough for our immediate purpose to recognize that capitalist society is an example of such a structure. That certain positions in a capitalist society have a hierarchical character is obvious. There is the hierarchy of power within the firm from the management down to the wage-earner, and the hierarchy of the corresponding groups in the society at large, in which power brings wealth and wealth buys power. But, although the outlines of the structure are clear, the details are not. And, although we may feel certain that economic positions rank themselves in terms of wealth, power and opportunity into something which looks like a system of superimposed strata or layers, we find it difficult to say exactly what these layers are and exactly who belongs to them. Here, too, the picture is incomplete, and in order to fill it out we may have to introduce some principle other than the objective test of position in the economic system.

All three systems have a certain objectivity, although the use of this word is fraught with the peril of misunderstanding. Caste membership is an indisputable and unalterable fact about which there is no room for differences of opinion. Estate, in its pure form, is equally factual; a man either possesses the rights or he does not. If the matter is in doubt, it is settled by a public authority, not by public opinion. Differences of class, in the technical sense in which we have been using the term, are also factual. That certain people occupy the same position in terms of wealth,

---

[5] L. Ducros: *French Social Life in the Eighteenth Century*, p. 61.
[6] H. H. Gerth and C. Wright Mills: *From Max Weber*, p. 405.

economic power and opportunity is something which an outside observer might discover even though the people themselves were not aware of it. It is this that we shall have in mind, and no more than this, when we refer to the objective facts of stratification.

# POWER, PRIVILEGE AND PRESTIGE

GERHARD LENSKI

When one seeks to build a theory of distribution on the postulates about the nature of man and society set forth in the last chapter, one soon discovers that these lead to a curious, but important, *dualism*. If those postulates are sound, one would predict that almost all the products of men's labors will be distributed on the basis of two seemingly contradictory principles, *need* and *power*.

In our discussion of the nature of man, it was postulated that where important decisions are involved, most human action is motivated either by self-interest or by partisan group interests. This suggests that power alone governs the distribution of rewards. This cannot be the case, however, since we also postulated that most of these essentially selfish interests can be satisfied only by the establishment of cooperative relations with others. Cooperation is absolutely essential both for survival and for the efficient attainment of most other goals. In other words, men's selfish interests compel them to remain members of society and to share in the division of labor.

If these two postulates are correct, then it follows that *men will share the*

Reprinted from Gerhard Lenski, POWER AND PRIVILEGE: A THEORY OF SOCIAL STRATIFICATION (New York: McGraw-Hill Book Company, 1966), pp. 44–46, 55, by permission of McGraw-Hill Book Company.

*product of their labors to the extent required to insure the survival and continued productivity of those others whose actions are necessary or beneficial to themselves.* This might well be called the first law of distribution, since the survival of mankind as a species depends on compliance with it.

This first law, however, does not cover the entire problem. It says nothing about how any *surplus*, i.e., goods and services over and above the minimum required to keep producers alive and productive, which men may be able to produce will be distributed. This leads to what may be called the second law of distribution. If we assume that in important decisions human action is motivated almost entirely by self-interest or partisan group interests, and if we assume that many of the things men most desire are in short supply, then, as noted before, this surplus will inevitably give rise to conflicts and struggles aimed at its control. If, following Weber, we define power as the probability of persons or groups carrying out their will even when opposed by others, then it follows that *power will determine the distribution of nearly all of the surplus possessed by a society.* The qualification "nearly all" takes account of the very limited influence of altruistic action which our earlier analysis of the nature of man leads us to expect.

This second law points the way to another very important relationship, that between our two chief variables, power and privilege. If privilege is defined as possession or control of a portion of the surplus produced by a society, then it follows that *privilege is largely a function of power, and to a very limited degree, a function of altruism.* This means that to explain most of the distribution of privilege in a society, we have but to determine the distribution of power.

To state the matter this way suggests that the task of explaining the distribution of privilege is simple. Unfortunately, this is not the case since there are many forms of power and they spring from many sources. Nevertheless, the establishment of this key relationship reduces the problem to more manageable proportions, since it concentrates attention on one key variable, power. Thus if we can establish the pattern of its distribution in a given society, we have largely established the pattern for the distribution of privilege, and if we can discover the causes of a given distribution of power we have also discovered the causes of the distribution of privilege linked with it.

To put the matter this way is to invite the question of how the third basic element in every distributive system, *prestige*, is related to power and privilege. It would be nice if one could say that prestige is a simple function of privilege, but unfortunately this does not seem to be the case. Without going into a complex analysis of the matter at this point, the best that can be said is that empirical evidence strongly suggests that *prestige is largely, though not solely, a function of power and privilege, at least in those societies where there is a substantial surplus.* If this is true, it follows that even though the subject of prestige is not often mentioned in this volume, its pattern of distribution and its causes can largely be deduced from discussion

of the distribution of power and privilege and their causes in those societies where there is an appreciable surplus.

Graphically, the relationship between these three variables, as set forth in the propositions above, can be depicted in this way with the solid lines indicating major sources of influence, the dashed lines secondary sources. To make this diagram complete, one other dashed line should probably be added, indicating some feedback from prestige to power. . . .

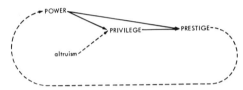

As the statement of the two laws indicates, the second law does not have any effect on the distributive process until the conditions specified in the first have been satisfied. Until the necessities of life have been made available to enough productive, mutually interdependent members of the group, there is no surplus to be fought over and distributed on the basis of power. Thus, as a first hypothesis we would be led to predict that *in the simplest societies, or those which are technologically most primitive, the goods and services available will be distributed wholly, or largely, on the basis of need.*

As the productivity of societies increases, the possibility of producing a surplus steadily increases, though it should be noted that the existence of a surplus is not a function of technological advance alone. Even though we cannot say that the surplus available to a society increases proportionately with advances in the level of technology, such advances increase the probability that there will be a surplus and also that there will be a sizable surplus. Hence, as a second hypothesis we are led to predict that *with technological advance, an increasing proportion of the goods and services available to a society will be distributed on the basis of power....*

On first consideration it may seem that the rule of right is merely the rule of might in a new guise, and therefore no real change can be expected in the distributive process. The fact is that, as the basis of power is shifted from might to right, certain subtle but important changes occur which have far-reaching consequences.

If the powers of the regime are to be accepted as rightful and legitimate they must be exercised in some degree, at least, in accord with the conceptions of justice and morality held by the majority—conceptions which spring from their self-interest and partisan group interests. Thus, even though the laws promulgated by a new elite may be heavily slanted to favor themselves, there are limits beyond which this cannot be carried if they wish to gain the benefits of the rule of right.

Second, after the shift to the rule of law, the interests of any single member of the elite can no longer safely be equated with the interests of the elite as a whole. For example, if a member of the new elite enters into a contractual arrangement with some member of the nonelite, and this turns out badly for him, it is to his interest to ignore the law and break the contract. However, this is not to the interest of the other members of the elite since most contractual arrangements work to their benefit. Therefore, it is to their interest to enforce the law in support of the claims of the nonelite to preserve respect for the law with all the benefits this provides them....

# THE NATURE OF CLASS CONFLICT

## T. H. MARSHALL

We think of 'a class' as a group of people. But we can also think of 'class' as a force or mechanism that operates to produce certain social attitudes. I like to begin my definition of class in this second sense by saying that it is a force that unites into groups people who differ from one another, by overriding the differences between them. It may sound paradoxical to stress in this way the differences within classes instead of

*Reprinted from T. H. Marshall,* CLASS, CITIZEN-SHIP, AND SOCIAL DEVELOPMENT, *copyright* © *1963 by T. H. Marshall (New York: Double-day & Company, Inc., 1965), pp. 180–90, by permission of Doubleday & Company, Inc.*

those between classes. But I believe it is salutary to do so. If you take in turn the class criteria that we have already discussed, income, property, education and occupation, you will find that every class contains within itself persons differently endowed in respect of each one of them. But the institution of class teaches the members of a society to notice some differences and to ignore others when arranging persons in order of social merit. In a word, social classes could not exist unless certain inequalities were regarded as irrelevant to the determination of social status. It follows that there are two main roads to the classless society. One leads through the abolition (as far as possible) of the social differences between individuals—which is roughly the way of communism—and the other proceeds by rendering all differences irrelevant to social status—which is roughly the way of democracy.

It is, of course, equally true that a class system notices, even emphasizes, certain forms of inequality, and uses them as a barrier to divide the classes. With respect to the points thus selected for attention members of the same class *are*—or believe they are—identical. But it is important to remember that they always differ in other respects. It is futile to argue that, because groups within a class are unlike in their circumstances or their interests, therefore the class itself is an 'artificial' group, or that because there is conflict within a class, therefore conflict between classes is 'unreal.'[1]

. . .

First, there is competition, where two or more persons offer the same service or desire the same object. This shows us at once that we cannot group people according to their resemblance to one another. In the case of competition it is similarity that divides; but let the competitors become partners, and the very same similarity will prove to be a bond of union. Secondly, there is the conflict that arises out of the division of labour, conflict, that is to say, over the terms on which co-operation is to take place, as illustrated by a wage dispute between employer and employed. The division here is a secondary product of a unity of interest based on difference. Thirdly, there is conflict over the system

itself upon which the allocation of functions and the distribution of benefits are based, as when a bargain about wages is converted into a revolt against capitalism.

Antagonism between competitors is clearly not incompatible with a community of interest between them. In fact such a community of interest is implied in the term 'competition.' For competition is a social process conducted through the medium of institutions which are equally indispensable to both competitors. The very existence of the service that is offered and its value in exchange are due to a social system and a civilization that are a common possession. The power of this common interest to produce common action will vary according to circumstances, but the interest always exists. In the second type of antagonism co-operation between the antagonists is part of the definition. It is sometimes suggested that the co-existence of the two relationships is illusory, on the grounds that the antagonism is not real and that the true interests of the parties are identical. But this is absurd. It is true that he who drives a hard bargain may injure himself by ruining his opposite. Nevertheless, a bargain is in essence a wrangle within limits set by the need to continue the offer of the service bargained for. There is no more difficulty in admitting that buyer and seller are at the same time friends and enemies than in asserting that bowler and batsman have a common interest in helping one another to play cricket, although their views as to the most desirable fate of each ball bowled are diametrically opposed. More important is the question how far co-operation between, say, employer and employed is an obstacle to the solidarity of labour *vis-à-vis* capital. That it *is* an obstacle is obvious, but this does not mean that it is the more real interest of the two. Here again we have the fact

---

[1] Such words have only a relative meaning. All group attitudes must be based, not only on facts, but also on the social meaning given to them. An attitude is only 'unreal' if the meaning is excessively farfetched or if, as in some types of propaganda, it is based on deliberate misrepresentation.

that labour is united by its common position in relation to the institutions through which the bargain of co-operation takes place. And to this I would add that, whereas the co-operative function of production by division of labour is sectional and specialized, the antagonism which is inherent in every bargain expresses itself in terms which are general to the class, in terms of wages and hours and the basic conditions of bargaining power.

To sum up: competition within the ranks of labour (or capital) does not render impossible or unnatural a conscious unity of labour (or capital), and sectional co-operation between labour and capital does not render impossible or unnatural a general antagonism between labour and capital.[2]

It is only in the third type of conflict that the common interest shared by the rivals dwindles to vanishing point. In extreme cases conflict of this kind becomes civil war, which is not a social process and in which, as the world knows only too well, little regard is paid even to the accepted rules of warfare. I suggest that we might well reserve the term 'conflict' for cases in which the presence of this last type of antagonism can be detected. Neither competition nor bargaining is conflict in this refined sense, but when either party feels that the process of competing or bargaining ought not to take place at all, or that it is of necessity being conducted under conditions of injustice, then conflict appears and may grow to revolution. Conflict therefore, implies, not merely disagreement as to what is to be done next, but dissatisfaction with what already exists. Two parties in parliament disagree as to policy, but conflict begins when one denounces parliamentary government. Two parents may disagree about the education of their child, but

conflict begins when the father denies that the mother has any say in the matter and the mother replies, 'I wish I had never married you.' And feelings of this kind may run as an undercurrent in the stream of disagreement for a long time before conflict breaks out, as has happened more than once in the history of trade unionism.[3]

I have been speaking so far, not about social classes, but about economic groups. I do not believe that the two are the same. I do believe in the reality of those social levels, distinguished by their culture and standard of living, which we discussed at our first two meetings. But differences of level are less likely to lead to conflict than differences of group interest. To that extent I accept the Marxian analysis of the nature of class conflict (though not the theory of its historic role), but I deny that it exhausts the subject of social stratification. Simplifying for the sake of brevity, I should say that class conflict occurs when a common interest unites adjacent social levels in opposition to more distant social levels. When the levels united by a common interest are not adjacent, as in international war, the conflict is not a class conflict. The fusion of levels is facilitated when the divisions between them are of unequal depth, when, for instance, the gulfs between levels one to four are shallower than that between levels four and five. There is another cause of fusion. Class conflict arises over social institutions. Often the same institutions dominate the division into levels. In such cases the two types of cleavage play into one another's hands. I imagine this was the case in feudal society. It is arguable that it is less true today. The wage-earner with savings finds that his social

[2] For an opposite view, see L. von Mises: *Socialism*, Part III, Section 1, Chapter 4.

[3] The 1926 General Strike in England showed well what confusion of mind results when the forms of bargaining are used for the purposes of conflict.

level urges him to defend the rights of property while his interests as a wage-earner prompt him to invade them. The issue depends partly on the nature of the conflict of interests, and on this point the analysis can be carried a stage further.

That resentment against inequality which is characteristic of class antagonism may spring from three processes, which I shall call comparison, frustration and oppression. Comparison sustains both the sense of superiority of the rich over 'the great unwashed' and the sense of resentment in the poor against 'the idle rich.' Such feelings may be shared by any number of persons from a single individual to a whole nation, and they are therefore most uncertain in their group-making effects. Yet they are the main force creating social levels, and they do this, not so much by provoking antagonism, as by perfecting the individual's awareness of himself and the group's consciousness of its own character. They are foundations of self-esteem. Perhaps that is why men seem to prefer to concentrate on comparing themselves with their inferiors. It is said that there is no caste in India so low that it cannot point to another beneath it. Comparison does not make contacts, it breaks them. It leads to isolation rather than to conflict. But if conflict is brewing, the attitudes born of comparison will stimulate it, and, when it matures, embitter it, and they are always there, ready to convert into a class struggle a dispute which is in essence no more than a disagreement about the terms of co-operation.[4]

Frustration adds to comparison a stronger motive for conflict by definitely imputing to the superior class responsibility for the injustice under which the inferior suffers. It arises, of course, wherever privilege creates inequality of

opportunity. But more important, because more distinctive, is the case where two classes represent, as it were, two different economic systems or two incompatible conceptions of social life. Pirenne has suggested that this is the normal way of economic progress. The creators of the new order rise up alongside of, not among, the decaying champions of the old.[5] The result is a lateral conflict, in which the old order appears more as an obstacle than as a tyrant. The process can be seen most clearly in the history of the *bourgeoisie* from the beginnings of the decline of feudalism to the perfection of capitalism in the nineteenth century, and especially in France. In the early days, says Pirenne, the *bourgeois* 'merely desired a place in the sun, and their claims were confined to their most indispensable needs.'[6] Subsequently it became clear that concessions to the *bourgeois* involved sacrifices by the aristocrat. Later, says Henri Sée, the *bourgeoisie* 'a intérêt au nouvel ordre de choses, à une organisation plus régulière, à la destruction des privilèges des deux premiers ordres, à la reconnaissance de l'égalité civile.'[7] Privilege was an obstacle because it was a cause of administrative inefficiency and financial mismanagement. How confused were ideas at the time of the Fronde as to the relations between social strata appears from the fact that the government's first act, when it realized the danger of disturbance, was to call on the *bourgeois* militia to stand by, while the revolutionary *bourgeoisie* organized a mercenary army of *compagnons* to relieve their portly selves of the burden of drilling and carrying arms.[8]

[5] H. Pirenne: *Les périodes de l'histoire sociale du capitalisme.*
[6] H. Pirenne: *Economic and social history of medieval Europe*, p. 51.
[7] *La vie économique au xviiie siècle*, p. 173.
[8] Charles Normand: *La bourgeoisie française au xviie siècle*, p. 349. In general see Joseph Aynard: *La bourgeoisie française*, Chapters 8 and 9.

[4] Subject, of course, to the reservations made above about the effect of social levels on class unity.

It might be argued that the position today is similar. The new middle class, composed mainly of the salariat and the lesser professions, is not writhing under the heel of a tyrant, but it is uncomfortably aware that the realization of its great ideal of a quiet life lived in security and with full enjoyment of the arts of civilization is being prevented by the incessant wranglings of capital and labour, which seem to it to be an essential part of the social system of the last century, and by the obsession of men's minds by a restless longing to speculate and to bargain in a ceaseless striving for profits. Either capitalism or socialism alone would be preferable, because both must use the services of this middle class in much the same way. But the conflict between the two is enough to goad it into revolution, with the natural, though not entirely wished for, result of Fascist dictatorship. Conflict against frustration is likely to include moral denunciation of the old order as corrupt, perverted or decadent. The modern middle-class movement shows this strain. It denounces materialism and the lack of a sense of social brotherhood, and, perhaps, the failure to appreciate the value of the artists and intellectuals. Fascism offers a new mind and a new spirit. 'The Fascist State... is a force, but a spiritual force, which embodies in itself all forms of the moral and intellectual life of man.... Its principle...implants itself in the heart of the man of action, the thinker, the artist and the scientist alike—it is the soul of the soul.'[9] This is not exactly what was asked for, but it may serve for a time.

Oppression describes a conflict between two parties engaged in unequal co-operation, the inequality being a product of the institutions of a stratified society. The word is not meant to define the motives or methods of the upper class, but only the situation as it appears to the lower. Whereas comparison breaks contacts and frustration produces contact by collision, oppression implies contact as an organic process. Obvious instances are the relations between serf and lord or labour and capital. When conflict breaks out, the attack is made against a group of persons wielding power. They may be referred to as 'the governing class.' This phrase is loosely used. The feudal aristocracy was literally a governing class. The modern capitalists are not. And yet the words express a truth. The implication is that the capitalist is using in the economic field a power that is partly political, in that it is derived from the laws and institutions of the society. If a class is strong enough to secure or to preserve those institutions that favour its activities, it may be said to be 'governing' to that extent. But, as we saw, in the modern world interest in the essential institutions is not confined to the capitalists who meet labour as employers. It is perhaps for this reason that the attack comes to be directed less against a group of persons than against an impersonal system. Relations between the co-operating groups relapse into bargaining. Conflict deals in theories. One would expect this to result in a decline in the influence of trade unionists, who bargain, as leaders of a working class, in favour of communists, who theorize. An alternative consequence may be an increase in what might be called 'level-consciousness' as compared with 'class-consciousness.' This seems to be what is happening in England.

Space remains for only one more point. We can ask whether conflict is more likely to arise in a static or a dynamic society. This involves contrasting estate with class, status with contract. In a society stratified into estates inequality is based on an accepted scheme of differential status and differential standards of living. One class is

[9] B. Mussolini: *La Dottrina del Fascismo*, Section 12.

utilized for the benefit of another, but within the limits of a plan of co-operation approved by custom. Disagreement over the terms of co-operation can hardly arise, since the terms are not open to question. Where status rules, bargaining, which belongs to contract, cannot prevail. Antagonism can find no expression except in conflict.[10] There is no middle course between acquiescence and rebellion. It might be argued that this must render conflict more likely, because there is no milder alternative. But it may equally be urged that the gravity of the step will act as a deterrent. It is easier to drift into danger than to jump into it. In addition, the very nature of a society based on estates is such as to favour the development in each group of the type of mentality suited to its position. Revolt is paralysed from within.

In a free contractual society disagreement as to the terms of co-operation is normal and chronic. It is implied in the bargaining process out of which the contract emerges. We notice, too, that the idea that every station in life has its proper standard, that every class has its culture, is at its weakest. Acquiescence is positively discouraged by the prevailing belief in the virtue of social ambition. Democracy professes to believe in equality and capitalism extols competition. A uniform standard for all kills competition, while differential standards deny equality. Capitalist democracy, therefore, at first accepts no standard, taking what is given it by the free play of economic forces. The English pauper was not to be fed according to the needs of the human body but according to what could be bought with a little less money than capitalism vouchsafed to the free worker. When the standard enters once more, as it did in the later

nineteenth century, it enters as a minimum, above which infinite variation is allowed and expected. In capitalist democracy, then, we have a perpetual state of friction between classes combined with a destruction of the psychological forces favouring acquiescence. Is there, we should ask, any positive force turning antagonism into conflict which is absent in the static society? I see a possible answer in the idea of exploitation.

In both types of society there appears to be utilization of one class by another for the benefit of the latter. But whereas in the society of estates it is according to plan, in the contractual society it is at will. To distinguish between these processes we may say that the second is exploitation and the first is not. The benefits accruing to lord and serf under feudalism cannot be compared, because they are different in kind. Those accruing to capital and labour seem to be measured by their money incomes, and they are manifestly unequal. A contract is ideally an agreement to co-operate for equal advantage. When it habitually produces unequal advantage, exploitation is suspected. The idea appeals strongly to the exploited, who quickly conclude that the power that is defeating them resides, not in the personal superiority of their oppressor, but in the unfair advantages he derives from the system. If the system renders contract a sham, the system must be changed.

Some people hold that social mobility affords a safety valve and helps to avert the threatened conflict. Although this is true up to a point, I think its importance can easily be exaggerated. Where individual mobility is automatic, or nearly so, class loyalty develops with difficulty. If every apprentice has a reasonable hope of becoming a master he will form his associations on the basis of his trade or profession rather

[10] Cf. K. Bauer-Mengelberg: 'Stand und Klasse,' in *Könerl Vierteljahrshefte für Soziologie* (1923).

than of his social level. Again, where a whole group can rise in social estimation and economic value, leaving no stragglers, the alliance of groups into classes is more difficult. This is no doubt the effect of the recent rise of many skilled occupations into the ranks of the professions. But where mobility is individual and not automatic, but depends on the results of competitive striving. I am doubtful whether the same result follows. When the race is to the swift, the slow, who are always in a majority, grow tired of their perpetual defeat and become more disgruntled than if there were no race at all. They begin to regard the prizes as something to which they are entitled and of which they are unjustly deprived. They declare that no man ought to be made to race for his bread and butter, and the argument is not without force. Especially is this so when society shows itself indifferent to the condition of the losers on the ground that the road to better things is ever open before them.[11] The use of mobility as an excuse for inequality is usually associated with a measure of self-deception. But, if I were to pursue that theme, I should be trespassing on the subject to be discussed at the next session of this Conference.

[11] Cf. C. H. Cooley: *Social Organization,* Chapter 27.

# PART TWO

# THE
# SOCIOLOGY
# OF
# WESTERN
# POLITICS

## A. Governmental Decision-Makers: Bureaucrats and Legislators

# BUREAUCRATIC STRUCTURE
# AND BUREAUCRATIC BEHAVIOR

### ROBERT K. MERTON

A formal, rationally organized social structure involves clearly defined patterns of activity in which, ideally, every series of actions is functionally related to the purposes of the organization.[1] In such an organization there is integrated a series of offices, of hierarchized status, in which inhere a number of obligations and privileges closely defined by limited and specific rules. Each of these offices contains an area of imputed competence and responsibility. Authority, the power of control which derives from an acknowledged status, inheres in the office and not in the particular person who performs the official role. Official action ordinarily occurs within the framework of preexisting rules of the organization. The system of prescribed relations between the various offices involves a considerable degree of formality and clearly defined social distance between the occupants of these positions. Formality is manifested by means of a more or less complicated social ritual which symbolizes and supports the "pecking order" of the various offices. Such formality, which is integrated with the distribution of authority within the system, serves to minimize friction by largely restricting (official) contact to modes which are previously defined by the rules of the organization. Ready calculability of others' behavior and a stable set of mutual expectations is thus built up. Moreover, formality facilitates the interaction of the occupants of offices despite their (possibly hostile) private attitudes toward one another. In this way, the subordinate is protected from the arbitrary action of his superior, since the actions of both are constrained by a mutually recognized set of rules. Specific procedural devices foster objectivity and restrain the "quick passage of impulse into action."[2]

### THE STRUCTURE OF BUREAUCRACY

The ideal type of such formal organization is bureaucracy and, in many respects, the classical analysis of bureaucracy is that by Max Weber.[3] As Weber

[1] For a development of the concept of "rational organization," see Karl Mannheim, *Mensch und Gesellschaft im Zeitalter des Umbaus* (Leiden: A. W. Sijthoff, 1935), esp. pp. 28 ff.

*Reprinted from Robert K. Merton,* SOCIAL THEORY AND SOCIAL STRUCTURE *(New York: The Free Press, 1949), pp. 151–60, by permission of The Macmillan Co.*

[2] H. D. Lasswell, *Politics* (New York: Mc-Graw-Hill, 1936), pp. 120–21.

[3] Max Weber, *Wirtschaft und Gesellschaft* (Tübingen: J. C. B. Mohr, 1922), Pt. III, chap. 6; pp. 650–678. For a brief summary of Weber's discussion, see Talcott Parsons, *The Structure of Social Action* (New York: The Free Press, 1949), esp. pp. 506 ff. For a description, which is not a caricature, of the bureaucrat as a personality type, see C. Rabany, "Les types sociaux: le fonctionnaire," *Revue générale d'administration,* LXXXVIII (1907), 5–28.

indicates, bureaucracy involves a clear-cut division of integrated activities which are regarded as duties inherent in the office. A system of differentiated controls and sanctions is stated in the regulations. The assignment of roles occurs on the basis of technical qualifications which are ascertained through formalized, impersonal procedures (e.g., examinations). Within the structure of hierarchically arranged authority, the activities of "trained and salaried experts" are governed by general, abstract, clearly defined rules which preclude the necessity for the issuance of specific instructions for each specific case. The generality of the rules requires the constant use of *categorization*, whereby individual problems and cases are classified on the basis of designated criteria and are treated accordingly. The pure type of bureaucratic official is appointed, either by a superior or through the exercise of impersonal competition; he is not elected. A measure of flexibility in the bureaucracy is attained by electing higher functionaries who presumably express the will of the electorate (e.g., a body of citizens or a board of directors). The election of higher officials is designed to affect the purposes of the organization, but the technical procedures for attaining these ends are carried out by a continuous bureaucratic personnel.[4]

Most bureaucratic offices involve the expectation of life-long tenure, in the absence of disturbing factors which may decrease the size of the organization. Bureaucracy maximizes vocational security.[5] The function of security of tenure,

[4] Karl Mannheim, *Ideology and Utopia* (New York: Harcourt, Brace, 1936), pp. 18n., 105 ff. See also Ramsay Muir, *Peers and Bureaucrats* (London: Constable, 1910), pp. 12–13.

[5] E. G. Cahen-Salvador suggests that the personnel of bureaucracies is largely constituted of those who value security above all else. See his "La situation matérielle et morale

pensions, incremental salaries and regularized procedures for promotion is to ensure the devoted performance of official duties, without regard for extraneous pressures.[6] The chief merit of bureaucracy is its technical efficiency, with a premium placed on precision, speed, expert control, continuity, discretion, and optimal returns on input. The structure is one which approaches the complete elimination of personalized relationships and nonrational considerations (hostility, anxiety, affectual involvements, etc.).

With increasing bureaucratization, it becomes plain to all who would see that man is to a very important degree controlled by his social relations to the instruments of production. This can no longer seem only a tenet of Marxism, but a stubborn fact to be acknowledged by all, quite apart from their ideological persuasion. Bureaucratization makes readily visible what was previously dim and obscure. More and more people discover that to work, they must be employed. For to work, one must have tools and equipment. And the tools and equipment are increasingly available only in bureaucracies, private or public. Consequently, one must be employed by the bureaucracies in order to have access to tools in order to work in order to live. It is in this sense that bureaucratization entails separation of individuals from the instruments of production, as in modern capitalistic enterprise or in state communistic enterprise (of the 1949 variety), just as in the post-feudal army, bureaucratization entailed complete separation from the instruments of destruction. Typically, the worker no longer owns his tools nor the

des fonctionnaires," *Revue politique et parlementaire* (1926), p. 319.

[6] H. J. Laski, "Bureaucracy," *Encyclopedia of the Social Sciences*. This article is written primarily from the standpoint of the political scientist rather than that of the sociologist.

soldier, his weapons. And in this special sense, more and more people become workers, either blue collar or white collar or stiff shirt. So develops, for example, the new type of the scientific worker, as the scientist is "separated" from his technical equipment—after all, the physicist does not ordinarily own his cyclotron. To work at his research, he must be employed by a bureaucracy with laboratory resources.

Bureaucracy is administration which almost completely avoids public discussion of its techniques, although there may occur public discussion of its policies.[7] This secrecy is confined neither to public nor to private bureaucracies. It is held to be necessary to keep valuable information from private economic competitors or from foreign and potentially hostile political groups. And though it is not often so called, espionage among competitors is perhaps as common, if not as intricately organized, in systems of private economic enterprise as in systems of national states. Cost figures, lists of clients, new technical processes, plans for production— all these are typically regarded as essential secrets of private economic bureaucracies which might be revealed if the bases of all decisions and policies had to be publicly defended.

## THE DYSFUNCTIONS OF BUREAUCRACY

In these bold outlines, the positive attainments and functions of bureaucratic organization are emphasized and the internal stresses and strains of such structures are almost wholly neglected. The community at large, however, evidently emphasizes the imperfections of bureaucracy, as is suggested by the fact that the "horrid hybrid," bureaucrat, has become an epithet, a *Schimpfwort.*

The transition to a study of the negative aspects of bureaucracy is afforded by the application of Veblen's concept of "trained incapacity," Dewey's notion of "occupational psychosis" or Warnotte's view of "professional deformation." Trained incapacity refers to that state of affairs in which one's abilities function as inadequacies or blind spots. Actions based upon training and skills which have been successfully applied in the past may result in inappropriate responses *under changed conditions.* An inadequate flexibility in the application of skills, will, in a changing milieu, result in more or less serious maladjustments.[8] Thus, to adopt a barnyard illustration used in this connection by Burke, chickens may be readily conditioned to interpret the sound of a bell as a signal for food. The same bell may now be used to summon the "trained chickens" to their doom as they are assembled to suffer decapitation. In general, one adopts measures in keeping with his past training and, under new conditions which are not recognized is *significantly* different, the very soundness of this training may lead to the adoption of the wrong procedures. Again, in Burke's almost echolalic phrase, "people may be unfitted by being fit in an unfit fitness"; their training may become an incapacity.

Dewey's concept of occupational psychosis rests upon much the same observations. As a result of their day to day routines, people develop special preferences, antipathies, discriminations and emphases.[9] (The term psychosis is used by Dewey to denote a "pronounced character of the mind.") These psychoses develop through demands put upon

[7] Weber, *op. cit.,* p. 671.

[8] For a stimulating discussion and application of these concepts, see Kenneth Burke, *Permanence and Change* (New York: New Republic, 1935), pp. 50 ff.; Daniel Warnotte, "Bureaucratie et Fonctionnarisme," *Revue de l'Institut de Sociologie,* XVII (1937), 245.

[9] *Ibid.,* pp. 58–59.

the individual by the particular organization of his occupational role.

The concepts of both Veblen and Dewey refer to a fundamental ambivalence. Any action can be considered in terms of what it attains or what it fails to attain. "A way of seeing is also a way of not seeing—a focus upon object A involves a neglect of object B."[10] In his discussion, Weber is almost exclusively concerned with what the bureaucratic structure attains: precision, reliability, efficiency. This same structure may be examined from another perspective provided by the ambivalence. What are the limitations of the organizations designed to attain these goals?

For reasons which we have already noted, the bureaucratic structure exerts a constant pressure upon the official to be "methodical, prudent, disciplined." If the bureaucracy is to operate successfully, it must attain a high degree of reliability of behavior, an unusual degree of conformity with prescribed patterns of action. Hence, the fundamental importance of discipline which may be as highly developed in a religious or economic bureaucracy as in the army. Discipline can be effective only if the ideal patterns are buttressed by strong sentiments which entail devotion to one's duties, a keen sense of the limitation of one's authority and competence, and methodical performance of routine activities. The efficacy of social structure depends ultimately upon infusing group participants with appropriate attitudes and sentiments. As we shall see, there are definite arrangements in the bureaucracy for inculcating and reinforcing these sentiments.

At the moment, it suffices to observe that in order to ensure discipline (the necessary reliability of response), these sentiments are often more intense than is technically necessary. There is a margin of safety, so to speak, in the pressure exerted by these sentiments upon the bureaucrat to conform to his patterned obligations, in much the same sense that added allowances (precautionary overestimations) are made by the engineer in designing the supports for a bridge. But this very emphasis leads to a transference of the sentiments from the *aims* of the organization onto the particular details of behavior required by the rules. Adherence to the rules, originally conceived as a means, becomes transformed into an end-in-itself; there occurs the familiar process of *displacement of goals* whereby "an instrumental value becomes a terminal value."[11] Discipline, readily interpreted as conformance with regulations, whatever the situation, is seen not as a measure designed for specific purposes but becomes an immediate value in the life-organization of the bureaucrat. This emphasis, resulting from the displacement of the original goals, develops into rigidities and an inability to adjust readily. Formalism, even ritualism, ensues with an unchallenged insistence upon punctilious adherence to formalized procedures.[12] This may be exaggerated to the point where primary concern with conformity to the rules interferes with the achievement of the purposes of the organization, in which

[10] *Ibid.*, p. 70.

[11] This process has often been observed in various connections. Wundt's *heterogony of ends* is a case in point; Max Weber's *Paradoxie der Folgen* is another. See also MacIver's observations on the transformation of civilization into culture and Lasswell's remark that "the human animal distinguishes himself by his infinite capacity for making ends of his means." See R. K. Merton, "The Unanticipated Consequences of Purposive Social Action," *American Sociological Review*, I (1936), 894–904.

[12] See E. C. Hughes, "Institutional Office and the Person," *American Journal of Sociology*, XLIII (1937), 404–413; R. K. Merton, "Social Structure and Anomie," *American Sociological Review*, III (1938), 6720681; E. T. Hiller, "Social Structure in Relation to the Person," *Social Forces*, XVI (1937), 34–44.

case we have the familiar phenomenon of the technicism or red tape of the official.

. . .

## STRUCTURAL SOURCES OF OVERCONFORMITY

Such inadequacies in orientation which involve trained incapacity clearly derive from structural sources. The process may be briefly recapitulated. (1) An effective bureaucracy demands reliability of response and strict devotion to regulations. (2) Such devotion to the rules leads to their transformation into absolutes; they are no longer conceived as relative to a given set of purposes. (3) This interferes with ready adaptation under special conditions not clearly envisaged by those who drew up the general rules. (4) Thus, the very elements which conduce toward efficiency in general produce inefficiency in specific instances. Full realization of the inadequacy is seldom attained by members of the group who have not divorced themselves from the "meanings" which the rules have for them. These rules in time become symbolic in cast, rather than strictly utilitarian.

Thus far, we have treated the ingrained sentiments making for rigorous discipline simply as data, as given. However, definite features of the bureaucratic structure may be seen to conduce to these sentiments. The bureaucrat's official life is planned for him in terms of a graded career, through the organizational devices of promotion by seniority, pensions, incremental salaries, *etc.*, all of which are designed to provide incentives for disciplined action and conformity to the official regulations.[13] The official is tacitly expected to and largely does adapt his thoughts, feelings and actions to the prospect of this career.

But *these very devices* which increase the probability of conformance also lead to an over-concern with strict adherence to regulations which induces timidity, conservatism, and technicism. Displacement of sentiments from goals onto means is fostered by the tremendous symbolic significance of the means (rules).

Another feature of the bureaucratic structure tends to produce much the same result. Functionaries have the sense of a common destiny for all those who work together. They share the same interests, especially since there is relatively little competition insofar as promotion is in terms of seniority. In-group aggression is thus minimized and this arrangement is therefore conceived to be positively functional for the bureaucracy. However, the esprit de corps and informal social organization which typically develops in such situations often leads the personnel to defend their entrenched interests rather than to assist their clientele and elected higher officials. As President Lowell reports, if the bureaucrats believe that their status is not adequately recognized by an incoming elected official, detailed information will be withheld from him, leading him to errors for which he is held responsible. Or, if he seeks to dominate fully, and thus violates the sentiment of self-integrity of the bureaucrats, he may have documents brought to him in such numbers that he cannot manage to sign them all, let alone read them.[14] This illustrates the defensive informal organization which tends to arise whenever there is an apparent threat to the integrity of the group.[15]

[13] Mannheim, *Mensch und Gesellschaft*, pp. 32–33. Mannheim stresses the importance of the "Lebensplan" and the "Amtskarriere." See the comments by Hughes, *op. cit.*, 413.

[14] A. L. Lowell, *The Government of England* (New York, 1908), I, 189 ff.

[15] For an instructive description of the development of such a defensive organization in a group of workers, see F. J. Roethlisberger and W. J. Dickson, *Management and the Worker* (Boston: Harvard School of Business Administration, 1934).

It would be much too facile and partly erroneous to attribute such resistance by bureaucrats simply to vested interests. Vested interests oppose any new order which either eliminates or at least makes uncertain their differential advantage deriving from the current arrangements. This is undoubtedly involved in part in bureaucratic resistance to change but another process is perhaps more significant. As we have seen, bureaucratic officials affectively identify themselves with their way of life. They have a pride of craft which leads them to resist change in established routines; at least, those changes which are felt to be imposed by co-workers. This nonlogical pride of craft is a familiar pattern found even, to judge from Sutherland's *Professional Thief*, among pickpockets who, despite the risk, delight in mastering the prestige-bearing feat of "beating a left breech" (picking the left front trousers pocket).

In a stimulating paper, Hughes has applied the concepts of "secular" and "sacred" to various types of division of labor; "the sacredness" of caste and *Stände* prerogatives contrasts sharply with the increasing secularism of occupational differentiation in our mobile society.[16] However, as our discussion suggests, there may ensue, in particular vocations and in particular types of organization, the *process of sanctification* (viewed as the counterpart of the process of secularization). This is to say that through sentiment-formation, emotional dependence upon bureaucratic symbols and status, and affective involvement in spheres of competence and authority, there develop prerogatives involving attitudes of moral legitimacy which are established as values in their own right, and are no longer viewed as merely technical means for expediting administration. One may note a tendency for certain bureaucratic norms, originally introduced for technical reasons, to become rigidified and sacred, although, as Durkheim would say, they are *laïque en apparence*.[17] Durkheim has touched on this general process in his description of the attitudes and values which persist in the organic solidarity of a highly differentiated society.

PRIMARY VS. SECONDARY RELATIONS

Another feature of the bureaucratic structure, the stress on depersonalization of relationships, also plays its part in the bureaucrat's trained incapacity. The personality pattern of the bureaucrat is nucleated about this norm of impersonality. Both this and the categorizing tendency, which develops from the dominant role of general, abstract rules, tend to produce conflict in the bureaucrat's contacts with the public or clientele. Since functionaries minimize personal relations and resort to categorization, the peculiarities of individual cases are often ignored. But the client who, quite understandably, is convinced of the "special features" of *his* own problem often objects to such categorical treatment. Stereotyped behavior is not adapted to the exigencies of individual problems. The impersonal treatment of

---

16 E. C. Hughes, "Personality Types and the Division of Labor," *American Journal of Sociology*, XXXIII (1928), 754–768. Much the same distinction is drawn by Leopold von Wiese and Howard Becker, *Systematic Sociology* (New York: John Wiley & Sons, 1932), pp. 222–25 *et passim*.

17 Hughes recognizes one phase of this process of sanctification when he writes that professional training "carries with it as a by-product assimilation of the candidate to a set of professional attitudes and controls, a *professional conscience and solidarity. The profession claims and aims to become a moral unit.*" Hughes, *op. cit.*, p. 762, (italics inserted). In this same connection, Summer's concept of *pathos*, as the halo of sentiment which protects a social value from criticism, is particularly relevant, inasmuch as it affords a clue to the mechanism involved in the process of sanctification. See his *Folkways* (Boston: Ginn & Co., 1906), pp. 180–181.

affairs which are at times of great personal significance to the client gives rise to the charge of "arrogance" and "haughtiness" of the bureaucrat. Thus, at the Greenwich Employment Exchange, the unemployed worker who is securing his insurance payment resents what he deems to be "the impersonality and, at times, the apparent abruptness and even harshness of his treatment by the clerks.... Some men complain of the superior attitude which the clerks have."[18]

Still another source of conflict with the public derives from the bureaucratic structure. The bureaucrat, in part irrespective of his position with*in* the hierarchy, acts as a representative of the power and prestige of the entire structure. In his official role he is vested with definite authority. This often leads to an actually or apparently domineering attitude, which may only be exaggerated by a discrepancy between his position within the hierarchy and his position with reference to the public.[19] Protest and recourse to other officials on the part of the client are often ineffective or largely precluded by the previously mentioned esprit de corps which joins the officials into a more or less solidary in-group. This source of conflict *may* be minimized in private enterprise since the client can register an effective protest by transferring his trade to another organization within the competitive system. But with the monopolistic nature of the public organization, no such alternative is possible. Moreover, in this case, tension is increased because of a discrepancy between ideology and fact: the governmental personnel are held to be "servants of the people," but in fact they are usually superordinate, and release of tension can seldom be afforded by turning to other agencies for the necessary service.[20] This tension is in part attributable to the confusion of the status of bureaucrat and client; the

18 " 'They treat you like a lump of dirt they do. I see a navvy reach across the counter and shake one of them by the collar the other day. The rest of us felt like cheering. Of course he lost his benefit over it.... But the clerk deserved it for his sassy way.' " (E. W. Bakke, *The Unemployed Man*, New York: Dutton, 1934, pp. 79–80). Note that the domineering attitude was *imputed* by the unemployed client who is in a state of tension due to his loss of status and self-esteem in a society where the ideology is still current that an "able man" can always find a job. That the imputation of arrogance stems largely from the client's state of mind is seen from Bakke's own observation that "the clerks were rushed, and had no time for pleasantries, but there was little sign of harshness or a superiority feeling in their treatment of the men." Insofar as there is an objective basis for the imputation of arrogant behavior to bureaucrats, it may possibly be explained by the following juxtaposed statements. "Auch der moderne, sei es öffentliche, sei es private, Beamte erstrebt immer und geniesst meist den Beherrschten gegenüber eine spezifisch gehobene, 'ständische' soziale Schätzung." (Weber, *op. cit.*, 652.) "In persons in whom the craving for prestige is uppermost, hostility usually takes the form of a desire to humiliate others." (K. Horney, *The Neurotic Personality of Our Time*, New York: Norton, 1937, pp. 178–79).

19 In this connection, note the relevance of Koffka's comments on certain features of the pecking-order of birds. "If one compares the behavior of the bird at the top of the pecking list, the despot, with that of one very far down, the second or third from the last, then one finds the latter much more cruel to the few others whom he lords it than the former in his treatment of all members. As soon as one removes from the group all members above the penultimate, his behavior becomes milder and may even become very friendly.... It is not difficult to find analogies to this in human societies, and therefore one side of such behavior must be primarily the effects of the social groupings, and not of individual characteristics." K. Koffka, *Principles of Gestalt Psychology* (New York: Harcourt, Brace, 1935), pp. 668–9.

20 At this point the political machine often becomes functionally significant. As Steffens and others have shown, highly personalized relations and the abrogation of formal rules (red tape) by the machine often satisfy the needs of individual "clients" more fully than the formalized mechanism of governmental bureaucracy. See the slight elaboration of this as set forth in Chapter I.

client may consider himself socially superior to the official who is at the moment dominant.[21]

Thus, with respect to the relations between officials and clientele, one structural source of conflict is the pressure for formal and impersonal treatment when individual, personalized consideration is desired by the client. The conflict may be viewed, then, as deriving from the introduction of inappropriate attitudes and relationships. Conflict within the bureaucratic structure arises from the converse situation, namely, when personalized relationships are substituted for the structurally required impersonal relationships. This type of conflict may be characterized as follows.

The bureaucracy, as we have seen, is organized as a secondary, formal group. The normal responses involved in this organized network of social expectations are supported by affective attitudes of members of the group. Since the group is oriented toward secondary norms of impersonality, any failure to conform to these norms will arouse antagonism from those who have identified themselves with the legitimacy of these rules. Hence, the substitution of personal for impersonal treatment within the structure is met with widespread disapproval and is characterized by such epithets as graft, favoritism, nepotism, apple-polishing, etc. These epithets are clearly manifestations of injured sentiments. The function of such "automatic resentment" can be clearly seen in terms of the requirements of bureaucratic structure.

Bureaucracy is a secondary group structure designed to carry on certain activities which cannot be satisfactorily performed on the basis of primary group criteria.[22] Hence behavior which runs counter to these formalized norms becomes the object of emotionalized disapproval. This constitutes a functionally significant defence set up against tendencies which jeopardize the performance of socially necessary activities. To be sure, these reactions are not rationally determined practices explicitly designed for the fulfillment of this function. Rather, viewed in terms of the individual's interpretation of the situation, such resentment is simply an immediate response opposing the "dishonesty" of those who violate the rules of the game. However, this subjective frame of reference notwithstanding, these reactions serve the latent function of maintaining the essential structural elements of bureaucracy by reaffirming the necessity for formalized, secondary relations and by helping to prevent the disintegration of the bureaucratic structure which would occur should these be supplanted by personalized relations. This type of conflict may be generically described as the intrusion of primary group attitudes when secondary group attitudes are institutionally demanded, just as the bureaucrat-client conflict often derives from interaction on impersonal terms when personal treatment is individually demanded.[23]

---

[21] As one of the unemployed men remarked about the clerks at the Greenwich Employment Exchange: " 'And the bloody blokes wouldn't have their jobs if it wasn't for us men out of a job either. That's what gets me about their holding their noses up.' " Bakke, op. cit., p. 80.

[22] Cf. Ellsworth Faris, The Nature of Human Nature (New York: McGraw-Hill, 1937), pp. 41 ff.

[23] Community disapproval of many forms of behavior may be analyzed in terms of one or the other of these patterns of substitution of culturally inappropriate types of relationship. Thus, prostitution constitutes a type-case where coitus, a form of intimacy which is institutionally defined as symbolic of the most "sacred" primary group relationship, is placed within a contractual context, symbolized by the exchange of that most impersonal of all symbols, money. See Kingsley Davis, "The Sociology of Prostitution," American Sociological Review, II (1937), 744–55.

## PROBLEMS FOR RESEARCH

The trend towards increasing bureaucratization in Western Society which Weber had long since foreseen, is not the sole reason for sociologists to turn their attention to this field. Empirical studies of the interaction of bureaucracy and personality should especially increase our understanding of social structure. A large number of specific questions invite our attention. To what extent are particular personality types selected and modified by the various bureaucracies (private enterprise, public service, the quasi-legal political machine, religious orders)? Inasmuch as ascendancy and submission are held to be traits of personality, despite their variability in different stimulus-situations, do bureaucracies select personalities of particularly submissive or ascendant tendencies? And since various studies have shown that these traits can be modified, does participation in bureaucratic office tend to increase ascendant tendencies? Do various systems of recruitment (e.g., patronage, open competition involving specialized knowledge or "general mental capacity," practical experience) select different personality types? Does promotion through seniority lessen competitive anxieties and enhance administrative efficiency? A detailed examination of mechanisms for imbuing the bureaucratic codes with affect would be instructive both sociologically and psychologically. Does the general anonymity of civil service decisions tend to restrict the area of prestige-symbols to a narrowly defined inner circle? Is there a tendency for differential association to be especially marked among bureaucrats?

The range of theoretically significant and practically important questions would seem to be limited only by the accessibility of the concrete data. Studies of religious, educational, military, economic, and political bureaucracies dealing with the interdependence of social organization and personality formation should constitute an avenue for fruitful research. On that avenue, the functional analysis of concrete structures may yet build a Solomon's House for sociologists.

# OCCUPATIONAL ROLE STRAINS: THE AMERICAN LEGISLATOR

WILLIAM C. MITCHELL

An important subject for behavioral research is the interplay between organizational structure and personality, between the peculiar conditions or demands of given occupations and the kinds of accommodations that individuals make to them. This analysis is concerned with the strains and conflicts associated with elected political office in the United States. Unfortunately

*Reprinted from William C. Mitchell, "Occupational Role Strains: The American Elective Public Official,"* ADMINISTRATIVE SCIENCE QUARTERLY, *3 (September 1958), 210–28, by permission of* ADMINISTRATIVE SCIENCE QUARTERLY *and the author.*

Weber's classic essay on politics as a vocation has not been widely read, nor is it influential among American scientists.[1] Politics is widely and intensively studied, but the practice of politics as an occupation has received little more than anecdotal treatment by journalists.[2] In this study role theory and role analysis are used to explore certain facets of the elective public official's occupational role. More precisely the paper is concerned with the development of a "middle-range" conceptual scheme for the analysis of the strains engendered by elective public office.

ROLE STRAINS

Briefly, we can define strain as the resultant of attempts to meet expectations that cannot be fully met either by a person or a social system. Neither social systems nor persons can ever be free of the problems of adjustment to new and difficult situations. Strain in some form will therefore accompany the process of adjustment.

The strains to which a person is subject are not randomized in the social system. Rather these strains are patterned along the structure of the roles or norms that make up the system. All incumbents of a particular role will therefore be subject to the same role strains, even though they may respond quite differently to them. If we know the role or norm structure of a given social system we ought to be able to predict where and how role strains will occur.

Whether a particular occupational strain is consciously felt by a given individual is problematical. Some politicians may recognize the existence of a strain for a colleague but not be personally bothered by that same strain. Certain personality types may demonstrate an immunity to strains that cause great anxiety among others. But even in the case of the person who does not recognize or admit to being disturbed by some strain, we have to recognize the possibility that his failure to do so is itself a response to the strain. Self-awareness of a role strain is not a criterion of its existence. If it were, psychoanalysis would have little to do.

The role strains of politics are not simply acquiesced in by the politician any more than is the case with other persons in the social structure. A variety of responses is possible, including passive acceptance and deviance; but typically the politician attempts to effectuate some control over the situation, even if only a partial form. Efforts, of course, are also made to reform the situation so that the strain can be eliminated, but for the most part politicians attempt to gain only a partial control as the more realistic course of action. Periodically rather full-scale transformations of the political situations are completed; one such transformation was the Legislative Reorganization Act of 1946, which made some significant changes in the situation of congressmen and senators.

I shall consider seven general sources of strain for the elected public official. The categories used are by no means exhaustive, but they are primary in the sense that any other role strains are products of those selected for discussion. In the order in which they will be analyzed they are (1) insecurity of tenure; (2) conflict among public roles; (3) conflict of private and public roles; (4) ambiguities in political situations; (5) diffused responsibility and limited control of situations; (6) time and pressure of demands; (7) and status in-

[1] A translation of Weber's "Politik als Beruf" can be found in H. H. Gerth and C. Wright Mills, eds. and trs., *From Max Weber* (London, 1948).

[2] The best but by no means the only writings of this type are those of Frank Kent, *Political Behavior* (New York, 1928), and J. H. Wallis, *The Politician* (New York, 1935).

security. Finally, it should be clear that I am writing not as a psychologist, but as a political sociologist. No attempt will be made, therefore, to analyze the effects of role strains upon the personality. My concern is solely with sources.

## SOURCES OF STRAIN

### Insecurity of Tenure

No occupational role guarantees perfact security of tenure, least of all, perhaps, that of the politician. The turnover in the ranks of elected public officials is very great as the investigations of Charles S. Hyneman have demonstrated.[3] His findings respecting tenure in ten state legislatures over a period of ten years (1925–1935) indicate that in only four of the twenty chambers studied had as many as 50 per cent of the members completed three sessions. And in seven chambers less than 25 per cent could show experience in three previous sessions. In "Tribulations of a State Senator" Duane Lockard claimed that "roughly half of the six thousand legislators you are going to elect will be entering the legislature for the first time. Most legislators cannot afford to serve more than one term."[4] Regardless of the reason fragmentary evidence indicates that tenure is far from being guaranteed in politics.

Although the insecurity of public office is a fact, it does, however, require an explanation. Whenever an occupational role is part of a competitive situation—as it normally is in politics—insecurity of tenure is bound to be felt. Tenure, of course, refers to the role itself and not to any other roles the person may occupy. A politician may have a guaranteed income from other sources so that his economic anxieties are allayed; yet his insecurity as a politician will force him to reduce the tensions of the political role. And this will not necessarily be done for selfish reasons. The reduction of tension will be an indicator of success as a politician, meaning that his work is being done more effectively. A person who has to devote considerable time and energy to the security of his tenure will be more responsive, both consciously and subconsciously, to the wishes of those governing his tenure than one who does not. The politician is in this position because he is elected. He is therefore peculiarly sensitive to the currents of public opinion in his constituency. The fickle nature of the crosscurrents of opinion adds to his insecurity, for the number of issues on which the constituency can be unified into significant, clear-cut majorities is rather small. The politician's mandate, then, is ambiguous on most issues and his insecurity heightened for that reason. No politician can ignore public opinion. Even when he feels it to be wrong, it is still a fact that he has to calculate when attempting to rule.

The strains of insecurity then stem from the periodic, usually rather short, terms of office that a politician can attain only by winning elections. Much of what a politician does can be viewed as varying forms of response to political insecurity. The very fact that American politicians respond more quickly and willingly to the demands of their constituencies than to those of their parties is a recognition, by them, of the source of the insecurity.[5] In devoting their attentions to the constituencies, they are hoping to relieve tension and its consequences.

Increases in salary and pension plans are also means of coping with the problem. Control over elections—ranging

[3] "Tenure and Turnover of Legislative Personnel," *Annals* 195 (Jan. 1938), 21–31.
[4] "Tribulations of a State Senator," *Reporter* (May 17, 1956), pp. 24–28.

[5] Julius Turner, *Party and Constituency: Pressures on Congress* (Baltimore, 1951), p. 179.

from the purely legal ones of intense campaigning and gerrymandering to the illegal buying of votes—are additional responses. Among the better-known means of control has been the resistance of politicians to the adoption of open primaries. Since the primary adds another hurdle, many policians obviously opposed it; when they could no longer prevent its development, they then moved to minimize its effects. They were aided in this by an indifferent electorate. No politician encourages competition, and certainly not at the primaries. There the effort is to eliminate as many potential competitors as possible before the formal election and to reduce the effectiveness of those who escape during the campaign.

Democratic forms of procedure, however, are designed to promote competition so that the politician can never be said to have complete control over his fate. And, as stated above, forces from without the constituency can and do affect tenure. Great social forces—and such well-known phenomenon as the "coattail" effect—all impinge upon the politician's tenure of office.[6] They are, almost of necessity, imponderable forces and difficult for the practical politician to control.

*Role Conflicts*

The fact that most politicians serve in more than one role as elective public officials guarantees conflicts among norms of performance. Expectations emanating from a variety of sources impinge upon the politician every time he is to make a decision. Various persons and groups constantly attempt to influence the decisions and the premises of the politician so that the actual decision will satisfy the interests of the

persons specifying the premises or decisions.

Talcott Parsons' pattern-variable scheme enables us to categorize the premises of decisions in terms of five dichotomous choices on the part of the actor in orienting himself to his situation.[7] Different orientations mean different decisions on the part of the politician—hence the great concern in shaping the politicians' orientation by other persons. If a politician chooses to accept or be guided in his decision making by one role in preference to another, he is forced to de-emphasize other roles he might be expected by some to perform. This matter of choosing certain premises rather than others brings out the problem of role conflict.

We can illustrate the point by characterizing two roles, the administrative and the partisan. When these roles are analyzed in terms of the pattern variables, one can readily see that the expectations concerning performances are contrary at every relevant choice point. The premises of action in each role are opposed. Whereas the administrator is expected to be affectively neutral, the partisan is expected to be affectively involved in the situation. Whereas the administrator's role is functionally specific, the partisan's is diffused. The administrator is expected to employ universalistic standards; the partisan, to employ particularistic criteria. Whereas administrators are expected to be achievement-oriented, the partisan has to be ascriptively oriented. And, finally, partisans are expected to be self-oriented, while administrators are expected to be collectivity-oriented.

The norms or premises of action ex-

---

[6] See V. O. Key, Jr., *American State Politics: An Introduction* (New York, 1956), chs. ii and viii; Samuel Lubell, *The Future of American Politics* (New York, 1951).

[7] The pattern-variable scheme is dealt with in most of Parsons' recent work. The best introduction, however, contained in the volume edited by Parsons and Edward A. Shils, *Towards a General Theory of Action* (Cambridge, 1952), pp. 76–91.

pected by others of the politician are not always in conflict. At some of the relevant junctures in decision making, the premises may be the same so that no role conflict ensues. We know that administrative and the judicial roles have much in common. The one role which, perhaps, conflicts the most with each of the other roles is that of the partisan. One should not deduce, therefore, that the partisan role is dysfunctional and to be suppressed. Whether it ought to be is a value judgment and not a scientific one.

The conflicts that theoretically exist among the four roles of the polity can be simply presented in tabular form. This means of presentation has the merit of bringing out the relationships among the norms in a clearer fashion.

One can proceed down the other columns in the same way and list the conflicts.

A fruitful question to pose at this time is: Under what conditions are role conflicts most likely to occur? On an impressionistic basis alone the answer suggests that the major variables are the office, the structure of the constituency, and the incumbent of the office.

Obviously those offices which combine the greater number of roles will engender the most conflicts, whereas the offices with the fewest number of roles develop the fewest conflicts. Offices such as the presidency, governorships, and mayoralties of the large cities are likely to be the source of more conflicts than both legislative and judicial offices. In the latter case litigants and interested

TABLE 1. THE PATTERN-VARIABLES AND ROLE CONFLICT

| Role | 1 | 2 | 3 | 4 | 5 |
|---|---|---|---|---|---|
| Admin. | Specific | Affective neutrality | Universalistic | Collectivity orientation | Achievement |
| Executive | Diffuse | Affective neutrality | Universalistic | Collectivity | Achievement |
| Partisan | Diffuse | Affective | Particularistic | Self-orientation | Ascription |
| Judicial | Specific | Affective neutrality | Universalistic | Collectivity | Ascription |

Table 1 illustrates the role structure and possible areas of conflict. Read horizontally, Table 1 describes in terms of the pattern variables the premises or norms of each of the four possible roles constituting an office. If instead of the rows the columns are read, we are presented with the points at which conflicts among the norms or premises of decisions are found. Thus in the first column the conflicts are found between the administrative role and both the executive and partisan roles. Again, the executive role conflicts with the judicial. In total there are four possible conflicts at this juncture in the decision-making process.

persons or groups have conflicting expectations about the outcome of a particular trial or decision, but the role of the justice is so clearcut, so isolated from the other role, and so protected from the public and retribution that role conflicts are minimized. The legislative and executive offices are not so protected; but since the legislator generally has fewer roles to play, he has fewer conflicts. His conflicts are of another type involving the same role, usually the partisan, in conflict with other partisans rather than with other roles. Republican and Democratic congressmen apply the same premises of action but come out with opposing decisions on a particular piece of legislation. One votes "yes" and the other "no."

It stands to reason that in the matter of constituencies, those districts which have the greatest heterogeneity in the voting population will cause the greatest number of conflicts for their elective public officials to resolve. Some voters will expect their officeholders to act as executives, and others will emphasize other roles. Generally speaking, the larger the constituency in terms of population, the greater will be the heterogeneity and the subsequent number of conflicts. Senators probably face more role conflicts than do congressmen, assuming other factors are constant. Because of the districting process some congressmen have larger constituencies than do many senators, so the former's problems may be magnified as a result. Congressman Celler is a good example, as he has more constituents than many western senators do. Among the executive offices role conflicts are greater on the national level than on the state and local levels.

### Private versus Public Roles

The type of role conflict discussed in the previous section dealt with conflicts originating within or among the various roles that constitute an elective public office. But these are not the only role conflicts a politician must face. The fact is that politicians while fulfilling public office must also play private roles, i.e., roles without formal public responsibilities. The distinction between the two types of roles is a convention, as are all roles, but it is a convention of the greatest significance in a democracy and especially in America.

In short, behavior which is regarded as acceptable or even admirable in private life may not be so regarded in public office. Let us compare, e.g., the role of the businessman with that of an elected public officeholder. The former is not only permitted to attempt to maximize his financial returns but is encouraged to do so; the public official, on the other hand, is not only discouraged from doing so but is sometimes required to divest himself of financial holdings. The politician is expected to work directly and at all times for the public interest, whereas the businessman is encouraged to serve his own ends. This contradiction between private, economic, and political roles would not be important if the politician could simply play one or the other role. In reality he must generally play both roles because public office seldom provides the incumbent his sole income. Insecurity of tenure and low salaries often force the politician to maintain other sources of income. As a result the politician has to live by a dual set of norms. To honor one set may mean the dishonoring of the other.

I should now like to consider another type of strain, one arising from this same source in the conflict of private and public roles. The previous illustration was one of a private and a public role conflict stemming from simultaneous adherence to both roles. Another type of strain results when a person transfers from one role to another but has difficulty in shedding his previous role and adopting the new one. This is particularly the case when at least one of the roles in sharply defined. A scholar, a military man, or a minister will probably have great difficulty in adjusting to the roles of a politician. Each role is not only sharply defined but defined in a way that is quite different from those of political life. Consider the notion of authority in each of these roles: the politician is expected to honor majorities; the minister the word of God; the scholar the canons of science; and the military man superior office or rank. A person who has devoted many years of obedience to any one set of these norms and who suddenly finds that he is expected to honor a new set is faced with very intense problems of adjustment. Political life subjects the person not only to a new set of norms but to different occupational problems, problems which it is not easy to prepare for through education or any other kind of experience. To be successful in a private role does not automatically guarantee success in public office. Illustrations are hardly necessary.

*Ambiguities in Political Situations*

Lest the discussion suggest that most political situations are characterized by clear-cut conflicting expectations, let me emphasize the fact that as many or even more are dominated by ambiguity. Instead of being pulled in opposite directions by well-known forces, the elected official is often in the position of a lost hunter seeking direction.

Both the administrative and partisan roles share in the ambiguity, but the latter experiences a somewhat different type. The ambiguities of the administrative role stem from a lack of knowledge concerning means, and the partisan has difficulty defining the goals of the community. Theoretically the former admit of scientific resolution; the latter only of compromise or power. Goals are, by definition, preferences, and in a democracy individual preferences are ideally weighted equally, as is testified by the practice of one man, one vote. While an administrator is concerned with the efficiency of means, the partisan focuses on the moral question of whether efficiency is the desired norm to apply. In a democracy efficiency may not be the proper end of social action.

Yet the value problems confronted by the politician are not insoluble. Politicians do have some relatively stable reference points in the American value systems. The problem is one of the practical application of general norms to specific social problems. The task is not easy because standards change, constituency pressures are conflicting and powerful, and the authoritative documents, like the Constitution, are not always crystal clear. Politicians lack the certainty of scientifically valid answers, because political situations are concerned with values that do not admit of scientific treatment.[8]

Response to ambiguous situations is uncertain response, whereas response to conflicting but unequal forces is generally certain. Politicians often have "no comment" to make when confronted by the former case. They are "waiting for the dust to settle," for the situation to clarify itself in terms of expectations and possibilities. Those situations in which the greatest amount of ambiguity exist are those in which both the greatest amount of strain and perhaps freedom are present. Depending upon the incumbent, the politician can either be immobilized or creative. Well-structured situations can permit independent action, as in a constituency where a given problem is of little concern; such is the case in many northern districts where the "Negro problem" is unimportant. But they may also deter independent action when the expectations are overwhelming in one direction. Such is the case with politicians in the South when faced with race issues.

Politicians react to ambiguity by attempting to reduce it. Public opinion polls, newspaper commentary, personal contact with constituents, reports from advisers, research bureaus, investigating committees, and "trial balloons" are a

8 The assertion is premised upon the notion that political systems are primarily concerned with the specification of societal goals and the mobilization of support for their implementation. And, finally, it is maintained that such goals are statements of preference and not factual assertions about reality.

few of the methods used to counteract uncertainty. But while politicians are utilizing more scientific processes to gather factual data for the structuring of situations, in the final analysis the data is never complete, nor can it resolve value questions, because logically an "ought" statement cannot be deduced from an "is" statement. The politician's responsibility to define system goals will always be fraught with ambiguity.

*Diffused Responsibility and Limited Controls*

Though the politician has to define his own sense of responsibility to some extent, it is probably safe to say that responsibility in all offices which have an executive role to play is diffused regardless of how the incumbent decides to structure his own role.[9] Executive responsibility is generalized rather than specific—as in most administrative roles or other nonpolitical, specialized roles. The focus in such a role is upon relationships with other persons rather than upon technical goals to be reached by the most efficient means. Men are to be treated less as instruments for the creation of things than as ends in themselves whose co-operation has to be sought before anything can be done. In a democracy diffused responsibility and limited controls over the situation are built into the situation of the leader. While the politician is often held responsible by someone for practically everything, he cannot control many of the variables that affect the outcome of the situation and its demands. This is, of course, more true of the executive role than of any other, and of national than of state and local offices. But politicians from all levels complain about the limited control they have to effectuate goals.

Most of the strain that comes from

this disparity of responsibility and control relates to the structure of government in the United States. The American polity disperses power to such an extent that no one official is able to accomplish a task without the co-operation of several other officials, who may have different values and goals and may, in addition, belong to a different party. Because the formal means for securing co-operation are not always sufficient, many informal means have grown up. I need not specify these means here, but merely indicate that role strains have encouraged them.

Politicians are constantly attempting to improve their control over their situations. Proposals are always being advanced to give the President more control, the Congress more control, the governors more control, and so on. I might quote a few politicians on the subject. Note how they claim inability to meet their functions as presently defined by themselves. Notice, too, that a simple reform of the structure of government is expected to improve their control. In general, while politicians always have good things to say about the American polity, they seldom deceive themselves about their own position within it. The governmental system, though outmoded in many respects, is never outmoded fundamentally. Efficiency can be introduced by enacting the necessary reforms.

Senator Kefauver has been quite articulate concerning reform of the governmental structure. In fact, he wrote a book on the subject, though restricting his analysis to the situation of congressmen. In the opening pages appears a straightforward statement about the strains of politics:

> Like many an average freshman congressman, I had my ideals and plans for worthwhile legislation. . . . I was anxious that Congress be equipped for the part it would have to play.

[9] See Talcott Parsons, *The Social System* (Glencoe, Ill., 1951), p. 100.

As the years passed, the results were disappointing. I found that the outmoded legislative machinery made it difficult to get much done. I soon realized that the Congress, intended by the Founding Fathers to be the predominate branch of the government, was ill-equipped to chart the legislative program of the nation and was surrendering too many treasured powers to the Executive. I also discovered that the numerous other services expected of a congressman left me little time to study or analyze legislation.[10]

Later, Senator Kefauver speculates on the reasons why men leave active political careers. One of the reasons was the "feeling of frustration due to the inefficiency that results from trying to run a twentieth-century Congress without adequate tools." The frustrations of office outweighed the contributions one could make.

The volume of work and responsibility is simply too taxing for the legislator to accept his job with equanimity. Practically every student of the legislative process has commented upon this fact and suggested reforms to improve the condition. Senator Kefauver was one of these people. Senator La Follette was another.[11] Those who assisted La Follette and Senator Monroney in the legislative reorganization of Congress in 1946 also wished to reduce the demands upon the legislator stemming from organizational sources.

*Time and the Pressure of Demands*

A persistent complaint of politicians at all levels is related to the number of demands being made on their time and influence. Voters commonly overestimate the influence of politicians; consequently

[10] Estes Kefauver and Jack Levin, *A Twentieth Century Congress* (New York, 1947), p. vii.

[11] Robert M. La Follette, Jr., "A Senator Looks at Congress," *Atlantic Monthly*, 172 (July 1943), 91–96.

they ask them to do the impossible. More burdensome are their time-consuming requests; the politician often feels this time could better be devoted to more important matters. Local politicians expect to perform chores and usually do not complain to the same extent as do politicians who are concerned with more significant policy matters. Senator Downey of California gives a vivid portrait of the burdens of a senator, burdens which, incidentally, are increasing:

Each day Senators have matters come before them which could, if they could spare the time, occupy their attentions for months...yet here we are compelled to dispose of weighty and complicated matters after being able to listen to arguments only for perhaps an hour or two.... Observe for a moment the volume of business that is done in my office alone. It is so great as almost to break me and my whole staff down. In mail alone we receive from 200 to 300 letters every 24 hours. And this in addition to telegrams and long-distance calls and personal visits. We do the best we can. We try to have every letter answered the day it is received. My staff is departmentalized. That is, each girl is an expert in some particular field.... If the office were not so organized, we could not possibly begin to carry the load. Yet, Mr. Chairman, I can say to you truthfully that even if I had four times the amount of time I have I could not possibly perform adequately and fully the duties imposed upon me as ambassador from my state. In the departments of government there are always delays or injustices or matters overlooked in which a Senator can be of very great assistance to his constituents. The flood of duties in my office has reached such proportions, and is so steadily increasing, that I am almost totally unable to enter into the study of any legislative matters. That means that frequently

I have to inform myself concerning matters of importance by listening to arguments on the floor of the Senate. And yet even my presence on the floor is only intermittent, so great is the burden of my office duties if I am to efficiently carry out my responsibilities with respect to the state of California.[12]

Senator Fulbright adds his lament in the following words:

But the fact is that the multitude of requests for minor personal services comes close to destroying the effectiveness of a great many capable representatives. The legislator finds himself in a dilemma. If he refuses to see the constant stress of visitors or to give personal attention to their requests, they may become offended and withdraw their support. In addition, it is personally gratifying to be able to be of help to one's friends. On the other hand, if he does give his attentions to these matters, he literally has no time left for the intelligent study and reflection that sound legislation requires.[13]

The senator further states that voters often will not accept the services of secretaries but insist on the personal attention of the politician. "They [the voters] feel that they elected the Senator and they are, therefore, entitled to his personal attention."[14] Senator Kennedy adds:

If we tell our constituents frankly that we can do nothing, they feel we are unsympathetic or inadequate. If we try and fail—usually meeting a counteraction from other Senators representing other interests—they say we are like all the rest of the politi-

cians. All we can do is retreat into the cloakroom and weep on the shoulder of a sympathetic colleague— or go home and snarl at our wives.[15]

Several of the quotations just given suggest rather strongly that politicians, at least those on the congressional level, feel frustrated in their mission by the press of time and conflicting demands in their situation. The politician often feels that he has a job of considerable responsibility and that petty demands prevent him from making the contribution which he was elected to do and ought to do. Young politicians are frequently disillusioned about politics in this respect. Senator Neuberger, then a newly elected state legislator in Oregon, wrote: "I arrived at our new marble Capitol expecting to spend most of my time considering momentous issues—social security, taxes, conservation, civil liberties. Instead, we have devoted long hours to the discussions of regulations for the labeling of eggs."[16]

*Status Insecurities*

Adequate performance on the part of role incumbents requires some form of compensation or appreciation for the services rendered. Most men like to believe that what they are doing is a contribution to others and that the relevant others know this and are grateful. Politicians are no different in this respect than are other people; if anything, they are even more sensitive to opinion about their work than are many other groups in the community. Although politicians occasionally voice dissatisfaction with their monetary rewards, more often the complaint is about an assumed low social status. According to T. V. Smith and L. D. White,

---

[12] George B. Galloway, *Congress at the Crossroads* (New York, 1946), p. 279.

[13] J. William Fulbright, "The Legislator: Duties, Functions, and Hardships of Public Officials," *Vital Speeches of the Day*, 12 (May 15, 1946), 470.

[14] *Ibid.*

[15] *New York Times Magazine*, Dec. 18, 1955, p. 34.

[16] I Go to the Legislature, *Survey Graphic*, 30 (July 1941), 374.

"The politician's faith in himself has been impaired by the people's distrust of him."[17] I have some doubts about the assumption of a low status for the politicians, but the important point is the assumption in the case of the politicians themselves. If they feel they are appreciated, they may act accordingly. "If he [the politician] believes in himself he'll devote himself to his high mission," Smith and White conclude.[18]

Senator Robert La Follette, Jr., voiced a common complaint in respect to the status of Congressmen:

Congress has been a favorite target for the disgruntled, the disappointed, the intellectual snobs, and the doubters of democracy alike. But most of this criticism is not constructive. It springs from personal prejudice, political bias, and above all from an utter lack of knowledge of the workaday problems with which a great legislative body must deal.[19]

After stating that "a legislator, like other people, has an ego that requires expression and recognition if it is to avoid becoming warped and eccentric," Senator Fulbright went on to say:

Honorable men in public life can take the abuse that is heaped upon them by the public so long, and then they succumb to a sense of futility and frustration. It is true that some of the frustration that afflicts the Member of Congress is due to the antique and obsolete organization of the Congress itself, and it should be remedied. But of far greater influence upon the decision of good men to remain in politics is the attitude of those whom they seek to serve.[20]

Senator Neuberger has also been quoted

as saying the vilification of politics is "one of the nation's basic problems."[21]

Status insecurities thus grow out of the ambivalent status accorded the politician by the voters. The politician is never quite certain whether he has a position of respect or not. If he is convinced that he has, he is still unsure about the reason for it. The reasons may not be particularly admirable ones, for the politician is subject to much selfish flattery. Some he can recognize, but not all. As a result many politicians are likely to manifest forms of behavior that indicate doubt about their prestige.

The foregoing quotations indicate some of the responses of the politician to his status insecurity. The first response is to give verbal expression to the fact, writing articles about the plight of the public official. Note, too, that the writers assert vigorously that the politician is mistakenly abused and that he serves a vital function in society. Typical in this respect is an article by Governor Bradford of Massachusetts entitled, "Politicians Are Necessary Too."[22] A congressman and scholar has written an article on "The Magnitude of the Task of the Politician" to prove that the politician deserves better treatment.[23] In *Profiles in Courage* a well-known present-day senator, John Kennedy, has defended the politician by citing historical examples of great politicians who lived up to their principles. There is a certain defensiveness about such articles and books, indicating that the politician is not only interested in correcting the public's view of him but in sustaining his own conception of himself as a useful member of society.

[17] *Politics and Public Service: A Discussion of the Civic Art in America* (New York, 1939), p. 228.

[18] *Ibid.*, p. 229.

[19] La Follette, *op. cit.*, p. 92.

[20] Fulbright, *op. cit.*, p. 472.

[21] Quoted by Maurice Klain, " 'Politics'— Still a Dirty Word," *Antioch Review* (Winter 1955–1956), 464.

[22] *Harvard Business Review*, 32 (Nov.–Dec. 1954), 37–41.

[23] Frederich M. Davenport, in *Harvard Business Review*, 11 (July 1943), 468–477.

Status insecurity can take other forms. One of the more obvious is for the politician simply to leave the realm of active politics. As noted earlier, Senator Kefauver believes some excellent congressmen are leaving government for precisely this reason. I have no statistics on the matter, but it seems certain that status insecurity does lead some men to leave politics. The writer knows of two individuals who paricipated in local politics but decided, with the approval of their wives, that they had taken enough abuse from unappreciative voters. Their resentment is considerable, even though other politicians have taken more abuse during the same period and in the same area.

Politicians form a sort of informal mutual admiration society to compensate for their insecurities. The often exaggerated deference that politicians show for one another, in spite of party affiliations, suggests a latent function in terms of maintaining morale. The politicians who appear on television and radio to debate various issues always pay high tributes to their opponents and colleagues. The same is true of much of the debate that takes place in legislative assemblies. The contributions of one politician are always cited by other politicians in their public appearances. Incidentally the politician generally refers to his colleagues as "statesmen," and seldom, except during a campaign and only in regard to the opposition, as "politicians."

Still another means of coping with status insecurity is for the politician to adopt a cynical attitude toward those who are responsible for his situation, the voters. Not infrequently, the politician becomes tough-minded and cynical. By distrusting other people and their motives, he immunizes himself from criticism and disappointment. The politician may attempt to convince himself that he is uninterested in the attitudes of others. In fact, he cannot be, but the delusion is comforting.

Some politicians adopt a stoic view to handle their status problems. Presidents Roosevelt, Truman, and Eisenhower have all been known to say that the varying degrees of abuse to which each has been subjected is petty and unimportant compared to the criticism suffered by some of the greatest of American Presidents. The detractors are, so Truman is reported to have once said, soon forgotten. The historical-minded politician is more concerned with what future generations will think of him than what his contemporaries do. The conviction that what one is doing will be of lasting importance sustains the politician through the rocky present.

The role of humor ought not to be underestimated as a means for handling the strains of politics, including that of status insecurity. Politicians like the late Senator Barkley were not only renowned for their gift of humor but also honored for the use which they made of it during times of great stress. The politician, as Senator Wiley has shown, is quite capable of laughing at himself.[24] The fact that he can and does may constitute an effort to minimize the difficulties of political life.

CONCLUSION

I have indicated some of the major sources of strain in the occupation of the elected public official. Instead of summarizing them, I want, now, to list a few propositions or, better, hypotheses about role strains in the hope that others may be stimulated to further research. The hypotheses are stated in an unqualified manner and without supporting evidence.

Hypothesis 1. The more complex the social system, the more numerous are the possible sources of role strains.

[24] *Laughing with Congress* (New York, 1947).

Hypothesis 2. The more sharply roles are defined in a system the more intense will be the resultant strains where role conflict occurs.

Hypothesis 3. In the American polity executive offices are subject to more role strains than are legislative and judicial offices.

Hypothesis 4. Legislative offices are subject to more role strains than are judicial offices.

Hypothesis 5. The higher the office, i.e., in terms of the local, state, and national division, the more numerous the role strains.

Two further subjects deserve emphasis. The first concerns the practical use of any information which might result from further studies in the area of occupational role strains in politics. We know very little about the way in which public officials respond to the conditions under which they labor. Yet, as democrats, we want them to perform their functions in a responsive and responsible manner. Traditional political theory has not offered much help in devising conditions that will produce the desired behavior. Since much of political behavior is conditioned by the strains to which it is subject, we might inquire into those strains, their sources, and the resultant behavior. If we can understand and, perhaps, control the strains, we will be in a better position to make the ideals of democratic rule possible. I do not wish to be understood as pleading for a reduction of the strains

of politicians, if indeed that were possible. American democratic theory has always emphasized the desirability of subjecting public officials to various strains, and no doubt there is much to be said for this position. But empirical evidence on the point is rare, and the problem remains. In any case it is worth entertaining the view that the elected official's work, like that of other organizational members, might be improved by bettering his conditions of employment.

The final point I want to make relates to research on role strains. Relationships need to be established—if there are any —among types of offices, personalities, awareness of strains among politicians, and their behavior. The research apparatus of the social sciences is sufficiently advanced to handle most of the problems involved. Questionnaires and interviews can be used quite effectively in getting at a politician's awareness of his occupational problems and frustrations. Harold Lasswell long ago demonstrated some of the possibilities. More recently certain political scientists have shown how legislators respond to conflicting expectations when they cast their votes. And, of course, we have a rich background of historical and biographical writing from which to derive hypotheses and data. Burns's study of Roosevelt and the Georges' personality analysis of Wilson contain excellent material on the role strains of these two Presidents.

B. *Political Parties*

# ORGANIZATION AND DEMOCRACY
# WITHIN POLITICAL PARTIES

JOHN D. MAY

This article marks an attempt to clarify the teachings of Robert Michels. It suggests that in *Political Parties: A Sociological Study of the Oligarchical Tendencies of Modern Democracy* (1915), Michels presented a *favorable* account of the compatibility of organization and democracy.

Other treatments attribute to Michels a thesis of the following kind: (1) Large, organizationally complex associations, compared with small, simple associations, are likely to be governed by cliques whose powers (disposable resources, freedom of action, security of tenure) are abundant and whose policies (use of official status and resources) deviate from the policy-preferences of their constituents. (2) Increments of Organization (of scale, or members, and of complexity, or procedural formality, functional differentiation, stratification, specialization, hierarchy, and bureaucracy) augment the powers and the policy-deviating propensities of leaders *vis-à-vis* followers.[1]

It probably is true that in Michels's terms, a system where leaders possess the means and the disposition to ignore their followers' will (or wills) is an undemocratic system.[2] It is not true that

challenges, see the following: P. M. Blau and W. R. Scott, *Formal Organizations* (Chandler, 1962), pp. 48, 228; R. A. Dahl and C. E. Lindblom, *Politics, Economics and Welfare* (Harper, 1953), pp. 279–85; A. W. Gouldner, ed., *Studies in Leadership*, pp. 418–35 (T. W. Adorno) and 477–504 (B. Barber); Arthur Kornhauser and others, eds., *Industrial Conflict* (McGraw-Hill, 1954), ch. 9 (L. H. Fisher and G. McConnell); H. D. Lasswell and A. Kaplan, *Power and Society* (Yale, 1950); R. T. McKenzie, *British Political Parties* (Praeger, 1964 ed.), pp. 15–17, ch. 11; Robert Presthus, *The Organizational Society* (Knopf, 1962), pp. 4, 41–52; Giovanni Sartori, *Democratic Theory* (Wayne State University Press, 1962), pp. 42, 82, 100, 120–28, 134; David Spitz, *Patterns of Anti-Democratic Thought* (Macmillan, 1949), esp. p. 27 and the treatment in Part II of James Burnham's *The Machiavellians*; D. B. Truman, *The Governmental Process* (Knopf, 1955), pp. 137–55.

[2] Michels does not use the terms "democracy," "oligarchy," and "organization" in a consistent or coherent manner. The terminological difficulties have been probed by C. W. Cassinelli, in "The Law of Oligarchy," *American Political Science Review*, Vol. 47 (Sept. 1953), p. 3 ff. However, Michels persistently associates democracy with equality, with conditions suggesting the notion of popular sovereignty, and with the "system in which delegates represent the mass and carry out its will." On the other hand, he speaks of "The notion of the representation of popular inter-

[1] See S. M. Lipset's introduction to the Collier Books edition (1962) of *Political Parties*, and the commentaries cited by Lipset. For additional statements or approximations of this version of Michels's thesis, and some

*Reprinted from John D. May, "Democracy, Organization, Michels,"* AMERICAN POLITICAL SCIENCE REVIEW, *59 (June 1965), 417–29, by permission of the publisher and the author.*

on Michels' showing, organization is relatively inhospitable to democratic leader-follower relations. It is not true that Michels portrays increments of Organization as breeders, persistently and proportionally, of counter-democratic changes. Instead, he argues (in a complex but not inconsistent manner) that Organization is incompatible with the attainment or maintenance of absolute democracy and yet can be a source, in many cases and in many ways, of democratization.

It is true that Michels deplored Organization. It is true that Michels voiced a profound pessimism about the fate of mankind, a pessimism rooted in conceptions of the indispensability and the consequences of Organization. It is not true that Michels's pessimism was the pessimism of a democrat.

Far from being a democrat, Michels was a Romantic Revolutionist. He deplored the "conservative" effects of Organization—its general tendency to facilitate the maintenance of a society which is not and cannot be perfectly democratic, and its particular tendency to dissipate "revolutionary currents" in society. But by his account, Organization is counter-revolutionary precisely because it facilitates the amelioration of discontents and injustices; it facilitates democratization.

Far from being a democrat, moreover, Michels was a Scientific Paternalist. He portrayed, and lamented, Organization as the nemesis of authority-systems wherein leaders possess the means and the disposition to voice the scientifically ascertained Interests of the "mass." But by his account, Organization facilitates the advent and the maintenance of leaders who are able and willing to ex-

press the manifest wills of their clients or constituents.

Such, at any rate, is the interpretation which seems consistent with the following analysis of (I) Michels's account of general historical trends, (II) his basic reasoning, and (III) his treatment of the Socialist experience.

## I

According to Michels's account of general trends, *democratization has persistently accompanied Organization.*

The modern era, in which "political and economic life" acquires increasingly "complex forms," and in which massive bureaucratization occurs in the state and industry and labor, is "what we know as the era of democracy."[3] Only the "blind and fanatical" fail to perceive that "the democratic current daily makes undeniable advance."[4]

Modern "state institutions" exhibit "increasing democratization." Human "freedoms and privileges" have broadened. The workers are enjoying "better conditions of labor;" their burgeoning aptitude for "criticism and control" is bound to increase further "in proportion as the economic status of the masses undergoes improvement and becomes more stable, and as the masses are admitted more effectively to the advantages of civilization."[5]

Michels stipulates that in "the sphere of party" as contrasted with "the sphere of the state," democracy is in a "descending phase." Yet he testifies that a "democratic external form" prevails among modern parties. The aristocratic parties have come to espouse "democratic" policies, and some liberal and conservative parties have worked "essentially" for "socialist ideas and for the victory of the proletariat." The Socialist International has changed from an "in-

ests, a notion to which the great majority of democrats...cleave...." *Political Parties,* trans. Eden and Cedar Paul (Dover Publications, 1959), esp. pp. 1–2, 27, 401. References hereafter will be to this edition unless designated otherwise.

3 Pp. 33, 40.
4 P. 402.
5 Pp. 329, 406.

dividual dictatorship" into "a federal republic consisting of several independent oligarchies." Nearly every Socialist and labor group has manifested "tendencies toward decentralization," tendencies which create pluralistic rather than monistic oligarchies. In the German Socialist and labor parties, an "enormous increase" in membership and in organizational development has been accompanied by changes from "dictatorship" to "oligarchy" and to "theoretical and applied democracy."[6]

The foregoing citations are not arbitrarily selective. Michels does not specifically name any associations in which democracy has been attenuated by Organization.

His contradictory testimony concerning party evolution may be ascribed to at least two sources. On the one hand, it may be ascribed to inconsistent, ambiguous use of the term "party." Sometimes "party" denotes an existential aggregate; sometimes if refers to a hypothetical aggregate. Thus, the so-called, existential 'parties' have not manifested counter-democratic changes, but hypothetical, authentic 'parties' must undergo such changes.

On the other hand, his contradictory testimony may be ascribed to inconsistent, ambiguous use of the term "democracy." Sometimes "democracy" signifies close control by followers over leaders; sometimes it signifies a distinctive associational character (an ideological, sociological, operational uniqueness) and a moral commitment to the cause of social-democratic revolution.

Only in the latter unconventional sense, and only with respect to hypothetical aggregates, does he sustain the argument that 'parties' necessarily undergo a counter-'democratic' transformation.

## II

According to Michels's basic reasoning, *Organization precludes democracy,*

6 Pp. 3, 5, 5n, 11, 63, 190, 194, 201.

*and can destroy democracy, and can facilitate democratization.*

These three propositions are not contradictory. The first pertains to what is ultimately attainable. The others pertain to what can happen in various situations.

ORGANIZATION PRECLUDES DEMOCRACY. Michels argues persuasively that the presence of Organization is incompatible with the presence of democracy:

Organization implies the tendency to oligarchy.... Immanent oligarchical tendencies [exist] in every kind of human organization which strives for the attainment of definite ends.... Oligarchy is...a preordained form of the common life of great social aggregates.... The majority of human beings, in a condition of eternal tutelage, are predestined...to submit to the dominion of a small minority, and must...constitute the pedestal of an oligarchy.... Leadership is a necessary phenomenon in every form of social life [and] every system of leadership is incompatible with the most essential postulates of democracy.... All order and civilization must exhibit aristocratic features.[7]

This reiterated proposition seems logically unassailable, so long as two considerations are kept in mind: (a) the proposition pertains only to the attainability of 'pure' democracy, or absolute equality; and (b) "oligarchy" signifies not the antithesis of democracy, but a condition occupying the ground between pure democracy and pure autocracy.

With these considerations noted, the basis of his proposition can readily be appreciated.[8] The presence of Organization signifies the presence of an associa-

7 Pp. 11, 32, 390, 400, 402.

8 We are excluding here Michels's arguments for the indispensability of Organization and his suggestions that the process of Organization tends to be self-accelerating. Attention is confined to the question of what arrangements can be compatible with the presence of Organization.

tion whose members are so numerous that it is technically difficult for all to participate equally in all decisions. This condition also is technically incompatible with the exercise by one member of direct control over the formulation and implementation of policies.

Similarly, the presence of Organization signifies the presence of a "system" of leadership, or of subordinate-superordinate relations, together with an established pattern of differentiated tasks, responsibilities, privileges and resources. These conditions are incompatible with equality—and with autocracy. There must be inequalities, and the inequalities must be multiple. Various tasks and resources are vested in various members of the association, each being endowed with a particular expertise and a particular decisional jurisdiction.[9]

In short, Organization necessitates "oligarchy"—that is, arrangements which are neither absolutely democratic nor absolutely autocratic.

Between the poles of pure democracy and pure autocracy lies an enormous range of variations. Although no "system of leadership" can be democratic, some can be less undemocratic than others. Variations can arise from differences in the rules, in the social composition, and in other traits of associations.

Michels does not say, nor does he imply, that the extent of deviation from pure democracy must be directly related to the size or complexity of organization. He does not exclude the possibility that increments of democratization can accompany increments of scale and complexity. Thus his proposition that Organization precludes (absolute) democracy is logically compatible with his reports that democratization has persistently accompanied Organization.

ORGANIZATION CAN DESTROY DEMOC-

RACY. Michels devotes most of his attention not to the proposition that Organization is a condition which precludes (absolute) democracy, but to the proposition that Organization is an agent which destroys (absolute) democracy:

Democracy leads to oligarchy, and necessarily contains an oligarchical nucleus. . . . When democracies have gained a certain stage of development, they undergo a gradual transformation, adopting the aristocratic spirit, and in many cases also the aristocratic forms, against which at the outset they struggled so fiercely. . . . Oligarchy . . . issues from democracy. . . . Organization is. . . the source from which the conservative currents flow over the plain of democracy. . . . The formation of oligarchies within the various forms of democracy is the outcome of organic necessity.[10]

The proposition contained in these passages has been persistently misunderstood. It is not that Organization breeds Oligarchy; it is that Democracy leads (through Organization) to Oligarchy. The difference is momentous.

Michels's proposition—his Iron Law of Oligarchy—is a statement about what must happen in groups which initially are democracies. Only when democracy is present initially can it be slain by Organization. Democracy is not self-evidently present in all groups which lack Organization. Some small, primitive groups may be run by bullies; others may be isocracies, or associations of equals. Only in the latter instances can the onset of Organization be blamed for the demise of Democracy.

Scholars have persistently inferred that Michels's Law applies, or can apply, to a much broader range of cases—perhaps to the generality of voluntary associations, or of social movements, or of human groups.[11] Michels has been credited with the broad proposition that

[9] For a sophisticated discussion of these processes and of some implications, see Langer, above, note 1, esp. ch. 3.

[10] Pp. viii, 22, 168, 402, 408.

[11] For example, David Easton, *The Political System* (Knopf, 1959), pp. 56–7.

increments of Organization invariably yield increments of Oligarchy. This misunderstanding may be due to a misapprehension concerning his use of key words. The key words are emphasized in the following passages:

> In every organization, whether it be a *political party*, a *professional union*, or any other *association of the kind*, the aristocratic tendency manifests itself very clearly. The mechanism of the organization, while conferring a solidity of structure, induces serious changes in the organized mass, completely inverting the respective position of the leaders and the led. As a result of organization, every *party* or *professional union* becomes divided into a minority of directors and a majority of directed.[12]

\* \* \*

Reduced to its most concise expression, the fundamental sociological *law of political parties* (the term "political" being used in its most comprehensive significance) may be formulated in the following terms: "It is organization which gives birth to the dominion of the elected over the electors, of the mandatories over the mandators, of the delegates over the delegators. Who says organization, says oligarchy."[13]

The crucial point here is that by "political parties" and "professional unions" Michels does not mean the generality of so-called, historical parties and unions. Instead, he uses these terms to designate the "kind" of association which is emphasized in Marxian thought: *association by social class*. This qualification is of vital importance.

According to the Marxian formulation, the members of a social class are equal to one another and are endowed with identical needs. If they actively associate, the initial relationship among them must be democratic. The leaders initially will be equal in resources to

the followers and will exemplify the policy-preferences of their followers. In Michels's terms, then, *who says "party" says initial democracy*. Thus,

> The term "party" presupposes that among the individual components of the party there *should* exist a harmonious direction of wills toward identical objective and practical aims. Where this is lacking, the party *becomes* a mere "organization."[14]

Similarly, in a "party,"

> Originally the chief is merely the servant of the mass. The organization is based upon the absolute equality of its members. Equality is here understood in its most general sense, as an equality of like men.... The democratic principle aims at guaranteeing to all an equal influence and an equal participation in the regulation of the common interests. All are electors, and all are eligible for office. ... All offices are filled by election. The officials, executive organs of the general will, play a merely subordinate part, are always dependent upon the collectivity, and can be deprived of their office at any moment. The mass of the party is omnipotent.[15]

From this romantic premise of "pure democracy," Michels unfolds his tragic tale of degeneration wrought by Organi-

---

[12] P. 32.
[13] P. 401.

[14] P. 376; emphasis added. He also says, "A party is neither a social unity nor an economic unity." (p. 387) His characterization of *change* in parties, however, presupposes initial unity. See section III below, under *Social Pluralism*.

[15] Pp. 27–8. Omitted from this quotation is a contradictory remark, illuminating Michels's chronic confusion about the difference between hypothesis and history. He remarks that the "equality of like men" is "manifested" in some cases (*i.e.*, Socialist labor groups) "by the mutual use of the familiar 'thou,' which is employed by the most poorly paid wage-laborer in addressing the most distinguished intellectuals." (p. 27) If poor laborers and intellectuals are associated, then "equality of like men" is absent. The group is not a social democracy, although it may employ equalitarian rituals and it may be pledged to the attainment of social democracy.

zation. In "the sphere of party," with "the advance of organization, democracy tends to decline." As far as party life is concerned,

> It may be enunciated as a general rule that the increase in the power of the leaders is directly proportional with the extension of the organization. In the various parties and labor organizations of different countries the influence of the leaders is mainly determined...by the varying development of organization. Where organization is stronger, we find that there is a lesser degree of applied democracy.[16]

Given this premise of initial democracy, Michels is logically free to argue that only at a "second stage" of organizational development (the stage of full-time, salaried, specialized officialdom) do leaders become "stable and irremovable."[17] Similarly, the assumption that the first leaders were indistinguishable from the followers enables him to say that the "first appearance of professional leadership" marks "the beginning of the end" for "democracy," since such leaders are said to be stronger than their followers and to be animated by deviant interests.[18]

This line of reasoning depends for its elemental plausibility on the validity of the premise of initial democracy. Michels's argument applies only to cases where "at first" the leaders are "no more than executive organs of the general wills," where the leaders first arise "spontaneously" to perform only "accessory and gratuitous" functions, where the leaders initially are "simple workmates" or "single molecule(s) of the mass."[19]

Such reasoning is conspicuous for the contingencies it does not cover. It does not cover associations initially run by bullies. It does not cover groups initially led by men who, instead of being "simple workmates," descend from upper social strata. Since it does not cover cases of this sort, it is neither sustained nor refuted by evidence that in many cases, including cases of so-called political parties, Organization has been accompanied by democratization.

ORGANIZATION CAN FACILITATE DEMOCRATIZATION. The propositions that Organization precludes absolute democracy and can destroy absolute democracy do not exclude the possibility that Organization can facilitate democratization. Two broad possibilities, within appropriate circumstances, are discernible from Michels's analysis.

(1) *Organization can facilitate 'external' democratization.* Michels teaches that Organization is the "weapon of the weak in their struggle with the strong"—an instrument which facilitates "economy of effort" and the political utilization of numerical strength.[20] He acknowledges that "Within certain narrow limits, the democratic party, even when subjected to oligarchical control, can doubtless act upon the state in a democratic sense."[21] (In the context, the phrase "democratic party" evidently denotes a kind of aim or interest, rather than an internal structure.) The chances for democratizing the state are relatively favorable "where there exists universal, equal, and direct suffrage, and where the working class is strongly organized and is awake to its own interests."[22]

In this argument Michels covers a contingency which he has been accused of overlooking. He acknowledges that the democratization of the state and of society can be promoted by, and can occur in the midst of, associations which are non-democratic.[23] Strong organization among society's lower strata impels

---

[16] P. 33.
[17] P. 401.
[18] P. 36.
[19] Pp. 31–2, 36, 206, 400.

[20] Pp. 21–2.
[21] P. 365.
[22] P. 365n.
[23] For example, see Sartori, above, note 1, pp. 121–26.

the ruling caste, for the sake of self-preservation, to make concessions in the form of policies and positions.[24]

The old political caste of society, and above all the "state" itself, are forced to undertake the revaluation of a considerable number of values—a revaluation both ideal and practical. The importance attributed to the masses increases, even when the leaders are demagogues. The legislature and the executive become accustomed to yield, not only to claims proceeding from above, but also to those proceeding from below.[25]

(2) *Organization can facilitate 'internal' democratization.* Michels does not deal explicitly with the possibility that Organization can facilitate the democratization of groups within society—that is, the equalization of resources among members and the conformity of leaders' policies to followers' wishes. Such a possibility may be inferred, however, from his testimony that counter-autocratic changes accompanied Socialist Organization. The same possibility may be inferred from the basis of his reasoning. Increments of Organization necessitate delegation and dispersal of authority. In the case of an association where all the members have exercised all authority on an equal basis, the effect of Organization will be counter-democratic. In the case of an association where one or just a few members have exercised all authority, the effect of Organization will be counter-autocratic. An appraisal of these possibilities may be gained from a review of Michels's treatment of Socialist history.

### III

According to Michels's account of Socialist experience in Western Europe before 1914,

ORGANIZATION   FACILITATES   DEMO-

CRATIZATION. He depicts Organization as the efficient cause of multitudinous changes in the 'character' of Socialism, changes that are alleged to be unavoidable and horrible. He spins a fable of innocence lost.

In the days of the so-called "socialism of the emigres," the socialists devoted themselves to an elevated policy of principles, inspired by the classic criteria of internationalism. Almost every one of them was...a specialist in this more general and comprehensive domain. The whole course of their lives, the brisk exchange of ideas on unoccupied evenings, the continued rubbing of shoulders between men of the most different tongues, the enforced isolation from the bourgeois world of their respective countries, and the utter impossibility of any "practical" action, all contributed to this result. But in proportion as, in their own country, paths of activity were opened for the socialists...the more did a recognition of the demands of the everyday life of the party divert their attention from immortal principles.[26]

With the advent of practical activities and professional activists, Socialism's "wider and more ideal cultural aims" were smothered by the "petty, narrow, rigid, and illiberal" bureaucratic spirit. The "logical audacities" and "revolutionary currents" suppressed, the once-bold champions displaced by routinizers whose "personal inclination towards quietism" could not be "neutralized" by "the preponderant energy of a comprehensive theory." Socialism's youthful promise to represent the "popular interests" was violated; the "democratic principle" of "THAT WHICH OUGHT TO BE" was suffocated by "that which is." Bureaucratization and vote-chasing ravished Socialism's "essential character"; having contracted "promiscuous

[24] See pp. 176, 185–87, 272, 392.
[25] P. 365.

[26] Pp. 187–8.

relationships with the most heterogeneous elements," Socialism lost "political virginity."[27]

Now let us dry our tears. Let us attempt to break the spell of the "metaphysical pathos" of organization.[28] Before agreeing with Michels that Socialism underwent a moral *and* a counter democratic degeneration because of the imperatives of Organization, let us attempt a more systematic canvass.

Below are listed ten changes which by Michels's account took place as the Socialist parties developed. Each will be discussed briefly for its broader theoretical implications.

(1) *Mitigation of formal dictatorship.* Genuine Socialist parties allegedly are, and some of the young Socialist parties allegedly were, corps of para-military combatants. Small, frail, ostentatiously seditious groups cannot afford the luxury of democratic procedures.[29] Socialist growth and development produced a new orientation, emphasizing legalism and electioneering. This marked a deviation from principle; it also facilitated and necessitated a measure of formal democratization.

In broader terms, Michels's analysis suggests that patterns of internal authority vary systematically according to associational aims and situations (or strategies) and sizes. Internal dictatorship is most likely to accompany revolutionary aims, extra-legal tactics, and smallness. Bigness necessitates allegiance, legalism, and a modicum of

internal democracy. Each factor helps to explain and engender the others.

(2) *Mitigation of informal dictatorship.* "Every great class movement in history has arisen upon the instigation, with the co-operation, and under the leadership of men sprung from the very class against which the movement was directed."[30] The Socialist movement allegedly consisted initially of two social strata: wage workers, or incipient proletarians, who in terms of "culture and of economic, physical and physiological conditions" are society's "weakest element"; and ex-bourgeois intellectuals, veritable "supermen," the "best instructed, most capable, and most adroit" products of society's most powerful class.[31] Such a composition is required because the workers, without help, are ignorant of their interests and their practical needs. It was "only when science placed itself at the service of the working class" that "the *proletarian* movement" became "a *socialist* movement." The men of "science" served at the head of the new movement. The early Socialist program was not a compromise between insight and ignorance; it was "a synthesis of the work of numerous learned men."[32]

Michels never claims the Socialist groups were democracies at *in*ception. He claims rather, that they were democratic in *con*ception—in the goals they espoused (rather than the procedures employed), and in the Interests they 'objectively' represented (as contrasted with the cause they actually promoted). Thus,

the socialist and revolutionary parties, ...in respect of *origin* and of *program*, represent the negation of any such tendency [as oligarchy], and have actually come into existence out of opposition thereto.... *In*

---

[27] Pp. 187, 189, 371, 307, 401 (his capitals), 376.

[28] See A. W. Gouldner, "Metaphysical Pathos and the Theory of Bureaucracy," *American Political Science Review*, Vol. 49 (1955), p. 3. Gouldner argues that Michels, Selznick (in *TVA and the Grass Roots*), and other modern theorists of group organization quite arbitrarily assume that the "unanticipated consequences" wrought by organization will be deplorable.

[29] Part I, ch. 3, esp. pp. 41–3.

[30] P. 238.

[31] Pp. 22, 237, 281.

[32] P. 238; emphasis his.

*theory*, the *principle* of the social and democratic parties is the struggle against oligarchy in all its forms.[33]

More generally, Michels suggests that history's great political movements must initially be internally oligarchic, even if their goals and results are democratic. Leaders of the great leveling movements descend from the upper echelons of society; followers are recruited from the most deprived strata. As the resources of leaders and followers become more equal, the drive for societal equalization loses momentum.

(3) *Social pluralism.* Whereas the Socialist groups initially consisted of a bourgeois and a proletarian stratum, they rapidly became heterogeneous. Many processes contributed to this differentiation:

(a) General social change. The social composition of the Socialist groups was differentiated in consequence of the general process which characterizes modern life—a process not of class polarization, *à la* Marx, but of "increasing differentiation."[34]

(b) Secular social change. Worker-Socialists became additionally differentiated among themselves, and within the working class, in consequence of their various political activities. These contributed to "an even greater accentuation of the differentiation which the proletarian groupings already present...."[35]

(c) Proletarian enterprise. Some worker-Socialists were transformed into petty-bourgeois in consequence of Socialist Organization. Of these, some were forced into small business in consequence of industrial blacklisting, while others exploited commercial opportu-nities (such as tavern-keeping) which developed in consequence of Socialist activities.[36]

(d) Bureaucratization. The advent of Socialist Organization enabled some worker-Socialists to become salaried officials. Organization served to "deproletarianize" workers, according to how "extensive" and "complicated" the "bureaucratic mechanism" of the Socialist movement became.[37]

(e) Immigration. Additional differentiation was produced by the influx of recruits drawn from various social strata. Such differentiation was facilitated by a number of factors and processes: formal accessibility of membership; the absence of repugnant slogans and policies; the increased availability of salaried posts and other vocational opportunities.[38]

In view of these changes, Michels suggests that bureaucratized associations in general, and politically sensitive associations in particular, cannot be (or long remain) socially homogeneous. Bureaucrats characteristically solicit new recruits, paying little attention to "quality." The "modern party, like the modern state, endeavors to give to its own organization the widest possible base," and to fortify the support attained by multiplying salaried posts.[39] Consequently, each mature Socialist party became, "from the social point of view," a "mixture of classes," being composed of elements fulfilling "diverse functions in the economic process."[40]

Such a social transformation might be deemed counter-democratic, from the standpoint of intra-group relations, *if* the transformation occurred in a once-homogeneous setting. In the Socialist

---

[33] P. 11; emphasis added. Elsewhere (esp. ch. 2) Michels voices doubt that such a commitment has ever truly animated a particular social group.

[34] P. 40; also pp. 289–90.

[35] P. 295.

[36] Pp. 283–88.

[37] Pp. 271–82.

[38] Pp. 265–70.

[39] Pp. 185–87.

[40] P. 387.

case, as Michels portrays it, the change was from polarized dualism to horizontal and vertical pluralism.

(4) *Petty-embourgeoisement.* Whereas the authentic or early Socialist groups were dualistic and polarized, social change involved chiefly an enlargement of middle-ranking strata. This occurred through the attraction of petty-bourgeois recruits and the "deproletarianization" of some worker-Socialists.

Michels summarizes this transformation as "the *embourgeoisement* of the working-class parties."[41] However, his label is not accurate, unless it is meant as a psycho-moral judgment rather than a sociological description. A bourgeois element was present at the beginning, and this element persisted. Socio-economic distance was not created or increased by Socialist Organization; it was 'filled in.'

The Socialist case cannot be cited to show that Organization invariably 'depolarizes' groups. The 'de-polarization' was conspicuous in the Socialist case because of a distinctive social origin. However, Michels does suggest unmistakably that *Organization facilitates the maintenance and enlargement of society's middle strata.*

Bureaucratic posts are middle-class in social status. These posts allegedly multiply faster than total populations. The proliferation of bureaucratic posts serves to counteract the effects of capital-concentration, effects which otherwise would drive bankrupt small businessmen into the ranks of the proletariat.[42]

Various bureaucracies cater to various social strata. The modern state's bureaucracy caters particularly to the sons of "small manufacturers and traders, independent artisans, farmers, etc."—the sons of people who are particularly discontented and articulate, because they feel the squeeze of "expropriative capitalism" and organized labor.[43] The Catholic Church enables talented sons of petty-bourgeois and peasant families to attain middle-class professional status, whereas this status normally is unattainable because it requires long formal education at private expense.[44] Similarly,

> For the German workers, the labor movement has an importance analogous to that of the Catholic Church for certain fractions of the petty bourgeoisie and of the rural population. In both cases we have an organization which furnishes opportunities for the most intelligent members of certain classes to secure a rise in the social scale.[45]

In no instance does Michels argue that Organization polarizes society. He depicts Organization, rather, as a built-in antidote to the worst consequences of capitalism. The processes of production and exchange under capitalism supposedly spur the creation of two radically distant classes, each increasingly homogeneous. But these processes also spur Organization. The processes generated by Organization facilitate (a) a general, but uneven, improvement in the socio-economic status of the lower strata ('deproletarianization'); (b) the maintenance and enlargement of the middle strata; and (c) a kind of "social exchange" whereby some people move upward socio-economically while others move (in a nonsocio-economic sense) downward.[46] Michels laments this

41 P. 268.
42 P. 275f.
43 Pp. 185–87.
44 P. 278.
45 *Ibid.*
46 Part IV, chs. 2, 3, 4. The downward movement involved in the "social exchange" is ideological and affiliational rather than socioeconomic. Idealistic or opportunistic bourgeois join Socialist groups, usually as leaders.

process, because it is counter-revolutionary.

(5) *Careers opened to talent.* Throughout his book, Michels emphasizes that the individuals most directly and substantially benefited by Organization (in terms of socio-economic elevation), are society's most talented, most intelligent individuals. Organization provides "facility for ascent in the social scale" by such individuals.[47] The peasants who attain middle-class status through the Church, the bourgeois who penetrate the Prussian nobility through the military corps, the workers who become petty-bourgeois through Socialist organizations, are not hacks. At one point, indeed, Michels declares that "democracy" (his fictional starting-point of Socialist development) "ends by undergoing transformation into a form of government by the best, into an aristocracy.[48]

Such a characterization of the men who attain bureaucratic eminence seems particularly remarkable in view of one of the meanings he assigned to democracy. Although he frequently identifies democracy with absolute equality, Michels also says that democracy "gives to each [citizen] the possibility of ascending to the top of the social scale ...annulling...all privileges of birth, and desiring that in human society the struggle for pre-eminence should be decided in accordance with individual capacity."[49]

On the other hand, Michels maintains that "the bureaucratic spirit corrupts character and engenders moral poverty."[50] This accusation is closely identified with his major accusation: that in elevating talented workers (along with other workers), Organization forestalls revolution.

(6) *Advent of diverse interests.* Whereas the early Socialists allegedly were endowed with a singular Interest (social-democratic revolution), social differentiation allegedly produced a conflict of Interests. Especially debilitating was the emergence of full-time, professional leaders endowed with a singular "conservative" Interest which diverges from the Interest of the "mass."

The party is created as a means to secure an end. Having, however, become an end in itself, endowed with aims and interests of its own, it undergoes detachment, from the teleological point of view, from the class which its represents. In a party, it is far from obvious that the interests of the masses which have combined to form the party will coincide with the interests of the bureaucracy in which the party becomes personified. ... By a universally applicable social law, every organ of the collectivity, brought into existence through the need for the division of labor, creates for itself, as soon as it becomes consolidated, interests peculiar to itself. The existence of these special interests involves a necessary conflict with the interests of the collectivity. Nay, more, social strata fulfilling peculiar functions tend to become isolated, to produce organs fitted for the defense of their own peculiar interests. In the long run they tend to undergo transformation into distinct classes.[51]

Michels rests his case for the oligarchical impact of Organization chiefly on the argument that the specialists' Interests clash with those of the "mass" and the specialists' powers are stronger. Thus the advent of "professional leadership" marks the beginning of democracy's end. This argument seems inapplicable to the generality of cases, in-

[47] P. 279.
[48] P. 89.
[49] P. 1.
[50] P. 189.

[51] P. 389. A very similar argument (omitting the "teleology" of "class" fidelity), is advanced by E. H. Carr in *The New Society* (1951) and is dissected by Langer, above, note 1, p. 263.

cluding the Socialist cases, for these reasons:

In the first place, with regard to Socialism it is necessary to accept uncritically the assumption that initial class differences did not involve a conflict of Interests. Michels seemingly covers this eventuality by depicting the pioneer Socialist intellectuals as "ideologues" who transcended the Interest peculiar to their class status.[52]

In the second place, the notion of a conflict of Interest between leaders and "mass" spuriously presupposes a homogeneous "mass." According to Michels's analysis, the advent of professional leadership coincides with the advent of a heterogeneous rank-and-file.

In the third place, the notion that a "conservative" Interest clashes with the Interest of the "mass" arbitrarily presupposes an innovatively oriented, revolutionary "mass." Only the proletariat, according to Michels's Marxian analysis, is objectively endowed with an unconscious Interest in revolution. But worker-Socialists are not fully proletarianised. And any other membership would be endowed with an 'objective' Interest which is not diametrically different from a "conservative" Interest.

In the fourth place, while a given caste of leaders might be endowed with an identical Interest, what is *in* the interest of one leader may contradict what is *in* the interest of another Michels devotes a chapter on "The Struggle Among the Leaders Themselves," to this chronic situation. He indicates that the policies championed by various leaders will differ *because* each leader is striving competitively to solidify his own position.

Finally, identity between the Interests of leaders and electors is not self-evidently a requisite of democratic representation. If there is a need which

can be expressed in the language of Interest, it is the need that the Interest of the leader be one which impels him to conform to the *will(s)* of his electors. As it happens, the "conservative" Interest ascribed by Michels to professional leaders seems to meet this requirement. The professional leader is "conservative" in the sense that he craves to maintain his status. To that end he is likely to conform to the wishes (rather than to the 'objective' Interests) of his electors, insofar as such behavior is the most efficacious or economical means of staying in office.

(7) *Emasculation of unpopular doctrines.* While the early Socialist program allegedly voiced the true "interests of the workers,"[53] Many elements of this program proved to be inexpedient politically. They were inexpedient for the game of "modern" party politics, the game of "electoral agitation" to secure votes and "direct agitation" to secure recruits.[54] In short, they were unpopular.

Socialist and aristocratic party experience mutually demonstrated that "principles" are "often a stumbling block to a party whose main desire is to increase its membership; and to disregard principles may bring electoral advantage, if at the cost of honor."[55] To "avoid alarming" potential "adherents" and "sympathizers" who are "still outside the ideal world of socialism or democracy, the pursuit of a policy based on strict principle is shunned...."[56] Similarly, since the aristocrat "recognizes" that in this "democratic epoch" he "stands alone" with his unpopular "principle," he "dissembles his true thoughts, and

[52] P. 280.

[53] The early Socialist platform was "the best one from which to advocate the interests of the workers...so that the renunciation of this platform almost always involves the loss of opportunity for defending working-class interests" (p. 116).

[54] P. 367.

[55] Pp. 398–9.

[56] P. 367.

howls with the democratic wolves in order to secure the coveted majority."[57]

The efficient cause of this doctrinal emasculation, as of all the other changes besetting the Socialist movement, is alleged to be Organization. With increments of scale and complexity, "every struggle on behalf of ideas within the limits of the organization is necessarily regarded as an obstacle to the realization of its ends"—the ends, that is, of the bureaucrats, who yearn for recruits and safety.[58]

(8) *Renunciation of unpopular policies.* Let us examine two examples.

(a) Legalism. The old Socialist determination "to demolish the existing state" was supplanted "by the new aim, to permeate the state with the men and ideas of the party."[59] This change allegedly was realistic, in the sense that it marked a response to the fact that "the forces of the party, however well-developed, are altogether inferior and subordinate to the forces of the government."[60] The realism was prompted, however, by Organization, which created thousands of livelihoods which would be jeopardized by governmental suppression. Socialist experience demonstrates the general and ironic fact that "the party becomes increasingly inert as the strength of its organization grows."[61] Numerical and financial affluence does not breed audacity. It produces a "need for tranquillity."[62] Thus "the last link in the long chain of phenomena which confer a profoundly conservative character upon the intimate essence of the political party" is the problem of gaining governmental indulgence.[63] However, Michels acknowledges that the advent of Socialist legalism was consistent with widespread popular sentiments. He also acknowledges that the laws which the Socialists came to obey were the laws of formally democratic states.

(b) Patriotism. In response to World War I, most of the Socialist leaders in Western Europe renounced policies which seemed consistent with their avowed principle of "proletarian internationalism." This change allegedly proved conclusively that the "oligarchical tendencies" infesting "modern political parties" impose a "regressive evolution": the "external form of the party, its bureaucratic organization, definitely gains the upper hand over its soul, its doctrinal and theoretical content." Be that as it may, Michels readily acknowledges that the leaders who opted for patriotism were conforming to prevailing rank-and-file sentiment. "Throughout the proletarian mass there has not been reported a single instance of moral rebellion" against the patriotic stance.[64]

(9) *Emergence of 'representative' leaders.* Whereas the ex-bourgeois intellectuals allegedly expressed the Interests of the proletarian "mass" without belonging to that stratum, the second-generation Socialist leaders allegedly conformed more closely to the values and attitudes of their electors. The new leaders came up from the ranks. Michels

---

[57] P. 6.

[58] P. 367.

[59] P. 374.

[60] P. 394; also pp. 367–74. Michels amended this assumption in the light of the Bolshevik and Fascist triumphs. He acknowledged the prowess of elitist-insurrectionary (non-"mass") parties during crisis periods. He also suggested that these parties alone can maintain a moral and social integrity, since they do not need to emasculate their doctrines for the sake of pluralistic electoral support. R. Michels, "Some Reflections on the Sociological Character of Political Parties," *American Political Science Review*, Vol. 21 (Nov. 1927), 3.

[61] P. 371.

[62] P. 374.

[63] P. 367.

[64] P. 393–5.

emphasizes the psychological transformation which must accompany a change in status. But his conception of a psychological transformation pertains to Interests, or underlying motivations, rather than to attitudes and values. As to the latter, he portrays a close correspondence between those of workers and those of ex-worker-bureaucrats.

> The leaders who have themselves been manual workers...are more closely allied with the masses in their mode of thought, understand the workers better, experience the same needs as these, and are animated by the same desires....[They commonly possess] a more precise understanding of the psychology of the masses....[65]

The ex-proletarian Socialist leaders deviated from official or sacred Socialist principles, not from rank-and-file attitudes and values. The typical workman's "ideal" is "to become a petty bourgeois"; his attitudes are "optimistic," accommodative toward other classes, and "conservative."[66] If the professional leader "continues to express 'reasonable opinions,' he may be sure of securing the praise of his opponents *and* (in most cases) the admiring gratitude of the crowd."[67]

(10) *Advent of 'responsive' leaders.* Whereas the early Socialist leaders allegedly responded to the Interests of a Collectivity, the second-generation leaders responded to the manifest will(s) of constituents. Michels castigates such behavior. The new leaders' "mania for promotion" found expression in "obsequiousness" toward employers, in "a semblance of obedience to the masses," and in "demagogy." Demagogues are "courtesans of the popular will. Instead of raising the masses to their own level, they debase themselves to the level of the masses."[68] Such deplorable responsiveness exemplified the characteristic Interest of professional leaders (a yearning for status-maintenance) and the characteristic situation of professional leaders, a situation in which deviations from constituents' wishes entail relatively great risks. The situational imperatives include the following:

(a) Financial dependence. "When the leaders...are attached to the party organism as employees, their economic interest coincides as a rule with the interests of the party"; the "practice of paying for... services rendered... creates a bond"—a control which is not available in the case of non-salaried volunteers.[69]

(b) Meager 'personal' resources. The professional leaders were relatively deficient in those non-technical resources which allegedly facilitate domination in the absence of tangible service. The principal "factors which secure the dominion of minorities over majorities" are "money and its equivalents (economic superiority), tradition and hereditary transmission (historical superiority)."[70] Also formidable are "prestige of celebrity," hypnotic eloquence, catonian self-righteousness, psycho-economic self-sufficiency, and "force of will which reduces to obedience less powerful wills."[71] Compared with their predecessors, the second-generation Socialist leaders were meagerly endowed with these resources. They were not suited to become "temporal divinities"

---

[65] P. 297. The second-generation Socialist leaders, in addition to being psychologically and sociologically more representative than their predecessors, also were 'ethnically' more representative. The early leaders (and many followers) were bourgeois, militant, and Jewish. (pp. 258–63, 28, 324, 342).

[66] Pp. 289, 319, 171.

[67] P. 306; emphasis added.

[68] Pp. 89, 165.

[69] Pp. 389, 114.

[70] P. 80.

[71] Pp. 71–2.

in the eyes of idolatrous masses.[72] Such idolatry, with all the authority it confers, is not likely to devolve upon "strict and prosaic" bureaucrats.[73]

(c) Alert constituents. Michels cites the "general immobility and passivity of the masses" as a major source of "oligarchy in the democratic parties." In such groups, drawn chiefly from the lower social strata, turnover among members is high and turnout for meetings is low. The "leaders, when compared with the masses, whose composition varies from moment to moment, constitute a more stable and constant element." The "gregarious idleness" of the rank-and-file facilitates "the influence of the leader over the masses" and the leaders' "independence" from the masses.[74] This condition varies among groups not according to organizational scale or complexity, but according to social composition and concern with the affairs of a group. The advent of professional Socialist leadership coincided with, and facilitated, an influx of petty-bourgeois members, an elevation of the socio-economic status of worker-Socialists, and an enlargement of the personal, tangible significance of Socialist affiliations.

(d) Non-available 'official' resources. The advent of professional leadership coincided with the establishment of regular, 'official' treasuries, organs of communication, files, agendas, meeting dates, mailing lists, and patronage. Michels discusses with keen insight the way such resources may be used by leaders to disarm challengers. But he does not indicate that these resources become more formidable, more available, in proportion to the scale or complexity of organization. He does testify

that "decentralization" of authority occurred, and this presumably involved a dispersal of control over the official resources. He also testifies that Organization entails procedural formalization; this presumably involves specification of legitimate uses of official resources.

(e) Individual technical expendability. Michels argues that the "technical indispensability of leadership" proved to be "the principal cause of oligarchy in the democratic parties."[75] This seemingly acknowledges that the leaders ultimately proved durable on account of their authentic utility to their followers, rather than their superiority in wealth, celebrity, oratory and other factors which promote obedience without necessarily rendering service. However, Michels's concept of "technical indispensability" is elusive; it merits an extended analysis.

In one sense, the "technical indispensability of leadership" signifies merely that a particular function, leadership, cannot be forsaken.[76] Since those who perform this function are likely to enjoy some advantage in one-to-one contests with challengers (the advantage, for example, of incumbency), there must be an element of Oligarchy in Organization. But this tells nothing about the relative advantages of leaders in various organizational and sociological contexts.

In another sense, Michels seemingly

---

[72] P. 67.

[73] P. 301.

[74] Pp. 400, 50–2, 79, 98.

[75] P. 400.

[76] "The mass *per se* is amorphous, and therefore needs division of labor, specialization, and guidance." This "incompetence" is "incurable." (p. 404). Sartori observes that what is rendered as "leadership" in the English translation of *Political Parties* appears as *Führerstum* and as *sisterma di capi* in the German and Italian editions. The latter terms allegedly connote "rulership," or "headship" or some sort of arrangement more sinister than what is conveyed by "leadership." Sartori, above, note 1, p. 110.

is suggesting that an individual's power (his freedom of action and security of station) depend ultimately upon the 'objective' utility of the skills at his disposal. One who is richly endowed with a skill which is rare and prized approaches technical indispensability. Such an endowment raises the problem of discretionary action. Gratitude for past service and diffidence toward current complexities may impel clients to grant their agents a broad range of discretion. Agents thought to possess rare skills may be retained even if they defy their clients' policy directives, on the expectation that in future the officials will prove to be technically adept *and* responsive.

On this subject Michels testifies that

This special competence, this expert knowledge, which the leader acquires in matters inaccessible, or almost inaccessible, to the mass, gives him a security of tenure which conflicts with the essential principles of democracy.

The democratic masses are...compelled to submit to a restriction of their own wills when they are forced to give to their leaders an authority which is in the long run destructive to the very principle of democracy. ...The history of the working-class parties continually furnishes instances in which the leader has been in flagrant contradiction with the fundamental principles of the movement, but in which the rank and file have not [drawn] the logical consequences of this conflict, because they feel that they cannot get along without the leader, and cannot dispense with the qualities he has acquired in virtue of the very position to which they have themselves elevated him, and because they do not see their way to find an adequate substitute. Numerous are the...leaders who are in opposition to the rank and file at once theoret-

ically and practically... [The rank and file] seldom dare to give [the] leaders their dismissal.[77]

If indeed the second-generation Socialist leaders could survive "practical" conflicts more readily than their predecessors, then one could not conclude that the new leaders were relatively responsive to the will(s) of their electors. But Michels does not systematically develop, or sustain, the charge that the new leaders could readily retain office in the face of "practical" conflicts (deviations from the policy-directives of their constituents). He confines himself almost exclusively to the charge that the new leaders persistently, and securely, retained office in spite of "theoretical" conflicts (deviations from the policies 'demanded' by Socialist doctrine).

That "practical" conflicts actually dwindled in the course of Socialist development seems evidenced by the nature of the changes in Socialist policies and by the growth of Socialist membership. The new leaders did the popular, rather than the theoretically 'correct,' thing.

That "practical" conflicts *necessarily* dwindled in the course of Socialist development—dwindled *in consequence of Organization*—seems likely in view of all the considerations advanced earlier in this article and in view of two more considerations.

First, Socialist Organization facilitated, and was accompanied by, material affluence. To that extent, the Socialist partisans acquired more resources with which they could search for agents who were technically qualified and psychologically disposed to be responsive.

Second, Socialist Organization involved task-specialization, and task-specialization often involves task-simplification. "It must not be supposed that

[77] Pp. 83–84, 86.

the technical competence of the leaders is necessarily profound. . . ."[78] Moreover, the "epoch" of Organization also is a time when "science puts at every one's disposal" such "efficient means of instruction" that "even the youngest may speedily bcome thoroughly well-instructed." Thus there is "less need for accumulated personal experience of life. ...Today everything is quickly acquired, even that experience in which formerly consisted the sole and genuine superiority of the old over the young."[79] To that extent, the supply of qualified technicians grows more abundant as organization develops. Consequently, the risks involved in defying an employer's policy-directives become more substantial.

On this showing—on Michels's showing—political survival in large-scale, complex organizations would seem to require that officials gratify the wishes of those they are hired to serve, regardless of the Interests of the latter. The result may be denounced as "obsequiousness" and as infidelity to popular interests, or it may be described as democratization.

SUMMARY AND CONCLUSION

Contrary to prevailing belief, then, Robert Michels actually provided a favorable account of the compàtibility of Organization and democracy. While maintaining that Organization is incompatible with pure democracy, and that increments of Organization produce

78 P. 83n.
79 P. 76.

counter-democratic changes in associations which initially are pure democracies, he also suggested (in the case of European Socialism and in broader theoretical terms), that Organization can and frequently does accompany and facilitate a multitude of changes which constitute or faciltate democratization.

Among the conditions he linked to Organization are augmented formal rights and privileges, a general increase in social wealth, more prosperity and security and leisure and education and sophistication among the lower social strata, increased horizontal but not vertical social differentiation, enhanced opportunities for talented individuals to ascend socially, and the advent within public and private associations of leaders who are conspicuously qualified technically, disposed socio-psychologically, and obliged circumstantially to conform to the policy-preferences of their electors.

Far from being a pessimistic democrat, Michels was a pessimistic Romantic Revolutionist and a pessimistic Scientific Paternalist.

He denounced Organization for promoting the amelioration instead of the radical purification of society. He detested Organization for promoting the manifest wishes rather than the 'objective' Interests of the "masses."

Michels's solicitude for the welfare of the "masses" evidently was linked with a profound disdain for the judgment of the "masses." In the light of his values and his beliefs, it seems understandable that Michels accommodated himself to Fascism.

# PARTY STRUCTURE AND SOCIO-ECONOMIC DUALISM: THE ITALIAN COMMUNIST PARTY

SIDNEY G. TARROW

The poverty of philosophy, for Marx, was its formalism. The social sciences, in contrast, are blessed with the ability to adjust theory to experience. In our study of Marxist movements, however, we lack precisely the marxian flexibility we need to overcome a patrimony of ideology, misinformation and rigidity. Writers like Duverger and Selznick, for example, talk about "devotee parties" and "organizational weapons" without considering that their terminology may in some cases be misleading.[1]

The devotee party, writes Duverger, "represents a change from the conception of the party as a class; it is the party conceived as the elite." Its members pledge their "whole human being" to the party while its structure focuses upon "unceasing propaganda and agitation," to the detriment of parliamentary activity.[2] Duverger leaves no doubt that his archetype of the devotee party is the Communist Party. What he never asks, however, is whether a Communist Party may be anything *but* a devotee party.

With a similar focus, Philip Selznick describes "the combat party," whose peculiar property is its "competence to turn members of a voluntary association into disciplined and deployable political agents," and its "adoption of subversion" and "penetration and manipulation of institutional targets."[3] While the model is most relevant in societies in which Communist doctrine is remote and unappealing to the population, Selznick, like Duverger, holds that it "provides a fair interpretation of the Communist vanguard or combat party, wherever it is found."[4]

Each of these approaches extrapolates a marxist party model out of a single political setting—the West before 1950 —and a single party strategy—the Leninist strategy of *What is to be Done?* Neither writer considers the elementary marxian proposition that both party strategy and political setting can vary greatly, and that a model of a marxist party can emerge only from the interaction of the two. This article is an attempt to elaborate this proposition in one rich empirical setting: Italy, and particularly southern Italy, where the Italian Communist Party (PCI) is very different from the party of devotion and combat envisaged by Duverger and Selznick.[5]

[1] Maurice Duverger, *Political Parties*, 2nd, rev. ed., North translation (New York: Science Editions, 1965); Philip Selznick, *The Organizational Weapon*, 2nd. ed. (Glencoe: The Free Press, 1960).

[2] *Op. cit.*, especially p. 70, p. 2, and p. 58.

*Reprinted from Sidney G. Tarrow, "Political Dualism and Italian Communism,"* AMERICAN POLITICAL SCIENCE REVIEW, *61 (March 1967), 39–53, by permission of the publisher and the author.*

[3] *Op. cit.*, pp. xii, xv.

[4] *Ibid.*, p. vi.

[5] These data are presented systematically in the author's *Peasant Communism in Southern Italy* (New Haven: Yale University Press, 1967.)

I hope to show (1) that the party's role differs sharply between advanced, industrial North and backward, traditional South; (2) that these variations can be ascribed both to Italy's dualistic political setting and to party strategy; and (3) that these two variables—political setting and party strategy—are the key to understanding marxist parties wherever they are found.[6]

## I. THE ITALIAN COMMUNIST PARTY

When we turn to the Italian Communist Party, we find most students close to the Selznick-Duverger view. For example, in his paper "European Political Parties: The Case of Polarized Pluralism," Giovanni Sartori shares Selznick's emphasis on the party's capacity to withdraw members from other group loyalties ("the ability of the party's organizational network to produce a culturally manipulated isolation of given social groups in given areas") and his concern with the dual nature of Communist organization—a party of elite with mass following. He also shares Duverger's emphasis upon organization but implicitly recognizes the weakness of the cells ("the organizational incapsulation and cultural saturation that a Communist *network* is capable of producing").[7] And while both Selznick and Duverger concentrate upon the subver-

sive aspects of Communist activity, Sartori concludes that the PCI is outside the system altogether. He writes, "We thus come to the uncomfortable paradox that the Communist party would make for an excellent opposition if it were an opposition, i.e., a possible alternative government. But since it would replace the *system* as well as the people, the net result is that the country is deprived of its best potential elites. . . ."[8]

While no one would deny the Italian Communist Party's opposition to the present Italian regime, we gain nothing by substituting the scientific word "system" for the less inclusive term "regime." Secondly, Sartori overstresses the disruptive effect of the PCI. In a series of manipulative hypotheses, he maintains that "an extreme centrifugal development is very likely wherever the political system accepts not only as legal but also as a legitimate and somewhat equal and normal competitor a party . . . which opposes the very system, such as a Communist Party." He adds that "Such a centrifugal development will not necessarily follow . . . if the existence of anti-system parties is legally prohibited."[9]

Apart from the fact that these "hypotheses," if realized, would not make for a very democratic theory,[10] are we justified in concluding that the PCI is a devotee party and an anti-system party simply because it is the PCI? I would argue that, so contrary is the evidence and so rare the historical

[6] Intra-nation comparative analysis is creatively used by Juan Linz and Amando de Miguel, "Eight Spains," in Richard Merritt and Stein Rokkan (eds.), *Comparing Nations: The Use of Quantitative Data in Cross-National Research* (New Haven: Yale University Press, 1966); also see Stein Rokkan and Henry Valen, "Regional Contrasts in Norwegian Politics," in Eric Allardt and Yijo Littunen (eds.), *Cleavages, Ideologies and Party Systems* (Helsinki: The Academic Book-Store, 1964).

[7] Giovanni Sartori, "European Political Parties: The Case of Polarized Pluralism," in Joseph LaPalombara and Myron Weiner (eds.), *Political Parties and Political Development* (Princeton: Princeton University Press, 1966), pp. 145–147, emphasis added.

[8] *Ibid.*, p. 147, emphasis added.

[9] *Ibid.*, p. 170.

[10] See Sartori's excellent *Democratic Theory* (New York: Praeger, 1965). The problem of the efficacy of a legal prohibition of anti-system parties may perhaps be settled by a consideration of the impact of prohibition upon the German Social-Democratic Party in the nineteenth century. The ban failed to interrupt its growth but did succeed in turning it into an anti-system party. See Douglas A. Chalmers, *The Social Democratic Party of Germany* (New Haven: Yale University Press, 1965), p. 4.

examples of flourishing parties of the type Duverger and Selznick describe, the burden of proof is on the other side.

What is the PCI like in very general terms?[11] Under the guidance of Togliatti and Longo its strategy since 1944 has been a broad national one, rather than the strategy of proletarian revolution and hegemony developed by Togliatti's predecessor, Antonio Gramsci. Returning from Moscow in 1944, Togliatti said "We are the party of the working class; but the working class has never been foreign to the nation," thereby launching what has come to be called the *Via Italiana al Socialismo*. Its general characteristics are: (1) constructive participation in parliament and in elections and local government; (2) a strategy of alliances which has at the same time emphasized the party's proximity to the Socialists, "sincere democrats" and the progressive wing of the Christian Democratic Party; (3) an ideology of "reform of structure" as the preferred means of constructing socialism in Italy; and (4) activity in local government, cooperative associations and stores, which both develops an efficient class of PCI administrators and ties the economic interests of large numbers of people to the party.[12]

Three general points should be made about the *Via Italiana al Socialismo*. First, it was developed by Togliatti as a strategic response to a particular political setting: a modern, industrial society which had been torn by twenty-two years of reactionary extremism. It was possible to interpret the party line in merely tactical terms in 1944 when the presence of Allied troops made revolution impossible, but the party's revisionism has, if anything, increased between that time and the present.

Second, it is not clear that there is anything about the PCI which would justify its classification as an anti-system party or a centrifugal force. I would argue that the symbiotic stability of the Italian political system (which is often confused with the instability of the French Fourth Republic) depends precisely upon the existence of a Communist Party like the PCI. Its broad, popular strategy and stress upon reform have both prevented the formation of radical leftist groups and forced a conservative government upon a path of reform that it would have avoided if left to its own devices.

Third, and most important, it is impossible to talk reformism for twenty years and then carry off a revolution. What we see in the PCI is something we may tentatively call the institutionalization of strategy.[13] The communication of its militants, its image among the population and the structure of loyalties at the local level have been conditioned by the party's strategy over the last two decades. Once a commitment to vote-getting is made, a political party, marxist or otherwise, routinizes certain roles and behaviors and endows them with legitimacy. Were these roles and behaviors to suddenly shift, a complicated structure of loyalties based upon personal and group interest, and not upon the devotion of militants, would come tumbling down.

[11] The party is analyzed in detail in Chapters Five and Six of *Peasant Communism, op. cit.* For a sensitive analysis of its external relations and policy line, see Donald Blackmer, *Italian Communism and the International Communist Movement* (Cambridge: M.I.T., mimeo.), 1966.

[12] Togliatti's important speeches and writings have been collected in three volumes: *Il Partito; La Via Italiana al Socialismo;* and *Sul Movimento Operaio Internazionale,* all published by Editori Riuniti of Rome in 1964. See in particular his "Promemoria sulle Questioni del Movimento Operario Internazionale e della sua Unita," published post-humously in 1964 in *Sul Movimento Operaio Internazionale,* pp. 361–376.

[13] The concept of institutionalization as used here is similar to its usage in Philip Selznick's *Leadership in Administration* (Evanston: Row, Peterson, 1957).

The party's strategy has had an impact upon its membership, its organization, its behavior and its internal unity. First of all, the typical party member is not a dedicated militant whose entire life is devoted to party work. Interviews and questionnaires carried out with PCI federal secretaries in 1964 showed that only 10 to 15 per cent of party members are full-time activists. Moreover, the number of party members has decreased sharply since 1956 and the ratio of members to voters has changed from one member for every three voters in 1956 to one member for every 4.8 voters in 1963.[14] Finally, the ideological preparedness of even the most militant party cadres is very weak. In 1962, a party report concluded that "the problem of launching an elementary activity of ideological education in the party on a wide scale remains an urgent one."[15]

Second, the classical unit of disciplined party activity—the cell—has been progressively weakened in the post-war years, while the party section has become more prominent. The shift is not coincidental; the *Via Italiana* is geared more closely to the loose, horizontally-linked party sections than to the narrow, vertically-linked cells. Between 1950 and 1963, the number of PCI cells decreased from 54,000 to 33,000 while party sections increased from 10,200 in 1951 to 11,000 in 1961.[16] Factory cells have become less important in contrast to the more heterogeneous neighborhood cells and sections.

Third, the PCI pays *primary* attention

to parliamentary and electoral activity and has not been observed to dedicate itself to conspiratorial activities more than any other Italian party in the rather Byzantine Italian Party system. The increased importance of the party section is related to this emphasis, for the traditional cell structure is useless in winning elections, while the section functions as a typical party club.[17] In the trade-union field, the party-dominated Confederazione Generale Italiano del Lavoro (CGIL) now shuns the political strike weapon and concentrates upon bread-and-butter union issues. The infiltration of non-Communist organizations, which Selznick postulates as an essential element of combat party strategy, is nowhere evident in Italy, despite the party's substantial popularity.

While the PCI is by far the most disciplined party group in Parliament,[18] its voting patterns in secret parliamentary committees are far less rigid. A research group at Bologna recently estimated that PCI parliamentary committee members vote with the government on a large majority of committee votes. This high level of compromise voting was maintained even during periods of maximum intransigence in the Chamber.[19]

The party administers over eighty

[14] See *Dati sull'Organizzazione del PCI* (Rome: PCI, 1964), p. 4.

[15] See *Organizzazione del Partito* (Rome: PCI, 1962), p. 59.

[16] See "Modificazioni Strutturali e Politiche del PCI al suo IX Congresso," *Tempi Moderni*, 2 (April, 1960), p. 50; also see the official party statistics in *Forza ed Attivitá del Partito* (Rome: PCI, 1954); *Organizzazione del PCI* (Rome: PCI, 1961); *Dati sull'Organizzazione del PCI* (Rome: PCI, 1964).

[17] "Modificazioni Strutturali e Politiche del PCI," p. 30.

[18] Giovanni Sartori, *Il Parlamento Italiano* (Naples: Edizioni Scientifiche Italiane, 1963), p. 105. Most of the interviewed Communist deputies felt that parliamentary discipline was not excessive, while the members of other parties interviewed were not at all satisfied with the constraints placed on their voting by the parties.

[19] The author is indebted to the Carlo Cattaneo Research Institute of Bologna for allowing him to refer to its as-yet unpublished study, *La Partecipazione Politica in Italia*. This multi-volume study will be published in the United States in shorter form under the auspices of the Twentieth Century Fund.

communes in the central provinces of the country—the so-called "Red Belt." These local units perform all the typical functions of local government and maintain majorities which depend upon the satisfaction of concrete personal and group interests. The party administers a whole range of profit-making cooperatives which are essential to relations with workers and peasants. Major dislocations would occur in the economic life of thousands should the PCI suddenly turn to revolutionary strategy. Despite the possible tactical origin of its pattern of participation in Italian politics, the institutionalization of these tactics transforms them into commitments.

Several attitude studies have suggested that Communist leaders and followers have developed political attitudes which correspond to the party's broad strategy. A study of Italian parliamentarians carried out in 1963 revealed that Communist deputies scored lower on the Rokeach dogmatism scale than Christian Democrats.[20] Further evidence was provided by a CISER public opinion survey in the same year which demonstrated, first, that PCI supporters reflect the reformist doctrinal line of the party and, second, that certain key divergencies may be seen within the sample with regard to their presumed support for the PCI in a hypothetical two-party system; for example, only 60 per cent of the sample would choose the PCI in a bipolar choice between their own party and the Socialists![21] Third, Almond and Verba have pointed out that supporters of the left are more likely to be "open partisans" than supporters of the right. They write, "Opposed to the Constitution is a left wing which, at least in part and at the rank-and-file voter level rather than among the party elite, manifests a form of open partisanship that is consistent with a democratic system."[22]

In other words, the following of the PCI is far more pluralistic than has been generally acknowledged. The same appears to be true of the leaders, if the factional strife currently raging in the party is any indication. The right, led by Giorgio Amendola, would go further than Togliatti in examining the crimes of Stalin, in condemning the Chinese and in adapting the PCI to a reformist strategy. The left, on the other hand, returns ideologically to Gramsci's emphasis upon the factory and the trade unions, but seeks more internal democracy in the party and wants to empower the party Congress to make theoretical decisions in place of the bureaucratic Central Committee.[23]

Two facts are indicative of the relationship of the two factions to the PCI's *Via Italiana al Socialismo*. First, the left is neither the old sectarian Stalinist left, nor, as is sometimes imagined, a pro-Chinese group. It arose out of the crisis generated by the anti-Stalin campaign and the Hungarian Revolution and does not criticize the fundamentals of the *Via Italiana*.[24] Second, the new left arose in part with a basis of support in the Communist Youth Movement (FGCI), in whose publication, *Nuova Generazione*, they found an excellent forum,

[20] Di Rienzo, *A Study in Political Dogmatism* (unpublished doctoral thesis, Notre Dame University, 1963).

[21] These data are reported in Istituto Carlo Cattaneo, *Il Comportamento Elettorale in Italia alla Luce di Alcune Ricerche Condotte Direttamente sugli Elettori* (Bologna, mimeo, n.d.), pp. 150–153.

[22] Gabriel Almond and Sidney Verba, *The Civic Culture*, rev. ed. (Boston: Little, Brown and Co., 1965), pp. 115–116.

[23] See Pietro Merli-Brandini, "La Crisi del Pensiero Comunista," *Conquiste del Lavoro*, 18 (November 14–20, 1965), pp. 9–20.

[24] See Blackmer, *op. cit.*, on the important distinction between the old sectarian left and the new left and on the contrast between left and right within the PCI today.

and in the trade unions, whose late leader, Giuseppe de Vittorio, was fond of telling Togliatti that the labor movement is *not* the transmission belt of the party. In other words, the internal diversification of a party which takes up the tasks of day-to-day operation in a parliamentary system encourages the development of internal differences which, if not themselves democratic, are at least competitive.

But the internal differentiation of the PCI is not merely ideological; it is structural and behavioral as well. The *Via Italiana* strategy opens the way to a variety of influences from the political setting. The most important such influence is the dualistic nature of the Italian political system itself. If the analysis up to this point has indicated that the PCI is not a devotee or combat party, it is only an analysis of what happens to the *Via Italiana* strategy in its two political settings which can suggest what the party *is*.

## II. THE CONTEXT: THE TWO ITALIES

"Italy," Joseph LaPalombara writes, "represents two distinct cultures, the relatively dynamic and industrial North and the relatively stagnant South."[25] The disparity between the regions is not merely one of degree; it is a structural cleavage, observed by generations of statesmen and intellectuals, extending into the economic, social and political systems and presenting concrete obstacles to political integration.[26] While

exhaustive analysis of Italian dualism is impossible in this context, several basic indicators may suggest the breadth of the economic, social and political gap between North and South.[27]

Economically, Italy has long been a "dual economy," with a dual labor market and a dual structure of industry.[28] The North is industrial, the South agricultural: out of fifty-eight northern provinces, thirty-five have more than half of the working population in nonagricultural activities, while in the South only four provinces out of thirty-two have more than 50 per cent of the active population outside agriculture.[29] In the industrial sector, most southern workers (500,000 in 1951) work in the small-scale traditional sector, while only 200,000 are employed in the large-scale modern sector.[30] In agriculture, the stable and productive commercial and family farms of the North contrast sharply with the unstable tenancies and *latifundia* of the South.

Socially, we find a rather mobile highly organized society in the North and a fragmented developing society in the South. Briefly, what the latter term designates is a social structure which has lost the functional coherence of tradition and has not yet achieved a modern organization of social roles. Historically, we can trace the emergence of modern social organization in the North to the typical western processes of commercialization and industrialization; commercialization set up a marketing and

[25] Joseph LaPalombara, *Interest Groups In Italian Politics* (Princeton: Princeton University Press, 1964), p. 37.

[26] The classical sources on the cutlural cleavage between North and South are found in Gaetano Salvemini, *Scritti Sulla Questione Meridionale* (Milan: Einaudi, 1955); Francesco Saverio Nitti, *Scritti Sulla Questione Meridionale* (Bari: Laterza, 1958); Giuseppe Fortunato, *Il Mezzogiorno e lo Stato Italiano* (Bari: Laterza, 1911).

[27] A statistical analysis of economic and social indices has been collected in *Un Secolo di Statistiche Nord e Sud, 1861–1961* (Rome: SVIMEZ, 1961).

[28] Vera Lutz, *Italy: A Study in Economic Development* (London: Oxford University Press, 1962), Ch. V.
*Development* (London: Oxford University
[29] Istituto Centrale di Statistica, *Compendio Statistico Italiano, 1958* (Rome: Istituto Poligrafico dello Stato, 1959), p. 17.

[30] Lutz, *op. cit.*, p. 94.

credit network while industrialization re-shaped social stratification through the discipline of the factory process.[31]

The South, in contrast, remains a fragmented developing society because commercialization, caused by the influx of northern goods after national unification in 1861, was not accompanied by industrialization; traditional social roles were undermined by commercialization, but in the absence of industrialization, they remained transitional and disorganized. Without industry, the attention of all major social groups focused upon the land, with results that soon became pathological.[32] The middle class, urban, aggressive and entrepreneurial in the North, was unproductive, provincial and land-oriented in the South.[33] The family retains an importance in socialization and economic allocation in the South far greater than its equivalent in the North; in a society in which modern forms of social organization have failed to crystallize, the family is a solidarity unit of almost pathological consistency.[34]

If we search for indicators of the South as a fragmented developing society, we can find them in the atomization of business enterprise and in the network of unstable and transitional roles in agriculture. The average industrial firm in the South employs 2.4

workers, as opposed to 7.5 workers in the North; only 13 per cent of southern firms have joint-stock ownership, as compared to 46 per cent in the North; and twice as many southerners (27.3 per cent) working in industry are owners and directors than in the North (12.8 per cent),[35] suggesting the dominance of the family enterprise over modern forms of business.

In agriculture, the situation is still more symptomatic. Until the agrarian reform of 1951, much of the land was operated by small renters, share tenants and day laborers on plots with no farmhouse or equipment. These marginal operating units are not "farms" in any significant sense of the word, nor are they commercial operations. Many peasants shift from one occupational role to another, while others (*figure miste*) hold several occupational roles at once.[36] The fragmentation of contractual ties between owners and peasants prevents the formation of horizontal secondary organization, inhibiting both economic development and political aggregation.

In the political system, the fragmented nature of southern Italian society has critical effects. Politics in the North have long been organized according to typical western patterns, with groups and parties growing out of the broad functional and class groupings of an industrial society. In the South, in contrast, a formal representative system disguised what amounted to a massive system of clienteles. *Clientelismo* grew out of the narrow vertical ties of a fragmented agricultural system. Organized by the liberal middle class of the prov-

[31] David Apter writes, "Industrialization is that aspect of modernization so powerful in its consequences that it alters dysfunctional social institutions and customs by creating new roles and social instruments, based on the use of the machine": *The Politics of Modernization* (Chicago: Chicago University Press, 1965), p. 68.

[32] See the analysis of southern Italian brigandage by Eric Hobsbawm in *Social Bandits and Primitive Rebels* (Glencoe: The Free Press, 1959).

[33] Gaetano Salvemini, "La Piccola Borghesia Intelletuale," in Caizzi (ed.), *Antologia della Questione Meridionale*, pp. 383–405.

[34] Edward Banfield and Laura Fasano Banfield, *The Moral Basis of a Backward Society* (Glencoe: The Free Press, 1958).

[35] SVIMEZ, *Un Secolo di Statistiche, op. cit.*, pp. 336–338.

[36] Vera Lutz writes: "The peasant is almost always what is called a mixed figure—small proprietor, tenant, share-cropper, wage earner. In the past, at least, the link between him and that part of the land which he farmed but did not own was in many cases a precarious one": *op. cit.*, p. 105.

inces, which held a strategic role in land-holding, it used the fulcrum of local government for patronage, and sent local notables to parliament to make up willing majorities for regional politicians. The ties between leader and follower are highly personal; an American research group found that in seventy-six towns of the South where the vote had shifted greatly,

> ...the voters were motivated by strictly local and personal issues, that ideology and national issues played little part in determining their voting behavior, and that many shifts were simply the result of *clientelismo*, voters following a personal leader from one party to another.[37]

Structurally, the clientele pattern means that broad functional interests are not readily represented in politics, where personal favors and patronage are dominant. The failures of the system are patent; one reaches the apex of authority not by merging one's demands in a horizontal membership group, but by linking up to a hierarchical chain of personal acquaintance which may begin in the network of neighborly relations and reaches up to the state bureaucracy with little adjustment in structure.[38] The clientele chain soon grows too long for effective political allocation. It is this, and not a conspiracy by the industrialists of the North, which has made the South ineffective in the national political arena; faced by the well-organized interest groups of Milan, Turin and Genoa, southern clienteles are unable to bargain effectively since they can trade only in personal favors. The lack of political integration between the regions is not simply a matter of political culture, but is a *structural* factor; the clientele system is actually congruent with the South's fragmented social structure and resists or modifies the forms and techniques of a modern party system. Even a "monolithic" party like the PCI is profoundly affected by the dualism of the political system in Italy.

### III. DUAL POLITY AND DUAL PARTY

Four dimensions are particularly interesting in comparing the PCI in nothern and southern Italy: (a) the composition of the membership; (b) the party organization; (c) the leadership; and (d) its ideology.

(a) *Membership.* The membership of the PCI in northern Italy is concentrated in the medium and large-sized cities, while party membership in the South is dispersed in the countryside. Northern membership is consistent as well as concentrated: new members in the North composed less than six per cent of regional membership in 1961. In the South, in contrast, the party suffers from rapid turnover, with new members amounting to 13.9 per cent in 1961, during a period in which it was losing an average of 45,000 members a year.[39]

The sharpest difference in the membership of the PCI in North and South stems directly from the different social composition of the two regions: a working class cadre is strong in the North and weak in the South, while the peasantry is the bulwark of the party in the South (with 42 per cent of the members) and much weaker in the North (30 per cent). A historical factor colors the composition of the PCI membership in the South: the absence of an important labor movement to provide the experience and the cadres for political activity today. In this reversal of historical roles, the Communist Party in southern Italy resembles many marxist

[37] Cited in Joseph LaPalombara, *Interest Groups in Italian Politics, op. cit.,* p. 65.

[38] Cf. Julian Pitt-Rivers, *People of the Sierra* (Chicago: Phoenix, 1961), p. 154.

[39] *Dati sull'Organizzazione del Partito, op. cit.,* p. 21.

parties in non-western nations. In northern Italy, the PCI profits from the long experience of labor organization in the region.[40]

Secondly, Communist Party membership in southern Italy differs radically in its composition from the northern wing of the party in the relative importance of intellectuals and students in its membership. While 25.8 per cent of the PCI's members live in the South, 40 per cent of the intellectuals registered in the party and 60 per cent of its student members are southerners.[41] The importance of intellectuals in the South increases as we move up the hierarchy from ordinary members to active cadres. Figures released in 1954 indicate that over 30 per cent of the members of the party's federal committees in the South were students, technicians, intellectuals or other professionals, as compared to less than 18 per cent in the North.

Turning to youth in general, we find that 34 per cent of the members of the party's Federations of Young Communists of Italy (FGCI) are found in the South, 10 per cent higher than the region's share of total party membership.[42] This factor perhaps reflects the deep frustration of youth in a developing society, where the symbols of affluence have recently become visible but the means of achieving them are not available. Women members of the party, in contrast, are concentrated in the North. Eighteen per cent of the party's female members live in the South as opposed to 82 per cent who live in the

North. These figures reflect the traditional role of women in the South and their relative emancipation in the North.[43]

TABLE 1. PCI FEDERAL COMMITTEES PROFESSIONAL DISTRIBUTION BY REGIONS, 1954*

| | | North | South | Italy |
|---|---|---|---|---|
| Workers | (N) | 1323 | 402 | 1725 |
| | (%) | 44.9 | 30.8 | 40.6 |
| Agricultural workers | (N) | 120 | 92 | 211 |
| | (%) | 4.1 | 7.1 | 5.0 |
| Peasants | (N) | 245 | 114 | 359 |
| | (%) | 8.3 | 8.7 | 8.5 |
| Artisans | (N) | 134 | 78 | 212 |
| | (%) | 4.5 | 6.0 | 5.0 |
| White Collar | (N) | 452 | 143 | 595 |
| | (%) | 15.4 | 11.0 | 14.0 |
| Professionals, students and technicians | (N) | 506 | 392 | 898 |
| | (%) | 17.2 | 30.1 | 21.1 |
| Housewives | (N) | 60 | 52 | 112 |
| | (%) | 2.1 | 4.0 | 2.6 |
| Others | (N) | 104 | 30 | 134 |
| | (%) | 3.5 | 2.3 | 3.2 |
| Total | (N) | 2943 | 1303 | 4264 |
| | (%) | 100.0 | 100.0 | 100.0 |

Source: PCI, Forza del Attivita del Partito (Rome, 1954), p. 67.
* More recent figures on the professional composition of federal committees are not available.

Perhaps because of its largely peasant composition, PCI membership in the South is less closely related to electoral success than in the North. Relating the percentage of the population registered in the PCI to the party's share of the provincial vote, we find that membership rises rapidly with electoral success in the North, while it is almost unresponsive to the polls in the South. Party membership ranges from 0.3 per cent of the provincial population in the lowest voting province to 17.4 per cent in the highest province in the North, but from 1.7 per cent in the lowest province to 3.5 per cent in the highest voting province in the South. Moreover,

40 While 42 per cent of the membership in the North are members of the working class, 32 per cent of the southern PCI members are workers. In the North, even in the agricultural regions, Emilia, Tuscany and the Marches, 36 per cent of the members are workers, more than the working class portion of the party in any southern region. See PCI, Dati Sull' Organizzazione del PCI (Rome: PCI, 1964).
41 Calculated from ibid., pp. 22–27.
42 Ibid., p. 74, pp. 15–17.

43 Ibid., pp. 22–27.

the rise in party members bears an almost geometric relation to the vote in the North when the vote is above 30 per cent, suggesting that the *Via Italiana* in that setting is a successful organizational and electoral strategy. In the South, in contrast, at no point in the electoral curve does membership rise above 4 per cent of the population, even when the vote is as high as 37 per cent.

The paradox of the *Via Italiana* in southern Italy is that the PCI has as its largest membership bloc a group with the poorest organizational potential. Rather than a popular mass party based upon the organized support of the urban proletariat, the PCI has the membership outline of a poor peasant's party in a fragmented developing society, with an intellectual leadership group and a scattering of worker and middle class groups on either side. Not only is its major membership group dispersed and poorly organized; unlike the urban and rural proletariat of the North, it is a group whose social aspirations belong to a rearguard and not a vanguard. The effects of this conservative center of gravity in the PCI membership group in the South can be noted in the inertia of its programs, which still insist upon the need for an agrarian reform at a time when thousands of peasants want only to escape from the land to the cities.

(b) *The Party Structure.* In its network of party sections, cells and factory cells, clear differences within the PCI between North and South are directly linked to the socio-political structure of each region. Seventy per cent of its party sections, 68 per cent of its cells and 92 per cent of its factory cells are found in the North.[44] In the large-scale industries of the major cities and the commercialized agriculture of the central provinces, these units operate with

relative regularity and precision. Moreover, a panoply of secondary units—recreational groups, adult classes, and economic organizations—are articulated around the nucleus of the party cell and section. The relevance of these secondary organizations to the economic life of the worker creates the natural basis for the differentiation of program between party and mass organization—one of the bases of the Leninist party.

In the South, party organizations are less numerous and less articulated than in the North, and the differentiation of program between party and mass organization is far less clear. While 30 per cent of the party sections are in the South, only 11.4 per cent of its cells, and less than 8 per cent of its factory cells are found there. The decrease in articulation from level to level means that the PCI organizational pyramid is virtually inverted with respect to that of the North. In many places, there are more sections than cells, and the cells are far too large to permit their political use.[45]

Secondly, the number of secondary and mass organizations surrounding the party cells and sections is far smaller than in the North. In the absence of these groups, the section is often the single manifestation of the party in the southern village. The party member goes there to meet his friends and gossip, to play cards and watch television. Surprisingly, 42 per cent of the PCI sections in this impoverished region have television sets, as opposed to only 16 per cent in the North.[46] It is significant that the only PCI units in which the southern portion of the party carries its organizational weight are the *Circoli* of the Communist Youth Federation: 22.1 per

[44] *Ibid.*, pp. 29–63, *passim.*

[45] *Ibid.;* also see Celso Ghino, "Aspetti della Struttura della Organizzazione," *Rinascita,* 7 (March, 1950), p. 163.

[46] *Dati sull'Organizzazione del Partito, op. cit.*, p. 45.

cent of the national total are found in the region. Women's cells, on the other hand, are extremely underrepresented in the South, with 7.1 per cent of the national total. To one party leader, this results not only from the modesty of women in the region, but from resistance from PCI leaders. He writes, "Conceptions which assign to women a subaltern and a marginal role in society are not yet overcome by the PCI."[47]

A third organizational characteristic of the PCI in southern Italy which contrasts sharply with the North is the lack of the strategic differentiation between the programs of the party and the policies of the mass organizations. Launched in the region in an organizational vacuum, the party was compelled to recruit many members spontaneously and to fulfill many of the functions which normally fall to labor and other mass secondary groups. A number of party front groups were formed, but these inevitably drew upon the same cadres, and "very often the Communist Party, the Socialist Party, the Chambers of Labor and the Cooperatives were nothing but different faces of a single popular movement."[48] In some provinces, the membership of the party exceeds that of the unions and in others the reverse is true. The division seems to depend upon which group arrived first after Fascism. "One of the defects in our organization is that the party today pursues directly many of the activities which should be fulfilled by the secondary mass organizations."[49]

Organizational difficulties are en-

countered by all militant political parties in their early phases, but the PCI in southern Italy appears to have been permanently affected by these problems. Why this should be so relates to the socio-political milieu of southern Italy. As a party document states: "Experience has shown the great difficulty in organizing the masses of the southern peasants and, above all, of grouping them in organizations by category, because of their indeterminate social character."[50] This is particularly true in the backward areas of the region. As a Sardinian leader writes, "Every social category is fragmented in a guise which is difficult to locate. . . . More than twenty or thirty people in a village who are tied to a clear identity of interests cannot be found."[51]

The Communist Party in southern Italy has developed a style of organization distinctly different from its style in northern Italy. A resolution of the Central Committee defines it: "A multiplicity of popular assemblies, of committees for the land and other democratic organizations of an elementary type are necessary to give a primary and simple form of organization to masses of the people who are not socially concentrated and homogeneous."[52] This pattern of organization reached its apogee in the PCI-led movement for the occupation of the *latifundia* in 1950. Yet twenty years after the party began its activity in the South, its organizations still have an amorphous and fluctuating character.

(c) *Leaders and Leadership Roles.* As might be expected when dealing with political leadership in dualistic political

[47] Pietro Valenza, "Alcuni problemi del Rinnovamento del PCI nel Mezzogiorno," *Cronache Meridionali*, 7 (January–February, 1960), p. 7.

[48] P. di Pasquale, "Dalla Politica di Salerno alla Crisi del Frontismo Meridionale," *Rinascita*, 13 (October, 1956), p. 543.

[49] Pietro Secchia, "Relazione," in *VII Congresso Nazionale, Atti e Risoluzioni* (Rome: PCI, 1951), p. 146.

[50] Comitato Centrale, PCI, *Documenti*, 1951, p. 197.

[51] Velio Spano, "La Sardegna alla Vigilia delle Elezioni Regionali," *Rinascita*, 6 (March, 1949), p. 103.

[52] Comitato Centrale, PCI, "Risoluzione della Direzione," *Documenti*, 1951, p. 230.

settings, the backgrounds and career patterns of Communist leaders in northern and southern Italy differ sharply. Southern Italian Communist leaders are mainly middle- or upper-middle-class individuals with urban backgrounds. In the North, 48 per cent of the party's national level leadership are of lower- or lower-middle-class origin, while only 34 per cent of the southern leaders come from these groups. Eighteen per cent of the northern leaders are of middle-class status, compared to 28 per cent in the South; and 19 per cent of the northern leaders are of upper-middle or upper-class origin, compared to 32 per cent in the South.[53]

TABLE 2. PCI NATIONAL LEADERSHIP SOCIAL STATUS OF FAMILY, BY REGION

|         |       | Lower | Lower Mid. & Up. Middle | Upper Middle | Upper Class | Total |
|---------|-------|-------|-------------------------|--------------|-------------|-------|
| North   | (203) | 18.2% | 41.4                    | 26.1         | 10.8        | 100.0% |
| Center  | (134) | 16.8% | 37.9                    | 28.5         | 10.2        | 100.0% |
| South   | (107) | 13.1% | 25.2                    | 35.5         | 23.4        | 100.0% |
| Islands | (66)  | 7.6%  | 22.7                    | 42.4         | 19.7        | 100.0% |

Source: Istituto Carlo Cattaneo, unpublished data collected from PCI parliamentarians and national officers, 1964.

Northern and southern leaders differ in the size of the city of their origin, too. Northern leaders parallel the distribution of the population of the North in the cities of their birth; 15 per cent come from villages up to 5,000 in population, 26 per cent are from towns of 5,000–20,000, 12 per cent are from cities from 20,000–100,000 and 36 per cent are from large cities of more than 100,000 population. Most southern national leaders were born in the large towns and the cities from 20,000–100,000 population (31 per cent in the former and 36 per cent in the latter)

with only 11 per cent from the small villages and only 20 per cent from cities over 100,000 in population. This distribution of southern leaders is hardly in keeping with the preponderantly rural membership of the party in the region.

Additional data on the leadership were collected by the author in a series of questionnaires and interviews with party secretaries on the provincial level.[54] Social origins on this level do not differ significantly between leaders in North and South, with lower-middle-class backgrounds predominant in each group. Educationally, however, marked contrasts are apparent; while provincial secretaries in the North are evenly divided between elementary or medium level education and secondary or college backgrounds, almost two-thirds of the southern leaders have graduated from high school or college, and little more than a third ended their education in elementary or high school; indeed, there is a chronic overabundance of intellectuals in the PCI in this backward region.

The geographic (and presumably social) mobility of the leaders differs between North and South, too. Forty-three per cent of the southern provincial leaders grew up in cities other than those of their birth, while 25 per cent of the northern leaders changed residence during the formative period of their youth. The northern leaders are characterized by greater career localism; 38 per cent hold positions in the cities and provinces of their childhood, 47 per cent work in a different city but in the same province, and 15 per cent hold a post outside the province of their childhood. In the South, half as many (19 per cent) work in the city and province of their childhood, 52 per cent hold posts in the same province but in different cities, and twice as many (29 per

---

[53] The data which follow on the PCI national elite were graciously provided me by Professor Gianfranco Poggi of the University of Edinburgh and of the Instituto Carlo Cattaneo.

[54] For a more extensive treatment of the data on the PCI provincial elite, see *Peasant Communism, op. cit.,* Ch. IX.

cent) have positions in entirely different provinces. Related to this factor is the greater breadth of experience of the southern leaders; 40 per cent have held positions in two or more provinces, while only 28 per cent of the northerners have worked in several provinces.

The southerner is a relative newcomer to politics. Turning again to the national leadership, we find that 58 per cent from the South are full-time professional politicians, as opposed to 67 per cent from the North. Half as many southern national leaders are the sons of Communist Party members, and very few have siblings, wives and children who are members of the party. On the provincial level once again we find that 53 per cent of the northern leaders entered the party from the Resistance movement, compared to 24 per cent in the South. The largest group of southern provincial leaders were recruited into politics while in college or during professional careers (28 per cent), or from the peasant or labor movement (36 per cent). In the North, in contrast, 11 per cent came from intellectual pursuits and 19 per cent joined the party from the labor movement.

The roles assumed by the leadership differ between North and South. Since fewer paid officials are available in the South, the provincial leaders in that region function more as generalists than in the highly-articulated federations of the North. Interview and questionnaire responses indicate that 45 per cent of the southern federations employ only one to five persons, 40 per cent employ six to ten persons and only 15 per cent employ over ten. In the North, in contrast, only 13 per cent of the federations employ less than five full-time officials, 45 per cent employ six to ten, and 42 per cent employ over ten.

While the southern membership of the party is spread out in the countryside, the leadership tends to cluster in the cities. The most dynamic party workers gravitate to the federations, where they can find greater social prestige and better positions. In fact, party leaders have often noted that the dispersion of party cadres in the villages has slowed up the process of formation of a leadership group, since organizers forced to live in the villages become demoralized and isolated, frequently becoming involved in "clientelistic relationships with local figures."[55] A disproportionate number of the full-time leaders of the PCI in the South are now stationed in the provincial capitals. Party sections in the villages often have a merely formal existence; they form and dissolve according to the issues of the moment and the season of the year—the peasant organizations are only truly militant in seasons when the planting and harvesting have been completed.

The disjunction between city and country-side, between middle class intellectual leaders and peasant members, is attitudinal as well as organizational. Southern leaders tend to view the peasants paternalistically. The failure of a substantial peasant cadre to develop in the party may be linked to such attitudes. As national leaders critical of the southern leadership maintain, "The party must advance further to liberate itself courageously from any elements of clientelism and paternalism which still exist here and there."[56] As one leader complained, "The formation of a new type of cadre of popular extraction is bound to meet or even instigate a certain resistance and danger of distortion from the residues of clientelism in the bosom of the popular movement."[57]

[55] Pietro Valenza, "Alcuni Problemi del Rinnovamento del PCI nel Mezzogiorno," op. cit., p. 10.

[56] PCI, IX Congresso Nazionale (Rome: PCI, 1960), Vol. I, p. 231.

[57] Pietro Valenza, "Aspetti del Fanfanismo in Lucania," Cronache Meridionali, 5 (December, 1958), p. 865.

Southern provincial leaders are far more "political"—understanding "political" as public activity-orientation—and less "organizational" than their northern colleagues. There appears to be considerably more flexibility, less ideological closure and more discussion than in the northern federations. Southern leaders, one informant suggested, "have more political sensitivity than leaders in the North."[58] Another informant, a member of the party secretariat said,

> The cadres in the South are more politically sensitive, more flexible, more sensitive to the political nature of their problems. In the South, traditionally, everything is decided politically, for in a disorganized society, it is the relations between individuals which solve problems. In the North, in contrast, we deal more with concrete classes and opposing groups, and less with contacts on a personal level. In the leaders of the South, therefore, political sensitivity and ideological subtleties are more important.[59]

Yet the greater political capacity of the southern leaders, according to these informants, is damaged by their organizational incapacity. As another informant in the national party organization said,

> The differences between northern and southern leaders are the differences in the characteristics of the regions. The northerner is more of a formalist; the southerner is more versatile but he is less organizationally oriented.[60]

The characteristic described as "political sensitivity" by party informants shades into personalism in relationships with followers and with the opposition. In interviews, provincial leaders in the South stressed such qualities as "prestige," "honesty," and "seriousness" as the factors which recommend them to the admiration of their fellow citizens. In the North, party leaders are more concerned with presenting a united face to the opposition. Southern leaders were far more conscious of the need to establish a network of ties with local elites than northerners, who interpret the Leninist policy of alliances as the affair of the party organizations themselves, pointing to relations with the Vatican rather than interaction with village priests.

In their relations with the rank and file, the southern leaders are personally oriented too. They spend much of their time helping job seekers, writing letters of recommendation for students and trying to resolve the legal disputes of the peasants. A leader writes, "There is a need to overcome the personalism, the tendency to divide into groups around one or another personality. This derives from the type of social organization of the South, and is a reflection of its social dis-aggregation in the files of our party."[61]

Southern leaders perceive their federations as more autonomous with relation to the party national office than do their northern colleagues. Each secretary was asked his opinion on the role a party secretary should play in relation to the national party organization. There were five alternatives presented, representing different degrees of autonomy or central direction. Northern leaders were ranged heavily on the side of central direction (66 per cent), with 17 per cent perceiving their role autonomously and another 17 per cent expressing moderate positions. In the South, in contrast, only 42 per cent were centralists, as many as 42 per cent were autonomists and 16 per cent were moderates.

In order to further explore the per-

[58] Interview F-1, Naples.
[59] Interview S-1, Rome.
[60] Interview S-4, Rome.

[61] *Cronache Meridionali*, 5 (May, 1958), p. 305.

ceptions of their roles held by northern and southern leaders, provincial secretaries were asked in questionnaires and personal interviews: "In your work as party secretary, what are the most important things you do, in the order of their importance?" Responses were not contextually coded because of the small number of respondents, but were classified according to their political orientation, their labor orientation and their organizational content. The results are recorded in Table 3.

TABLE 3. PCI FEDERAL SECRETARIES INDIVIDUAL ROLE PERCEPTIONS (N=80)

| | | Political | Labor Oriented | Organizational | DK NA | Total |
|---|---|---|---|---|---|---|
| North | (N) | 8 | 4 | 31 | 4 | 47 |
| | (%) | 16% | 9% | 66% | 9% | 100% |
| South | (N) | 20 | 3 | 5 | 5 | 33 |
| | (%) | 61% | 9% | 15% | 15% | 100% |
| Italy | (N) | 28 | 7 | 36 | 9 | 80 |
| | (%) | 35% | 9% | 45% | 11% | 100% |

Source: *Peasant Communism, op. cit.*, Chapter IX.

Naturally, all the responses contained a strong political element, but many incorporated elements which were specifically labor oriented, while many others were organizationally oriented. As the Table shows, two-thirds of the northern respondents perceive their roles predominantly in organizational terms, while almost two-thirds of the southerners include mainly political factors in their role perceptions.

(d) *Ideology.* Unlike French communism, which has been wholly dependent upon imported theory, the PCI was fortunate to possess its own theorist in Antonio Gramsci, whose writings in prison under the Fascists later became an important source for today's leaders.[62] What is most interesting, however, is the extent to which the *Via Italiana al Socialismo* in both North and South was formulated *without* Gramsci's aid, for he died in prison and his writings were not publicly disinterred until 1948.

Gramsci contributed two important ideas to his party's future ideology: the idea of the party as the modern Prince, and the concept of the alliance of northern workers and southern peasants. Both were Leninist in inspiration if not in tone.

Gramsci saw in *The Prince* "a creation of concrete imagination which could work upon a dispersed and disintegrated society to stimulate and organize its general will."[63] The modern equivalent of Machiavelli's Prince is the political party and its sublime role is organizing a new collectivity.

> The modern Prince, the myth-prince, cannot be a real person, a concrete individual; it can only be an organism...the political party, which, time and again...knows how to form a new type of state.[64]

The party is a creative agent of education and revolution, "a collective intellectual," developing a new class of leaders out of an old and divided society.

A second aspect of Gramsci's thought regarded the backward and "dis-aggregated" nature of southern Italian society and its role in the future revolution. To Gramsci, North and South were not united nationally, but colonially; "The bourgeoisie of the North," he wrote, "has subjected the South of Italy and the Islands to the status of colonies for exploitation."[65] The South is ruled by

study of Gramsci's influence on the early period of the party is John M. Cammet, *Antonio Gramsci and the Origins of the Italian Communist Party*, (Stanford: Stanford University Press, 1967).

[63] Gramsci, *Note sull Machiavelli* (Torino: Einaudi, 1955), p. 3.

[64] *Ibid.*, p. 5.

[65] *Antologia degli Scritti*, vol. II, p. 50.

[62] Gramsci's works are collected in the six-volume series, *Opere di Antonio Gramsci* (Torino: Einaudi, 1955), and selected in Carlo Salinari and Mario Spinella (eds.), *Antonio Gramsci: Antologia degli Scritti* (Rome: Editori Riuniti, 1963). A recent

an agrarian bloc of landed proprietors and intellectuals who are paid off by their northern bosses through parliamentary deals. The peasant is helplessly tied to the agrarian bloc through clientele relations with the landholders. Semi-feudal contractual relations dominate economic life, preventing the peasantry's emergence as a modern social force.

Left to themselves, the peasants of the South will dissolve into a "disorganized mass, a chaotic disorder of exasperated passions." Organized by the proletariat of the North, they are the motor force of the revolution. "The proletariat," Gramsci wrote, "will destroy the southern agrarian bloc in the degree that it succeeds, through its party, in organizing ever larger masses of poor peasants in autonomous and independent organizations."[66]

Several points are significant about this formulation of Gramsci. First, it separates North and South theoretically and admits that special factors condition the organization of the southern peasant. Second, the relationship is bilateral. "The workers of the factory and the poor peasants," he writes, "are the *two energies* of the proletarian revolution."[67] Third, the alliance is revolutionary and socialist, rather than tactical and democratic and there is no doubt about proletarian hegemony. Instead of what he calls the "magic formula" of the division of the *latifundia*, Gramsci proposes a "political alliance between workers of the North and peasants of the South to overthrow the bourgeoisie from the power of the state."[68]

The "organizational weapon" which emerged from these two central ideas— the party as the modern Prince and the alliance of northern workers and southern peasants—would have had a strong potential for revolution in an underdeveloped area like the South. Gramsci wanted the peasants to start an insurrection in the countryside to occupy the army, thereby leaving a clear field for a proletarian revolution in the cities. With allowance made for his unique style and sensitivity to Italian conditions, he is quite close to Lenin's model for a revolutionary party in a backward society. "Spontaneity" is rampant in the "dis-aggregated" southern peasantry, while the party as modern Prince is the embodiment of "consciousness." The parallel to Lenin's model, we may assume, was not lost on Gramsci.

In the North, Gramsci concentrated upon the factory. He wanted to transform society *from within*, as a preparation for the revolution. Gramsci's group in Turin wanted to establish the *Consigli di Fabbrica*, workers' councils which aimed at eventual assumption of the control of production. In 1919, he wrote:

> The socialist state already exists potentially in the institutions of the social life of the exploited working class. To tie these institutions together...means creating from then on a true and real workers' democracy.[69]

These ideas, actually of anarcho-syndicalist derivation, were denounced as "reformist experiments" by Gramsci's extremist opposition in the party.

The essence of PCI ideology since 1945 is the cross-fertilization of Gramsci's ideas with Togliatti's *Via Italiana al Socialismo*. And since the latter is essentially reformist in nature— calling for action within the constitutional system through structural reform —the combination ranges from the comic to the bizarre, with a good deal of practical common sense in between.

---

[66] *Ibid.*, p. 79.
[67] *Ibid.*, vol. I, p. 52, emphasis in the original.
[68] *Ibid.*, vol. II, p. 51.

[69] *L'Ordine Nuovo*, Torino: Einaudi, 1955, p. 10.

Gramsci's idea of the party as the modern Prince has, in North and South, lost its Leninist components and is now interpreted almost entirely in terms of Togliatti's emphasis upon national solidarity. Togliatti wrote in 1944:

> The central idea of the political action of Gramsci was the idea of unity: unity of the working class parties in the defense of democratic institutions and the destruction of Fascism;...unity of the socialist working masses with the Catholic working masses of the city and countryside; unity of the workers; unity of workers and peasants; unity of workers of the arm with those of the mind....[70]

In the North we find the PCI operating with an increasingly reformist political ideology, with excellent results. For the *Via Italiana* is a strategy for industrialized societies. Emphasis is increasingly placed upon trade union action and structural reform within the capitalist system. Theoreticians have virtually adopted revised views on the evolution capitalism, and party leaders talk of "insertion" in the processes of neo-capitalism to influence its direction. As a leading labor intellectual writes:

> The CGIL does not try to prevent the modernization of Italian capitalism. Instead of opposing neo-capitalist solutions *a priori*, we each time oppose more advanced and equally realistic and concrete solutions.[71]

In the South, the synthesis of the *Via Italiana* with Gramsci's formulations has been less happy. The party has obliterated his concept of a creative working class impelling a peasant motor force to revolutionary action in a bilateral relationship directed by the party as a modern Prince. Instead, it calls for a pluralistic *system* of alliances between many social groups which *suppresses* the insurrectionary force of the peasants. A partnership-turned-coalition is expanded into "a system with the working class at its head...and an alliance with the southern peasants, first, with the petit bourgeoisie, the intellectuals and the progressive medium bourgeoisie, isolating the conservative and the large bourgeoisie."[72]

The alliance also loses its revolutionary character. We learn retrospectively that "Gramsci reaffirmed the real unity between workers and peasants in the common battle for the *structural renewal* of the Italian state."[73] There is a theoretical problem in the admixture of Gramsci and Togliatti: the first is revolutionary, the second reformist; taken together they are contradictory.

For example, the party inevitably impels the peasant "motor force" to action which is not revolutionary, for it simultaneously seeks the support of social groups whose interests would be threatened by a peasant insurrection. Moreover, lacking the "organizational weapon" of the Leninist party, PCI initiatives for the peasants do not enlist them in the battle for socialism, but support the peasants' own struggle to become petit bourgeois landowners. Hence, the limited agrarian reform which the party demanded in 1950 has aided the peasants of the South immeasurably, but not the party.

With neither a Leninist organizational weapon nor its revolutionary goals, the PCI in the South falls prey to the "objec-

---

[70] *Rinascita*, August 29, 1944.
[71] "Report on the Debate of the Central Committee of the PCI on the Twenty-Second Congress of the CPSU," *New Left Review*, nos. 13–14 (June, 1962), p. 153. For the re-interpretation of capitalism, see Istituto Gramsci (ed.), *Tendenze nel Capitalismo Moderno* (Rome: Ed. Riuniti), 1962.

[72] Mauro Scoccimaro, "Dottrina Marxista e Politica Comunista," *Rinascita*, May–June, 1945, p. 138.
[73] Franco Ferri, "Questione Meridionale e Unità Nazionale," *Rinascita*, 9 (January, 1952), p. 10, emphasis added.

tive conditions" of its political setting in a backward and fragmented society. The whole concept of the party changes from the creative catalytic agent envisaged by Gramsci into an amorphous movement which casts its net through diverse social strata, seeking issues which can unite them. As Togliatti wrote in a key theoretical article:

> Because of the social disorganization of the South, we need an organization of a conspicuously broad, popular nature, more than is necessary in the large industrial centres.[74]

As a result, the PCI in southern Italy shares the personalism, disorganization and ideological weakness of other political parties in that setting. Having applied a strategy well-designed for the industrial North to the backward South, *where the same conditions do not obtain*, the PCI in the South is *neither* an effective Leninist party *nor* a well-organized mass party, but something very different again.

IV. AN INTERPRETATION

Neither in North nor South does the Italian Communist Party have the attributes of the devotee-combat party described by Duverger and Selznick. This illustrates two things, one that we should have known all along and another that requires a great deal more thought and elaboration. First, the role and structure of Marxist parties cannot be derived abstractly as Duverger and Selznick attempt to do. Second, a theory of Marxist parties will only result, in true dialectical fashion, from analysis of the interaction of party strategy and political setting under many different conditions. Turning to this second consideration, we may well ask, "What then are the 'models' with which we may understand the Italian Communist Party in North and South?" In the North,

Duverger provides us with an answer: the mass party. In the South, we must turn to the experience of Marxist parties in the underdeveloped world.

It is ironic that Communism in northern Italy at mid-twentieth century should vindicate the nineteenth century Western European Social-Democratic tradition. By 1900, the advances made in western society had negated many of the assumptions of Marx in the *Communist Manifesto*. These assumptions had "presupposed a pattern of events which experience had shown to be no longer possible in Europe—*or indeed in any advanced country.*"[75] The chauvinistic behavior of the Social-Democratic parties in 1914 and the failure of the revolution to spread to Western Europe in 1917 gave the finishing touch to Western European revolutionary socialism. Since then, every flourishing western socialist party has been a constitutional mass party, recruiting broadly and emphasizing parliamentary and electoral activity instead of the barricades and the *putsch*. The idea of the vanguard party, with which Marx had toyed in 1850 and Blanqui developed more fully, did not appear again until 1905 in Russia.[76]

For just as advancing conditions in Western Europe caused the transformation of European Socialism, "the obverse also applied: where the pre-1848 situation still existed, the fire that had gone out in the West might still burst into flames."[77] Lenin's double-edged contribution was to recognize the connection between political backwardness and revolution, and to develop an organizational weapon and a strategy tailored to these conditions. The Leninist party was the ideal weapon for making the revolution in a backward country, for it bypassed the weak and "spontane-

[74] Palmiro Togliatti, "L'Azione Democratica e Socialista nel Mezzogiorno," *Cronache Meridionali*, 1 (June, 1954), p. 412.

[75] George Lichtheim, *Marxism* (New York: Praeger, 1965), p. 125, emphasis added.
[76] *Ibid.*, pp. 124–127.
[77] *Ibid.*, p. 125.

ous" proletariat and seduced the disorganized but potentially revolutionary poor peasantry. This is essentially the strategy Gramsci wanted to develop for southern Italy.

Lenin was convinced that the conditions of all backward societies demanded the strategy he had utilized in Russia. He told a group of Asian Communists:

> It is imperative for you to make a success of applying Communist theory and practice under conditions where the peasant is the primary class of the masses, where the task of struggle pending solution lies in the fight against the remnants of mediaevalism, but not in the fight against capitalism. . . .
>
> The solution to the above tasks. . . can . . .be seen in the over-all struggle already started in Russia.[78]

Yet he failed to conclude the obvious corollary: that the strategy used in Russia *would no longer do* in the advanced nations of the West, where capitalism and liberal democracy had already proceeded too far in satisfying the masses.

It is Togliatti's great contribution to have recognized this "bright side" of Leninism and to have responded with the idea of the *Via Italiana al Socialismo*. His statement that "It is impossible to conceive realistically of the advance towards socialism outside the fabric of Italian democratic life, outside of the struggle for the objectives that interest the whole society,"[79] is typical of this attitude.

When we examine the membership, the organization, the leadership and the ideology of the Communist Party in northern Italy, we can only be impressed by its successful adaptation and struck by its essential similarity to the "sociological type" of the mass party presented by Duverger: membership is broad and relatively unselective; loyalty is class-based and weak as compared to the religious loyalty of the devotee party; the cell is replaced in importance by the section, and formal centralization disguises factionalism and ideological rivalry; and party strategy focuses upon parliament, the trade unions and the mass media, in contrast to conspiracy and infiltration.

The proof of the essential compatability of the PCI's *Via Italiana* with the conditions of an advanced industrial setting is found in its incompatability with the conditions of the backward agricultural South. Here membership is inconsistent and weak; commitment is personal and interest-oriented; neither the cells nor the sections are well articulated; leadership reflects the clientelistic nature of southern politics; and party ideology is dispersive and "catch-all" in nature.

If the PCI in the South cannot be described as either a Leninist party or a mass labor party, what then is its nature? Here we must turn to the experiences of marxist parties in today's developing areas; in the combination of an underdeveloped setting and a non-Leninist strategy, the PCI in southern Italy has emerged as a type very similar to political movements in the new nations. David Apter writes:

> The central characteristics of the movements, whatever their forms, are their spontaneous and populist qualities, the direct relationship between the leadership and the people, the high degree of emotional appeal of their programs, and the simplicity of their aims.[80]

Not only does the PCI in southern Italy reflect many of these character-

---

[78] V. I. Lenin, "Report Before the Second All-Russian Representatives Congress of the Communist Organizations of the Eastern Peoples," *Sochinenya* (Works) (Moscow: 1932), vol. XXIV, pp. 542–551, quoted in Lucian Pye, *Guerilla Communism in Malaya* (Princeton: Princeton University Press, 1956), p. 26.

[79] *Rinascita*, August 29, 1944.

[80] *The Politics of Modernization, op. cit.*, p. 205.

istics, it also reflects the failure of this type of movement to grapple successfully with many of the needs of the under-developed areas. The problem is one which a careful reading of Lenin could have predicted to party leaders: a marx-ist party in a backward country which lacks a Leninist organization will advance the (not necessarily progres-sive) goals of the peasant population without advancing the goals of the party. It thus appears as a sophisticated struc-ture of patron-client relations fortified by an ideology that is more populist than marxist and led by intellectuals who are more bourgeois than prole-tarian.

All this leads us back to the question of the relevance of Duverger and Selz-nick and other western theorists to the study of marxist movements. The fore-going analysis shows that *neither* in northern nor southern Italy do we find the devotee or combat party. In the first, the combination of a highly developed setting and an open strategy have led to the emergence of the PCI as a mass party. In the second, the same open strategy in a fragmented developing society leads to another sociological type —one closely related to the political movements we now see in the new nations. Had the party in southern Italy been more rigorously Leninist in its strategy, as Gramsci was, we would have seen a third sociological type: the van-guard party, which can overcome the "spontaneity" of a backward society with the "consciousness" of a revolu-tionary leadership.

Where does this leave the devotee or combat model developed by Duverger and Selznick? It leaves it a poor fourth, a historical mutant in which a strategy designed for underdeveloped societies was mistakenly applied to the West in its high stage of industrialization. That this combination was an unhappy one may be seen in the sorry history of the Communist Party in both Germany and the United States, where an elite of revolutionaries became a sect of devotees persecuted for their beliefs and "outside the system" in a scientific, as well as in a political way. Such a pattern is not inevitable however, as is evident upon examination of marxist parties in places like Italy.

## C. Voting Behavior

# VOTING: THE EXPRESSION OF THE DEMOCRATIC CLASS STRUGGLE

SEYMOUR MARTIN LIPSET

In every modern democracy conflict among different groups is expressed through political parties which basically represent a "democratic translation of the class struggle." Even though many parties renounce the principle of class conflict or loyalty, an analysis of their appeals and their support suggests that they do represent the interests of different classes. On a world scale, the principal generalization which can be made is that parties are primarily based on either the lower classes or the middle and upper classes. This generalization even holds true for the American parties, which have traditionally been considered an exception to the class-cleavage pattern of Europe. The Democrats from the beginning of their history have drawn more support from the lower strata of the society, while the Federalist, Whig, and Republican parties have held the loyalties of the more privileged groups.

. . .

The simplest explanation for this widespread pattern is simple economic self-interest. The leftist parties represent themselves as instruments of social change in the direction of equality; the lower-income groups support them in

*Reprinted from Seymour Martin Lipset,* POLITICAL MAN, *copyright © 1960 by Seymour Martin Lipset (New York: Doubleday & Company, Inc., 1959), pp. 220, 229–258 by permission of Doubleday & Company, Inc.*

order to become economically better off, while the higher-income groups oppose them in order to maintain their economic advantages. The statistical facts can then be taken as evidence of the importance of class factors in political behavior.

This relationship between class position (as measured by education, income, status, power, occupation, or property status) and political opinions or party choice is far from consistent, however. Many poor people vote conservative and some wealthy ones are socialists or Communists. Part of the explanation of these deviations has already been pointed out: other characteristics and group affiliations such as religious belief are more salient in particular situations than high or low social and economic position. But the deviations are also a consequence of the complexity of the stratification system itself. In modern society, men are subjected to a variety of experiences and pressures which have conflicting political consequences because men have disparate positions in the class structure. Men may hold power, like some civil servants, but have a low income or status; they may enjoy high occupational prestige, like many intellectuals, but receive low income; they may enjoy a relatively high income, but have low social status like members of some ethnic minorities or *nouveaux riches* businessmen, and so forth. Some of their social positions may predispose them to be conservative, while others favor a more leftist political outlook. When faced with such conflicting social pressures, some men will respond more to one than to another, and therefore appear to deviate from the pattern of class voting.

These conflicting and overlapping social positions probably injure the leftist lower-class-based parties more than they do the conservative right. Men are constantly struggling to see themselves favorably, and some of their status-attributes will produce a favorable self-evaluation, others a negative one. It seems logical to assume that men will arrange their impressions of their environment and themselves so as to maximize their sense of being superior to others. Thus the white-collar worker will stress the identification of white-collar work with middle-class status (a point to be discussed further later) ; the low-income white worker will regard himself as superior to the Negro, and so forth. A variety of evidence gathered in the course of research on social mobility indicates that those who are occupationally upwardly mobile seek to get rid of the characteristics which still link them to their past status. The man who succeeds will in fact often change his neighborhood, seek to find new, higher-status friends, perhaps leave his church for one whose members are higher in status, and also vote more conservatively. The more conservative parties have the advantage of being identified with the more prestigeful classes in the population, an asset which helps to overcome the left's appeal to the economic interests of the lower strata.

Although it is not always possible to predict whether a right or a left political direction will result from specific status-discrepancies, the concept itself points up sources of change in political values flowing from the tensions of contradictory social positions. A discrepancy in status may even lead an old but declining upper class to be more liberal in its political orientation. For example, most observers of British politics have suggested that the emergence of Tory socialism, the willingness of British nineteenth-century conservatism to enact reforms which benefited the working class, was a consequence of the felt hostility of the old English landed aristocracy to the rising business class, which was threatening its status and power. . . .

But although variations in the political behavior of the more privileged strata constitute one of the more fascinating problems of political analysis, the available reliable evidence which permits us to specify why people differ in their political allegiances is largely limited to the largest segments of the population, particularly workers and farmers. Public opinion surveys and studies of the voting patterns of different rural districts can deal statistically with different types of workers and farmers in ways that cannot as yet be done on a comparative international level for most sections of the urban middle and upper classes. Discussion, therefore, . . . focuses primarily on the politics of the lower and more numerous strata.

Table 1 presents a summary of the social characteristics that are related to these variations within the lower-income group, i.e., those whose standard of living ranges from poor to just adequate by local middle-class standards—most workers, working farmers, lower white-collar workers, etc. In comparing international political behavior, it is difficult to make a more precise classification.

These generalizations are made on the basis of having examined public opinion or survey data from a large number of countries including the United States, Argentina, Chile, Brazil, Canada, Aus-

TABLE 1. SOCIAL CHARACTERISTICS
CORRELATED WITH VARIATIONS
IN LEFTIST VOTING IN THE
LOWER-INCOME GROUPS
WITHIN DIFFERENT
COUNTRIES*

| Higher Leftist Vote | Lower Leftist Vote |
|---|---|
| Larger cities | Smaller towns, country |
| Larger plants | Smaller plants |
| Groups with high unemployment rates | Groups with low unemployment rates |
| Minority ethnic or religious groups | Majority ethnic or religious groups |
| Men | Women |
| Economically advanced regions | Economically backward regions |
| Manual workers | White-collar workers |
| Specific occupations: Miners Fishermen Commecial farmers Sailors, longshoremen Forestry workers | Specific occupations: Servants, service workers Peasant, subsistence farmers |
| Less skilled workers | More skilled workers |

* The major exceptions to some of these
patterns are discussed below.

tralia, Japan, India, Finland, Norway,
Sweden, Denmark, Germany, the Nether-
lands, Belgium, France, Austria, Italy,
Great Britain, and Hungary.

LEFT VOTING: A RESPONSE TO
GROUP NEEDS

Leftist voting is generally interpreted
as an expression of discontent, an indication that needs are not being met.
Students of voting behavior have suggested the following needs as central:

1. The need for security of income.
This is quite closely related to the desire
for higher income as such; however,
the effect of periodic unemployment or
a collapse of produce prices, for example, seems to be important in itself.

2. The need for satisfying work—
work which provides the opportunity for
self-control and self-expression and
which is free from arbitrary authority.

3. The need for status, for social recognition of one's value and freedom
from degrading discrimination in social
relations.

In terms of this list, let us see how various groups vote.

*Insecurity of Income*

Certain occupational groups in the
lower-income category suffer from extreme insecurity of income—one-crop
farmers, fishermen, miners, and lumbermen—and these groups have histories of
high rates of leftist voting.

The prototype of a "boom-and-bust"
agricultural economy is the North
American wheat area. Depression or
drought, or both, have hit the wheat
belt in every generation since it was
settled. Many studies of the political
behavior of this region have been made,
and all agree that the wheat farmers are
the most leftist of all farmers in times of
economic crisis. They have formed the
core of the great agrarian radical movements—the Greenbackers, Populists, and
Non-Partisan League in the United
States, and in Canada the Progressives,
Social Credit, and the Cooperative Commonwealth Federation.[1] The only socialist government in North America above
the local level is the Cooperative Commonwealth Federation provincial government of Saskatchewan, a one-crop
wheat area.

Studies of one-crop commercial
farmers in other parts of the world show
that they too tend to support periodic
protest movements which are often

---

[1] S. M. Lipset, *Agrarian Socialism* (Berke-
ley: University of California Press, 1950);
J. D. Hicks, *The Populist Revolt* (Minneap-
olis: University of Minnesota Press, 1931);
S. A. Rice, *Farmers and Workers in American
Politics* (New York: Columbia University
Press, 1924), Chap. II; V. O. Key, Jr., *Poli-
tics, Parties, and Pressure Groups* (New
York: Crowell, 4th ed., 1952), Chap. II; C. B.
MacPherson, *Democracy in Alberta* (Toronto:
University of Toronto Press, 1953).

authoritarian in character.[2] In contrast, farmers whose crops are diversified, who depend on local rather than world markets, and even very poor subsistence farmers whose level of income is steady and reliable tend to support conservative parties.

Fishermen selling to national or international markets are in much the same position as the wheat farmers, and commercial fishermen vote left around the world. In Norway, the first labor representatives in the Storting were elected from a fishing district.[3] In Iceland, the fishermen support the second strongest Communist party in Scandinavia.[4] André Siegfried in his pioneer study of voting statistics in western France in 1913 found the fishermen to be a strong leftist group.[5] The fishermen of British Columbia are a strong source of support for the leftist unions.[6] In the United States the West Coast fishermen are tradition-

ally militant and have been organized in a Communist-dominated union, even though they are mostly owners or part owners of their own boats. Great Lakes fishermen have been disproportionately Democratic. And in Great Britain fishing districts are Labor party strongholds.[7]

Miners are among the working-class groups most exposed to unemployment, and the fact that they are one of the strongest leftist groups throughout the world has already been noted. In the British elections of 1950, the thirty-seven Labor party candidates sponsored by the National Union of Mineworkers were elected with a median vote of 73 per cent.[8] In Canada, the only eastern district which has elected a socialist on different occasions is a coal-mining area in Nova Scotia; the only Quebec constituency ever to elect a socialist to the provincial legislature was a metal-mining area. Studies in the United States show that coal miners are among the most consistent supporters of the Democratic party.[9]

In France, where workers in nationalized industries elect representatives to Works Councils, the underground workers in coal mines gave the Communist-controlled C.G.T. 80 per cent of their votes—a higher figure than that

---

[2] A. Siegfried, *Tableau politique de la France de l'ouest sous la troisieme république* (Paris: Librairie Armand Colin, 1913), Chap. 44; R. Heberle, *From Democracy to Nazism* (Baton Rouge: Louisiana State University Press, 1943), Chap. III; Charles P. Loomis and J. Allen Beegle, "The Spread of German Nazism in Rural Areas," *American Sociological Review*, 2 (1946), pp. 724–34; S. S. Nilson, *Histoire et sciences politiques* (Bergen: Chr. Michelsens Institut, 1950); S. S. Nilson, "Aspects de la vie politique en Norvege," *Revue française de science politique*, 3 (1953), pp. 556–79.

[3] E. Bull, *Arbeiderklassen i Norsk Historie* (Oslo: Tilden Norsk Forlag, 1948).

[4] S. S. Nilson, "Le Communisme dans les pays du nord—les élections depuis 1945," *Revue française de science politique*, 1 (1951), pp. 167–80. Rudolf Heberle reports on the success of the leftist parties among the fishermen in Schleswig-Holstein in *From Democracy to Nazism, op. cit.*, p. 104.

[5] See also B. Leger, *Les opinions politiques des provinces françaises*, 2d ed. (Paris: Recuiel Sirey, 1936), pp. 49–50.

[6] S. Jamieson and P. Gladstone, "Unionism in the Fishing Industry in British Columbia," *Canadian Journal of Economics and Political Science*, 16 (1950), pp. 1–11 and 146–71.

[7] J. K. Pollock and S. J. Eldersveld, *Michigan Politics in Transition* (Ann Arbor: University of Michigan Press, Michigan Governmental Studies, No. 10, 1942), p. 54. For the behavior of British fishermen see *The Economist* (Aug. 15, 1959), p. 435.

[8] H. G. Nicholas, *The British General Election of 1950* (London: Macmillan, 1951), pp. 42, 61. See also J. F. S. Ross, *Parliamentary Representation* (New Haven: Yale University Press, 1944), pp. 58–77.

[9] H. F. Gosnell, *Grass Roots Politics: National Voting Behavior of Typical States* (Washington: America Council on Public Affairs, 1942), pp. 31–32; see also Malcolm Moos, *Politics, Presidents, and Coattails* (Baltimore: The Johns Hopkins Press, 1952), pp. 47–48.

for any other group, including railroad, rapid transit, public utility, shipyard, aircraft, and automobile workers. Data from Germany indicate that in pre-1933 elections as well as in elections to Works Councils in the 1950s, mining areas gave heavy support to the Communists.[10] An ecological analysis of voting in Chile in 1947 showed that the small Communist party had its greatest strength in mining areas. In the coal, copper, and other mineral mining areas the Communists received from 50 to 80 per cent of the votes as compared to only 10 per cent in the country as a whole.[11]

Lumber workers are also subject to severe cyclical fluctuations. In Sweden lumbering areas give the Communists a higher vote than do the large industrial centers.[12] Analysis of the results of an Austrian provincial election in 1952 showed that 85 per cent of the forestry workers voted for the Socialist party.[13] California and Michigan data indicate that lumber areas give more support to leftist candidates than do other areas,[14] and lumber workers were prominent in the old Industrial Workers of the World (I.W.W.).

· · ·

A general depression makes economic insecurity widespread, and in the elec-

tions of 1932 and 1936 the counties in the U.S. which were hardest hit by the Depression were the most strongly pro-Roosevelt. Survey data pinpoint the fact that in 1936 and 1940, of all low-income people, those on relief were the most strongly Democratic—over 80 per cent.[15] A study of political attitudes in 1944 found that among American manual workers who had never been unemployed, 43 per cent were "conservative" as compared with only 14 per cent were "conservative" as compared with only 14 per cent conservative among those who had experienced more than a year of unemployment.[16]

Comparable findings are reported from Great Britain—the higher the unemployment in an area, the stronger the Labor vote. Moreover, the extent of unemployment in the 1930s was still affecting voting during the full-employment year of 1950—the districts that showed the least decline in Labor vote between 1945 and 1950 were those with the most depression-time unemployment.[17] Similarly in Finland, areas with the most depression-time unemployment gave highest support to the Communist party in 1951–54.[18] In Germany, the extent of unemployment was directly related to the size of the Communist vote in the 1932 elections. A French public opinion poll of 1956 states that 62 per cent of the members of the Communist trade-union movement, the C.G.T., report having been unemployed at some time in the past, as compared to 43 per

---

[10] O. K. Flechtheim, *Die Kommunistische Partei Deutschlands in der Weimarer Republik* (Offenbach Am Main: Bollwerk-Verlag Karl Drott, 1948), p. 211, for pre-1933 data; for statistics on Works Councils elections in the 1950s see Michael Fogarty, *op. cit.*, p. 213.

[11] Richardo Cruz Coke, *Geografia electoral de Chile* (Santiago de Chile: Editorial del Pacifico, S.A., 1952), pp. 53, 81–82.

[12] S. S. Nilson, "Le Communisme dans les pays du nord—les élections depuis 1945," *op. cit.*, pp. 167–80.

[13] Walter B. Simon, *The Political Parties of Austria* (Ph.D. thesis, Department of Sociology, Columbia University, 1957, Microfilm 57–2894 University Microfilms, Ann Arbor, Michigan), p. 263.

[14] H. F. Gosnell, *op. cit.*, p. 77, and J. K. Pollock and S. J. Eldersveld, *op. cit.*, p. 54.

[15] H. F. Gosnell, *op. cit.*, pp. 3, 32, 37, 90.

[16] R. Centers, *The Psychology of Social Classes* (Princeton: Princeton University Press, 1949), pp. 177–79.

[17] H. G. Nicholas, *op. cit.*, pp. 297–98; Wilma George, "Social Conditions and the Labor Vote in the County Boroughs of England and Wales," *British Journal of Sociology*, 2 (1951), pp. 255–59.

[18] Erik Allardt, *Social Struktur och Politisk Aktivitet* (Helsingfors: Söderstrom and Co., 1956), p. 84.

cent of the members of the socialist *Force Ouvrier*, and 33 per cent of the members of the Catholic C.F.T.C.[19]

The relative conservatism of white-collar workers in the United States may be due to their greater job security during the Depression. Only about 4 per cent of the white-collar workers were unemployed in 1930, as compared to 13 per cent of urban unskilled workers. In 1937, 11 per cent of the former and a quarter of the latter were out of work.[20] In Germany this middle-class group was much more affected by the postwar economic crisis than in the United States. The German white-collar workers tended to turn to the fascist movement rather than to the leftist parties with their doctrinaire emphasis on the proletariat.[21]

. . .

*Status*

Feelings of deprivation and consequent political radicalism on the part of those in lowly occupations are not solely due to the objective economic situation. All societies are stratified by status (prestige) as well as by economic rewards, and while status and income tend to be related, they are far from identical. Status involves invidious distinctions— men and groups defined as superior or inferior to others—and it does not follow from what we know about human behavior that men will accept a low social evaluation with equanimity. Wherever the possibility exists, therefore, people will try either to improve their prestige position through individual efforts (social mobility) or to

improve the position of their group through collective action of some sort. And if self-interest describes the motivation flowing from the desire to improve the material conditions of existence, then *resentment* describes the feelings of lowly placed persons toward the social system and those who are high in prestige.[22]

The lack of respect with which workers are treated by office personnel, salespeople, clerks, minor officials, etc., and the general failure of middle-class society to recognize the workers' economic contributions and personal abilities undoubtedly contribute to dissatisfaction with the *status quo* and to political leftism.

While low prestige plus low income and high prestige plus high income join together to reinforce leftist or conservative political motivation, situations in which one factor places the individual much higher or lower on relative ranking scales help, as has been already noted, to account for seemingly deviant patterns of behavior. In all societies for which we have data, white-collar workers receive more prestige than manual workers, and identify in many ways (dress, speech, family patterns) with those higher in the system, even when their income is not higher than that of skilled manual workers.[23] And many studies show that the white-collar workers in different countries are much more likely to vote for the more conservative parties than are manual workers—in general, taking a position midway between that of the higher busi-

[19] *Réalités*, No. 65, April 1956.
[20] C. W. Mills, *White Collar* (New York: Oxford University Press, 1951), p. 281.
[21] T. Geiger, *Die Soziale Schichtung des Deutschen Volkes* (Stuttgart: Ferdinand Enke, 1932), pp. 109–22; Samuel Pratt, *The Social Basis of Nazism and Communism in Urban Germany* (unpublished M.A. thesis, Department of Sociology, Michigan State University, 1948), Chap. 8.

[22] For a more detailed discussion of the reactions to position in the status structure see S. M. Lipset and Hans Zetterberg, "Social Mobility in Industrial Societies," in S. M. Lipset and R. Bendix, *Social Mobility in Industrial Society* (Berkeley: University of California Press, 1959), pp. 60–64.
[23] For a detailed summary of evidence bearing on this point from many countries, see *ibid.*, pp. 14–17.

ness strata and the manual workers on the left-right continuum.[24] This greater conservatism is not due solely to higher income. A study of voting in the 1949 Norwegian election showed that the vote for leftist parties (Communist and socialist) was almost twice as high among manual workers as it was for white-collar workers on each income level (see Table II). A survey study of political affiliation in Germany gave similar results.[25]

TABLE 2. PERCENTAGE VOTING FOR LABOR AND COMMUNIST PARTIES BY OCCUPATIONAL GROUP AND INCOME IN NORWAY—1949*

| Yearly income in Kroner | Industrial workers | White-collar workers |
|---|---|---|
| Under 4,000 | 56 | 35 |
| 4,000–7,000 | 70 | 28 |
| 7,000–12,000 | 69 | 24 |
| Over 12,000 | —† | 13 |

* A. H. Barton, *Sociological and Psychological Implications of Economic Planning in Norway* (unpublished Ph.D. thesis, Department of Sociology, Columbia University, 1954), p. 327.
† Too few cases.

Direct evidence of the importance of the status motive in white-collar political behavior is provided by a study of "class identification" in the United States where 61 per cent of white-collar workers called themselves "middle-class," as against only 19 per cent of manual workers. Among the white-collar

workers this self-labeling made a great difference in political attitudes—65 per cent of those who considered themselves "middle-class" had conservative attitudes, compared with 38 per cent of the "working-class" white-collar workers. Among manual workers, subjective class identification made much less difference in attitudes—37 per cent of "middle-class" manual workers had conservative attitudes, compared with 25 per cent of the "working-class" workers.[26]

The political role of the white-collar workers was studied intensively in Germany, but unfortunately before the days of sampling surveys.[27] Studies using available area voting statistics suggest that the white-collar vote swung from the centrist parties to the Nazis under the impact of the Depression of 1929.[28] A strong correlation existed between the proportion of the unemployed among the white-collar workers in German cities and the Nazi vote.[29] The usual explanation offered by Germans for this is that the Nazis represented a hope for solving the economic crisis and at the same time for maintaining the status position of the white-collar workers, while the Marxist parties offered them economic gains only at the cost of "proletarianization."[30]

Some of the variations in the way workers vote in different countries may possibly be explained by differences in the rigidity of the status-hierarchy. The data on political party choices of Australian, British, American, French, and

[24] G. Gallup, *The Gallup Political Almanac for 1948* (Princeton: American Institute of Public Opinion, 1948), p. 9; R. Centers, *op. cit.*, p. 38; E. G. Benson and Evelyn Wicoff, "Voters Pick Their Party," *Public Opinion Quarterly*, 8 (1944), pp. 165–74; L. Harris, *Is There a Republican Majority?* (New York: Harper & Bros., 1954); H. Cantril, *op. cit.*

[25] Institut für Marktforschung und Meinungsforschung, E.M.N.I.D., *Zur Resonanz der Parteien bei Männer und Frauen in den Soziologischen Gruppen* (Bielefeld: mimeographed, no date), pp. 5, 7, 9.

[26] R. Centers, *op. cit.*, pp. 130–32.

[27] T. Geiger, *op. cit.*, pp. 109–22.

[28] W. Dittman, *Das Politische Deutschland vor Hitler* (Zurich: Europa Verlag, 1945); A. Dix, *Die Deutschen Reichstagswahlen, 1871–1930, und die Wandlungen der Volksgliederung* (Tübingen: J. B. C. Mohr, Paul Siebeck, 1930); W. Stephan, "Zur Soziologie der Nationalsozialistischen Deutschen Arbeiterpartei," *Zeitschrift für Politik*, 20 (1931), pp. 293–300. See also Chap. V.

[29] S. Pratt, *op. cit.*, Chap. 8.

[30] T. Geiger, *op. cit.*, p. 114.

Italian workers all suggest that the lower the socioeconomic position of a worker, the more likely he is to vote for a party of the left. On the other hand, in Germany and Sweden the lowest stratum of workers is most likely to back the non-labor oriented parties. In these countries the higher strata within the working class are more prone to support left parties.[31] For each level of skill in a sample of workers in Germany, the workers earning over 250 marks per month more likely to support left (Socialist and Communist) parties than workers earning less than that amount. Nearly half of the workers in every group supported these parties, but the lowest support was found in the un-skilled, low-income group (45 per cent going to those parties) and the highest (65 per cent) in the skilled, better-paid group (see Table 3).

In absence of more detailed investigations of the varying situation of workers in these two countries as compared with others, it would be foolhardy to attempt to explain these striking differences. The one hypothesis which some people more familiar with life in different parts of Europe than I am have suggested is that there is more frustration among the upper levels of the working class in Germany and perhaps Sweden precisely because these nations remain among the most status-differentiated countries in the Western world. The nobility retained

TABLE 3. PROPORTION OF MALE WORKERS SUPPORTING THE SOCIAL DEMOCRATIC AND COMMUNIST PARTIES IN GERMANY—1953*

| Skill Level and Income | | |
|---|---|---|
| All Skilled Workes | 61% | (230) |
| Over 250 Marks per Month | 65 | (140) |
| Under 250 Marks per Month | 55 | (94) |
| All Semiskilled | 58 | (209) |
| Over 250 Marks per Month | 65 | (113) |
| Under 250 Marks per Month | 50 | (96) |
| All Unskilled | 51 | (97) |
| Over 250 Marks per Month | 59 | (42) |
| Under 250 Marks per Month | 45 | (55) |

* Computations made for the purposes of this study from IBM cards kindly supplied by the UNESCO Institute, Cologne, Germany, from their survey of the 1953 German population.

[31] Similar German findings are also reported in Institut für Marktforschung und Meinungsforschung, E.M.N.I.D., op. cit., and in Divo Institut, Umfragen 1957 (Frankfurt: Europaiische Verlaganstalt, 1958), p. 53. Thus three different research institutes report that the more skilled in Germany are more radical than the less skilled. The Divo Institut found these results in both its surveys of the 1953 and 1957 elections. In the latter year 62 per cent of the skilled workers who voted were for the Social Democrats as contrasted with 43 per cent among the semiskilled and unskilled, p. 5. For Sweden see Elis Hastad, et al., eds., "Gallup" och den Svenska Vajarkaren (Uppsala: Hugo Gebers Forlag, 1950), pp. 157–70.

power and influence in these countries until well into the twentieth century, and interpersonal relations still reflect a considerable explicit emphasis on status. Superiority and inferiority in status position are expressed in many formal and informal ways. Conversely, Australia, Britain, America, and France are nations in which these status differences have declined in importance, given the decline or absence of aristocracy. And an emphasis on status differentiation should affect the more skilled and better-paid workers more than their less privileged class brethren. While the more skilled are better off than other workers, their very economic success makes more obvious to them their rejection by the middle classes. They are in a sense like successful Negroes or Jews in societies which discriminate socially against members of these groups. The more successful among them are more likely to be aware of, and consequently resentful of, their status inferiority. The lower group of workers, Negroes, or Jews, will be less likely to feel deprived of status.

Thus the tentative hypothesis may be offered that the more open the status-linked social relations of a given society, the more likely well-paid workers are to become conservatives politically. In an "open" society, relative economic deprivation will differentiate among the workers as it has traditionally done in the United States and Australia. In a more "closed" society, the upper level of the workers will feel deprived and hence support left-wing parties. Whether these hypotheses correspond to the actual facts is a moot question. It is a fact, however, that these differences in political behavior exist. We need more research to account for their sources.

A second prestige hierarchy is based on religious or ethnic differences. Minority religions, nationalities, and races are usually subjected to various forms of social discrimination, and the low-income member of a minority group consequently faces additional obstacles to economic and social achievement. The poor majority group member, on the other hand, may find substitute gratifications in his ethnic or religious "superiority." High-income members of a low-status ethnic or religious group are therefore, as we have noted, in a situation comparable to the upper level of the working class in those countries with "closed" status systems.

In the English-speaking countries, studies show that among the various Christian denominations, the more well to do the *average* socioeconomic status of the church members, the more likely the lower-status members are to vote for the more conservative party. In Britain, Australia, Canada, and the United States, workers belonging to the more well-to-do churches like the Anglican (Episcopal in the U.S.) are more likely to back the more conservative party than workers belonging to poorer churches.

Similarly, middle-class voters who belong to a relatively less well-to-do church like the Catholic or the Baptist are more prone to be Laborites or Democrats than their class peers in other denominations. One British study reports that among industrial workers voting in the 1951 elections, the percentage backing the Labor Party was 73 among Catholics, 64 among Nonconformists, and 43 among Anglicans. "The proportion of Anglicans who voted Conservative is almost exactly twice as great as the proportion of non-Anglicans who did so; and three-fifths of all the industrial workers who voted Conservative were Anglicans."[32]

In Australia in 1951 and 1955, Gallup Poll data indicate that approximately 50 per cent of the Catholics in urban nonmanual jobs backed the Labor party, as contrasted with less than 30 per cent of the Anglicans in comparable positions. Similarly, among manual workers, Australian Catholics have been more heavily Laborite than any other denomination.[33]

In all of the above countries, Jews, although relatively well to do, are politically the least conservative denomination, a pattern which holds as well in many non-English-speaking Western na-

[32] A. H. Birch, *Small-Town Politics* (London: Oxford University Press, 1959), p. 112; for national data on British voting see H. J. Eysenck, *The Psychology of Politics* (London: Routledge and Kegan Paul, 1954), p. 21, and M. Benney, A. P. Gray, and R. H. Pear, *How People Vote: A Study of Electoral Behavior in Greenwich* (London: Routledge and Kegan Paul, 1956), p. 111; for data dealing with Britain and the United States see Michael Argyle, *Religious Behavior* (Glencoe: The Free Press, 1959), pp. 81–83; for published Australian data see Louise Overacker, *The Australian Party System* (New Haven: Yale University Press, 1952), pp. 166–70, 298, 305–6, and Leicester Webb, *Communism and Democracy in Australia* (Melbourne: F. W. Cheshire, 1954), pp. 91–100.

[33] All the Australian Labor parties are considered as Labor for the purposes of this analysis, although the dissident right-wing Labor parties are largely based on the Catholics.

tions. Electoral data in Austria show that the Jewish districts of Vienna, although middle class, were disproportionately Socialist in many elections before 1933.[34] A study of voting in Amsterdam, the Netherlands, also indicated that the predominantly Jewish district of that city was a strong Social Democratic center.[35] The leftist voting patterns of the Jews have been explained as flowing from their inferior status position (social discrimination) rather than from elements inherent in their religious creed.[36]

The differential impact of religious affiliation on political allegiances does not flow solely from the current status position of the different denominations. In a number of countries churches which have been established, protected by the state, and linked to the landed aristocracy often provide the base for a religious political party which seeks to defend or restore religious rights and influence against the attacks of more left-wing and anticlerical political movements. Thus in Catholic Europe working-class Catholics have disproportionately voted for the more conservative and Catholic parties, while middle-class Protestants, Jews, and free-thinkers have been more leftist, even to the point of backing Marxist parties.[37]

. . .

Many ethnic and religious minorities suffering social or economic discrimina-

tion support the more left parties in different countries, although this pattern is most commonly found in the Jews. In the United States, the Negro minority tends to be more Democratic than whites on a given income level; indeed, within the Negro group economic status makes little difference in voting.[38] Other examples can be found in Asia. In India the Andhras, a large linguistic minority, have been among the strongest supporters of the Communist party,[39] while in Ceylon the Communists are disproportionally strong among the Indian minority. In Japan the Korean minority gives considerable support to the Communists.[40] In Israel the Arab minority and in Syria the Christian minority have been relatively pro-Communist.[41]

SOCIAL CONDITIONS AFFECTING
LEFT VOTING

Granted that a group of people is suffering from some deprivation under the existing socioeconomic system, it does not automatically follow that they will support political parties aiming at social change. Two conditions facilitate such a response: effective channels of

Communist or Socialist in 1951, as against only 35.1 per cent in the Catholic communes. On the whole, the Protestant communes are more well to do than the Catholic ones. For the best discussion of the characteristics of Catholic and other religious political parties in Europe, see Michael Fogarty, *op. cit.,* Chap. 22.

[34] Walter B. Simon, *op. cit.,* pp. 335, 338–41.

[35] J. P. Kruijt, *De Onkerkelikheid in Nederland* (Groningen: P. Noordhoff, N. V., 1933), pp. 265, 267.

[36] See Robert Michels, *Political Parties* (Glencoe: The Free Press, 1949), pp. 261–62, for an analysis of the sources of Jewish radicalism in Wilhelmine Germany that still seems applicable to other countries.

[37] See Stuart R. Schram, *Protestantism and Politics in France* (Alençon, France: Corbiere and Jugain, 1954), pp. 183–86. For example, 55.5 per cent of the registered voters in the Protestant communes (in the *Gard*) voted

[38] J. A. Morsell, *The Political Behavior of Negroes in New York City* (Ph.D. thesis, Department of Sociology, Columbia University, 1951).

[39] S. S. Harrison, "Caste and the Andhra Communists," *American Political Science Review,* 50 (1956), pp. 378–404.

[40] R. Swearingen and P. Langer, *Red Flag in Japan: International Communism in Action, 1919–1951* (Cambridge: Harvard University Press, 1952), pp. 181–84.

[41] Bureau of Applied Social Research, *Syrian Attitudes Toward America and Russia* (New York: Columbia University, 1952), mimeographed.

communication, and low belief in the possibility of individual social mobility.

### Channels of Communication

Perhaps the most important condition is the presence of good communications among people who have a common problem. Close personal contacts between such people further awareness of a community of interests and of the possibilities of collective action, including political action, to solve the common problems. When informal contacts are supplemented by formal organization in trade-unions, farm groups, or class political movements, with all their machinery of organizers, speakers, newspapers, and so forth, political awareness will be intensified still more.

For example, Paul Lazarsfeld has shown that membership in social or other organizations reinforces the tendency to vote Republican among upper- and middle-class people. Similarly, among the lower socioeconomic groups "only 31 per cent of those who were union members, but 53 per cent of those who were not union members voted Republican." The greater political interest and more leftist vote of trade-union members has been frequently documented by studies in a number of countries.

We have already discussed several occupational groups which suffer from severe insecurity of income and which vote strongly leftist in different countries—one-crop farmers, fishermen, miners, sheepshearers, and lumbermen. In each of these groups there was not only a strong reason for social discontent but also, as has been pointed out in detail earlier, a social structure favorable to intragroup communications and unfavorable to cross-class communications, an "occupational community."

In contrast to such groups the service industries generally are composed of small units scattered among the well-to-do populations they serve, and their workers tend to be not only less politically active but also more conservative. The white-collar workers' well-known lack of organization and class consciousness may also be partly due to the small units in which they work and to their scattering among higher-level managerial personnel.[42]

Two general social factors that correlate with leftist voting are size of industrial plants and size of city. We have already noted that there was a correlation between size of plant and leftist vote in German elections before 1933, a finding which was reiterated in a 1953 German survey. Among wrokers the combined Socialist and Communist vote increased with size of the plants. Twenty-eight per cent of the workers in plants with under ten workers voted left; as contrasted with 57 per cent of those in establishments of over a thousand. Similarly, the vote for the Christian Democrats and the conservative parties was smaller for each larger category of plant size. Interestingly enough, the percentage of workers preferring no party also decreased with increasing plant size, indicating both social pressure to vote left, and simply pressure to vote. The earlier study also found a relation between over-all city size and leftist vote.[43]

A later German study (1955) showed that among men the leftist vote increased with size of city in every occupational group except that of people with independent means. But the increase was greatest among manual workers.[44] Similar results are indicated by an analysis of the election returns for Works Coun-

[42] C. Dreyfuss, "Prestige Grading: A Mechanism of Control," in R. K. Merton, *et al.*, eds., *Reader in Bureaucracy* (Glencoe: The Free Press, 1952), pp. 258–64.

[43] S. Pratt, *op. cit.*, Chap. 3.

[44] See also Juan Linz, *op. cit.*, pp. 347 ff. Both men and women and male workers at each skill level were more leftist in larger cities.

cils in Italy in 1954 and 1955. The larger the city and the larger the factory, the more votes received by the Communist-controlled C.G.I.L. (General Confederation of Italian Labor) in elections to Works Councils. The Communist union federation secured 60 per cent of the vote in cities with less than 40,000 population and 75 per cent in cities with over a million people. The same pattern held up when comparing union strength by size of factory for the entire country, and even within most specific industries. For example, in the textile industry, the Communist-controlled union secured 29 per cent of the vote in plants employing 50–100 people (the smallest size reported for this industry) and 79 per cent in plants employing over 2,000.[45]

The same relationship between size of community and party choice is to be found in France, Australia, and the United States.

· · ·

In all these cases the communications factor may be involved. A large plant makes for a higher degree of intra-class communication and less personal contact with people on higher economic levels. In large cities social interaction is also more likely to be within economic classes. In certain cases the working-class districts of large cities have been so thoroughly organized by working-class political movements that the workers live in a virtual world of their own, and it is in these centers that the workers are the most solidly behind leftist candidates, and, as we have already seen, vote most heavily.

*Belief in Opportunities for Individual Mobility*

Instead of taking political action,

[45] For detailed statistical breakdowns of specific cities and plants see *L'Avanzata della C.I.S.L. nolle commissioni interne* (Rome: Confederazione Italiana Sindacati Lavoratori, 1955), pp. 46–95.

some discontented individuals attempt to better their lot within the existing economic system by working their way up the ladder of success. If such a possibility seems to exist, there will be a corresponding reduction in collective efforts at social change, such as the support of unions and leftist parties.

This has long been the major explanation offered for the fact that American workers tend to vote for mildly reformist parties, while European workers normally vote socialist or Communist. Supposedly living in an open-class society, with a developing economy which continually creates new jobs above manual-labor level, the American worker is presumably more likely to believe in individual opportunity. His European counterpart, accepting the image of a closed-class society which does not even pretend to offer the worker a chance to rise, is impelled to act collectively for social change. While these stereotypes of the relative degree of social mobility in Europe and America do not correspond to reality, their acceptance may well affect voting.[46]

Unfortunately, it is not easy to give precise statistical validation for this explanation, since there are so many other ways in which European and American society differ. In America the working

[46] A recent survey of the literature and research relating to mobility in many different countries found that the total vertical mobility (movement from lower- or working-class occupations to nonmanual or higher-prestige occupations) in the United States was not substantially different (30 per cent of the population) than in most other relatively developed countries. Other rates were Germany, 31 per cent; Sweden, 29 per cent; Japan, 27 per cent; France, 27 per cent; Denmark, 31 per cent; Great Britain, 29 per cent. Slightly lower was Switzerland, 23 per cent, and the lowest country in Western Europe was Italy at 16 per cent. These studies are fully reported in S. M. Lipset and R. Bendix, *op. cit.*, Chap. II.

class as a whole has risen, through a large long-term increase in real wages, to a position which in other countries would be termed "middle class." There is a good deal of evidence that American workers believe in individual opportunity; various surveys show about half the workers saying that they have "a good chance for personal advancement in the years ahead."[47] A study in Chicago in 1937 during the Great Depression found that no less than 85 to 90 per cent of every economic group believed that their *children* had a good chance to be better off economically.[48] The most recent data indicate that *actual* social mobility in Europe is as high as it is in the United States but the *belief* in mobility differs. A relatively high rate of actual social mobility appears to be characteristic of all industrial societies.

Two factors are involved in the differential *belief* in mobility: the differences between the United States and Western Europe in total national income and its distribution and, second, the different value systems of the American and European upper classes. As I have put it elsewhere: "Income, in every class, is so much greater in America, and the gap between the living styles of the different social classes so much narrower, that in effect the egalitarian society envisaged by the proponents of high social mobility is much more closely approximated here than in Europe. While Europeans rise in the occupational scale as often as we [Americans] do, the marked contrast between the ways of life of the different classes continues to exist.

[47] E. Roper, "Fortune Survey: A Self-Portrait of the American People," *Fortune*, 35 (1947), pp. 5–16.

[48] A. W. Kornhauser, "Analysis of Class Structure of Contemporary American Society," in G. W. Hartmann and T. M. Newcomb, eds., *Industrial Conflict* (New York: The Cordon Co., 1939), pp. 199–264.

Thus, in the United States workers and middle-class people have cars, while in Europe only the middle class can own an automobile."[49]

But divergent value systems also play a role here, since the American and European upper classes differ sharply in their conceptions of egalitarianism. The rags-to-riches myth is proudly propagated by the successful American businessman. Actual differences in rank and authority are justified as rewards for demonstrated ability. In Europe aristocratic values and patterns of inherited privilege and position are still upheld by many of the upper class, and therefore the European conservative wishes to minimize the extent of social mobility.

Given the much wider discrepancy in consumption styles between the European and American middle and working class, one would expect the upwardly mobile European of working-class origin to have somewhat greater difficulties in adjusting to his higher status, and to feel more discriminated against than his American counterpart, much like the successfully upwardly mobile Negro or other minority ethnic member in America comparing himself with a native-born Protestant white. The comparative materials bearing on the effect of mobility on party choice are, in fact, consistent with the hypothesis that Europeans remain more dissatisfied or retain more ties with their previous status. Surveys in five European nations —Sweden, Finland, Germany, Norway, and Britain—find that upward-mobile Europeans are more likely to vote for left parties than are their fellow countrymen who were born into the middle class, while in the United States, three different survey studies report that the upward mobile are more conservative

[49] S. M. Lipset and Natalie Rogoff, "Class and Opportunity in Europe and the United States," *Commentary*, 18 (1954), pp. 562–68.

(Republican) than those who grew up in middle-class families.[50] Some indication that the propensity to adjust to the cultural style of the class into which one moves is associated with political views is suggested by Swedish data which indicate that men in nonmanual occupations who have risen from the working class will continue to vote for the left party unless they change their consumption styles. Conversely, among those still in the class in which they grew up, variations in consumption style seem to have no relationship to voting choice.

The American version of this difference in "consumption styles" may be the move to the suburb, and several studies have shown the differences in the political behavior of lower-status persons who make such a move. A re-analysis of the 1952 survey conducted by the Survey Research Center at Michigan (and analyzed generally in *The Voter Decides*) along lines of suburban-urban differences found that there were indeed shifts in party loyalties which could not be explained simply as the movement of already conservative people to the suburbs. Both hypotheses suggested by the authors of this study are consistent with the thesis suggested here of the impact of social mobility upon lower-class people. Whether self-selection is the crucial factor (implying that the new suburbanites are upwardly mobile and anxious to become socialized into a higher environment, which means voting Republican) or whether the effects of being exposed to a more Republican environment—friends and neighbors—accounts for greater conservative voting,

the data show that mobility of this kind produces higher Republican voting on the part of previously Democratic voters.[51] When occupation was held constant, in both "medium" and "high" status occupations there was considerably more Republican voting in the suburbs.[52]

While most discussions of the impact of mobility on the political and social systems emphasize the supposed consequences of different rates of upward mobility, considerable evidence indicates that there is a substantial degree of downward movement from one generation to another in every modern industrial society—a father's high position is no guarantee of a similar position for his children. And the most recent American data do in fact indicate that about one third of the sons of professionals, semi-professionals, proprietors, managers, and officials—the most privileged occupations—are in manual employment.[53] Similarly, there is extensive movement from rural to urban areas in most societies, much of which helps to fill the ranks of the manual workers.

These rather extensive movements into the industrial proletariat are one of the major sources of conservative politics within that class. In every country for which data are available—Germany, Finland, Britain, Sweden, Norway, and the United States—workers of middle-class parentage are much more likely to vote for the conservative parties than are workers whose fathers are of the same class. Those of rural background are

[50] See S. M. Lipset and Hans Zetterberg, *op. cit.*, pp. 64–72, for a detailed report on the political consequences of social mobility. Data which indicate that the relationship between upward mobility and vote choice in England is like that in other European countries rather than the United States may be found in R. S. Milne and H. C. Mackenzie, *op. cit.*, p. 58.

[51] See Fred I. Greenstein and Raymond E. Wolfinger, "The Suburbs and Shifting Party Loyalties," *Public Opinion Quarterly*, 22 (1958), pp. 473–83.

[52] Samuel Lubell, *The Revolt of the Moderates* (New York: Harper & Bros., 1956) and William H. Whyte, *The Organization Man* (New York: Simon and Schuster, 1956) discuss the political impact of suburbia.

[53] S. M. Lipset and R. Bendix, *op. cit.*, pp. 87–91.

also relatively more conservative. The difference is even more accentuated when variations in background over three generations are compared. In Germany a 1953 survey found that 75 per cent of the workers whose grandparents were workers voted for the Socialists or the Communists, but only 24 per cent of the workers with a middle-class father did.[54] In Finland, a similar study in 1948 showed that 82 per cent of the workers whose father and paternal grandfathers were workers voted for left parties as compared with 67 per cent of those with a rural background, and 42 per cent of those of middle-class parents.

Given the fact of extensive social mobility in all industrial societies, perhaps the most important effect of mobility on politics which should be noted is that the bulk of the socially mobile, whether their direction be upward or downward, vote for the more conserva-tive parties. In Germany, where over three quarters of the manual workers of middle-class parentage voted for the nonsocialist parties in 1953, almost 70 per cent of those in nonmanual positions of working-class family background also opted for the "middle-class" parties. Similarly in Finland, two thirds of the workers of middle-class origin remained loyal to nonleftist parties, while less than a quarter of those who had risen into middle-class occupations from working-class family background voted for the Socialists or Communists.[55] These find-ings illustrate the pervasive influence of contact with superior status on attitudes and behavior. Those subject to a cross-pressure between the political values congruent with a higher and a lower status as a result of having been in both positions are much more likely to resolve the conflict in favor of the former.

---

[54] Data computed from materials supplied by the UNESCO Institute in Cologne, Germany.

[55] Both German and Finnish studies are re-ported in more detail in Lipset and Bendix, *op. cit.*, pp. 69–71.

# CLASS IDENTIFICATION AND VOTING:
# THE WORKING-CLASS TORIES
# IN ENGLAND

### ERIC A. NORDLINGER

In the last ten years political scientists have come to attribute major signifi-cance to people's self-evaluation of their

*Reprinted from Eric A. Nordlinger,* THE WORK-ING-CLASS TORIES: AUTHORITY, DEFERENCE, AND STABLE DEMOCRACY *(Berkeley: University of California Press, 1967), pp. 160–75, by per-mission of the publisher.*

class position as this influences their voting behaviour. The influence of sub-jective class identification upon the workers' electoral behaviour, with spe-cial reference to those workers who consider themselves middle class, has received a good deal of attention in Eng-land. However, as Goldthorpe and Lockwood have pointed out, the hypotheses relating the workers' subjective class to their voting behaviour have not been developed in a systematic way, nor are these authors ready to place much reliance on the manner in which subjective class has been measured.[1] Here an attempt will be made to analyse some of the possible inter-relationships between subjective class and voting behaviour in a systematic manner, but before launching into this problem it is necessary to outline the methodology used in assessing the respondents' subjective class position.

There are basically two possible strategies to be followed. The respondents may simply be presented with a list of social classes and asked which class they belong to. This method is followed in the great majority of survey studies; it requires the minimum of time and expense. The second strategy relies upon a series of intensive and broad ranging interviews of an open-ended nature. Information is gathered about the respondents' perceptions and evaluations of the entire class and status systems, which then serves as the relational context within which the respondents' own subjective class position can be located. This method is expensive and requires a great deal of the respondents' time. However, it is a more powerful and valid tool of social analysis than is the former method relying solely upon a completely structured interview schedule. Most importantly, a frame of reference is provided for interpreting the respondent's *meaning* when placing himself in a particular class. For example,

some workers who define themselves as middle class may have as their frame of reference not the entire class system, but only the objective working class, and within that strata they believe themselves to be 'middle class', i.e. they are in the 'middle' of the working class. Or to take another example, some workers assign themselves middle-class status when that term is taken to refer to all those people who 'work for a living', and since they too are working people, they define themselves as middle class. Someone using the first method would conclude that these two types of workers are claiming objective middle-class membership for themselves, having identified themselves as such, but this would immediately appear to be an unwarranted interpretation to the social scientist using the second method.

While admitting that the second method is the optimum one if it could be applied to a sufficiently large sample,[2] in a national survey the problem becomes one of maximizing the validity of the interpretations placed upon the respondents' class identifications, while minimizing the proportion of the interviewing session devoted to this problem. The survey strategy employed here is something of a hybrid, combining the main features of the two basic methods. Following the usual procedure, the respondents were asked: 'Here is one type of list of the various social classes found in this country. People are sometimes placed in these classes. Which one would you say you belonged to?' The list contained five classes: labouring working class, skilled working class,

---

[1] John H. Goldthorpe and David Lockwood, 'Affluence and the British Class Structure', *The Sociological Review*, Vol. XI, No. 2, July 1963. However, this assertion was made before the appearance of W. G. Runciman's study, *Relative Deprivation and Social Justice: 1966*, pp. 170–187.

[2] In one of the leading studies employing an extensive and intensive series of interviews only twenty husband and wife couples constituted the sample. See Elizabeth Bott, *Family and Social Network: 1957*. So far as this writer is aware the intensive method has never been applied in a large survey study.

lower middle class, middle class and upper middle class.[3] In order to minimize the possibility of these responses being misinterpreted the sample was also asked to describe the class structure, mentioning the number of classes to be found in England and the types of people making up each class.[4] The free answers given to this question served as the frames of reference within which the workers' subjective class positions were interpreted, i.e. given a meaning. In 10 per cent of the cases there was a clearcut divergence between the respondents' definitions of the working and middle classes and the common definitions given these terms by social scientists. For example, some workers conceive of the working class as 'people who live off the government', as 'lazy lay-abouts', or 'rough and ready types', and when asked which class they belong to they replied 'middle class'. Such responses were then altered to subjective working class.[5] In

another instance, a man who defined the middle class as 'just ordinary people of the world', consequently assigning himself to the middle class, was also placed in the subjective working-class category. In these instances the respondents' frames of reference regarding the class structure were markedly different from the frame of reference used by most social scientists, and when subjectively placing themselves in the class structure they consequently have in mind a different conception of their class position than indicated by the terms working class and middle class as they are commonly employed. In order to take this discrepancy into account, the respondents' frames of reference were first aligned with the one used by social scientists, and their subjective class positions were then altered accordingly. This hybrid method of identifying the respondents' subjective class position both reduces the danger of misinterpreting the responses to the single subjective class question, and allows its application to a large sample.[6]

---

[3] Another difficulty in using a structured list of responses is that the class appearing at the bottom of the scale might take on negative connotations in the respondents' minds. This usually happens when the terms 'unskilled working class' or 'lower class' are used. It was therefore thought best to employ the term 'labouring working class' which does not usually imply a negative valuation.

[4] The wording of this item is: 'People usually agree that there are such things as social classes. Now if a friend of yours from Australia were to ask you to describe the different social classes in this country, how would you do it? You would want to tell him how *many* different social classes there are, and what *kind of people* are in each class.'

[5] It is recognized that in some cases of this sort the respondents are indeed attempting to elevate their own status by defining the working class in such a way as to differentiate themselves from its less desirable elements, and by positing the existence of a class lower than the one to which they belong. Yet an attempt to raise one's status through an invidious comparison does not necessarily entail the desire to be recognized as a member of the middle class.

[6] Runciman has also recognized the difficulty of assigning any particular meaning to subjective class identification given the fact that a significant number of people define the working class and the middle class in terms that are most peculiar to social scientists. He has attempted to get around this problem by employing a technique similar to the one used here. The respondents were asked 'What sort of people do you mean when you talk about the middle class (the working class)?' After a careful analysis of these responses, Runciman concluded that subjective class is a meaningless concept when applied to about 10 per cent of the respondents—the exact figure which appears in the present study. There is however, one important difference between the two techniques for handling this difficulty. Given the relatively small proportion of respondents involved, Runciman thought it best to carry out his analysis of subjective class without either dropping the 10 per cent from the analysis or altering their subjective class identifications to conform to the more orthodox definitions. In the present study it was

## I. THE 'MIDDLE-CLASS' TORIES[7]

A perusal of English voting studies will show no lack of comments about the observation that manual workers who think of themselves as middle class vote Conservative more frequently than do those workers whose subjective and objective class positions coincide. As with the findings of other surveys, the data in Table 1 indicate that middle-class identification strongly predisposes the workers to vote Conservative.[8] More than twice as many working-class identi-fiers vote Labour as vote Tory, whereas among the 'middle-class' workers a slightly larger proportion actually vote Conservative. To be more specific, 29 per cent of the working-class subjectives compared to 53 per cent of the middle-class identifiers vote Tory. However, to note the correlation between these two variables is only the beginning. If this phenomena is to be properly understood and its political relevance appreciated, it would be necessary to know what it is about subjective class which affects vot-ing behaviour (i.e. what leads 'middle-class' workers to vote Tory); and to take the analysis back one step further, there is the fundamental problem of specifying the factor(s) that lead

TABLE 1. CLASS IDENTIFICATION AND VOTING BEHAVIOUR[9]

|              | Working class | Middle class |
|--------------|---------------|--------------|
| Conservative | 29            | 53           |
| Labour       | 71            | 47           |
| Total per cent | 100         | 100          |
| Total number | 340           | 99           |

manual workers to think of themselves as middle class (i.e. deciding what it is about middle-class membership that allows some workers to identify them-selves in this way).

Within academic, journalistic and Labour Party circles it has been argued that either economic affluence or status aspirations have induced a sizeable proportion of workers to claim middle-class membership for themselves; and at the same time, their perception of them-selves as middle class has led the larger proportion of these workers into the Tory fold. Yet notwithstanding the atten-tion that this subject has received, until the recent appearance of Runciman's work its sociological meaning has hardly been touched upon in any rigorous analysis. In the estimation to two care-ful students of the problem, 'There is in fact as yet little evidence which would help in deciding how far the Conserva-tive vote of the manual worker (exclud-ing the "deference voter")[10] is due to

decided to do the latter. In Runciman, op. cit., pp. 152–164, and esp. p. 177, it is seen that the correlation between Conservative voting and middle-class identification does not hold among those workers who maintain a peculiar defini-tion of the middle class.

[7] Whenever the respondents are described as 'middle class' in quotes this should be taken as a shorthand reference to the manual workers who replied that they are middle class.

[8] The sampling technique used here is described in pp. 55–62 of the study from which this selection is taken. In brief, the sample in made up of male, urban, manual workers who regularly vote Conservative or Labor. Since the study focuses primarily upon the working-class Conservatives, the latter have been oversampled—320 Tories vs. 127 Labour voters. [ED.]

[9] The weighting index, according to which the number of Labour respondents has been multiplied by five, is used here.

[10] The authors do not state why the defer-entials are disregarded in this connection. The implication is that the deference voter is thought to be content with his traditional place in the social hierarchy and therefore middle-class identification is not characteristic of him. However, our data indicate this not to be the case; deferentials and pragmatists ex-hibit almost identical rates of middle-class identification. Seymour M. Lipset also makes this unwarranted assumption. He suggests that except for the deferentials, all Tory manual workers are middle-class aspirants. ('Must Tories Always Triumph?' *Socialist Commen-tary*, November 1960.)

his conception of himself as "middle class" simply in material terms (the hypothetical "prosperity" voter), or how far it represents a claim to be accepted as a middle-class person in a full social sense (the hypothetical "identification" voter)'.[11]

The first interpretation of the relation between middle-class identification and Conservative voting to be tested is the most commonly accepted one amongst English political scientists and sociologists: a significant proportion of the manual workers actively aspires to become members of the objectively defined middle class;[12] and since one mark of middle-class status is Conservative voting, these workers support the Tories in order to better their claim for such status and to allow themselves to identify with the middle class. In the words of Mark Abrams, 'They see themselves as merging with the middle class and, by voting Conservative, they hope to consolidate their new class (i.e. status) aspirations.'[13]

On an *a priori* basis this argument ought to be approached in a sceptical manner. Notwithstanding the overlap between the incomes of the highly paid workers and those of the lower middle class leading to certain common consumption patterns which certain writers have interpreted as an indication of status-seeking—it does not appear overly

plausible that a significant number of manual workers are actively aspiring for middle-class status.[14] The workers' increasingly widespread adoption of what was previously considered a lower middle-class life style is hardly an indication of status strivings on their part; televisions, cars and washing machines may be bought to make life easier and more pleasurable, not to imitate a higher status. Even if an innate aspiration for higher social status were found among manual workers its expression would be very much discouraged. The peer-group pressures felt by workers putting on middle-class 'airs';[15] the formal and informal work-place segregation of the manual 'works' people from the non-manual 'staff'; and the high acceptance barriers erected by the lower middle class against any aspirations for middle-class membership on the part of manual

[11] Goldthorpe and Lockwood, op. cit., p. 145.

[12] In the words of David Butler and Richard Rose, they are 'on the threshold of the middle class'. (*The British General Election of 1959:* 1960, p. 15. Also see p. 2.) According to Ferdinand Zweig, 'The whole working class finds itself on the move, moving towards new middle class values and middle class existence.' ('The New Factory Workers', *Twentieth Century*, May 1960). For additional references, see Goldthorpe and Lockwood, op. cit.

[13] 'Party Politics After the End of Ideology', in E. Allardt and Y. Littunen, eds. *Cleavages, Ideologies and Party Systems:* 1964, p. 57, parentheses added.

[14] Although writing of a less prosperous working class than that of the middle 'sixties', Richard Hoggart thinks that the workers are concerned with avoiding the 'Fall' into the depths of the unrespectable working class, rather than with pushing themselves up to middle-class heights. "Cleanliness, thrift and self-respect arise more from a concern not to drop down, not to succumb to the environment than from an anxiety to go up...Even the urge for children to "get on" and the respect for "booklearning" is not most importantly produced by the wish to reach another class out of snobbery. It is associated much more with the thought of a reduction in the numerous troubles which the poor have to meet, simply and because they are poor.' *The Uses of Literacy:* 1957, p. 67. Josephine Klein stresses the 'contempt and disapproval' which the workers have for the "unrespectable" working class, and their fear of becoming part of that group. *Samples From English Cultures:* 1965, Vol. I, p. 5.

[15] 'Acting beyond the ideas of the group "acting posh", "giving y'self airs", "getting above y'self", "being lah-de-dah", "thinking y'self too good for other people", "being stuck up", "turning y'nose up at other people", "acting like Lady Muck"—all these are much disliked and not very sensitively discriminated.' Hoggart, op. cit., p. 73. Also see Klein, op. cit., p. 89.

workers[16]—these are only some of the factors mitigating against any manifest strivings for middle-class status on the part of the working class.

The belief that a working man cannot appreciably elevate his status, thereby making any such aspirations unrealistic, even if he had money or a responsible position, finds expression in a number of interviews. When asked 'How do you feel about people moving from one class to another?', a Birmingham house painter who votes Tory replied: 'Quite frankly, I don't think they can move. I'm working class now, but if I won the pools tomorrow I might have a swimming pool in the garden, but I'd still be working class.' A deferential respondent living as an old-age pensioner in Putney believes that with 'good qualifications you can rise up in the firm you work for—from worker to manager. I'd say yes to this. But the man oughtn't to go into a club (that) his manager belongs to. The manager can't hold his usual conversation and neither can the worker. None of them can be truthful. They've got to build up their conversation.' The fact that this particular worker thinks of himself as lower middle class, while denying the possibility of social as opposed to occupational mobility, foreshadows one aspect of the conclusion we are moving towards.

These responses are cited simply as two examples of the workers' beliefs about social mobility—beliefs whose representativeness need to be established by testing the hypothesis of the middle-class identification voter with the survey data. It is reasoned here that if the

'middle-class' workers are concerned with becoming *bona fide* members of the middle class, they should exhibit certain attitudes having a decidedly middle-class flavour more frequently than do the working-class identifiers. They would hold such attitudes in order to 'prove' their status claims both to themselves and to others, and because the middle class would serve as their normative reference group to whose values they would conform in anticipation of their entry into that social strata.

One attribute of a middle-class life style is a respect for education, both as a status symbol and as a means for social and economic mobility. In order to measure the value placed upon education the respondents were asked: 'If you had your life to live over again, would you have tried to stay on in school longer than you did?' Since only a small fraction of the respondents attended secondary school, they are being asked whether they would have desired such an education, presumably for reasons of economic or social betterment. The data indicate that the middle-class identifiers answered with the proper middle-class reply only to a slightly greater degree than the respondents who see themselves as working class, only 6 percentage points separating the two groups on this measure.[17] A similar finding emerges from the data collected by F. M. Martin in his study of the subjective aspects of social stratification. After dividing the manual workers in his sample into those who identified as working class and middle class, the respondents were asked: 'Up to what age would you like to see your children continue full-time education?' The mean age selected by the 'middle-class' workers was 16.7 years, compared to the 16.6-year mean

---

[16] Peter Willmott and Michael Young, *Family and Class in a London Suburb:* 1960, p. 122. At times the high acceptance barriers are replaced by an even more effective device; the status conscious middle class sometimes simply move out of the predominantly working-class neighbourhood. See Peter Willmott, *The Evolution of a Community:* 1963, Chapter V.

[17] This also applies to both Tory and Labour voters separately. Wherever the two groups are combined it may be assumed that there are no differences between them.

of the working-class subjectives.[18] Taken together, these two findings indicate there to be only an insignificant difference in the importance and desirability attributed to education by the two types of workers.

A second way in which middle-class aspirations can be gauged is to ask the respondents what kind of social connections they would desire for their children. Even if the manual workers cannot hope to achieve middle-class status themselves, if this ambition were present they could entertain it for the next generation. The workers were asked: 'Let us say that you have a son at a grammar school. Would you prefer that he become friendly with the son of a cabinet maker or the son of a bank clerk?' Among the working-class subjectives 6 per cent replied that the bank clerk's son would be preferable, compared to 7 per cent of the 'middle-class' workers. These figures can then hardly be said to support the middle-class identification hypothesis.[19] In fact they show the working class as a whole to have few aspirations for middle-class social status—even for their children. However, these data must not be interpreted to mean that only some 7 per cent of the male manual workers want their children to 'rise' out of the working class through their own efforts and achievements. When asked what *occupation* they would prefer for their sons, fully one-third of the workers interviewed in the Martin study indicated their choice of a clerical, business or professional occupation.[20] What is claimed here is that only a small per-centage of workers are concerned with the social status aspects of middle-class membership for their children (i.e. associating with people of higher status as opposed to becoming middle class through occupational mobility), and that there is no difference in this regard between the working-class and middle-class identifiers. And even when we examine the workers' occupational preferences for their children the middle-class identifiers turn out not to have any greater aspirations than the working-class subjectives; there is only 2 per cent difference between the two groups in the proportion desiring non-manual occupations for their children.[21]

If the commonly held assumption that women are more status conscious than men is accepted, then we find further evidence for the argument in another survey study. Runciman reports that the proportion of men and women in the working class who described themselves as middle class is exactly the same.[22] But if middle-class identification were a manifestation of status strivings, the data ought to have indicated a higher proportion of 'middle-class' women than 'middle-class' men.

Taking all these data together, it is clear that the 'middle-class' workers do not think of themselves in such terms because of any stirrings for membership in the middle class.[23] It then also follows that the tendency for the middle-class subjectives to vote Conservative is not due to a desire on their part to increase their social status. Since they do not view the middle class as a reference group, imparting its standards of behaviour to the workers, there is no rea-

---

[18] F. M. Martin, 'Some Subjective Aspects of Social Stratification', in Glass, ed., op. cit., p. 68. The mean age selected by the professional middle class was 18.8 years and 17.5 years for the salaried middle class.

[19] It must be admitted that the response pattern might have been different if a bank manager had been substituted for a bank clerk in the formulation of the question.

[20] Op. cit., p. 69.

[21] Ibid.

[22] Op. cit., p. 166.

[23] W. G. Runciman reaches this conclusion by a different path in his ' "Embourgeoise-ment", Self-Rated Class and Party Preference', *The Sociological Review*, July 1964, pp. 144–145.

son to believe that these workers vote Conservative in order to appear middle class. The hypothetical 'identification' voter is then just that—hypothetical.

The second factor which is commonly used to explain social upgrading and Conservative voting is the working class' new-found affluence. On the face of it this hypothesis is eminently plausible. Compared to the 'traditional' pre-1939 working class whose primary concern was the maintenance of a minimal standard of living, the contemporary workers' relative prosperity obviates any untold concern for income and economic security.[24] Furthermore, compared to the pre-1939 situation when a significant gap separated working-class wages from lower middle-class salaries, there is today an overlap between the two, with not a small percentage of skilled workers earning more than the lower-echelon 'black-coated' and 'white-collared' workers. Then, too, with the coming of the welfare state, the beginnings of voluntary pension schemes and a full-employment economy, the workers are approaching the degree of economic security enjoyed by the lower middle class. And finally, the combination of high wages and opportunities for hire purchase has resulted in the workers' acquiring a standard of life comparable to that of many lower middle-class people. Thus it would seem plausible to argue that the workers' new-found prosperity (in absolute and relative terms)

[24] Notice should be taken of the warning given by David Lockwood about such comparisons. When contrasting the pre-1939 working class with its post-1950 counterpart, the error of comparing the most distinctive part of the 'old' working class (the unemployed) with the most distinctive section of the 'new' working class (the £20-a-week wage earners) is an easy one to fall into. For in an 'unemployed society people are interested in how the worker survives in poverty; in a full employed one how he reacts to prosperity.' ('The "New Working Class"' *Archives Européenes de Sociologie*, 1960, Number 2, p. 251.)

has led many of them to identify as middle class, and having achieved their new level of prosperity under the *aegis* of Conservative Governments, they have been ushered into the Tory fold.

The obvious test of the latter half of the argument is to relate income to voting behaviour in order to see whether or not the more prosperous workers tend to vote Conservative. This is done in Table 2, where the hypothesis is clearly seen to be unwarranted. The rate of Tory voting does not increase as income increases. In fact, just the opposite is true: 39 per cent of the workers earning below average incomes vote Conservative, compared to 30 per cent of the above average earners.[25] The 'prosperity' voter, as such, who enters the polling booth with a thank-you note in his pocket addressed to Central Office is clearly not a significant factor in English politics.

Since the hypothesis that higher incomes result in Tory voting is based on a crude economic determinism there ought to be little surprise in its disconfirmation. Material prosperity alone does not shape party preferences. It is only after material prosperity is related to personal economic expectations, resulting in economic satisfaction or dissatisfaction, that income level helps to pattern voting behaviour. The crucial variable is not income, but the degree to which the workers are satisfied or dissatisfied with their economic situation. Table 3 indicates that greater economic satisfaction does help to explain Conservative voting behaviour. The rate

[25] In his study of West German workers Juan Linz also found an inverse relationship between income and voting for the Socialists. See *The Social Bases of German Politics*: unpublished Ph.D. thesis, Department of Sociology, Columbia University, 1958, p. 325. For similar data on the French working class during the Fourth Republic, see Richard F. Hamilton, *Affluence and the French Worker*: 1967.

of Tory voting increases from 26 per cent among the economically dissatisfied, to 34 per cent among the partly satisfied, to 40 per cent of the economically contented workers.

On the one hand we have found Tory voting to decrease as income increases, and on the other, to increase with greater economic satisfaction. These seemingly contradictory patterns are accounted for by the higher economic expectations held by the Labour supporters, which consequently remain unfulfilled more often that the Conservatives' economic expectations. The evidence for this argument is found when income is related to economic satisfaction. In the preceding chapter it was seen that within all three income groups the proportion of Labour voters who are unsatisfied is greater than the corresponding proportion of Conservatives. Thus given the fact that it is more difficult to satisfy the Labour voters than the Conservatives' economic expectations, notwithstanding the somewhat higher average income of the Labour voters, affluence alone does not lead to an increase in Tory voting.

Having shown that economic satisfaction is associated with the workers' Tory preferences, it remains to be seen how the other half of the argument—the effect of subjective class upon voting

TABLE 2. INCOME AND VOTING BEHAVIOUR[26]

|  | £10 and below | £11–£15 | £16 and above |
|---|---|---|---|
| Conservative | 39 | 31 | 30 |
| Labour | 61 | 69 | 70 |
| Total per cent | 100 | 100 | 100 |
| Total number | 115 | 184 | 121 |

[26] The weighting index, according to which the number of Labour respondents has been multiplied by five, is used here in order to neutralize the statistical effects or the overrepresentation of the Tories in the sample.

TABLE 3. ECONOMIC SATISFACTION AND VOTING BEHAVIOUR[27]

|  | Satisfied | So-so | Unsatisfied |
|---|---|---|---|
| Conservative | 40 | 34 | 26 |
| Labour | 60 | 66 | 74 |
| Total per cent | 100 | 100 | 100 |
| Total number | 194 | 104 | 139 |

behaviour—is related to this finding. It is then first necessary to specify what it is that leads a sizeable proportion of workers to think of themselves as middle class. The overlap between the more prosperous workers and the lower economic strata of the middle class suggests that the 'middle-class' workers think of themselves in these terms because of their absolute and relative affluence. This hypothesis is partly supported by the data; there is a relationship between income and class identification (see Table 4). None of the Labour voters earning below average incomes identify as middle class, the proportion increasing to 18 per cent of those with above average incomes. Thus affluence does tend to induce them to view themselves as middle class. Presumably they conceive of themselves as such because middle class people are thought of as prosperous types, and seeing themselves in this light, they too become middle class.

This conclusion is not, however, applicable to the Conservatives, even though there is a correlation between income and subjective class among these workers. For in Table 5 it is seen that economic satisfaction is a more powerful explanatory variable in accounting for middle-class identification than is income alone. Of those Tories who are economically contented 39 per cent are middle-class subjectives, the proportion dropping to 15 per cent of those who are economically dissatisfied. The weaker correlation between the Tories'

[27] The weighting index, according to which the number of Labour respondents has been multiplied by five, is used here.

TABLE 4. INCOME AND CLASS IDENTIFICATION

|  | Tories | | | Labour | | |
|---|---|---|---|---|---|---|
|  | £10 and below | £11–£15 | £16 and above | £10 and below | £11–£15 | £16 and above |
| Working class | 80 | 69 | 66 | 100 | 88 | 80 |
| Middle class | 17 | 28 | 31 | 0 | 11 | 18 |
| DK, other | 4 | 3 | 2 | 0 | 2 | 3 |
| Total per cent | 100 | 100 | 100 | 100 | 100 | 100 |
| Total number | 88 | 127 | 83 | 27 | 57 | 40 |

income and their class identification then becomes only a limited explanation; for it is the sense of economic well-being rather than income alone which leads the Tories to identify as middle class. The data in Table 5 indicates that in the case of the Labour voters there is no relationship between economic satisfaction and middle-class identification. Whatever the reasons may be for this negative finding, the problem is extraneous to the present analysis. For one thing only 12 per cent of the Labour voters identify as middle class, compared to 35 per cent of the Conservatives. But more important, the Labour group can now be disregarded because the object of the exercise is to understand how economic satisfaction and middle-class identification are specifically related to Conservative voting.

We have found correlations between all three variables, but this does not tell us by which path the three are interconnected. The two most plausible possibilities are set out diagrammatically in Figure 1.

In Pattern A economic satisfaction results in middle-class identification presumably because these manual workers think of middle-class people as being economically secure and contented, and since they share this perceived middle-class attribute they are led to envision themselves in just such terms. The other half of the hypothesis depicted in Pattern A—economic satisfaction resulting in a Conservative vote—is presumably due to the workers' belief that Conservative leaders and policies are best suited for the realization of their economic expectations. In Pattern B the same relationship between economic satisfaction and middle-class identification as in Pattern A is posited. However, here Tory voting is not independently affected by economic contentment as it is in Pattern A. Rather, economic satisfaction is a condition of Conservative voting in so far as it *first* results in middle-class identification, which then results in Conservative voting independently of the economic variable. This latter relationship is probably structured by the middle-class subjectives' belief that Conservative voting is in the economic interests of 'middle-class' people like themselves—a belief bolstered by the objective middle-class' solid support for the Tory Party.

If Pattern A correctly depicts the inter-relationship then it must be shown that economic satisfaction leads to Conservative voting amongst both working-

Figure 1

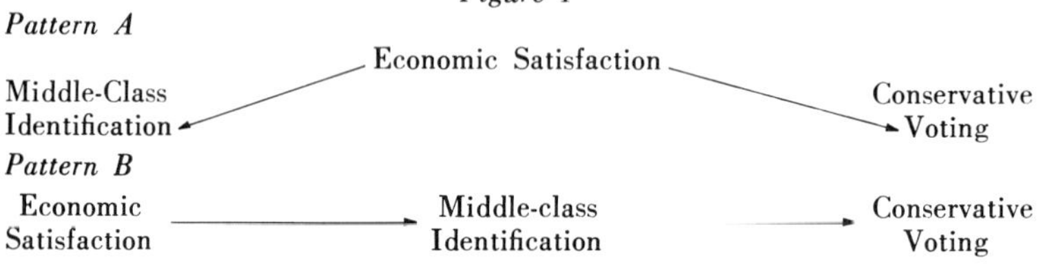

Pattern A

Middle-Class Identification ← Economic Satisfaction → Conservative Voting

Pattern B

Economic Satisfaction → Middle-class Identification → Conservative Voting

TABLE 5. ECONOMIC SATISFACTION AND CLASS IDENTIFICATION

|  | *Tories* | | | *Labour* | | |
|  | *Satisfied* | *So-so* | *Unsatisfied* | *Satisfied* | *So-so* | *Unsatisfied* |
|---|---|---|---|---|---|---|
| Working class | 58 | 81 | 82 | 87 | 93 | 86 |
| Middle class | 39 | 16 | 15 | 13 | 7 | 14 |
| Other, DK | 4 | 3 | 3 | 0 | 0 | 0 |
| Total per cent | 100 | 100 | 100 | 100 | 100 | 100 |
| Total number | 141 | 75 | 88 | 47 | 29 | 51 |

TABLE 6. ECONOMIC SATISFACTION AND VOTING BEHAVIOUR WITH CLASS IDENTIFICATION CONTROLLED FOR[28]

|  | *Working Class* | | | *Middle Class* | | |
|  | *Satisfied* | *So-so* | *Unsatisfied* | *Satisfied* | *So-so* | *Unsatisfied* |
|---|---|---|---|---|---|---|
| Conservative | 28 | 31 | 25 | 66 | 57 | 26 |
| Labour | 72 | 69 | 75 | 34 | 43 | 74 |
| Total per cent | 100 | 100 | 100 | 100 | 100 | 100 |
| Total number | 127 | 89 | 116 | 65 | 15 | 19 |

class and middle-class identifiers. If this condition is not met Pattern A would be disconfirmed since subjective class is not posited as an intervening variable as it is in Pattern B. Table 6 has been constructed to settle this matter. It is seen that economic satisfaction does lead to Conservative voting amongst the *middle-class* identifiers, 66 per cent of these workers who are also economically contented voting Tory, with the proportion dropping to 57 per cent and 26 per cent amongst the partly satisfied and dissatisfied middle-class identifiers respectively. In contrast, there is no relationship between economic satisfaction and voting behaviour amongst the working-class identifiers. Since economic satisfaction is not associated with the voting behaviour of the working-class identifiers, the conclusion emerges that there is not a direct relationship between economic satisfaction and Tory voting. Pattern A is thereby invalidated and the strong suggestion emerges that Pattern B with class identification as the intervening variable, correctly posits the three variables' inter-relationship.

In fact, the validity of Pattern B has already been established, and it is just left to bring the strands of two previous arguments together. It has already been shown that economic satisfaction results in middle-class identification, although this applies solely to the Conservative supporters, the 'middle-class' Labour supporters tending to view themselves as such because of a high income level. And the second inter-relationship in Pattern B is the one which we set out to explain at the outset—namely, the tendency for those workers who conceive of themselves as middle-class to vote Conservative. To state the conclusion in a sentence, a sense of economic well-being frequently leads to middle-class identification because the workers define middle-class people as economically secure and comfortable and see themselves as such; and in turn, middle-class identification often results in Tory voting due to the dual belief that this is the 'proper' way for middle-class people to behave and that Tory measures are most likely to maintain their economic well-being.[29]

[28] The weighting index, according to which the number of Labour respondents has been multiplied by five, is used here.

[29] This conclusion ought not to be taken to mean that economic satisfaction is the single factor patterning class identification. Region, neighbourhood and the class position of one's parents are also relevant. See Runciman, op. cit., pp. 165–167.

# SOCIAL CLASS AND
# POLITICAL PARTICIPATION

ROBERT E. LANE

Class status is indicated by objective criteria (such as income, occupation, and education), plus a network of social relations, plus a person's conception of his own place in society.[1] It both defines and serves as the instrument of a man's aspirations and ambitions. Where one lives, what church one belongs to, one's style of life are usually functions of social class. The position of a person's class in the total class structure determines the benefits he receives from his class membership. A social class is a life space with various ranks and restrictions and pressures of its own; its non-mobile members, therefore, come to grips with life largely within the terms of their own class.[2] Yet, like other groups, it has a reference function both for members and for those who are not, by objective criteria, members. Thus people in working-class occupations who think of themselves as middle-class may pattern their behavior after middle-class norms.[3]

Social classes develop characteristic attitudes, belief, and goals, indicating a kind of class differentiation of sub-national culture patterns.[4] For example, people in different social classes read different magazines. The Yankee City study shows that while 83 per cent of the *New Yorker* subscribers in that community were members of the upper class (and 17 per cent upper-middle), 54 per cent of the *True Story* subscribers were members of the lower class (and 46 per cent middle class).[5] Television appears to be a great equalizer in this respect, but if television is like the radio, where there are marked class differences in

[1] For a bibliography of social stratification see *Current Sociology*, Vol. II, Number 1, 1953–54 (a UNESCO publication). For an excellent review of current theory, see Kurt Mayer, "The Theory of Social Classes," *Harvard Education Review*, 23 (1953), pp. 149–57. See also, Reinhard Bendix and Seymour M. Lipset, eds., *Class Status and Power* (Glencoe, Ill.: Free Press, 1953).

[2] G. W. Hartman makes the point that competition for status occurs largely within classes, rather than between them. See "The Prestige of Occupations," *Personnel Journal*, 13 (1934).

*Reprinted from Robert E. Lane,* POLITICAL LIFE *(Glencoe: The Free Press, 1959), pp. 220–34, by permission of the Macmillan Co.*

[3] On the general subject of subjective class status, see Richard Centers, *The Psychology of Social Classes* (Princeton: Princeton University Press, 1949); also Heinz Eulau, "Perceptions of class and Party in Voting Behavior, 1952," *American Political Science Review*, 49 (1955), pp. 364–84.

[4] See Arthur W. Kornhauser, "Public Opinion and Social Class," *American Journal of Sociology*, 55 (1950), pp. 333–45.

[5] See W. Lloyd Warner's Yankee City series, especially Warner and Lunt, *The Social Life of a Modern Community* (New Haven: Yale University Press, 1941), pp. 390–93.

listening habits the appearance of uniformity is deceptive.[6]

It has long been known that political participation in the United States increases with increasing status. This is illustrated in Woodward and Roper's findings on the socio-economic groups who rate high on a composite index of political participation:[7]

"A" Economic Level
Executives
Professional people
Stockholders
College educated

Those who scored lowest were:
Laboring people
Housewives
People with only grade school education
Negroes
"D" economic level

The "A" economic level had twelve times as great a proportion of very active participants (top 10 per cent on index) as did the "D" economic level. Why are social status and political participation so closely linked in the United States?

The gains from governmental policy for lower income groups must be collective gains, gains granted to classes or groups of people, which may or may not accrue to any one individual. In contrast to this, a large category of middle-income persons, businessmen, are in a position to gain some specific individual advantage from government such as a fast tax write-off, a paving contract, or a real estate deal. As a consequence, the relationship between political effort and personal gain is usually closer for

businessmen than for working-class people.

Beyond this, however, the means available for participation are different in the different status groups. The poor man can contribute no significant sums of money, nor is his individual social and occupational position likely to give him, as an individual, much influence over governmental actions. Poor people can exert influence only by collective action; really, only through organizations designed for this purpose. The more prosperous individual, however, can make larger financial contributions and can use his personal and professional influence to some effect. The working-class person must speak through an agent; the business or professional person may delegate his politics in the same way, but he may also exercise personal influence.

Among the objective criteria which we have said are indices of socio-economic status, is it education, income, or occupation which makes the greatest difference? Connelly and Field, with reference only to voting, find that when a cross-analysis of income and education is made, the differences between the income levels for each educational classification are greater than the differences among the educational level for each income classification.[8] Foskett, on the other hand, finds that indices of more general community participation reveals greater differences among educational groups when income is held constant than among income groups when education is held constant.[9] Perhaps for a simple conventional act such as voting, income is more important, while more

[6] Paul F. Lazarsfeld and Patricia L. Kendall, *Radio Listening in America* (New York: Prentice-Hall, Inc., 1948); see also, Genevieve Knupfer, "Portriat of the Underdog," *Public Opinion Quarterly, 11* (1947), pp. 108–9.

[7] Julian L. Woodward and Elmo Roper, "Political Activity of American Citizens," *American Political Science Review, 44* (1950), p. 877.

[8] Gordon M. Connelly and Harry M. Field, "The Non-Voter—Who He is, What He Thinks," *Public Opinion Quarterly, 8* (1944), p. 179.

[9] John M. Foskett, "Social Structure and Social Participation," *American Sociological Review, 20* (1955), p. 434.

complex forms of participation are more dependent upon qualities associated with education. Occupation is hard to grade along a similar, single dimensional continuum, but from inspection of the 1952 Survey Research Center data, it is apparent (for what it is worth) that differences among standard occupational classifications are smaller than differences among the educational or income classifications.[10]

Education affects attitudes toward political participation in several directions at once. A preliminary study of 400 students at Ohio Wesleyan University and others in the local community showed that college students (particularly those who had political science courses) were significantly more willing than high school students to work for a political party, but among the college students those who were most willing to work for a political party were the Freshman and those generally least willing to do so were the college Seniors.[11] Furthermore, these attitudes of willingness or unwillingness were supported in the various college class groups by "appropriate" differences in attitudes toward the political system: more cynical among Seniors and more hopeful and conscientious among Freshmen. Thus, the micro-processes whereby the gross experiences of education are converted into a higher sense of duty and willingness to participate remain still to be made clear.

Returning to the more molar level of explanation, however, the substantial social class differences in political activity require a general social analysis. Why should persons in higher socio-economic status positions in the United States engage more actively in the political process than those with lower status positions? A number of answers have been brought forward and of these, eleven deserve examination.

In the first place, there is sometimes offered a simple answer in terms of time and energy available for matters not immediately related to the daily problems of living. Saenger points out, for example, that political activity is not merely a matter of awareness of what is going on, but is also affected by the "amount of time and energy specific activities require."[12] It takes an amount of leisure above the minimum to ring doorbells, write letters, read magazine articles, go to forums, and serve on committees, and a differential in leisure may account for some of the differential in activity. Bryce attributes many of the differences between British and American politics to the lack of a leisure class in the United States.[13] Lipset and associates consider that leisure time differences help explain the discrepancies in voting rates in different income groups.[14]

At least for men, the leisure theory fails to explain class differences in participation in the United States at this time, however useful it may have been in other cultures at other times. Leisure has a wide variety of contexts and mean-

---

[10] Angus Campbell, Gerald Gurin, and Warren E. Muler, *The Voter Decides* (Evanston, Ill.: Row, Peterson, 1954), p. 72.

[11] *The Development of Attitude Scales in Practical Politics* (Delaware, Ohio: The Evaluation Service, Ohio Wesleyan University, 1955, mimeographed), pp. 21, 26. See also a subsequent report by the Ohio Wesleyan Evaluation Service, *Changes in the Political Attitudes of Students at Ohio Wesleyan University During Their First Two Years* (1957). Apparently two additional years of college increases willingness to participate in politics.

[12] Gerhart H. Saenger, "Social Status and Political Behavior," *American Journal of Sociology*, 51 (1945), p. 105.

[13] James Bryce, *The American Commonwealth* (New York: Macmillan, 1910), pp. 62, 67.

[14] Seymour M. Lipset, Paul F. Lazarsfeld, Allen H. Barton, and Juan Linz, "The Psychology of Voting: An Analysis of Political Behavior," in Gardner Lindzey, ed., *Handbook of Social Psychology* (Cambridge, Mass. Addison-Wesley, 1954), pp. 1124–75.

ings among which are isolation from working companions; retirement, and hence a more tenuous relation to economic strivings; unemployment and the depression and apathy which this often entails; travel with its loosening of community bonds; and so forth. If, all other things remaining equal, the hours of work are varied, probably there is an inverted "u-shaped" curve relating leisure and political participation.

Also, there is no clear relation between working hours and income. For example, in Connecticut (February, 1956, and also generally throughout the year), workers in the apparel industry worked an average of thirty-six hours a week and received the lowest hourly wage rate and the lowest weekly earnings of all manufacturing production workers, while those in primary metal industries worked an average of forty-seven hours a week, and had among the highest hourly rates. The most prosperous workers had the least leisure.[15] Although the data are not available, it is equally uncertain that the executive or professional man today works less hours than the factory worker. And perhaps he carries his occupational burdens with him rather more than the manual or clerical worker—he is more preoccupied.

Furthermore, those with the most leisure, the retired, seem to be less politically active than others of their age bracket. Arneson and Eells, for example, found that out of seventy categories of people analyzed, the "retired" group had the lowest voting rate in 1948, far lower than those classified as "over 70 years of age."[16] Furthermore, in Erie County in 1940, of those who reported that they had attempted to convince someone of

their political ideas or had been asked for political advice, the unemployed, next to the housewives, revealed the lowest rate of participation of this kind.[17]

For reasons of this nature the availability of time and leisure does not seem to account for the variation in class participation among men, although allowance should be made for the inconvenience to working men of the opening and closing times of the polls.[18] But among women, the situation may be different. Katz and Lazarsfeld found not only that upper-status women are more likely to be political opinion leaders than lower-status women, but that women with small families are also more likely than women with large families to be opinion leaders of this kind.[19] These authors suggest that greater leisure to increase social contacts outside the home is an important factor in accounting for these differences. Thus, for women, if not for men, class differences in participation may, indeed, reflect differences in amount of leisure.

If time and leisure seem to be ambiguously related to different rates of political participation in different socioeconomic classes, what of economic security? Here the basis for a reliable class difference seems somewhat better supported. In Albany, New York (1949), upper income persons were found to be substantially less worried about the possibility of a depression and about their own personal finances than

[15] Connecticut Labor Department Monthly Bulletin, 21 (April, 1956), p. 6.

[16] Ben A. Arneson and William H. Eells, 'Voting Behavior in 1948 as Compared with 1924 in a Typical Ohio Community," American Political Science Review, 44 (1950), p. 434.

[17] Paul F. Lazarsfeld, Bernard Berelson, and Hazel Gaudet, The People's Choice, 2nd ed. (New York: Columbia University Press, 1948), p. 50. But, note that, for some reason, the retired, as distinct from the unemployed, were among the highest participants in this study.

[18] See Charles E. Merriam and Harold F. Gosnell, Non-Voting (Chicago: University of Chicago Press, 1924), pp. 78–108.

[19] Elihu Katz and Paul F. Lazarsfeld, Personal Influence (Glencoe, Ill.: Free Press, 1955), pp. 273, 291.

persons of lower income.[20] But worry of this kind seems to have various results. On the one hand, it does not seem to absorb attention and time so that an interest in foreign affairs is made less likely.[21] On the other hand, another study shows that people who "feel quite secure financially" are likely also to feel that they are politically effective and have an effective voice in the affairs of the republic.[22] These attitudes, we know, form a solid basis for political activity. On the whole, it seems justifiable to say that the lack of financial worry which is generally associated with a better income provides one cause for substantial socio-economic class differences in political activity.

Turning now to a third argument which seeks to explain why members of upper-status groups participate more than do members of lower-status groups, one comes to an essentially economic concept. This argument, following the familiar lines of the Federalist papers,[23]

[20] Survey Research Center, *Interest, Information, and Attitudes in the Field of World Affairs* (Ann Arbor, Mich., 1949, mimeographed), p. 100.

[21] *Ibid.*, p. 38.

[22] Elizabeth Douvan and Alan M. Walker, "The Sense of Effectiveness in Public Affairs," Ann Arbor, Mich., Survey Research Center, c. 1954, (mimeographed), p. 17. The question was: "Some people feel quite secure financially: others have many worries about how they will get along. How is it in your case?"

[23] "Government is instituted no less for protection of the property, than of the persons, of individuals. The one as well as the other therefore, may be considered as represented by those who are charged with the government. Upon this principle it is that in several of the States, and particularly in the State of New York, one branch of government is intended more especially to be the guardian of property, and is accordingly elected by that part of the society which is most interested in this object of government." Moreover, "If the law allows an opulent citizen but a single vote in the choice of his representative, the respect and consequence which he derives from his fortunate situation very frequently guide the

states that those with property (or larger incomes?) have a greater stake in the society and therefore not only do but should have greater influence on governmental policy-making. Leaving out of account the moral phase of the argument, there is a theory, which we believe false, that men do naturally participate in politics somewhat in proportion to their stake in society and further, that the more prosperous have a greater stake in society.

Since the idea of "stake in society" is a chimerical argument leading into premiseless debate, let us consider the proposition to mean stake in governmental policy. With the rise of the welfare state, the proportion of policy designed to be of immediate assistance to the working class has clearly increased. Just as the bearing of public policy upon fair employment practices brought the Northern Negro increasingly to the polls, so the increase of welfare legislation helped to increase the rate of participation of the urban worker. If there ever was a time when ownership of property or greater income necessarily gave a man greater status in governmental decisions than lack of such property or income, that time is fast disappearing.

Nevertheless, there are differences in the way in which the government impinges on individuals in different income groups. It is psychologically more painful to be threatened with deprivation of something you have than it is psychologically rewarding to be offered something you want but have never experienced. On such grounds as these, perhaps, more emotion is invested in a 10 per cent increase in taxation than in

votes of others to the objects of his choice; and through this imperceptible channel the rights of property are conveyed into the public representation." Federalist Paper No. 54 (Hamilton or Madison), see E. M. Meade, ed., *The Federalist* (New York: Random House, c. 1937), p. 357.

a 10 per cent increase in standard of living due to federal subsidy of housing. This difference between social classes in the nature of the rewards and punishments of government policy may help to explain differential turnout among these social classes.

Perhaps even more important than the extent and nature of the relevant policies and the means available to affect them is the degree to which they are visible to the affected groups. We have argued that the society distributes education and access to sources of information unequally to the several social classes, and that the media make visible the relevance of governmental policy to upper status groups when they do not do so to the same degree for the lower status groups. This argument is borne out by the fact that education is positively related to a perception of "whether the outcome of an election would make any difference or not," but it must be confessed that the relationship is not so great as one would expect (67 per cent grammar school to 77 per cent high school and college).[24] In any event, if domestic politics are related to a distribution of rewards and punishments on a socio-economic status basis and the parties favor different status-groups, as most observers believe, the fact that the proportion of the working class voting Republican is larger than the proportion of the middle class who vote Democratic suggests (but does not prove) a lower visibility of objective group interests in the working class.

A fourth approach to class differentials lies through a complex of attitudes of self-confidence and effectiveness and the correlates of these views. Genevieve Knupfer puts this position clearly in focus: "the economic and educational limitations accompanying low status produce a lack of interest in and lack of self-confidence in dealing with certain important areas of our culture; as a result, there is reduced participation— a withdrawal from participation in these areas."[25] This lack of self-confidence in the lower-status groups is, in fact, reflected in the lower sense of political effectiveness which already has been noted; and interest in politics follows the same class pattern. It is seen in the higher percentage of "don't knows" among the lower-status groups in the survey responses. Lack of self-confidence is, moreover, associated with fewer group memberships, inasmuch as a refusal to join parent-teacher organizations or even fraternal groups where persons of different status mingle, often is the product of fear of how one will appear to others of somewhat higher status.[26]

When the democratic illusion—all men are powerful; all men are informed —comes into conflict with the realities of the politically powerless lower-status situation, the working man or woman is caught and made to feel uncomfortable. It is this situation that Riesman and Glazer confront when they speak of the dangers of divorcing opinions from influence. Contending that this is a relatively recent condition, they point to the unrealistic nature of opinion lodged in the minds of those who have no experience with the relevant situations and have no reason to expect that their views will ever be tested.[27] These are, by and large, lower-status persons, and the discrepancy helps to explain qualitative differences in participation—the marginal character of the views expressed, the ineffective measures employed, and the fringe movements which draw their

---

[24] G. H. Saenger, *op. cit.*, p. 104.

[25] G. Knupfer, *op. cit.*, pp. 104–105.

[26] *Ibid.*, p. 105.

[27] David Riesman and Nathan Glazer, "The Meaning of Opinion," *Public Opinion Quarterly*, 12 (1948), pp. 631–48.

clientele from the lower socio-economic classes.

There are those, like C. W. Mills, who dispute that the working class is actually the group with these deficiencies of influence. For them, it is the white collar middle class:[28]

> The white-collar people slipped quietly into modern society. Whatever history they have had is a history without events; whatever common interests they have do not lead to unity; whatever future they have will not be of their own making.... Internally, they are split, fragmented; externally, they are dependent on larger forces. Even if they gained the will to act, their acts, being unorganized, would be less a movement than a tangle of unconnected contests.... The white collar man is the hero as victim, the small creature who is acted upon but who does not act, who works along unnoticed in somebody's office or store, never talking aloud, never talking back, never taking a stand.

But in many ways the evidence tends to run against this view. The middle classes belong to more organizations, are better informed, have greater facility with the verbal means of influence, and participate in elections more than do the working classes. Indeed, in 1948, the white collar group had the highest voting record of any group in the nation, including the professorial and managerial group.

A fifth line of argument seeks to explain class differentials in political participation in terms of class differences in child-rearing practices. Middle-class child-training, say Davis and Havighurst, is characterized by the insistence of parents on certain typically restrictive values, such as cleanliness, punctuality, responsibility, and so forth. The effort

to instill these values in the growing child creates a sense of anxiety and desire to conform, a stricter regulation of impulses, and an over-developed conscience.[29] These qualities, so the argument goes, are carried over from private life to public life where they appear as a civic conscience, and are reflected in attendance at forums, a dutiful reading of the "duller" section of the paper dealing with distant policy questions and electoral participation. The lower-class child, according to Davis and Havighurst, is brought up with less restrictions on his bodily functions, fewer inhibitory commands, and hence a different attitude toward indulgence of impulses and an unwillingness to impose a sense of duty over a sense of what would be more fun. Therefore, given the choice, they read those newspapers which give play to their instinctual life, prefer television comedy to the forum, and consider that it is too much trouble to go and vote.

There are two difficulties with this argument. The first deals with the presumption that strict training encourages those attitudes which we have lumped together as "civic conscience." There is no evidence to support this view and as discussed earlier, on theoretical grounds one might more plausibly argue that a controlled permissiveness, and a relaxed attitude toward weaning and elimination would lead to a set of civic attitudes which might more appropriately be termed "conscientious," and to greater civic participation. Erikson, for example, argues that strict toilet training encourages the child to believe that he has no "say" in the important decisions which affect him.[30] The second difficulty with this argument, deals with the evidence of class differences in wash-

---

[28] C. Wright Mills, *White Collar: The American Middle Classes* (New York: Oxford University Press, 1951), pp. ix, xii.

[29] W. Allison Davis and Robert J. Havighurst, *Father of the Man* (Boston: Houghton Mifflin, 1947), pp. 186–87, 217.

[30] Erik H. Erikson, *Childhood and Society* (New York: Norton, 1950), pp. 269–70.

ing and toilet training procedures. On the whole these seem to be minimal and not generally in the direction suggested by Davis and Havighurst in their original Chicago study.[31]

But there are other suggestions in the data on child-rearing which may account for higher middle-class political and social participation. In both Boston and Chicago, "middle class children (are) allowed more freedom of movement away from home during day."[32] Middle-class parents, more than working-class parents, seem to understand and permit a kind of controlled aggression among their children. The techniques of imposing discipline suggest greater reliance on building up the super-ego regulating devices. Parents expect greater educational attainments for their children. In general, the middle-class child seems to receive at the same time, greater encouragement to explore and be ambitious, and greater capacity for internal regulation and purposive action.

A further (sixth) difference between the various socio-economic class groups lies in the political roles which persons in each group are expected to play. Is there such a difference? On the whole, it seems clear that there is. Descriptively, we find in Elmtown that a five class system reveals:

> Class II focuses its attention upon the aggressive manipulation of economic and political processes; consequently, its members are hyperactive in the power wielding associations, such as Chamber of Commerce, Rotary, Masons, country club, and the major political parties. The women are as active as the men within their own sphere. . . .
>
> Although political activity [in class

III] is more widespread than in any other stratum, and from two-thirds to three-fourths of the several county offices are staffed by persons either elected or appointed from this class, these facts do not lead to the conclusions that Class III is politically powerful. On the contrary it looks to Classes I and II for its leadership.[33]

The sociologist's profile does not include political activity for Classes IV and V; here politics is sporadic and not a part of the cultural roles as they appeared in a Middle Western town of about 6,000.

The Elmira study of Berelson and his associates, tends to confirm this picture of the location of political participation roles in the class just under the small closed elite at the top: "Class I" for Hollingshead, "upper-upper" in Warner's terminology.[34] This study finds that active political roles are rarely assumed by Class I individuals, but instead such persons delegate this function to those at an intermediate level of society who serve their interests in return for various psychic (and sometimes economic) rewards. Financial participation, on the other hand, is more appropriate for Class I persons, whose per capita rate of giving was the highest in Elmira. On the other hand, the lower economic groups tend to delegate their political responsibilities to those who have somewhat more education and somewhat more income than they themselves possess. Thus, there is a principle of social proximity for political activities in that each of the major parties and allied classes delegates toward the middle. To some extent, perhaps, this may

[31] See Robert J. Havighurst and Allison Davis, "A Comparison of the Chicago and Harvard Studies of Social Class Differences in Child Rearing," *American Sociological Review*, 20 (1955), pp. 438–42.

[32] *Ibid.*, p. 441.

[33] August B. Hollingshead, "Selected Characterization of a Middle Western Community," *American Sociological Review*, 12 (1947), pp. 385–95.

[34] Bernard R. Berelson, Paul F. Lazarsfeld, and William N. McPhee, *Voting* (Chicago: University of Chicago Press, 1954), pp. 156–60.

explain the pragmatic similarity of the major parties. In any event, it is clear that the working and upper classes define political roles somewhat differently; there is a tendency to push these obligations toward middle-class groups, and the net result is that the expectations of active participation in each group differ in such a way as to encourage middle-class more than working-class participation.

There are exceptions to the proposition that upper status people avoid overt political leadership, as some of the great names in politics indicate: Roosevelt, Harriman, Lodge, Stevenson, Byrd. In analyzing the upper-class complexion of the Progressive movement leadership, Hofstadter throws some light on the motivation of political leaders from this social group.[35] The Progressive movement somehow enlisted the active support of a number of men, whose economic interests, narrowly interpreted, seemed not to lie in the direction of this movement. Among the selecting factors which Hofstadter finds important for the wealthy Progressive leaders are their Protestant faiths and, to a large extent, their New England origins with their emphasis upon conscience and duty; the fact that they represented "old" wealth as contrasted to the new plutocracy whose politics reflected their economic mode of life; and, less altruistically, their fear that if they did not capture the reform movement, radicals might do so to their (and society's) lasting detriment. In some ways this was an extension of the stewardship doctrine which Carnegie expressed in the economic sphere: success showed that they had

been called by Divine powers to govern the economy—why not also the same mission with respect to the political life of the nation. But also, as Almond has shown, behind the division between plutocracy and progressive reform, were personality factors attributable to the differences in the nature of their earliest training.[36]

Nor is this elite sense of responsibility for the state of the nation (a seventh factor) limited to the very wealthy or to the early years of this century. In that sophisticated panegyric of the American Way produced by the Editors of *Fortune* and Russell M. Davenport,[37] there is evidence that among the grass roots elite, the business leaders of small communities, something of the same attitude prevails. Looking into the "busy, busy" lives of such men, these authors find them constantly active in civic and political groups of all kinds, partly from self-interest, but partly also from a sense of responsibility for their communities and a desire to pour non-material meaning into their lives. They are quoted as saying: "It seems to me that none of us can look forward with hope over the years unless all of us can find solutions to problems bigger than our immediate interests," "I was brought up to serve the community," and, referring to participation in civic affairs, "paying our civic rent."[38] The authors, uniquely qualified as spokesmen for business interests, report their conclusion that "The basis of American economic development has been private initiative in economic matters; the basis for American social development must be private in social matters."[39]

[35] Richard Hofstadter, *The Age of Reform, from Bryan to F.D.R.* (New York: Knopf, 1955), pp. 132–212, also Hofstadter, *The American Political Tradition* (New York: Knopf, 1948), pp. 204–222. I am indebted to Raymond Wolfinger for bringing this theme to my attention.

[36] Gabriel Almond, "The Political Attitudes of Wealth," *Journal of Politics*, 7 (1945), pp. 213–55.

[37] *U.S.A., The Permanent Revolution* (New York: Prentice-Hall, 1951).

[38] *Ibid.*, pp. 128, 137, 145.

[39] *Ibid.*, p. 200.

As an eighth consideration, we may look at the cross pressures which tend to reduce partisanship and emotional commitment to politics. If it could be established that there are class differences in the incidence of such conflicts, a further reason for differences in political participation in different social classes would follow. There is some evidence for believing that working-class groups are in the midst of such cross pressures in four respects. First, much of the politics of metropolitan areas with large ethnic populations presents a picture of conflicting ethnic and class identifications. In New Haven, for example, the large Italian population tends to vote Republican in local elections when their ethnic loyalties are aroused, but their class status tends to confirm them in their identification with the national (New Deal, Fair Deal) democratic programs. Such conflicts may operate to reduce their wholehearted commitment to either party and hence weakens their inducement to participate in electoral matters.

A second kind of cross pressure with a heavier incidence in the working class lies in the conflict between the stimuli which reaches them in the union press, or in the addresses directed to them by liberal political leaders, and the more conservative (Republican) stimuli of the daily press, television, and radio. As noted above, the media raise to visibility the attractions of Republican identification and voting more than the attractions of Democratic identification, hence working-class persons are in the stream of conflicting propaganda. The middle-class voter, due to his, one is tempted to say "natural," selection of reading matter, does not experience this conflict.

Third, as MacRae points out, there is a tendency in non-working class districts for lower status people to identify more with the community and the community leaders than with their own class-linked spokesmen.[40] These leaders are, by and large, upper-or middle-class persons, and the possible conflict of identifications in such instances might further be said to depress political participation.

Finally, there is more of a tendency for members of the working class, objectively defined, to think of themselves as middle class (36 per cent) than for the middle-class members (objectively defined) to think of themselves as working class (24 per cent).[41] Such a conflict between objective class position and subjective identification would lead to a cross-pressured situation, and hence, like other cross pressures, could lead to a failure of partisanship and weakening of political interest. The different incidence of such a conflict, then, would help to account for lower working-class participation.[42]

A ninth reason for class differentials in political participation turns upon the previously discussed factor of group memberships. Nationally, and perhaps in every local community to some degree among some groups, the number of group memberships tends to be associated with greater political participation. Since middle-class and upper-class people tend to belong to more groups than working-class people, greater mutual contact makes for greater awareness of political problems, and greater reinforcement of class values and partisanship among upper-strata groups than lower-strata groups.

In this connection, an extremely important modification of the prevailing lower-class pattern should be pointed out—the rise of labor unions, which have the effect of increasing the political

[40] Duncan MacRae, Jr., "Occupations and the Congressional Vote, 1940–1950," *American Sociological Review, 20* (1955), pp. 332–44.

[41] Heinz Eulau, "Identification with Class and Political Perspective," *Journal of Politics, 18* (1956), p. 242.

[42] But on the influence of such cross pressures, see pp. 197–203.

activity of their members.[43] In Pennsylvania, for example, the widespread indifference to politics among workers was substantially modified by the great organizing drives of the thirties.[44]

For any social class, joining homogeneous groups tends to reinforce political beliefs and stimulate political interests. But joining heterogeneous class groups has different effects upon lower-status members than it does upon high-status members.

For lower-status persons, inter-strata contact establishes a cross pressure which the upper-strata person does not feel, since he does not experience the divergent views of the lower-stratum person (when expressed) as a "pressure."[45]

Not only is it true that lower-status people have fewer group memberships, it is also true that they have fewer friends and informal social contacts. Evidently the "warmth" and solidarity of the working class is a product of the romantic notions of the middle-class observer, projective in origin and filled with pathos for what it implies about the observers. In Middletown, for example, while one-eighth of the "business class" women said they had no intimate friends, one-third of the working class made this statement.[46] Other studies on other communities tend to support this relationship. Without such informal clique group reinforcement, political partisanship tends to wither and political discussion which feeds interest is made impossible.

A tenth consideration, which has some prima facie value, deals with the skills required for participation and their distribution among the social classes. Here certain discriminations must be made between those qualities whose distribution has a linear relation to class status and those which do not. Education falls in the first category and has a clear effect upon capacity to understand and deal with the kinds of issues which are present in national politics—particularly foreign policy issues.[47] But there are other qualities which seem present in the middle ranges of the working class, although not in the lowest group. Among these are, apparently, capacity to serve as opinion leaders in informal discussion. Skilled workers in Erie County had among their group almost as many opinion leaders as did the professional and clerical groups.[48] Furthermore, although in general the evidence shows that lower-status people are less aware of the features of their environment which affect them intimately, such as price control during the war, one suspects that this ignorance is largely concentrated in the lower ranges of the working class.[49] The skill differential and the allied information and "alertness" differentials among classes may help to explain the lower rates of participation among the lower-status groups, but some relevant skills are apparently absent only in what Warner would call the "lower-lower" class.

Finally (eleventh), we come to the question of identification with society or its absence, sometimes termed alienation. Is this class-linked? Alienation, in the sense of personal dissatisfaction with one's job and life prospects, is indeed more prevalent in low-status groups.[50] Also, those in the upper-status groups

---

[43] Angus Campbell and associates, *op. cit.*, p. 73.

[44] Harold F. Gosnell, *Grass Root Politics* (Washington, D. C.: American Council on Public Affairs, 1942), pp. 21–37.

[45] Lazarsfeld and associates, *op. cit.*, pp. 146–47.

[46] See Robert and Helen Lynd, *Middletown* (New York: Harcourt, Brace, 1929), p. 272.

[47] Survey Research Center, *op. cit.*, p. 34.

[48] Lazarsfeld and associates, *op. cit.*, p. 50.

[49] G. Knupfer, *op. cit.*, p. 111.

[50] See Donald Super, "Occupational Level and Job Satisfaction," *Journal of Applied Psychology*, 23 (1939), p. 550.

are generally more satisfied with their community, or better integrated in it, than those on lower-status levels.[51] Since both satisfaction with one's own life prospects and one's community (with status held constant) tend to increase participation, the distribution of these attitudes helps to explain lower turnout in lower-status groups. Yet the possibility of mobilizing these dissatisfactions in the service of extremist political movements is always present.

The eleven reasons for class differentials in political participation given above operate through some of the attitudes originally shown to be related to political participation. In most instances they tend to depress for one status and elevate for another stratum the sense of political effectiveness, the sense of citizen duty, partisanship, perception of and concern for group stakes in an election, satisfaction with the society in which they live and work, interest in political affairs, or partisan identification with some politically connected group. Furthermore, some of the class differentials tend to facilitate political expression, while others inhibit or erect barriers to such expression. In the American society wherever status is marked, therefore, some or all of these variables will be in operation—although, of course, in European societies where group memberships and cross pressures and attitudes are differently distributed status may operate in a quite different fashion.

Of course, class status is not a fixed assignment in the United States, and is decreasingly so in Europe.[52] Consequently the forces operating upon the person who moves from one status level to another may assume significant proportions. Among these forces is the weakening of group and community attachments. Vertical mobility may very well require a change of residence, from tenement to suburban development or from exclusive suburb to middle-class apartment. Furthermore, changes in social status often imply changes from union membership to Rotary Club membership, or from fraternal order to street corner society, depending upon whether the movement is up or down. These kinds of changes tend to weaken the forces making for active political life.

On the other hand, the norms of the group to which a person moves or from which he moves will have other effects, possibly complementary but possibly also conflicting. In general the upwardly mobile person seeks to adopt the norms of the group toward which he is moving; the downwardly mobile person retains, so far as possible, the norms of his former associates.[53] Both of these tendencies tend to increase participation—increasing class differentials for the upwardly mobile, decreasing them for the downwardly mobile.

In summary, then we may set forward the following hypotheses on the influence of socio-ecenomic status upon political activity.

A socio-economic status group (social class) is: (1) a significant reference group for many persons because of the many ties which link them with their class, and (2) a sub-national culture because of the common experiences, attitudes, interests, and values which are significantly different for the different socio-economic classes.

Identifying socio-economic status groups by income, education, and occupation, we can discover in each of these

[51] Alice S. Kitt and David B. Gleicher, "Determinants of Voting Behavior," *Public Opinion Quarterly, 14* (1950), pp. 393–412.

[52] See Seymour M. Lipset and Natalie Rogoff, "Class and Opportunity in Europe and the U.S.," *Commentary,* 18 (1954), pp. 562–68.

[53] See Eleanor E. Maccoby, Richard E. Matthews, and Anton S. Morton, "Youth and Political Change," *Public Opinion Quarterly,* 18 (1954), pp. 34–36.

factors contributions to differential political behavior.

The lesser degree of political participation and interest in lower status groups is partly accountable by the following factors: (1) Lower-strata women (but not men) have less leisure available for political activity. (2) Lower status persons have less economic security, and, partly for that reason, feel less of a sense of control over their (political) environment. (3) The threat of deprivation to upper-strata groups present in the politics of the welfare state provides greater motivation than the promise of reward to the lower-status groups.

The relation of public policy to the group stakes at issue in that policy is made more visible to upper-status groups than to lower-status groups.

Lower-status individuals can influence and benefit from governmental action only socially, by group activity and membership, while upper-class persons can influence and benefit from such action individually. Therefore, upper-class persons have a higher incentive to participate.

Lower-status people, feeling at a disadvantage compared to upper-status people, tend to avoid social contact in mixed groups, withdraw interest, defer to others in "difficult" matters, and generally reveal a lack of self-confidence. Actually, lack of experience and influence combined with pressures to be "opinionated" leads to unrealistic participation in some instances.

Child-rearing practices in the lower-status groups tend to provide a less adequate personality basis for appropriately self-assertive social participation.

The social norms and roles in the lower-status group tend to emphasize political participation less than do the norms and roles of the upper-status groups. There is a tendency for these political roles to be concentrated in middle-class rather than upper-class or working-class groups.

High status sometimes implants attitudes of social and civic responsibility in persons who enjoy this status, depending upon moral, religious, and cultural reinforcement for such attitudes, i.e., "with privilege goes responsibility."

Lower-status persons experience greater cross pressures with respect to (a) ethnic versus class identifications, (b) divergent political appeals of the media to which they are exposed, and conflict between media and status identification, (c) community leadership and own-group leadership, and (d) subjective versus objective class identification.

Lower-status persons belong to fewer formal organizations and have fewer intimate personal friends. However, union membership tends to modify this pattern.

Lower-status persons have less capacity to deal with abstract issues and less awareness of their larger social environment.

Lower-status persons are less satisfied with their lives and communities, leading, in a minimally class conscious society, to withdrawal from civic activities, or, alternatively, to participation in deviant politics.

Inter-class mobility tends to weaken the forces for political participation, a tendency modified by identification with upper-status (participant) norms by both upwardly mobile and downwardly mobile groups.

# POVERTY, SUSPICIOUSNESS AND POLITICAL PASSIVITY: A SOUTHERN ITALIAN TOWN

EDWARD C. BANFIELD

A very simple hypothesis will make intelligible all of the behavior about which questions have been raised and will enable an observer to predict how the Montegranesi will act in concrete circumstances.[1] The hypothesis is that the Montegranesi act as if they were following this rule:

> Maximize the material, short-run advantage of the nuclear family; assume that all others will do likewise.

One whose behavior is consistent with this rule will be called an "amoral familist." The term is awkward and somewhat imprecise (one who follows the rule is without morality only in relation to persons outside the family—in relation to family members, he applies standards of right and wrong; one who has no family is of course an "amoral individualist"), but no other term seems better.

In this chapter, some logical implications of the rule are set forth. It will be seen that these describe the facts of behavior in the Montegrano district. The coincidence of facts and theory does not "prove" the theory. However, it does

show that the theory will explain (in the sense of making intelligible and predictable) much behavior without being contradicted by any of the facts at hand.

1. *In a society of amoral familists, no one will further the interest of the group or community except as it is to his private advantage to do so.* In other words, the hope of material gain in the short-run will be the only motive for concern with public affairs.

This principle is of course consistent with the entire absence of civic improvement associations, organized charities, and leading citizens who take initiative in public service.

A teacher who is a member of a leading family explained,

> I have always kept myself aloof from public questions, especially political ones. I think that all the parties are identical and those who belong to them—whether Communist, Christian Democrat, or other—are men who seek their own welfare and well-being. And then too, if you want to belong to one party, you are certain to be on the outs with the people of the other party.

Giovanni Gola, a merchant of upper-class origins, has never been a member of a political party because "It isn't convenient for me—I might lose some business."

Gola does not think of running for office because:

> I have all I can do to look after my own affairs. I do enough strug-

---

[1] This selection attempts to interpret and integrate the variegated behaviors of the people of Montegrano which have been described in the preceding chapters of the study from which this chapter is taken.—[ED.]

*Reprinted from Edward C. Banfield,* THE MORAL BASIS OF A BACKWARD SOCIETY *(New York: The Free Press, 1958), pp. 83–101, by permission of The Macmillan Co.*

gling in my business not to want to
add to it in any political struggling.
Once in office there would be a constant demand for favors or attentions.
I'd have to spend all my time looking
after other people's affairs...my own
would have to be neglected. I don't
feel like working hard any more. I
am no longer young. [He is in his
late forties.]

Those who run for office, Gola says,
do so for private advantage.

They get the office, and then they
look after themselves. Some take office
so as to be able to say, "I am the
mayor." But really there isn't much
honor attaching to an office; people
here don't even respect the President
of the Republic. In F—, the mayor
wants to be mayor so that he can
keep the population down.

2. *In a society of amoral familists
only officials will concern themselves
with public affairs, for only they are
paid to do so. For a private citizen to
take a serious interest in a public problem will be regarded as abnormal and
even improper.*

Cavalier Rossi, one of the largest
landowners of Montegrano, and the
mayor of the nearby town of Capa, sees
the need for many local public improvements. If he went to the prefect in
Potenza as mayor of Capa, they would
listen to him, he says. But if he went as
a private citizen of Montegrano, they
would say, "Who are you?" As a private citizen he might help a worker get
a pension, but as for schools, hospitals,
and such things, those are for the authorities to dole out. A private citizen
can do nothing.

The trouble is only partly that officials
will not listen to private citizens. To a
considerable extent it is also that private
citizens will not take responsibility in
public matters. As Rossi explains,

There are no leaders in Montegrano. People's minds are too unstable; they aren't firm; they get

excited and make a decision. Then
the next day they have changed their
minds and fallen away. It's more or
less the same way in Capa. There is
lots of talk, but no real personal interest. It always comes to this: the
mayor has to do it. They expect the
mayor to do everything and to get
everything—to make a world.

Farmuso, the director of the school
district and formerly the Communist
mayor of a town in another province, is
earnest, energetic, and intelligent. He
listed several things which might be
done to improve the situation in Montegrano, but when he was asked if he
could bring influence to bear to get any
of them done, he said that he could not.
"I am interested only in the schools,"
he explained. "If I wanted to exert influence, with whom would I talk? In
Vernande there are six teachers in two
rooms, but no money for improvements.
I have talked to the mayor and others,
but I can't get anything even there."

The feeling that unofficial action is an
intrusion upon the sphere of the state
accounts in some measure both for
Mayor Spomo's haughty officiousness
and for the failure of private persons to
interest themselves in making stop-gap
arrangements for a school and a hospital. In nearby Basso a reclamation project will increase vegetable production
and make possible the establishment of
a canning factory. The large landowners
of Basso will not join together to build
a factory, however, even though it might
be a good investment. It is the right
and the duty of the state to build it.

3. *In a society of amoral familists
there will be few checks on officials, for
checking on officials will be the business
of other officials only.*

When Farmuso, the school director,
was asked what he would do if it came
to his attention that a public official took
bribes, he said that if the bribery were
in his own department he would expose

it at once. However, if it occurred outside his department, he would say nothing, for in that case it would be none of his concern.

A young schoolteacher, answering the same question, said that even if he could prove the bribery he would do nothing. "You are likely to be made a martyr," he explained. "It takes courage to do it. There are so many more dishonest people than honest ones that they can gang up on you...twist the facts so that you appear to be the guilty one. Remember Christ and the Pharisees."

A leading merchant would not expose bribery, because "Sooner or later someone would come to me and tell me it would be good if I didn't."

4. *In a society of amoral familists, organization (i.e., deliberately concerted action) will be very difficult to achieve and maintain. The inducements which lead people to contribute their activity to organizations are to an important degree unselfish (e.g., identification with the purpose of the organization) and they are often non-material (e.g., the intrinsic interest of the activity as a "game"). Moreover, it is a condition of successful organization that members have some trust in each other and some loyalty to the organization. In an organization with high morale it is taken for granted that they will make small sacrifices, and perhaps even large ones, for the sake of the organization.*

The only formal organizations which exist in Montegrano—the church and the state—are of course provided from the outside; if they were not, they could not exist. Inability to create and maintain organization is clearly of the greatest importance in retarding economic development in the region.[2]

2 Max Weber remarked in *The Protestant Ethic and the Rise of Capitalism* (Allen and Unwin edition, London, 1930, p. 57) that "the universal reign of absolute unscrupulousness in the pursuit of selfish interests by the mak-

Despite the moral and other resources it can draw upon from the ouside, the church in Montegrano suffers from the general inability to maintain organization. There are two parishes, each with its priest. Rivalry between the priests is so keen that neither can do anything out of the ordinary without having obstacles placed in his way by the other, and cooperation between them is wholly out of the question. (On one occasion they nearly came to blows in the public square; on another the saint of one parish was refused admittance to the church of the other when the *festa*-day procesion stopped there on its route.) When some young men tried to organize a chaper of Catholic Action, a lay association to carry Catholic principles into secular life, they encountered so much sabotage from the feuding priests, neither of whom was willing to tolerate an activity for which the other might receive some credit, that the project was soon abandoned....

Lack of attachment even to kindred has impeded emigration and indirectly economic development. In the half century prior to 1922, there was heavy emigration from Montegrano to the United States and later to Argentina. In general, however, ties between the emigrants and those who remained at home were not strong enough to support "chains" of emigration. Hundreds of Montegranesi live in the hope that a brother or uncle in America will send a "call," but such calls rarely come. People are perplexed when their rela-

ing of money has been a specific characteristic of precisely those countries whose bourgeois-capitalistic development, measured according to Occidental standards, has remained backward. As every employer knows, the lack of *coscienziosita* of the laborers of such countries, for instance Italy as compared with Germany, has been, and to a certain extent still is, one of the principal obstacles to their capitalistic development."

tives in America do not answer their letters. The reason is, probably, that the letters from Montegrano always ask for something, and the emigrant, whose advantage now lies elsewhere, loses patience with them. The relative absence of emigration, as well as of gifts from persons who have emigrated, is a significant impediment to economic development. Some Italian towns, whose ethos is different, have benefited enormously from continuing close ties with emigrants who have prospered in the New World.

5. *In a society of amoral familists, office-holders, feeling no identification with the purposes of the organization, will not work harder than is necessary to keep their places or (if such is within the realm of possibility) to earn promotion. Similarly, professional people and educated people generally will lack a sense of mission or calling. Indeed, official position and special training will be regarded by their possessors as weapons to be used against others for private advantage.*

In southern Italy, the indifference of the bureaucracy is notorious. "A zealous official is as rare as a white fly," a man who had retired after 49 years in the public service remarked.

"From the President of the Republic down to the last little Italian," a landowner said, "there is a complete lack of any sense of duty—especially of the sense of duty to do productive work."

The schoolteachers of Montegrano notably lack a sense of calling. It is not uncommon for a teacher to come late to class or to miss class altogether. At best the teacher teaches four hours a day and takes no further part in the lives of the children. An engineer from northern Italy was shocked at what he saw in Montegrano. "During the summer vacation," he said, "a teacher in the north may hold informal classes. He will take the children on walks into the country

and explain a bit about nature. Or they will go on picnics and sing together. The teacher is a part of the children's lives out of school as well as in." In Montegrano, he found teachers spend the summer loafing in the *piazza* and they do not speak to their pupils when they see them.

"Study and education," a young teacher who was himself of an artisan family explained, "has helped some people to succeed. It has helped them by giving them an advantage over the ignorant. With their knowledge, they are better able to exploit ignorance. They are able to cheat more dexterously."

With other professionals the situation is more or less the same. The pharmacist, a left-wing socialist who enjoys a government monopoly and is one of the richest men in town, feels himself under no obligation to stock the antibiotics and other new medicines which the doctor prescribes or to extend credit to those desperately in need. The doctor himself, although an outstanding man in many ways, does not feel under an obligation to provide himself with the bare essentials of equipment for modern medical practice.

6. *In a society of amoral familists, the law will be disregarded when there is no reason to fear punishment. Therefore individuals will not enter into agreements which depend upon legal processes for their enforcement unless it is likely that the law will be enforced and unless the cost of securing enforcement will not be so great as to make the undertaking unprofitable.*

This, of course, is another impediment to organization and to economic and other development.

It is taken for granted that all those who can cheat on taxes will do so. Minimum wage laws and laws which require the employer to make social security payments on the wages of domestic servants are universally ignored.

An employer who can get away with it is almost sure to cheat his employees. If the employer is a local man, the worker can get justice by appealing to the Marshal, whose informal powers are great. Otherwise the worker is usually cheated. The new municipal building was built by contractors from Matera who paid Montegrano laborers less than the legal minimum and left town owing several of them wages for their last month's work. Since the employer was not a local man, the Marshal could do nothing. In principle the workers could appeal to a labor commission in Potenza. In practice they had to reconcile themselves to the fact that they had been cheated.

Frequently the worker is prevented by self-interest from taking his case to the Marshal. He cannot afford to be on bad terms with the employer: it is better to be cheated than to be deprived of employment altogether. Accordingly, it is the custom for the employer to pay only at his convenience. A peasant may have to go, hat in hand, to the *signore* month after month to ask politely for the dollar or two that is owed.

Mutual distrust between landlords and tenants accounts in part for the number of tiny, owner-operated farms in Montegrano. Rather than work a larger unit on shares, an arrangement which would be more profitable but which would necessitate getting along with a landlord, the peasant prefers to go it alone on his uneconomic holding. Twenty-one peasants were asked which they would prefer, to own eight hectares of land or to sharecrop 40. One said he would prefer to sharecrop the larger holding "because even if I had to be under another and to work a little harder, the gain would be much more." None of the others thought the gain from the larger holding would offset the burden of having to get along with a landlord. Their explanations showed how anxiety, suspi-

cion, and hate make cooperation burdensome.

> I would prefer to be the owner of eight hectares rather than have the rental of 40 because if you are an owner no one commands you and furthermore you are not always worried that tomorrow your half may not be yours and so always under the necessity of being careful.

> I would prefer to be the owner of eight hectares or even less than to work someone else's land. I've had experience with that already and it is really unbearable because the owners always think you are stealing from them. . . .

7. *The amoral familist who is an office-holder will take bribes when he can get away with it. But whether he takes bribes or not, it will be assumed by the society of amoral familists than he does.*[3]

[3] An interview with the Communist mayor of Grottole, another village of Lucania, by E. A. Bayne of the American Universities Field Staff, reveals the same selfishness and distrust that are evident in Montegrano.

After explaining to Bayne that the peasants of Grottole would not work together—that all wanted something for themselves—the mayor asked if the Americans would give the village a tractor. After he had been discouraged in this hope, the mayor said,

"When you leave here I will go down in the street with my people, and they will ask me, 'Did you get any help for us?' And I will try to explain that you are not officials—not even rich tourists—but journalists. 'Why then,' they will say, 'have you bought them wine and coffee with our money and now have nothing to show for it?' "

At the conclusion of his interview Bayne laid a few thousand *lire* on the mayor's desk and asked if he would distribute it where it would do the most good. Perhaps there was a Christmas fund for children? The mayor's consternation was immediate. With politeness but with unmistakable firmness he refused.

"You do not understand my people [he protested]. If I were to accept this gift which *I* understand, those people in the street would soon ask if there had not been more and how

There is no way of knowing to what extent bribery actually exists in Montegrano. There is abundant evidence, however, that it is widely believed to be common. The peasants are sure that the employment officer gives preference to those who bring him presents. They believe, too, that Mayor Spomo made a fortune by selling the communal forest without competitive bids. Better informed people say that it is highly unlikely that there is graft in the administration of the commune: its affairs are too closely supervised from Potenza. However, many upper class people agree that bribery and favoritism are widespread in southern Italy at large. A teacher said,

> Today one gets ahead only by bribes and recommendations. All of the examinations are infected with this disease and those who get ahead are the ones with the most drag. To me this is odious. I would do anything not to have to see it.

The principal merchant is building a cinema. Before it goes into operation he must have a permit from the proper authority. After months of waiting, his request for a permit had not been acted upon. "If I took an envelope with $160 and slipped it into the right pocket, I would have my permission right away," he told an interviewer. "It's the little yellow envelope that gets things done. Big and small, they all take bribes."

"Why don't you do it, then?"

"Because I don't have $160 to spare."

8. *In a society of amoral familists the weak will favor a regime which will maintain order with a strong hand.*

Until it involved them in war, Fascism appealed to many peasants—at least so they now say—because by enforcing the laws rigorously, it protected them. Here are some answers given by peasants to the question, "What did the Fascists claim to stand for?"

> The Fascists said they wanted to be commanders of all. We had no free speech under them, but Mussolini was a good administrator. The Fascists were very bad, but you could send a child any distance unmolested when they were in power. Now you have to walk with a hand on your pocket and a hand on your hat to keep from being robbed.

> The Fascists wanted the peasants to have a better life. There was an eight-hour day and a standard rate of pay. It was a published rate. If a proprietor made you work ten hours you went to the employment office and they would force him to pay the right wage. Now it is everyone for himself, and everyone tries to get the most work for the least pay out of the peasant.

> I don't know what they wanted, but they did make severe laws. There was order and you had rights and duties. You had the right to be paid when you worked and it was a duty to pay workers for work done. They looked after the children too. There were subsidies for large families and help when a new baby was born. Nowadays there is supposed to be help, but it is not enforced.

> I do not remember what it was the Fascists wanted. I only remember that in those days one made out better than today. In those days the worker was well off and not unhappy. Also there were many more aids. Instead, today, nobody cares. If it were during the days of Fascism, the

---

much I had kept for myself. We have no Christmas fund, for who would contribute to it?..."

Two years later Bayne revisited Grottole and found that the mayor had been defeated for re-election and had taken to drink. "He didn't do anything for the people and they became tired of him," someone explained. "Now we have a new mayor—this one is really a fascist. He won't do anything either."

Quoted with permission from American Universities Field Staff letters of December 17, 1954, and February 21, 1957.

things that happen now would not happen. Today a worker must wait to be paid...must wait for the convenience of his employer. Many times months pass without his being paid. During Fascism, this would never have happened.

A landowner made a similar explanation:

> During Fascism, parents were really forced to send their children to school. There could be no excuses, like lack of clothes or books, because the government really provided those where necessary. There was an official who stood outside the school building each morning at 8:30. He gave the children bread and cheese or marmalade and the children would go into the school to eat. School would begin at nine. Now if ten suits are sent to the commune for the children, we are lucky if a cuff of one suit realy gets here...it just melts by the wayside. The laws are all there, but no one enforces them.

A merchant argued that the consumer was better off under Fascist regulation than under present-day competition. "Cloth was grade-labelled and marked with a fixed price along the selvedge. Everything was controlled. You knew what you were getting for your money. Now, unless you really understand cloth, a merchant can sell you inferior material at high prices. It was good for the customer and good for the merchant too. The customer knew what he was getting and the merchant could count on his twenty or thirty percent. Some people get one hundred percent today."

• • •

9. *In a society of amoral familists, the claim of any person or institution to be inspired by zeal for public rather than private advantage will be regarded as fraud.*

A young man said,

> If I decided that I wanted to do something for Montegrano, I would

enter my name on the list at election time, and everyone would ask, 'Why does he want to be mayor?' If ever anyone wants to do anything, the question always is: what is he after?

Anti-clericalism is widespread in Montegrano, and the usual objection to priests is that they are "money grubbers" and "hypocrites." In fact, the priests seem to be no more concerned with gain than are other professionals, and their level of living is no higher than that of the others. They are *peculiarly* liable to attack, however, because the church professes to be unselfish.

Socialists and Communists, like priests, are liable to be regarded as pious frauds. "There are socialists of the mouth and socialists of the heart," a peasant woman explained.

The extraordinary bitterness and, as it seems to an outsider, unfairness with which so many peasants accuse others of hypocrisy is to be understood, in part, perhaps, as an expression of guilt feelings. As is explained elsewhere, the peasant is not unaware that charity is a virtue. Not practicing it himself, he feels some guilt therefore, and he projects this as hostility against those institutions, especially the church, which preach the virtue of charity and through which, perhaps, he would like to be vicariously virtuous.

10. *In the society of amoral familists there will be no connection between abstract political principle (i.e., ideology) and concrete behavior in the ordinary relationships of every day life.*

In Montegrano, the principle left-wing socialists are the doctor and the pharmacist, two of the town's most prosperous gentlemen. The doctor, although he has called upon the government to provide a hospital, has not arranged an emergency room or even equipped his own office. The pharmacist, a government-licensed monopolist, gives an absolute minimum of service at extremely high prices (Signora Prato paid five cents for a single aspirin tablet!) and is wholly unconcerned with local affairs, i.e., those which would have implications for action by him.

The discrepancy between ideology and behavior in practical affairs tends to discredit ideology in the eyes of the peasants. Prato was one of those who assembled in the *piazza* when Dr. Gino tried to organize a branch of the Socialist Party.

> I went a few times and it all sounded very good [he said later]. But that Spring Don Franco hired a mule to cultivate his vineyard, and I thought to myself, What can this be? What can Socialism mean? Why does Don Franco, who is such a believer in it, hire a mule instead of the ten workers he used to hire? There are ten people out of work. And it wouldn't cost him any more to use them than to use the mule.

> What ignorance! [the doctor exclaimed when he was told what Prato said]. Cultivation well done by hand is better than cultivation done with a mule. But the workers here must be watched all the time because they don't really know their jobs, and it is a nuisance to have to be on hand to keep watch. With a mule, you can at least see that the whole row has been done the same way.

11. *In a society of amoral familists there will be no leaders and no followers. No one will take the initiative in outlining a course of action and persuading others to embark upon it (except as it may be to his private advantage to do so) and, if one did offer leadership, the group would refuse it out of distrust.*

Apparently there has never been in Montegrano a peasant leader to other peasants. Objectively, there is a basis for such leadership to develop: the workers on road gangs, for example, share grievances and one would expect them to develop feelings of solidarity.

Suspicion of the would-be leader probably reduces the effectiveness of the doctor, the midwife, and the agricultural agent as teachers. When a peasant was asked whether she could get birth control information from the midwife, she replied, "Of course not. It is not to her interest that I limit the size of my family."

The nearest approximation to leadership is the patron-client relationship. By doing small favors (e.g., by lending a few bushels of grain during the winter, by giving cast-off clothing, or by taking a child from a large family as a housemaid), a well-to-do person may accumulate a clientele of persons who owe him return favors and, of course, deference. Such clients constitute a "following," perhaps, but the patron is not a "leader" in any significant sense. In Montegrano, moreover, none of the well-to-do has troubled to develop much of a clientele. One reason is, perhaps, that the leading families are not engaged in factionable squabbles, and so the advantage to be had from a clientele does not outweigh the expense and inconvenience of maintaining it.

12. *The amoral familist will use his ballot to secure the greatest material gain in the short run. Although he may have decided views as to his long-run interest, his class interest, or the public interest, these will not effect his vote if the family's short-run, material advantage is in any way involved.*

Prato, for example, is a monarchist as a matter of principle: he was born and brought up one and he believes that monarchy is best because Italy is too poor to afford frequent elections. These principles do not affect his vote, however. "Before elections," he explains, "all the parties send people around who say, 'Vote for our party.' We always say 'Yes,' but when we go to vote, we vote for the party we think has given us the most." The Christian Democratic party has given Prato a few days work on the roads each year. Therefore he votes for it. If it ceased to give him work and if there were no advantage to be had from voting for another party, he would be a monarchist again. If Mayor Spomo has influence with the Minister of Agriculture, he should be kept despite his haughtiness and his stealing. But if Councilmen Viva and Lasso can get a larger project than the mayor can get, or if they can get one quicker, then down with him.

13. *The amoral familist will value gains accruing to the community only insofar as he and his are likely to share them. In fact, he will vote against measures which will help the community without helping him because, even though his position is unchanged in absolute terms, he considers himself worse off if his neighbors' position changes for the better. Thus it may happen that measures which are of decided general benefit will provoke a protest vote from those who feel that they have not shared in them or have not shared in them sufficiently.*

In 1954, the Christian Democratic party showed the voters of Basso that vast sums had been spent on local public works. Nevertheless the vote went to the Communists. There are other reasons which help to account for the vote (the Christian Democratic candidate was a merchant who would not give credit and was cordially disliked and distrusted), but it seems likely that the very effectiveness of the Christian Democratic propaganda may have helped to cause its defeat. Seeing what vast sums had been expended, the voters asked themselves: Who got it all? Why didn't they give me my fair share?

No amoral familist ever gets what he regards as his fair share.

14. *In a society of amoral familists the voter will place little confidence in the promises of the parties. He will be apt to use his ballot to pay favors already received (assuming, of course, that more are in prospect) rather than for favors which are merely promised.*

Thus Prato, in the statement quoted above, attaches weight to past performance rather than to promises. "All the parties make promises," he says. "The Christian Democratic party had a chance and it has done a great deal. Why change?" And thus the writer of the letter quoted in Chapter One, after describing the enthusiasm with which the new mayor was received after Spomo's defeat, remarks significantly, "We will wait and see."

The principle of paying for favors received rather than for ones merely promised gives a great advantage to the party in power, of course. Its effect, however, is often more than offset by another principle, as follows:

15. *In a society of amoral familists it will be asumed that whatever group is in power is self-serving and corrupt. Hardly will an election be over before the voters will conclude that the new officials are enriching themselves at their expense and that they have no intention of keeping the promises they have made. Consequently, the self-serving voter will use his ballot to pay the incumbents not for benefits but for injuries, i.e., he will use it to administer punishment.*

Even though he had more to gain from it than from any other, the voter may punish a party if he is confident that it will be elected despite his vote. The ballot being secret, he can indulge his taste for revenge (or justice) without incurring losses. (Of course there is some danger that too many will calculate in this way, and that the election will therefore be lost by error.)

Addo's switch from Christian Democrat to Communist and back again to Christian Democrat is to be explained in this way. The priest in Addo was slightly mad. Some of his eccentricities nobody minded (he arrayed himself as a cardinal and required a chicken as part payment for a marriage), but when he left town a few days before the election taking with him the *pasta*, sugar, and other election-day presents that had been sent them from the Vatican, the voters of Addo were outraged. Afterward, a new priest soon made matters right.

16. *Despite the willingness of voters to sell their votes, there will be no strong or stable political machines in a society of amoral familists. This will be true for at least three reasons: (a) the ballot being secret, the amoral voter cannot be depended upon to vote as he has been paid to vote; (b) there will not be enough short-run material gain from a machine to attract investment in it; and (c) for reasons explained above, it will be difficult to maintain formal organization of any kind whatever.*

Prato says "Yes" to all who ask for his vote. Since they cannot trust him to vote as he promises, none of the parties will offer to buy his vote. The *pasta* and sugar that are distributed by the parties are good-will offerings rather than bribes. The amounts given are, of course, trivial in comparison to what would be paid if there were some way of enforcing the contract.

17. *In a society of amoral familists, party workers will sell their services to the highest bidders. Their tendency to change sides will make for sudden shifts in strength of the parties at the polls.*[4]

The sudden conversion of the secretary of the Montegrano branch of the Monarchist Party to Communist occurred because Monarchist headquarters in Naples was slow in paying him for his services. When he turned Communist, the Monarchists made a settlement. He then returned to his duties as if nothing had happened.

[4] That voter behavior in the Montegrano district is closely similar to that in much of rural Italy is suggested by the data in an undated report by the Office of Intelligence Research, based on data secured by International Research Associates, Inc., of New York, which includes "profiles" of the political situation in 76 communes ranging in size from 200 to 7,000 electors and located in all parts of Italy.

# POLITICAL PARTICIPATION AND DEMOCRATIC STABILITY

GABRIEL A. ALMOND AND SIDNEY VERBA

## POWER AND RESPONSIVENESS

The maintenance of a proper balance between governmental power and gov-

*Reprinted from Gabriel A. Almond and Sidney Verba,* THE CIVIC CULTURE: POLITICAL ATTITUDES AND DEMOCRACY IN FIVE NATIONS, *(Princeton, N.J.: Princeton University Press, 1963), pp. 476–93, by permission of Princeton University Press.*

ernmental responsiveness represents one of the most important and difficult tasks of a democracy. Unless there is some control of governmental elites by non-elites, it is hard to consider a political system democratic. On the other hand, nonelites cannot themselves rule. If a political system is to be effective—if it is to be able to initiate and carry out policies, adjust to new situations, meet internal and external challenges—there must be mechanisms whereby governmental officials are endowed with the power to make authoritative decisions. The tensions produced by the need to pursue the opposing goals of governmental power and governmental responsiveness become most apparent in times of crisis. Wars, for instance (hot or cold), have often shifted the balance so far in the direction of governmental power and authority as to cause concern about the preservation of democratic responsiveness. Yet if the balance is not so shifted, it is argued that democratic governments may succumb to external challenges.

Crises bring to the fore the problem of maintaining an adequate balance, but the problem exists in the day-to-day running of a democracy. How can a governmental system be constructed so that a balance is maintained between power and responsiveness? As E. E. Schattschneider has put it, "The problem is not how 180 million Aristotles can run a democracy, but how we can organize a community of 180 million ordinary people so that it remains sensitive to their needs. This is a problem of *leadership, organization, alternatives, and systems of responsibility and confidence.*"[1] In trying to resolve this problem, political scientists have usually spoken in terms of the structure of electoral conflict. An electoral system, designed to turn power over to a particular elite for a limited period of time, can achieve a balance between power and responsiveness: the elites obtain power, yet this power is limited by the periodic elections themselves, by the concern for future elections during the interelection period, and by a variety of other formal and informal checks. For a system of this sort to work, there must obviously be more than one party (or at least some competing elite group with the potentiality of gaining power) to make the

choice among elites meaningful; and at the same time there must be some mechanism wherby an elite group can exercise effective power—perhaps by the giving of all power to the victorious party in a two-party system, or by the formation of workable coalitions among a group of parties. Most of the debate on the most appropriate electoral system for a democracy (proportional representation, single member districts, or some mixed form) has revolved around two questions: how to maximize the competing goals of power and responsiveness, and how to decide which goal deserves greater stress.[2] There has also been much concern over the proper organization of political parties to maximize both of these goals. This concern clearly motivated the members of the American Political Science Association's Committee on Political Parties, when, in their report, they called for a political party system that is "...democratic, responsible, and effective—a system that is accountable to the public, respects and expresses differences of opinion, and is able to cope with the great problems of modern government."[3]

The tension between power and responsiveness can be managed to some extent by the structure of partisan conflict. But our main interest is in the relationship between this tension and political culture. Can the set of attitudes held by citizens help to maintain the delicate balance between the contradictory demands placed on a democratic

[1] E. E. Schattschneider, *The Semi-Sovereign People*, New York, 1960, p. 138. Italics in original.

[2] On this continuing debate, see, among others, Enid Lakeman and James D. Lambert, *Voting in Democracies*, London, 1955; F. A. Hermens, *Democracy or Anarchy*, South Bend, Ind., 1941, and M. Duverger, *Political Parties*, London, 1954.

[3] "Toward a More Responsible Two Party System," a report of the Committee on Political Parties, of the American Political Science Association, *American Political Science Review*, XLIV (1950), Special Supplement, p. 17.

system? This concentration upon the political attitudes of ordinary citizens does not imply a rejection of the important role of political structures or of elite attitudes and behavior. These are important as well, and we shall return to them below when we consider the way in which the attitudes of ordinary citizens and of elites interact.

The tension between governmental power and responsiveness has a parallel in the conflicting demands made upon the citizens of a democratic system. Certain things are demanded of the ordinary citizen if elites are to be responsive to him: the ordinary citizen must express his point of view so that elites can know what he wants; he must be involved in politics so that he will know and care whether or not elites are being responsive, and he must be influential so as to enforce responsive behavior by the elites. In other words, elite responsiveness requires that the ordinary citizen act according to the rationality-activist model of citizenship. But if the alternate pole of elite power is to be achieved, quite contradictory attitudes and behavior are to be expected of the ordinary man. If elites are to be powerful and make authoritative decisions, then the involvement, activity, and influence of the ordinary man must be limited. The ordinary citizen must turn power over to elites and let them rule. The need for elite power requires that the ordinary citizen be relatively passive, uninvolved, and deferential to elites. Thus the democratic citizen is called on to pursue contradictory goals: he must be active, yet passive; involved, yet not too involved; influential, yet deferential. [This is the civic culture.]

MAINTAINING THE BALANCE
BETWEEN PARTICIPATION AND
PASSIVITY

The data presented in this book suggest some ways in which these conflict-

ing demands might be managed. The crucial cases for our analysis are clearly Britain and the United States, for if there is some pattern of attitudes that can allow this tension to be managed, one might expect it to act most effectively within the relatively more stable democracies. It is in these two nations that we found the closest approximation to the civic culture. Our data suggest that in two broad ways the civic culture maintains the citizen's active-influential role as well as his more passive role: on the one hand, there is in the society a *distribution* of individuals who pursue one or the other of the *conflicting* citizen goals; on the other hand, certain *inconsistencies in the attitudes of an individual* make it possible for him to pursue these seemingly conflicting goals at the same time. Let us first consider the inconsistencies within the individual.

As our survey showed, there exists a gap between the *actual political behavior* of our respondents, on the one hand, and their *perceptions of their capacities to act* and their *obligations to act*, on the other. Respondents in Britain and the United States manifest high frequencies of what we have called subjective political competence. As was reported in Chapter 7, a large proportion considers itself able to influence the decisions of the local government, and a substantial, though not quite as large, proportion feels the same way about the activities of the national government. Yet this high estimation of one's competence as an influential citizen is certainly not matched by actual political behavior. In the first place, only a small proportion of those respondents who say they could influence the government report that they have ever attempted such influence. And even if those who think they could influence governmental decisions were to attempt to do so—which is unlikely—they would almost certainly not have the success that they believe they would have. It is clearly an exaggeration when forty per cent of American respondents or twenty-four per cent of the British say that there is some likelihood that an attempt of theirs to influence the national legislature would be successful.

A similar gap exists between the sense of obligation to participate in political life and actual participation. As reported in Chapter 6, a much higher proportion of respondents says that the ordinary man has some obligation to participate in the affairs of his local community than in fact does participate; and again the pattern is clearest in the United States and Britain. As one respondent, quoted in Chapter 6, put it, "I'm saying what [one] ought to do, not what I do." And there is evidence that this position is far from rare. Certainly, the sense of obligation to take some part in one's community affairs is not matched by the importance attributed to such activity by respondents. The proportion saying that one has such obligations is in each nation much larger than the proportion that, when asked to report on its free-time activities, reports participation in community affairs. Fifty-one per cent of the American respondents report that the ordinary man ought to take some active part in the affairs of his community. But when asked what they do in their free time, only about ten per cent of the American respondents mention such activities. . . . This suggests that though there is a widespread norm that one ought to participate within the community, active participation is far from the most significant activity to most people. It is not what most people do in their spare time, nor is it the major source of satisfaction, joy, and excitement.

These two gaps—between a high perception of potential influence and a lower level of actual influence, and between a high frequency of expressed obligation to participate and the actual importance and amount of participation —help explain how a democratic political culture can act to maintain a balance between governmental elite power and governmental elite responsiveness (or its complement, a balance between nonelite activity and influence and nonelite passivity and noninfluence). The comparative infrequency of political participation, its relative lack of importance for the individual, and the objective weakness of the ordinary man allow governmental elites to act. The inactivity of the ordinary man and his inability to influence decisions help provide the power that governmental elites need if they are to make decisions. But this maximizes only one of the contradictory goals of a democratic system. The power of the elites must be kept in check. The citizen's opposite role, as an active and influential enforcer of the responsiveness of elites, is maintained by his strong commitment to the norm of active citizenship, as well as by his perception that he can be an influential citizen. This may be in part a myth, for it involves a set of norms of participation and perceptions of ability to influence that are not quite matched by actual political behavior. Yet the very fact that citizens hold to this myth— that they see themselves as influential and as obligated to take an active role— creates a potentiality of citizen influence and activity. The subjectively competent citizen, as was pointed out in Chapter 7, has not necessarily attempted to influence the government, but he is *more likely* to have made such attempts than is the citizen who does not consider himself competent.[4]

A citizen within the civic culture has, then, a reserve of influence. He is not constantly involved in politics, he does

[4] On the importance of the democratic myth, see, V. O. Key, Jr., *Public Opinion and American Democracy*, New York, 1961, p. 547.

not actively oversee the behavior of political decision makers. But he does have the potential to act if there is need. This reserve of influence—influence potential that is inactive and uncommitted to the political system—was best illustrated by the data, presented in Chapter 7, on the ability of citizens to create political structures in time of need. The citizen is not a constant political actor. He is rarely active in political groups. But he thinks that he can mobilize his ordinary social environment, if necessary, for political use. He is not the active citizen: he is the potentially active citizen.

Yet the intermittent and potential character of the citizen's political activity and involvement depends upon steadier, more persistent types of political behavior. By living in a civic culture, the ordinary man is more likely than he would be otherwise to maintain a steady and high rate of exposure to political communications, to be a member of an organization, and to engage in informal political discussion. These activities do not in themselves indicate an active participation in the decision-making process of a society; but they do make such participation more possible. They prepare the individual for intervention in the political system; and more important perhaps, they create a political environment in which citizen involvement and participation are more feasible.

We have been saying that inconsistencies within attitudes and inconsistencies between attitudes and behavior, rather than the one-sided attitudes of the rationality-activist model, can maintain the tension between citizen activity and citizen passivity. But now we must ask whether these inconsistencies cause instability in the civic culture. Much of the recent theorizing about attitude formation emphasizes the strain toward consistency or consonance among the be-

liefs, attitudes, and behavior of an individual; there now exists a large body of data to support the theory that cognitive inconsistencies will produce a stress toward the reduction of these inconsistencies.[5] But as we have seen, the balance between citizen influence and citizen passivity *depends upon the inconsistencies* between political norms and perceptions, on the one hand, and political behavior, on the other. This inconsistency, however, creates no undue strain within the citizen; for politics, as much of our data suggest and as the data from many other studies confirm, is not the uppermost problem in his mind. Compared with other concerns, politics is usually invested with relatively little affect or involvement. Thus inconsistencies among attitudes or between attitudes and behavior can be more easily tolerated, for they can be overlooked or ignored. As Rosenberg and Abelson have put it, "...potential imbalance will remain undiscovered by an individual unless he is motivated to think about the topic and in fact does so."[6] Because politics has little importance for them, few citizens are motivated to think about their influence or their political activities.

That politics has relatively little importance for citizens is an important part of the mechanism by which the set of inconsistent political orientations keeps political elites in check, without

[5] Some of the important literature developing this theory includes: Leon Festinger, *A Theory of Cognitive Dissonance*, Evanston, Ill., 1957; F. Heider, *The Psychology of Interpersonal Relations*, New York, 1958; C. E. Osgood, C. J. Suci, and P. H. Tannenbaum, *The Measurement of Meaning*, Urbana, Ill., 1957, and M. J. Rosenberg *et al.*, *Attitude Organization and Change*, New Haven, Conn., 1960. See also the special issue of the *Public Opinion Quarterly* on attitude change, XXIV (Summer 1960), especially the articles by Zajonc, Cohen, Rosenberg, and Osgood.

[6] Milton J. Rosenberg and Robert F. Abelson, "Analysis of Cognitive Balancing," in Rosenberg *et al.*, *op. cit.*, chap. iv, p. 121.

checking them so tightly as to make them ineffective. For the balance of inconsistent orientations would be more difficult to maintain if the issues of politics were always considered important by the citizens. If issues arise that individuals consider important, or if some relatively severe dissatisfaction with government occurs, the individual will be motivated to think about the topic and thus will be under greater pressure to resolve the inconsistency— to make attitudes and behavior consonant with each other. One way he may do this is to bring his behavior into line with norms and perceptions by becoming politically active. Thus the inconsistency between attitudes and behavior acts as a latent or potential source of political influence and activity.

To say that the civic culture maintains the balance between power and responsibility suggests a further point about democratic politics. It suggests why unresolved political issues of great importance eventually create instability in a democratic political system. The balance between activity and passivity can be maintained only if the issues of politics are relatively mild. If politics becomes intense, and if it remains intense because of some salient issue, the inconsistency between attitude and behavior will become unstable. But any relatively permanent resolution of the inconsistency is likely to have unfortunate consequences. If behavior is brought into line with attitudes, the amount of attempted control of elites by nonelites will create government ineffectiveness and instability. On the other hand, if attitudes change to match behavior, the resulting sense of impotence and noninvolvement will have damaging consequences for the democratic quality of the political system.

However, this does not suggest that all important issues damage a democratic political system. It is only when issues become intense and remain intense that the system may be made unstable. If significant issues arise only sporadically *and* if the government is able to respond to the demands stimulated by these issues, an equilibrium can be maintained between citizen influence and government influence. In ordinary times, citizens are relatively uninterested in what governmental decision makers do, and the latter have the freedom to act as they see fit. However, if an issue becomes prominent, citizen demands on officials will increase. If officials can respond to these demands, the importance of politics will fall again and politics will return to normal. Furthermore, these cycles of citizen involvement, elite response, and citizen withdrawal may tend to reinforce the balance of opposites needed for democracy. Within each cycle, the citizen's perception of his own influence is reinforced; at the same time the system adjusts to new demands and thereby manifests its effectiveness. And the system may become generally more stable through the loyalty engendered by participation and effective performance.

These cycles of involvement are an important way of maintaining the balanced inconsistencies between activity and passivity. If the constant involvement and activity associated with salient issues would eventually make the maintenance of the balance difficult, so, too, would the complete absence of involvement and activity. The balance can be maintained over time only if the gap between activity and passivity is not too wide. If the belief in one's political competence is not reinforced occasionally, it is likely to fade. Or, if the belief is maintained in a purely ritual manner, it will not represent potential influence or be a check on decision makers. This, perhaps, is what characterizes the "aspirational" political competence observable in Mexico. Mexican respondents manifest relatively high levels of subjective political competence, especially in comparison to their very low levels of "administrative" competence, exposure to communications, and the like. Furthermore, they quite frequently mention group-forming strategies. But as we have seen, their sense of competence is not matched by experience in political action. There is a gap between the subjective perception of competence and actual political behavior, as there is in the United States and Britain. But the gap is much wider. In the United States, for instance, thirty-three per cent of those respondents who say they believe they can influence the local government have actually tried to do so, as have eighteen per cent of the British local competents. But among the Mexican local competents, only nine per cent report such experience. Thus the perception-behavior gap may be so wide as to make difficult the performance of the dual functions of furthering citizen control and maintaining citizen passivity. For the democratic "myth" to be an effective political force, it cannot be pure myth. It must be an idealization of real behavioral patterns. Where, as perhaps in Mexico, it has very little relation to reality, it cannot function as part of a balanced civic culture.[7]

We have so far dealt with the way in which activity and passivity may be balanced within the individual citizen. But this balance is maintained, not merely by the set of attitudes individuals have, but by the distribution of attitudes among different types of political actors

in a system: some individuals believe that they are competent and some do not; some individuals are active and some are not. This variation in beliefs and activity among individuals also helps enforce the power-responsiveness balance. This can be seen if we consider the equilibrium mechanism described above: an issue becomes salient, activity rises, and balance is restored by a governmental response that reduces the salience of the issue. One reason that an increasingly prominent issue and the consequent rise in political activity are kept from straining the political system is that the prominence of the issue rarely increases for all citizens at once. Rather, it is particular groups that show a rise in political activity, while the rest of the citizens remain inactive. In this way the amount of citizen activity at any one point in time is not so great as to strain the system.

The above discussion is based upon our data on the attitudes of ordinary citizens. But if a mechanism such as the one we postulate is to work, the attitudes of elites must complement those of nonelites. The decision maker must believe in the democratic myth—that ordinary citizens ought to participate in politics and that they are in fact influential. If the decision maker accepts this view of the role of the ordinary citizen, his own decisions serve to maintain the balance between governmental power and responsiveness. On the one hand, he is free to act as he thinks best because the ordinary citizen is not pounding on his door with demands for action. He is insulated by the inactivity of the ordinary man. But if he shares the belief in the influence potential of the ordinary man, his freedom to act is limited by the fact that he believes there *will* be pounding on his door if he does not act in ways that are responsive. Furthermore, if he shares the view that the ordinary man ought to participate

---

7 If the ordinary man's belief in his competence is to be reinforced, it may not be necessary for him to be personally involved in successful influence activity vis-a-vis the government. It may be enough simply that he be aware of others engaged in such activity. But the likelihood that an individual will see others attempting to influence the government will naturally depend upon how frequently people make such attempts.

in decisions, he is under pressure to act responsively because he believes that such citizen influence is legitimate and justified. Though our data cannot demonstrate this, there is reason to believe that political elites share the political culture of the nonelite; that in a society with a civic culture they, as well as nonelites, hold the attitudes associated with it.[8] Elites are, after all, part of the same political system and exposed to many of the same political socialization processes as are nonelite. And studies have shown that political and community leaders, as well as those of higher social status, are more likely than those of lower status to accept the norms of democracy.[9]

The consideration of elite attitudes suggests another mechanism whereby elite responsiveness can be enforced while the activity and involvement of the ordinary citizen remain low. The pattern of citizen influence is not always, or even predominantly, one of stimulus (the citizen or group of citizens make a demand) followed by response (the governmental elite acts to satisfy the demand). Rather, the well-known "law of anticipated reactions" may operate here. A good deal of citizen influence over governmental elites may entail no activity or even conscious intent of citizens. On the contrary, elites may anticipate possible demands and activities and act in response to what they anticipate. They act responsively, not because citizens are actively making demands, but in order to keep them from becoming active.[10]

Within the civic culture, then, the individual is not necessarily the rational, active citizen. His pattern of activity is more mixed and tempered. In this way he can combine some measure of competence, involvement, and activity with passivity and noninvolvement. Furthermore, his relationship with the government is not a purely rational one, for it includes adherence—his and the decision maker's—to what we have called the democratic myth of citizen competence. And this myth has significant consequences. For one thing, it is not pure myth: the belief in the influence potential of the average man has some truth to it and does indicate real behavioral potential. And whether true or not, the myth is believed.

## PARTICIPATION AND EMOTIONALISM

We have discussed the way in which the civic culture balances involvement and activity with indifference and passivity. But the balance achieved by the civic culture goes further. Not only

[8] Yet there are important ways in which elites differ from the general population in their political attitudes; see chap. i, p. 27. Further, there are probably differences in autonomy between British and American political elites; see below, for some comments on these differences.

[9] Relevant here are our data on the effect of educational differences on the differences in attitudes among respondents. Also relevant is the finding in Samuel Stouffer's, *Communism, Conformity, and Civil Liberties,* New York, 1955, to the effect that community leaders are more tolerant and more accepting of democratic norms than are nonleaders. Several studies of German public opinion support this general finding. See, for instance, Erich Reigrotski, *Soziale Verflechtungen in der Bundesrepublik,* Part 2, and *Basic Orientation and Political Thinking of West German Youth and Their Leaders,* DIVO Institute Frankfurt am Main-Bad Godesberg, 1956.

Political leaders in democracies must express agreement with the democratic myth in public. Of course, much of this may be lip service. But the requirement that they give public support to this set of beliefs also puts pressure on them to accept the beliefs—unless hypocrisy is a conscious value among political elites. As the studies in cognitive dissonance have shown, the requirement that an individual make a certain kind of public declaration creates pressures to change his private beliefs in that direction. See Rosenberg *et al., op. cit.,* and Festinger, *op. cit.*

[10] See chap. 7 for a discussion of "anticipatory" and other forms of influence.

must involvement and activity be balanced by a measure of their opposites, but the *type* of political involvement and activity must itself be balanced. In particular, there appears to be a need for a balanced affective orientation to politics; or rather, there must be a balance between instrumental and affective orientations to politics. Politics must not be so instrumental and pragmatic that participants lose all emotional involvement in it. On the other hand, the level of affective orientation to politics ought not to become too intense.

There are several reasons why this balance, rather than a maximization of either pragmatism or passion, is needed in an effective democracy. In the first place, political commitment, if it is to be dependable, cannot be completely unemotional. Loyalty to a political system, if it is based on purely pragmatic considerations of the effectiveness of that system, represents, as Lipset has suggested, a rather unstable basis of loyalty, for it is too closely dependent upon system performance.[11] If it is to remain stable in the long run, the system requires a form of political commitment based upon more general attachment to the political system—a commitment we have called "system affect." Furthermore, as Eckstein suggests, a purely pragmatic and unemotional political involvement implies a politics of opportunism; a politics that will probably lead to cynicism.[12] On the other hand, if an affective commitment to politics or to a particiular political group is too intense, this can have unfortunate consequences for a democracy. In the first place, an intense emotional involvement in politics endangers the balance between activity and passivity, for that balance depends on the low salience of politics. Second, such intense involvement tends to "raise the stakes" of politics: to foster the sort of mass, messianic movements that lead to democratic instability.[13] Furthermore, the consequences can be harmful whether the commitment is to the system as a whole and the incumbent elites or only to particular subgroups in society. It is clear that intense commitment to particular political parties or groups can produce an unstabilizing level of fragmentation in the system. But even an intense commitment to the political system and to the incumbent elites is likely to have harmful effects. If citizens are to maintain some control over political elites, their loyalty to the system and to the elites must not be complete and unquestioning. Furthermore, the civic culture implies the maintenance of the more traditional parochial roles along with the role of citizen. The preservation of a sphere of activity that is outside of politics is important if one is to have the balanced participation of the civic culture.

Participation in politics, this suggests, ought to be neither purely instrumental nor purely affective. The political participant ought to receive both instrumental and emotional gratifications from his participation. And this balanced involvement in politics again appears to characterize the civic culture in the two more successful democracies. As was discussed in Chapter 8, in the United States and Britain the more the respondent considers himself capable of participating in politics, the more likely he is to receive affective satisfaction from the political system and to evaluate posi-

[11] Seymour Martin Lipset, *Political Man*, New York, 1959, pp. 77–83.

[12] Harry Eckstein uses as an example of this the politics of *Trasformismo* of pre-World War I Italy. See his *Theory of Stable Democracy*, Princeton, 1961, p. 33.

[13] See William Kornhauser, *The Politics of Mass Society*, Glencoe, 1959.

tively the instrumental performance of that system. In contrast, the other three nations show patterns of unbalanced participation. In Germany and Italy the sense of ability to participate is accompanied by a higher evaluation of the instrumental effectiveness of the system but not by a deeper general commitment. In Mexico the opposite is true: sense of participation is accompanied by greater pride in the system but not a higher evaluation of its performance. In Italy and Germany, commitment to the political system is largely pragmatic, and is based on little emotional commitment. In Mexico there may be an unrealistic attachment to symbols, coupled with the absence of a belief in instrumental rewards of politics.

SOCIAL TRUST

Our data suggest another way in which the political cultures of the more successful democracies are characterized by a balanced type of commitment. As was reported at various places throughout this volume, respondents in the United States and Britain more frequently than respondents in the other three nations express pride in their political system and feel satisfaction when voting. They are more likely to report interest in politics and actually to discuss politics. And they are more likely to report some emotional involvement in political campaigns. All these indicate a comparatively high level of political involvement. Yet the political involvement in these two countries is tempered in intensity by its subordination to a more general, overarching set of social values. As the data in Chapter 10 suggest, attitudes of interpersonal trust and cooperation are more frequent in the United States and Britain than in the other nations. More important, these general social attitudes penetrate into the realm of politics. The role of social trust

and cooperativeness as a component of the civic culture cannot be overemphasized. It is, in a sense, a generalized resource that keeps a democratic polity operating. Constitution makers have designed formal structures of politics that attempt to enforce trustworthy behavior, but without these attitudes of trust, such institutions may mean little. Social trust facilitates political cooperation among the citizens in these nations, and without it democratic politics is impossible. It probably also enters into a citizen's relation with political elites. We argued earlier that the maintenance of elite power was essential in a democracy. We would now add that the sense of trust in the political elite—the belief that they are not alien and extractive forces, but of the same political community—makes citizens willing to turn power over to them.

Furthermore, these general social attitudes temper the extent to which emotional commitment to a particular political subgroup leads to political fragmentation. This general set of social attitudes, this sense of community over and above political differences, keeps the affective attachments to political groups from challenging the stability of the system. Furthermore, it acts as a buffer between the individual and the political system, and thereby reduces the "availability" (in Kornhauser's use of the word) of the ordinary citizen for involvement in unstabilizing mass movements.[14] These norms—particularly those that say that political criteria are not to be applied to all situations—place a limit on politics. They indicate that certain social relationships are not to be dominated by political considerations. And in this way they allow the individual to maintain a certain degree of independence from the political system.

[14] *Ibid.*, Chap. 2.

CONSENSUS AND CLEAVAGE

This brings us to a further balance that must be maintained within a democratic political system: that between consensus and cleavage.[15] Without some meaningfully structured cleavage in society, it is hard to see how democratic politics can operate. If democracy involves at some point a choice among alternatives, the choice must be about something. If there were no cleavage, if people did not combine into meaningfully opposed political groupings, this would suggest "...a community in which politics was of no real importance to the community,"[16] and one in which the alternation of political elites meant little. Too much agreement would mitigate against the enforcement of elite responsiveness. Yet if cleavage went too far, "...a democratic society...would probably be in danger of its existence. The issues of politics would cut so deeply, be so keenly felt, and, especially, be so fully reinforced by other social identifications of the electorate..." as to threaten democracy.[17] There must be what Parsons has called a "limited polarization" of society.[18] If there is no consensus within society, there can be little potentiality for the peaceful resolution of political differences that is associated with the democratic process. If, for instance, the incumbent elite considered the opposition elite too threatening, it is unlikely that the incumbents would allow a peaceful competition for elite position.

This balance between consensus and cleavage is managed within the civic culture by a mechanism similar to the one that managed the balance between activity and passivity: that is, an inconsistency between norms and behavior. This is illustrated by the data presented on attitudes toward primary group membership and partisan affiliation (reported in Chapters 5 and 10). On the one hand, as all studies of voting behavior indicate, primary groups tend to be homogeneous in the partisan sense; families, friendship groups, workplace groups tend to be composed of people of like political views. And, what may be more important evidence for their partisan homogeneity, if there is some heterogeneity of political views within the group, there will be pressure toward attitude change to produce homogeneity.[19] This existent homogeneity attests to the existence of cleavage in the political system. If partisan affiliation was not closely correlated with primary group affiliation, it is hard to see how there could be any basis for meaningful political competition, for partisan affiliation would then be unimportant as well as unrelated to basic social groupings in society. On the other hand, the cleavage produced by this existent correlation between primary group affiliation and partisan affiliation is tempered in the United States and Britain by the consensual norm (discussed in Chapters 5

[15] The significance of this balance is also stressed by Eckstein, op. cit., Bernard Berelson, et. al., Voting, Chicago, 1954, and Talcott Parsons, "Voting and the Equilibrium of the American Political System," in Burdick and Brodbeck, eds., American Voting Behavior, Glencoe, Ill., 1959.

[16] Berelson et al., op. cit., p. 319.

[17] Ibid.

[18] Parsons, in Burdick and Brodbeck, eds., American Voting Behavior, p. 92.

[19] This homogeneity is partly due to the fact that members of a primary group tend to share similar social characteristics that affect their vote. They tend to be members of the same class, residential area, and so forth. But even when these characteristics are held constant, the political composition of the primary group has a strong residual effect on the individual's political attitudes; see Berelson et al., op. cit., pp. 88–93 and 137–38; and Herbert McCloskey and Harold E. Dahlgren, "Primary Group Influence on Party Loyalty," American Political Science Review, LIII (1960), pp. 757–76.

and 10) that one's primary group *ought not* to be politicized. Though one's most intimate associates tend to be of like political affiliation (and if they are not, there will be pressure for attitudes to change until they are), this cleavage is balanced by a general social norm that places some relationships (in theory, if not in practice) above politics. Again, the civic culture allows a balance between apparently contradictory demands through the mixture of a set of norms (that primary groups be nonpartisan) and actual behavior (that primary groups are indeed homogeneous in the partisan sense) that are themselves in contradiction one with the other.

This is but one example of the way in which the civic culture manages cleavage in society. In general, this management of cleavage is accomplished by subordinating conflicts on the political level to some higher, overarching attitudes of solidarity, whether these attitudes be the norms associated with the "rules of the democratic game" or the belief that there exists within the society a supraparty solidarity based on nonpartisan criteria.[20]

This balance, furthermore, must be maintained on the elite as well as the citizen level. Though our data are not relevant here, it is quite likely that similar mechanisms operate on the elite level as well. The elaborate formal and informal rules of etiquette in the legislatures of Britain and the United States, for example, foster and indeed require friendly relations (or at least friendly words) between the supporters of the opposing parties. And this tempers the intensity of partisanship. It is not that partisanship is destroyed as a significant force; rather, it is kept in its place by more general norms of social relationships.

In sum, the most striking characteristic of the civic culture as it has been described in this volume is its mixed quality.... There is political activity, but not so much as to destroy governmental authority; there is involvement and commitment, but they are moderated; there is political cleavage, but it is held in check. Above all, the political orientations that make up the civic culture are closely related to general social and interpersonal orientations. Within the civic culture the norms of interpersonal relationships, of general trust and confidence in one's social environment, penetrate political attitudes and temper them. The mixture of attitudes found in the civic culture, we have argued in this chapter, "fits" the democratic political system. It is, in a number of ways, particularly appropriate for the mixed political system that is democracy.

[20] See Parsons, *op. cit.*, p. 100.

F. *Community Power*

# COMMUNITY POWER STUDIES

WILLIAM SPINRAD

Since Floyd Hunter published his study of "Regional City" about a decade ago, many social scientists have devoted their attention to the study of community power.[1] Whatever comments we will make on some of the specific material, we would initially like to welcome this trend in the allocation of the professional resources of the social science fraternity. Particularly in the area of community research, this had been a relatively neglected subject, with the conspicuous exception of the Lynds' monumental study of Middletown.[2] The detailed cataloguing of the status structure was too often the dominant, in fact sometimes the only, theme. Longing for a simple stratification model in which everyone fits, more or less, into an obviously assignable place, the students of American communities tended to avoid the more complicated task of striving to learn "who got things done," why and how. It was, therefore, especially pleasing to read that in the old New England city of New Haven very few of the "social notables," the members of status-exclusive clubs, had any crucial role in the community decision-making process under review.[3]

The efforts at community power analysis have been many, the findings plentiful, the interpretations challenging. But, despite several suggestive attempts, thorough systematization is still wanting; the relation between the "power variable" and the entire community social structure is barely sketched. Let this preliminary appraisal not be misconstrued. The critique which follows is prefaced not only with praise for a worthwhile direction of social scientific inquiry but an appreciation of the valuable material that already exists. It is offered as a modest set of directives for future work in the area.

. . .

A meaningful organization of the field would be a posing of the major contending analyses. This, in essence, is the function of a symposium entitled *Power and Democracy in America*.[4] Despite its rather grandiose title and the variety of subjects considered by the major contributors and the editors, the core of the

[1] Floyd Hunter, *Community Power Structure: A Study of Decision Makers*, Chapel Hill: The University of North Carolina Press, 1953.
[2] Robert S. Lynd and Helen M. Lynd, *Middletown in Transition*, New York: Harcourt, Brace, 1957.
*Reprinted from William Spinrad, "Power in Local Communities,"* SOCIAL PROBLEMS, *12 (Winter 1965), 335–56, by permission of the publisher and the author.*

[3] Robert Dahl, *Who Governs? Democracy and Power in an American City*, New Haven and London: Yale University Press, 1961, pp. 63–69.
[4] *Power and Democracy in America*, edited by William V. D'Antonio and Howard J. Ehrlich, Notre Dame, Indiana: University of Notre Dame Press, 1961.

book is the debate between two students of community power, Delbert Miller and Robert Dahl. Utilizing their own researches and other relevant material, the two scholars generally represent and expound the two opposite sides of the methodological and analytical conflict that has characterized recent community power discussion. Miller favors the "reputational" form of investigation and finds a pyramidal, quasi-monolithic structure dominated by a "business elite" more or less typical. He is thus quite in accord with the findings of Hunter's original study. Dahl, utilizing "event analysis," searches for evidence of specific decision makers on particular issues, and concludes that a relatively pluralistic power structure is more prevalent. Of course, the divergencies are more complex and detailed, but these are the summary statements around which the discussion evolves.

The reputational technique, which has, with many variations, become fairly widespread in use, seeks to get knowledgeable informants to select, from a list of leading figures in community organizations and institutional areas, those whom they considered most powerful in "getting things done." Those chosen were then interviewed to learn about the personal and social relations among them, and which people they would themselves solicit if they wanted something adopted or achieved. Reviewing many studies with this research emphasis, including his own "Pacific City," Miller's conclusions are, essentially, the following:[5]

1) Businessmen are overrepresented among "key influentials" and dominate

community policy-making in most communities.[6]

2) Local governments are weak power centers. The elected officials are mostly small businessmen, local lawyers, and professional politicians. Policy on important questions is formulated by organized interests groups under the influence of the economic dominants. City councils merely respond to their pressures.

3) Representatives of labor, education, religious, and "cultural" groups are rarely key influentials, are underrepresented in city councils.

4) In vivid contrast, Miller reports his investigations of "English City," like "Pacific City" a seaport community of about 500,000 population. Businessmen constitute only a minority of the "key influentials." Labor is significantly represented. There is also an appreciable number from educational, religious, welfare, and "status" leaderships. Furthermore, the city council is the major arena of community decision making, the party organizations the directing groups.

Noting differences between "Regional City" and "Pacific City," Miller does not insist that the power pattern is identical in all American communities. In fact, he develops a typology of possible structures which will be later considered. But the modal type is clearly sketched, particularly in contrast with the findings of his British study.

Dahl's counter propositions are based primarily on his study of New Haven, summarized in the symposium and more fully elaborated in his book *Who Governs?*[7] The power structure of New Haven is seen as relatively pluralistic or, to use his terminology, one of "dispersed inequalities," a metamorphosis from earlier days of oligarchal dominance by "aristocratic patricians" and

[5] Actually, the major bulwarks for his thesis are his own and Hunter's research, plus a series of inquiries by Charles Loomis and his associates in Southwestern United States for which no published citations are given. The other references offered actually reveal much more complex patterns. See *Ibid.*, pp. 38–71.

[6] *Ibid.*, p. 61.

[7] Dahl, *op. cit.*

"entrepreneurs" successively. This is initially indicated in the change in political leadership with the rise of the "ex plebeians" from various ethnic groups, often with proletarian backgrounds. The attention is, however, more to the examination of decision-leadership in three issue areas—political nominations, public education, and urban redevelopment, which Dahl insists are both representative and salient. The method in such "event analysis" is typically one of chronological narration of who did what, when, and what effect it had, in this instance supplemented by a more precise systematic tabulation of the kinds of people who held formal positions in the organizations concerned with the above issues and of those who initiated or vetoed significant decisions.

The refutation of the business dominance thesis is quite explicit. Some two hundred "economic notables" were located. Within the issue-areas studied, a significant number occupied formal positions only in connection with urban redevelopment (about fifty), of which seven were actually considered decision leaders. None were formally involved in public education, a handful in political parties.

Even within the area of urban redevelopment, the decision-making role of businessmen was considered minor. Their contributions came largely through their participation in the "Citizens Action Committee," organized by the Mayor with the objective of legitimizing decisions and providing an arena in which objections to the program could be anticipated and avoided. Neither the Committee, nor individual businessmen or business groups, were responsible for many crucial decisions. Dahl believes that they could, if vigorously in opposition, have blocked proposals, but the political officials, led by the Mayor, prevented such contingencies by a "capacity for judging with con-

siderable precision what the existing beliefs and the commitments of the men on the CAC would compel them to agree to if a proposal were presented in the proper way, time, and place."[8] In general, business groups possess many "resources," but they are also limited by many power "liabilities," so that they simply appeared as "one of the groups out of which individuals sporadically emerge to influence the policies and acts of city officials."[9] "Like other groups in the community, from the Negroes on Dixwell Avenue to teachers in the public school, sometimes the Notables have their way and sometimes they do not."[10]

In the decision areas studied, the "inequalities" are not so widely "dispersed." Only a few people make the key decisions in each issue area, but they achieve their hegemony by accepting the indirect influence of larger groups. Nominations are genrally determined by a few party leaders, but with attention to the wishes of their followers within the party organizations, especially subleaders and representatives of ethnic groups. Most important redevelopment decisions were made by the Mayor and appropriate staff officials, with full sensitivity to the need for getting support from business and other groups. Major public education policy was directed by the Mayor and his appointees on the Board of Education; superintendents, principals, and teachers' organizations played some part, but mostly to mobilize support for public education. A few public and party officials thus constituted the directing leadership, each in his own province, with the office and personality of the dynamic Mayor, Richard Lee, supplying the unifying force. We have advisedly called the leading group a "directing" rather than a "dominating" oligarchy. It apparently got its way

8 Dahl, *op. cit.*, p. 137.
9 *Ibid.*, p. 72.
10 *Ibid.*, p. 75.

less from authority or influence, in the communication sense, than from the ability to please others, particularly potentially opposing groups. In fact, the political leaders favored the existence of organized groups as a means of legitimizing their decisions and mobilizing support, as well as providing an arena where various sentiments could be expressed and somewhat satisfied. The Citizens Action Committee in the urban redevelopment field was one such example. Similarly, school principals and the Board of Education utilized PTAs "to head off or settle conflicts between parents and the school system."[11]

Dahl does not maintain that the New Haven pattern he describes is the only one possible or existent. Like Miller, he offers a model of power types which will be later discussed. But the New Haven analysis provides the basic elements around which most of the varied forms are structured.

The dispute between the two major contending approaches to American community power is thus, more or less, joined. Partly methodological, it is, at least initially, a disagreement between a business-elite dominance thesis and an acceptance of a relative pluralism. It is also a disagreement about the role of local government and political leadership. Dahl believes that mayors and their staff have increasingly become the initiators and organizers of important community decisions. Miller insists that the political leaders are uncertain about themselves and wait for the cues of others, while businessmen have a clearly defined image "and thus act with more assertion."[12]

A third recent volume further helps locate the principal disputes on the subject. Edward Banfield's *Political Influence*, utilizing event analysis, narrates,

with a detailed chronology, how decisions involving six very specific community problems were arrived at or, in most cases, blocked or compromised.[13] In all cases, there was a divided opinion around significant forces and individuals. The actual list of issues should be of some interest: proposals for extending a particular hospital's facilities, reorganization of welfare administration, a state subsidy for the Chicago Transit Authority, a plan for a vast business center, the creation of a large Chicago branch of the University of Illinois, the building of an extensive Exhibition Hall. At the time of publication, only the last had been achieved. The welfare reorganization plans had produced a compromise; in all other cases, the contending elements had forced a general stalemate.

Banfield's accounts are in the nature of the best type of scholarly journalistic history. They contain extensive details, but little systematic treatment. However, his interpretations are organized around several summary ideas. Initially, he does not discount the possibility of business dominance. In essence, he believes that the resources of the leading Chicago businessmen, representing the top officials of leading national corporations and prominent regional commercial and banking institutions, offer an apparently unlimited power potential. Yet, he insists that, in his investigations, the "richest men in Chicago are conspicuous by their absence."[14] In fact, "big businessmen are criticized less for interfering in public affairs than for 'failing to assume their civic responsibilities.' "[15]

Businessmen do not dominate community decisions because of lack of unity, lack of interest, and because of the "costs" of intervening on any issue,

[11] *Ibid.*, p. 156.
[12] D'Antonio and Ehrlich, *op. cit.*, p. 136.

[13] Edward C. Banfield, *Political Influence*, New York: The Free Press of Glencoe, 1961.
[14] *Ibid.*, p. 288.
[15] *Ibid.*, p. 287.

including the encouragement of counter pressures. Their vital interests are not at stake and they are relatively satisfied with what is done. When their interests are more aroused, either because of some visible economic stake or because of personal predilections, particular business organizations may become heavily involved and be very influential. For instance, the disputed Exhibition Hall was built because it was a pet project of Colonel Robert McCormack and his successors on the Chicago *Tribune*. But, usually businessmen are only casually concerned or on all sides of most of the questions studied.

Typically, the most influential people in the community-decision making in Chicago are: "the managers of large organizations, the maintenance of which is at stake, a few 'civic leaders' whose judgment, negotiating skill, and disinterestedness are unusual and above all, the chief elected officials."[16] The organizations referred to are specified as those supported by "customers" rather than "members."[17] They may be profit-making businesses, public agencies which give free services, or public and semi-public agencies which sell services. In most cases, the involved organizations are public and the executives are civil servants, though Banfield describes them as "fighting politicians" rather than "bureaucrats."[18]

However, the most influential leaders in this megalopolis, as in the medium-sized city of New Haven, are the elected political officials, especially the Mayor. Banfield is thus on the side of Dahl against Miller. But, the leadership of Mayor Richard Daley, so frequently bracketed with Mayor Lee of New Haven as one of the "strong" mayors of

our times, appears to be less forceful. Though both chief executive and official leader of the powerful Democratic machine, he is faced with many limitations on the exercise of power, even within the political realm. He needs the cooperation of other elected officials, "irregulars" within his own party, elected officials of the other party (especially the Republican Governor in the period under study). He may be, and in this study actually was, blocked by the courts. Voters may veto proposals, as on a bond referendum, and, of course, the possibility of electoral opposition in the next election must always be considered. Above all the Mayor and his associates, like anyone who seeks to wield power in specific situations, has limited resources of "working capital." These cannot be "used up" for every challenge that arises.

Like the business dominants, Banfield seems to consider the political leaders as potentially omnipotent when they go "all out" on any question. But this would require depleting their limited working capital. They have to contend with other power groups besides those mentioned—national government in some cases, businessmen, other strong community elements that may be affected or aroused. They are, therefore, in practice, slow to take up issues and seek compromises. The initiative on most questions thus comes from the maintenance and enhancement needs of the type of formal organization listed. Other organizations may then support, oppose, or strive for modification. The following are some examples: A hospital tries to expand. Another hospital, for its own reasons, opposes. The *Tribune* wants an Exhibition Hall, the owners of another Hall oppose. The state, city, and county Welfare Departments have varying positions on reorganization plans. Attempts are made to line up different

---

16 *Political Influence*, p. 288.
17 *Ibid.*, p. 265.
18 *Ibid.*, p. 266.

elements of the "public" on each side. The political leaders may then adjudicate or support one side or the other, but rarely with all their resources.

The varying positions of Miller, Dahl, and Banfield have been presented in some detail not so much to assess their ideas and their work at this juncture, but because their combined efforts do suggest the kinds of questions that have to be probed. These include the following:

1) Of what does community power consist and how does one locate it? This involves the general question of methodology.

2) Who attempts to wield power in which situation? Power motivation is generally ignored by Miller, is of great importance to Dahl and Banfield.

3) How are important community decisions made? Miller appears to see most community-relevant decisions as a simple reflection of the values and efforts of the business elite and its subordinates. Dahl and Banfield pay attention to the motivation, resources and tactics of specific groups and individuals.

4) What is the power position of particular groups? Emphasis has been on business and local government.

5) What is the prevailing power picture in the community? Corollary questions include the relation between power and other features of particular communities. Comparisons among communities is thus an inherent element of such analyses.

The remainder of this discussion is an attempt to elaborate and, to some extent, answer those questions, utilizing the material already reviewed as well as those of other students in the area. Our formulations are, of course, very tentative; we hope, in any case, that they can be guides for those looking for more complete answers, either in the research already undertaken or in the subsequent investigation which, we hope, is forthcoming.

ORIENTATION AND METHODOLOGY: WHAT IS COMMUNITY POWER AND HOW IS IT LOCATED?

WHAT IS COMMUNITY POWER? Initially, the term "community power" demands clarification. Appending the concept of "influence," which is, more or less, assumed to be synonymous, adds to the confusion. The traditional theoretical emphasis, summarized in Weber's formula—"the chance of a man or of a number of men to realize their own will in a communal action even against the resistance of others who are participating in the action"—is generally irrelevant to most discussions of American community power.[19] The orientation actually utilized is more in line with Bertrand Russell's description of power as "the production of intended effects."[20] Investigations have concentrated on the ability to and/or the practice of deciding what is to be done in, for, by the community. Power over people is thus an implicit, but rarely explicit, feature of the investigations. Furthermore, a "Machiavellian" model of power, which depicts individual power maintenance and enhancement as ends in themselves, must yield to approaches which seek to relate the exercise of power to other interests and values. Similarly, the long list of descriptions of types of power, bases of power, mechanisms of power, the distinctions among "power," "authority," "social control," et al., seem operationally outside the scope of the

[19] *From Max Weber: Essays in Sociology*, translated, edited, and with an introduction by H. H. Gerth and C. Wright Mills, New York: Oxford University Press, Galaxy Book, 1958, p. 180.
[20] Bertrand Russell, *Power: A New Social Analysis*, London: Unwin Books, 1962, p. 25.

literature on American community power analysis.[21]

In essence, the focus is characteristically on community decisions, actual or potential, even if the methodology is "reputational." The basic question becomes who has more to say, or can have more to say, about things which are important to many people in the community. . . .

METHODOLOGY The variations in the findings are often, but not always, correlated with the method of inquiry— *reputation* vs. *event* analysis. A more obvious set of criteria, *formal position,* has been attempted and rejected. One study disclosed that the economic and political "office holders" were not typically community leaders by reputation.[22] Another revealed that the formal leaders were not directly involved in decision-making.[23] Research-wise, these conclusions may be pertinent, but they are subject to further probing as analytical interpretations, as later discussed.

Both of the major approaches have obvious virtues and defects, as apparent in their application. The "reputation" material is relatively codifiable and systematic, allows for ready replication and comparison. The criticisms are also

obvious and often enough noted: the arbitrary choice of informants which can initially bias the findings, the "circularity" of the interviews (influentials talking about "influentials"), the acquired information suggesting "power potential" rather than "power utilization," the vagueness of the question wording, the possibility that the informant's observations may reflect folklore rather than knowledge, the possibility that "status" is automatically identified with power.[24] The tone is frequently a kind of groping inside-dopester exposé rather than a depiction of the institutional complexities of the contemporary American community.

The event analysis has more of the feel of the precise socio-political processes. It dwells on what has been done, not about what could be done, though ad hoc discussions of resources available are significantly added, in many cases, as additional variables. Some of the institutional arrangements, conflicts and coalitions, problems and issues are available to the reader. At least, up to now, the defects and dangers are also glaring. Choice of issues involves neglecting others. Are those which are chosen representative? Are they salient to the functioning of the city, to the analysis of the power structure, or even to the specific purposes of the inquiry? Are the cases generalizable to the entire city decision-making process or only to particular types of decision-making?

One study did strive for an elaborate systematization of specific decisions.[25]

[21] Game models of decision-making, which pose analogies of combatants striving to win out over each other, are apparently as inapplicable as other orientations which emphasize "power over" rather than "power to." Dahl, for instance, has offered such a theoretical model, which he does not seem to utilize in his own community power analysis. See Robert A. Dahl, "The Concept of Power," *Behavioral Science,* 3 (July, 1957), pp. 201–215.

[22] Robert O. Schulze and Leonard U. Blumberg, "The Determination of Local Power Elites," *American Journal of Sociology,* 63 (November, 1957), pp. 290–296.

[23] Linton C. Freeman, Thomas J. Fararo, Warner Bloomberg Jr., and Morris H. Sunshine, "Locating Leaders in Local Communities: A Comparison of Some Alternative Approaches," *American Sociological Review,* 28 (October, 1963), pp. 791–798.

[24] For a thorough criticism see Raymond E. Wolfinger, "Reputation and Reality in the Study of Community Power," *American Sociological Review,* 25 (October, 1960), pp. 636–644.

[25] Linton C. Freeman, et al., "Local Community Leadership," Publications Committee of University College, Syracuse University, 15, 1960; Linton C. Freeman, et al., "Metropolitan Decision Making," Publications Committee of University College, Syracuse University, 28, 1962.

Examining action on almost forty issues in the city of Syracuse, the researchers, through documentation and interviews, were able to locate the crucial decision-makers in each case. The quest was for a precise statistical summation of the more relevant social characteristics of these "influentials." Through factor analysis of these characteristics, a large proportion of the decisions could be grouped, i.e., the same types of people were involved in these types of decisions. The technique warrants continued applications and the results, referred to from time to time in this paper, were suggestive. But serious deficiencies remain. All the issues seem to have been given equal weight, and the problems of generalizability, pertinence, etc. still remain.

If the reputation approach sometimes resembles a quantification of a gossip column, some event descriptions appear like detailed journalistic case histories, good and comprehensive examples of the genre, but all with inherent dangers. The New Haven and Syracuse studies do offer more precise and ordered material, but they are not constructed so as to give us a clear-cut systematic picture of power in the community. The ideas are seminal, the evidence is there, but the data are still subject to the charge of selective choice.

In summary, the reputation approach appears to be comprehensive and methodologically neat; the question to be posed is: how relevant are the answers to meaningful hypotheses about community power. Event studies present the proper queries, search in the right directions, and provide tentative answers. But the answers remain partial and, usually, insufficiently systematized. Yet the author's predilection is towards the event approach, somehow systemized. It tends to be more concrete, to be accompanied by greater attention to the socio-political life of the community, to suggest more

suitable insights into such elements as motivation for power utilization and power potential and, generally, to produce more fruitful results. However, our objective is not principally to appraise methodology. The discussion which follows utilizes material however obtained, though the method of acquiring the data is, necessarily, at least an implicit feature of our evaluation.

. . .

MOTIVATION FOR DECISION-MAKING

In the relatively pluralistic American community, power over decisions is not an automatic reflection of a prescribed hierarchal role description. A significant variable that emerges from the literature is the motivation to intervene in a particular decision-making process. Such motivation is simply a product of the extent to which that decision is salient to the group and/or the individual.

*Group Saliency Factors*

Several types of group saliency factors are listed here, not with any logical organization, which does not seem obvious at this point, but as a list of the kinds of elements observed in the literature. They include: group power maintenance or enhancement in specific areas, furtherance of economic "interests" in the traditional sense, defense and extension of values. Contrariwise, nonintervention may imply that relative power, economic interests, and values are being achieved without such decision intervention.

GROUP POWER IN COMMUNITY The general lines of this type of motivation are indicated in the methodological note and the review of Banfield's narratives. A community decision which may limit or enhance the relative power of groups will impel intervention by the leaders of such groups. This rather simplistic formula may be better understood by noting the converse, the non-intervention by potentially powerful groups when their power positions are not at stake. Returning again to our methodological note, this is one reason why business groups do not throw their resources into every question that arises. For instance, one of the discussants in the *Power and Democracy in America* volume, noting that businessmen collect philanthropic funds but leave the question of disbursement, the genuine decision-making aspects, to welfare professionals, remarks: "Perhaps the crucial issue is whether or not the allocation of funds is of relevance to the businessmen. If, in fact, they have no interest in, or are satisfied with, the allocation, their lack of concern may reflect not their weakness or fear of defeat but the realization that there is little power challenge involved."[26]

Similarly, the oft-noted ambivalence of officials of large absentee corporations toward participation in community activities, except when middle-management is prodded by the company for public relations reasons, is partly a reflection of the fact that their local and, of course, their national power positions, are rarely affected.[27] On the other hand, local government officials were among the few citizens actively concerned about metropolitan government reorganization plans, for the future of their "domains" might be at stake.[28]

[26] D'Antonio and Ehrlich, *op. cit.*, p. 125.

[27] Peter H. Rossi, "The Organizational Structure of an American Community," in *Complex Organizations*, edited by Amitai Etzioni, New York: Holt, Rinehart and Winston, Inc., 1962, pp. 301–312; Ronald J. Pellegrin and Charles H. Coates, "Absentee-Owned Corporations and Community Power Structure," *American Journal of Sociology*, 61 (March, 1956) pp. 413–419; Robert O. Schulze, "The Role of Economic Dominants in Community Power Structure," *American Sociological Review*, 23 (February, 1958), pp. 3–9.

[28] Scott Greer, *Metropolitics: A Study of Political Culture*, New York: John Wiley and Sons, Inc., 1963.

One other power motivation may be noted, the search for power in some areas to compensate for powerlessness in other areas of the potentially powerful. The dominant role of businessmen in civic and philanthropic organizations may thus be seen as an outlet for power loss in local government.[29]

In summary, power groups will intervene in decisions when their bases of power are the issue. There seems to be little evidence of a drive towards generic power imperialism in American communities. Rather, the impulsion seems to be towards the maintenance and enhancement of the group's position in these particular "areas" of power within which it operates, which, to repeat, may involve an inherent power over many "areas."

ECONOMIC INTERESTS The literature likewise supports the almost truistic statement that intervention in decision-making will vary with the extent to which an issue has definite economic relevance to a group. In Banfield's discussion of proposed Chicago projects, those businessmen who would clearly gain business advantages were most vigorous in pushing for them, those who might lose a competitive position thereby were actively, if sometimes surreptitiously, in opposition.[30] Absentee corporations may have little concern about local problems which have little effect on the enterprises; however, in the communities where they have large home offices they may be actively involved in redevelopment decisions. In the Syracuse study, the local "aristocratic commercial leadership" were heavily represented in "Downtown Development" decisions, the "new management" elite of industrial corporations in those of

[29] Peter H. Rossi, "Theory and Method in the Study of Power in the Local Community," paper presented at meetings of American Sociological Association, New York, August, 1960.

[30] Banfield, *op. cit., passim.*

"Industrial Interest."[31] In a study of the politics of a small town, merchants who would be adversely affected by a re-routing of traffic were decisive in defeating an attempt to change a highway through town.[32] Unions may be only tangentially concerned about community problems except when the economic interests of members are directly involved.[33]

Urban renewal offers a particular area in which economic interests may be at stake. Therefore, observers, with the possible exception of Dahl, find that many business groups are, quite appropriately, conspicuously engaged in decision-making about such questions.[34] An additional type of power exercise around economic interests is the ever present striving to lower governmental expenditures and to maintain lower taxes. Much of the intervention in small town or suburban community politics is concerned with little else.[35]

VALUES Such "interests" may or may not be closely identified with group values, particularly those which are manifestly politically relevant, and especially when some aspect of the group's legitimacy in the social structure is at issue. Public welfare expenditures can be considered an ideological challenge to a private business approach to solving community problems. Therefore, businessmen oppose such expenditures, actively work at private philanthropic alternatives, or get into official government positions where they can combat the "welfare state" philosophy.[36] People will spend as much on private activities as it would cost in taxes if the same effort were undertaken by government agencies.[37] Businessmen will push for a tax-supported subsidy to a private bus company rather than sanction a publicly-owned bus line.[38]

Perhaps the converse again reveals the nub of the question more clearly. Intervention by potential power wielders is less likely when neither the legitimacy nor the resources of the power base is threatened. Especially is this true of businessmen. Why bother with the effort, and costs, of trying to marshal resources on every decision, even of business relevance? As long as you can run your business, let the others have their particular decision-areas. This has been part of the traditional attitude of big business towards "corrupt" municipal political machines. Such a non-intervention orientation will, of course, be even more likely when there is a general satisfaction, or at least minimal antagonism towards what others are doing, especially if it may help your "interests." Why should New Haven businessmen spend their valuable time in the details of urban renewal planning, except when prodded by the Mayor? He and his staff seem to be doing a good enough job.

Somewhat surprisingly, the literature contains few other explicit examples of

[31] Freeman, *et al.*, "Local Community Leadership," *op. cit.*

[32] Werner E. Mills Jr. and Harry R. Davis, *Small City Government: Seven Cases in Decision Making*, New York: Random House Studies in Political Science, 1962, pp. 31–43.

[33] Dahl, *Who Governs? op. cit.*, pp. 253–255.

[34] Peter H. Rossi and Robert A. Dentler, *The Politics of Urban Renewal: The Chicago Findings*, New York: The Free Press of Glencoe Inc., 1961; Robert C. Wood, *1400 Governments: The Political Economy of the New York Metropolitan Region*, Cambridge, Mass.: Harvard University Press, 1961, pp. 158–160; Salisbury, *op. cit.*

[35] Robert C. Wood, *Suburbia: Its People and Their Politics*, Boston: Houghton Mifflin Co., 1959, pp. 161–197, *passim*; Arthur J. Vidich and Joseph Bensman, *Small Town in Mass Society*, Princeton, New Jersey; Princeton University Press, 1958, pp. 109–136.

[36] Pellegrin and Coates, *op. cit.*; Hunter, *op. cit.*, pp. 207–227.

[37] Vidich and Bensman, *op. cit.*, pp. 128–136.

[38] Mills and Davis, *op. cit.*, pp. 55–72.

intervention in decisions because of group values beyond those of business groups. There are descriptions of those who get involved in decisions because of group "tastes" (art, mental health), professional orientation (health), life style (home owners striving to maintain a neighborhood).[39] Especially surprising is the comparative absence of accounts of group "ideological" motivation, secular and religious.

CONCLUSION...The research and analytical directive can almost be summed up as: find out why the leaders of a particular group should care about a particular controversy, find out why it does or does not mean enough to the group to warrant marshalling resources in the light of the possible contending forces.

*Personal Factors*

ROLE The specific individual role requirements may be as consequential as the group aspects in determining the degree of intervention in decision-making.This has been the point of the many analysts who emphasize the central power position of the Mayor, his staff, and the responsible professionals in government agencies. In the context of the problems and structure and public expectations of the contemporary American cities, to do their jobs, especially to do them well, they have to become actively involved in many important decisions, have to utilize their power resources. In former times, when their role expectations were less demanding, they could more readily avoid power utilization and decision responsibility.

CAREER Attempts at power utilization may not be inherent in the role, but may enhance the possibility of success in that role and resultant career oppor-

tunities. It becomes an estimate of how to "do the job well," which may mean trying to foster or alter particular decisions. This could characterize some "go-getting officials," bureaucrats, professionals, perhaps some city managers. The mayor who wants to make a "name for himself," whatever the purpose, would be such an example, as in the case of Mayor Lee of New Haven. The pressure of corporations to get middle management to participate in civic organizations has been previously described. This is apparently the principal reason why many do participate, for it can become an appropriate mechanism for a favorable judgment in the corporation hierarchy or, in some cases, the opportunity to get known and thus shift to a position outside the corporation.

PERSONALITY Because of the nature of the inquiries, there has been little explicit attention to personality factors, which are frequently central in some general models of "power striving." It is appropriate to suggest, however, that motivations for exercise of power include this variable. It may be related to career strivings, to role performance, to group power maintenance, or to some combination thereof, as, for instance, the attempted use of power by anxious individuals who feel that their individual roles and careers are threatened by an assumed threat to their group's power. How this can be meaningfully studied is not readily answerable.

CONCLUSION Motivation for an effort at decision-making, or power wielding, in a situation where there is controversy, or possibility of controversy, is a product of, among other things, the extent to which the issue is deemed salient to the appropriate actors. Among the elements involved, as noted in the literature, are: the possible effects on the relative power position of a group; the economic interests of a group (or individual); the

---

[39] Freeman, *et al.*, "Local Community Leadership," *op. cit.*, Dahl, *op. cit.*, pp. 192–199; Banfield, *op. cit.*, *passim*.

relevance to legitimacy, values, and life styles; the role demands and career aspirations of individuals.

## WHO ARE THE "POWERFUL," HOW, AND WHY?

As spelled out, those who have most to say about community relevant decisions are appropriately motivated to intervene in that decision. The measure of their "power," to what extent they will have their "way," requires some consideration of the following elements:

### Formal Features

FORMAL POSITION The formal position of groups of individuals within the social structure involves being assigned the ultimate function of making the relevant decisions. With the popularity of "invisible government" approaches implicit in so much of the Hunter-Miller type of finding, it is important that this be initially emphasized. Even Vidich and Bensman, who frequently use the "invisible government" label in depicting the structure of a rural community, actually describe a "power elite" quartet which has important formal positions in the local government and party.[40]

The formal function of particular organizations is related to the kinds of decisions in which such organizations are involved. Thus, it should not be surprising that government officials play more of a role in decisions which have to be made by a government agency, have less to say when they are not officially assigned this responsibility. Private philanthropy projects are illustrative. Those with money collect from others with money. The money collectors, or rather the directors of money collections, are in the obvious position of deciding what is to be done with the money if they so wish. Similarly, since businessmen have to build private re-

development and private civic projects, they will have much to say about those projects, whoever else may be involved.

If the formal position, or formal organization, require decisions on a subject, and if the issue is salient to the position or organization, the occupant is likely to be, in some manner, an important participant in the decision-making process. Thus, in the contemporary context, school superintendents are important in school decisions, expert officials in municipal departments are assigned decision responsibilities within their sphere and, above all, the "wishes" of the leaders of city governments today inherently carry great weight. In contrast, the officials of small towns and suburbs are not, by constitutional requirement or popular expectations, presumed to have much of an independent decision role, and few issues are very salient to them.[41] Therefore, their governments tend to be "weak."

However, as already indicated, some studies reveal that the formal leaders may not be either those who have power by reputation or those directly involved in important decisions. Their roles may be limited to that of "lending prestige or legitimizing the situations provided by others."[42] Those others, labeled as the "Effectors," are generally the underlings—particularly government personnel and the employees of the large private corporations.

Such interpretations tend to confuse "formal position" with "formal organizations." Comparatively lower range personnel of organizations may be involved in the actual decision process, but it is the position in the entire social structure of their organizations which gives them the ability and the motivation

[40] Vidich and Bensman, *op. cit.*, especially pp. 217–221.

[41] Wood, *Suburbia, op. cit.*, pp. 153–255, *passim*.

[42] Freeman, *et al.*, "Locating Leaders," *op. cit.*, pp. 797–798.

to make decisions. Furthermore, this decision-making potential and impetus would not exist without and cannot, in most instances, be counter to the more formal leadership of the organization. In essence, power-wielding hardly exists outside organization role. Whether the reputation or decision approach is used, the decision-makers are thus usually found rooted in some formally organized matrix.

There remains one formally assigned decision-making entity in a democracy with open contests—the electorate. Elections for office are rarely emphasized in the literature. In most of the communities studied, the incumbents or their likely successors seem fairly secure in tenure. But there are several indications of need to make a "good showing" in elections, as a popular legitimizing of their policies, a way of enhancing careers, a method of mobilizing followers, or simply because the role of a politician requires getting more votes. The "power" of the electorate, in this widespread situation of municipal government continuity, is that of a variety of publics toward whom politicians somehow try to appeal even if any comparative lack of appeal may not mean loss of political power. Referenda present a different picture. A formal requirement for popular approval limits the decision-making capabilities of any political leader or anyone else involved in such a decision. In the extreme case of suburban school officials, the decision-making option becomes very narrow.[43] The communication "appeals" then become of vital concern, the response to those appeals a direct expression of power by the electorate or sections thereof.

As a final consideration, the background of formal decision-makers, the element so frequently emphasized in traditional "elite" analysis, is rarely emphasized in community studies. Such features are occasionally stated, more frequently implied, but are rarely explicitly considered. In essence, such an approach states that because of common interests and values, the orientation of formal decision-makers is directed towards the reference group of those of similar origin, who, therefore, become powerful. It is not utilized because contemporary role, organization, etc. of those in formal positions seems to provide a more meaningful focus.

ACCESS TO FORMAL DECISION-MAKERS The notion of "access" to those who formally make decisions, particularly government officials, is evident in many studies of national and state politics. All discussions of "pressure groups" in local affairs dwell on, except when referenda are involved, some means of "getting to" and thus affecting those who have the official decision-making responsibility. This is the assigned task of the "effectors" in corporations.[44] But, in most reputational studies and typical accompanying business dominance emphasis, as well as in various notions of "invisible government," much more is implied. The government is assumed to be a weak power center. Businessmen, as well as other groups "behind the scenes," possess formal and informal communication channels to government officials. Since the former represents "strength," the communications will be heeded.[45] To the extent that this process does occur, it should not be interpreted as a symptom of decision by intrigue. It is merely a reflection of the existing power relationship.

FORMAL STRUCTURE The propensity and ability to make decisions may be related to the formal *structure* of the group and the formal relations with

[43] Wood, op. cit., pp. 192–194.

[44] Freeman, et al., "Locating Leaders," op. cit.

[45] Hunter, op. cit., pp. 83–113, 171–205.

other groups. The power of local government, for instance, may be greater if staffed by full-time rather than part-time officials, and if elections are partisan rather than "non-partisan."[46] The existence of a structure for making decisions and formal resources for implementing them may be other variables. Thus, Dahl describes how earlier attempts at urban redevelopment proved unsuccessful because there was no available political process for agreement, nor appropriate financial sources.[47] The Federal Housing Act of 1949 provided both. The "strong mayor" tendency is partly buttressed by the city charter provisions which give the chief executive authority and responsibility for so many decisions. Small towns and suburban governments frequently decide little because they are not constitutionally so assigned and would not have the formal means for executing such decisions if they were made.

Banfield describes two contrasting types of groups with varying formal decision-making potentials. "Civic organization" leaders do not have a mandate to take positions on certain controversial issues, it would be difficult to get the membership to make such decisions, and the organizations could not be readily mobilized to support them if adopted. Leaders of private corporations and the type of public bodies he describes can make such decisions and, to some degree, commit their organizations to them.[48]

The list of formal limitations to power exercise can be readily extended. Local governments have to receive state and Federal approval for many actions. As already described, electorate support is a definite limitation when referenda are required, a latent control in candidate elections. Courts may act as a check on many political decisions. Corporation employees operating in community affairs may require corporation approval for their actions.[49] In summary, in American communities today, effective exercise of power is partially dependent on the existence of appropriate formal mechanisms and the lack of formally restricting structures.

. . .

POWER POSITION OF BUSINESS AND LOCAL GOVERNMENT

In summary, who makes the community relevant decisions or has more say about them? First of all, those who make them are those who are supposed to make them, because of their officially assigned positions or because this is their approved legitimate bailiwick. When the decision is not directly within their formally-designed domain, the appropriate formula should be along these lines: those who are properly motivated by the saliency of an issue, capable of committing and mobilizing their groups, having access to those who have the ability and the impulsion to make the appropriate formal decisions, possessing some form of legitimacy in the decision-area, capable of and utilizing appeals to the values and interests of many publics, able further to mobilize either large numbers or those in strategic positions (using whatever resources can be called upon), and somehow having an opposition with as few as possible of these advantages, will win out, i.e., will exercise their power over a particular area around a specific decision.

Although many groups thus can and do exercise power in American communities, the major contentions are, quite appropriately about the two major institutional groups, business and local gov-

[46] Rossi, "Theory and Method," *op. cit.*, pp. 26–29.

[47] Dahl, *op. cit.*, p. 116.

[48] Banfield, *op. cit.*, pp. 288–295.

[49] Pellegrin and Coates, *op. cit.*

ernment. The foundations of their respective power positions are accordingly appraised in line with the previous formulations.

BUSINESS Banfield offers this conjecture about possible behavior of leading Chicago businessmen: "In some future case—one in which their vital interests are at stake—they may issue the orders necessary to set in motion the lower echelons of the alleged influence hierarchy."[50] Whatever the results of such an effort, this would imply a crucially divisive issue in the community, a quasi "revolutionary" conflict in which some aspect of legitimacy is debated. None of this appears in the literature. Business power within its own institutional area is hardly an issue in contemporary American communities. Beyond this, the following emerges from the literature.

The most important resources of businessmen are obviously the possession of money—their own and of others whose money can be utilized—and status. For many who postulate business elite dominance, these are the only factors involved, for there is the casual assumption that, in American society, wealth, status, and power are automatically correlated. Additionally, there is the generally accepted legitimacy of business values and the expertise of businessmen. Material interest in the city compels concern about many decisions. There is frequently close internal communication among businessmen.

But the inherent limitations to their exercise of power are also evident, as already suggested. The legitimacy of businessmen and their values is not accepted in all areas of community life and by all people.[51] Conflict of interest and opinion among businessmen is as evident as cohesion. Communication

may not be as easy as assumed, especially through their far-flung organizations.[52] The process of formal decision-making on an issue is not always readily available, and potentially divisive decisions, within business organizations or in the community, are avoided. Public relations may be more important than power wielding for its own sake. There is little desire for political activity by corporation officials unless pushed by the companies desire for a proper public image.

Businessmen expect public officials to handle the political problems and, unless seriously dissatisfied with what is done, will rarely intervene with any vigor. When economic interests are involved, they may participate, but often as supporters and legitimizers of the outspoken proponents. Their role in political affairs may be more extensive when local government is weak or when intervention does not brook serious opposition. In essence, they would then be responding to a "power vacuum," even though it is one of long standing. Their "citizen" activity may tend to be in civic, service, and philanthropic organizations, where objectives are clear, methods "clean," and controversy minimal, and the thorny arena of political conflict avoided. The exceptions, to repeat, are situations when *direct economic interests are involved*. Small local businessmen and professional people may be more involved in political affairs, particularly in smaller communities, because of more direct material interest, status strivings, or greater value concerns about the community.

LOCAL GOVERNMENT The basis for the power position of local government can be sketched more briefly. Despite the growing nationalization of government and politics and the checks that automatically follow, municipal government

---

[50] Banfield, *Political Influence, op. cit.*, p. 288.
[51] See Dahl in D'Antonio and Ehrlich, *op. cit.*, p. 109.

[52] Banfield, *op. cit.*, pp. 295–296.

power has grown within the following context: the necessary functions of the government in solving complex contemporary problems and the accompanying role of professionals; a popularly supported plebeian-based political organization, typically with some ties to labor organizations and ethnic groups; a formal political structure which accents the power potential of the mayor and "partisan" organizations and elections. Traditional political machines are typical, though often diminished in power and appeal, but they are rarely involved in major policy decisions. Relative lack of power of political leaders and their staff professionals is correlated with the comparative absence of the above and the power of business groups, because of specific community configurations and historical antecedents, including the dominant position of local-based business and the slowness of change.

## THE POWER STRUCTURE OF AMERICAN COMMUNITIES

Despite their disagreement about the prevailing power picture, Miller and Dahl offer models of possible power structures which are not too dissimilar. Both allow for completely pluralistic patterns, with either particular spheres of influence for particular groups, or open struggles by relatively equal groups on the same issue. To Miller, these are subordinate aspects in most American communities. To Dahl, they exist but are less likely possibilities than a system of comparative pluralism with *coordination by the political leadership* in different ways in different communities, a variant not specifically indicated by Miller. Finally both accept the possibility of domination by an economic elite, but Dahl generally relegates such situations to the past while Miller insists that this pattern, with all its variations, is most common in the United States today.

A more composite replica of these typologies is that of Rossi, with his simple division into "monoliths" and "polyliths."[53] The former is typically business elite dominant. In a polylith, local government is the province of the political leaders, backed by strong parties and working class associations.[54] The rest of his formulation is in accord with our previous discussion. Civic associations and community chests are in the hands of the leaders of business and staff professionals. A polylith is associated with strong political parties, based upon class political attitudes, frequently with ethnic concomitants. In response, economic leaders (and others), may advocate changes in government structure (non-partisan elections) to thwart some of the power of political parties. Absentee corporation officials will tend to set themselves off from purely local political concerns. In monoliths, conflicts tend to take on the character of minor revolts, like the revolutionary postures of the powerless in authoritarian countries.

All this can be restated in terms of what has already been spelled out. Business elite dominance appears most characteristic of communities when the dominant businessmen are most motivated to participate in community decisions (company towns, established commercial aristocracies, etc.) and/or when there are fewer rival power centers. The polylith is characterized by both the leadership of government officials and relative pluralism. Decision-making is widespread among many groups, depending upon motivation, resources, and the other listed ingredients. Businessmen are an important part of the

---

[53] Rossi, "Theory and Method", *op. cit.*, pp. 24–43.

[54] A good example is provided in the description of Lorain, Ohio, by James B. McKee, "Status and Power in the Industrial Community," *American Journal of Sociology*, 58 (January, 1939), pp. 364–370.

power picture, but only as part of the above formula. In fact, a large section avoids the arena of political decisions, except when very pressing, because of the efforts demanded and risks inherent, and concentrates on the private areas of community decision-making, such as civic associations and philanthropic activities, where there is little opposition in power or ideology. The political leaders are the necessary coordinators in such a complex pattern and their power rests on the fairly strong power position of many groups—especially political parties, trade unions, ethnic groups, staff professionals, etc.—and the importance of governmental decisions today.

To complete our review, one additional presentation must be described. Political Scientist Robert Salisbury states that what others would consider polylithic structures are, in most cases, evidence of a "new convergence."[55] A new power triumvirate has arisen to solve the vital problems of the contemporary city. Its elements have already been sufficiently identified: the business interests directly dependent on the condition of the city, particularly the downtown area; the professionals, technicians, experts engaged in city programs; the mayor, generally secure in his tenure. What Salisbury emphasizes is that this constitutes a coordinate power group; the mayor is the most influential, but he appears to be only the first among equals.

The leadership convergence directs most mayor decisions, particularly those that involve allocation of scarce resources; some of these, like redevelopment and traffic control, can determine the future of the city. The rest of the population—other organized groups, other politicians, and unorganized publics—are part of the process in three

ways: they must be "sold" on certain issues, especially if referenda are in order; their interests and needs must be somewhat satisfied and/or anticipated; some demands must be responded to, such as race relations. Salisbury, however, believes that the importance of the last process can be exaggerated. Specifically, he insists that Banfield's selection of issues tends to magnify the initiative of the groups outside the "convergence." The more vital questions should, with few exceptions such as race relations, reveal the initiating, as well as decision-making position, of the triumvirate.

Salisbury's analysis can thus supply the basis for the concluding statements of this essay. Power over community decisions remains a matter of motivation, resources, mechanisms of decision-making, mobilization of resources, etc. On many, many decisions, various groups may initiate and win out, as in Banfield's account and in some of the descriptions of Dahl and others. Current disputes about race relations offer a fitting example where this more pluralistic interpretation, including both the ideas of spheres of influence and competing pressures around a common issue, may be readily applicable. But on the most salient community issues a directing leadership can be observed. In some communities, for the reasons outlined, the decision leaders have been, and may still be, particular business interests. In most of them, a new pattern has emerged, a polylithic structure in which business groups and local government each lead in their own domains. But the urgent problems of the past World War II era in most large cities have brought some business groups into the same decision area as the local government and the ever growing crop of experts. The extent to which the businessmen are involved may vary, as in the different accounts of the role of businessmen in urban renewal in different cities.

[55] Salisbury, *op. cit.*

Does the rest of the population, organized and unorganized, become merely an audience called on occasionally to affirm and applaud these "big decisions?" Salisbury may have overstated his case. Many groups may initiate, veto, modify, pressure in all decision areas, in accord with the ingredients frequently listed. But those who are part of the new power convergence cannot be circumvented. In some manner, they have the responsibilities and will generally have to assume a decision-making role in all major decisions.

To return to the original debate, whatever evidence is available tends to support Dahl's emphasis against Miller's. Most American communities reveal a relatively pluralistic power structure. On some community-relevant questions, power may be widely dispersed. On the most salient questions, many groups may have an effect on what is decided, but the directing leadership comes from some combination of particular business groups, local government, and, in recent developments, professionals and experts. Communities differ and communities change in the power relations among these elements. A suggestive hypothesis holds that the tendency has been towards their coordination into a uniquely composite decision-making collectivity.[56]

[56] One type of community does not seem to fit any model described—the ever growing residential suburb. Perhaps, the reason is that it does not constitute a genuine "community."

# PART THREE

# THE
# SOCIOLOGY
# OF
# POLITICAL
# CHANGE

# POLITICAL AND SOCIAL
# INTEGRATION: FORMS AND STRATEGIES

MYRON WEINER

It is often said of the developing nations that they are "unintegrated" and that their central problem, often more pressing than that of economic development, is the achievement of "integration." The term "integration" is now widely used to cover an extraordinarily large range of political phenomena. It is the purpose of this article to analyze the various uses of this term, to show how they are related, then to suggest some of the alternative strategies pursued by governments to cope with each of these "integration" problems.

DEFINITIONS

(1) Integration may refer to the process of bringing together culturally and socially discrete groups into a single territorial unit and the establishment of a national identity. When used in this sense "integration" generally presumes the existence of an ethnically plural society in which each group is characterized by its own language or other self-conscious cultural qualities, but the problem may also exist in a political system which is made up of once distinct independent political units with which

*Reprinted from Myron Weiner, "Political Integration and Political Development,"* THE ANNALS OF THE AMERICAN ACADEMY OF POLITICAL AND SOCIAL SCIENCE, *358 (March 1965), 52–64, by permission of the Academy and the author.*

people identified. National integration thus refers specifically to the problem of creating a sense of territorial nationality which overshadows—or eliminates—subordinate parochial loyalties.[1]

(2) Integration is often used in the related sense to refer to the problem of establishing national central authority over subordinate political units or regions which may or may not coincide with distinct cultural or social groups. While the term "national integration" is concerned with the subjective feelings which individuals belonging to different social groups or historically distinct political units have toward the nation, "territorial integration" refers to the objective control which central authority

[1] This is perhaps the most common use of the term. For a precise view of the many attempts to define "nationality," see Rupert Emerson, *From Empire to Nation* (Boston: Beacon Press, 1960), especially Part 2: "The Anatomy of the Nation." K. H. Silvert, the editor of a collection of studies of nationalism prepared by the American Universities Field Staff, *Expectant Peoples: Nationalism and Development* (New York: Random House, 1963), suggests as a working definition of nationalism "the acceptance of the state as the impersonal and ultimate arbiter of human affairs" (p. 19). See also Karl W. Deutsch, *Nationalism and Social Communication* (New York: John Wiley and Sons, 1953) and Karl W. Deutsch and William J. Foltz (eds.), *Nation-Building* (New York: Atherton Press, 1963).

has over the entire territory under its claimed jurisdiction.[2]

(3) The term "integration" is often used to refer to the problem of linking government with the governed. Implied in this usage is the familiar notion of a "gap" between the elite and the mass, characterized by marked differences in aspirations and values.[3] The "gap" may be widest in society with a passive population and modernizing elite, but a relatively stable if frustrating relationship may exist. More often the masses are beginning to become organized and concerned with exercising influence, while the elite responds with attempts to coerce, persuade, or control the masses. It is under these conditions of conflict and often internal war that we customarily speak of "disintegration."

(4) Integration is sometimes used to refer to the minimum value consensus necessary to maintain a social order. These may be end values concerning justice and equity, the desirability of economic development as a goal, the sharing of a common history, heroes, and symbols, and, in general, an agreement as to what constitutes desirable and undesirable social ends. Or the values may center on means, that is, on the instrumentalities and procedures for the achievement of goals and for resolving conflicts. Here the concern is with legal norms, with the legitimacy of the constitutional framework and the procedures by which it should operate—in short, on desirable and undesirable conduct.

(5) Finally, we may speak of "integrative behavior," referring to the capacity of people in a society to organize for some common purposes. At the most elementary level all societies have the capacity to create some kind of kinship organization—a device whereby societies propagate themselves and care for and socialize their young. As other needs and desires arise within a society we may ask whether the capacity grows to create new organizations to carry out new purposes. In some societies the capacity to organize is limited to a small elite and is only associated with those who have authority.[4] Only the state, therefore, has a capacity to expand for the carrying out of new functions. In still other societies organizational capacities are more evenly spread throughout the population, and individuals without coercive authority have the readiness to organize with others. Societies differ, therefore, in the extent to which organizational proclivities are pervasive or not, and whether organizations are simply expressive in character—that is, confined to kinship and status—or purposive.

The term "integration" thus covers a vast range of human relationships and attitudes—the integration of diverse and discrete cultural loyalties and the development of a sense of nationality; the integration of political units into a common territorial framework with a government which can exercise authority; the integration of the rulers and the ruled; the integration of the citizen into a common political process; and, finally,

---

[2] For a discussion on some of the problems of territorial control in Africa see James S. Coleman, "The Problem of Political Integration in Emergent Africa," *Western Political Quarterly* (March 1955), pp. 44–57.

[3] For an explanation of this use of the term integration in the literature see Leonard Binder, "National Integration and Political Development," *American Political Science Review* (September 1964), pp. 622–631. Elite-mass integration is also one of the usages in James S. Coleman and Carl G. Rosberg (eds.), *Political Parties and National Integration in Africa* (Berkeley: University of California, 1964).

[4] For an analysis of the attitudes which inhibit organized activity see Edward Banfield, *The Moral Basis of a Backward Society* (Glencoe, Ill.: Free Press, 1958). Though Banfield's study is confined to a single village in Italy, he raises the general problem of analyzing the capacities of a people to organize for common purposes.

the integration of individuals into organizations for purposive activities. As diverse as these definitions are, they are united by a common thread. These are all attempts to define what it is *which holds a society and a political system together.* Scholars of the developing areas have groped for some such notions of integration, for they recognize that in one or more of these senses the political systems they are studying do not appear to hold together *at a level commensurate with what their political leadership needs to carry out their goals.* If each scholar has in his mind a different notion of "integration," it is often because he is generalizing from one or more specific societies with which he is familiar and which is facing some kind of "integration" problem. Since there are many ways in which systems may fall apart, there are as many ways of defining "integration."

To avoid further confusion we shall use a qualifying adjective hereafter when we speak of one kind of integration problem. We shall thus speak of national integration, territorial integration, value integration, elite-mass integration, and integrative behavior and use the term integration alone when we are referring to the generalized problem of holding a system together.

FORMS AND STRATEGIES

Transitional or developing political systems are generally less integrated than either traditional or modern systems. This is because these systems cannot readily perform the functions which the national leadership—or in some instances, the populace too—expects them to perform. In other words, as the functions of a system expand or the political leadership aspires to expand the functions of the system—a new level of integration is required. When we speak of political development, therefore, we are concerned first with the

expanding functions of the political system, secondly with the new level of integration thereby required to carry out these functions, and, finally, with the capacity of the political system to cope with these new problems of integration. It is necessary, therefore, that we now take a more concrete look at the kinds of expanding functions which occur in the course of political development, the specific integrative problems which these pose, and the public policy choices available to governmental elites for coping with each of these integrative problems.

*National Integration*

It is useful to ask why it is that new nations with pluralistic social orders require more national integration than did the colonial regimes which preceded them. The obvious answer is that colonial governments were not concerned with national loyalties but with creating classes who would be loyal to them as a colonial power. Colonial governments, therefore, paid little or no attention to the teaching of a "national" language or culture, but stressed instead the teaching of the colonial language and culture. We are all familiar with the fact that educated Vietnamese, Indonesians, Nigerians, Indians, and Algerians were educated in French, English, and Dutch rather than in their own languages and traditions. Although the colonialist viewed the development of national loyalties as a threat to his political authority, the new leadership views it as essential to its own maintenance. Moreover, since the colonial rulers permitted only limited participation, the parochial sentiments of local people rarely entered into the making of any significant decisions of essential interest to policy makers. Once the new nations permit a greater measure of public participation, then the integration requirements of the system are higher. Moreover, the new elite in the new nations have higher standards of national integration than those of their former colonial rulers and this, too, creates new integration problems.

So long, for example, as export-import duties were imposed by a colonial ruler whose primary concern was with the impact of commercial policies upon their trade and commerce, then no questions of national integration were involved. Once these areas of policy are in the hands of a national regime, then issues immediately arise as to which sections of the country—and therefore which communities—are to be affected adversely or in a beneficial fashion by trade policies. Once educational policy is determined by national rather than colonial needs, the issues of language policy, location of educational facilities, the levels of educational investment, and the question of who bears the costs of education all affect the relations of culturally discrete groups. Finally, once the state takes on new investment responsibilities —whether for roads and post offices or for steel mills and power dams—questions of equity are posed by the regions, tribes, and linguistic groups which make up plural societies. Even if the assent of constituent groups is not necessary for the making of such decisions—that is, if an authoritarian framework is maintained—at least acquiescence is called for.

How nations have handled the problems of national integration is a matter of historical record. Clifford Geertz[5] has pointed out that public policy in the first instance is effected by patterns of social organization in plural societies. These patterns include (1) countries in which a single group is dominant in numbers and authority and there are

one or more minority groups; (2) countries in which a single group is dominant in authority but not numbers; (3) countries in which no single group by itself commands a majority nor is a single group politically dominant; and (4) countries of any combination in which one or more minorities cut across international boundaries. Examples of the first group are prewar Poland (68 per cent Polish), contemporary Ceylon (70 per cent Sinhalese), and Indonesia (53 per cent Javanese). The dominant minority case is best exemplified by South Africa (21 per cent "white"). The best examples of complete pluralism with no majorities are India, Nigeria, and Malaya and, in Europe, Yugoslavia and Czechoslovakia. And finally, among the minorities which cross international boundaries, the most troublesome politically have been the Kurds, the Macedonians, and Basques, the Armenians, and the Pathans. In contemporary Africa, there are dozens of tribes which are cut by international boundaries, and in Southeast Asia there are substantial Chinese and Indian minorities.

In general there are two public policy strategies for the achievement of national integration: (1) the elimination of the distinctive cultural traits of minority communities into some kind of "national" culture, usually that of the dominant cultural group—a policy generally referred to as assimilationist: "Americanization," "Burmanization," "detribalization"; (2) the establishment of national loyalties without eliminating subordinate cultures—the policy of "unity in diversity," politically characterized by "ethnic arithmetic." In practice, of course, political systems rarely follow either policy in an unqualified manner but pursue policies on a spectrum somewhere in between, often simultaneously pursuing elements from both strategies.

The history of ethnic minorities in

[5] See Clifford Geertz, "The Integrative Revolution: Primordial Sentiments and Civil Politics in the New States," *Old Societies and New Nations*, ed., Clifford Geertz (New York: Free Press of Glencoe, 1963).

national states is full of tragedy. If today the future of the Watusi in East Africa, the Hindus in East Pakistan, the Turks in Cyprus and the Greeks in Turkey and Indians in Burma and Ceylon is uncertain, let us recall the fate of minorities in the heterogeneous areas of East Europe. Poland in 1921 had minorities totalling 32 per cent of the population. Since then 2.5 million Polish Jews have been killed or left the country and over 9 million Germans have been repatriated. Border shifts and population changes have also removed Ruthenian, white Russian, and Lithuanian minorities, so that today only 2 per cent of the population of Poland belongs to ethnic minorities. Similarly, the Turkish minority in Bulgaria was considerably reduced at the end of the Second World War when 250,000 Turks were forced to emigrate to Turkey in 1950; and three million Germans and 200,000 Hungarians have been repatriated from Czechoslovakia since the war. Killings, the transfers of populations, and territorial changes have made most Eastern European countries more homogeneous today than they were at the beginning of the Second World War. Yugoslavia and Czechoslovakia are the only remaining East European countries which lack a single numerically dominant ethnic group.[6]

It is sad to recount an unpleasant historical fact—that few countries have successfully separated political loyalties from cultural loyalties. The dominant social groups have looked with suspicion upon the loyalty of those who are culturally different—generally, though not always (but here, too, we have self-fulfilling prophecies at work) with good reason. Where killings, population transfers, or territorial changes have not occurred, the typical pattern has been

[6] These figures are taken from Lewis M. Alexander, *World Political Patterns* (Chicago: Rand McNally), pp. 277–325.

to absorb the ethnic minority into the dominant culture or to create a new amalgam culture. Where cultural and racial differences continue in Europe or the United States, they are generally accompanied by political tensions. No wonder that so many leaders of the new nations look upon assimilation and homogenization as desirable and that strong political movements press for population transfers in Cyprus, India, and Pakistan, and are likely to grow in importance in sub-Sahara Africa. It remains to be seen whether the ideal of unity and diversity, that is, *political* unity and *cultural* diversity, can be the foundation for modern states. Perhaps the most promising prospects are those in which no single ethnic group dominates—Nigeria, India, and Malaysia. The factors at work in prewar Eastern Europe seem tragically in the process of being duplicated in many of the developing nations: the drive by minorities for ethnic determination, the unsuccessful effort by newly established states to establish their own economic and political viability, the inability of states to establish integration without obliterating cultures—and often peoples—through assimilation, population transfers, or genocide, and, finally, the efforts of larger more powerful states to establish control or absorb unintegrated, fragile political systems.

## Territorial Integration

The association of states with fixed territories is a relatively modern phenomenon. The fluctuating "boundaries" of historic empires, and the fuzziness at the peripheries where kinship ties and tributary arrangements marked the end of a state are no longer acceptable arrangements in a world where sovereignty is characterized by an exclusive control over territory. In time the control over territory may be accompanied by a feeling of common nationality—our "national integration," but there must first of all be territorial integration. For most new states—and historic ones as well—the establishment of a territory precedes the establishment of subjective loyalties. A Congo nation cannot be achieved, obviously, without there being a Congo state, and the first order of business in the Congo has been the establishment by the central government of its authority over constituent territorial units. Some scholars have distinguished between the state and the nation, the former referring to the existence of central authority with the capacity to control a given territory and the latter to the extent of subjective loyalty on the part of the population within that territory to the state. There are, of course, instances where the "nation" in this sense precedes the "state"—as in the case of Israel and, according to some, Pakistan—but more typically the "state" precedes the "nation." "Nation-building," to use the increasingly popular phrase, thus presumes the prior existence of a state in control of a specified—and, in most instances, internationally recognized—territory. Territorial integration is thus related to the problem of *state-building* as distinct from *nation-building*.

Colonial rulers did not always establish central authority over the entire territory under their *de jure* control. The filling of the gap between *de jure* and *de facto* control has, in most instances, been left to the new regimes which took power after independence. Thus, the areas under *indirect* control by colonial authorities have been placed under the *direct* control of the new governments—in India, Pakistan, Malaya and in many areas of Africa. This process has been accomplished with relatively little bloodshed and international disturbance—although the dispute over Kashmir is an important exception—largely because the colonial regimes denied these quasi-independent pockets

of authority the right to create their own armies.

The more serious problem of territorial integration has been the efforts of the new regimes to take control over border areas which were, in effect, unadministered by the colonial governments. Since both sides of a boundary were often governed by the same colonial power—as in French West Africa—or by a weak independent power—as in the Indian-Tibetan and Indian-Chinese borders—the colonial government often made no effort to establish *de facto* authority. Moreover, some of these areas are often occupied by recalcitrant tribes who forcefully resisted efforts toward their incorporation in a larger nation-state.

Some of the new governments have wisely not sought to demonstrate that they can exercise control over all subordinate authorities—wisely, because their capacity to do so is often exceedingly limited. But no modern government can tolerate for long a situation in which its laws are not obeyed in portions of its territory. As the new regimes begin to expand their functions, their need to exercise control grows. As an internal market is established, there is a need for a uniform legal code enforceable in courts of law; as state expenditures grow, no area can be exempt from the tax collectors; with the growth in transportation and communication there is a need for postal officers and personnel for the regulation in the public interest of communication and transport facilities. Finally, there is pride, for no government claiming international recognition will willingly admit that it cannot exercise authority in areas under its recognized jurisdiction, for to do so is to invite the strong to penetrate into the territory of the weak.

*Value Integration*

The integration of values—whatever else it encompasses—at a minimum means that there are acceptable procedures for the resolution of conflict. All societies—including traditional societies—have conflicts, and all societies have procedures for their resolution. But as societies begin to modernize, conflicts multiply rapidly, and the procedures for the settlement of conflict are not always satisfactory. There are societies where the right of traditional authority to resolve conflict remained intact during the early phases of modernization—Japan comes readily to mind—and were thereby able to avoid large-scale violence. But these are the exceptions. Why does the system require a new level of value integration?

First of all, the scale and volume of conflict increase in societies experiencing modernization. The status of social groups is frequently changed, even reversed, as education opens new occupational opportunities, as the suffrage increases the political importance of numbers, and as industrial expansion provides new opportunities for employment and wealth. A caste or tribe, once low in status and wealth, may now rise or at least see the opportunity for mobility. And social groups once high in power, status, and wealth may now feel threatened. Traditional rivalries are aggravated, and new conflicts are created as social relationships change.

The modernization process also creates new occupational roles and these new roles often conflict with the old. The new local government officer may be opposed by the tribal and caste leader. The textile manufacturer may be opposed by producers of hand-loomed cloth. The doctor may be opposed by a traditional healer. To these, one could add an enormous list of conflicts associated with modernization; the conflicts between management and labor characteristic of the early stages of industrial development, the hostility of landlords to government land-reform legislation, the hostility of regions, tribes, and

religious groups with one another as they find it necessary to compete—often for the first time—in a common political system where public policies have important consequences for their social and economic positions. Finally, we should note the importance of ideological conflicts so often found in developing societies as individuals try to find an intellectually and emotionally satisfying framework for re-creating order out of a world of change and conflict.

There are two modal strategies for integrating values in a developing society. One stresses the importance of consensus and is concerned with maximizing uniformity. This view of consensus, in its extreme, emphasizes as a goal the avoidance of both conflict and competition through either coercion or exhortation. A second view of the way integrative values may be maximized emphasizes the interplay of individual and group interests. Public policy is thus not the consequence of a "right" policy upon which all agree, but the best policy possible in a situation in which there are differences of interests and sentiments.

Since most developing societies lack integrative values, political leaders in new nations are often self-conscious of their strategies. In practice, of course, neither of these two strategies is pursued in a "pure" fashion, for a leadership which believes in consensus without conflict may be willing to permit the interplay of some competitive interests while, on the other hand, regimes committed to open competition often set limits as to which viewpoints can be publicly expressed.

Though movements often develop aimed at the elimination of conflict—Communists, for example, see class harmony as the culmination of a period of struggle—such movements in practice simply add another element of conflict. The problem has been one of finding acceptable procedures and institutions for the management of conflict. It is striking to note the growth of dispute-settling institutions in modern societies. When these bodies are successful, it is often possible to prevent conflicts from entering a country's political life. Here we have in mind the social work agencies, churches and other religious bodies, lawyers and the courts, labor-management conciliation bodies and employee councils, and interracial and interreligious bodies. The psychiatrist, the lawyer, the social worker, and the labor mediator all perform integrating roles in the modern society. In the absence of these or equivalent roles and institutions in rapidly changing societies in which conflict is growing, it is no wonder that conflicts move quickly from the factory, the university, and the village into political life.

A modern political system has no single mechanism, no single procedure, no single institution for the resolution of conflict; indeed, it is precisely the multiplicity of individuals, institutions, and procedures for dispute settlement that characterizes the modern political system—both democratic and totalitarian. In contrast, developing societies with an increasing range of internal conflict, typically lack such individuals, institutions, and procedures. It is as if mankind's capacity to generate conflict is greater than his capacity to find methods for resolving conflict; the lag is clearly greatest in societies in which fundamental economic and social relationships are rapidly changing.

### Elite-Mass Integration

The mere existence of differences in goals and values between the governing elite and the governed mass hardly constitutes disintegration so long as those who are governed accept the right of the governors to govern. British political culture stresses the obligations of citizens toward their government; the

American political culture stresses the importance of political participation. In both, a high degree of elite-mass integration exists. At the other extreme are societies faced with the problem of internal war, and in between are many countries whose governments are so cut off from the masses whom they govern that they can neither mobilize the masses nor be influenced by them. The integration of elite and mass, between governors and the governed, occurs not when differences among the two disappear, but when a pattern of authority and consent is established. In no society is consent so great that authority can be dispensed with, and in no society is government so powerful and so internally cohesive that it can survive for long only through the exercise of cohesive authority. We need to stress here that both totalitarian and democratic regimes are capable of establishing elite-mass integration and that the establishment of a new pattern of relations between government and populace is particularly important during the early phase of development when political participation on a large scale is beginning to take place.

It is commonplace to speak of the "gap" between governors and the governed in the new nations, implying that some fundamental cultural and attitudinal gaps exist between the "elite" and the "mass," the former being secular-minded, English- or French-speaking, and Western-educated, if not Western-oriented, while the latter remain oriented toward traditional values, are fundamentally religious, and are vernacular-speaking.[7] In more concrete political terms, the government may be concerned with increasing savings and investment and, in general, the post-

[7] For a critique of "gap" theories of political development, see Ann Ruth Willner, "The Underdeveloped Study of Political Development," *World Politics* (April 1964), pp. 468–482.

ponement of immediate economic gratification in order to maximize long-range growth, while the public may be more concerned with immediate gains in income and, more fundamentally, equitable distribution or social justice irrespective of its developmental consequences. Often the governmental elite itself may be split with one section concerned with satisfying public demands in order to win popular support while the other is more concerned with maximizing growth rates, eliminating parochial sentiments, establishing a secular society, or achieving international recognition. The elite-mass gap also implies that communications are inadequate, that is, that the elite is oriented toward persuading the mass to change their orientation, but the feedback of political demands is not heard or, if heard, not responded to.

Perhaps too much is made of the attitudinal "gap" between governors and governed; what is more important perhaps is the attitude of government toward its citizens. Nationalist leaders out of power are typically populist. They generally identify with the mass and see in the "simple peasant" and the "working class" qualities which will make a good society possible. But once the nationalist leadership takes power and satisfies its desire for social status it tends to view the mass as an impediment to its goals of establishing a "modern," "unified," and "powerful" state. From being the champion of the masses the elite often becomes their detractor.

In all political systems, those of developing as well as developed societies, there are differences in outlook between those who govern and those who are governed. In a developed system, however, those who govern are accessible to influence by those who are governed— even in a totalitarian system—and those who are governed are readily available

for mobilization by the government. In modern societies governments are so engaged in effecting the economy, social welfare, and defense that there must be a closer interaction between government and the governed.[8] Governments must mobilize individuals to save, invest, pay taxes, serve in the army, obey laws. Modern governments must also know what the public will tolerate and must be able to anticipate, before policies are pursued, what the public reaction to a given policy might be. Moreover, the modern government is increasingly armed with sophisticated tools of economic analysis and public opinion surveys to increase its capacity to predict both the economic and political consequences of its actions. In contrast, the elites of new nations are constantly talking to the masses; it is not that they do not hear the masses, but what they hear is often so inappropriate to what they wish to do. To ban opposition parties, muzzle the press, and restrict freedom of speech and assembly does indeed close two-way channels of communication, but often this is precisely what is intended.

But whatever their fear of the masses, governmental elites in new nations cannot do without them. While the elite may be unsympathetic to mass efforts to exercise influence, the elite does want to mobilize the masses for its goals. In some developing societies an organizational revolution is already under way as men join together for increasingly complex tasks to create political parties, newspapers, corporations, trade unions, and caste and tribal associations. Governmental elites are confronted with a choice during the early stages of this

---

[8] Karl Deutsch has pointed out that governments of industrial societies, whether totalitarian or democratic, spend a larger proportion of their GNP than do governments in underdeveloped economies, irrespective of their ideologies.

development. Should they seek to make these new organizations instruments of the authoritative structures or should these organizations be permitted to become autonomous bodies, either politically neutral or concerned with influencing government? When the state is strong and the organizational structures of society weak—a condition often found in the early phases of postcolonial societies with a strong bureaucratic legacy—then government leadership clearly has such an option.[9] It is at this point that the classic issue of the relationship of liberty and authority arises, and the elite may choose to move in one direction rather than the other.

The choices made are often shaped by dramatic domestic or international crises of the moment. But they are also affected by the society's tradition of elite-mass relations. The traditional aloofness, for example, of the mandarin bureaucracy toward the Vietnamese populace and the traditional disdain of the Buddhist and Catholic Vietnamese toward the *montegnards* or "pagan" hill peoples have probably been more important factors affecting elite-mass relations in contemporary Vietnam than any strategic or ideological considerations on the part of the Vietnamese government. Similarly, the behavior of many African leaders can often be understood better by exploring the customary patterns of authority in traditional tribal society than by reference to any compulsions inherent in the development process.

In the analysis of elite-mass relations much attention is rightly given to the development of "infra-structures"—that is, political parties, newspapers, universities, and the like—which can provide a two-way communication channel between government and populace.[10] Much attention is also given to the development of "middle strata" of individuals who can serve as links—newspapermen, lobbyists, party bosses, and precinct workers. While in the long run these developments are of great importance, in the short run so much depends upon the attitude of the governmental elites, whether the elites fundamentally feel—and behave—as if they were alienated from and even antagonistic to the masses as they are, or whether the elites perceive the values of the masses as essentially being congruent to their own aims.

*Integrative Behavior*

The readiness of individuals to work together in an organized fashion for common purposes and to behave in a fashion conducive to the achievement of these common purposes is an essential behavioral pattern of complex modern societies. Modern societies have all encountered organizational revolutions —in some respects as essential and as revolutionary as the technological revolution which has made the modern world. To send a missile into outer space, to produce millions of automobiles a year, to conduct research and development, to manage complex mass media all require new organizational skills. During the last few decades we have begun to understand the nature of managerial skills and the complexity of organizations—how they carry out their many purposes, how they adapt themselves to a changing environment, and how they change that environment. We know less about why some societies are more successful than others in creating men and women capable of establishing,

[9] This theme is amplified by Fred W. Riggs, "Bureaucrats and Political Development: A Paradoxical View," *Bureaucracy and Political Development*, ed., Joseph LaPalombara (Princeton, N. J.: Princeton University Press, 1963).

[10] For a discussion of the role of infrastructures in political development, see Edward Shils, *Political Development in the New States* (The Hague: Mouton, 1962).

maintaining, and adapting complex organizations for the achievement of common purposes.

The consequences of an organizational lag as an impediment to development are, however, quite apparent. The inability of many political leaders to maintain internal party and government unity in many new nations has resulted in the collapse of parliamentary government and the establishment of military dictatorships. The much vaunted organizational skill of the military has also often failed in many new nations. In Ceylon a planned military coup collapsed when several of the conspirators spoke of their plans so openly that even a disorganized civilian government had time to take action, and in many Latin-American countries, and now in Vietnam, the military has proven to be as incapable of maintaining cohesive authority as their civilian predecessors.

The capacity—or lack of capacity—to organize with one's fellow men may be a general quality of societies. A society with a high organizational capacity appears to be organizationally competent at creating industrial organizations, bureaucracies, political parties, universities, and the like. Germany, Japan, the United States, the Soviet Union, Great Britain come quickly to mind. In contrast, one is struck by a generalized incompetence in many new nations where organizational breakdowns seem to be greater bottlenecks to economic growth than breakdowns in machinery. In some new countries technological innovations—such as industrial plants, railways, telegraph and postal systems—have expanded more rapidly than the human capacities to make the technologies work, with the result that mail is lost, the transport system does not function with any regularity, industrial managers cannot implement their decisions, and government administrative regulations impede rather

than facilitate the management of public sector plants. Though some scholars have argued that the skill to create complex institutions will accompany or follow technological innovation, there is good reason to think that organizational skills are a prerequisite for much political and economic development. In fact, the pattern of interpersonal relations appears to be more conducive to organization-building in some traditional societies than in others. Just as the presence of entrepreneurial talents in the traditional society is a key element in whether or not economic growth occurs, so may the presence of organizational talents be an important element in whether or not economic growth occurs, so may the presence of organizational talents be an important element in whether there emerges a leadership with the capacity to run a political party, an interest association, or a government.[11]

Surprisingly little is known about the conditions for the development of effectual political organizations. If the modernization process does produce political organizations, why is it that in some societies these organizations are effectual and in others they are not? By effectual, we mean the capacity of an organization to establish sufficient internal cohesion and external support to play some significant role in the decision-making or decision-implementing process. The multiplication of ineffectual political organizations tends to result either in a highly fragmented unintegrated political process in which government is unable to make or implement

[11] For an attempt to relate traditional patterns of social and political relations to modern party-building, see Myron Weiner, "Traditional Role Performance and the Development of Modern Political Parties: The Indian Case," *Journal of Politics* (November 1964). The problems of party-building in a new nation are treated in my *Party-Building in a New Nation: The Indian National Congress* (in preparation).

public policy, or in a political system in which the authoritative structures make all decisions completely independently of the political process outside of government. In the latter case we may have a dual political process, one inside of government which is meaningful and one outside of government which, in policy terms, is meaningless.

Some scholars have suggested that political organization is a consequence of increased occupational differentiation which in turn results from economic growth and technological change—an assumption, incidentally, of much foreign economic assistance. The difficulty with viewing political change as a consequence of social changes which in turn are the consequence of economic development is that, however logical this sequence may appear to be, in the history of change no such sequence can be uniformly found. Indeed, political organization often precedes large-scale economic change and may be an important factor in whether or not there is large-scale economic change.

In recent years greater attention has been given to the psychocultural components of political organization. Attention is given to the existence of trust and distrust and the capacity of individuals to relate personal ambition with some notion of the public good and of moral behavior. For explanations, psychologists focus on the process of primary socialization.

While psychologists focus on the working of the mind, sociologists and social anthropologists have been concerned with the working of society, and focus on the rules that affect the relationship among men—why they are kept and why they are broken. Sociologists have given attention to the complex of rules that organize social relationships, the patterns of superordination and subordination as among and between groups and individuals, how these change, and

what effects they have on political and social relationships. While psychologists give attention to the primary process of socialization, sociologists and social anthropologists are concerned with the way in which the individual, during his entire life, comes to learn the rules and, under certain circumstances, to break them. It is from these two complementary views of man that we may expect the more systematic study of politically integrative and disintegrative behavior.

CONCLUSION

We have tried to suggest in this essay that there are many different kinds of integration problems faced by developing nations, for there are innumerable ways in which societies and political systems can fall apart. A high rate of social and economic change creates new demands and new tasks for government which are often malintegrative. The desire of the governing elite or the governed masses, for whatever reasons, to increase the functions of government are often causes of integration problems. Since modern states as well as modernizing states are often taking on new functions, it would be quite inappropriate to view integration as some terminal state. Moreover, the problems of integration in the developing areas are particularly acute because so many fundamentally new tasks or major enlargements of old tasks are now being taken on. Once the state actively becomes concerned with the mobilization and allocation of resources, new patterns of integration between elite and mass are called for. Once the state takes on the responsibilities of public education and invokes sentiments of "national" solidarity, then the integration of social groups to one another becomes an issue. And once men endeavor to create corporations, newspapers, political parties, and professional associations because they perceive their individual interests served by common actions, a new set of values is called for which provides for the integration of new structures into the political process. The challenges of integration thus arise out of the new tasks which men create for themselves.

# PRIMORDIAL SENTIMENTS AND CIVIL POLITICS IN THE NEW STATES

CLIFFORD GEERTZ

Multiethnic, usually multilinguistic, and sometimes multiracial, the populations of the new states tend to regard the immediate, concrete, and to them inherently meaningful sorting implicit in such "natural" diversity as the substantial content of their individuality. To subordinate these specific and familiar identifications in favor of a generalized commitment to an overarching and somewhat alien civil order is to risk a loss of definition as an autonomous person, either through absorption into a culturally undifferentiated mass or, what is even worse, through domination by some other rival ethnic, racial, or linguistic community that is able to imbue that order with the temper of its own personality. But at the same time, all but the most unenlightened members of such societies are at least dimly aware—and their leaders are acutely aware—that the possibilities for social reform and material progress they so intensely desire and are so determined to achieve rest with increasing weight on their being enclosed in a reasonably large, independent, powerful, well-ordered polity. The insistence on recognition as someone who is visible and matters and the will to be modern and dynamic thus tend to diverge, and much of the political process in the new states pivots around an heroic effort to keep them aligned.

A more exact phrasing of the nature of the problem involved here is that, considered as societies, the new states are abnormally susceptible to serious disaffection based on primordial attachments.[1] By a primordial attachment is meant one that stems from the "givens" —or, more precisely, as culture is inevitably involved in such matters, the assumed "givens"—of social existence: immediate contiguity and kin connection mainly, but beyond them the givenness that stems from being born into a particular religious community, speaking a particular language, or even a dialect of a language, and following particular social practices. These congruities of blood, speech, custom, and so on, are seen to have an ineffable, and at times overpowering, coerciveness in and of themselves. One is bound to one's kinsman, one's neighbor, one's fellow believer, ipso facto; as the result not merely of personal affection, practical

Reprinted from Clifford Geertz, "The Integrative Revolution: Primordial Sentiments and Civil Politics in the New States," in Clifford Geertz, ed., OLD SOCIETIES AND NEW STATES, (Glencoe, Ill.: The Free Press, 1963), pp. 108–13, 119–28, by permission of the publisher.

[1] E. Shils, "Primordial, Personal, Sacred and Civil Ties," British Journal of Sociology, June, 1957.

necessity, common interest, or incurred obligation, but at least in great part by virtue of some unaccountable absolute import attributed to the very tie itself. The general strength of such primordial bonds, and the types of them that are important, differ from person to person, from society to society, and from time to time. But for virtually every person, in every society, at almost all times, some attachments seem to flow more from a sense of natural—some would say spiritual—affinity than from social interaction.

In modern societies the lifting of such ties to the level of political supremacy—though it has, of course, occurred and may again occur—has more and more come to be deplored as pathological. To an increasing degree national unity is maintained not by calls to blood and land but by a vague, intermittent, and routine allegiance to a civil state, supplemented to a greater or lesser extent by governmental use of police powers and ideological exhortation. The havoc wreaked, both upon themselves and others, by those modern (or semimodern) states that did passionately seek to become primordial rather than civil political communities, as well as a growing realization of the practical advantages of a wider-ranging pattern of social integration than primordial ties can usually produce or even permit, have only strengthened the reluctance publicly to advance race, language, religion, and the like as bases for the definition of a terminal community. But in modernizing societies, where the tradition of civil politics is weak and where the technical requirements for an effective welfare government are poorly understood, primordial attachments tend to be repeatedly, in some cases almost continually, proposed and widely acclaimed as preferred bases for the demarcation of autonomous political units. . . .

It is this crystallization of a direct conflict between primordial and civil sentiments—this "longing not to belong to any other group"—that gives to the problem variously called tribalism, parochialism, communalism, and so on, a more ominous and deeply threatening quality than most of the other, also very serious and intractable problems the new states face. Here we have not just competing loyalties, but competing loyalties of the same general order, on the same level of integration. There are many other competing loyalties in the new states, as in any state—ties to class, party, business, union, profession, or whatever. But groups formed of such ties are virtually never considered as possible self-standing, maximal social units, as candidates for nationhood. Conflicts among them occur only within a more or less fully accepted terminal community whose political integrity they do not, as a rule, put into question. No matter how severe they become they do not threaten, at least not intentionally, its existence as such. They threaten governments, or even forms of government, but they rarely at best—and then usually when they have become infused with primordial sentiments—threaten to undermine the nation itself, because they do not involve alternative definitions of what the nation is, of what its scope of reference is. Economic or class or intellectual disaffection threatens revolution, but disaffection based on race, language, or culture threatens partition, irredentism, or merger, a redrawing of the very limits of the state, a new definition of its domain. Civil discontent finds its natural outlet in the seizing, legally or illegally, of the state apparatus. Primordial discontent strives more deeply and is satisfied less easily. If severe enough, it wants not just Sukarno's or Nehru's or Moulay Hasan's head it wants Indonesia's or India's or Morocco's.

The actual foci around which such discontent tends to crystallize are various, and in any given case several are usually involved concurrently, sometimes at cross-purposes with one another. On a merely descriptive level they are, nevertheless, fairly readily enumerable.[2]

1] *Assumed Blood Ties.* Here the defining element is quasikinship. "Quasi" because kin units formed around known biological relationship (extended families, lineages, and so on) are too small for even the most tradition-bound to regard them as having more than limited significance, and the referent is, consequently, to a notion of untraceable but yet sociologically real kinship, as in a tribe. Nigeria, the Congo, and the greater part of sub-Saharan Africa are characterized by a prominence of this sort of primordialism. But so also are the nomads or seminomads of the Middle East—the Kurds, Baluchis, Pathans, and so on; the Nagas, Mundas, Santals, and so on, of India; and most of the so-called "hill tribes" of Southeast Asia.

2] *Race.* Clearly, race is similar to assumed kinship, in that it involves an ethnobiological theory. But it is not quite the same thing. Here, the reference is to phenotypical physical features—especially, of course, skin color, but also facial form, stature, hair type, and so on—rather than any very definite sense of common descent as such. The communal problems of Malaya in large part focus around these sorts of differences, between, in fact, two phenotypically very similar Mongoloid peoples. "Negritude" clearly draws much, though perhaps not all, of its force from the notion of race as a significant primordial property, and the pariah commercial minorities—like the Chinese in Southeast Asia or the Indians and Lebanese in Africa—are similarly demarcated.

3] *Language.* Linguism— for some yet to be adequately explained reasons—is

particularly intense in the Indian subcontinent, has been something of an issue in Malaya, and has appeared sporadically elsewhere. But as language has sometimes been held to be the altogether essential axis of nationality conflicts, it is worth stressing that linguism is not an inevitable outcome of linguistic diversity. As indeed kinship, race, and the other factors to be listed below, language differences need not in themselves be particularly divisive: they have not been so for the most part in Tanganyika, Iran (not a new state in the strict sense, perhaps), the Philippines, or even in Indonesia, where despite a great confusion of tongues linguistic conflict seems to be the one social problem the country has somehow omitted to demonstrate in extreme form. Furthermore, primordial conflicts can occur where no marked linguistic differences are involved, as in Lebanon, among the various sorts of Batak-speakers in Indonesia, and to a lesser extent perhaps between the Fulani and Hausa in northern Nigeria.

4] *Region.* Although a factor nearly everywhere, regionalism naturally tends to be especially troublesome in geographically heterogeneous areas. Tonkin, Annam, and Cochin in prepartitioned Vietnam, the two baskets on the long pole, were opposed almost purely in regional terms, sharing language, culture, race, etc. The tension between East and West Pakistan involves differences in language and culture too, but the geographic element is of great prominence owing to the territorial discontinuity of the country. Java versus the Outer Islands in archipelagic Indonesia; the Northeast versus the West Coast in mountain-bisected Malaya, are perhaps other examples in which regionalism has been an important primordial factor in national politics.

5] *Religion.* Indian partition is the outstanding case of the operation of this type of attachment. But Lebanon, the

---

[2] For a similar but rather differently conceived and organized listing, see R. Emerson, *From Empire to Nation*, Cambridge, Mass., Harvard University Press, 1960, Chapters 6, 7, and 8.

Karens and the Moslem Arakenese in Burma, the Toba Bataks, Ambonese, and Minahassans in Indonesia, the Moros in the Philippines, the Sikhs in Indian Punjab and the Ahmadiyas in Pakistani, and the Hausa in Nigeria are other well-known examples of its force in undermining or inhibiting a comprehensive civil sense.

6] *Custom.* Again, differences in custom form a basis for a certain amount of national disunity almost everywhere, and are of especial prominence in those cases in which an intellectually and/or artistically rather sophisticated group sees itself as the bearer of a "civilization" amid a largely barbarian population that would be well advised to model itself upon it: the Bengalis in India, the Javanese in Indonesia, the Arabs (as against the Berbers) in Morocco, the Amhara in—another "old" new state—Ethiopia, etc. But it is important also to point out that even vitally opposed groups may differ rather little in their general style of life: Hindu Gujeratis and Maharashtrians in India; Baganda and Bunyoro in Uganda; Javanese and Sundanese in Indonesia. And the reverse holds also: the Balinese have far and away the most divergent pattern of customs in Indonesia, but they have been, so far, notable for the absence of any sense of primordial discontent at all.

. . .

The reduction of primordial sentiments to civil order is rendered more difficult, by the fact that political modernization tends initially not to quiet such sentiments but to quicken them. The transfer of sovereignty from a colonial regime to an independent one is more than a mere shift of power from foreign hands to native ones; it is a transformation of the whole pattern of political life, a metamorphosis of subjects into citizens. Colonial governments, like the aristocratic governments of premodern Europe in whose image they

were fashioned, are aloof and unresponsive; they stand outside the societies they rule, and act upon them arbitrarily, unevenly, and unsystematically. But the governments of the new states, though oligarchic, are popular and attentive; they are located in the midst of the societies they rule, and as they develop act upon them in progressively more continuous, comprehensive, and purposeful manner. For the Ashanti cocoa farmer, the Gujerati shopkeeper, or the Malayan Chinese tin miner, his country's attainment of political independence is also his own attainment, willy-nilly, of modern political status, no matter how culturally traditional he may remain nor how ineffectively and anachronistically the new state may in practice function. He now becomes an integral part of an autonomous and differentiated polity that begins to touch his life at every point except the most strictly private. "The same people which has hitherto been kept as far as possible from government affairs must now be drawn into them," the Indonesian nationalist Sjahrir wrote on the eve of World War II, defining exactly the character of the "revolution" that was in fact to follow in the Indies over the next decade—"That people must be made politically conscious. Its political interest must be stimulated and maintained."[3]

This thrusting of a modern political consciousness upon the mass of a still largely unmodernized population does indeed tend to lead to the stimulation and maintenance of a very intense popular interest in the affairs of government. But, as a primordially based "corporate feeling of oneness," remains for many the *fons et origo* of legitimate authority —the meaning of the term "self" in "self-rule"—much of this interest takes

[3] S. Sjahrir, *Out of Exile,* New York, John Day, 1949, p. 215.

the form of an obsessive concern with the relation of one's tribe, region, sect, or whatever to a center of power that, while growing rapidly more active, is not easily either insulated from the web of primordial attachments, as was the remote colonial regime, or assimilated to them as are the workaday authority systems of the "little community." Thus, it is the very process of the formation of a sovereign civil state that, among other things, stimulates sentiments of parochialism, communalism, racialism, and so on, because it introduces into society a valuable new prize over which to fight and a frightening new force with which to contend.[4] The doctrines of the nationalist propagandists to the contrary notwithstanding, Indonesian regionalism, Malayan racialism, Indian linguism, or Nigerian tribalism are, in their political dimensions, not so much the heritage of colonial divide-and-rule policies as they are products of the replacement of a colonial regime by an independent, domestically anchored, purposeful unitary state. Though they rest on historically developed distinctions, some of which colonial rule helped to accentuate (and others of which it helped to mod-

erate), they are part and parcel of the very process of the creation of a new polity and a new citizenship.

For a telling example in this connection one may look to Ceylon, which, having made one of the quietest of entries into the family of new states is now the scene of one of its noisiest communal uproars. Ceylonese independence was won largely without struggle; in fact, without even very much effort. There was no embittered nationalist mass movement, as in most of the other new states, no loudly passionate hero-leader, no diehard colonial opposition, no violence, no arrests—no revolution really, for the 1947 transfer of sovereignty consisted of the replacement of conservative, moderate, aloof British civil servants by conservative, moderate, aloof British-educated Ceylonese notables who, to more nativistic eyes at least, "resembled the former colonial rulers in everything but the color of their skin."[5] The revolution was to come later, nearly a decade after formal independence, and the British governor's valedictory expression of "profound satisfaction that Ceylon has reached its goal of freedom without strife or bloodshed along the path of peaceful negotiation,"[6] proved to be somewhat premature: in 1956 wild Tamil-Sinhalese riots claimed more than a hundred lives, in 1958, perhaps as many as two thousand.

The country, 70 per cent Sinhalese, 23 per cent Tamil, has been marked by a certain amount of group tension for centuries.[7] But such tension has taken

---

[4] As Talcott Parsons has pointed out, power, defined as the capacity to mobilize social resources for social goals, is not a "zero-sum" quantity within a social system, but, like wealth, is generated by the working of particular, in this case political rather than economic, institutions. "The Distribution of Power in American Society," *World Politics*, 10:123–143, 1957. The growth of a modern state within a traditional social context represents, therefore, not merely the shifting or transfer of a fixed quantity of power between groups in such a manner that aggregatively the gains of certain groups or individuals match the losses of others, but rather the creation of a new and more efficient machine for the production of power itself, and thus an increase in the general political capacity of the society. This is a much more genuinely "revolutionary" phenomena than a mere redistribution, however radical, of power within a given system.

[5] D. K. Rangenekar, "The Nationalist Revolution in Ceylon," *Pacific Affairs*, 33:361–374, 1960.

[6] Quoted in M. Weiner, "The Politics of South Asia," in G. Almond and J. Coleman, *The Politics of the Developing Areas*, Princeton, N.J., Princeton University Press, 1960, pp. 153–246.

[7] About half the Tamils are stateless "Indian Tamils"—that is, individuals transported to Ceylon in the nineteenth century to

the distinctively modern form of an implacable, comprehensive, and ideologically instigated mass hatred mainly since the late S. W. R. D. Bandaranaike was swept into the premiership on a sudden wave of Sinhalese cultural, religious and linguistic revivalism in 1956. Himself Oxford-educated, vaguely Marxist and essentially secularist in civil matters, Bandaranaike undermined the authority of the English-speaking (and bi-ethnic Colombo) patriciate by appealing openly, and one suspects somewhat cynically, to the primordial sentiments of the Sinhalese, promising a "Sinhala-only" linguistic policy, a place of pride for Buddhism and the Buddhist clergy, and a radical reversal of the supposed policy of "pampering" the Tamils, as well as rejecting Western dress for the traditional "cloth and banian" of the Sinhalese countryman.[8] And if, as one of his more uncritical apologists claims, his "supreme ambition" was not "to set up an outmoded, parochial, racialist government," but to "stabilize democracy and convert his country into a modern welfare state based on Nehru-style socialism,"[9] he soon found himself the helpless victim of a rising tide of primordial fervor, and his death, after thirty hectic and frustrating months in power, at the hands of an obscurely motivated Buddhist monk was merely that much more ironic.

The first definite move toward a resolute, popularly based, social reform government led, therefore, not to heightened national unity, but to the reverse—increased linguistic, racial, regional, and religious parochialism, a strange dialectic whose actual workings have been well described by Wriggins.[10] The institution of universal suffrage made the temptation to court the masses by appealing to traditional loyalties virtually irresistible, and led Bandaranaike and his followers to gamble, unsuccessfully as it turned out, on being able to tune primordial sentiments up before elections and down after them. The modernizing efforts of his government in the fields of health, education, administration, and so on, threatened the status of consequential rural personages—monks, ayurvedic doctors, village schoolteachers, local officials—who were thereby rendered that much more nativistic and insistent upon communal tokens of reassurance in exchange for their political support. The search for a common cultural tradition to serve as the content of the country's identity as a nation now that it had become, somehow, a state, led only to the revivification of ancient, and better forgotten, Tamil-Sinhalese treacheries, atrocities, insults, and wars. The eclipse of the Western-educated urban elite, within which class loyalties and old-school ties tended to override primordial differences, removed one of the few important points of amicable contact between the two communities. The first stirrings of fundamental economic change aroused fears that the position of the industrious, frugal, aggressive Tamils would be strengthened at the expense of the less methodical Sinhalese. The intensified competition for government jobs, the increasing importance of the vernacular press, and even government-instituted land-reclama-

---

work on British tea estates, and now rejected as citizens by India on the ground that they live in Ceylon, and by Ceylon on the ground that they are but sojourners from India.

[8] Commenting on the spectacular failure of Sir Ivor Jennings's 1954 prediction that Bandaranaike was unlikely to win the leadership of the nationalist movement because he was a "political Buddhist," having been educated as a Christian, Rangenekar shrewdly remarks, "In an Asian setting a Western-educated politician who renounces his Westernization and upholds indigenous culture and civilization wields a much greater influence than the most dynamic local thoroughbred can ever hope to do." Rangenekar, op. cit.

[9] Ibid.

[10] H. Wriggins, "Impediments to Unity in New Nations—the Case of Ceylon," American Political Science Review, 55:2, 1961.

tion programs—because they threatened to alter population distribution and so communal representation in the parliament—all acted in a similarly provocative manner. Ceylon's aggravated primordial problem is not a mere legacy, an inherited impediment to her political, social, and economic modernization; it is a direct and immediate reflex of her first serious—if still rather ineffective—attempt to achieve such modernization.

And this dialectic, variously expressed, is a generic characteristic of new state politics. In Indonesia, the establishment of an indigenous unitary state made the fact that the thinly populated but mineral-rich Outer Islands produced the bulk of the country's foreign-exchange earnings, while densely populated, resource-poor Java consumed the bulk of its income, painfully apparent in a way it could never become in the colonial era, and a pattern of regional jealousy developed and hardened to the point of armed revolt.[11] In Ghana, hurt Ashanti pride burst into open separatism when, in order to accumulate development funds, Nkrumah's new national government fixed the cocoa price lower than what Ashanti cocoa growers wished it to be.[12] In Morocco, Riffian Berbers, offended when their substantial military contribution to the struggle for independence was not followed by greater governmental assistance in the form of schools, jobs, improved communications facilities, and so on, revived a classic pattern of tribal insolence—refusal to pay taxes, boycott of market places, retreat to a predatory mountain life—in order to gain Rabat's regard.[13] In Jordan, Abdullah's desperate attempt to strengthen his newly sovereign civil state through the annexation of Cis-Jordan, negotiation with Israel, and modernization of the army provoked his assassination by an ethnically humiliated pan-Arab Palestinian.[14] Even in those new states where such discontent has not progressed to the point of open dissidence, there has almost universally arisen around the developing struggle for governmental power as such a broad penumbra of primordial strife. Alongside of, and interacting with, the usual politics of party and parliament, cabinet and bureaucracy, or monarch and army, there exists, nearly everywhere, a sort of parapolitics of clashing public identities and quickening ethnocratic aspirations.

What is more, this parapolitical warfare seems to have its own characteristic battlegrounds; there are certain specific institutional contexts outside the customary arenas of political combat into which it has a strong inclination to settle. Though primordial issues do, of course, turn up from time to time in parliamentary debates, cabinet deliberations, judicial decisions and, more often, in electoral campaigns, they show a persistent tendency to emerge in purer, more explicit, and more virulent form in some places where other sorts of social issues do not ordinarily, or at

[11] H. Fieth, "Indonesia," in G. McT. Kahin (ed.), *Government and Politics of Southeast Asia*, Ithaca, N.Y., Cornell University Press, 1959, pp. 155–238; and G. McT. Kahin (ed.), *Major Government of Asia*, Ithaca, N.Y., Cornell University Press, 1958, pp. 471–592. This is not to say that the crystallization of regional enmities was the sole motivating force in the Padang rebellion, nor that the Java-Outer Islands contrast was the only axis of opposition. In all the quoted examples in this essay, the desire to be recognized as a responsible agent whose wishes, acts, hopes, and opinions matter is intertwined with the more familiar desires for wealth, power, prestige, and so on. Simple primordial determinism is no more defensible a position than economic determinism.

[12] D. Apter, *The Gold Coast in Transition*, Princeton, N.J., Princeton University Press, 1955, p. 68.

[13] W. Lewis, "Feuding and Social Change in Morocco," *Journal of Conflict Resolution*, 5:43–54, 1961.

[14] R. Nolte, "The Arab Solidarity Agreement," American University Field Staff Letter, Southwest Asia Series, 1957.

least so often or so acutely, appear. One of the most obvious of these is the school system. Linguistic conflicts, in particular, tend to emerge in the form of school crises—witness the fierce dispute between Malay and Chinese teachers' unions over the degree to which Malay should replace Chinese in Chinese schools in Malaya, the three-way guerrilla war between partisans of English, Hindi, and various local vernaculars as instruction media in India, or the bloody riots staged by Bengali-speaking university students to block the imposition of Urdu by West on East Pakistan. But religious issues, too, tend to penetrate educational contexts quite readily. In Moslem countries there is the enduring question of the reform of traditional Koranic schools toward Western forms; in the Philippines there is the clash between the American-introduced tradition of the secular public school and the intensified clerical effort to increase the teaching of religion in such schools; and in Madras there are the Dravidian separatists announcing sanctimoniously that "education must be free from political, religious or communal bias," by which they in fact mean that it "must not stress Hindu writings such as the epic Ramayana."[15] Even largely regional struggles tend to engulf the school system: in Indonesia the rise of provincial discontent was accompanied by a competitive multiplication of local institutions of higher learning to the point where, despite the extreme shortage of qualified instructors, there is now a faculty in nearly every major region of the country, monuments to past resentments and perhaps cradles for future ones; and a similar pattern may now be developing in Nigeria. If the general strike is the classical political expression of class

warfare, and the *coup d'état* of the struggle between militarism and parliamentarianism, then the school crisis is perhaps becoming the classical political—or parapolitical—expression of the clash of primordial loyalties.

There are a number of other poles around which parapolitical vortices tend to form, but so far as the literature is concerned they have been more noted in passing than analyzed in detail. Social statistics, for example. In Lebanon there has not been a census since 1932, for fear that taking one would reveal such changes in the religious composition of the population as to make the marvelously intricate political arrangements designed to balance sectarian interests unviable. In India, with its national language problem, just what constitutes a Hindi speaker has been a matter of some rather acrimonious dispute, because it depends upon the rules of counting: Hindi enthusiasts use census figures to prove that as many as a half of India's people speak "Hindi" (including Urdu and Punjabi), while anti-Hindiists force the figure down as low as 30 per cent by considering such matters as script differences, and evidently even religious affiliation of the speaker, as linguistically significant. Then, too, there is the closely related problem of what, in connection with the strange fact that according to the 1941 census of India there were 25 million tribal peoples but in the 1951 one only 1.7 million, Weiner has aptly called "genocide by census redefinition."[16] In Morocco, published figures for the percentage of the population that is Berber run all the way from 35 to 60 per cent, and some nationalist leaders

15 P. Talbot, "Raising a Cry for Secession," American University Field Staff Letter, South Asia Series, 1957.

16 M. Weiner, "Community Associations in Indian Politics," unpublished MS. The reverse process, "ethnogenesis by census redefinition," also occurs, as when in Libreville, the Gabon capital, Togolese and Dahomeans are lumped statistically into a new category, "the Popo," or in Northern Rhodesia copperbelt towns

would like to believe, or have others believe, that the Berbers are a French invention altogether.[17] Statistics, real or fancied, concerning the ethnic composition of the civil service are a favorite weapon of primordial demagogues virtually everywhere, being particularly effective where a number of local officials are members of a group other than the one they administrate. And in Indonesia a leading newspaper was banned, at the height of the regionalist crisis, for printing, in mock innocence, a simple bar graph depicting export earnings and government expenditure by province.

Dress (in Burma hundreds of frontier tribesmen brought to Rangoon for Union day to improve their patriotism are cannily sent home with gifts of Burmese clothing), historiography (in Nigeria a sudden proliferation of tendentious tribal histories threatens to strengthen the already very powerful centrifugal tendencies plaguing the country), and the official insignia of public authority (in Ceylon, Tamils have refused to use automobile license plates marked with Sinhala characters, and in South India they have painted over Hindi railroad signs) are other as yet but impressionistically observed spheres of parapolitical controversy.[18] So, also, is the rapidly expanding complex of tribal unions,

caste organizations, ethnic fraternities, regional associations, and religious sodalities that seems to be accompanying urbanization in virtually all the new states, and has made the major cities in some of them—Lagos, Beirut, Bombay, Medan—caldrons of communal tension.[19] But, details aside, the point is that there swirls around the emerging governmental institutions of the new states, and the specialized politics they tend to support, a whole host of self-reinforcing whirlpools of primordial discontent, and that this parapolitical maelstrom is in great part an outcome—to continue the metaphor, a backwash—of that process of political development itself. The growing capacity of the state to mobilize social resources for public ends, its expanding power, roils primordial sentiments because, given the doctrine that legitimate authority is but an extension of the inherent moral coerciveness such sentiments possess, to permit oneself to be ruled by men of other tribes, other races, or other religions is to submit not merely to oppression but to degradation—to exclusion from the moral community as a lesser order of being whose opinions, attitudes, wishes, and so on, simply do not fully count, as those of children, the simple-minded and the insane do not fully count in the eyes of those who regard themselves as mature, intelligent, and sane.

Though it can be moderated, this tension between primordial sentiments and civil politics probably cannot be entirely dissolved. The power of the "givens" of

---

Henga, Tonga, Tambuka, and so on, are "by common consent" grouped together as Nyasalanders, these manufactured groupings then taking on a real "ethnic" existence. I. Wallerstein, "Ethnicity and National Integration in West Africa," *Cahiers d'etudes africaines,* 3: 129–139 October, 1960.

[17] The 35 per cent figure can be found in N. Barbour (ed.), *A Survey of North West Africa,* New York, Oxford University Press, 1959, p. 79; the 60 per cent figure in D. Rustow, "The Politics of the Near East," in Almond and Coleman, *op. cit.,* pp. 369–453.

[18] On Burmese dress, see H. Tinker, *The Union of Burma,* New York, Oxford University Press, 1957, p. 184. On Nigerian tribal histories, see Coleman, *op. cit.,* pp. 327–328.

On Ceylonese license plates, see Wriggins, "Ceylon's Time of Troubles, 1956–8," *Far Eastern Survey,* 28: 33–38 (1959). On Hindi railroad signs, see Weiner, "Community Associations...," *op. cit.*

[19] For a general discussion of the role of voluntary associations in the urbanization process in modernizing societies, see Wallerstein, "The Emergence of Two West African Nations," *op. cit.,* pp. 144–230.

place, tongue, blood, looks, and way-of-life to shape an individual's notion of who, at bottom, he is and with whom, indissolubly, he belongs is rooted in the non-rational foundations of personality. And, once established, some degree of involvement of this unreflective sense of collective selfhood in the steadily broadening political process of the national state is certain, because that process seems to touch on such an extraordinarily wide range of matters. Thus, what the new states—or their leaders—must somehow contrive to do as far as primordial attachments are concerned is not, as they have so often tried to do, wish them out of existence by belittling them or even denying their reality, but domesticate them. They must reconcile them with the unfolding civil order by divesting them of their legitimizing force with respect to governmental authority, by neutralizing the apparatus of the state in relationship to them, and by channeling discontent arising out of their dislocation into properly political rather than parapolitical forms of expression. This goal, too, is not fully achievable or at least has never yet been achieved in Canada and Switzerland. But it is relatively so, and it is upon the possibility of such relative achievement that the hope of the new states to turn the attack upon their integrity and their legitimacy by unfettered primordial enthusiasms rests. As with industrialization, urbanization, restratification, and the various other social and cultural "revolutions" these states seem fated to undergo, the containment of diverse primordial communities under a single sovereignty promises to tax the political capacity of their peoples to its utmost limits—in some cases, no doubt, beyond them.

# ETHNICITY AND NATIONAL INTEGRATION IN WEST AFRICA

IMMANUEL WALLERSTEIN

Many writers on West Africa, whether academic or popular, assert that there is currently a conflict between tribalism and nationalism which threatens the stability of the new West African nations. In fact, the relationship between tribalism and nationalism is complex. Although ethnicity (tribalism) is in some

Reprinted from Immanuel Wallerstein, "Ethnicity and National Integration in West Africa," CAHIERS D'ETUDES AFRICAINES, No. 3 (October 1960), 129–38, by permission of the publisher and the author.

respects dysfunctional for national integration (a prime objective of nationalist movements), it is also in some respects functional. Discussion of the presumed conflict might be clarified by discussing this hypothesis in some detail. Before doing so, it should be noted that we deliberately use the term ethnicity in preference to tribalism, and we shall preface our remarks by carefully defining our use of the term ethnicity.

· · ·

Membership in an ethnic group is a

matter of social definition, an interplay of the self-definition of members and the definition of other groups. The ethnic group seems to need a minimum size to function effectively, and hence to achieve social definition.[1] Now it may be that an individual who defined himself as being of a certain tribe in a rural area can find no others from his village in the city. He may simply redefine himself as a member of a new and larger group.[2] This group would normally correspond to some logical geographical or linguistic unit, but it may never have existed as a social entity before this act.

Indeed, this kind of redefinition is quite common. Two actions give such redefinition permanence and status. One is official government sanction, in the form of census categories,[3] or the recognition of "town chiefs"; the other is the formation of ethnic (tribal) associations which are described more accurately by the French term, *association d'originaires*. These associations are the principal form of ethnic (tribal) "government"[4] in West African towns today.

Some of these ethnic associations use clearly territorial bases of defining membership, despite the fact that they may consider their relationship with traditional chiefs as their *raison d'être*. For example, in the Ivory Coast, Amon d'Aby has described the process as follows:

> L'un des phénomènes les plus curieux enregistrés en Côte d'Ivoire au lendemain de la Libération est la tendance très marquée des élites autochtones vers la création d'associations régionales. . . .
>
> Ces associations groupent tous les habitants d'un cercle ou de plusieurs cercles réunis. Leur objet est non plus le sport et les récréations de toutes sortes comme les groupements anodins d'avant-guerre, mais le progrès du territoire de leur ressort. Elles ont le but d'apporter la collaboration des jeunes générations instruites aux vieilles générations représentées par les chefs coutumiers accrochés aux conceptions périmés, à une politique surannée.[5]

It should be observed that the administrative units in question (les cercles) are the creation of the colonial government, and have no necessary relationship to traditional groupings. Such ethnic associations, formed around non-traditional administrative units, are found throughout West Africa.[6] A pre-

---

[1] Mercier observes: "Il faut noter également que, moins un groupe ethnique est numériquement important dans la ville, plus la simple parenté tend à jouer le rôle de liens de parenté plus proches." (P. Mercier, "Aspects de la société africaine dans l'agglomération dakaroise: groupes familiaux et unités de voisinage," p. 39, in P. Mercier *et al.*, "L'Agglomération Dakaroise," in *Études sénégalaises*, No. 5, 1954, p. 22.

[2] In Dakar, Mercier notes: "Un certain nombre de personnes qui étaient manifestement d'origine Lébou...se déclaraient cependant Wolof, preuve de la crise de l'ancien particularisme Lébou." (*Op. cit.*, p. 17.)

[3] For example, G. Lasserre writes: "L'habitude est prise à Libreville de recenser ensemble Togolais et Dahoméens sous l'appellation de 'Popo.'" (*Libreville*, Paris, Armand Colin, 1958, p. 207.)

Epstein notes a similar phenomenon in the Northern Rhodesian Copperbelt towns, where one of the major ethnic groups, sanctioned by custom and by census, the Nyasalanders. Nyasaland is a British-created territorial unit, but people from the Henga, Tonga, Tumbuka, and other tribes are by common consent grouped together as Nyasalanders. (A. L. Epstein, *Politics in an Urban African Community*, Manchester, Manchester University Press, 1958, p. 236.)

[4] By government we mean here the mechanism whereby the norms and goals of the group are defined. There may or may not be an effective formal structure to enforce these norms.

[5] F. Amon d'Aby, *La Côte d'Ivoire dans la cité africaine*, Paris, Larose, 1952, p. 36.

[6] Similar phenomena were reported in other areas undergoing rapid social change. Lewis reports the growth in Somalia of a "tribalism founded on territorial ties [in] place of clanship," at least among the southern groups (I. M. Lewis, "Modern Political Movements

sumably classic example of the significance of tribalism in West African affairs is the role which traditional
Yoruba-Ibo rivalry has played in
Nigerian politics. Yet, Dr. S. O. Biobaku
has pointed out that the very use of the
term "Yoruba" to refer to various peoples in Western Nigeria resulted largely
from the influence of the Anglican mission in Abeokuta in the nineteenth century. The standard "Yoruba" language
evolved by the mission was the new
unifying factor. Hodgkin remarks:

> Everyone recognizes that the notion
> of "being a Nigerian" is a new kind
> of conception. But it would seem that
> the notion of "being a Yoruba" is not
> very much older.[7]

Sometimes, the definition of the ethnic
group may even be said to derive from
a common occupation—indeed, even
dress—rather than from a common language or traditional polity. For example,
an Accra man often tends to designate
all men (or at least all merchants) coming from savannah areas as "Hausa-
men," although many are not Hausa, as
defined in traditional Hausa areas.[8]
Similarly, the Abidjan resident may

designate these same men as Dioula.[9]
Such designations may originate in
error, but many individuals from savannah areas take advantage of this confusion to merge themselves into this grouping. They go, for example to live in the
*Sabon Zongo* (the Hausa residential
area), and even often adopt Islam, to
aid the assimilation.[10] They do so because, scorned by the dominant ethnic
group of the town, they find security
within a relatively stronger group
(Hausa in Accra, Dioula in Abidjan,
Bambara in Thiès), with whom they feel
some broad cultural affinity. Indeed,
assimilation to this stronger group may
represent considerable advance in the
prestige-scale for the individual.[11]

Thus we see that ethnic groups are
defined in terms that are not necessarily
traditional but are rather a function of
the urban social situation. By ethnicity,
we mean the feeling of loyalty to this
new ethnic group of the towns. Epstein
has urged us to distinguish between two
senses of what he calls "tribalism": the
intratribal, which is the "persistence of,
or continued attachment to, tribal custom," and tribalism within the social

---

in Somaliland, I," in *Africa*, XXVIII, July,
1958, p. 259). In the South Pacific, Mead
observes: "Commentators on native life shook
their heads, remarking that these natives were
quite incapable of ever organizing beyond the
narrowest tribal borders, overlooking the fact
that terms like 'Solomons,' 'Sepiks' or
'Manus,'" when applied in Rabaul, blanketed
many tribal differences." (M. Mead, *New
Lives for Old*, New York, Morrow, 1956,
p. 79.)

The article by Max Gluckman, which appeared since this paper was delivered, makes
the same point for British Central Africa. Cf.
"Tribalism in British Central Africa," in
*Cahiers d'Etudes Africaines*, I, Jan. 1960, pp.
55-70.

[7] T. Hodgkin, "Letter to Dr. Biobaku," in
*Odù*, No. 4, 1957, p. 42.

[8] J. Rouch, "Migrations au Ghana," in
*Journal de la Société des Africanistes* XXVI,
No. I/2, 1956, p. 59.

[9] A. Kobben, "Le planteur noir," in *Études
éburneennes*, V, 1956, p. 154.

[10] The religious conversion is often very
temporary. N'Goma observes: "L'Islam résiste
mal à la transplantation des familles musul-
manes de la ville à la campagne. On a
remarqué que le citadin qui retourne à son
groupement d'origine revient souvent au culte
de la terre et des Esprits ancestraux." (A.
N'Goma, "L'Islam noir," in T. Monod, ed.,
*Le Monde noir* Présence africaine, No. 8–9,
p. 342.) The motive for the original conversion may in part explain this rapid reconver-
sion.

[11] G. Savonnet observes in Thiès, Sénégal:
"Le nom de Bambara est employé générale-
ment pour désigner le Soudanais (qu'il soit
Khassonké, Sarakollé, ou même Mossi). Ils
acceptent d'autant plus volontiers cette dé-
nomination que le Bambara (comme tout à
l'heure le Wolof) fait figure de race évoluée
par rapport à la leur propre." ("La Ville de
Thiès," in *Etudes sénégalaises*, No. 6, 1955,
p. 149.)

structure, which is the "persistence of loyalties and values, which stem from a particular form of social organization."[12] This corresponds to the distinction we made above between loyalty to tribal government and loyalty to the tribal community. In using the term ethnicity, we are referring to this latter kind of loyalty. This distinction cannot be rigid. Individuals in West Africa move back and forth between city and rural area. Different loyalties may be activated in different contexts. But more and more, with increasing urbanization, loyalty to the ethnic community is coming to supersede loyalty to the tribal community and government. It is the relationship of this new ethnic loyalty to the emergent nation-state that we intend to explore here.

There are four principal ways in which ethnicity serves to aid national integration. First, ethnic groups tend to assume some of the functions of the extended family and hence they diminish the importance of kinship roles; two, ethnic groups serve as a mechanism of resocialization; three, ethnic groups help keep the class structure fluid, and so prevent the emergence of castes; fourth, ethnic groups serve as an outlet for political tensions.

First, in a modern nation-state, loyalties to ethnic groups interfere less with national integration than loyalties to the extended family. It is obvious that particularistic loyalties run counter to the most efficient allocation of occupational and political roles in a state. Such particularistic loyalties cannot be entirely eliminated. Medium-sized groups based on such loyalties perform certain functions—of furnishing social and psychological security—which cannot yet in West Africa be performed either by the government or by the nuclear family. In the towns, the ethnic group is to some extent replacing the extended family in performing these functions.

The role of the ethnic group in providing food and shelter to the unemployed, marriage and burial expenses, assistance in locating a job has been widely noted.[13] West African governments are not yet in a position to offer a really effective network of such services, because of lack of resources and personnel. Yet if these services would not be provided, widespread social unrest could be expected.

It is perhaps even more important that ethnic associations counter the isolation and anomy that uprooted rural immigrants feel in the city. Thus Balandier has noted in Brazzaville the early emergence of ethnic associations tends to indicate a high degree of uprootedness among the ethnic group, which tends to be found particularly in small minorities.[14]

But from the point of view of national integration is the ethnic group really more functional than the extended family? In the sense that the ethnic group, by extending the extended family, dilutes it, the answer is yes. The ties are particularistic and diffuse, but less so and less strong than in the case of kinship groups. Furthermore, such a development provides a precedent for the principle of association on a non-kinship

[12] Epstein, op. cit., p. 231.

[13] Mercier notes: "Nombreux sont ceux qui, dans l'actuelle crise de chômage, ne peuvent se maintenir en ville que grâce à l'aide de leurs parents. Cela aboutit à une forme spontanée d'assurance contre le chômage." (Op. cit., p. 26.)
See also passim, K. A. Busia, Report on a Social Survey of Sekondi-Takoradi, Accra, Government Printer, 1950; I. Acquah, Accra Survey, London, University of London Press, 1958; O. Dollfus, "Conakry en 1951–1952. Etude humaine et économique," in Etudes guinéennes, X–XI, 1952, pp. 3–111; J. Lombard, "Cotonou, ville africaine," in Etudes dahoméennes, X, 1953.

[14] G. Balandier, Sociologie des Brazzavilles noires, Paris, Armand Colin, 1955, p. 122.

basis. It can be seen perhaps as a self-liquidating phase on the road to the emergence of the nuclear family.[15] Thus, it can be said with Parsons, that ethnic groups "constitute a focus of security beyond the family unit which is in some respects less dysfunctional for the society than community solidarity would be."[16]

The second function suggested was that of resocialization. The problem of instructing large numbers of persons in new normative patterns is a key one for nations undergoing rapid social change. There are few institutions which can perform this task. The formal educational system is limited in that it is a long-range process with small impact on the contemporary adult population. In addition, universal free education, though the objective of all West African governments at the present time, is not yet reality in any of these countries. The occupational system only touches a small proportion of the population, and a certain amount of resocialization is a prerequisite to entry into it. The government is limited in services as well as in access to the individuals involved (short of totalitarian measures). The family is in many ways a bulwark of resistance to change.

The ethnic groups, touching almost all the urban population, can then be said to be a major means of resocialization. They aid this process in three ways. The ethnic group offers the individual a wide network of persons, often of very varying skills and positions, who are under some obligation to retrain him and guide him in the ways of urban life.

By means of ethnic contacts, the individual is recruited into many non-ethnic nationalist groupings. Apter found evidence of this in Ghana, where he observed a remarkable number of classificatory brothers and other relatives working together in the same party, kinship thus providing a "reliable organizational core in the nationalist movement."[17] Birmingham and Jahoda similarly suggest the hypothesis that kinship (read, ethnic) links mediated Ghana political affiliation.[18]

And lastly, members of the ethnic group seek to raise the status of the whole group, which in turn makes it more possible for the individual members to have the mobility and social contact which will speed the process of resocialization.[19]

The third function is the maintenance of a fluid class system. There is in West Africa, as there has been historically in the United States, some correlation between ethnic groups and social class, particularly at the lower rungs of the social ladder. Certain occupations are often reserved for certain ethnic groups.[20] This occurs very obviously because of the use of ethnic ties to obtain jobs and learn skills.

It would seem then that ethnicity contributes to rigid stratification. But this view neglects the normative context. One

15 Forde suggests that "This multiplicity of association, which is characteristic of the Westernization procedure, is likely to preclude the functional persistence of tribal organisations as autonomous units in the economic or political sphere." (D. Forde, "The Conditions of Social Development in West Africa," Civilisations, III, No. 4, 1953, p. 485.)

16 T. Parsons, The Social System, New York, Free Press, 1951, p. 188.

17 D. Apter, The Gold Coast in Transition, Princeton, Princeton University Press, 1955, p. 127.

18 W. B. Birmingham and G. Jahoda, "A Pre-Election Survey in a Semi-Literate Society," in Public Opinion Quarterly, XIX, Summer, 1955, p. 152.

19 Glick explains the role of Chinese ethnic groups in Chinese assimilation into Hawaiian society in just these terms. (C. Glick, "The Relationship between Position and Status in the Assimilation of Chinese in Hawaii," in American Journal of Sociology, XLVII, September, 1952, pp. 667–679.)

20 P. Mercier, "Aspects des problèmes de stratification sociale dans l'Ouest Africain," in Cahiers internationaux de sociologie, XVII, 1954, pp. 47–55; Lombard, op. cit., pp. 57–59.

of the major values of contemporary West African nations is that of equality. Individuals may feel helpless to try to achieve this goal by their own efforts. Groups are less reticent, and as we mentioned before, its members usually seek to raise the status of the group. The continued expansion of the exchange economy means continued possibility of social mobility. As long as social mobility continues, this combination of belief in equality and the existence of ethnic groups striving to achieve it for themselves works to minimize any tendency towards caste-formation. This is crucial to obtain the allocation of roles within the occupational system on the basis of achievement, which is necessary for a modern economy. Thus, this is a self-reinforcing system wherein occupational mobility contributes to economic expansion, which contributes to urban migration, which contributes to the formation of ethnic associations and then to group upward mobility, which makes possible individual occupational mobility.

The fourth function we suggested was the ethnic groups serve as an outlet for political tensions. The process of creating a nation and legitimating new institutions gives rise to many tensions, especially when leaders cannot fulfill promises made. Gluckman's phrase, the "frailty in authority"[21] is particularly applicable for new nations not yet secure in the loyalty of their citizens. We observed before that ethnic groups offered social security because the government could not. Perhaps we might add that this arrangement would be desirable during a transitional period, even were it not necessary. If the state is involved in too large a proportion of the social action of the individual, it will be burdened by concentrated pressure and demands which it may not be able to meet. It may not yet have the underlying

diffuse confidence of the population it would need to survive the non-fulfillment of these demands.[22] It may therefore be of some benefit to divert expectations from the state to other social groups.

The existence of ethnic groups performing "an important scapegoat function as targets for displaced aggression"[23] may permit individuals to challenge persons rather than the authority of the office these persons occupy. Complaints about the nationalist party in power are transformed into complaints about the ethnic group or groups presumably in power. This is a common phenomenon of West African politics, and as Gluckman suggests:

> These rebellions, so far from destroying the established social order [read, new national governments] work so that they even support this order. They resolve the conflicts which the frailty in authority creates.[24]

Thus, in rejecting the men, they implicitly accept the system. Ethnic rivalries become rivalries for political power in a non-tribal setting.

The dysfunctional aspects of ethnicity for national integration are obvious. They are basically two. The first is that ethnic groups are still particularistic in their orientation and diffuse in their obligations, even if they are less so than the extended family. The ethnic roles are insufficiently segregated from the occupational and political roles because of the extensiveness of the ethnic group. Hence we have the resulting problems of nepotism and corruption.

The second problem, and one which worries African political leaders more, is separatism, which in various guises is

---

21 M. Gluckman, *Custom and Conflict in Africa*, Oxford, Basil Blackwell, 1955, ch. 2.

22 Unless, of course, it compensate for lack of legitimation by increase of force as a mechanism of social control, which is the method used in Communist countries.

23 Parsons, *op. cit.*, p. 188.

24 Gluckman, *op. cit.*, p. 28.

a pervasive tendency in West Africa today.[25] Separatist moves may arise out of a dispute between élite elements over the direction of change. Or they may result from the scarcity of resources which causes the "richer" region to wish to contract out of the nation (e.g., Ashanti in Ghana, the Western Region in Nigeria, the Ivory Coast in the ex-federation of French West Africa). In either case, but especially the latter, appeals to ethnic sentiment can be made the primary weapon of the separatists.

In assessing the seriousness of ethnicity as dysfunctional, we must remember that ethnic roles are not the only ones West Africans play. They are increasingly bound up in other institutional networks which cut across ethnic lines. Furthermore, the situation may vary according to the number and size of ethnic groupings. A multiplicity of small groups is less worrisome, as Coleman reminds us, than those situations where there is one large, culturally strong group.[26]

The most important mechanism to reduce the conflict between ethnicity and national integration is the nationalist party. Almost all of the West African countries have seen the emergence of a single party which has led the nationalist struggle, is now in power, and dominates the local political scene.[27]

[25] Separatism, of course, arises as a problem only after a concept of a nation is created and at least partially internalized by a large number of the citizens.

[26] J. S. Coleman, "The Character and Viability of African Political Systems," in W. Goldschmidt, ed., *The United States and Africa*, New York, The American Assembly, 1958, pp. 44–46.

[27] There is normally room for only one truly

In the struggle against colonial rule, these parties forged a unity of Africans as Africans. To the extent that the party structure is well articulated (as, say, in Guinea) and is effective, both in terms of large-scale program and patronage, the party does much to contain separatist tendencies.

Linguistic integration can also contribute, and here European languages are important. It is significant that one of the Ghana government's first steps after independence was to reduce the number of years in which primary schooling would be in the vernacular. Instruction in English now begins in the second year. We might mention, too, that Islam and Christianity both play a role in reducing centrifugal tendencies.

Lastly, there is the current attempt to endow pan-Africanism with the emotional aura of anti-colonialism, the attempt to make Unity as much a slogan as Independence. Even if the objective of unity is not realized, it serves as a counterweight to ethnic separatism that may be very effective.

Thus we see that ethnicity plays a complex role in the contemporary West African scene. It illustrates the more general function of intermediate groups intercalated between the individual and the state, long ago discussed by Durkheim. It points at the same time to the difficulties of maintaining both consensus and unity if these intermediate groups exist.

nationalist party in a new nation. Other parties in West African countries, when they exist, tend to be formed on more particularistic (ethnic, religious, regional) bases.

# THE RISE AND ROLE
# OF CHARISMATIC LEADERS

ANN RUTH WILLNER AND DOROTHY WILLNER

The term "charismatic leader" has recently attained widespread and almost debased[1] currency. In the past, it was occasionally applied to Gandhi, Lenin, Hitler, and Roosevelt. Now nearly every leader with marked popular appeal, especially those of new states, is indiscriminately tagged as charismatic. In the absence of clearcut specifications of traits of personality or behavior shared by the many and apparently diverse men[2] to whom charisma has been attributed and of any inventory of the common characteristics of the publics who have been susceptible to charismatic appeal, it is not surprising that scholars should question the meaning and utility of the concept of charismatic leadership.[3]

To avoid such indiscriminate and therefore meaningless use of the term, we should know what is or should be included in the category of charismatic leadership to distinguish it from other forms of leadership. Such knowledge might help us recognize whether the phenomenon—as distinct from the term —has really been particularly frequent in recent years. If it has, it is important to understand how and when charismatic leadership appears and what it can or cannot contribute to political change.

Max Weber adapted the term *charisma*[4] from the vocabulary of early Christianity to denote one of three types of authority in his now classic classification of authority on the basis of claims to legitimacy. He distinguished among (1) traditional authority, whose claim is based on "an established belief in the sanctity of immemorial traditions," (2) rational or legal authority, grounded on the belief in the legality of rules and in the right of those holding authoritative positions by virtue of those rules to issue commands, and (3) charismatic or

---

[1] When a recent book groups together as "charismatic statesmen" Sukarno, Abdul Rahman, Macapagal, Diem, Sihanouk, Captain Kong Le, General Ne Win and the King of Thailand, one wonders whether every leader who achieves any sort of prominence in Southeast Asia is automatically charismatic or whether Southeast Asia simply boasts a perpetually charismatic climate. See Willard A. Hanna, *Eight Nation Makers: Southeast Asia's Charismatic Statesmen* (New York: American Universities Field Staff, 1964).

[2] Peron, Nehru, Ben Gurion, Nkrumah, Magsaysay, Churchill, DeGaulle, Sukarno, Castro, Touré, Lumumba, Eisenhower, Kenyatta, Kennedy, and Khrushchev are just a few of the political leaders who have been called charismatic in recent years.

*Reprinted from Ann Ruth Willner and Dorothy Willner, "The Rise and Role of Charismatic Leaders," THE ANNALS OF THE AMERICAN ACADEMY OF POLITICAL AND SOCIAL SCIENCE, 358 (March 1965), 77–88, by permission of the Academy and the authors.*

[3] See K. J. Ratnam, "Charisma and Political Leadership," *Political Studies*, Vol. XII, No. 3 (October 1964), pp. 341–354 for one of the more cogent critiques of contemporary uses of the concept.

[4] The term is of Greek origin, meaning "gift," and was originally identified as a "gift of grace" or a divinely inspired calling to service, office or leadership.

personal authority, resting on "devotion to the specific sanctity, heroism, or exemplary character of an individual person, and of the normative pattern or order revealed by him."[5]

Of these types—and it must be emphasized that they are "ideal types" or abstractions—charismatic authority, according to Weber, differs from the other two in being unstable, even if recurrent, and tending to be transformed into one of the other two types.[6] While elements of charismatic authority may be present in all forms of leadership,[7] the predominantly charismatic leader is distinguished from other leaders by his capacity to inspire and sustain loyalty and devotion to him personally, apart from his office or status. He is regarded as possessing supernatural or extraordinary powers given to few to have. Whether in military prowess, religious zeal, therapeutic skill, heroism, or in some other dimension, he looms "larger than life." He is imbued with a sense of mission, felt as divinely inspired, which he communicates to his followers. He lives not as other men. Nor does he lead in ex-

pected ways by recognized rules. He breaks precedents and creates new ones and so is revolutionary. He seems to flourish in times of disturbance and distress.[8]

The somewhat misleading search for the source of charisma in the personalities of such leaders may have resulted from misreading of Weber's frequently cited definition of charisma as "a certain quality of an individual personality by which he *is set apart* from ordinary men and *treated as endowed* with supernatural, superhuman, or at least specifically exceptional powers or qualities."[9] For, as the words deliberately italicized here suggest and Weber repeatedly emphasized, it is not so much what the leader is but how he is regarded by those subject to his authority that is decisive for the validity of charisma. His charisma resides in the perceptions of the people he leads.

There are those who deny that the term can be properly applied to leaders whose "call" neither comes from God nor can be considered divinely inspired in the specifically religious sense. On the grounds that one ought not to class together the works of a Luther and a Hitler, they deplore Weber's extension of an originally Christian concept to include leaders who are seized with and communicate a darkly secular fervor.[10] As individuals, we can commend the motives of those who wish to distinguish on moral or esthetic grounds between men whose mission leads to Heaven and men whose mission leads to Hell. But as social scientists we must recognize that the empirical or earthly manifestation of inspired and inspiring leadership

[5] Max Weber, *The Theory of Social and Economic Organization*, ed. by Talcott Parsons (New York: Oxford University Press, 1947), p. 328.

[6] This notion of transformation or "routinization" has led to criticism that Weber uses the concept of charisma ambiguously, that is, on the one hand as a characteristic of certain classes of people in certain situations, on the other as a more general quality that can be transmitted to and identified with institutions such as the family and the office; see *Ibid.*, p. 75 and Carl J. Friedrich, "Political Leadership and the Problem of Charismatic Power," *The Journal of Politics*, 23 (February 1961), p. 13. Such criticism overlooks the possibility that *during the course of* charismatic leadership, a transfer can be effected of aspects of the belief induced by the leader toward another object, especially if designated by him.

[7] Authority is here defined as the sanctioned basis for the exercise of a leadership role, whereas leadership refers to the individual seen as capable of exercising the role for the situation in which direction is called for.

[8] Weber, *op. cit.*, pp. 358–362; also H. H. Gerth and C. Wright Mills, *From Max Weber: Essays in Sociology* (New York: Oxford University Press, 1946), pp. 245–250.

[9] Weber, *op. cit.*, p. 358.

[10] For a striking example of this point of view, see Friedrich, *op. cit.*, pp. 14–16, 19.

is one and the same whether in the service of good or evil.

We therefore can redefine charisma—without departing from Weber's intrinsic intention—as a leader's capacity to elicit from a following deference, devotion, and awe toward himself as the source of authority. A leader who can have this effect upon a group is charismatic for *that* group. An analysis of *how* leaders achieve such an effect of the means by which and the conditions under which this kind of loyalty is generated and maintained, might give us a better intellectual grasp of charismatic leadership.

It may be that systematic comparison of political leaders who have been regarded by their peoples as superhumanly inspired and inspiring would reveal certain traits common to all of them. Further systematic comparison of the societies where and the conditions under which such leaders have come to the fore might eventually take the concept of charismatic leadership out of the realm of speculation into that of empirically based social science. The lack of such systematic research since Weber familiarized us with the concept is somewhat surprising. In its absence we can offer no firmly based findings. We hope the following reflections may be relevant to such an investigation.

First we consider the conditions that appear to have been conducive to the rise of charismatic leadership in new states. Then we attempt to explain how the charismatic leader emerges and gains recognition. Finally, we try to assess the functions and significance of charismatic leadership for the kinds of changes which are customarily called "development."

## NEW STATES AND THE EMERGENCE OF CHARISMATIC LEADERSHIP

Weber gave little attention to the conditions under which charismatic leadership can emerge, merely mentioning times of psychic, physical, economic, ethical, religious, or political distress.[11] Since he defined this phenomenon as abnormal and intermittent—indeed he considered that the pure form of charismatic authority existed only at the time of origin[12]—he was more interested in its routinization. We attempt to expand Weber's treatment, and perhaps depart from it in some respects, by concentrating on what might be termed the other pole of the developmental continuum.

Charismatic leadership seems to flourish today particularly in the newer states that were formerly under colonial rule. Their very attainment of independence generally signified that the old order had broken down and the supports that sustained it had disappeared or were rapidly being weakened. We might more correctly distinguish two "old" orders in postcolonial countries: (1) the precolonial traditional system, many of whose elements survived during colonial rule and (2) the colonial system, a close approximation of Weber's rational-legal type, which was superimposed upon but did not completely efface the traditional system. Particularly under the "indirect rule" type of colonial regime, much of traditional belief and observance, political as well as socioeconomic, existed beneath the order imported from and imposed by the metropolitan country and in the more rural areas side-by-side with it.

The basis of traditional authority, however, was eroded by colonialism and indigenous nationalism, and the basis of legal authority was undermined by indigenous nationalism. Traditional authority, whether exercised through kingship and dominant caste, chieftainship and special lineage, or whichever of the many and varied institutions

11 Gerth and Mills, *op. cit.*, p. 245.
12 Weber, *op. cit.*, p. 364.

found in the many traditional societies, had been part of and based upon indigenous patterns of social organization, land tenure, economic activity, and other elements of a relatively integrated social system. Traditional social systems tended to disintegrate or be transformed under the impact of institutions imposed by the colonial power. Concomitantly, traditional prescriptions and procedures for the selection of rulers, for the control of conflict and the settlement of disputes, and for the maintenance of what had been considered appropriate relations between rulers and ruled were modified and in varying degrees displaced by colonial systems of authority. Even where colonial administrations supported or tolerated some maintenance of traditional authority, this was restricted to traditional contexts.

The attitude that traditional authority systems were inadequate to cope with the urban and industrial institutions introduced into colonies by Europeans was transmitted to and absorbed by the native elites educated in accordance with European standards and values and recruited into the colonial bureaucracies and business organizations. Nationalist intellectuals among the native elites also came to deprecate their own traditions, seeing them as weaknesses which had made colonialism possible and which were used by their colonial rulers to keep them in subjection.

We consider the typical colonial order to have been a fair approximation of the Weberian ideal type of legal-rational authority. For an administrative bureaucracy formulated and applied a system of rules, in accordance with what it considered rational criteria, relatively free from the constraints and controls of domestic political pressures. Problems ultimately arose, as they frequently do, when such rules are imposed upon people who cannot either participate in their making, or accept the norms on which they are based, or

successfully resist or modify their application.

In retrospect, it is clear why one of the major difficulties faced by leaders of successful national independence movements as they sought to establish their own governmental systems was the lack of respect for impersonal legal authority based on rational norms. For in successfully having discredited the colonial rulers and their works, they also unwittingly discredited the rule of law introduced by the colonial powers. However, the certainty of the traditional order had already been shattered during the colonial period. Thus there were no longer clear-cut and generally acceptable norms for the legitimacy of authority and the mode of its exercise. Their absence created the need for leadership that could serve as a bridge between the discredited past and the uncertain future. A climate of uncertainty and unpredictability is therefore a breeding ground for the emergence of charismatic leadership.

## SOURCES AND VALIDATION OF CHARISMA

Having indicated the conditions propitious for the emergence of charismatic leadership, we now describe how it comes into existence and what sustains it. To suggest, as we have, that when other bases for authority are discredited, charismatic leadership can arise by default is to state merely the necessary but not the sufficient conditions for its emergence. We need to know what the charismatic leader does to assert and impose his authority over those he presumes to lead and how he does it. Since his charisma has been defined as validated through the perceptions of a following, we are concerned with the process by which this validation occurs. We also wish to understand how some leaders, rather than others, can gain this validation.

The process, broadly stated, is one of

interaction between the leader and his followers. In the course of this interaction the leader transmits, and the followers accept, his presentation of himself as their predestined leader, his definitions of their world as it is and as it ought to be, and his conviction of his mission and their duty to reshape it. In actuality, the process is more complicated, involving several groups of followers and several stages of validation. There is the small group of the "elect" or "disciples," the initial elite whom the leader first inspires or who throw up from among themselves one who can inspire others. There is the public at large which, in turn, can be divided into those of predominantly traditional orientation and those oriented toward a newer order. In the societies with which we are concerned, further divisions may exist along ethnic, tribal, religious, regional, and linguistic lines. The point to be made is that the nationally significant charismatic leader can command the loyalty of all or most of these groups.

To understand how he can do so, it seems advisable to distinguish two levels on which his appeal is communicated and responded to. The first level is that of special grievance and special interest of each group; its significance is probably greatest during the stage in which the charismatic leader mobilizes the population in opposition to a prevailing order and in assertion of the possibility of a new order. In the situations of transition with which we deal, this stage is that of opposition to the rule of a colonial power.

Changes during the colonial period resulted in losses and uncertainties for many groups in the colonized population. Traditional agrarian land rights were interfered with, and unfamiliar forms of taxation were imposed on peasants. The monetary gains of those pushed or pulled out of their traditional agricultural, pastoral, or handicrafts oc-cupations to become plantation and industrial workers may have been more than offset by the problems of adapting to unfamiliar environments. Traditional merchants and traders often lost out to the competition of imported manufactures. Traditional ruling groups may have given outward obedience to colonial overlords who allowed them to retain their titles and some vestiges of their past powers, but often resented their loss of real power. Those who gained from the new opportunities generated by the colonial system—and there were many—chafed at the limits placed upon their continued advancement. Native embryonic capitalists could not easily compete on equal terms with European businesses backed by the facilities of the metropolitan country. Native officials of the governmental and business bureaucracies often felt themselves unfairly excluded from the high-level posts. The intellectuals, especially those who were trained at European universities, became bitter at the disparity between the expectations aroused by their education and the blocks that appeared in the way of maximizing this education. For all of these groups, the colonial system was or could be made to appear the cause of their grievance.

While the attraction exercised by the charismatic leader can, in part, be attributed to his ability to focus and channel diverse grievances and interests in a common appeal, unifying a segmented population in pursuit of a common goal, this explanation is insufficient to account for the acceptance of a given leader. Nor does it tell us how a leader maintains charisma in the conditions of uncertainty and fractionalization following the attainment of the goal of independence.

To turn to a deeper level, we suggest that the charisma of a leader is bound up with and, indeed, may even depend upon his becoming assimilated, in the thought and feelings of a populace, to its sacred figures, divine beings, or heroes. Their actions and the context of these actions, recounted in myth, express the fundamental values of a culture, including its basic categories for organizing experience and trying to resolve basic cultural and human dilemmas.

Of the overlapping and conflicting theories of myth to be found in the recent anthropological literature, all seem to agree in regarding myths as tales referring to events that took place in the past, usually a legendary past. However, as Lévi-Strauss points out, "what gives the myth an operational value is that the specific pattern [i.e., combination of elements] is timeless; it explains the present and the past as well as the future." Immediately following this statement is the comparison, significant for our purposes, "between myth and what appears to have largely replaced it in modern societies, namely politics." The comparison is really no more than a statement that the French Revolution, while a nonreversible sequence of past happenings, also constitutes for the French politician and his followers "a timeless pattern which can be detected in the contemporary French social structure and which provides a clue for its interpretation, a lead from which to infer future developments."[13]

We wish to suggest that recent events in a people's politics, particularly those marking a major transition or extraordinary occurrence in public life, can become endowed with the quality of myth if they fit or can be fitted into the pattern of a traditional myth or body of myths. Furthermore, insofar as myths can be regarded as charters for action, validating ritual and moral acts,[14] or, indeed, any culturally prescribed behavior, the assimilation of a historical event to the pattern of traditional myth or of a given individual to a mythic figure endows the event or individual with the aura or sanction of the myth itself.

The charismatic leader, we suggest, is able to communicate to his followers a sense of continuity between himself and his mission and their legendary heroes and their missions. Since "a myth remains the same as long as it felt as such,"[15] he and his claims are legitimated by his ability to draw on himself the mantle of myth. How a particular leader does this can be considered his strategy of "cultural management,"[16] in part conscious and deliberate, in part probably unconscious and intuitive.

The particular strategies of individual charismatic leaders are a subject for empirical investigation.[17] Elements of such strategies might be broken down into such categories as: rhetoric employed in speeches, including rhythm;[18] use of simile and metaphor and allu-

---

13 Claude Lévi-Strauss, "The Structural Study of Myth," *The Journal of American Folklore*, Vol. 68 (October–December 1955), p. 430.

14 Bronislaw Malinowski, "Myth in Primi-

tive Psychology," *Magic, Science and Religion* (Boston: Beacon Press, 1948), pp. 96–108.

15 Lévi-Strauss, *op. cit.*, p. 435.

16 See Lloyd A. Fallers, "Ideology and Culture in Uganda Nationalism," *American Anthropology*, Vol. 63 (August 1961), pp. 677–678 and McKim Marriott, "Cultural Policy in New States," in Clifford Geertz, ed., *Old Societies and New States* (New York, 1963), p. 29.

17 We deliberately refrain from giving concrete examples of strategies here; for, as is suggested below, to make meaningful the illustration of even a single strategy of a single leader would require an elaboration of the myths and values of his culture which lack of space prohibits.

18 For example, it might be worth examining the frequency of Biblical allusions in the speeches of FDR, such as the reference in his first inaugural address to driving the money-changers out of the temple, and the extent to which his rhetoric parallelled the cadences of the St. James Bible. Similarly, it would be interesting to compare the rhythmic patterns of the speeches of Nkrumah and other African leaders with the predominant drum and dance rhythms of their societies.

sions to myth and history; use of gesture and movement; employment of ritual and ceremony; manner of dealing with felt doubt and opposition; and mode of handling crises. While this list can be refined and extended, it suggests some of the categories in terms of which the charismatic appeal of leaders can be analyzed.

It should be stressed that the elements of behavior indicated by such categories vary from culture to culture. This, of course, would be true of the behavior of any leader, charismatic or not, who seeks to mobilize popular support. Specific to the charismatic leader, according to our theory, is the role of myth in validating his authority. His appeal, therefore, can best be understood by reference to the body of myth in a given culture that his strategy taps and manipulates, and the actions and values associated with and sanctioned by these myths.[19] In brief, the charismatic leader is charismatic because, in the breakdown of other means of legitimizing authority, he is able to evoke and associate with himself the sacred symbols of his culture.

It follows that the charismatic appeal of a leader is, by definition, limited to those who share the traditions of a given culture, that is, to those who understand and respond to the symbols expressed in the myths a charismatic leader evokes.[20] It further follows that the attributes of the charismatic leader will vary from society to society.[21] Concomi-

tantly, within any society, the charismatic appeal of competing leaders will depend on their relative strength in evoking myths with the broadest common appeal, and in maintaining the association of themselves and their actions with mythical figures and their actions.

We do not, however, suggest or wish to imply that a charismatic leader either achieves power or retains it on the basis of charisma alone. Charismatic appeal provides the source of and legitimates his authority. Other supports may be needed and are frequently employed to gain and maintain power, especially when charismatic appeal begins to decline.[22]

CHARISMATIC LEADERSHIP AND
THE DILEMMAS OF DEVELOPMENT

As we have earlier indicated, the mission of the charismatic leader in the societies with which we deal is two-fold, incorporating two distinct, although somewhat overlapping,[23] stages. The first is the destruction of the old order; the second, which might be termed "political development," is the building of the promised new and better order.

Political development, whether considered as a goal or as a process, can be viewed in the context of new countries as encompassing two distinct goals or processes. One is that of achieving and maintaining an autonomous and viable

---

[19] See Malinowski, *op. cit.*

[20] We cannot here examine the means by which the binding force of mythology is maintained and transmitted, although obviously involved are the socialization and educational practices obtaining in a society.

[21] Precisely because of this cultural variation, criticisms by Ratnam, *op. cit.*, and others of the concept of charismatic leadership on the basis that clear statements of the personality qualities of charismatic leaders do not exist are neither relevant nor tenable.

[22] As David Apter points out in *Ghana in Transition* (New York: Atheneum, 1963), pp. 328–29, charisma can decline in favor of secular authority or, as he found in Ghana, as a result of conflict with traditional authority.

[23] These stages may overlap in several ways. The formation of a political unit that can gain external recognition can take place while the struggle against the old order continues. For some leaders, such as those of Indonesia and the United Arab Republic, the old order is not extinct, despite political independence, as long as former rulers retain ownership or control of important segments of the new country's economy.

state or political community that can be recognized as such by, and participate with, other states in the international political community. The second is that of gaining and maintaining central government capacity to manage technological modernization and cope with its socioeconomic concomitants.[24]

These goals or processes are not necessarily synonymous or complementary, as is often assumed. While they may be interrelated and interdependent in some respects, they can be antipathetic and incompatible in others. What appear to be rational policies pursued in support of one goal may only serve to inhibit or prevent the attainment of the other.

Many new countries cannot begin either form of development at the point where their predecessors left off. In the first place, they start with less internal cohesion than existed in the same territories under colonial control or during nationalist mobilization against it. The very tactics of nationalist mobilization confront the new governments with new sets of expectations and conditions, limiting the alternatives open to it.

As recent Asian and African history has demonstrated, the preindependence solidarity forged in the common struggle of diverse groups against their common ruler does not long survive the departure of that ruler. The vision of a single nation submerged under colonial control fades before the reality of competitive subsocieties, each of which tends to view independence as

a mandate to reassert its traditional heritage and strengthen its claims against those of other groups.

No longer can the conflicting interests and ambitions of different ethnic groups and, cross-cutting these, the different economic segments of the population be merged in the single overriding goal of freedom. Now they are couched in the concrete terms of more land and lower taxes for peasants, higher wages for workers, subsidies for small businessmen, boosts in status and salary for bureaucrats, or whatever particular benefits people had sought or been led to expect as the immediate and inevitable fruits of successful anticolonialism.

Moreover, nationalist leaders were committed to representative government, whether through personal conviction or because explicit adherence to democracy in its Western institutional forms was the implicit condition of American support for their cause. Soon new parliaments, parties, unions, and associations provide new forums to articulate expectations and arouse new aspirations.[25] Rival contenders for ethnic, regional, and national roles of intermediate political leadership press upon the central government the rival claims of those they lead.

But the already hard-pressed new governments have less capacity to provide even the expected services than had their colonial counterparts. This is not merely a matter of limited financial

[24] We use technological modernization rather than a more inclusive concept of modernization, not only because technological advance is the core of other forms, but because there are universally accepted and nonethnocentric criteria to define and measure technological change. This leaves open the types of social, economic, and cultural systems which are or can be compatible with the development of a modern technology.

[25] In place of the conventional concept of demand, we prefer to distinguish between expectation and aspiration which are differently derived and have different potential for violence when frustrated. Expectations constitute claims made on the basis of prevailing norms whose satisfaction is felt as owed by right; aspirations are hopes of future gains not previously enjoyed which are seen as desirable but not necessarily due one. Whereas unrealized aspirations result in disappointment, frustrated expectations produce an often intolerable sense of deprivation.

resources or unanticipated needs to re-habilitate refugees and reconstruct installations destroyed by military action. The replacement of skilled administrators and technicians by less trained or unskilled ones, especially where nationalist zeal and political reliability are the major criteria of appointment,[26] means that preindependence norms of governmental performance are difficult to restore, much less improve upon to meet the new aspirations. In this respect, India perhaps suffered least and the Congo most.

At almost any stage of planning policies and programs or implementing them, dilemmas multiply and internal conflict increases. Basic dilemmas over how to allocate scarce resources as between long-run investment goals and short-run consumption requirements and between projects stimulating industrial growth and those needed to maintain levels of employment[27] are further complicated by struggles over the distribution of the available pie.[28] Satisfaction of one set of claims, even in terms of national developmental goals rather than particularistic ones, produces, at mini-mum, accusations of favoritism leveled against the central government and counter-claims from those feeling themselves disadvantaged. At maximum, it produces large-scale violence and even overt insurrection.

The charismatic leader can conceivably use his appeal to integrate the state and to create strong central government institutions to modernize the society, that is, to further development in both senses of the term as defined earlier. But the extent to which he can focus simultaneously on both will depend on the particular conditions and resistances in his society.[29] In circumstances of acute subgroup competition, many national modernization goals weaken or tend to be shelved. Of necessity, the leader concentrates his charisma on holding together a potentially fragmenting country. Priority is given to maintaining and unifying the state or gaining some semblance of solidarity whatever the cost.

In a society fissioned by parochial identifications and particularistic goals, the charismatic leader may be the single symbol of unity surmounting the diversity and the primary means of creating consensus on objectives. To the many who need some tangible referent for a loyalty still somewhat beyond their comprehension, he is the visible embodiment of the nation come into being. And to those confused by the loosening of familiar ties and the profusion of new groups and activities claiming their attention, he provides the reassurance that links them with the old and sanctions the new.

Of the many devices used by charismatic leaders to create cohesion, only a few can be briefly mentioned here. Analogous to the process earlier men-

---

[26] The provision of government jobs to the disciplines and their followers may be seen as booty distribution, noted by Weber as one of the means of support of charismatic leaders.

[27] For fuller treatment of this and preceding points, see B. F. Hoselitz and A. R. Willner, "Economic Development, Political Strategies, and American Aid," in M. A. Kaplan, *The Revolution in World Politics* (New York: John Wiley & Sons, 1963), pp. 357–71.

[28] Even the implementation of a universal goal, such as education, can provoke dissent and conflict. The advantages of a single language of instruction that will also serve as a unifying force has often been countered by demands for education in the local languages. The very groups who have requested vernacular schools, after gaining their objectives, may often exhibit resentment when their members do not easily have access to posts and occupations that demand fluency in the dominant national language.

[29] This has been far more possible in India, Israel, and the United Arab Republic than in Indonesia or Ghana.

tioned in which the leader is clothed in the mantle of myth, he seeks to endow the state with a quasi-mythology.[30] To link together both those of predominantly modern orientations and those of traditionalist leanings, the quasi-myths, whether expressed in ideology and ritual or utilized by organizations, are synthetic or syncretic blends of the indigenous and the imported. Reinterpretations of socialism and democracy are yolked to traditional institutions often resurrected from a romanticized past.[31]

The charismatic leader can be seen as a double-visaged Janus, projecting himself on the one hand as the omniscient repository of ancient wisdom and on the other as the new man of the people, not only leading them toward, but sharing with them, the trials of revolutionary renewal.[32] Similarly, the increasingly politicized organizational life that is promoted when the charismatic leader seeks to conserve his charisma[33] and subdue factionalism under the umbrella of the single-party regime[34] serves a double function. The

sense of community is restored in partly traditional terms but embracing far more inclusive membership units than previously. And joint participation in regime-sponsored organizational activities, even if partially or originally coerced, can create a sense of solidarity among people who work together, a sense of identification with similar goals —even when originally imposed upon them rather than generated by them— and a sense of accomplishment that gives some meaning to their hardships.

Of major significance in the creation of a national identity can be the use by the charismatic leader of the international stage. Part of the sense of self derives from the measurement of self against others and much of the feeling of strength comes from the awareness of one's impact on others. The presence and prominence of their leaders in distant capitals and exerting obvious influence on international conferences, spelled out to their peoples through all the media of mass communication, give the latter a sense of national identity and pride.

There is another way in which charismatic leaders tend to have an impact on the international stage which often annoys and outrages the leaders and peoples of more established countries. This is the constant raising of such issues as cryptocolonialism, "disguised" imperialism, and perceived foreign "interference." These may strike outside observers as unwarranted and dangerous shadow battles. But they, too, serve the function of maintaining internal cohesion. The sacrifices demanded of the disciples and the populace in the preindependence period could be dramatized in terms of the ordeals that the mythic hero and his followers must undergo to overcome their visible colonial enemy. But inadequate social overhead, budget deficits, poor planning, scarcity of skills, and the like are diffi-

[30] We use the term "quasi-mythology" here to distinguish the attempts to create new myths and symbols from the genuine body of myth in the society. It is, of course, possible that some of these quasi-myths will over time become incorporated into the culture and form part of the deeply embedded reservoir of myth.

[31] Sukarno's "gotong-rojong" parliament is an excellent example of this.

[32] This double-projection is frequent in the speeches of Sukarno and can also be found in some of Nasser's statements.

[33] Paradoxically, the charisma of the leader often seems to be both diffused and dispersed in the structures he sets up yet rechannelled and returned in his direction. This may be the consequence of his role as founder and final arbiter.

[34] Apter's imaginative designation of the basis of such regimes as "political religion" is a compelling metaphor but perhaps somewhat overextended. See David Apter, "Political Religion in the New Nations," *Old Societies and New States, op. cit.*, pp. 57–104.

cult to dramatize in concrete and meaningful terms as explanations of the delay of the anticipated millennium. And so symbolic enemies must be created to serve as the scapegoat for the continued frustrations of the people.

While charismatic leadership may contribute in many ways to the consolidation of the state, its exercise may also delay the kind of institutionalization and continuity of authority needed for concrete tasks of development. The charismatic leader may become trapped by his own symbols and substitute symbolic action as ends instead of means. Viewing himself as the indispensable prop of his country's existence and the only one in whose hands its destiny can be trusted, he may treat constructive criticism as treason. Those surrounding him may do little more than echo him and vie for his favor while awaiting his demise and hoping for the mantle to descend on themselves. Charismatic leadership does not provide for orderly succession. In its absence the crisis of succession may undo much that was built up and conserved.

Admittedly, it is difficult for outsiders to determine which of the choices made or the directions taken by any particular charismatic leader are the product of inexorable necessity and which result from expediency or concern with self over nation. From the vantage point of membership in states whose political systems are relatively intact and integrated, it is easy to look askance at the frequent extremism of these men. Yet the historian of the future may well conclude that the charismatic leader of today provided the basic foundations on which their countries may achieve tomorrow's development.

# B. Tradition and Change

# TRADITIONAL AND MODERN STYLES OF LEADERSHIP: NORTHERN NIGERIA

C. S. WHITAKER, JR.

This paper has two principal objects: 1) to show that on a central issue of speculative political thought, namely the proper basis and structure of political

Reprinted from C. S. Whitaker, Jr., "Three Perspectives on Hierarchy: Political Thought and Leadership in Northern Nigeria," JOURNAL OF COMMONWEALTH POLITICAL STUDIES, 3. (March 1965), 1–19, by permission of Leicester University Press and the author.

participation, the three leading Northern Nigerian political figures take three different positions, each compatible with the practice of government within a democratic framework; 2) to contend that the ideological differences between these men may be explained, in part at least, by the fact that each occupies a different position within a common traditional political culture, the structure of which is hierarchical. The contention, in other words, is that the decisive influence on each man's view of the desirable structural implications of a modern democratic political system has been his particular relationship to, and experience of, a certain kind of traditionally stratified policy. Implicitly this contention touches on a controversial theoretical issue concerning political behaviour which in this paper is not pursued as such: whether socio-cultural situations engender political ideologies.[1] It is hoped, however, that in this respect the paper will be suggestive and that it may in particular encourage consideration of the influence of traditional society on the contemporary political thinking of other African leaders.

The paper may incidentally shed light on certain political roles which might well befuddle the casual observer. Thus, the Northern Nigerian political leader who most conspiciously identifies himself with the cause of traditional rulers is also the person most responsible for certain measures patently contrary to their own true wishes and inclinations.

[1] According to Professor Gabriel Almond, 'political systems tend to perpetuate their structures through time, and...they do this mainly by means of the socializing influences of the primary and secondary structures through which they pass in the process of maturation...Political socialization is the process of induction into the political culture. Its end product is a set of attitudes—cognitions, value standards, and feelings—towards the political system, its various roles and role incumbents'. *The Politics of the Developing Areas*, (Princeton, 1960), 27. The concepts of political socialisation and political culture, which appear to bear resemblance to the concepts of 'national character' and perhaps also to the Marxian notion of a relationship between 'structure' and 'superstructure', are implicitly applicable in the context of this paper. It is not to be inferred, however, that the relationship of such general factors as these concepts point to in the case herein discussed is, in the view of the author, either inevitably decisive or universally operative.

In this curious championship this leader's most important ally is a man who at one time held an extremely disparaging opinion of the traditional system—in which his personal status is decidedly inferior. The office he now holds in Nigeria's modern scheme of government is in principle the paramount one; yet he has shown no inclination to use his power to undermine traditional authority. The third leader was a colleague of the other two for purposes of operating the coalition of political parties that governed Nigeria in its first five years of independence, notwithstanding the fact that professedly he absolutely rejects important traditional values which the others proclaim should be upheld.

The inference that such apparently anomalous roles merely represent the sacrifice of convictions to ambition, or, alternatively, the lack of any clear political conceptions in the first place, would be consistent with frequently encountered interpretations of leadership in African and other new independent states. The analysis in this paper should indicate, however, that either inference in this case would be inadequate to the reality involved. Specifically, it may help to explain, as such inferences do not, persistent interparty and intraparty cleavages in Northern Nigeria which to a large extent reflect the coherent views which separate these three leaders.

Alhaji Sir Ahmadu Bello, Sardauna of Sokoto (Sardauna, like Earl, is a traditional title), is the Premier of the Northern Region of the Federal Republic of Nigeria, and President-General of Nigeria's largest single party, the Northern People's Congress (NPC). The NPC forms both the Government of Northern Nigeria and, in coalition with the National Council of Nigerian Citizens (NCNC), that of the Federal Republic (this at the time of writing—just prior to the 1964 Federal election). Alhaji

Sir Abubakar Tafawa Balewa is the First Vice-President of the NPC and Prime Minister of the Federal Republic. Malam Aminu Kano is the Life-President of the Nigerian Elements Progressive Union (NEPU) which has bitterly opposed the NPC within the Northern Region, although it has been linked to it in the Federal Government by virtue of an alliance with the NCNC, in which Aminu Kano holds the office of Vice-President. All three are natives of the distinctive political culture area made up of the thirty-odd, mostly Hausa-Fulani peopled, states or emirates which together dominate Northern Nigeria in population and territory.

These emirates are traditional political entities whose salient common characteristics are hierarchical and quasi-theocratic authority, a high degree of social stratification, well-developed bureaucratic machinery, and, in several instances, extensive demographic scale. They have flourished in their present form since being conquered in a *jihad* or Islamic holy war led by a Fulani devout, Shehu Usman dan Fodio, early in the nineteenth century, although the characteristics of emirate government noted above antedate Fulani rule by centuries.[2]

The advantages of political organisation these traditional states offer were primarily responsible for their becoming the classic case of the British colonial policy of indirect rule or 'native administration' in Africa.[3] This policy

greatly contributed, in turn, to the survival of emirate political culture in the present era, with the result that it has profoundly influenced the course of the parliamentary system of government and politics which the British introduced into Nigeria before its independence,[4] the political outlooks of the three Northern leaders being not the least of that influence.

## II. FORMATIVE EXPERIENCES

### Alhaji Sir Ahmadu Bello

Ahmadu Bello might well have attained as eminent a position in a pristine traditional society as he occupies as Northern Premier. The pinnacle of traditional leadership in the emirate system— the Sultanship of Sokoto—is reserved to prominent descendants of dan Fodio, who founded the Sokoto (emirate) ruling dynasty along with the Fulani empire. Ahmadu's father, a District Head of Rabah, in Sokoto, was the son of the eighth Sokoto Sultan; the first Sultan, Muhaman Bello, son of dan Fodio, was Ahmadu's great-grandfather. He is otherwise well-connected on his maternal side, his grandmother being the daughter of the fourth Fulani Emir of Kano, most populous and wealthy of the emirates. (In *My Life*, Bello's autobiography, he asserts a claim, the merits of which need not detain us here, to descent, on both sides, from the Holy Prophet.[5])

Such a pedigree obviously justifies regarding Bello as an exemplification of leadership continuity in modern Africa. Merely to attribute his present station and views to a silver spoon, however, would do injustice both to the political

[2] See M. G. Smith, 'The Beginnings of Hausa Society: A.D. 1000–1500' in J. Vansina *et al.* (ed.), *The Historian in Tropical Africa*, (London, 1964), 339–54.
[3] For recent illuminating discussions of indirect rule and its architect in Northern Nigeria, see M. Perham, *Lugard: The Years of Authority*, 1898–1945, (London, 1960), 138–73; M. Bull 'Indirect Rule in Northern Nigeria, 1906–1911', in K. Robinson and F. Madden (ed.), *Essays in Imperial Government*, (Oxford, 1963), 47–87.

[4] The impact of the traditional emirate system of government and politics on the modern system is the subject of C. S. Whitaker, Jr., *The Politics of Tradition: A Study of Continuity and Change in Northern Nigeria, 1946–60 (PT)* (Unpublished Ph. D. thesis, Princeton University, 1964).
[5] Alhaji Sir Ahmadu Bello, *My Life*, (London, 1962), 239.

dynamics of a traditional emirate and to his pivotal role as at once modern politician and traditional ruler.

With no custom of primogeniture or any other rule determining a strict order of succession, the office of emirship (like many lesser ones in the state hierarchy) is in principle open to all male members of the royal dynasty—inevitably a large group, since the ruling stratum values maximum procreation of males, and practices both polygamy and concubinage. In practice, *isa*, the Hausa word for 'influence', in this context meaning wealth and followers to sway the kingmakers, determines success. The critical units in the competition are corporate groups rather than individuals, for the dynasty of each emirate is split for these purposes into one or more lineages (a few emirates also have multiple dynasties). The collective intensity, indeed, frequent bitterness, which characterises contests for a throne is partly attributable to the fact that customarily the victorious candidate is expected eventually to bestow state offices and titles on his kinsmen and clients, which often necessitates more or less arbitrary removal of incumbents associated with a rival lineage or dynasty.

The British outlawed the practice of forcible confiscation (*wasau*) of rivals' possessions, including offices, and they also threw into the balance of rivalry the criteria of western educational qualification and administrative competence. But the very logic of British policy, which involved upholding a certain discretionary power on the part of traditional rulers, precluded elimination of that ample measure of royal patronage around which the government of an emirate largely revolves to this day. Indeed, concerning the milieu of the typical native administration in the colonial phase, Bello himself has written: 'There was obviously a great deal of jealousy and intrigue—and I don't say

there isn't any now.'[6] He also acknowledges the impact of that milieu on his own career.[7]

Having completed primary school in Sokoto, the young Ahmadu earned distinction as a student at the famous Katsina College, the Northern secondary school the British had established with the explicit aim of equipping the emirate ruling class with western education. After graduating in 1931, he taught in the Sokoto Middle School for three years, resigning to succeed his deceased father as District Head of Rabah. The death of the Sultan in 1938 occasioned the usual struggle for the Sokoto throne, and Ahmadu, as a grandson of the eighth Sultan and by British standards one of the most promising District Heads, was one of several contestants. However, his first cousin, Abubakar, the present Sultan, won.

A common ancestor of Ahmadu and Abubakar was Muhamman Bello, whose descendants form a royal lineage group, called Bellawa. The Bellawa duly competed in 1938 with their main rivals, the Atikawa (descendants of the second Sultan). However, the energetic candidacies of the two Bellawa prospects reduced solidarity in that lineage. The new Sultan, perhaps as an outward show of reconciliation, awarded his own former title, Sardauna, to Ahmadu, who also became the first holder of that title to be appointed to the Sultan's traditional council of advisers. Simultaneously, the new Sardauna was given the novel assignment of supervising the eastern portion of the Emirate, from the important commercial town of Gusau. An interesting question is whether a premeditated motive of this assignment was to entangle the Sardauna in difficulties; the Sardauna's own account clearly implies as much.[8] Another ver-

[6] *Ibid.*, 102.
[7] *Ibid.*, 58–9.
[8] *Ibid.*

sion of the story, not necessarily in conflict with the first, is that the Sardauna's energetic and efficient administrative performance in Gusau was deemed a potential threat to the Sultan's own reputation and position. In any case, the undisputed facts are that he was tried and convicted in 1944, in the Sultan's Court, on a charge of having embezzled the *jangali* or cattle tax, with the collecting of which he was officially concerned at Gusau; yet on appeal to the British High Court he was completely exonerated. Subsequently he was reinstated as a Sultan's councillor (an office he still holds) in which capacity he is known to have served faithfully and indeed, it is said, with evident effort to cultivate the Sultan's goodwill.

The Sardauna's reaction to his ordeal seems a harbinger of his later political posture. Thus, appealing against the judgement of a judicial council of the Sultan was by customary standards an exceedingly unconventional act, more especially coming from a Sokoto subordinate official (the English translation of the Sultan's traditional title, *Sarkin Musulmi*, is 'Commander of the Faithful,' i.e. spiritual head of all the Muslims in Northern Nigeria). It was undoubtedly indicative of determined personal ambition, extending to a willingness to invoke secular authority against the highest sanctions of religion and tradition. On the other hand, the vicissitudes of traditional politics had nearly dealt the Sardauna's career a fatal blow. Similar experiences produced in other young aristocrats a disaffection with the traditional system, in some cases to the point, later on, of willingness to serve the cause of radical democratic change. The Sardauna's superior scholastic and administrative abilities set him apart from the ordinary princely title-holder. Yet, far from disaffection, his response to his experience (as suggested in his

seeking reconciliation with the Sultan) was in effect to reaffirm his belief in the fundamental legitimacy of the traditional order.

### Alhaji Sir Abubakar Tafawa Balewa

The Prime Minister of Nigeria's status in traditional terms is as humble as the Sardauna's is exalted. He was born in Bauchi Emirate in 1912, a son of Yakubu, whose minor traditional title (*Garkuwan Shamaki*—literally 'bodyguard' or 'keeper' of the horses) was at the time reserved strictly to members of slave lineages.[9] Unlike certain other slave-titles, that of his father, who was a menial of the *Ajiya* (traditional title of the usually Fulani District Heads of Lere), did not carry political power or authority. An apocryphal version that he was the District Head of *Ajiya*'s son has been published in several places in Nigeria and abroad (*Who's Who in Nigeria, West Africa, Time*, Ronald Segal's *Political Africa*, etc.). That Balewa has apparently seen fit to leave

[9] As a legal status, slavery in Northern Nigeria was abolished in principle by Lugard's Proclamation, 1 January 1900. However, the designation of individuals as slaves or descendants of slaves is a social usage which persists in Northern Nigeria, thanks in no small measure to the fact that Lugard's Proclamation in effect allowed those slaves who failed to apply for legal manumission to continue functioning as before. The progeny of such slaves were automatically free at birth before the law, but Hausa society has emphasised slave parentage, as reflected in use of the terms *dimajo* (pl. *dimajai*) or *bacucune* (*cucunawa*—used especially in Kano). Hence, as the author has witnessed, in Bauchi Emirate the Prime Minister is sometimes referred to in these terms. In and outside Bauchi, however, most people appear to be either ignorant of the facts of Balewa's background or anxious to conceal them, perhaps particularly from foreign researchers. For fuller discussion and interesting analysis of the Hausa institution of slavery and the British impact on it see M. G. Smith, *Government in Zazzau* (*GZ*) (London, 1960), 253 ff.; and 'Slavery and Emancipation in Two Societies (Jamaica and Zaria)', 3 *Social and Economic Studies* (1954), 239–88.

this error uncorrected may be taken as a sign of his society's profound preference for the person who retains his hereditary status over the 'self-made' man whom western societies applaud.[10]

Bauchi lore relates that Abubakar, like several other now prominent Northerners, owes his start in western secular education to the fact that the Muslim emirates' ruling classes, being in those days implacably hostile to that innovation, often contrived to placate the British by sending to school the sons of their retainers in place of their own. Whatever the true facts in Balewa's particular case, it is certain that few if any of his class were, at the time, knowingly recruited for the kind of education he received: first at Bauchi, then at Katsina College, where, like Bello, he confirmed an earlier scholastic promise. A career in education, probably the only suitable one readily available to him then, followed; he first taught in 1933 at Bauchi Middle School, of which he became Headmaster less than two years later.

In keeping with post-war British policies that opened up Government education departments to Africans and native administration (emir's) councils to commoners, Balewa was, successively, one of a handful of Northern Nigerians sent abroad in 1945 to study for a diploma (Institute of Education, London University) and then, after his return in 1946, the first traditionally non-eligible person ever appointed to the venerable institution of the Emir of Bauchi's Council. Instead of directly entering Government service, Balewa accepted the option of comparable rank and salary within the native administration education department.

Educated, highly articulate in English, and familiar with British customs,

Balewa was a natural choice to serve as the Bauchi Native Administration's nominee in the new Northern legislature (established initially with strictly advisory powers under the 1946 Constitution) and later to attend the series of consultative meetings that preceded promulgation of the 1951 Constitution. This instrument introduced a Northern Assembly (with legislative authority), to which Balewa was elected. That institution in turn offered Balewa a realm of leadership that transcended traditional society, in the form first of simultaneous membership in the Nigerian legislature at Lagos, then a federal (or central as it was then styled) ministry, and eventually the highest national office.

The central feature of Balewa's experience then is upward social mobility, thanks to modernity. He almost certainly would have remained fastened in obscurity were it not for the historical contingencies of western contact and Nigerian nationhood under parliamentary forms. A singularly low-born member of an emphatically ascriptive society that change has incorporated rather than displaced, Balewa's sociopolitical point of vantage is truly that of the 'new man.'

## Malam Aminu Kano

Aminu Kano was born into the Fulani clan of Kano Emirate called Genawa. In the structure of that state, the Genawa are prominent, even patrician, but they are not royalty or ordinary nobility. Rather they are renowned for pursuing the specialised Islamic vocations: jurists, priests, and scholars. Aminu Kano was reared in this tradition. His father, Malam Yusufu, was for a time Acting Chief *Alkali*, or Muslim judge, of Kano. His grandfather was Hassan Abdulaziz, a celebrated *malam* or religious scholar; his grandmother's reputation for religious learning earned her the respectful title, *Modibo*. Before Aminu was educated in western-type

[10] See M. G. Smith, 'The Hausa System of Social Status', 39 *Africa* (1959), 239–52.

schools, his mother, who was literate in Arabic and Hausa, a rare accomplishment among women of her generation, taught him to read and write and introduced him to Koranic study.

The peculiar aspects of this heritage would seem to furnish insight into Aminu Kano, the leader of a modern, radical democratic party. *Alkalai, malamai,* and *Limani* ('Imams' or 'priests') constitute the principal transmitters of the spiritual and moral values of Islamic society, and the *bona fide* interpreters of its laws. In theory 'Islam knows only one law, the divinely revealed *Shari'a,* which holds sway over political no less than over social, economic and cultural life.'[11] It follows that those officially concerned with its exposition and dissemination not only hold high and respected positions in orthodox Islamic communities like the emirates but they are also in principle the ultimate source of authoritative political judgement.

While in theory the *Shari'a* admits of no separation between temporal and spiritual authority, it of course does not prevent the emergence of purely *de facto* political power, nor guarantee that rulers' behaviour will conform to its prescriptions. If there is to be any legitimate criticism of the conduct of the state, obviously it must come from the Muslim clerics, scholars, and judges, who historically have been disposed to scrutinise, evaluate, and even censure the acts of rulers in the light of ideal prescriptions. Furthermore, they constitute persons to whom victims of oppression naturally look for redress of grievances, for 'apart from actual rebellion, extralegal recourse against (individual acts of) the government is had only through the protests and admonitions of the religious elite.'[12]

However, like their counterparts in medieval Christendom (e.g. Becket), these defenders of the faith lack both independent machinery to enforce their assessments and means of 'protecting against governmental reprisal.'[13] The result is a sociopolitical role which entails responsibility to a concept of higher law and its derivative standards of earthly justice and moral probity, but imposes severe limitations of action on those who assume the role. That such personal orientation towards traditional state authority tends to be either indignant hostility or abject resignation is only to be expected. The Kano Genawa, it is pertinent to note, customarily take pride in preferring service in independent or *Alkali* courts to subordinate membership of the Emir's Court, a custom nowadays not always individually honoured in the observance.

To be sure, influences other than those of the family were at work in Aminu Kano's earlier life: in particular western education (also partly at the Northern elite secondary school, which having been relocated at the Northern capital was accordingly renamed Kaduna College) and travel to England, where he was in touch with personalities on the left-wing of the Labour Party and exposed to the writings of Marx, Laski, and Gandhi. Surely it is not without significance, however, that his earliest modern political mentor was one Malam Sa'adu Zungur. Zungur, whose great-grandfather is said to have studied under dan Fodio, was himself a noted Koranic scholar and, by the time Aminu met him, the most outspoken Northern detractor of the system of native authority and indirect rule.

In an interview with the author Aminu Kano traced the roots of a deep

[11] E. I. J. Rosenthal, *Political Thought in Medieval Islam* (London, 1958), 23.

[12] G. E. Von Grunebaum, *Islam: Essays in the Nature and Growth of a Cultural Tradi-tion* (Memoir No. 81) 57 pt. 2, *American Anthropologist* (1955), 133–4.

[13] *Ibid.*

enmity between himself and the Kano Native Authority to the six months when his father was Acting Chief Alkali. He related that on several occasions his father found himself at variance with the throne on questions of justice. One such incident he cited as a turning point personally: a servant of the late Emir (Bayero) had fallen out of royal favour and was to be ejected from the palace. His father insisted that justice required compensation to the servant for labour and money spent on improving his house located within the palace walls. The Emir refused and there ensued a bitter dispute which eventually drew in the sons of the principal adversaries, Sanusi, then *Ciroma* (heir apparent) and later a powerful Emir of Kano, and Aminu. The incident illustrates the friction between traditional authority and the sort of ideals that engaged Aminu Kano's attention from his youth.

III. MODERN POLITICAL FOUNDATIONS

The three leaders' divergent backgrounds and future political views are reflected in the very manner and occasion of their entrance into the realm of modern politics. We have already noticed that Balewa began his political career in 1946 as a nominee of the Bauchi Native Authority (in effect the Emir of Bauchi) in a regional legislature then devoid of decision-making powers. In 1949 the Sokoto Sultan nominated the Sardauna to that same body in place of his deceased *Waziri* (Hausa corruption of 'vizier' or prime minister). Neither Balewa nor the Sardauna associated himself openly with any overtly political organisation until late 1951, when the provisions of the new Constitution induced the NPC to convert from a self-styled 'cultural society' to a political party. Elsewhere the point has been made that at this juncture the NPC virtually shed its original identity as a

forum essentially for western educated, reform minded, 'progressives' and became in essence a parliamentary caucus dominated by holders of traditional offices and titles in the emirates.[14]

This last development was in part a consequence of the 1951 constitutional provisions governing elections, which utilised various tiers of traditional councils as a chain of electoral colleges, and in effect helped emirs to control the results by authorising them to appoint 10 per cent of the membership of the highest level college. Modified systems of indirect election on this pattern were in force during the 1954 (federal) and 1956 (Northern regional) elections: direct voting and adult male suffrage being introduced for the first time in the federal ("independence") election of 1959.

The 1955 Annual Party Convention of the NPC, of which the Sardauna had in the meantime become President-General and Balewa First Vice-President, voted to freeze its roster of officers for five years. (In the event, by the end of 1963 no further election of party officers and only a few party conventions had actually been held.)

The sum significance for our purposes of the circumstances described in the last three paragraphs is that during the whole period of Northern Nigeria's advance to self-government (1959) the Sardauna and Tafawa Balewa operated independently of direct mass political support, and of any real popular accountability. In fact they were modern politicians only in the quite limited sense that they were parliamentarians. As such they were free to formulate their own political roles—within the limits set by virtual dependence on the political spon-

[14] R. L. Sklar and C. S. Whitaker, Jr., 'Nigeria', in J. S. Coleman and C. G. Rosberg (ed.), *Political Parties and National Integration in Tropical Africa* (Berkeley and Los Angeles, 1964), 607–9.

sorship of traditionally composed native authorities.

Leading NPC members of the period state that originally the favourite candidate for the Presidency-General among the pre-1951 or 'young Turk' wing of the party was Balewa, but that the party as a whole became persuaded that the Sardauna must occupy this office if the party was to enjoy the confidence of traditional rulers and their politically orthodox subjects. (Much the same line of reasoning was responsible for his selection by the British as the first Northern Minister for Local Government.) As head of the party commanding a majority in the regional legislature, the Sardauna later naturally assumed the post of Northern Premier. His attitude toward the forces mainly responsible for his position was summed up in an inimitable paraphrase of Churchill widely attributed to him: that he had not become Premier of the Northern Region in order to preside over the disintegration of his great-grandfather's empire. In a 1950 speech, otherwise famous for its incisive criticisms of the shortcomings of native administration, Balewa had already given some hint of his own inclination: 'I do not wish to destroy, I call for reform.'[15]

In contrast to the others, Aminu Kano did not occupy a seat in any Parliament before 1959. Along with Malam Sa'adu Zungur, he was forced out of the Executive Committee of the NPC in 1950 by the vote of a majority, who already by that date considered their radical slant inimical. To win support for his political programme, Aminu Kano was compelled to foster a mass political movement. An opportunity was presented in the form of the Northern Elements Progressive Union (NEPU), founded in August 1950; he joined and quickly thereafter assumed leadership. His newspaper article explaining the motive for this action, which entailed his resignation from a relatively secure position as a teacher in government service, made very plain the passions underlying his intention to employ NEPU as an uncompromising foe of traditionally constituted authority:

> I resigned because I refuse to believe that this country is by necessity a prisoner of the Anglo-Fulani autocracy or the unpopular indirect rule system.
>
> I resigned because there is no freedom to criticize this most unjust and anachronistic and un-Islamic form of hollow institutions promulgated by Lugard. I resigned because I fanatically share the view that the Native administrations, as they stand today, coupled with all their too trumpeted 'fine tradition,' are woefully hopeless in solving our urgent educational, social, economic, political, and even religious problems...
>
> I cannot tolerate these institutions because of their smell. I cannot tolerate them because they do not tolerate anyone. They even go to the extent of dooming the future of their critics. I am prepared to be called by any name. Call me a dreamer or call me a revolutionary, call me a crusader or anything you will. I have seen a light on the far horizon and I intend to march into its full circle either alone or with anyone who cares to go with me.[16]

To complete this background to contemporary Northern Nigerian political controversy it is important to observe the suddenness with which the traditional society was confronted with modern western institutions of government. Indirect rule had assisted the survival into the present era of an extraordinarily resilient system of political autocracy.

[15] Northern Nigeria, *R. C. Deb.*, 19.8.50, 4.

[16] 'My Resignation', *Daily Comet* (Kano), 11.11.50, 1 and 4.

It was not primarily ferment from within that system but British colonial policy —revised under the pressure of African nationalism elsewhere (notably in southern Nigeria and Ghana)—that led to the introduction of democratic forms in Northern Nigeria, for the British invariably made acceptance of these forms a precondition to the transfer of power. The same influence determined the pace and timing of change, with the outcome that virtually within seven years (1952–59) Northern Nigeria spanned the enormous distance separating European medieval political institutions from those of modern representational government.

The democratic apparatus was introduced at the regional level of government, which did not, however, supplant local traditional systems. In fact the framework of emirate government was retained for the express purpose of a gradual transition to democratic local government. Apart from this deliberate 'caution,' the mere superimposition of representational forms was in itself powerless to eradicate the substance of a people's political habits, expectations, beliefs, and values.

The net result has been to rule out explicit consideration, from first principles, as it were, of the merits of democratic institutions; doubtless a general desire to attract western investment capital further helps to obviate that issue still. Instead, the working ground of political contention in Northern Nigeria has been whether, or to what extent, those institutions are reconcilable with pre-established political norms, notably the traditional emirates' basis and structure of political participation. In essence, this has meant a dialogue, or rather trialogue, as we shall see, on the place, if any, of hierarchy in a putatively democratic society.

IV. THREE VIEWS

The Sardauna's roots and experience dispose him to be concerned primarily with values appropriate to the state as such, not particularly with those of the democratic variety. Thus, he is preoccupied with obedience, order, stability, and discipline; and these are key words in almost all his important speeches. 'Among the traditions we have inherited from our forefathers and which we intend to transmit to our descendants' he asserted in an address marking the attainment of Northern self-government, 'there is none we prize more highly than respect for lawful constituted authority.'[17] That the respect whereof he speaks has been inculcated by a century of rule under an autocratic regime based on conquest apparently represents in his eyes not the slightest debasement of its quality.

On the contrary, he takes enormous pride in the fact that the new democratic institutions of Northern Nigeria have so far derived their legitimacy and security from being linked, through himself and a considerable number of others in the new positions of power,[18] to the Sokoto Empire. Thus he deliberately chose March 15, the date of the fall of Sokoto to British troops in 1903, to celebrate the resumption, as it were, of Northern self-government. A year later he confirmed that 'to follow in the footsteps of my ancestors' was his ideal.[19]

However conspicuous is the element of sentiment in the Sardauna's visions of the past, it would be mistaken to conclude that these are devoid of political realism or resolved into indifference to

[17] *Northern Nigeria's Day of History: Speeches made by H. E. the Governor, Sir Gawain W. Bell and the Hon. Premier, Alhaji Sir Ahmadu Bello, on Sunday, 15th March, 1959* (NNDH) (Kaduna, 1959), 2.

[18] See Whitaker, *PT*, 389–90, which contains a tabulation, based on intensive interviews and surveys, showing that from 72 to 84 per cent of the emirate members of the Northern House of Assembly in 1959 belonged to the traditional ruling class. The corresponding figure for Northern Ministers is 17 out of 19.

[19] Northern Nigeria, *H. A. Deb.*, 16.4.60, 291.

modernity. He has repeatedly stressed the importance of social discipline in the task of economic development, which his government has in fact been pursuing seriously.[20] But many of the generally useful qualities for which he applauds ancient Fulani rule—the ability to command obedience, maintain order and stability, tax, administer, and even innovate[21]—plainly are also relevant to that task. Hence the Sardauna sees no good reason why the advantages of traditional hierarchy should be repudiated.

At the 1950 Ibadan Conference on the Nigerian Constitution, the fiery southern Nigerian nationalist, Mbonu Ojike, alluded to what he termed the universal decline of hereditary monarchy in this 'the century of the common man.' 'If my friend might live for centuries,' retorted the Sardauna coolly, 'he might still find natural rulers in the North.'[22] This remark, made in the context of negotiating the introduction of the democratic forms which, to the surprise of many observers, the Sardauna's regime increasingly welcomed, clearly did not mean espousal of the *status quo ante*. Evidently, what he meant to deny was that the right to choose representatives, or the injection of novel governmental functions, must require a wholly transformed structure of leadership.

In reckoning that a newly enfranchised people may affirm the supremacy of its established rulers—that it may cling to belief in an innate capacity to govern—the Sardauna does not, of course, lack the comfort of historical

precedent, that of the British being nearest to hand: 'I am told that this belief [in continuity] has helped other nations to greatness, God willing it will do so for us.'[23] With respect to the premise of Hausa-Fulani (and related) culture(s), which, as already indicated, evinces 'a general preference for social continuity and for stability in the status order,'[24] he is on equally solid ground. In a mood of African self-discovery and self-affirmation, he even enjoys the grudging admiration of some of his strongest ideological assailants, who take pride in the emirate phenomenon as evidence of African ability to sustain a complex society.

But the Sardauna does not appear content to rely indefinitely on such propitious reflexes, however essential they may be to his initial opportunity to shape the future, in regard to which he approvingly cites the Hausa proverb 'it is better to repair than to build afresh.'[25] Rather, he seems to envisage a regime of aristocratic composition which will, like himself, accept the conditions and restraints of a framework of modernising and democratic institutions, and within it *earn*, as it were, the right to go on ruling.

An integral part of this vision is the insistent encouragement he has given the ruling classes to ensure that their offspring acquire the qualifications and skills of modern leadership. A number of emirs and hereditary nobles have responded by continuing in the practice, initiated in colonial days, of sending their sons to English public schools. The Sardauna's grasp of the long-term political significance of western education also underlies the gratitude he has often expressed to the founders of Katsina College, graduates of which, he points out with pride, 'hold almost all the

---

[20] See Ministry of Trade and Industry, Northern Nigeria, *The Industrial Potentialities of Northern Nigeria* (Kaduna, 1963), 11–14.

[21] For an account of the incorporation of modern technical functions and departments of administration into the traditional bureaucracy during the colonial period see M. G. Smith, *GZ*, 230–4.

[22] *Proceedings of the General Conference on Review of the Nigerian Constitution*, January 1950 (Lagos, 1950), 142.

[23] *NNDH*, 6.

[24] M. G. Smith, 'The Hausa System of Social Status', *loc. cit.*, 248.

[25] *NNDH*, 6.

key positions in the administration of the Region today.'[26]

The same vision has also led him to censure the behaviour of emirs far more frequently and forcefully than might otherwise be expected. His government, he warned early in 1961, 'would not hesitate to remove any chief who is found guilty of oppression or of neglect of his duty.'[27] Two years later came the abdication, under threat of deposition for maladministration, of the most powerful recent Northern Emir, Sanusi of Kano.[28] Such utterances and actions have naturally gone a long way towards reconciling the 'young Turk' faction of the NPC to his stewardship. Seemingly lest he create the impression of having lost faith in the traditional order, however, in the legislative commons he has more recently returned to expressions that leave little room for doubting his basic stand:

> Now all of us here are butterflies, we come and go but the Emirs are there. I wonder if any of those people who think that we are trying to downgrade the Chiefs or make them rubber stamps, can be called as *Sarkin Musulmi* or the Sardauna. (Applause). I am a member of the royal family and it will be a great shame and down-fall for me to see that Chieftaincy is degraded and if that should happen in this Region, I pray to God to do away with my life.[29]

The allusion to a connection between his personal destiny and that of traditional authority is more than fanciful. Indeed, cultivation of the style of ancestral figures in his role as Premier is pronounced and calculated. His dress (exquisite gowns and brocaded cloaks, the high turban—tied behind with the flourish reserved by custom to princes) and his magisterial physical bearing are only part of this. Lavish gift-giving, annual pilgrimages to Mecca accompanied in his aircraft by favoured associates, evening meals taken in his private residence with a large permanent inner circle, regularly widened by more occasional attenders (the scene's resemblance to that of dan Fodio and disciples is compelling), all help to build the image.

Opportunities for more pointed references are seldom lost. Campaigning for the first time in Bauchi Emirate, in connection with the 1959 election, he gloried in the parallel that—with Tafawa Balewa acting as the Northern Premier's 'biggest lieutenant in the present day set-up of Nigeria'—the relationship between Sokoto and Bauchi was as it had been 'since the beginning of Fulani rule in the Region.' (Yakubu, first Bauchi Emir, was one of dan Fodio's early pupils and later a principal liegeman of the first Sokoto Sultan, Bello.)[30] When, at a post-election rally in Kaduna, the Sardauna announced a decision (since rescinded) to retire soon from politics, he compared this to dan Fodio's action in renouncing earthly power in favour of his son Bello and brother Abdullahi. 'When the current political battle is over,' he stated, 'I, too, will divide this country between two trustworthy lieutenants'; he then presented, in the manner of an emir conducting an investiture, an *alkyabba* (traditional cloak signifying bestowal of authority) to his 'lieutenant in the South,' Balewa.[31] The presentation of a horse to each of his ministers on the occasion of the first of a series of cabinet meetings at his Sokoto residence in January 1961 was in like vein.

[26] *Ibid.*, 2.
[27] *Daily Times* (Lagos), 30.1.61, 1.
[28] See the brief summation of the background to this case in B. J. Dudley, 'The Nomination of Parliamentary Candidates in Northern Nigeria', 2 *Journal of Commonwealth Political Studies* (1963), 58 (note 51).
[29] Northern Nigeria, *H. A. Deb.*, 9.9.63, 66.

[30] *Nigerian Citizen* (Zaria), 11.11.59, 16.
[31] *Ibid.*, 19.12.59, 1.

Thus by 1963 the Premiership had already in certain quarters acquired a pseudonym (*Sarkin Arewa*—Emir of the North), although the Sardauna's ultimate personal ambition remains in Northern Nigeria a matter of some speculation, complicated by his often reiterated desire eventually to become Sultan of Sokoto. An ambition to ascend to that still lofty office is obviously inconsistent with an intention to reduce its dignity or impair its integrity. Whatever the future course of the Sardauna's role, clearly it serves at present not just to acknowledge but to reinforce his society's acceptance of the premise of hierarchy.

Succinctly put, the Sardauna's conception of democratic development is steady improvement and widening popular acceptance of governmental performance without essential damage to the elite composition of those who govern. In contrast, Aminu Kano's profound wish is to see the present basis and structure of authority, leadership, and political participation transformed. His understanding of democracy extends to government 'by,' rather than just 'for' and 'of,' the people. Whereas the Sardauna propounds in effect a doctrine of hierarchy based on a supposed natural harmony of interests between rulers and the ruled, Aminu Kano subscribes to the view that social hierarchy inevitably embodies conflict of divergent social class interests. Democracy to him is therefore the antithesis of hierarchy. Its development connotes a levelling process, indeed provides a necessary channel for the ultimate resolution of class conflicts.[32]

Distaste for the lordly comportment of aristocracy led Aminu Kano, as long ago as 1944, to place an advertisement in the Northern vernacular newspaper, *Gaskiya Ta Fi Kwabo*, calling on commoners (*talakawa*) to abandon such traditional habits of deference as taking off their shoes and prostrating themselves in the presence of *sarakuna* (royalty, nobility, and indeed all holders of traditional title and office). In one of his first speeches as NEPU leader, he asserted, before an astonished audience at Sokoto, that for emirs to defer to the *talakawa* whose taxes paid emirs' salaries would be more appropriate than the other way round.[33] At his insistence NEPU petitioners to emirs' judicial and executive councils nowadays usually keep their feet shod, their backs erect, and withhold the traditionally prescribed praise-greetings (such as '*Zaki*' 'Lion' or '*Rankya dade*' 'May your life be prolonged') on the grounds that these gestures are offensive to human dignity.

One of the first and probably most successful of NEPU campaigns under Aminu Kano's leadership was directed against the practice of compulsory labour, for noncommunal purposes, that in the North survived the enactment of the Nigerian Labour Code. Until the recent (1960) enactment of a new Penal Code the Northern legal set-up, in which Native Authorities were in effect authorised to define and adjudicate native law and custom, protected these and other popularly detested official practices. Characteristically, Aminu Kano's response to such legal immunities to prosecution for maladministration was to try and inculcate in his followers respect for the doctrines of *satyagraha*, or non-violent civil disobedience as developed in India.[34] Although the principle of non-violence seems not to have penetrated, justifiable resort to action outside or even contrary to presently constituted authority represents an important if un-

---

[32] *NEPU/SAWABA Declaration of Principles* (Jos, 1950), articles 2 and 3.

[33] First-hand account of speech in possession of the author.

[34] *Daily Comet* (Kano), 2.10.51, 1.

publicised tenet of NEPU's political creed. At the same time Aminu Kano was a forceful advocate of legal limitations on government, such as prerogative writs (most of them were suspended between 1956 and 1959 in Northern courts), separation of judicial, legislative, and executive authority (they still coalesce in the Native Authority system,)[35] constitutional guarantees of civil liberties and due process of law. In keeping with the last principle, he was also closely identified with the successful movement to write the provisions of fundamental human rights, based on the UN Declaration, into the Nigerian Constitution. (The Sardauna not long ago expressed the view that the Fundamental Human Rights section of the Nigerian Constitution hinders 'dealing with subversive elements in an emergency' and ought accordingly to be amended.)[36]

The crux of Aminu Kano's outlook is its transcendence of received socio-political arrangements, however viable these may now be in the circumstances of Northern Nigeria. It appears to stem, rather, from an *a priori* conception of man, in a manner consistent with a habit of deducing political institutions from religious premises and pitting their ideal sanctions against an opposing reality. Whether Islam actually endorses Aminu Kano's central political values, as he in fact contends,[37] is less important in the present context than the intellectual and

moral *process* they reflect. His anti-hierarchical presuppositions apparently rest on a belief in universal perfectability—hence his abhorrence of a servile human posture. NEPU poems and songs, many of them written by Aminu Kano personally, are full of eschatological images, expressing his perception of a desperate plight of the masses (e.g. 'as skewered meat before the fire') and promising deliverance, a 'new day,' a basic re-ordering of the system of roles and rewards.[38]

While his party's programmes reflect the prevailing enthusiasm among contemporary African political leaders for economic development, his objective would appear to be an optimum point between material progress and active popular control; short of the ideal, might he in practice sacrifice a measure of the former goal for the sake of the latter? The possibility is suggested by the fact that, despite what has been called the African leader's belief in a divine right of the educated to lead, Aminu Kano has often said that the attraction of new leadership opportunities frequently leads the newer educated elite to compromise with political principle, hence to forfeiture of a claim to democratic leadership.[39] Ironically, this is a judgement to which his role in the

---

[35] *Native Authority Law*, 1954 (as amended) (Kaduna, n.d.), Part III and, for a discussion of its provisions, Whitaker, *PT*, 234 ff.

[36] Northern Nigeria, *H. A. Deb.*, 9.8.63, 46.

[37] A persistent theme in mass-rally political speeches of Aminu Kano and other NEPU religious 'specialists' is, in essence, that the modern ideals of political accountability and popular participation are implicit in the Islamic concept of *'ijma'* (consensus of the community in being) as a source of law and legitimacy. Interviews in Kano, Zaria, and Kaduna, May and October 1959; Tunis, January 1960; New York, November 1961; Kano and Kaduna, August 1963.

[38] The name of a NEPU ancillary organisation, inaugurated by Aminu Kano, is *Nujumu Zaman* ('start of a new day'); others include *Zaharal Haq* ('truth is revealed'), and *Tab'iunal Haq* ('the masses will rule those now ruling').

[39] The verse of one NEPU song-poem about the educated elite reads:

You through hankering for a salaried job
your attitude has made a volte-face,
so that continually you take the way of
    corruption.
On the day of resurrection, the day of
    settlement,
you will be cast into the fire.

Abba Maikwaru, 'The song: we recognize those who have wronged us', pamphlet (Kano, n.d.)

Federal government has made him personally vulnerable, whether or not the role was assumed in order to combat the national political isolation and financial debility of NEPU as an organisation, as he insists.[40] However, his refusal to join other former opposition leaders in support of the NPC, or in a moratorium on criticism of Northern political life, together with his recent leadership of NEPU into a Northern Progressive Front in active opposition to the NPC, all suggest persistence of a political vision, once concisely expressed by him in these words:

> We interpret democracy in its more traditional, radical sense, and that is the rule of the common people, the poor, the illiterate, while our opponents (the NPC) interpret it in its modern Tory sense, and that is the rule of the enlightened and prosperous minority in the supposed interest of the common people.[41]

Like the Sardauna, Balewa is highly conscious of the special requisites of leadership in a modernising state, and, like Aminu Kano, he clearly recognises the change in the scope of participation and source of political authority such a state may involve. Balewa's reaction to these matters differs, however, from that of either of the other two.

Thus, he assumes that in the long run new conditions will give rise to a new class whose attributes and self-interests do not coincide with those of even 'enlightened' traditional rulers. The assumption was articulated in a now famous speech, in the Northern legislature, calling for reforms in the system of native administration:

The Natural Rulers of the North should realise that Western education and world conditions are fast creating a new class of people in the North. That this new class must exist is certain, and the Natural Rulers, whom the North must retain at all costs, should instead of suspecting it, try to find it proper accommodation.[42]

As probably the most outstanding of this 'emergent' class, Balewa might have been expected to welcome the development even at the expense of 'Natural Rulers.' This and other speeches definitely show otherwise, however. To the remarks above, he added:

> I will personally prefer to see such changes coming first from the Natural Rulers rather than from the new class. Things are rapidly changing and much trouble and bitterness could be avoided if those in high positions of authority would keep their eyes open and agree to move with the times.

At the same time, his indictment, in the same speech, of a propensity on the part of native administration for 'putting square pegs in round holes' revealed a disbelief in the claims to inherent superiority made by the traditional class.

The clue to this speech and to Balewa's general outlook would appear to lie in his perception of a dilemma confronting him and others like him in developing societies. In brief, the dilemma is that, while a person like Balewa is aware that objectively his talents and skills are potentially beneficial to his society in terms of economic progress, he is also aware that the overwhelming majority of his society's people are illiterate, relatively isolated from the outside world, and otherwise in no position fully to appreciate his potential contribution, or even to share his aspirations for them. He understands, in other words, that democratic control of polit-

---

[40] Interview in Tunis, January 1960, Kaduna, August 1963.

[41] 'Presidential Address to the Fifth Annual Conference of the Northern Elements Progressive Union', quoted in R. L. Sklar, *Nigerian Political Parties: Power in an Emergent African Nation* (Princeton, 1963), 372.

[42] Northern Nigeria, *H. C. Deb.*, 19.8.50, 4.

ical recruitment under these circumstances may prejudice both the progress of his society and his own chance for leadership. In the case of western societies the dilemma was obviated, or at least alleviated, by the protracted extension of the franchise and other devices that delayed exercise of popular sovereignty. Balewa appears to have sensed that the suddenness of institutional change rendered far more vulnerable the position of the 'new class' in Northern Nigeria. The misgiving underlies his remarks concerning the initial proposal to install elected representatives as government ministers in the North:

> There are men, as I say, Mr. Chairman, who can shoulder these responsibilities, but do we all believe that it is those type of people whom I have in mind who will be given the opportunity of shouldering those responsibilities?[43]

Active participation and control on the part of the peasant masses of Hausaland might take one of two forms, equally deplorable from Balewa's point of view: acquiescence in autocracy and despotism, or the embrace of revolutionary programmes of change and of leaders productive of chaos. Thus, distrust of politicians and anxiety about the response of the masses are the two recurrent major themes in Balewa's reflections on the coming of democracy.[44] 'Even when Nigeria is ripe for responsible government' he argued 'leadership ...should not be granted through the medium of its people who are agitating.'[45] 'The few of us here,' he remarked on another occasion in the Legislature,

'represent millions of people, the majority of whom, apart from being illiterate, is still very incapable of understanding what we are doing.'[46] To the radical critics of traditional authority he demonstrated: 'Now let me warn them...that if they abuse authority, in the same way the people of whom they expect to be masters will abuse their authority in their time.'[47]

For these problems, Balewa's solution has been a partnership patterned on his personal history. Traditional rulers can use their hold on popular loyalties to elevate new men of talent to responsible positions of power. In return, traditional leaders may be reassured, as he has repeatedly insisted, that modern and traditional leadership need not be antagonistic.[48]

In contrast to the Sardauna, Balewa's commitment to traditional authority is essentially instrumental or pragmatic; the partnership between the new men of talent and the knights of traditional legitimacy might in due course be happily liquidated. In keeping with his experience, Balewa's conception of the proper basis and structure of authority in the modern state is in essence bureaucratic, or, to use a more current term, meritocratic. Indeed, it may be this element in his thinking, rather than personal taste for dead ideological centre, that makes him a disappointment to the Northern Nigerian far right and far left alike.

CONCLUSION

The three leaders' different perspectives on hierarchy might be traced in their attitudes on other currently unresolved controversies in Northern Nigeria, such as socialism, female suffrage, constitutional reform, pan-

---

[43] *Proceedings*, 1950, *loc. cit.*, 68; c.f. Nigeria, *L. C. Deb.*, 16.3.49, 47.

[44] Nigeria, *L. C. Deb.*, 24.3.47, 212; 21.8.48, 193; 16.3.49, 474; 30.3.49, 723–4; Northern Nigeria, *R. C. Deb.*, 21.1.47, 17–18; Northern Peoples' Congress, *Minutes: Emergency Convention*, 1953 (mimeographed, n.d.), 1.

[45] Nigeria, *L. C. Deb.*, 24.3.47, 212; c.f. Northern Nigeria, *H. A. Deb.*, 20.2.54, 242–4.

[46] Nigeria, *H. R. Deb.*, 20.3.52, 325.

[47] Nigeria, *L. C. Deb.*, 30.3.49, 724.

[48] Northern Nigeria, *R. C. Deb.*, 11.12.50, 105; see also note 44 above.

Africanism, foreign policy, and the implications of Islamic faith in the modern world. The analysis here of their positions on one central issue may at least suggest, however, their respective approaches to other matters.

The contention here has not been that the traditional culture alone has influenced them, nor that it has done so in mechanistic fashion. Islamic doctrine, western education, Katsina College, careers in teaching, European contact and travel, to mention only those factors alluded to above, are doubtless separable and important. It is worth observing, however, that each appears to have reacted selectively to this set of common experiences, seizing on different possible interpretations of it. Thus, Aminu Kano fastened on the egalitarian implications of Islam and was drawn to the more radical strains in English politics represented by Laski and the left wing of the Labour Party, while pre-democratic aspects of Islamic doctrine and English

society were perceived by Balewa and the Sardauna.[49] The essence of the argument is that traditional political culture has constituted for these leaders a special kind of 'cognitive map,' pointing each in a different direction of thought and action.

While the political thinking and behaviour of these men may have been oriented by the character of an indigenous African society, the substance of the issue discussed here is hardly unfamiliar to western societies. Without overstressing the parallel, one may, for instance, find in the predilections of the Sardauna, Balewa, and Aminu Kano clear echoes of Adams, Jefferson, and Tom Paine. Indeed, the current Northern Nigerian scene serves to remind that, far from resolving all important issues, the formal adoption of democratic institutions leaves open to choice some of the most basic political values and objectives.

[49] Upon the occasion of British Prime Minister Macmillan's visit to Northern Nigeria, just after the British and Nigerian Federal elections of 1959, the Sardauna remarked that 'the conservatives had won in England and the conservatives also won in Nigeria'. *Northern Nigeria Daily Press Service*, No. 87, 16.1.60. Most likely the Sardauna had in mind a parallel in socio-political history, not a comparison of party manifestoes!

# THE POLITICAL ROLE OF INDIA'S CASTE ASSOCIATIONS

LLOYD I. RUDOLPH AND SUSANNE HOEBER RUDOLPH

It is one of the paradoxes of Indian politics that India's *ancien régime*,

Reprinted from Lloyd I. Rudolph and Susanne Hoeber Rudolph, "The Political Role of India's Caste Associations," PACIFIC AFFAIRS, 33, No. 1 (1960), 5–22, by permission of the publisher.

surely one of the oldest and most deeply rooted in the world, produced no reaction. In three-fifths of India the nationalist middle classes which emerged out of the British colonial experience aimed not only at independence but also at the transformation of Indian society. The

Rebellion of 1857 is the only historical event in which the old order attempted to preserve itself, but its causes and objectives were so ambiguous that its meaning remains open to serious dispute even today. At Independence, the vestigial political expression of the *ancien régime*, the princely states, which covered two-fifths of India's territory, swiftly collapsed. This event was as much the result of the atrophied condition of the institutions and wills of the ruling order as of the skill with which the Indian Government (through Sardar Patel) managed the negotiations. Only a few minor local parties today stand for a full return to the rule of Brahmans and *Kshatryas** according to the precepts of *dharma* or traditional duty, and they are ineffectual.[1]

There is one perspective in which the absence of a reaction in the European sense is not surprising: within Hinduism, conflict (at the level of theology, philosophy and law) has generally been dealt with less by confrontation of adversaries, struggle and decision, than by compartmentalization, absorption or synthesis. And absorption appears likely to be the fate of the *ancien régime's* most central and durable institution—caste. Within the new context of political democracy, caste remains a central element of Indian society even while adapting itself to the values and methods of democratic politics. Indeed, it has become one of the chief means by which the Indian mass electorate has been attached to the processes of democratic politics.

The appeal of India's relatively weakly articulated voluntary associations is confined to the urban-educated who are more or less attuned to the modern political culture. Caste, however, provides channels of communication and bases of leadership and organization which enable those still submerged in the traditional society and culture to transcend the technical political illiteracy which would otherwise handicap their ability to participate in democratic politics. Caste has been able to perform this novel role by developing a new form for political activity, the caste association (*sabha* or *sangham*). Caste associations were already visible in the mid-nineteenth century. Over the last forty or fifty years, they have proliferated, their number and strength paralleling the growth of political literacy. After Independence, it became increasingly apparent that they would be a central feature of Indian politics for some time to come.

The political role and characteristics of the caste association resemble in many ways those of the voluntary association or interest-group familiar to European and American politics. On the other hand, the caste association is distinguishable in a number of important respects not only from the voluntary association but also from the natural association of caste out of which it has developed.

Membership in a caste is completely ascriptive: once born into a caste, a man has no way to change social identity insofar as the social structure and cultural norms recognize caste.[2] Caste norms prescribe the ritual, occupational, commensal, marital and social relationships of members, and caste organization

---

* Traditionally, these are the two highest castes, which provided the priests and scholars and the warriors and rulers.—Ed.

[1] Not even the *Jan Sangh*, strongest of the right-wing parties, espouses such a program. It is much more a rightist radical party than a traditionalist one.

[2] Alternative status systems which parallel that of caste are also visible in contemporary India. See for example S. C. Dube, *Indian Village*, London, 1956, pp. 161–6; see also our discussion of aspects of this problem in "Indian Political Studies and the Scope of Comparative Politics," *Far Eastern Survey* (XXVII) No. 9, September 1959, pp. 134–8.

and authority enforce these norms within the group and with other caste groups. Caste members are culturally and socially quite homogeneous since they share the same occupation, social status and ritual position.[3] This social homogeneity results in a sense of exclusiveness and identity which tends to subsume all social roles to that of caste membership. The unit of action and location of caste has been, until recently, the sub-caste in the village or group of villages. Traditionally, it has been concerned with settling problems at the village level, both internally and in relation to other castes. At most, its geographic spread took account of the reach of intra-caste (endogamous) marriages which often extended to other villages, but the village unit was crucial. Leaders were hereditary, generally the senior members of a specific lineage group. Social integration, the relationship of the caste to other castes, was governed by *dharma*, the sacred and traditional prescriptions of duty which permeate Hindu life. Finally, its organization was latent, embedded in habit and custom, rather than manifest and rationalized.

The emergence of caste associations seems to have been associated with the spread of communications and a market economy under British rule.[4] On the one hand, these forces undermined the hold of the traditional culture and society as it was organized in relatively autonomous local units; on the other hand, they created the conditions under which local sub-castes could be linked together in geographically extended associations. Caste associations, particularly those of lower castes, frequently undertook to upgrade the position of the caste in the social hierarchy. They pressed for the extension of privileges and rights to the caste either by turning to the state or by emulating the social or ritual behavior of higher castes. Thus, for example, in the South, where the caste culture has been conspicuously dominated by Brahmanical norms, the rising castes have emulated those norms by "sanskritizing" their caste practices; they have encouraged vegetarianism, abstention from liquor, the adoption of Brahman rituals, and the prevention of widow re-marriage.[5] Caste associations have often expedited and coordinated such emulative activities.[6]

[5] It may be that "sanskritization," while also practiced in the North, may offer less compelling emulation patterns there than in the South because of the strength of *Kshatrya* norms in many areas.

[6] The caste association has not been alone in this type of activity. More parochial village caste groups have also pursued emulation as a vehicle for improving status, sometimes successfully. See for example the progress of the Boad Distillers, in F. G. Bailey, *Caste and the Economic Frontier*, Manchester, 1957. But McKim Marriott has pointed out that any caste group operating in an intimate local setting, where relative status positions are well understood and jealously protected, might have trouble advancing itself by emulation: "A mere brandishing of Brahmanical symbols by a well-known village group can scarcely hope to impress a village audience in its own parochial terms...." See his "Interactional and Attributional Theories of Caste Ranking," *Man in India* (39), April–June, 1959. Conversely, the caste association, operating in the wider, more impersonal setting of a district or a state, may encounter less resistance to its emulative claims because in the wider setting there is no clear standard for assessing its "true" position.

[3] Occupational heterogeneity of castes is already well advanced, however, in towns and urban areas. The materials of the older caste ethnographers indicate that the breakdown of social and occupational homogeneity was apparent in the ninteenth century. Both Edgar Thurston, in his *Castes and Tribes of Southern India*, Madras, 1909, and William Crooke in his *The Tribes and Castes of the North West Provinces and Oudh*, Calcutta, 1896, bear this out.

[4] See M. N. Srinivas' articles bearing on the issues raised here: "A Note on Sanskritization and Westernization," *Far Eastern Quarterly* (XV), August 1956; "Caste in Modern India," *Journal of Asian Studies* (XVI), August 1957.

When the caste associations turned to the state for furthering their purposes, their initial claims were aimed at raising caste status in terms of the values and structure of the caste order. But as liberal and democratic ideas penetrated to wider sections of the population, the aims of the caste association began to shift accordingly. Instead of demanding temple entry and prestigious caste names and histories in the Census, the associations began to press for places in the new administrative and educational institutions and for political representation. Independence and the realization of political democracy intensified these new concerns. Caste associations attempted to have their members nominated for elective office, working through existing parties or forming their own; to maximize caste representation and influence in state cabinets and lesser governing bodies; and to use ministerial, legislative and administrative channels to press for action on caste objectives in the welfare, educational and economic realms. Perhaps the most significant aspect of the caste association in the contemporary era, however, is its capacity to organize the politically illiterate mass electorate, thus making possible in some measure the realization of its aspirations and educating large sections of it in the methods and values of political democracy.

The caste association is no longer a natural association in the sense in which caste was and is. It is beginning to take on features of the voluntary association. Membership in caste associations is *not* purely ascriptive; birth in the caste is a necessary but not a sufficient condition for membership. One must also "join" the (*Rajput*) *Kshatrya Mahasabha* or the (*Jat*) *Kisan Sabha* through some conscious act involving various degrees of identification—ranging from attendance at caste association meetings or voting for candidates supported by caste

association leaders, to paying membership dues. The caste association has generally both a potential and an actual membership; when it speaks, it often claims to speak for the potential represented in the full caste membership. While the purposes of caste are wide-ranging and diffuse, affecting every aspect of members' life paths, the caste association has come to specialize in politics. The traditional authority and functions of the sub-caste are declining, but the caste association's concern with politics and its rewards serves to sustain caste loyalty and identification.[7] This loyalty and sense of identification tend to retain the exclusive quality of the natural association; the caste association seems to have a more complete and intense command of its members' commitments than is usually the case with voluntary associations.

Since modern means of transportation and communication have had the effect of broadening caste, binding together local sub-castes which had been relatively autonomous into geographically extended associations, caste associations today usually parallel administrative and political units—states, districts, sub-districts and towns—whose offices and powers of legislation or decision-making are the object of the caste associations' efforts.

Leadership in the caste association is no longer in the hands of those qualified by heredity—the senior or more able members of the lineage group which traditionally supplied village sub-caste leadership. The "availability" of association leaders is conditioned by their ability to articulate and represent the purposes of the caste association, and

[7] For confirmation of these and other points, see also Selig Harrison, "Caste and the Andhra Communists," *American Political Science Review* (L), June 1956; M. L. P. Patterson, "Caste and Politics in Maharashtra," *Economic Weekly*, (VIII) 29, July 21, 1956.

for this purpose they must be literate in the ways of the new democratic politics. Men whose educational and occupational backgrounds assure these skills have moved into the leadership positions. The new leaders stand in a more "accountable" and responsible relationship to their followers; their position depends to a great extent on their capacity to represent and make good the association's claims.

Finally, at the organizational level, the caste association is moving away from the latent structure of caste, towards the manifest structure characteristic of the voluntary association. It has offices, membership, incipient bureaucratization, publications, and a quasi-legislative process expressed through conferences, delegates and resolutions. On the other hand, the shared sense of culture, character, and status tends to create a solidarity of a much higher order than is usually found among voluntary associations where the multiplicity of social roles and the plurality of interests of its members tend to dilute the intensity of commitment and sense of identification.

The caste association brings political democracy to Indian villages through the familiar and accepted institution of caste. In the process, it is changing the meaning of caste. By creating conditions in which a caste's significance and power is beginning to depend on its numbers, rather than its ritual and social status, and by encouraging egalitarian aspirations among its members the caste association is exerting a liberating influence.

Liberties in the west have a dual paternity. They arose on the one hand from an assertion of political philosophy which placed the reason and interests of the individual in a central position. On the other hand, they were the end-product of a historical process in which the rights and liberties of a variety of corporate groups and orders in traditional feudal society were gradually extended to ever-widening sections of the population until many rights and liberties became available to all. In India, as formerly in 18th century Europe, one attack on tradition and the old order came from the modern middle classes who succeeded in writing into the new nation's constitution the values of 18th century liberalism.[8] But the modern middle classes' attack constituted only one aspect, and a formal and impersonal aspect at that, of the challenge to the old order.

The other challenge has come from the caste association; its successful assertions of privilege and rights are in many ways comparable to the extension of corporate feudal liberties which characterized the development of English liberalism. They are perhaps the more truly indigenous assertions of liberties than the liberalism of the modern Indian middle classes. Thus, for example, the *Shanans*, traditionally low caste southern tappers of palm-wine (toddy), asserted as early as 1858 that their women had a right to go about with an upper cloth, even though customary rules restricted such apparel to the higher castes. After a series of riots, the Maharaja of Travancore was persuaded to concede the claim: "We hereby proclaim that there is no objection to *Shanan* women either putting on a jacket like the Christian *Shanan* women, or to *Shanan* women of all creeds dressing in coarse cloth, and tying themselves round with it as the *Mukkavattigal* (Fisherwomen) do, or to covering their bosoms in any manner whatever, but not like women of higher castes."[9]

[8] They also included the often conflicting values of popular sovereignty and political democracy and the "socialist" goals of economic and social justice.

[9] Edgar Thurston, *Castes and Tribes*, Vol. VI, p. 265.

The caste's assertion, which could be multiplied many times with reference to other issues (such as extending the rights of temple entry to lower castes), exemplifies the caste association's liberating role. It also suggests that the corporate assertion of rights challenged the old order at points in which the "liberal" modern middle classes took rather little interest. Indian analyses of these developments have tended to attribute the entire credit for such victories to the state which concedes the right rather than to the group which agitates for it —a point of view which gravely underestimates the role of liberating forces within the old society.

The very considerable extent to which caste associations are performing a liberating function has been obscured by the fact that the modern Indian middle classes tend to see caste (in any form) as a part of the old order which they hope to destroy. That a new social and political force clad in the institutions of the old order is to an extent collaborating in this activity, that caste is in a sense anti-caste, appears to them incomprehensible. Because the caste association presses home the interests of its followers, it is also seen as pursuing a form of group selfishness which is deplored in the name of social duty and discipline. Finally, the caste association is condemned along with other interest groups of both the natural and voluntary variety, by those economic planners, civil servants and political ideologues who deduce policy from theories of economic development, conceptions of the public good and utopian visions of a new society. Such persons see the goals and interests pressed by caste associations and other groups as self-interested, confusing and partial. That the public good should in some measure be worked out from the interaction and accommodations of many group purposes is seen as morally degrading, intellectually

unsatisfactory or aesthetically displeasing. For them, the political community includes only the state on the one hand and the citizen on the other, with the state having an exclusive (or at least primary) role in the formulation and execution of the public good. They fail to see that associations, both voluntary and natural, have a vital role to play in the exercise of political freedom through group self-government which contributes to the process of finding an approximation of the public good, provides a means for furthering group purposes independent of, as well as supplementary to, the state, and helps to protect the liberties of both associations and individuals.

None of this is meant to imply, however, that the caste association is an unqualified asset in Indian politics. Its tendency to place group loyalties above merit and competence, and caste patriotism above the public interest, runs counter to both liberal and democratic values and jeopardizes the effectiveness of the government's vital functions. In the final analysis, the meaning of the caste association in politics is ambiguous. Up to the present its role has been seriously misunderstood and its positive contribution neglected.

The caste association's main impact on politics within the Indian federal systems is at the state level. Caste associations do not generally extend across state boundaries. Castes do not, as a rule, include persons of different linguistic-cultural backgrounds, and most Indian states today are organized on a linguistic-cultural basis.[10] The interest groups which seem to be most effective at the national level are voluntary as-

[10] Bombay and Punjab are exceptions. Castes with approximately similar origins do exist in different states. *Jats* live in the Punjab, Uttar Pradesh and Rajasthan. But inter-state organization is weak both in caste structure and in the caste associations.

sociations (such as trade unions or chambers of commerce which have national constituencies) and natural associations like linguistic-cultural subnationalisms and religious communities.

At the state level, the strength of caste associations varies with the numbers that a particular association can attempt to mobilize, with the degree of self-consciousness and effectiveness of leadership, with the degree of internal cohesiveness, and with the power of countervailing interest-group forces. The balance of these factors has to be assessed separately in each state. Thus, in Rajasthan, a state which was formerly part of Princely India, the power of the *Jat* peasant caste, which constitutes 9 percent of the population of that state, may be explained by the particular constellation of all these factors. In part, the *Jats* profit from vigorous and effective leadership. The untouchable *Chamars* in the same state approach the *Jats* in numbers, but are relatively ineffectual politically because their level of self-consciousness and the quality of their leadership leave them for the moment merely a latent political force.[11] Among the organized castes, the *Rajputs* (a warrior caste) have served to check the power of the *Jats* by the lively activity of their association. The *Rajputs* are numerous, ranking fifth among castes in the state with 6 percent of population, very self-conscious politically, fairly well-led, and they still retain some of the authority of their traditional caste and class rank as *Kshatryas* (warrior rulers who constituted Rajasthan's monarchical-feudal order until 1947). But the *Rajput* caste association has not been able to exploit its full powers, in part because its internal cohesion suffered

when *Rajputs* who were great feudal landholders and those who were petty landlords disagreed on the acceptability of the post-Independence land reforms.

The *Jats*, in addition to benefiting from these dissensions among the *Rajputs*, are also able to capitalize on the relative backwardness of the state. With very little industry or commerce and with a very high level of political illiteracy, neither voluntary associations nor other caste associations are particularly strong. In Bombay and Madras, which are more advanced economically and have higher levels of political literacy, the countervailing forces, both voluntary and natural, are considerably stronger. In addition then to the natural limitation to caste political power inherent in the fact that castes generally hold a minority status (at both the national and the state level) there are other possible checks—lack of cohesiveness, a low level of self-consciousness, ineffective leadership and the countervailing power of other caste associations or interest groups.[12]

The caste association differs from the other natural associations found in India —tribal, linguistic and religious—in its relationship to the political community, i.e., the nation-state. Tribal, religious and linguistic groups on the Indian scene represent *potential* political communities, which may claim (and often have claimed) a separate political identity, either in the form of a sovereign state or an autonomous unit in a federal system.[13] Caste, and its political expres-

---

[11] The *Chamars* profit from the reservation of seats for untouchables in the Rajasthan legislative assembly; but even this crutch is not enough to make them influential in the absence of able leadership.

[12] Of course India's constitutional structure, including the party system, also plays a crucial role. Space limitations prevent an exploration of this facet of the problem.

[13] Many religious groups (the Christians and the post-Independence Muslims) and many tribal groups (the Bhils for example) have not in fact posed such problems of integration. But others have, at various levels: the pre-Independence Muslims sought and found their political identity in the nation-

sion, the caste association, have no such aspiration. Caste is a part of Hindu society; its meaning as a social institution is found in the values of Hindu culture. In this sense, all castes share a common culture, purpose and identity. The caste association is concerned with the distribution of values, status and rewards within a larger unit of action. It does not have a sense of nationality or aspire to separate political identity. It would be foolish, however, to suggest that such a development is out of the question. A caste like the Rajasthan *Jats*, with a tribal rather than an occupational caste origin, with a reasonably identifiable territorial base and a fairly recent (18th century) political history, might conceivably develop such aspirations. However, so far there is no evidence of such a development.

One of the key means in Indian democratic politics for "brokering" and integrating diverse social forces is the political party; at present, it is the parties, particularly the Congress Party, that link together the caste associations which tend to play so vital a role in state politics. The relationship of caste to party (i.e., to the institutional means of political integration) has been markedly different from the relationship of other natural associations to party. Party has subsumed caste, acting as a broker for caste association interests and accommodating in some measure its demands for representation on party tickets. In rela-

tion to other types of natural associations, however, the party has often been subsumed by them. The most outstanding example of this appeared in Bombay where the *Samyukta Maharashtra Samiti* and the *Maha Gujerat Parishad* (associations of the two linguistic groups of the state) subsumed the parties to their larger "national" drives for political identity.[14] So long as a religious, linguistic or tribal drive for political identity is in full swing, the party has been harnessed to it. The lesson of states reorganization in India, from the demand for Andhra state onward, was that the demand for linguistic-cultural autonomy through some form of separate political identity could not be compromised or accommodated, nor could the demand for religious-cultural autonomy and identity, as the case of the Muslims and Sikhs clearly indicates.

In their relationship to parties, caste associations play a role more akin to voluntary interest-groups than do the other natural associations. They have specific program and personnel demands which can be accommodated at the levels of policy formation, "ticket balancing" in constituencies and in the cabinet, and legislation.

The *Vanniyars*, or *Vanniya Kula Kshatryas*, illustrate the development of caste associations. They are primarily a caste of agricultural laborers, but also include substantial numbers of cultivating owners and petty landlords in Madras state. They make up slightly less than 10 percent of the population of Madras, but in the four northern districts of the state (North Arcot, South Arcot, Chingleput and Salem) where they are concentrated, the caste consti-

state of Pakistan; the various Indian linguistic groups successfully pressed for a political identity and some measure of autonomy within the federal system; the Naga tribes rebelled in an effort to gain some form of political identity; and the Sikhs found a measure of political identity in the compromise achieved in the Punjab legislature whereby two intrastate Regional Committees with broad recommendatory powers were established for Sikh and Hindu legislators respectively. See Joan V. Bondurant, *Regionalism versus Provincialism*, Berkeley, 1958, pp. 114–124.

[14] See Marshall Windmiller, "The Politics of State Reorganization in India: The Case of Bombay," *Far Eastern Survey* (XXV), No. 9, September 1956, pp. 129–143; and Phillips Talbot, "The Second General Elections: Voting in the States," American Universities Field Staff, New York, 1957 (India, PT-6-1957).

tutes about a fourth of the population.[15] As early as 1833, the *Pallis*, as they were then called, had ceased to accept their status as a humble agricultural caste and tried to procure a decree in Pondicherry that they were not a low caste.[16] In anticipation of a census-taking in 1871, they petitioned to be classified as *Kshatryas* (high-caste warrior-rulers) — a claim which found support in their traditional caste histories if not in their then low occupational status. Twenty years later the community had established seven schools for its members, and an enterprising *Palli* who had risen to the status of a High Court *vakil* (lawyer) had produced a book on the caste, which he followed with another some years later, supporting the caste's claim to be *Kshatryas* and connecting *Pallis* by descent with the great Pallava dynasty.[17] Oral histories simultaneously were stressing descent from the traditional "fire races," which *Kshatryas* both north and south often claim as ancestors. This attempt to press history into the service of social mobility, to counter current ritual and occupational definition of caste status by a historically derived definition, has been a quite frequent practice among rising castes.

By 1901 the *Pallis* had not won any battles but everyone was aware of their efforts. The Madras Census Commissioner noted that "they claim for themselves a position higher than that which Hindu society is inclined to accord them," and added that they were attempting to achieve this status via "a widespread organization engineered from Madras."[18] The organization's sporadic seventy-year activities to make *Pallis* conscious of their dignified and glorious history was bearing fruit. Instead of giving the old name, *Palli*, many were beginning to refer to themselves as *Agnikula Kshatryas* or *Vannikura Kshatryas* (i.e. *Kshatryas* of the fire race). The associations of the caste were spreading and becoming increasingly effective in various districts, enforcing a higher "sanskritized" standard of social conduct:

> They have been closely bound together by an organization managed by one of their caste, who was a prominent person in these parts... and their *esprit de corps* is now surprisingly strong. They are tending gradually to approach the Brahmanical standard of social conduct, discouraging adult marriage, meat-eating, and widow remarriage.... In 1904 a document came before one of the courts which showed that, in the year previous, the representatives of the caste in 34 villages in this district had bound themselves in writing, under penalty of excommunication to refrain (except with the consent of all parties) from the practices formerly in existence of marrying two wives, and of allowing a woman to marry again during the lifetime of her first husband.[19]

When these new caste associations turned to politics at the turn of the cen-

[15] These figures are necessarily tentative because they are based on the 1931 census, the last Indian census to enumerate caste. At that time, the *Vanniyars* numbered 2,944,014 and almost all of the *Vanniyars* were located in those parts of Madras which remained within the state after Andhra was detached in 1953. Presumably the *Vanniyar* population has increased substantially since then, at a rate not too different from the average population increase. In Chingleput, North Arcot, Salem and South Arcot there were 2,340,920 *Vanniyars* in 1931 in a total population for these districts of 8,810,583. See *Census of India*, 1931, Vol. XIV, Madras, Part II, Imperial and Provincial Tables.

[16] On this and some of the material which follows, see Thurston, Vol. VI, pp. 1–28.

[17] T. Ayakannu Nayakar, *Vannikula Vilakkam: A Treatise on the Vanniya Caste*, 1891, and *Varuna Darpanam* (Mirror of Castes), 1901.

[18] *Census of India*, 1901, Madras, Part I, Report, p. 171.

[19] W. Francis in *Gazetteer of South Arcot District*. Cited in Thurston, Vol. VI, p. 12.

tury, their main target was the census office, for its listing of caste and caste descriptions became more "real" than reality itself, carrying as it did the authority of official imprint. Mr. J. Chartres Moloney, of the Indian Civil Service, having survived the decennial onslaught of petitions from castes who wanted to be reclassified, remarked in the Census of 1911:

> The last few years, and especially the occasion of the present census, have witnessed an extraordinary revival of the caste spirit in certain aspects. For numerous caste *sabhas* have emerged, each keen to assert the dignity of the social group which it represents.[20]

The rising castes continued to persuade their members to give a new name to the census enumerators, and to persuade the census commissioners to list this new name when the old one bore some odium. They also urged the census officers either to revise the description of traditional caste occupations, where these were thought undignified, or to drop them altogether. The Madras Census dropped caste occupations in 1921 as a result of these pressures.[21] The effectiveness of the *Pallis* in influencing the official recorders on the one hand and their own members on the other was

considerable. By 1931 the *Pallis* had disappeared altogether from the Census, and only the *Vanniya Kula Kshatryas* remained.

The explicit organization of the *Vanniya Kula Kshatryas* in an association called the *Vanniya Kula Kshatrya Sangham* dates back at least thirty years in some districts, although the 1901 census commissioner indicated that some organizational stirrings were visible then, and the efforts of 1833 indicate even earlier (probably sporadic) activity. The *Vanniya Kula Kshatrya Sangham* of North Arcot District held its 34th annual conference in 1953, and the South Arcot *Sangham* held its tenth in 1954.[22] For the *Vanniya Kula Kshatrya Sangham*, the district unit was initially more important than the larger, Madras-wide organization which developed somewhat later. In 1952, the *Vanniya Kula Kshatryas* published a volume,[23] the introduction of which gave expression to the *sabha*'s attempt to build a sense of caste patriotism and solidarity which would make it a more effective force:

> The Vanniya Kula Kshatryas who till now were proverbially considered to be backward in education have made long strides in a short space of time and have come almost on a level with other communities...the community has not realized its deserving status in society.... A cursory view of the book will show every reader how many a desirable fruit of the community was veiled by the leaves...(it) will stimulate the younger generation to greater deeds and will fill the hearts of the older with just pride in the achievements of the community....[24]

---

[20] *Census of India*, 1911, Madras, Part I, Report, p. 178.

[21] *Ibid.*, Vol. XIII. This successful agitation reflected the fact that some castes were abandoning the traditional occupations. They presumably felt that from a descriptive point of view this fact deserved recognition. Even where the caste still kept to its traditional tasks, the census description (i.e., "*Shanars* are oil pressers") carried a normative application. From the point of view of mobile castes, the census looked like a new agency for sacred classification, an impression hardly alleviated by the fact that Brahmans, the traditional compilers of sacred classifications, tended to dominate the Indian cadres in the bureaucracy. In a society of flux, the problem of maintaining "objective" official social records becomes particularly difficult.

[22] *Hindu* (Madras), June 18, 1953; *Mail* (Madras), June 21, 1954.

[23] *Graduates and Diploma Holders among the Vanniya Kula Kshatrya,* Triplicane, Madras, 1952.

[24] *Graduates and Diploma Holders*, Introduction.

That the *Sangham* still had some work ahead may be inferred from the fact that it listed 298 names, or about .01 percent of the community, as holders of degrees or diplomas.[25]

After the war, when the electorate was expanding but had not yet reached the adult suffrage proportions which came with the 1952 general elections, the *Vanniya Kula Kshatrya Sangham* began to press the Congress Party state ministry with two demands: it wanted the appointments to the civil services (which are based on competitive examinations and merit) to reflect the *Vanniyars'* percentage in the population, and it wanted Congress itself, through party nominations, to assure the election of *Vanniyars* on a population basis to all elected bodies—municipal corporations, district boards, and the state legislature. The request was Jacksonian in its optimism concerning the universal distribution of the capacity to hold office. But it was not altogether unreasonable in view of the constitutional, statutory and administrative provisions both at the central and the state levels, which are designed to give special consideration to scheduled castes (untouchables) and backward classes (usually low castes) in the public services and educational institutions, and the Congress' known disposition to give some special consideration in candidate selection to "depressed" elements in the population. It assumed also that the authority of caste no longer depended on traditional rank but rather on numbers in the context of democratic authority. However, the Congress ministry of Madras did not respond favorably to the *Vanniyar* demand, nor did the nominating bodies

of the Congress party. From that time, the *Vanniyars* decided that they could rely only on themselves, dropped the attempt to work through the Congress or any other party, and began to contest for public office as independents.

Their first major electoral efforts were exerted in district board elections in the districts where their greatest strength lay. In fact, the district boards became one of their main targets, not only because they represented a convenient geographic unit within which caste influence could be maximized, but because the subjects falling under the competence of district boards, especially educational and medical facilities and road building, were of the greatest local and political interest. In 1949, the *Vanniyars* did well in the district elections, capturing, for example, 22 of the 52 seats in the South Arcot District Boards, and defeating many Congress Party candidates. They almost succeeded in electing the President of the board.[26]

In 1951, with the prospect of the 1952 elections before them, the *Vanniyars* convened a major conference of the *Vanniya Kula Kshatrya Sangham* on a state-wide basis. The conference resolved that the *Vanniyars* should contest the elections "in cooperation with the toiling masses," and formed a political party called the Tamilnad Toilers' Party. The leading spirits in the conference were men with modern and cosmopolitan qualifications rather than hereditary and traditional ones. Two of the most significant were Mr. W. A. Manikkavelu Naicker, a lawyer with experience in earlier state-wide party activities, notably the Swarajya Party, and Mr. S. S. Ramaswami Padayachi, a young man (33 in 1951), a high school graduate, Chairman of the Cuddalore Municipal Council, member of the South Arcot

[25] A diploma holder is about the equivalent of an American high school graduate, while a graduate is one who has finished college. It is probably safe to assume that most of those listed were diploma holders rather than graduates.

[26] See interview with S. S. Ramaswami Padayachi, a prominent *Vanniyar* leader, in *Mail*, April 27, 1954.

District Board and the man who was narrowly defeated for its presidency in 1949.[27] The names of Padayachi and Naicker, especially the former, provided an effective signal for caste solidarity in voting. Padayachi's youth is an interesting commentary on leadership patterns in castes coming to political self-consciousness; older members of lower castes generally do not command the necessary skills in communication and education for state-wide organization.

Organizationally, the conference represented a capstone in the expansion of the association, since it mobilized the *Vanniyars* on a state-wide basis. It sought at once to centralize control and to bring about a proliferation of operating sub-units, working toward a more rationalized campaign organization which could mobilize the potential membership. Mr. Padayachi was elected Chairman of the Central Election Comitee, established to supervise *Vanniyar* candidate selections throughout the state, and District Election Committees were established for twelve districts.[28]

Subsequently, the unified state-wide effort represented by the conference broke down when the caste *sabhas* of North and South Arcot districts, which had always rested on local loyalties, failed to agree. The Tamilnad Toilers as a party remained strong in South Arcot and Salem under Mr. Padayachi's guidance, while the North Arcot and Chingleput *Vanniyars* rallied to a second caste party, the Commonweal Party, under Mr. Naicker.

At election time, the caste *sabhas*-cum-parties utilized the older village organization, mobilizing *Vanniyar* village leaders to assure solid caste voting for one or the other party. This mobilization device was effective because it

defined the electoral issues in terms meaningful to an unsophisticated electorate: governmental services, especially roads and educational and medical services, could surely be more firmly secured for poor *Vanniyars* if men familiar with their plight (i.e., other *Vanniyars*) were elected to office. Watching Nehru speak to uncomprehending thousands, one might assume that there is an unbridgeable gap between the ordinary Indian voter and his government, but observers watching village election meetings, in which local caste headmen engage in running debate with aspiring or incumbent legislators, cannot come to the same conclusion. Common caste background is not essential to these exchanges but the fact that candidate and village headman often share a common caste culture provides a context in which discourse is natural and easy.

The Commonweal Party, representing the older caste *sabha* of North Arcot and Chingleput, which had no program to speak of (much less an ideology), won six seats in the state legislative assembly, while the Tamilnad Toilers, speaking for the younger South Arcot *sabha* and stressing a more leftist socialist platform, captured 19. This gave the *Vanniyars* 25 of the 190 seats in the legislature of post-1953 Madras, or 13 percent (though they numbered only 10 percent of the population).

In the same 1952 General Elections, the Congress Party failed to win a majority in the Madras state legislature, and in its search for enough legislative support to form a cabinet, persuaded the six Commonweal Party members to support a Congress ministry, but it could not persuade them to join the Congress. In return, Mr. Naicker, the Commonweal leader, was given a seat in the Cabinet, an event which delighted many *Vanniyars* but won him public catcalls from the Tamilnad Toilers, who

[27] *Mail*, April 13, 1954; *Indian Express* (Madras) April 14, 1954.

[28] *Mail*, October 13, 1951.

decided to remain in opposition.[29] Shortly thereafter, the Tamilnad Toilers also opened "negotiations" with Congress, presumably to see what offices might be offered in return for support.[30] The negotiations came to nothing until 1954 when Mr. C. Rajagopalachari, a Brahman statesman with a long and distinguished history in the nationalist movement, resigned as Chief Minister and was replaced by the shrewd and competent but less cosmopolitan and lower caste Kamraj Nadar. He had made his reputation as chief of the Madras Congress Party over more than a decade, and belonged to a large and prosperous peasant caste.[31]

The Tamilnad Toilers decided to support Mr. Kamraj's ministry, and Mr. Padayachi joined the cabinet, consisting of eight persons. Mr. Naicker too remained in the Cabinet, so that the *Vanniyars* could now call two of eight cabinet seats their own. Mr. Padayachi reported to the press that he was happy to see that the Ministry was so much more representative of the backward classes than any previous one. With two ministers in the Cabinet and cordial relations with Congress assured, the Commonweal and the Tamilnad Toiler parties were dissolved, their members joining the Congress.[32]

[29] *Indian Express* and *The Hindu*, May 13, 1952.

[30] *Mail*, October 21, 1952.

[31] The *Nadars* were formerly called *Shanans* and were once oil pressers. See Thurston, *op. cit.*, Vol. VI, pp. 363–378. Their caste *sabha* was influential in getting the old, odious name replaced (in 1921). They persuaded the census authorities to drop traditional caste descriptions, since many had moved out of oilpressing, which had low status repute, into agricultural, commercial and financial pursuits. Mr. Nadar's strength is based on a combination of long service with the nationalist movement and on the faith which lower castes repose in him as "one of them."

[32] *Mail*, July 30, 1956. The parties were in fact dissolved before 1956. At that time, the

The procedure followed by the *Vanniyars* is not unusual. In Rajasthan, the (*Rajput*) *Kshatrya Mahasabha* pursued an almost identical tactic in 1952, campaigning successfully for the legislature, extracting not cabinet offices but concessions on land-reform from Congress, and then joining the party, which needed members to strengthen its very precarious majority. The *Jat* caste *sabhas* in Rajasthan very nearly did the same when many members in 1950 considered converting the Rajasthan branch of the *Krishikar Lok* Party into a *Jat* branch. But the *Jats*, with politically literate leaders and a self-conscious and effectively mobilized following, saw the expediency of infiltrating the weak Rajasthan Congress, gave up the idea of a separate party, and contested the elections for the most part under the Congress Party label.

Throughout this period, both before and after the dissolution of the two caste parties, the demands of the *Vanniya Kula Kshatrya Sangham* continued to find active expression. The *Sangham* had three primary objectives. The first was educational services. What was at stake were scholarships which might allow a village student to pay for room at the hostel of a distant secondary institution, fee concessions at institutions which still charged tuition, and reservation of seats for *Vanniyars* in institutions of higher learning. The second objective was places in the civil service; these conferred status as well as a job. The third was winning Congress "tickets" (i.e., nominations) for seats in lower governing boards as well as in the legislature and places in the cabinet. The *Sangham* was also interested in various economic services affecting *Vanniyars*. That they could hope for government help in several respects was clear from

election commission merely recognized their dissolution officially.

the fact that they had been officially classified as a Backward Class, that is, a caste above the Untouchable level but one whose status and condition was nevertheless so weak that it deserved special consideration under the policy of "progressive discrimination" which has been a central feature of Indian social policy.[33]

The way these demands were pursued and the responses of the two ministers to them is apparent from the proceedings of *Sangham* meetings and conferences. Shortly after his appointment in 1954, Mr. Padayachi explained to a *Sangham* conference why he had joined the Kamraj ministry when he had not joined the earlier one of Mr. Rajagopalachari. The *Vanniyars'* demands for educational facilities and representation in the civil services had not been met by the Rajagopalachari ministry, he said, and implied that he expected a more generous attitude from the Kamraj ministry.[34] At a North Arcot conference in 1955, he could report that the government had been doing its best to give school fee concessions, scholarships and employment preference to the *Vanniya Kula Kshatryas*.[35] At that time, 5 out of every 20 seats in the state civil service were reserved for "qualified candidates of the backward classes," in addition to the reservations for scheduled castes and tribes. These reservations were established by administrative order in cooperation with the Public Service Commission. (Unfortunately no figures are available on whether enough "qualified" candidates were found to fill these posts —formal reservation and actual seats filled by members of backward classes

have by no means always coincided.)[36] In any case, Mr. Padayachi apparently kept an eye on the situation, and presumably his and Mr. Naicker's views on how this difficult problem might be handled were always available to the government. The frequency with which both men reported to *Vanniyar* meetings indicates that they considered themselves to some extent special agents of *Vanniyar* interests; drawing a line between this role and their role as cabinet members responsible for the formulation and administration of public policy is of course difficult.

The quality of the *Sangham's* economic demands is illustrated by another North Arcot conference, addressed by Mr. Naicker in 1953. The resolutions present a striking illustration of the fact that the *Vanniya Kula Kshatrya Sangham* operated as an economic interest group—one might expect similar resolutions from western farm groups in the U.S. They urged better irrigation in North Arcot district; electricity for agricultural areas; better roads; expansion of the Krishna Pennar multi-purpose water project; relief to tenants for rain failure; and (recalling the fact that many *Vanniyars* were tenants and laborers) making tillers owners of the soil.[37]

Negotiations with the Congress concerning the number of nominations which would be given to the *Vanniyars* in local board elections became very lively late in 1954, just before the District Board elections. One result of the negotiations concerning seats in North Arcot was the promise, given by the officers of the state Congress Party, that once the District Board was elected, it would choose a *Vanniyar* chairman. This promise came in response to *Vanniyar*

---

[33] Progressive discrimination, especially in the services, was already a policy of the old Justice Party governments in pre-Independence Madras.

[34] *Indian Express*, April 28, 1954; *Mail*, May 30, 1954.

[35] *Mail*, January 5, 1955.

[36] See Government of India, *Report of the Backward Classes Commission* (3 Vols.), Delhi, 1955, especially Vol. I, p. 131.

[37] *Hindu*, June 18, 1953.

pressure to extend to District Boards the principle of "community rotation" in the selection of officers, a principle which has long been recognized in the Madras Municipal Corporation Presidency. In this case, the promise caught the state party in a difficult situation: the non-*Vanniyar* Congress Party members of the North Arcot District Board, many of whom belonged to the higher caste of *Reddiars*, saw no reason why they should be bound at the district level by negotiations carried on by the state party with the *Vanniyars*. They accordingly decided not to vote for a *Vanniyar*, and elected a *Reddiar* president, in cooperation with non-Congress members of the board. The Madras Congress Party, knowing that they might not be able to count on *Vanniyar* support in the general elections in 1957 if they did not keep faith with the *Vanniyars*, took strict disciplinary action and suspended a number of the recalcitrant *Reddiar* members from the party. According to the newspaper report:

> Sri Karayalar (President of the state Congress organization) said that indiscipline in Congress ranks should not be tolerated as it would weaken the organization.... In the North Arcot case, Sri Karayalar said, the idea was that the Presidentship this time should go to a member of the Vanniyar community as in South Arcot. All along the Reddiars had been presidents there. The Vanniyar community had supported the Congress in the Board elections and the understanding all along had been that the Congress nominee for the Presidentship should be a member of the Vanniyar community....[38]

Throughout this period, the *Sangham's* organizational structure was being elaborated and expanded. Local branches sprang up in many places, often at the level of smaller administra-

[38] *Mail*, November 20, 1954.

tive units such as *taluks* (districts) and towns. Usually one of the ministers graced the occasion with his presence.[39] At all these sessions, the ministers and others sought to strengthen the *Sangham's* solidarity, to increase the sense of unity and of mission. Mr. Padayachi reminded a conference that his ministership was the result of the united efforts and sacrifices of the community over a long period, and the caste flag was ceremonially unfurled at the 34th annual conference of the *Sangham* at North Arcot.

It is clear that today the *Vanniya Kula Kshatrya Sangham* plays an important role in Madras politics. Village subcastes persist, but their relative role in the new democratic culture is gradually declining. It is the caste associations (*sabhas* or *sanghams*) which have given caste a new vitality, and it is political democracy which has transformed caste and enabled it to play its paradoxical role in India today. Rather than providing the basis for a reaction, caste has absorbed and synthesized some of the new democratic values. Ironically, it is the caste association which links the mass electorate to the new democratic political processes and makes them comprehensible in traditional terms to a population still largely politically illiterate. Caste has been able to play this curious political role as bearer of both India's *ancien régime* and its democratic political revolution by reconstituting itself into the *sabha*, with characteristics of both the natural and the voluntary association, of caste defined in terms of both *dharma* and democracy.

[39] Thus, the first conference of the North Madras *Vanniya Kula Kshatrya Sangham*, the conference of the Uttiramerur sub-*taluk Sangham*, the tenth annual meeting of the South Arcot *Sangham*, the second annual conference at Perambur, and a conference at Ayyumpet. See *Hindu*, May 23, 1955; *Mail*, June 21, 1954, and January 10, 1956; *Indian Express*, July 23, 1956.

# TRADITIONAL STRUCTURES AS OBSTACLES TO REVOLUTIONARY CHANGE: THE CASE OF SOVIET CENTRAL ASIA

GREGORY J. MASSELL

## INTRODUCTION[1]

This study is concerned with a problem central to comparative politics in a world of new nations pursuing stupendous goals: how, and to what extent, political power—and specifically, legal engineering—may be deliberately used in the revolutionary transformation of societies, especially those we generally call "traditional societies." It pursues that concern through a study of the

[1] I have not taken for granted in this paper any previous acquaintance with the literature on Soviet Central Asia—the socio-cultural context from which the data for this study are drawn. Section I, in particular, is provided here largely as background and stage-setting material. While this, in part, accounts for the paper's length, it should be of help to the reader in following critically the argument as a whole.

For some recent general studies by Western scholars, dealing at least in part with Soviet Central Asia, *see* R. Pipes, The Formation of the Soviet Union: Communism and Nationalism, 1917–1923 (1964); S. Zenkovsky, Pan-Turkism and Islam in Russia (1960); E. Allworth (ed.), Central Asia: A Century of Russian Rule (1967); G. Wheeler, The Modern History of Soviet Central Asia (1964); A. Bennigsen & C. Lemercier-Quelquejay, Islam in the Soviet Union (1967); O. Caroe, Soviet Empire: The Turks of Central Asia and Stalinism (1967).

*Reprinted from Gregory J. Massell, "Law as an Instrument of Revolutionary Change in a Traditional Milieu: The Case of Soviet Central Asia,"* law and society review, 2 (February 1968), 179–226, by permission of the publisher and author.

interaction between central power and local traditions in one of the peripheral areas of the Soviet land mass, Soviet Central Asia. And it is most especially concerned with the meaning and impact of large, abstract, impersonal political blueprints of great movements and figures when pursued by ordinary men in the small, concrete, and intimate worlds of human relations, on the manipulation of which the achievement of all revolutionary goals ultimately depends.

Specifically, this study examines the role of legal rules and institutions (pertaining to personal status and family relationships, and hence, in this context, to sexual equality) in inducing, in conjunction with a series of other political drives, a full-scale revolution in traditional Islamic societies under Soviet rule in the late 1920s—*i.e.* in the early, experimental stages of communist revolutionary attempts in Central Asia.[2]

[2] The substantive material in the text that follows, including direct quotations as well as specific references to Soviet views and to events in Central Asia, is based almost entirely on Soviet sources—all of them in Russian, and none of them available in English translation.... Due to limitations of space, specific references to these sources have been omitted in the text. Detailed bibliographical references will be found in the author's forthcoming book, The Strategy of Social Change and the Role of Women in Soviet Central Asia: A Case-Study in Modernization and Control, to be published under the auspices of the Center of International Studies, Princeton University.

## THE QUEST FOR REVOLUTIONARY ACCESS AND INFLUENCE IN A TRADITIONAL MILIEU

At the inception of Soviet experiments in social engineering (mid-1920s) Central Asia combined enormous size (almost half the size of the United States) with a relatively small population (circa fifteen million). The population included three principal ethnic groups: Turkic (Uzbeks, Turkmens, Kirghiz, and Kazakhs); Iranian (mainly Tadzhiks); and—about 10 per cent of the total—Slavic (Russians, Ukrainians, and Belorussians). Formally, most of the indigenous population had been Moslem ever since the Arab invasions in the eighth century. The structure of traditional occupations in the area comprised sedentary pursuits of the oases and lowlands (agriculture, commerce, and artisan trades), and nomadic pastoralism of the steppes, deserts, and high plateaus (stock-breeding and caravan trade). The educational pattern was overwhelmingly traditionalist in nature; the few schools were staffed and controlled by Moslem clergymen. The illiteracy rate at the time of the October Revolution was almost 100 per cent. The social structure of indigenous communities tended to reflect basic subsistence patterns: local traditional societies were organized around kinship units in relatively self-sufficient communities, by and large along patriarchal, patrilineal, and patrilocal lines, with residues of tribal organization most pronounced among the pastoral nomads and, to a lesser extent, among the mountaineers.

A highly complex pattern of social and cultural pluralism was amply reflected in the region's legal institutions. What is very important, Tsarist colonial administrators had made no significant deliberate and concerted attempt to transform the prevailing socio-cultural and legal patterns, after Russia completed the conquest of the area toward the end of the nineteenth century. This meant that, at the inception of the Soviet experiment, the revolutionary regime confronted in the legal realm no less than in others a heterogeneous and multilayered universe. Aside from Russian statutory law (governing primarily the relationships of the region's European newcomers), two major categories of law were in operation here, affecting especially in the civil realm the bulk of the indigenous population: codified Moslem law *(shariat)* and local customary law *(adat)*. As a rule, *shariat* was administered by formal canonical courts staffed by qualified Moslem religious personages. In this form, the system was operative primarily in urban and sedentary-agricultural locales. The *adat* depended neither on a written code nor on formal administration; the resolution of disputes tended to be entrusted to tribal leaders, to clan and village notables, and/or to local Moslem clergymen. This system tended to be operative primarily in tribal, nomadic-pastoral milieus. In terms of Georges Gurvitch's legal typology, the legal systems of Central Asia's traditional Islamic principalities (such as Bukhara and Khiva) had a "theocratic-charismatic" base; the legal systems of primitive, "polysegmentary" social organizations (especially among nomads and mountaineers) had a "magical-religious" base.[3] Yet even these two broad categories of judicial legitimation and arrangements are ideal-typical in nature. Reality was considerably more complex. Central Asia subsumed an extremely variegated patchwork of religious and tribal tribunals, usages, and laws. In such a context, conflict resolution could be formal or highly informal, public or private, and the

[3] *See* G. Gurvitch, Sociology of Law ch. 4 (1942); *cf.* G. A. Almond & G. P. Powell, Jr., Comparative Politics: A Developmental Approach chs. VI and IX (1966).

prevailing legal forms, norms, and practices depended to a large extent on the particular region, communal organization, and ethno-cultural milieu, as well as on the personal charisma of the particular judicial mediator.

This social pattern could hardly offer serious direct resistance to the establishment of Soviet power in the period between 1917 and 1921. Yet as bolshevik strategists were shortly to realize with growing unease, the very pattern of local traditional solidarities and orientations that had made the cluster of Central Asia's traditional societies so fragmented, communocentric, and insular, and thus so accessible and vulnerable to the determined thrust of modern Soviet power, tended also to make them particularly elusive to attempts not merely to "establish" a mechanism of power but to use it for rapid revolutionary transformation and efficient integration.

The modernization process, even when relatively sedate, always contains elements of suspenseful confrontation. In few cases, however, has it been quite so dramatic as in the attempted modernization of Central Asia under Soviet auspices. One reason for this is that the drive toward modernization did not, by and large, come out of Central Asia itself, not primarily from a local elite nor even a local counter-elite commanding the support of an "expectant people." The outside powers, moreover, had an exceptionally extravagant vision and explicit ideology, as well as remarkable revolutionary elan and impatience. Per contra, the societies to be transformed were at an especially low level of social and economic development, as different from that postulated by the Marxist theory of revolution as they could possibly have been; they were also, relatively speaking, highly intact and integrated, that is, lacking in relatively large, significant, and politically experienced groups that were both alienated

and marginal. The drama of modernization in Soviet Central Asia thus arose from a huge gap between the social structures existing and those envisioned; from the lack of significantly disintegrated structures ready-made for refashioning; and from great verve and urgency on one side and a deep imperviousness to manipulation on the other.

· · ·

At first, then, we have in Soviet Central Asia a rather simple encounter between revolution and tradition, reflecting the simplicities of early Soviet politics in the large. There was a belief that disadvantaged men (and most men in traditional society were "disadvantaged") would readily take to a social transformation carried out by dedicated reformers operating new formal and legal institutions superior to the old. This belief was encouraged by the apparent ease with which the revolutionary takeover was accomplished in Central Asia; by the Marxist-Leninists' apocalyptic view of revolution itself, a view considering violent revolution as a final and definitive act, a consummation rather than a mere beginning; and the belief, shared by communists with other children of the Enlightenment, in the great strength of rationally devised social machinery as against the implicit norms and networks of informal expectations of prerational society. There was to be revolutionary machinery, and revolutionary products would issue from it as a matter of course.

The failure of that wonderfully hopeful approach, perhaps more crushing in Central Asia than anywhere else, was the first great trauma of Soviet rule. It was not so much that the revolutionary machinery was attacked and incapacitated by reactionary strata. Rather it was that the new institutions could not even begin to permeate the vast regions of society outside of the urban administrative centers, and that, in so far as they did gain entrance, they tended not to transform accustomed ways but to be themselves "traditionalized," to provide merely a new setting in which affairs proceeded much as before. As Marx and Engels would have visualized this, Central Asia's traditional elites (religious, tribal, and communal) turned out to stand "in the midst of society," in that they continued to command respect and authority at the grassroots. The agents of the Soviet state stood "outside and above" that society.[4]

There were several possible responses. One was to use the coercive power of the regime to excise the more manifest obstructive elements (especially the traditional elites) and to force the general population into compliance with revolutionary ways, thus accomplishing quickly revolutionary ends. Another was to find a weak link in society, a surrogate proletariat where no proletariat in the real Marxist sense existed, to recruit from it reliable native cadres and to use them, by slow and systematic processes, first to loosen and disintegrate traditional social relationships, then to rebuild society when its very dissolution compelled reconstitution. Access to the traditional structures to be transformed could then be viewed either as a negative process of forcibly removing obstructions or as a positive one of finding willing and useful collaborators, or as a combination of the two. But both approaches have a crucial point in common, one that has wide significance for the deliberate transformation of any and all societies: transforming social institutions that still are going concerns presupposes a prior weakening, if not utter destruction, of the institutions to be transformed, and hence the discovery of crucial actors whose deliberately engineered alienation and separation from

the institutions will cause these to be drained of vitality.

The initial Soviet political reflex in this case was essentially an orthodox one, reverting to a hard, fundamentalist bolshevik bias—to attack the obstructive elements head-on, and to excise them from the local body politic. Without waiting for either political, or economic, or cultural development to take its course, the party decided to attack directly the network of traditional authority relationships, and to strike it at a point that could logically be considered its nerve-center and its head. It called upon its cadres to subordinate everything to the requirements of "class struggle" in the traditionalist countryside, and to concentrate, first of all, on "undercutting...isolating...[and then physically] removing" the traditional elites of Soviet Central Asia. Such a decision involved more or less explicit expectations: that the liquidation of traditional elites would presumably amount to a political decapitation of the traditional command system; that it would thus serve to remove the linchpin from the formal organizational structures of local communities and tribes. As a result, local social structures would presumably collapse, the hold of primary and local groups upon their members would break down, and minds as well as bodies would be released from the previous equilibrium and set adrift, as it were, and be delivered into the Soviet fold.

Yet, what seemed to disturb the regime above all while the attack was in progress was that the separation of traditional leaders from their followers, even when successfully carried out—which was not everywhere the case—did not make a community automatically available for Soviet-sponsored mobilization. Far from being supplanted by considerations of property and bureaucratic status, the old unities based on kinship,

---

[4] F. Engels, The Origin of the Family, Private Property, and the State 156 (1942).

custom, and belief showed signs of persisting even in the absence of traditional figureheads and presented just as great an obstacle to the diffusion of Soviet influence as before. As perceived by Soviet analysts, these obstacles continued to group themselves around two basic, and intimately correlated, traditionalist propensities in the dealings of local groups with outsiders: secrecy and solidarity. If anything, intensified Soviet pressures upon tribal and communal leadership seemed, at least in the short run, to strengthen the resolve of communities and groups—or even to activate fresh or previously dormant dispositions—to guard the walls of secrecy and internal solidarity.

What came to be perceived in this context, at the apex of the party, as a crucial desideratum in Central Asian conditions was nothing less than a "cultural revolution." As communist organizers saw it, the blow dealt to tribal-patriarchal elites was but one blow, and possibly not the most crushing and important one. One needed to deliver "a second blow," one that would destroy the residues of "tribal-patriarchal... ideology"—an ideology that, through persistent loyalties and habits, made it possible for old kin and custom-based unities to survive even when the old elites were gone. One needed approaches that would reliably disengage human beings from the matrix of traditional ties, values, and beliefs. Where was one to begin? The answer, as one party analyst saw it, could be as dramatically unorthodox as it was apparently simple: "the real battle against harmful... tribal-patriarchal residues... [against] the survivals of the old order... [blocking the path of Soviet development], must begin from the destruction of the old... family—of that primary cell of the conservative [Central Asian] village, [a cell] that refuses to surrender its positions to [the forces of] the new...

[world]." Moreover, if the key to a genuine cultural revolution was in the destruction of traditional family structures, the undermining of the kinship system itself could most speedily be accomplished through the mobilization of those of its members who were the most consistently "humiliated... [and] exploited," who were, as a rule, segregated, secluded, and constrained, who were, in effect, "the lowest of the low," "the most enslaved of the enslaved": its women.

Accordingly, while the overall Soviet assault on Central Asia's Moslem traditional societies proceeded on a number of levels, and with widely varying degrees of success, one essential facet of that assault came to be the deliberate attempt to stimulate and manipulate sexual and generational tensions that would help to induce an upheaval in a traditional system of values, customs, relationships, and roles, beginning with the primary cell of that system: the extended, patriarchal Moslem family.

THE QUEST FOR STRATEGIC
LEVERAGE POINTS IN A
TRADITIONAL MILIEU:
MOSLEM WOMEN AS A SURROGATE
PROLETARIAT

### Revolutionary Action as Strategic Leverage

At least three basic propositions were implicit in the decision to use women to break up Moslem traditional societies. First, that "class struggle," in some societies, did not need to express itself exclusively through social strata conventionally designated on the basis of property and relation to the means of production. Second, that "patriarchism" characterized authority relationships not only in large and complex social organizations in Central Asia but also, and perhaps most strikingly, in the primary cell of the native traditional world, i.e. in the extended family. Third, that in such a milieu, social status, and hence potentially social tensions, could be based as much on sexual as on economic or other roles.

There was at least one congenial ideological precedent for such a view. Marx and Engels had written:

> *The first division of labor* is that between man and woman for the propagation of children. . . . *The first class opposition* that appears in history coincides with the development of the antagonism between man and woman in monogamous marriage. . . . *The first class oppression* coincides with the enslavement of the female sex by the male. . . . The modern family contains in germ not only slavery *(servitus)* but also serfdom, since from the beginning it is related to agricultural services. It contains *in miniature* all the contradictions which later extend throughout society and its state.[5]

One factor made such an analysis particularly relevant where Central Asia was concerned. Marxist references to female inferiority in a capitalist industrial system were relatively marginal illustrations of the hypocrisy and inequality accompanying the struggle between the classes. In the case of the emergence of the patriarchal family, however, the thrust and imagery of the analysis placed male-female relationships at the center of the class struggle.

It helped to strengthen conclusively the arguments of those who had been insisting all along that there were highly unusual opportunities for revolutionary action in Moslem traditional societies, and that women were the key to those opportunities. To deliberately proceed on the assumption of a woman's dumb, isolated, subordinated, exploited, depersonalized, will-less, and loveless existence could presumably help the party find more than merely additional social leverage in Central Asia. Deliberate and

planned utilization of this issue could prove to be social dynamite par excellence. It could attack what might be potentially the weakest link in the solidarities of native kinship systems, and could thus speed up immensely the processes both of social disorganization and of reintegration under Soviet auspices.

In this sense, it seems fruitful to visualize Soviet experience in Central Asia as a complicated search for strategic factors in a revolutionary transformation—for techniques, instrumentalities, and targets that would provide the regime with relatively high leverage in undermining and transforming a Moslem traditional milieu. In other words, it was a quest for a structural weakpoint through which particularly intense conflict could be engendered in society and leverage provided for its disintegration, the recruitment of sympathetic elements from its ranks, and, finally, its reconstitution.

. . .

*Revolutionary Action As Activation of a Surrogate Proletariat*

Where a Moslem woman was concerned, party activists could reason—certainly not without some psychological justification—that under the seeming bedrock of her traditional entrapment there seethed deep currents of humiliation, frustration, and hatred; and that these currents could be shaped into elements not just combustible in the short term but inherently and fundamentally subversive to the entire spectrum of traditional behavior, relationships, and norms. It was not of decisive significance whether a woman's fate was, in her own perception, as bleak as the party saw it, or wished it to be seen. More relevant: there was a possibility that the very terms of contact with unprecedented concepts of human existence would hold up an extraordinary mirror to a

[5] *Ibid.* at 51, 58 ff.

woman's eyes, letting her see herself as she had never seen herself before; that they would activate currents of unaccustomed restlessness, agitating minds and feelings into a search for ways to establish the newly perceived identity, to realize a novel sense of human worth and potentialities; that they would, in effect, raise to a conscious level the sense of outrage on account of an existence that could not fail but be perceived as being, relative to men, dramatically inferior. A woman might endure perpetual inferiority, degradation, and segregation, but only as long as she lacked the capacity to visualize, and the opportunity to grasp, alternative possibilities. As soon as the psychological and organizational barriers were breached—as soon as the past and future were perceived in a radically new light—a dramatic turnabout could not fail to take place.

The party's tasks were thus twofold. To maximize female revolutionary potential, it was necessary to maximize female discontent, and to minimize the obstacles in the way of a woman's perceiving, articulating, and acting upon that discontent. Along with this, it was the party's task to find the right keys to the latent revolutionary currents, and the right molds for harnessing the unleashed forces and channeling them in desirable directions—*i.e.* to find optimal social controls for unleashed social energies. This would require careful engineering: as good an estimate as possible of the linkages, in every conceivable sphere, between female mobilization and broader social transformation; of the specific advantages and forms of utilizing female revolutionary energy; and of the ways in which the latter could contribute to, or endanger, the stabilization, legitimation, and development of the revolutionary regime itself.

Given such requisites, what were Soviet expectations regarding the actual operational opportunities and potentials? How could women be used to help in the revolutionary transformation of a traditional society, and what impact could such use be expected to have? The Soviet plan of action (a plan that crystallized only gradually, and that was by no means consistent and continuous) may, perhaps, best be visualized in a series of propositions—propositions that constitute a brief and selective projection of the imperatives and premises underlying the Soviet action-scheme, that relate immediate means to ultimate ends, that are interdependent, and that fluctuate in emphasis within a spectrum from moral to instrumental considerations, from revolutionary idealism to cold political pragmatism.

1. *To emancipate women as individuals—and, with women, the young generation*—from "slavery in the feudal-patriarchal order" of kinship, custom, and religion, and thereby fulfill the egalitarian strictures of Marxism with respect to the family, as well as engage the humanitarian and reformist impulses of important segments of the emerging male and female elites in Russia and Central Asia.

2. *To undermine the prevailing patterns of traditional authority*—based on lineage, kinship, conquest, custom, religion, and age, as well as on the absolute superiority of men—by endowing women with unprecedented socio-political roles, and backing these roles with an organizational framework, with educational and material opportunities, and with the legal and police-power of the new state. By the same token, to undermine the backbone of a traditional community's political cohesion, and ease and hasten, thereby, the grafting and assimilation of new Soviet authority patterns at the grassroots.

. . .

3. *To undermine the kinship system*

*and the village community*—revolving around clan-loyalties, and ties of family and custom—by endowing women with unprecedented social, cultural, and economic roles, by encouraging and sponsoring divorces initiated by women, and by involving them in massive and dramatic violations of traditional taboos, such as mass-unveiling in public, playing of dramatic female roles on stage, open competition with males in sports events, and assumption of martial roles in paramilitary formations, including the operation of airplanes, the use of parachutes, and the handling of guns.

As a corollary, *to compound the power of attraction upon male as well as female youth*—by stressing a new accessibility of the sexes to each other, an accessibility based on free choice and no longer dependent on customary and religious rules, or on tribal, communal, or paternal authority, an accessibility involving unprecedented dimensions of contact, courtship, and romantic love. By the same token: either to subvert the traditional realms and hierarchies of loyalty and socialization, and thus release women and/or youth into Soviet socializing media, or gain inside those realms exceedingly important allies in bringing up the young generation—present or future mothers.

4. *To significantly weaken some crucial moorings of Islam in native societies*—especially the codified religious laws of *shariat*, and the main repository of local customary laws, the *adat*—by endowing women with unprecedented civil rights, by backing those rights with a new and especially tailored judicial system, and by staffing that system, in part, with women. To revolutionize traditional attitudes toward the clergy, by suggesting, among other things, that the latter's presumed spiritual guidance of a man's wives and daughters could easily go hand in hand with sexual exploitation; and by wooing especially women—

traditionally the most numerous and submissive clients—away from the influence of Moslem "teachers," village "wise men" and "holy men," and tribal shamans.

As a corollary, *to break the monopoly of knowledge, and of political, adjudicative, intellectual, educational, spiritual, and consecrative functions*, held by males in general, and by traditional elites—religious, tribal, and communal—in particular, thus helping to undermine the status, authority, as well as livelihood of these elites. To help subvert, thereby, not only the claims of religion and custom upon human beliefs, values, commitments, and ties, but, also, the hold of religious and customary institutions upon the hierarchies of society and family, the administration of justice, the system of education, property relations, and the overall pattern of daily life.

5. *To disorient and weaken the prevailing concepts of property*—by bringing into question the woman's role as, in bolshevik interpretation, her father's means of exchange, and her husband's beast of burden, chattel, and property in marriage; by forcefully stressing and challenging the entire range of her legal and customary inferiority, particularly with respect to her control and inheritance of property, including land; and by endowing her with unprecedented roles and capabilities in the sphere of economic activity.

As a corollary, *to compound the power of attraction upon poor and socially disadvantaged males*—by stressing a new availability of brides that would no longer be dependent on the social status of a man and his family or clan, or on the requirements of property in the form of the locally traditional bride-price *(kalym)* and thus endowing the males' sense of sexual deprivation with overtones of social, economic, and political deprivation, making the conflict over women into a potential fulcrum for a sharpening class-conflict.

6. *To gain, in the heretofore secluded female masses, a large and reliable labor pool, and a potentially important reservoir of technical cadres*—so as, in the short run, to maximize the scope and tempo of economic development (particularly in the growing of cotton, the production of silk, and the expansion of textile, clothing, and food industries) and, over the longer term, to release the productive and creative potentials of a traditional society.

.   .   .

REVOLUTIONARY LEGALISM AND
SOCIAL ENGINEERING: THE USES
AND LIMITS OF SUPERIMPOSED
RULES

The multifaceted justifications for work with Moslem women were, of course, designed to secure the party's acquiescence in ideologically unorthodox initiatives, as well as its maximum support with cadres and funds. But, if the party's high command came to see the promise of such action, and accordingly proceeded to set in motion a number of initiatives on this account, it also came to perceive sharply the dangers implicit in such an undertaking. To attempt a sudden and full-fledged mobilization and emancipation of Moslem women, to stage an all-out, undifferentiated assault on the realities and symbols of sexual apartheid and female inferiority in a traditional Islamic world, was to initiate what was perhaps the most overtly illegitimate action in that world.

.   .   .

*Potential Functions of a Heretical Model*

In its norms, forms, procedures, and personnel, and in its massive and detailed concentration on sexual equality, the new legal system in Soviet Central Asia constituted a fundamental challenge to the structure and life-style of local communities. Indeed, it constituted a powerful *heretical model.*

It was heretical in that (a) in and of itself, it constituted deliberate and absolutely autonomous legislative action by secular authority in any and all, including the most sacred, realms of life— something that Islamic orthodoxy has long regarded as by definition not only heretical and illegal but a contradiction in terms, given the avowedly revealed, comprehensive, and perfect nature of Moslem law; (b) rather than merely questioning the interpretation of one or another belief, it called into question the basic assumptions underlying the prevailing belief and value systems, and thus invited radical skepticism about the moral basis of society; (c) rather than merely calling for some adjustment in one or another dimension of social esteem, it threatened a *total* abrogation of the primordial status system, beginning with the structure and hierarchy of sexual and generational roles; (d) by assigning drastically new meanings to authority and domination, and to religious, communal, and affinal obligations, it negated ancient paradigms of solidarity and trust, sanctioned the abrogation of traditional social controls, and cast grave doubt on the justice, utility, and hence legitimacy of the entire social order; (e) in addition to engendering a revolutionary interpretation of the present and the past, it formulated radically new goals for the future, thus engendering unprecedented aspirations with respect not only to rights but also to roles, possibilities, and opportunities, and hence encouraging individual concerns deeply at variance with and apart from those of the local group; (f) in making tabooed issues a matter of open concern, it threatened, in effect, to make many latent conflicts manifest.

While, in this sense, the new legal system was profoundly heretical, it could also serve as a tangible model in that (a) rather than involving merely the sporadic propagation of whispered or printed doubts on the part of deviant men or groups of men, it was a negation of the social order embodied in a system of laws and courts forcefully grafted and backed by the overwhelming power of a state; (b) in marking not only a departure from particular precedents but a complete abolition of all antecedent judicial channels and procedures, it claimed a monopoly of the legal universe; (c) in turn, no matter what its intrinsic merits in the eyes of the population, it was always visible and available, perennially calling for utilization, and thus serving as a constant catalyst and exerting constant leverage; (d) insofar as Moslem women, for example, pioneered in using its services, enacting its precepts and, most important, joining the ranks of its personnel, it constituted a palpable standard, a consistent alternative, for comparison and choice.

. . .

There might have been expected to be at least four basic categories of clients affected in diverse ways by the function of Soviet law as a heretical model. If short-term Soviet operational objectives—based at least in part on female mobilization and emancipation—involved the productive intensification of class struggle in the traditional milieu and the resultant unraveling of the traditional social fabric, the attitudes and responses of these four client-categories had to be taken into account. (1) *A principal beneficiary client group*, including of course primarily women. (2) *A secondary beneficiary client group*, including primarily unmarried young and poor men, owning neither land nor flocks, *i.e.* men socialized in traditional values and solidarities, but lacking authoritative standing both in private and in public realms, lacking significant access to material and spiritual goods,

and lacking significant access to women as well, such access having been traditionally delimited by ritual, hereditary, authoritarian, and financial considerations. (3) *A secondary adversary client group*, including primarily married (monogamous) men, either poor or moderately well off, *i.e.* men with a large but limited stake in the traditional order in the sense of having access to women and commanding patriarchal authority in the kin group, but having relatively little authoritative influence at the suprafamilial level of community or society, and relatively narrow access to material and spiritual goods. (4) *A principal adversary client group*, including primarily polygamous, well-to-do, or socially esteemed patriarchs, and the surviving authoritative traditional elites (religious, tribal, and communal), *i.e.* men with a very high stake in the traditional order in the sense of having relatively broad access to, or actually controlling the allocation of, a community's social and political statuses as well as material, spiritual, and sexual objects.

On purely rational grounds, the Soviet regime could expect to find in the first group not only natural followers and friends but also enthusiastically devoted agents. In turn, the successful mobilization of the first group might have been expected to intensify the adherence and participation of the second group, and its delivery of what could be viewed as the regime's natural allies. While the third group had relatively greater cause than the first two to be repelled by Soviet initiatives and goals, it might have been expected to have commensurately little incentive to stake its life on the defense of the status quo; it could be expected to remain at least cautiously neutral and tacitly accommodationist to Soviet revolutionary approaches through law. For obvious reasons, the fourth group could certainly be expected to muster the regime's staunchest and natural enemies. Yet, given its originally small size, the thinning of its ranks through Soviet-sponsored deportations and executions, a measure of internal division (*e.g.* into red/progressive and black/reactionary *mullahs*), the shattering impact of large-scale defections from tradition on the part of kinswomen, kinsmen, parishioners, and countrymen, as well as the ever growing threat of draconic Soviet sanctions, it might have been confidently expected that the fourth group would find itself increasingly isolated and shorn of influence, and that it could in any case do very little damage.

The cumulative effect could thus be assumed to be obvious: a marked acceleration of a shift in the psycho-cultural and political orientations of virtually *all* clients. Explicitly or implicitly, nuances of precisely such expectations were advanced by communist field-organizers in justifying Soviet revolutionary initiatives. The concurrence of the highest echelons of the party was indeed reflected, in part, in official proposals that the revolution in Central Asia be spearheaded by a political alliance of "landless farmhands...poor peasants [and nomads]...and women."

Yet, even this relatively subtle turn of political judgment ran afoul of social reality. It turned out to be exceedingly difficult, if not impossible, to distinguish friend from foe in any meaningful or reliable way. First, the perceptions and responses of the women themselves turned out to be far from homogeneous in intensity, orientation, and value. Second, the attitudes and behavior of male clients turned out to be determined at least as much by old unities based on kinship, custom, and belief as by new, legally ensured considerations of property, bureaucratic status, and sex. Third, and perhaps most important in the short run, the performance of the new Soviet apparatus—the "sponsor system"—com-posed in the lower echelons of largely native cadres was itself subject to the same complex parallelogram loyalties. In other words, it was found to be difficult to replicate in reality the simple, "rational" dichotomy between "we" and "they," between "sponsors" and "targets" of action, between the worlds of "revolutionary agents" and "traditional clients...."

## Initial Moves

Soviet approaches to revolutionary change through law proceeded on two planes: (1) the decreed abolition of traditional court structures, including religious and customary tribunals, and their replacement by a secular, uniform, centralized, bureaucratic, and hierarchical system of Soviet courts; and (2) the decreed abolition of religious and customary law, applying (for the purposes of this study) to personal status and family matters, and their replacement by a secular, egalitarian, uniform, and written code of statutory laws.

In the period between 1918 and 1927 traditional courts were subjected to gradually increasing pressure. This included (a) growing competition from a parallel Soviet court structure, (b) separation from sources of material support, (c) infiltration of judicial personnel, and (d) delimitation and successive amputation of jurisdictional realms. In September 1927, traditional courts were formally proscribed and abolished.

In the course of the same decade, successive legislative enactments gradually extended the list of proscribed customary relationships and conduct. In April 1923, a new and fairly exhaustive code of laws—*On Crimes Constituting the Relics of the Tribal Order*—was enacted by the Russian republic (for the non-European minorities on its territory) and incorporated within a few months, with only minor variations, in the legal systems of the Central Asian republics. In addition to proscribing a number of customary forms of inter-tribal and interclan relations (such as blood-vengeance and blood-money for claimed loss, damage, or dishonor) the new code addressed itself virtually to the entire range of manifestations denoting status-inferiority on the part of women. The catalogue of proscribed acts included bride-price (*kalym*, carrying sanctions against both giver and receiver of payment), child-marriage, forced marriage (involving either physical or psychological coercion), marriage by abduction, rape (with or without intent to marry), polygamy, levirate, as well as mistreatment and killing of wives. The sanctions ranged from a year of hard labor for polygamy, to up to three years of jail for forcing a girl into marriage, to death for the murder of a wife.

A separate series of decrees and constitutional guarantees were promulgated with the express purpose of ensuring the absolute equality of the sexes. Thus, on the one hand, marriages concluded under traditional-religious auspices were declared to be invalid; only registration in appropriate Soviet state agencies, accompanied by proper evidence regarding age, health, and mutual consent of the marital partners, could make the unions legal. On the other hand, a number of women's rights were spelled out, contravening the very core of religious and customary prescriptions regarding sexual apartheid and female inferiority: the right to initiate divorce (as against a Moslem male's prevailing right to unilateral divorce action through simple repudiation); the right to equal succession (as against religious or customary provisions for female inequality in the inheritance of property); the right to equal witness in court (as against specific Islamic stipulations that the testimony of two female witnesses be required in contesting the testimony of one man); as well as the right to full-fledged participation in public life—including general education, professional training, and participation in all socio-cultural, economic, and political pursuits, services, and organizations on equal terms with men. The latter denoted not only voting but also service in all, including the highest, elective and appointive public offices in the land—with early and special emphasis given to service in judicial roles in the new Soviet court system. In recognition of the obvious possibility that overt acceptance of legal rights might go hand in hand with covert denial of real opportunities to exercise these rights, Central Asian republican constitutions incorporated explicit provisions for sanctions in cases of "resistance [by anyone and in any form] to the actual emancipation of women."

At the same time, an attempt was made to set three interrelated processes in motion outside of the legal realm, all designed as enabling vehicles to spur female mobility and self-assertion, and thus to undermine the mainstays of female dependence, segregation, and seclusion not only in public life but also in the private realms of family and home. (1) Cadres of the Party's *zhenotdel* (Department for Work with Women) were instructed to commence, in cooperation with appropriate industrial, agricultural, labor, trade, health, education, and welfare agencies of the state, the organization of "Councils of Women's Delegates," clubs, stores, vocational centers, literacy and hygiene circles, and health centers catering especially to women, and to use such new associational foci as forums for political agitation and recruitment. (2) *Zhenotdel* cadres were assigned to the task of personally encouraging Moslem women to sue for divorce from cruel, unloved, polygamous, or otherwise unacceptable husbands, and personally supervising and assisting them toward this end in court. (3) The entire party and state apparatus in Central Asia, including *zhenotdel* cadres, was instructed (a) to elicit public demands, especially on the part of Moslem women, to ban female veiling; to float such demands as trial balloons in all mass media, and to determine the feasibility of a legal prohibition of the veil; (b) to organize (beginning with March 8—Soviet Woman's Day—1927) mass meetings and demonstrations of women in a number of Central Asia's larger population centers; at these meetings to encourage—through the personal example of native communists' wives and daughters, through the example of especially assembled Turkic (particularly Tatar, and hence unveiled) women from outside the region, and through special provisions for police protection—the massive and dramatic unveiling of Moslem women in public, and the burning of their veils in great bonfires on village and city squares, including squares bordering on Central Asia's holiest Islamic shrines.

*Initial Results: The Pattern of Popular Response—Females*[6]

The response of indigenous Moslem women to the norms and thrust of Soviet legal engineering was varied in the extreme. It tended, at least at first, to be dependent on the attitudes and actions of males in general and the tug-of-war between traditionalist and Soviet forces in particular. Broadly speaking, female response may be said to have ranged from what might be called avoidance and selective participation to militant self-assertion and uncontrolled involvement.

[6] It should be kept in mind that not even a rough quantitative distribution of modes of response on the part of the relevant actors can be attempted at this point. Accessible Soviet sources have so far given no meaningful cues on this account. When Soviet Central Asian archives are opened to scholarly perusal, some rough estimates might become feasible.

1. AVOIDANCE. During the initial period of Soviet emancipatory initiatives in Central Asia in legal and extra-legal fields (1925–1926), what appears to have been the majority of Moslem women showed few if any signs of being interested in, or affected by, the unprecedented developments. They did not unveil; they failed to vote or otherwise assert their newly proffered rights; they avoided contact with Soviet agents and institutions; and, most importantly, they failed to bring their grievances to Soviet courts.

In attempting to explain this peculiar lack of response, communist field-organizers came to the following conclusions:

Moslem women in the traditional hinterland were not really aware of the new Soviet legislation and of the rights and opportunities it promised. In most cases the only people who could inform them about their civil rights, and urge them to utilize these rights, were native (*i.e.* male) Soviet officials, and they in particular were not going out of their way to do so. Thus, the disadvantaged either did not know about, or did not know how to take advantage of, the new world embodied in the new law.

The psychic world in which a Moslem woman lived constituted a "primordial wall" which one needed to break through. This wall was made up of "primordial habits and religious fanaticism," of "wild customs and superstitions," and it stood guard over a "slough of darkness and culturelessness." That world had made the woman "passive," engendering the feeling that "her slave-like position in the family and her isolation from society were predetermined from above [were decreed in heaven], were eternal and inviolable." Laws alone—"no matter what kind... and how good...they were"—could hardly be expected to make a dent in such a world.

Precisely because—without "long-term preparatory enlightenment work" by the party—these women were "not fully aware of their own slave-like existence," they considered all contacts with strangers as a "[mortal] sin," compounded by their living in perpetual fear of their fathers, husbands, brothers, or guardians, and of condemnation by the community as a whole.

In certain situations a woman had especially pressing, concrete reasons not to bring her grievances to a Soviet, or any other court. This was especially true in cases of human interaction in intimate situations. Thus, if a woman was abducted with intent to marry, and raped on the way, she either had to marry her abductor or risk becoming an outcast in her own community, since she had no other place to go. Under these circumstances, she was not likely to report the violation in a Soviet court lest she burn all her bridges behind her.

2. SELECTIVE PARTICIPATION. Under certain circumstances, and in certain locales (especially in urban and within close proximity to urban locales), women did show signs of willingness to assert, albeit selectively, their new rights. If contacted by a woman (especially by a kinswoman or a woman of the same ethnic and cultural background) and in circumstances considered natural and harmless by the dominant male in the family, they were disposed to bring up relatively frankly their grievances, needs, and hopes, If provided with segregated electoral districts, they appeared, even if hesitantly at first, at the polls. If provided with tangibly practical incentives (such as scarce consumer's goods, vocational and household counsel, medical assistance for themselves and their children, a chance to earn extra income or merely a chance to enjoy and participate in collective entertainment), and if assured of a secluded (*i.e.*, segregated) situation, they showed an interest in joining a Soviet-sponsored club, a handicraft or consumer's cooperative, or a literacy circle in close vicinity of their homes.

But in all cases they tended to retain their veils—at least on the way to and from the new milieu—to remain completely within the confines of their traditional community, and to shun communication, commitments, and actions that would in any way violate traditional taboos and provoke opprobrium or wrath from the community or kin group.

3. MILITANT SELF-ASSERTION. In relatively urbanized locales, in especially engineered emotional situations, and under close personal guidance by congenial leaders, some women (especially maltreated wives, wives of polygamous men, recent childbrides, menial employees in well-to-do households, orphans, and divorcees) showed themselves willing to exercise their rights and challenge the traditional status quo through massive, public, and dramatic violation of traditional taboos. Encouraged and trained in the relative isolation of the first women's clubs, some indigenous women were persuaded to enact (unveiled) female roles in the theater, and to give concerts and to dance in public. Especially recruited by female agents of the communist party's *zhenotdel* (Department for Work with Women), some Moslem women volunteered to run on the party's ticket and to be elected to public posts in "Councils of Women's Delegates," in soviets and in the administrative and judicial apparati. Some, albeit relatively few, joined the party.

Befriended, supported, and coached by *zhenotdel* representatives, a rapidly growing number of women in Soviet courts initiated divorce proceedings, accompanied by demands for equitable division of property and assignment of children. By mid-1926 communist organizers reported a veritable "divorce wave" in some Central Asian districts, or simply "massive...epidemic [abandonment]" of husbands by their wives. In March 1927, the party succeeded in organizing in Central Asia, the first great marches of female crowds in public. Exhorted by fiery recitations, revolutionary songs and music, and agitators' calls for immediate female liberation and sexual desegregation, great crowds of women not only entered into public quarters traditionally reserved for men, but also marched into locales sanctified for special religious purposes. There, thousands were moved into collective, simultaneous, and public burning of their veils, and then surged through the streets unveiled, chanting challenges to the old order. Throughout 1927 and early 1928, groups of women appeared at labor exchanges in Central Asia's major cities demanding jobs and equal employment opportunities. Other groups, led by communist *zhenotdel* officials, and accompanied by Soviet militiamen, roamed city streets, tearing veils off other women, hunting for caches of food and cotton hidden by peasants and traders, and hunting as well for members of traditional elites subject to arrest and deportation. Some reported to the Red Army and the secret police the hideouts of remaining local guerrillas. Even in some isolated outposts in the hinterland, party officials reported cases of especially aggressive Moslem women arriving in local party headquarters, offering their services as village organizers, and only asking for "guns, secretaries [and bodyguards]" to settle old accounts in the countryside.

4. UNCONTROLLED INVOLVEMENT. By 1928 communist officials in Central Asia reported with increasing frequency and unease that in locales where divorce proceedings, public unveiling, and overall female mobilization had gone farthest, conditions were "verging on [mass] prostitution." They offered two basic reasons for such an unprecedented turn of events: economic and psychocultural. Women abandoning—or being obliged to leave—their communities and kin groups, with or without a divorce,

had neither the means and skills nor the requisite attitudes and opportunities to support themselves. Women emerging suddenly from a Moslem traditional milieu, and coming into unrestricted contact with men in a variety of social situations, were emotionally unprepared for the occasion. . . .

*Initial Results: The Pattern of Popular Response—Males*

The pattern of male response within the traditional milieu may be said to have ranged from evasion and selective accommodation to limited retribution and massive backlash.

1. EVASION. Moslem males, in both traditionally authoritative and nonauthoritative roles, were found as a rule to evade the newly imposed rules and to avoid entanglement with the new judicial institutions. The reasons were manifold. As in Islamic contexts elsewhere, their cultural reflex was to pay, overtly, elaborate and even reverent obeisance to formal requisites imposed by a predominant outside power, but, at the same time, covertly, to expend inordinate energies on evading the law, including even the laws of the *shariat*—whenever the latter conflicted with locally valued mores and customs or with the perceived self-interest of individuals, local communities, and groups. The rules, procedures, and structures of the new legal system could be viewed, especially in this case, as directly antithetical to legitimate institutions. In addition to being, on general grounds, profoundly heretical and fundamentally subversive in traditional Moslem and customary tribal contexts, the new system embodied three specific features making it especially repellent. Its institutions were rigidly formal, bureaucratic, and impersonal, hence lacking the familiar, flexible, sacred, and charismatic attributes of mediation and control long considered

requisite and legitimate in local communities. It was sponsored and staffed by aliens and infidels—Russians, communists, and native reformers. And its emphasis on sexual equality was tantamount to subversion and regulation of the most deeply embedded, sensitive, intimate and sacred aspects of private life. Thus, as Soviet court officials reported uneasily from Central Asia, native males not only regarded the new laws as "sinful," and hence evaded them, but when apprehended and indicted for "crimes based on custom"—"crimes constituting survivals of a tribal way of life"—they "[experienced] no sense of guilt...[and]...could not understand why they were being punished." In some instances, to follow the new rules meant to incriminate oneself immediately and automatically. For example, two fathers (representing two extended families or clans) planning the marital union of their children and arriving in a Soviet agency to register the union, could at once be liable to imprisonment and fine —if, as was customary, a bride-price was involved, if the explicit consent of both marital partners was not secured, or if the boy's, or more usually the girl's, age was under the legal limit. Further, a male planning to acquire a second or third wife, who agreed to register his new marriage in a Soviet agency, would likewise be subject to prosecution. Under such circumstances, Moslem men tended not to utilize the legal auspices of formal Soviet institutions, not even to report the birth of a child, lest its age be thus incontrovertibly established. They continued, instead, to use the services of a *mullah* in traditionally sanctioned, private ceremonies. And if it was impossible to hide the fact of a traditional marriage, for example, and if pressed to register it under the law, male heads of families and clans simply invented new modes of negotiations for a bride-price that evaded official detection. They also supplied as many false witnesses as needed, including false grooms and brides, in order to legalize a traditional union in a Soviet institution.

2. SELECTIVE ACCOMMODATION. Under some circumstances, and in some realms, males in general and traditional elites in particular, showed signs of interest in responding to the challenge of female emancipation through selective accommodation....

Aroused by the visible and potential consequences of Soviet-sponsored mobilization among women, some Moslem clergymen and village and clan notables launched what was in effect the first conscious organizational effort in local cultural history directed along tribal and religious lines to "win back" women and youth. It included tribal and village sponsorship of "women's meetings" and elaborate celebrations—*toy* and *ash*— prominently involving women; material help in furthering cooperative arrangements in the community, *e.g.* simple machinery for the manufacture of dairy products; the formation under clerical auspices of Moslem youth groups, for boys as well as girls, to rival the Komsomol; the establishment of special girls' schools for "religious enlightenment"; the attraction of women into the mosque; the denial, at least in some cases, that the *shariat* necessarily ordained the veiling of women and their inequality in marriage, divorce, inheritance, and court proceedings; and even the establishment, in what were projected as centers of Moslem administration, of special "Women's Departments" under a female *kadi*, to rival the party's *zhenotdel*. This was a series of awkward, isolated, small-scale attempts, in self-defense, to formulate a response to the challenge of a secularist revolution under communist auspices. It was an effort to introduce some flexibility into the customary and Islamic view of social relations and roles, and to provide some alternatives to the rights proffered and the opportunities promised by the Soviet regime.

3. LIMITED RETRIBUTION. When faced with growing female participation, or pressure to participate, in the public realm, males responded—albeit largely as individuals, and largely private—by applying proscriptive counterpressures. Their motives were explicitly reported by Soviet organizers. They were, primarily, the fear of female economic and political competition; the fear of the effect that social participation would have on the attitudes, morality, and fidelity of daughters and wives (and hence the fear of other men's sexual competition); and the fear, ultimately, of the loss of authoritative male dominance over females.

In widely scattered locales, especially in the countryside, girls and women were persuaded, sometimes forcefully, to keep away from schools, clubs, and voting booths. Heads of families tended to permit a modest degree of such participation only when assured of complete sexual segregation in these realms, or when confronted, as on voting days, by police and the Red Army. While some husbands and fathers were tempted by the promise of extra income, they were reported to have deep misgivings about their females' going to work in a factory. Here the degree of the community's supervision over its members was bound to be much lower, and the chances of unrestricted contact with other men much higher than usual. In parallel fashion, while unmarried and relatively poor males showed signs of welcoming greater access to females, they were reported to feel deeply threatened by women's arrival in the economic market place in general and in factories in particular.

When faced with divorce proceedings initiated by women, and with the first acts of female unveiling, Moslem husbands and kinsmen responded with privately administered beatings, and to a growing extent, with the expulsion of these women from home. What seemed particularly ominous in the eyes of Soviet officials was the fact that, with or without a divorce, women were being thrown out unceremoniously into the streets, and were left without property that legally belonged to them, "without a roof over their heads, and without a piece of bread... [to keep body and soul together]." Likewise, when apprehended and pressed to dissolve a polygamous marriage, native males tended simply "to throw the [extra] wife [or wives]— in most cases the old ones and the cold ones—out the door, denying them even the least bit of property." It appeared, then, that by pressing the issue the regime was likely to wind up with a vast throng of old, lonely, and destitute women on its hands.

4. MASSIVE BACKLASH. When faced with a mounting wave of divorces and organized public unveiling, and with the concomitants of women's spatial and social mobility, including widespread desegregation, political denunciations, and prostitution, Moslem men responded with an explosion of hostility and violence unequaled in scope and intensity until then on any other grounds.

Two sets of mutually reinforcing perceptions seem to have been set in motion here. First, under the umbrella of Soviet rule a native male's opportunities for martial, acquisitive, and hegemonic self-assertion had been severely circumscribed. This meant that the act of asserting himself vis-a-vis a woman was one of the very few realms—if not the last one—left to him for the assertion of authority and virility. Under these circumstances, *khudzhum*—the "cultural revolution" launched through legal and extra-legal channels—by suddenly and powerfully intensifying men's apprehensions and anxiety stemming from the threat of impotence, apparently precipitated a crisis in the male's self-esteem. Moreover, the sudden threat to the nexus of authority relationships in the most intimate circle of a man's life—the sense of being *dispossessed* in sexual and generational realms—served to provide the vehicle that fused men's unease and resentment stemming from the entire spectrum of Soviet-inspired actions in the traditional milieu. By the same token, despondency, hatred, and violence heretofore devoid of clearly identifiable objects for blame could suddenly focus upon the sponsors of *khudzhum:* female defectors from tradition, male communists, infidels, and aliens.

Secondly, both the Islamic and customary components of Central Asian folkways had always carried expectations that unrestricted female mobility and unveiling would inevitably lead to widespread social disorganization, demoralization, promiscuity, and harlotry. Some aspects of female mobilization seemed to confirm these traditional expectations, thus providing the makings of a self-fulfilling prophecy.

The resulting backlash, beginning on a large scale in the spring of 1927 (*i.e.* immediately after the first organized public unveilings), marked the massive consummation of two interrelated trends: the radicalization of male attitudes to women and the radicalization of native male attitudes toward the Soviet regime.

The backlash patterns included the following manifestations which in turn constituted stages following each other in rapid succession and reaching their most violent forms within weeks of the pattern's inception: an insidious rumor campaign by *mullahs* associating Soviet-sponsored emancipatory and related activities with whatever actual or potential calamities might befall individuals or entire communities of believers; framing or casting out (amounting to excommunication) of men who acquiesced in their womenfolk's participation in public unveiling; public prophesying that bolsheviks would turn all Moslem women into harlots; shaming, raping, and killing of unveiled women in the streets (including the disemboweling of pregnant women) as traitors to tradition and prostitutes; vilification, persecution, and murder (including lynching) of female activists and organizers, and of their families; wholesale murder of anyone even distantly connected with the "cultural revolution"; indiscriminate generalized violence—*i.e.* "a wave of terror" directed against any and all representatives of the Soviet regime, male or female, native or Russian.

As Soviet organizers reported from the field, both the causes and the process of the backlash tended to lead to the closing of traditionalist ranks and to the hardening of traditionalist attitudes. The specter of massive and dramatic emancipatory activities in public seemed to drive traditionalist males—"poor" as well as "rich"—and the sacred Moslem intelligentsia and clan notables closer together, for all of them felt challenged as Moslems, as heads of kin groups, and as males. This meant that, instead of sharpening the class struggles, as the communists had hoped, precipitate Soviet initiatives tended to mitigate that struggle. Instead of leading to the alienation of substantial segments of society from the traditional way of life, sudden and massive female mobilization tended to lead to widespread and intense alienation from the Soviet system and its works, accompanied by cleavages running along primarily sexual and ethnic lines. Instead of helping to induce conflicts that would be socially, culturally, politically, and economically productive

from the Soviet point of view, precipitate female mobilization was activating
conflicts that were highly destructive.

. . .

## IMPLICATIONS OF MASSIVE
## ENFORCEMENT AND REPRESSION

Even as repression proceeded, doubts
in communist ranks, including the
highest echelons, multiplied. As reports
from the field poured in, a number of
specific problems came to be perceived
with varying degrees of clarity, and
their ramifications were given due
weight.

1. In a revolutionary and developmental period, indiscriminate and draconic repressions tended to have a
decidedly negative effect on the scarcest
political commodity at the regime's disposal: native cadres. (a) The greater
were the pressures to enforce the new
code among the native Soviet cadres,
the greater was the tendency among
them toward local mutual-protection associations—often in alliance with surviving local traditional elites—which
served to complicate immensely the
problems of detection, not only of the
cadres' but also of the masses' transgres-
sions. (b) The harsher were the regime's
reprisals against the cadres' circum-
locution and deviance, and their sabotage of the "cultural revolution" and
female emancipation, the more likely
was antagonism and the disposition toward evasion and sabotage to spill over
into other realms of official performance; thereby, otherwise useful and
loyal political servants tended to become
irretrievably alienated, compounding the
weaknesses of fledgling Soviet institutions. (c) The more consistent and widespread were the regime's attempts (especially if successful) to apply the new
rules to native cadres, the stronger was
the imperative, and the greater the risk,
of precipitous and wholesale purges of
those cadres (involving both the loss of

actual and the repulsion of potential
personnel).

2. In dealing with traditionalist
males, massive enforcement and repression geared to the objectives of the
"cultural revolution" tended to negate
some of the regime's other crucial commitments. The greater was the regime's
emphasis on absolute compliance in the
realm of female emancipation, the
stronger tended to be the traditionalist
males' determination to resist, and disposition to turn to violence and terror,
and the less their cooperation and participation in vital Soviet enterprises in
all other spheres. The more uncompromising was the regime's disposition to
contain and repress traditionalist outbreaks, and to extirpate all deviant behavior in one vast surgical operation,
the greater tended to be its need to
counter mass-malaise with mass-terror.
The logical concomitants of generalized
violence were civil war and, given Soviet
military capabilities, mass-extermination
of Central Asia's indigenous population.
Commensurately, at a certain point of
cost-benefit calculations, the imperatives
of extermination tended to threaten or
irretrievably subvert the communist
party's implicit and explicit commitments to (and expectations of) conversion and assimilation.

3. Paradoxically, even the regime's
successes in female mobilization entailed
decidedly dysfunctional effects both for
the women involved and for the regime.
*The implications were dysfunctional
because the successes were, so to speak,
unidimensional.*

(a) The shorter was the time-limit set
by Soviet authorities for female mobilization, and the more massive and dramatic were female demonstrations, unveilings, and veil-burnings in public,
the more intensive and generalized became male hostility, violence and terror
against those women. Yet, while this
made the need to protect women from

retribution commensurately greater, the regime's capacity to provide such protection proved to be utterly unequal to the need. For that matter, the greater the need, the smaller was the relative capacity to meet it, and the more problematic and dysfunctional the implications of meeting it. It proved utterly impossible to protect each and every "liberated" woman from insult, intimidation, and lynching. . . .

(b) The greater was the rate of female-initiated divorces in court, the rate of impulsive unveiling and of spontaneous abandonment by girls and women of households and husbands, and the rate of retaliatory outcasting of women by men from home, the greater tended to be those women's dependence on the regime's support, and the less the regime's relative capacity to extend such support. As it turned out, *no significant tie-in existed between legal action conferring legal rights and extra-legal initiatives permitting the utilization of these rights in real roles and situations.* No significant buildup of supportive structures and arrangements (in social, economic, cultural, and political spheres) had taken place in the course of Central Asia's "cultural revolution," and certainly no buildup commensurate with the volume and rate of unidimensional female emancipation. Way-stations for converts from tradition— institutions where new identities, relationships, capabilities, and skills would enable women to make a fresh start in life—were largely lacking. While laws and courts encouraged in women iconoclastic dispositions, unprecedented expectations, and mass participation, hardly any tangible channels had been prepared to reinforce their new attitudes, to usefully harness their involvement, and to fulfill their expectations. By the same token, the greater was the woman's dependence on new support, and the less the regime's capacity to

extend it, the heavier was the regime's burden in shouldering responsibility for masses of destitute women, some with infant children and no place to go but the street.

. . .

To sum up: (1) The realization through Soviet law of new ideal norms in Central Asia tended to be inversely related to the degree of forcible attempts to apply it in reality.[7]. . . (2) While law successfully elicited, reinforced, and focused grievances, it tended to be dysfunctional to the extent that it encouraged hopes it could not satisfy. (3) The functioning of law as an instrument of mobilization (as both a repository of ideal norms and a focus of grievances), while powerful in its revolutionizing impact, tended to be directly related to the degree that extra-legal integrative and supportive arrangements were provided for, and coordinated with the mobilizational thrust. . . .

(4) Having to function not only as a

[7] This is not to say, simply, that the less coercive the policy—in the Soviet case—the greater the possibility for revolutionary change. What the evidence does permit us to infer is this: (a) Coercion, even in the hands of a determined and powerful regime which is both authoritarian and revolutionary, cannot be an autonomous and decisive factor in inducing change; (b) The amount of coercion in the process of enforcement constitutes only one of many determinants in the success or failure of law as an instrument of revolutionary change; (c) Just as sudden, indiscriminate, and draconic application of force in the sacred realms of human existence tends to trigger a variety of forms of resistance and hence of hindrances to overall change, so does the de-emphasis of coercive measures serve to remove these specific hindrances. But the *positive* factors in effecting radical social change may be assumed to be a function, not so much of relatively permissive policies, as of the latter's correlation with a network of requisite supportive attitudes, actions, and structures that serve as a tangible and acceptable underpinning for an alternative way of life.

conveyor of new norms but also as an instrument to extirpate the entire antecedent legal system, Soviet law enjoyed the advantages of (a) a formal monopoly of the legal universe; (b) a formal monopoly and overwhelming superiority of force; (c) a centralized and potentially efficient bureaucratic apparatus; and (d) the backing of an authoritarian party-state committed to an overarching ideology and uninhibited by moral and democratic constraints. It was at a disadvantage, however, and hence was congenitally unattractive, or at least not immediately useful, in that (a) it lacked the sacred qualities and personalities of the antecedent system; (b) it tended to be abstract, rigid, and impersonal; (c) it could not easily gain access to traditional communities either because the latter were physically distant, or nomadic-pastoral (hence elusive), or because they were governed by a combination of religious and customary law, and could thus be independent of, and elusive to, formal legal structures. (5) To the extent that it had to function as a protective shield for revolutionary agents and converts, Soviet law tended to be not only useless (in that it could do little or nothing to protect defecting Moslem women from violent retribution), but decidedly dysfunctional (to the extent that it obliged the Soviet regime to risk the lives of valuable and scarce political activists in the impossible task of protecting the rights and lives of masses of individuals scattered in an extremely hostile milieu).

(6) Viewed as an heretical model, the impact of Soviet law on the traditional milieu was exceptionally great. Perhaps no other instrument could hold out to the traditional community, and especially its women, revolutionary standards of human relationships and potentialities as palpably, consistently and authoritatively as Soviet laws did. Perhaps no other instrument could in the short run, be as powerful a catalyst of systematic alienation in, and fundamental transformation of, the traditional milieu. But law as a heretical model tended also to be dysfunctional to the extent that (a) it was felt to be forced upon traditional communities by men who were ethnically or ideologically outsiders; (b) it not only posed a threat to the traditional unities and values, but impinged directly upon the most intimate and sacred realms of local lifestyles; (c) it stimulated the self-assertion of both Soviet-oriented heresy and traditionalist orthodoxy; (d) it put a discipline-oriented, implicitly authoritarian system in the position of encouraging iconoclastic and libertarian propensities that showed themselves capable of turning just as easily against the Soviet regime as against the traditional order. (7) As a regulative mechanism in a revolutionary situation, Soviet law was at one particularly pronounced disadvantage, apart from all those already mentioned. It had neither the legitimate authority, nor the judicial resources, nor yet the extra-legal supportive structures to be able to control tensions as widespread, pervasive, and corrosive as those induced by the heretical model. A revolutionary instrument that was itself not easily controllable, and was itself seeking legitimation in a traditional world, could not very well control tensions and ensure order in that world while it was enforcing with all the power at its command the very quintessence of illegitimacy: heresy.

(8) Therefore, in its role as a specialized tension-management system designed to induce and control revolutionary change, Soviet law turned out to be an exceedingly volatile, imperfect, inexpedient, and in certain circumstances, dangerous instrument. It tended to be volatile in the sense that it could just as easily go too far as not far enough in inducing and managing

change. It was imperfect in the sense that, if devoid of supportive institutions and arrangements that would permit the translation of legal rights into real roles and opportunities, it tended to define new goals while failing to supply the means to reach them. It was inexpedient in the sense that it could undermine the traditional status quo, but could not really transform it. It tended also to be dangerous in that, as a heretical model, it maximized undesirable as well as desirable tensions, while, as a regulative mechanism, it could not minimize the impact of those tensions on the political structures and developmental objectives of the incumbent Soviet regime.

. . .

Faced with the full panoply of implications of massive enforcement and repression, the Soviet regime had the following options: to continue inducing revolutionary tensions as before, to con-tain them by selective rather than indiscriminate enforcement, to deflect them by retaliating primarily against selected targets, to suppress them at all cost and with all the means at its disposal, or to reduce them at the source. While predispositions to all these choices continued to assert themselves in Soviet ranks, the regime's chief reaction was to attempt to mitigate the tensions at their source—through a deliberate reduction of legalistic pressures and a calculated attempt to construct a complex infrastructure of social-service, educational, associational, expressive, and economic facilities.

By early 1929, only two and one half years after the inception of the "cultural revolution" in Central Asia, the communist party felt obliged to bring the "storming" activities on behalf of female emancipation and the massive and overt forms of the cultural revolution itself to an abrupt halt.

*C. Political Instability:*
*Revolution and Violence*

# ON THE CAUSES OF INTERNAL WARS

HARRY ECKSTEIN

THE CONCEPT "INTERNAL WAR"

The term "internal war" denotes any resort to violence within a political order to change its constitution, rulers, or

Reprinted from Harry Eckstein, "On the Etiology of Internal Wars," HISTORY AND THEORY, 4 (1965), 133–63, by permission of Wesleyan University Press and the author.

policies.[1] It is not a new concept; distinctions between external and internal

[1] Elsewhere I have used more cumbersome specifications for the term, holding that internal war is "a kind of social force that is exerted in the process of political competition, deviating from previously shared social norms, 'warlike' in character (that is, conducted

war (*guerre extérieure* and *guerre intérieure*) were made already in the nineteenth century by writers on political violence. Nor does it mean quite the same thing as certain more commonly used terms, such as revolution, civil war, revolt, rebellion, uprising, guerrilla warfare, mutiny, *jacquerie, coup d'état*, terrorism, or insurrection. It stands for the genus of which the others are species.

Using the generic concept alongside, or even in place of, the more specific terms is justifiable on several grounds. Most obviously, all cases of internal war do have common features, however much they differ in detail. All involve the use of violence to achieve purposes which can also be achieved without violence. All indicate a breakdown of some dimension in legitimate political order as well as the existence of collective frustration and aggression in a population. All presuppose certain capabilities for violence by those who make the internal war and a certain incapacity for preventing violence among those on whom it is made. All tend to scar societies deeply and to prevent the formation of consensus indefinitely. There is, consequently, at least a possibility that general theories about internal war may be discovered— general theories which may also help to solve problems posed by specific instances.

. . .

THE PROBLEM OF ETIOLOGY

The theoretical issues raised by internal wars can be classified according to the phases through which such wars pass.

practically without mutually observed normative rules), and involving the serious disruption of settled institutional patterns." *Internal War: Problems and Approaches* (New York, 1964), 12. The differences between the two formulations are due to the fact that here I am defining a term, while in the other essay I was delimiting a theoretical subject. (For what I mean by delimiting a theoretical subject, see *ibid.*, 8–11).

They include problems about their preconditions, the way they can be effectively waged, the courses they tend to take, the outcomes they tend to have, and their long-run effects on society.

Curiously enough, the later the phase, the less there is to read about the issues involved. Despite the protracted normative argument between pro-revolutionaries and anti-revolutionaries, initiated by Paine and Burke, almost nothing careful and systematic has been written about the long-run social effects of internal wars, least of all perhaps about some of the most poignant and practical problems they raise: how political legitimacy and social harmony may be restored after violent disruption, what makes internal wars acute or chronic, and what the comparative costs (and probabilities) are of revolutionary and evolutionary transformations. Little more is available on the determinants of success or failure in internal wars. A fair amount has been written about the dynamic processes of revolutions, above all in some older comparative historical studies and in a very few more recent books, like Crozier's *The Rebels*.[2] But in regard to etiology, to "causes," we are absolutely inundated with print.

This abundance of etiological studies is not, however, an unmixed blessing. If studying other aspects of internal wars poses the basic problem of thinking of theoretical possibilities, studying their etiology poses a difficulty equally great: how to choose among a rare abundance of hypotheses which cannot all be equally valid nor all be readily combined. This problem exists because most propositions about the causes of internal wars have been developed in historical studies of particular cases (or very limited numbers of cases) rather than in broadly comparative, let alone genuinely

[2] Brian Crozier, *The Rebels: A Study of Post-War Insurrections* (London, 1960), Parts III–V and Postlude.

social-scientific, studies. In historical case-studies one is likely to attach significance to any aspect of pre-revolutionary society that one intuits to be significant, and so long as one does not conjure up data out of nothing one's hypotheses cannot be invalidated on the basis of the case in question.

That most studied of all internal wars, the French Revolution, provides a case in point—as well as examples in abundance of the many social, personal, and environmental forces to which the occurrence of internal wars might be attributed. Scarcely anything in the French *ancien régime* has not been blamed, by one writer or another, for the revolution, and all of their interpretations, however contradictory, are based on solid facts.

Some interpreters have blamed the outbreak of the French Revolution on intellectual causes, that is to say, on the ideas, techniques, and great public influence of the *philosophes* (who were indeed very influential). This is the standard theory of post-revolutionary conservative theorists, from Chateaubriand to Taine, men who felt, in essence, that in pre-revolutionary France a sound society was corrupted by a seductive and corrosive philosophy.

Other writers have blamed the revolution mainly on economic conditions, although it is difficult to find very many who single out as crucial the same conditions. The revolution has been attributed to sheer grinding poverty among the lower classes (who were certainly poor); to financial profligacy and mismanagement on the part of the government (of which it was in fact guilty); to the extortionate taxation inflicted on the peasants (and peasant taxation verged upon brutality); to short-term setbacks (which actually occurred and caused great hardship) like the bad harvest of 1788, the hard winter of 1788–89, and the still winds of 1789

which prevented flour from being milled and made worse an already acute shortage of bread; to the over-abundant wine harvests of the 1780's (one of the first historic instances of the harmful effects of overproduction); to the increased wealth and power of the bourgeoisie in a society still dominated to a significant extent by aristocrats, the growth of the Parisian proletariat and its supposedly increasing political consciousness, and the threatened abrogation of the financial privileges of the aristocracy, particularly their exemption from taxation —all unquestionable facts producing manifest problems.

Still another set of writers locates the crucial cause of the revolution in aspects of social structure. Much has been made, and with sufficient reason, of the fact that in the last years of the *ancien régime* there occurred a hardening in the lines of upward mobility in French society—for example, a decline in grants of patents of nobility to commoners and the imposition of stringent social requirements for certain judicial and administrative positions and the purchase of officerships in the army. This, many have argued (following Mosca's and Pareto's famous theory of the circulation of elites), engendered that fatal yearning for an aristocracy of wealth and talent to which the *philosophes* gave expression. Much has also been made, with equal reason, of popular dissatisfaction with the parasitic life of the higher nobility, with its large pensions and puny duties, its life of hunting, love-making, watch-making, and interminable conversation. And much has been attributed to the vulnerability of the privileged classes to the very propagandists who wanted to alter the system that supported them ("How," asked Taine, "could people who talked so much resist people who talked so well?"), reflected in the Anglomania which swept through the higher aristocracy toward the end of the *ancien régime* and in the rush of many aristocrats to the cause of the Americans in their war of independence.

There are also certain well-founded "political" explanations of the French Revolution: that the revolution was really caused by the violation of the tacit "contract" on which the powers of the monarchy rested (a contract by which the aristocracy surrendered its powers to the monarchy in return for receiving certain inviolable privileges), or that the revolution was simply a successful political conspiracy by the Jacobins, based on efficient political organization. Personalities, needless to say, get their due as well: the revolution has been blamed, for example, on the character, or lack of character, of Louis XVI (who was in fact weak, vacillating and inconsistent), the supposed immorality of the Queen (who indeed was the subject, justly or not, of many scandals), the effect on the public of the dismissal of Necker, and, of course, on the "genius," good or evil, of unquestionable geniuses like Mirabeau, Danton, Marat, and Robespierre.

We could take other internal wars and arrive at the same result—similarly large lists of explanations, most of them factual, yet inconclusive. The more remote in time and the more intensively analyzed the internal war, the longer the list of hypotheses. Yet even so recent a case as the Chinese Communist Revolution has given rise to a fearful number of plausible hypotheses, many directly contradictory.

. . .

How can this embarrassment of interpretative riches (one hesitates to say theoretical riches) be reduced? If the examination of any single case allows one to determine only whether an interpretation of it is based on facts, then broad comparative studies in space and/

or time are needed to establish the significance of the facts on which the interpretations are based. Was a blockage in the channels of social mobility a significant precondition of the French Revolution? We can be reasonably confident that it was only if it can be shown that elite circulation and political stability are generally related. Was the Chinese population explosion really an important cause of the Chinese revolution? Surely this is unlikely if demographic pressures do not generally affect the viability of regimes.

This is the simplest conceivable methodology, and easy to indicate abstractly. But actually to find the broad general relationships on the basis of which particular interpretations can be assessed is not so easy. For this purpose we need a tremendous amount of historical work that comparative historiographers of internal wars have hardly even begun to do. There are so many possibilities to be tested against so many cases. A general etiology of internal wars, at this stage, can only be a remote end of inquiry, and neither limited comparative studies nor interpretations of particular instances of internal war should pretend otherwise.

But even prior to undertaking that work, theoretical reflection can introduce some order into the chaos that internal war studies present. Most important, it can produce useful judgments as to the more economic lines to pursue in empirical inquiry. We can in a small way approach an etiology of internal wars by classifying the theoretical possibilities available, indicating the analytical choices they require and do not require to be made, and attempting to determine what lines of analysis are most likely to prove rewarding. Where the theoretical possibilities are as varied and chaotic as in the case of internal war, such reflection, to organize and restrict inquiry, is a necessary preliminary to the more definitive work of rigorously testing well-formulated propositions.

## "PRECONDITIONS" OR "PRECIPITANTS"?

Perhaps the first thing that becomes apparent when one tries to classify causal explanations of the sort sketched above is that many of the explanations do not really require a choice to be made by the analyst. The propositions do not always contradict one another; often, in fact, they are complementary, differing only because they refer to different points in the time-sequence leading to revolution, or because they refer to different kinds of causality, or because they single out one factor among many of equal significance.

The most important distinction to make in this connection is between preconditions and precipitants of internal wars. A "precipitant" of internal war is an event which actually starts the war ("occasions" it), much as turning the flintwheel of a cigarette lighter ignites a flame. "Preconditions" of internal war, on the other hand, are those circumstances which make it possible for the precipitants to bring about political violence, as the general structure of a lighter makes it possible to produce a flame by turning the flintwheel. Some of the causal explanations of the French Revolution already mentioned clearly fall into the first category, while others fall equally clearly into the second; and between explanations singling out precipitants and explanations emphasizing preconditions of internal war there obviously is no genuine contradiction. The distinction between precipitants and preconditions can therefore prevent much pointless argument between those who stress short-run setbacks and those who emphasize long-term trends in the etiology of civil strife. Clearly no inter-nal war can occur without precipitant events to set it off; and clearly no precipitants can set off internal war unless the condition of society makes it possible for them to do so.

The greatest service that the distinction between precipitants and preconditions of internal war can render, however, is to shift attention from aspects of internal war which defy analysis to those which are amenable to systematic inquiry. Phenomena which precipitate internal war are almost always unique and ephemeral in character. A bad harvest, a stupid or careless ruler, moral indiscretion in high places, an ill-advised policy: how could such data be incorporated into general theories? They are results of the vagaries of personality, of forces external to the determinate interrelations of society, of all those unique and fortuitous aspects of concrete life which are the despair of social scientists and the meat and drink of narrative historians.

. . .

However, certain kinds of precipitants of internal war have a special importance of their own in what one might call "practical etiology"—the anticipation of internal wars for policy purposes. A precipitant may be found so frequently on the eve of internal wars that its existence can be treated as a particularly urgent danger signal, particularly if its effects are delayed sufficiently to allow some adaptation to the danger. As far as we know, both of these conditions are satisfied by economic precipitants of internal war. The point deserves some elaboration, particularly in view of the persistent emphasis on economic conditions in writings on internal war.

It now seems generally agreed that persistent poverty in a society rarely leads to political violence. Quite the contrary. As Edwards points out, following an argument already developed by de Tocqueville, economic oppression, indeed all kinds of oppression, seems to wane rather than increase in pre-revolutionary periods.[3] Brinton makes the same point. While not underestimating the amount of poverty in the societies he analyzes in *The Anatomy of Revolution*, he does point out that all of these societies were economically progressive rather than retrograde. He points out also that revolutionary literature, at any rate in the pre-Marxist period, hardly ever dwelt on economic misery and exploitation—one hears about economic grievances, to be sure, but not the sort of grievances which arise out of "immiseration."[4] Even some Marxists seem to share this view. Trotsky, for example, once remarked that if poverty and oppression were a precipitant of revolution the lower classes would always be in revolt, and obviously he had a point.

It is equally difficult to establish a close link between economic improvement and internal war. Pre-revolutionary periods may often be economically progressive, but economic progress is not always (or even often) connected with internal war. From this, however, one need not conclude that economic tendencies are simply irrelevant to the occurrence of political violence. Only the long-term tendencies seem, in fact, to be irrelevant. The moment one focuses on short-term tendencies, a fairly frequently repeated pattern emerges—and one which tells us why it is that some writers adhere stubbornly to the immiseration theory of internal war and others, with just as much conviction, to the economic progress theory. It so happens that before many internal wars, one finds both economic improvement and immiseration; more precisely, many internal wars

are preceded by long-term improvements followed by serious short-term setbacks.[5] The bad harvests and unfavorable weather conditions in pre-revolutionary France, the American recession of 1774–1775, the bad Russian winter of 1916–1917 (not to mention the economic impact of the war on Russia) and the marked rise of unemployment in Egypt before Naguib's *coup* are cases in point. All dealt serious short-term blows to economic life and all followed long periods of economic progress, especially for those previously "repressed."

It is this dual pattern which really seems to be lethal, and it is not difficult to see why. In times of prolonged and marked economic progress, people become accustomed to new economic standards and form new economic expectations, which previously they could scarcely imagine. Confidently expecting continuous progress, they also tend to take risks (like accumulating debts) which they might not take otherwise. All this greatly exaggerates the impact of serious temporary setbacks; both psychologically and economically the costs of such setbacks are bound to be greater than if they occurred after long periods of stagnation or very gradual progress.

Occasionally, perhaps, the study of precipitants of internal war may play a minor role in "theoretical" as well as "practical etiology." It could conceivably shed some light on the preconditions themselves in that there might be a connection between revolutionary conditions and how internal wars are actually brought about. For example, someone may blame internal war on dissatisfactions in the rural population of a society; but if we find peasants playing no role in the fomenting of violence,

---

[3] L. P. Edwards, *The Natural History of Revolutions* (Chicago, 1927) 33.

[4] Crane Brinton, *The Anatomy of Revolution* (New York, 1958) 29–37.

[5] See James C. Davis, "Toward a Theory of Revolution", *American Sociological Review*, 27 (1962), 5–19. This paper traces the pattern in Dorr's Rebellion, the Russian Revolution, and the Egyptian Revolution.

then we have good reason to doubt the interpretation. Precipitants may not directly tell us what the preconditions of internal war are, but they can sometimes indicate what they are not—be useful for falsifying hypotheses, or at least shedding doubt on them. But this does not alter the basic point: that the task of an etiology of internal wars is to discover their preconditions.

COMMON HYPOTHESES ABOUT
THE PRECONDITIONS OF INTERNAL
WAR

We can profitably relegate to a secondary role most of those greatly varying, unique, and largely fortuitous events which occasion the outbreak of internal wars. But even if we do, a great variety of hypotheses remains—great enough if we confine ourselves to general treatments of internal war, and greater still if we deal with hypotheses formulated to deal with particular cases. In this connection, it might be useful to supplement the explanations of particular revolutions listed above with a sample of propositions frequently found in the more general literature on internal war. These include:[6]

a) *Hypotheses emphasizing "intellectual" factors*:
  1. Internal wars result from the failure of a regime to perform adequately the function of political socialization.
  2. Internal wars are due to the co-existence in a society of conflicting social "myths."

[6] The hypotheses come from a large variety of sources, including: Lasswell and Kaplan, *Power and Society* (New Haven, 1950); the works by Edwards and Brinton cited above; Rudé, *The Crowd in the French Revolution* (Oxford, 1959); Trotsky, *The History of the Russian Revolution* (Ann Arbor, Michigan, 1957); De Grazia, *The Political Community* (Chicago, 1948); Gaetano Mosca, *The Ruling Class* (New York, 1939); Vilfredo Pareto, *The Mind and Society* (New York, 1935); George S. Petee, *The Process of Revolution* (New York, 1938).

  3. Internal wars result from the existence in a society of unrealizable values or corrosive social philosophies.
  4. Internal wars are caused by the alienation (desertion, transfer of allegiance) of the intellectuals.

b) *Hypotheses emphasizing economic factors*:
  1. Internal wars are generated by growing poverty.
  2. Internal wars result from rapid economic progress.
  3. Internal wars are due to severe imbalances between the production and distribution of goods.
  4. Internal wars are caused by a combination of long-term economic improvement and short-term setbacks.

c) *Hypotheses emphasizing aspects of social structure*:
  1. Internal wars are due to the inadequate circulation of elites (that is, inadequate recruitment into the elite of the able and powerful members of the non-elite).
  2. Internal wars result from too much recruitment of members of the non-elite into the elite, breaking down the internal cohesion of the elite.
  3. Internal war is a reflection of *anomie* resulting from great social mobility.
  4. Internal war is a reflection of frustration arising from little general social mobility—from general social stagnation.
  5. Internal wars result from the appearance in societies of new social classes.

d) *Hypotheses emphasizing political factors*:
  1. Internal wars are due to the estrangement of rulers from the societies they rule.
  2. Internal war is simply a response to bad government (government

which performs inadequately the function of goal-attainment).

3. Internal wars are due, not to the attacks of the governed on those who govern, but to divisions among the governing classes.

4. Internal wars are responses to oppressive government.

5. Internal wars are due to excessive toleration of alienated groups.

e) *Hypotheses emphasizing no particular aspects of societies, but general characteristics of social process:*

1. Political violence is generated by rapid social change.

2. Political violence results from erratic and/or uneven rates of social change, whether rapid or not.

3. Internal war occurs when a state is somehow "out of adjustment" to society.

From this sample of propositions, all of them at least plausible, we can get some idea of the overwhelming ambiguities that general studies of the preconditions of internal war have created to supplement those originating in case studies. These ambiguities arise most obviously from the fact that many of the propositions are manifestly contradictory; less obviously, from the sheer variety and disparity of factors included, not all of which, surely, can be equally significant, or necessary, in the etiology of internal wars. For this reason, even when precipitants are subtracted, a considerable range of choices between theories remains to be made.

INSURGENTS OR INCUMBENTS?

One crucial choice that needs to be made is whether to put emphasis upon characteristics of the insurgents or incumbents, upon the side that rebels or the side that is rebelled against. Not surprisingly, the existing literature concentrates very largely on the rebels, treating internal war as due mainly to changes in the non-elite strata of society to which no

adequate adjustment is made by the elite. This would seem to be only natural; after all, it is the rebels who rebel. At least some writings suggest, however, that characteristics of the incumbents and the classes that are usually their props must be considered jointly with characteristics of the insurgents, indeed perhaps even emphasized more strongly. Pareto, for example, while attributing revolution partly to blockages in a society's social mobility patterns, considered it equally necessary that certain internal changes should occur in an elite if revolution was to be possible; in essence, he felt that no elite which had preserved its capacity for timely and effective violence, or for effective manipulation, could be successfully assailed, or perhaps assailed at all. One must, according to this view, seek the origins of internal war not only in a gain of strength by the non-elite, but also in the loss of it on the part of the elite. Brinton makes the same point: revolutions, in his view, follow the loss of common values, of internal cohesion, of a sure sense of destiny and superiority and, not least, of political efficiency in elites, and thus must be considered results as much as causes of their disintegration. And in Edwards's and Pettee's studies as well, revolutions emerge as affairs of the elites (if not always directly of the actual rulers): the crucial roles in them are played by intellectuals, by men rich and powerful but "cramped" by their lack of status or other perquisites, and by the gross inefficiency of the ruling apparatus.

Significantly enough, this view is stated perhaps more often in the writings of actual revolutionaries than in those of students of revolution. Trotsky, for example, believed that revolution requires three elements: the political consciousness of a revolutionary class, the discontent of the "intermediate layers" of society, and, just as important, a ruling class which has "lost faith in itself," which is torn by the conflicts of groups and cliques, which has lost its capacity for practical action and rests its hopes in "miracles or miracle workers."[7]

The joint consideration of insurgent and incumbent patterns thus would seem to be the logical way to proceed in the early stages of inquiry into the causes of revolution. But one should not overlook the possibility that sufficient explanations of the occurrence of many internal wars might be found in elite characteristics alone. A ruling elite may decay, may become torn by severe conflict, may be reluctant to use power, may come to lack vital political skills—and thus make it perfectly possible for a relatively weak, even disorganized, opposition of a sort that may exist in any political system to rise against it and destroy it. Indeed, there are theories which maintain that internal wars are always caused solely or primarily by changes in elite characteristics, and that one can practically ignore the insurgents in attempting to account for the occurrence of internal wars.

One such theory is propounded in Mosca's *The Ruling Class*. If the elementary needs of human life are satisfied, argued Mosca, one thing above all will cause men to rebel against their rulers, and that is their feeling that the rulers live in a totally different environment, that they are "separated" from their subjects in some profound sense. In other words, the estrangement of the elite from the non-elite is inseparable from the alienation of the latter; only the elite itself, consequently, can undermine its political position. In this regard Mosca made much of the feudal societies of Poland, Ireland, England, and Russia. The Polish nobles of the Middle Ages, for example, practiced extreme economic extortion, taking in levies almost all the peasant produced; they were ruthless

and violent; they scrupulously extracted the *droit du seigneur*; and despite all that, and more, the peasants never rebelled—as long as the nobles "lived among them, spoke their language, swore the same oaths, ate the same kind of food, wore the same style of clothes, exhibited the same manners or lack of them, had the same rustic superstitions."[8] But a drastic change occurred when the nobility acquired French manners and tastes, "gave luxurious balls after the manner of Versailles and tried to dance the minuet." Despite more humane treatment, vicious and frequent revolts attended the estrangement of the nobles from their people.

This interpretation certainly makes sense in light of French experience: the French Revolution was far more an attack upon the refined and parasitic court nobility than upon the coarse, and little less parasitic, provincial nobility. It makes sense also in the case of Britain, for the British nobility (in the main) always preserved close ties to the soil and to the manner and morals of its tenantry; Squire Western is the embodiment of that fact. That is why it was for so long the butt of jokes among the more sophisticated, and shorter-lived, continental aristocracies.

Perhaps the most prolonged period of civil unrest in American history, the late nineteenth century, can be, and has been, interpreted in much the same manner—not only by political sociologists like De Grazia, but also by acute literary observers like Mark Twain and historians like Miriam Beard.[9] One of the more conspicuous features of that period was the compulsive attempt of the American plutocracy to imitate European "society." At no other time in American history was the elite so pro-

---

[7] Trotsky, *The Russian Revolution*, 311.

[8] De Grazia, *The Political Community*, 74–75.

[9] De Grazia, *The Political Community*, esp. 117 ff. and Miriam Beard, *A History of the Business Man* (New York, 1938).

foundly estranged from American life. Mark Twain gave this period a name which fits exactly and has stuck to it ever since. It was the Gilded Age, the age of English clothes and accents, Roman orgies, continental travel, title-mongering, art-collecting, butlers and footmen, conspicuous consumption of every sort—the age which invented those now much more Americanized institutions, the debutante and the society page. Not until the American plutocracy had returned to its old habits of thrift and earthiness, of being plain Americans, was there a return to relative civil calm in the United States.[10]

More examples of the instability that ensues from the estrangement of elites are furnished in profusion by the westernized elites of many currently underdeveloped areas. The elites referred to in this case are not those who learn Western skills but remain identified with their native context; rather it is the westernized in lifeways, the visitors to the Riviera and the riders in Cadillacs, who try to lead a life totally different from that of their people. For such estranged elites, living abroad may indeed be a course preferable to the imitation of alien ways at home; at any rate, they are in that case rather less conspicuous.

It is worth noting that in the postwar period internal wars have been relatively rare in two kinds of societies: either thoroughly modernized countries or very underdeveloped countries whose elites have remained tied closely to the traditional ways and structures of life.[11] Of course, a generalization of this kind is becoming increasingly harder to test, since the number of societies without a

gulf between highly modernized elites and much less modernized masses seems to be rapidly shrinking. Nevertheless the notion is given credibility by the fact that, while transitional societies seem to suffer more from internal wars than either traditional or modern societies— as one would expect upon many hypotheses—a very few seem to have strikingly low rates of violence compared to the rest. Egypt is one example, and Pakistan another. These societies seem to differ from the rest in one main respect. They have had "secondary" revolutions, so to speak, in which men of rather humble origins and popular ways (colonels' regimes) have unseated previously victorious transitional elites.

All this is not meant to validate the idea that elite estrangement is the main cause of internal war but only to show why it should be taken very seriously. The possible consequences of elite estrangement are not, however, the only reason for emphasizing studies of the incumbents at least as much as studies of insurgents in the etiology of internal wars. Another is the fact that internal wars are almost invariably preceded by important functional failures on the part of elites. Above all is this true of difficulties in financial administration—perhaps because finance impinges on the ability of governments to perform all their functions.[12] And finally, insurgent groups seem rarely to come even to the point of fighting without some support

---

[10] For evidence of acute unrest in the United States in this period, see De Grazia, *The Political Community.*

[11] Cases in point are the stable, highly developed democracies on the one hand, and countries like Ethiopia and Somalia on the other.

[12] One of the most common conditions found before large-scale political violence is the financial bankruptcy of government, due to profligacy, over-ambitious policies, or the failure of a traditional tax structure in an inflationary situation, followed by an attack upon the financial privileges of strata which were previously the main props of the regime. R. B. Merriman, in *Six Contemporaneous Revolutions, 1640–1660* (Oxford, 1938) points out that the seventeenth-century revolutions in England, France, the Netherlands, Spain, Portugal, and Naples all had this point in common.

from alienated members of incumbent elites. On this point, agreement in the literature on internal war is practically unanimous.

## STRUCTURAL OR BEHAVIORAL HYPOTHESES?

A second strategic choice to be made in constructing an etiology of internal wars is between structural and behavioral hypotheses. A structural hypotheses singles out, so to speak, "objective" social conditions as crucial for the occurrence of internal war: aspects of a society's "setting," such as economic conditions, social stratification and mobility, or geographic and demographic factors. A behavioral hypothesis, on the other hand, emphasizes attitudes and their formation—not setting, but "orientations" (such as degrees of strain and *anomie* in societies, the processes by which tension and aggression are generated, and the processes by which human beings are "socialized" into their communities). The great majority of propositions regarding the causes of internal war are, on the basis of these definitions, structural in character. But, in concentrating upon structural explanations have writers on internal war taken the more promising tack?

At first glance, there would seem to be little to choose between structural and behavioral approaches. Since most human action is motivated, not reflexive, one always wants to know, if one can, about attitudes underlying men's actions. At the same time, there can be little doubt that attitudes are always formed somehow in response to external conditions. The difference between structural and behavioral theories would therefore seem to be, at best, one of emphasis or point of view. Yet emphasis can make a difference. Certain research results do seem to be associated with one point of view or the other. Behavioral approaches, for instance, may lead to theories stressing "intellectual" and

voluntaristic factors in the etiology of political violence, or to theories attributing internal war mainly to efficient revolutionary indoctrination or inadequate value-formation by the incumbents. Structural explanations may lead to theories of mechanical imbalance in society, or to theories attributing internal war mainly to specific situational conditions, attitudes being treated as mechanical responses to such conditions.

Which approach is preferable? Despite the fact that there is a danger that the behavioral approach might lead to naive conspiracy theory (the belief that internal wars are always the results of insidious indoctrination by subversive elements, and could therefore always occur or always be avoided) the arguments against a primary emphasis on structural theories are very strong.

One such argument derives from the general experience of modern social science. Purely structural theories have generally been found difficult to sustain wherever they have been applied, and one fundamental reason for this is that patterns of attitudes, while responsive to the settings in which men are placed, seem also to be, to an extent, autonomous of objective conditions, able to survive changes in these conditions or to change without clearly corresponding objective changes. This is one of the basic insights underlying the sociological theory of action, which, to be sure, assigns an important role to the situations in which human action occurs, but treats "culture" largely as a separate variable and attaches particularly great significance to agencies of socialization and acculturation. It underlies as well the relatively successful use of mediational models, the S–O–R models rather than the simple S–R models, in behavioral psychology.

No doubt this point should be much elaborated.[13] But one can make a cogent

13 Useful summaries of action and behavior

case for stressing behavioral theories of the causes of internal wars without going lengthily into the general nature and past experiences of social science.

The most obvious case for behavioral theories of internal war derives from the very fact that so many different objective social conditions seem capable of generating it. We may have available many interpretative accounts of internal wars simply because an enormous variety of objective conditions can create internal-war potential. Certain internal wars do seem to have followed economic improvement, others seem to have followed closely the Marxist model of internal wars, however many more have followed some combination of the two. Some internal wars have in fact been preceded by great, others by little social mobility; some regimes have been more oppressive and others more liberal in the immediate pre-revolutionary period, some both and some neither. Is it not reasonable to conclude that one should not seek explanations of the occurrence of internal wars in specific social conditions, but rather in the ways in which social conditions may be perceived? Instead of looking for direct connections between social conditions and internal war, should one not look rather for the ways in which an existing cognitive and value system may change, so that conditions perceived as tolerable at one point are perceived as intolerable at another; or, concomitantly, look for the ways in which old systems of orientation are in some cases maintained rather than adapted in the face of social change, so that changes which one society absorbs without trouble create profound difficulties in another?

The point is not that objective conditions are unrelated to internal war.

Rather it is that orientations mediate between social setting and political behavior, and—because they are not simply mirrors of environment—so that different objective conditions may lead to similar political activities, or similar conditions to different activities in different contexts; that in a single context a considerable change in political activity may occur without significant changes in objective conditions or changes in objective conditions without changes in activity. What should be avoided is linking aspects of social setting *directly* to internal war or *mechanically* to orientations. Internal wars are best conceived as responses to political disorientation (such as "cognitive dissonance," *anomie*, and strains in the definition of political roles), particularly in regard to a society's norms of legitimacy; and political disorientation may follow from a considerable variety of conditions, due to the variable nature of the orientations themselves and of the agencies that implant them in different societies.

One conspicuous point of agreement in comparative studies of revolution gives further credence to this argument. This is that revolutions are invariably preceded by the "transfer of allegiance" of a society's intellectuals and the development by them of a new political "myth." If intellectuals have any obvious social "functions," in the sense social scientists understand the term function, they are surely these: to socialize the members of a society outside of the domestic context, in schools and adult learning situations; to reinforce and rationalize attitudes acquired in all social contexts; and to provide meaning to life and guidelines to behavior by means of conscious doctrines where events have robbed men of their less conscious bearings. Intellectuals are particularly important in the education of adolescents and young people, and it has

theories can be found in Roland Young, ed., *Approaches to the Study of Politics* (Evanston, Illinois, 1958), 217–243 and 285–301.

been shown quite definitely that political socialization occurs (or fails) mainly in the years between early childhood and full maturity.[14] It could also be shown that among revolutionaries the young tend to predominate, sometimes quite remarkably. Together these points go far to explain why the alienation of intellectuals is, in Edwards's language, a "master-symptom" of revolution: a condition that makes revolutionary momentum irreversible.

Another point that speaks for behavioral propositions is that internal wars can, and often do, become chronic. In some societies, the most manifest cause of internal war seems to be internal war itself, one instance following another, often without a recurrence of the conditions that led to the original event. This means that political disorientation may be followed by the formation of a new set of orientations, establishing a predisposition toward violence that is inculcated by the experience of violence itself. In such cases, internal wars result not from specifiable objective conditions, and not even from the loss of legitimacy by a particular regime, but from a general lack of receptivity to legitimacy of any kind. Violence becomes a political style that is self-perpetuating, unless itself "disoriented."

The very fact that elite estrangement so often precedes acute political unrest itself fits the case for behavioral propositions. It fits in part because the Establishment of any society includes its intellectuals, but also for a more important, rather technical, reason. Orientations, particularly as treated in action theory, are not purely internal and self-sufficient, as it were, but involve expectations from others ("alters")—mutualities or complementarities in behavior. Hence men are likely to become disoriented and

alienated when those with whom they interact become aliens to them, even if the alien ways involve, from abstract moral standpoints, a change for the better. The Polish peasant probably did not positively like to be beaten, but he *expected* to be, and he himself undoubtedly committed a good deal of institutionalized mayhem on anyone subordinated to his authority. A liberal aristocrat would appear to him not only to act strangely but arbitrarily, and, in a way, as a constant personal reproach.

To give still more support to the argument for behavioral theories there is the object lesson provided by the sad history of Marxist theory. Marxism singles out certain objective social conditions as underlying internal wars. It also singles out certain social groups as indispensable to the making of internal war. But Marxist revolutions themselves have been made neither under the social conditions nor by the groups emphasized in the theory. What is more, these revolutions have been made in a large variety of conditions, with a large variety of means, by organizations constituted in a large variety of ways. This is true even if one can show that the appeal of Marxism is greatest in transitional societies, for the term transition, in its very nature, denotes not a particular social state but a great many different points on whatever continuum social development may involve.

PARTICULAR CONDITIONS OR
GENERAL PROCESSES?

This argument has a close bearing upon a third strategic choice to be made in analyzing the causes of internal war. Even if one emphasizes behavioral characteristics in theories of internal wars, one must, as I have said, always relate these characteristics to the social setting. The question is how to do this. Should one, in the manner of most of the hypotheses listed above, develop proposi-

---

[14] For evidence, see Herbert H. Hyman, *Political Socialization* (Glencoe, Illinois, 1959).

tions emphasizing particular social conditions or, in the manner of a few of them, select propositions about general characteristics of social process? In the first case, one would relate internal war to particular socio-economic changes, in the second to characteristics of the general phenomenon of social change itself, such as rapid change or erratic change in any sectors of society, or conditions that may result from any social change whatever, such as imbalances between social segments (e.g., between elites of wealth and elites of status) or incongruities among the authority patterns of a society.

The proper choice between these alternatives is already implied in the arguments of the previous section. If many particular social conditions may be connected with internal wars, then clearly one should stress broad propositions about social processes and balances that can comprehend a variety of such conditions. The same position results if disorientation is conceived, in large part, as a breakdown in mutualities and complementarities of behavior. Not least, there is overwhelming evidence to show that "*anomie*," the feeling that one lacks guidelines to behavior, is increased by rapidity of change in any direction (for example, by rapid economic betterment no less than rapid economic deterioration) and that "strain," the feeling that one's roles make inconsistent demands, is aggravated by uneven or incongruent changes in different social sectors (for example, when the economic sector of society becomes significantly modern while the political remains largely traditional).

What has been said about economic conditions preceding internal wars fits the argument particularly well. It is not just that cases can be found to support both immiseration and improvement theories of revolution, hence the view that internal wars are related to economic

changes as such, not to change in any particular direction; more suggestive still is the fact that internal wars most frequently follow an irregular—an anomalous—course of economic change, long-term trends being interrupted by abrupt and short-lived reversals. Such a course exhibits at least two of the general characteristics of social processes that would, upon earlier arguments, seem to be related to the occurrence of internal wars: rapidity of change and eccentricity of change.

From this standpoint it would be most interesting to investigate whether *any* rapid and eccentric course of economic development tends to be related to internal war, perhaps even one involving long-term stagnation or deterioration followed by abrupt short-term improvement. This idea is not as farfetched as may seem; after all has not Durkheim fully documented the argument that "*fortunate crises*, the effect of which is abruptly to enhance a country's prosperity, affect suicide like *economic disasters*"?[15]

Undoubtedly there is a danger that broad formulations concerning general social processes will turn into empty and untestable generalizations, trivialities like the much-repeated proposition that political violence tends to accompany social or economic change. But this danger is avoidable; one can, after all, be specific and informative about general social processes as well as about their substantive content.

OBSTACLES TO INTERNAL WAR

So far I have tried to make two related points. The first is that one is most likely to gain understanding of the forces impelling societies toward internal war if one avoids preoccupation with the more visible precipitants of internal wars,

---

[15] Emile Durkheim, *Suicide* (London, 1952), 243 (my italics).

including conspiracies, and directs one's efforts to the analysis of their preconditions, stressing disorientative general social processes and particularly taking into account elite behavior, performance, and cohesion. The second point is in a sense the converse of this: that existing etiologies of internal wars are chaotic and inadequate precisely because studies have so far concentrated on precipitants rather than preconditions, insurgents rather than incumbents, and particular aspects of social structure rather than the effects on orientations of general social processes.

An important point must now be added. Even if we had better knowledge of the forces which push societies toward political violence, a crucial problem relating to the etiology of internal wars would remain, one that is generally ignored in the studies available to us. This problem concerns forces that might countervail those previously discussed: "obstacles" to internal war, as against forces which propel societies toward violence.

In the real world of phenomena, events occur not only because forces leading toward them are strong, but also because forces tending to inhibit, or obstruct, them are weak or absent; . . . internal wars may fail to occur solely or mainly because of certain hindrances to their occurrence. Some of these hindrances may be absolute in character, in that wherever they exist internal war fails to materialize; hence their obverse may be considered "requisites" of internal war (necessary, but not sufficient, conditions). In the main, however, obstacles to internal war, like forces making for internal war, are better conceived as factors making such wars more or less likely, rather than either inevitable or impossible—their actual significance depending, at least in part, on the strength of forces pulling in a contrary direction. It certainly seems unlikely that we shall ever find a condition that makes internal war quite inevitable under any circumstances, and equally unlikely that we could discover conditions that always rule it out (except perhaps purely definitional ones: e.g., the absence of any perceived frustrations). In real life, internal war, like other concrete events, results from the interplay of forces and counterforces, from a balance of probabilities pulling toward internal war and internal peace.

REPRESSION. The most obvious obstacle to internal war is, of course, the incumbent regime. It goes almost without saying that by using repression the established authorities can lessen the chances of violent attack upon themselves, or even reduce them to nil. Internal wars, after all, are not made by impersonal forces working in impersonal ways, but by men acting under the stress of external forces. This much at least there is in the conspiracy theory of revolution: wholly spontaneous riots by wholly unstructured and undirected mobs may occur, but hardly very frequently or with much effect. Actual cases of internal war generally contain some element of subversion, some structure for forming political will and acting upon decisions, however primitive and changeable. On this point, if no other, the great enemies of revolution (Burke, Chateaubriand, Taine) are at one with the great revolutionaries (Lenin, Trotsky); it is also this point, rather than some more subtle idea, which underlies Pareto's and Brinton's argument that revolutions are due to elites as much as non-elites. And anything with a structure can of course be detected and repressed, though not always very easily.

The matter, however, is not quite so simple. Repression can be a two-edged sword. Unless it is based upon extremely good intelligence, and unless its application is sensible, ruthless, and continuous, its effects may be quite opposite to those intended. Incompetent repression leads to a combination of disaffection and contempt for the elite. Also, repression may only make the enemies of a regime more competent in the arts of conspiracy; certainly it tends to make them more experienced in the skills of clandestine organization and *sub rosa* communication. No wonder that botched and bungled repression is often a characteristic of pre-revolutionary societies. The French *ancien régime*, for example, had a political censorship, but it only managed to make French writers into masters of the hidden meaning, and whet the appetite of the public for their subversive books. "In our country," a French aristocrat said, "authors compete with one another for the honors of the bonfire"; even the Queen seems to have spent many delicious evenings reading the forbidden Encyclopedia with her ladies.[16] Russia, under the later Czars, was practically a model of repressive bumbledom; her policy of exile, for example, created close-knit communities of revolutionaries more than it destroyed their cohesion.

The worst situation of all seems to arise when a regime, having driven its opponents underground, inflamed their enmity, heightened their contempt, and cemented their organization, suddenly relaxes its repression and attempts a liberal policy. The relaxation of authority is a part of the pre-revolutionary syndrome, no less than other forms of social amelioration; in that sense, repression in societies with high internal war potential is little more than a narcotic, intensifying the conditions it seeks to check and requiring ever larger doses to keep affairs in balance—if other things are equal. We can see this dynamic at work in the development of

totalitarian rule, particularly if we remember that blood-letting, while certainly the ultimate in repression, is only one form that coercion can take.

From this standpoint, repression may be both an obstacle to and precipitant of internal war. Repression is of course least likely to prevent internal war in societies which, unlike totalitarian regimes, have a low capacity for coercion. In such societies, adjustive and diversionary mechanisms seem to check revolutionary potential far better. Indeed, they may in any society.[17]

DIVERSIONS AND CONCESSIONS. Diversionary mechanisms are all those social patterns and practices which channel psychic energies away from revolutionary objectives—which provide other outlets for aggressions or otherwise absorb emotional tensions. If Elie Halévy's theory is correct, then English nonconformist evangelicalism, especially the Methodist movement, furnishes an excellent case in point.[18] Halévy, being French, was deeply puzzled by the fact that England did not have any serious revolution in the early nineteenth century, despite conditions which, on their face, seem to have contained very great revolutionary potential—conditions resulting from the industrial revolution and from the fact of endemic revolution throughout the Western world. His interpretation was that English evangelicalism, more than anything else, performed a series of functions which greatly lowered the revolutionary level of British politics. Among these functions were the provision of outlets for emotional expression and the inculcation of a philosophy which reconciled the lower

---

[16] For much information relevant to this point, see Hyppolite Taine, *Origines de la France contemporaine*, rev. ed., 12 vols. (Paris, 1899–1914), vol. 1.

[17] "Power", says Merriam, "is not strongest where it uses violence, but weakest. It is strongest where it employs the instruments of substitution and counter-attraction, of allurement, of participation..." C. E. Merriam, *Political Power* (New York, 1934), 179–80.

[18] Elie Halévy, *A History of the English People*, 6 vols. (London, 1960), vol. 1.

classes to their condition, made that condition seem inevitable, and made patient submission to it a sacred obligation. In England, at least at the time in question, religion seems indeed to have been the opiate of the people, as Marx and Engels, no less than later and different-minded historians, seem to have realized.

England may have been spared major political violence since the seventeenth century for other reasons too: for example, because at least twice in English history, just when she seemed to be on the very brink of civil war, external war opportunely occurred, unifying the country as external wars will: at the time of the Napoleonic wars, and again in 1914 after the mutiny in the Curragh threatened to develop into something much more serious. Indeed, diverting popular attention from domestic troubles by starting foreign wars is one of the most venerable dodges of statecraft. This too, however, is a weapon that cuts two ways. Military adventures are excellent diversions, and military successes can marvellously cement disjoined societies, but military failure, on the evidence, can hardly fail to hasten revolution in such cases. Russia may well have entered the first World War to distract domestic unrest, but, if so, the outcome was revolution rather than the contrary.

Orgiastic excitements—festivals and dances, parades and circuses, *Reichsparteitäge* and mass gymnastics—also provide diversionary outlets for popular discontent. "If the late czardom," says Edwards, "instead of abolishing vodka, had made it more plentiful and very cheap—if, in addition, they had stimulated to the utmost those forms of religious frenzy and excitement to which the Russian populace appear to be so susceptible—then it is at least possible that the people would have been so exhausted mentally, emotionally, and financially by their alcoholic and reli-

gious orgies that they would not have had sufficient energy left to carry out a successful revolution.[19]

Totalitarian regimes seem to be shrewder about such matters, as well as being more coercive. The massive sports programs which are a feature of every totalitarian regime (German, Russian, or Chinese) may have a variety of purposes—physical fitness as preparation for war, or the inculcation of discipline—but one of them assuredly is to absorb the energies of the young and the interest of the not-so-young. No less than eschatological ideology, sport is the opiate of the masses in totalitarian countries, and not in these alone.

Adjustive mechanisms reduce, or manage, tensions, rather than providing surrogate outlets for them. Concessions are perhaps the most obvious of such mechanisms. It is banal, but probably true, to say that timely concessions have been the most effective weapons in the arsenal of the British ruling class, and one of Halévy's more cogent points about the pacific effects of avangelicalism on nineteenth-century England is that it made the elite extraordinarily willing to ameliorate the lot of the masses. It enjoined upon them philanthropy as a sacred duty and educated them in the trusteeship theory of wealth —remember Wesley's counsel "gain all you can, save all you can, give all you can"—at the same time as it made the masses extraordinarily willing to suffer their burdens in peace. (For this reason, we can of course regard all functioning institutions for adjusting conflict as barriers to internal war.) But concessions too may work in two directions, no less than repression and certain diversionary tactics. They may only lead to further and greater demands, further and greater expectations of success, and must

---

[19] Edwards, *The Natural History of Revolution*, 49.

therefore, like repression, be continuous, and continuously greater, to succeed. "There is no bettter way [than a conciliatory policy]" according to Clemenceau, "of making the opposite party ask for more and more. Every man or every power whose action consists solely in surrender can only finish by self-annihilation. Everything that lives resists..."[20]

FACILITIES FOR VIOLENCE. A final set of obstacles to internal war are conditions that affect the capacities of alienated groups to use violence at all, or, more often in real life, to use it with fair prospects of success. These conditions do not always prevent violence. But they can prevent its success. For this very reason, they help determine the likelihood of decisions to use violence at all. What are some of these conditions? Perhaps the first to come to mind is terrain. While practically all kinds of terrain can be used, in different ways, for purposes of rebellion, not all can be used to equal advantage. The ideal, from the viewpoint of the insurgents, seems to be an area which is relatively isolated, mountainous, overgrown, criss-crossed by natural obstacles (hedges, ditches, etc.), and near the sea or other sources of external supply—terrain which affords secure bases to the insurgents in their own territory, gives them the advantage of familiarity with local conditions, and allows ready access to them of external supporters.[21]

The communications facilities of a society are another relevant condition.

Marx, among many others, seems to have realized this when he argued that urbanization increases the likelihood of revolution, if only in that it makes men accessible to one another and thus makes revolutionary organization easier to achieve. "Since the collective revolutionary mentality is formed by conversation and propaganda," writes the French historian Lefebvre, "all means that bring men together favor it."[22] In this one case, a condition which may heighten the chances of successful internal war (bad communications) may also discourage its outbreak. There may be nothing more mysterious to the celebrated peaceability of peasants, as compared to city-dwellers, than the physical difficulty in rural life, especially if fairly primitive, to form a "collective revolutionary mentality."

Terrain and communications are physical obstacles to (or facilities for) internal war. There are human obstacles as well. For example, internal wars seem rarely to occur, even if other conditions favor them, if a regime's instruments of violence remain loyal. This applies above all to the armed forces. Trotsky for one, and Lenin for another, considered the attitude of the army absolutely decisive for any revolution;[23] so also did Le Bon.[24] Pettee, on the other hand, dissents, but for a rather subtle reason: not because he considers the attitude of the armed forces insignificant, but because he feels that armies never fail to join revolutions when all other causes of revolution are present, and that they never fail to oppose them when this is not the case.[25] We could

[20] Quoted in G. Sorel, *Reflections on Violence* (New York, 1915), 71.
[21] For examples of how such terrain benefits insurgents, see Peter Paret, *Internal War and Pacification: The Vendée, 1793–1796* (Princeton, 1961); W. E. D. Allen, *Guerrilla War in Abyssinia* (London, 1951), 19; Chalmers Johnson, "Civilian Loyalties and Guerrilla Conflict", *World Politics*, July 1962; and Ernesso Guevara, *Che Guevara on Guerrilla War* (New York, 1961)—among many others.

[22] G. Lefebvre, "Foules Révolutionnaires", *Annales Historiques de la Révolution Française*, 1934, 23.
[23] Trotsky, *The Russian Revolution*, 116.
[24] Gustave Le Bon, *The Psychology of Revolution* (New York, 1913), 29.
[25] G. S. Pettee, *The Process of Revolution*, 105.

enlarge this point to read that internal wars are unlikely wherever the cohesion of an elite is intact, for the simple reason that insurgent formations require leadership and other skills, and are unlikely to obtain them on a large scale without some significant break in the ranks of an elite. Even if elites do not always "cause" their own downfall by becoming rigid or foreign to their people, they can certainly hasten their own demise by being internally at odds. From this standpoint, if not from that of Mosca's theory, elite cohesion is a factor which should be classified among the obstacles to internal war, as well as among their causes.

A final human obstacle to internal war —perhaps the greatest of all—is lack of wide popular support for rebellion. It seems generally accepted among modern writers on internal war, indeed it is the chief dogma of modern revolutionaries, that without great popular support the insurgents in an internal war can hardly hope to win (and with it are hardly likely to lose)—unless by means of a *coup d'état*. So vital is this factor that some writers think that the distinctive characteristic of internal war is the combination of violent techniques with psychological warfare, the latter designed, of course, to win the active support of the non-combatants; this is asserted in the much repeated pseudo-formula of the French theorists of *guerre révolutionnaire*: revolutionary warfare = partisan war + psychological warfare.[26] To be sure, psychological warfare occurs nowadays also in international wars. Its role in these, however, is not nearly so

[26] G. Bonnet, *Les guerres insurrectionelles* (Paris, 1958), 60. The point that in guerrilla warfare almost everything turns on popular support is argued in many sources, most strongly perhaps in C. A. Johnson, "Civilian Loyalties and Guerrilla Conflict", *World Politics*, July 1962.

crucial as in internal war; it is incidental in one case but seems to be decisive in the other.

One reason for this is that in internal wars, unlike international wars, there is generally a great disparity in capacity for military effort between the incumbents and insurgents. The former tend to be in a much stronger position—not always, of course, for this is where the loyalties of the established instrumentalities of violence enter the picture, but more often than not. The insurgents are therefore forced, in the normal case, to supplement their capabilities by taking what advantage they can of terrain and the cooperation of the non-combatant population. Like terrain itself, a well-disposed population affords a secure base of operations to rebels, as well as providing them with indispensable logistical support. Rebels who can count on popular support can lose themselves in the population (according to Mao "the populace is for revolutionaries what water is for fish"), count on the population for secrecy (in wars in which intelligence is practically the whole art of defense), and reconstitute their forces by easy recruitment; if they can do all of these things, they can be practically certain of victory, short of a resort to genocide by the incumbents.

Great popular support is necessary also because internal wars, precisely because the common disparity of forces rules out quick victory by the insurgents (except by *coup*), tend to be long drawn out wars of attrition—perhaps better, either very prolonged or very quickly settled. In such wars, when victory always seems remote, when, at times, impasse is the best that can be hoped for, when the disruption of normal life is greater even than in external war, the morale of the revolutionaries, their ultimate trump card against their opponents, can hardly be sustained if they feel themselves isolated from their own people.

For all of these reasons, calculations about popular loyalties normally play a role in the decision to resort to political violence. The calculations may be mistaken but they are almost always made, sometimes, as in the case of the Algerian nationalist struggle, in ways approaching the survey research of social science.[27]

TOWARD AN ETIOLOGY OF
INTERNAL WARS

Needless to say, these arguments do not amount to anything like a finished etiology of internal wars. My concern here has been with preliminary, but fundamental and neglected, questions of strategy in theory-building, no more. Nevertheless, taking it all in all, this study does imply something more than that certain lines of inquiry are more promising than others in internal-war studies. When its arguments are added up, there emerges at least a considerable clue to the *form* that an adequate etiology of internal wars should take, even if little of a very specific nature can as yet be said about content. We have arrived at a paradigm, if not a full-fledged theory.

Two points can serve as summary, as well as to spell out the nature of the paradigm I have in mind. One is that internal-war potential (the likelihood that internal war in some form will be precipitated)[28] should be conceived formally as a ratio between positive

27 Interview with M. Chanderli, F. L. N. Observer at the United Nations, December, 1961.

28 I stress internal-war *potential* because this is all one can assess if the actual occurrence of internal wars depends on precipitants beyond the scope of systematic analysis or even the predictive capacities engendered by practical wisdom. Needless to say, however, the actual occurrence of internal wars gives the best assurance that the societies concerned indeed had great internal-war potential.

forces making for internal war and negative forces working against it—with the *possibility* that internal war of some kind may be fomented no matter what the overall potential, and the *probability* of its occurrence increasing as internal-war potential rises. This is certainly elementary, but it is in fact far more usual, in both general theories and specific interpretations of internal war, to speak of revolutionary or pacifying forces alone, and to depict rebelliousness as either absolutely present or absolutely lacking in societies. The other, and more important point, is that the forces involved should be conceived in both cases as functions of four factors. The positive forces are produced by the *inefficacy of elites* (lack of cohesion and of expected performance), *disorienting social processes* (delegitimization), *subversion* (attempts deliberately to activate disorientation, to form new political orientations and to impede the efficacy of elites), and the *facilities* available to potential insurgents. Countervailing these factors are four others: the *facilities* of incumbents, *effective repression* (not any kind of repression), *adjustive concessions* and *diversionary mechanisms*—the first referring to the incumbents' perceived capacity to fight if internal war occurs, the others to preventative actions.

This summation provides at least the minimum that one expects from paradigms: a formal approach to study and a checklist of factors that should be particularly considered whether one is interpreting specific cases or constructing general theory. But a minimum is not much. It is necessary to go further, particularly in the direction of determining the relative values of the factors and their relations to one another. After being stated, the variables must be ordered. Consequently, to conclude, I should like to add some suggestions that indicate how one might proceed from the mere cataloguing of promising variables toward their systematization.

In the first place, it seems, from what has been said about possible obstacles to internal war, that the negative forces vary within a much smaller range than the positive ones, so that beyond a point, internal-war potential can be reduced only with geometrically decreasing effectiveness, if at all. Take, for example, adjustive concessions. These cannot be indefinitely increased, for, in the end, they would be tantamount to surrender, and long before that point, would only serve to increase the insurgents' capabilities (not to mention the probable effects on the insurgents' demands and the incumbents' cohesion). Repression is intrinsically limited as well, among other reasons because it requires repressors and because its use will tend to intensify alienation; as in the case of concessions there may be an optimum of repression, but a maximum of it is as bad as none at all. And one can doubt the efficacy of diversions where disorientation is very widespread and goes very deep; besides, intrinsic limitations operate in the case of this factor too, for a society that lives on diversions to the extent of, say, the Roman Empire, is for that very reason in decay. The factors that make for internal-war potential clearly are less inherently circumscribed. More clearly still, certain of them, like the crucial facility of popular support, belong to the realm of zero-sums, so that an increase of forces on the positive side implies a concomitant decrease on the other. In this sense, the variables involved in internal-war potential have a certain hierarchical order (an order of "potency"): one set is more significant than the other.

Such an order seems to exist within each set as well. For example, no one rebels simply because he has appropriate facilities—otherwise, the military and police would be everywhere and constantly in rebellion. At the very least, internal war presupposes some degree of subversion as well as brute capabilities. Subversion in turn, however, presupposes something that can be subverted— disorientations to activate and to reshape toward new legitimizations. And much evidence suggests that, whatever forces may be at work in a society, in whatever fashion, disorientation and subversion are both unlikely where the elite performs well, is highly cohesive, and is deeply enough attuned to the general spirit of social life to provide the mutualities and complementarities that settled social orientations require— granted that certain social processes make this extremely improbable. Per contra, elite inefficacy in itself always invites challenge, from within or without, no matter what other forces may be at work in the non-elite; in one form (incohesion), it implies the likelihood of internecine elite conflict, in others the probability of alienation of the non-elite. If disorientation arising from other sources is added, the brew obviously becomes more lethal (and its explosion tends to take a different form), with or without much concerted subversion. The latter, and insurgent facilities, are essentially extra addatives, the more so since insurgents can hardly lack facilities on some scale where elite inefficacy and political disorientation are great; these factors may intensify internal-war potential, but do not create it.

The factors that reduce internal-war potential can be arranged (with rather more ambiguity, to be sure) in a similar order of potency. The essential criterion that establishes their weight is the extent to which they are intrinsically limited, either because they can become self-defeating or because they are zero-sums that do not allow increases on the positive side to be balanced by increases on the other. Diversions, while certainly not unlimited, are probably the most potent of the factors, for they can apparently be carried very far before they thoroughly devitalize societies. Repression and concessions seem to have a much lower optimum point. It is difficult at present to say which of them is the less potent; in all probability, however, it is repression—if only because concessions may increase the legitimation of authority among potential dissidents (that is, serve as surrogates for other kinds of elite "performance") while acts of repression, as well as being inherently self-denials of legitimacy, are well-tailored to cope only with the less potent factor of subversion. Incumbent facilities, finally, while being by all odds the most ambiguous factor, seem to belong somewhere between diversions on one hand and concessions on the other. The reasons for this are three: First, since the most vital of them are zero-sums, they can be, in a sense, either very weak or very potent, a decrease in them implying a corresponding increase in insurgent facilities and the reverse holding as well (a sort of inherent limitation different from that operating in the case of the other factors). Secondly, it seems, on the evidence, more difficult for incumbents to regain lost facilities (especially lost loyalties) than for insurgents to multiply their stock of them, even if "logical" reasons for this are not readily apparent. And thirdly, while an increase in incumbent facilities most clearly reduces one of the positive factors, that factor happens to be least potent of the four.

The catalogue of forces making for internal-war potentials thus takes on a certain preliminary order—even if this order is as yet far from precise.

A further element of order can be introduced into the list of variables by noting that, to an extent, they can be paired with one another, specific negative and positive forces being particu-

larly closely related. This is manifest in the case of insurgent and incumbent facilities—clearest of all where the facilities in question are zero-sums. All else being equal, it is obviously not the absolute value of facilities on either side that matters, but the ratio of the facilities concerned. Just as obviously, as already stated, there is a special relation between subversion and repression. Disorientation or elite inefficacy can hardly be repressed; only subversion can.[29] Less manifestly, but pretty clearly still, adjustive concessions bear a particular relation to certain elite failures, particularly in performance, and diversions can, to an extent, provide gratifications that alleviate the psychic stresses of disorientation; but neither is likely to counteract anything else.

One final point that bears more indirectly upon the ordering of the variables listed above requires consideration. It is an appropriate theme on which to conclude, for it is the point with which we started. Throughout the discussion, no distinction has been made between types of internal war, and this not without reasons. The fact remains, however, that internal wars, although in some ways similar, are in most respects greatly various. An adequate etiology of internal wars should therefore be able to tell one more than whether internal war in some form will occur in a society. It should also enable one to account for the specific forms internal wars take in different circumstances.

Any discussion of this mattter is at present greatly handicapped by the lack of a settled, well-constructed typology of internal wars—and constructing such a typology is a task great enough to require another, and rather extensive, study. This much can be said, however,

[29] To avoid misunderstanding, it should be clearly understood that repression here refers not to putting down rebels in internal wars but preventative actions by the incumbents.

without settling on specific typological categories: Approaching the etiological study of internal wars in the manner suggested here makes it possible to deal with the many different phenomena covered by the term internal war within a single theoretical framework, yet in a way that yields quite different accounts of clearly disparate events. And this is surely desirable where phenomena that differ in many respects have also much in common.

The point is that two things can be done with the paradigm I have sketched. By weighing the general balance of positive and negative forces, one can arrive at an assessment of the overall degree of internal-war potential in a society. By considering the *particular* forces, combinations of forces, and ratios of forces that are strong or weak—the forces that are especially instrumental in determining the overall result—one can arrive at definite ideas of what kinds of internal war are likely to occur (quite apart from the possibility that the general degree of internal-war potential may itself set limits to the varieties that internal war can take). For example, where elite inefficacy, especially incohesion, greatly predominates among the positive forces, something like what many have called palace revolution is a very likely result. Where disorientation is very great but other positive factors are negligible, one might expect relatively unorganized, sporadic rioting as the normal response. Where subversion looms large relative to other factors, *coups, Putsches* or terrorism are more likely. Where incumbent and insurgent facilities are rather equally matched and elite cohesion is particularly tenuous, the stage is probably set for full-scale civil war. One could, in fact, contrive a useful, although very

complex, typology of internal wars by working out probable results for the various possible constellations of factors included in the paradigm; and one could similarly take any typology otherwise worked out and produce for it a set of appropriately corresponding combinations of the factors.

The signal advantage of this procedure is that it avoids what defaces the whole corpus of historical studies of internal war available to us, the *ad hoc* piling up of unrelated theories, and prevents also the most conspicuous flaw of unhistorical, abstract models of revolutionary processes, the disregarding of special forces in particular cases. As well, the procedure I suggest can deal coherently with another eminently historical and theoretical matter, the transformation of many internal wars in the course of their development—the revolutionary "process." It can do so simply by applying typological theories dynamically. For the constellations of forces that provide initial impetus to internal wars are likely to undergo constant transformation in their course, much as such constellations may vary in the pre-revolutionary period. Subversion may become more intense, more purposeful; the balance of facilities may shift; incumbent elites may become more cohesive or disunited under fire; mild disorientation may become severe as authority is challenged and society disrupted by violence; the insurgents may win power, but at the cost of their own cohesion and without being able to provide effective new legitimations—and thus internal wars may proceed from stage, from type to type, in unique or characteristic, continuous or spasmodic, dynamic patterns.

# INEQUALITY AND INSTABILITY:
# THE RELATION OF LAND TENURE
# TO POLITICAL INSTABILITY

## I

At least since the ancient Greeks many thinkers have regarded great diversity of wealth as incompatible with stable government. According to Euripides:

In a nation there be orders three:—
The useless rich, that ever crave for more;
The have-nots, straitened even for sustenance,
A dangerous folk, of envy overfull,
Which shoot out baleful stings at such as have,
Beguiled by tongues of evil men, their "champions":
But of the three the midmost saveth states;
They keep the order which the state ordains.[1]

Alexis de Tocqueville, writing many centuries later, declared: "Remove the secondary causes that have produced the great convulsions of the world and you will almost always find the principle of inequality at the bottom. Either the poor have attempted to plunder the rich, or the rich to enslave the poor. If, then, a state of society can ever be founded in which every man shall have something to keep and little to take from others, much will have been done for the peace of the world."[2]

Many modern writers echo the same thought. Merle Kling, for example, blames political instability in Latin America on the extreme concentration of economic bases of power in what he terms "colonial economies." Land ownership, he says, is so heavily concentrated that no individual not already possessing great tracts of agricultural land can reasonably hope to achieve wealth through farming. Foreign exploitation of mineral resources effectively blocks the ambitious native from that source of wealth. Industry remains rudimentary. Of the possible sources of enrichment, only government is open to competition. Political office provides such a unique source of gain that "large segments of the population are prepared to take the ultimate risk of life, in a revolt, in a *coup d'état*, to perpetuate a characteristic feature of Latin American politics—chronic political instability."[3]

[1] "The Suppliants," *The Tragedies of Euripides*, trans. by Arthur S. Way (London 1894), 373.

*Reprinted from Bruce M. Russett, "Inequality and Instability: The Relation of Land Tenure to Politics," WORLD POLITICS, 16 (April 1964), 442–54, by permission of the publisher and the author.*

[2] Alexis de Tocqueville, *Democracy in America* (Vintage edn., New York, 1954), II, 266.

[3] Merle Kling, "Toward a Theory of Power and Political Instability in Latin America," *Western Political Quarterly*, IX (March 1956), 21–35. Note that land distribution is only one element of the "colonial economy" defined by Kling.

Both Plato and Karl Marx so despaired of the pernicious effects of wealth that they saw no way to abolish the evil except to abolish private property itself. Tocqueville, on the other hand, thought that he found in America a society which had been able to reach another solution: "Between these two extremes [very few rich men and few poor ones] of democratic communities stands an innumerable multitude of men almost alike, who, without being exactly either rich or poor, possess sufficient property to desire the maintenance of order, yet not enough to excite envy. Such men are the natural enemies of violent commotions; their lack of agitation keeps all beneath them and above them still and secures the balance of the fabric of society."[4]

Yet if we check the matter empirically with present-day polities the answer is not so clear-cut. Wealth is everywhere distributed unequally; even in the most egalitarian societies the income of the rich is many times that of the poor. And one can readily point to a number of instances—such as Spain—where, despite an impressionistic judgment that goods are distributed highly unequally, the polity is seemingly stable under the rule of a dictator.

Part of the difficulty stems from a conceptual problem, a lack of clarity about just what is the dependent variable. Is economic inequality incompatible with *stable* government, or merely with *democratic* or "*good*" government? If we mean stable government, do we mean regimes in which the rulers maintain themselves in power for long periods despite the chronic outbreak of violence (Colombia and South Vietnam), or simply the avoidance of significant violence even though governments may topple annually (France throughout most of the Third and Fourth Republics)? Or must "stable" government be

both peaceful and reasonably long-term? Finally, what do we mean by the government? A particular individual (Spain), a particular party (Uruguay), the essential maintenance of a particular coalition (France under the system of "replastering"), or the continued dominance of a particular social stratum (Jordan)?

Another part of the difficulty stems from the absence of comparative study. Numerous authors have examined the distribution of agricultural land in particular countries or areas, and its contribution to a particular political situation. Several books have drawn together studies giving attention to many different nations.[5] But none of these have been based on the same concepts or have presented data for the same variables in a manner necessary for true comparative analysis. Case studies are essential for providing depth and insight, but generalization requires eventual attention to many cases.

Comparative analysis is dependent on the provision of comparable data. For instance, one may know that in contemporary England the upper 5 per cent of income earners receive over 15 per cent of all current income, even after taxes.[6] Is this high or low compared with other nations? All too often the necessary data simply are not available or, if they are, they are not in comparable form. For another country one may, for instance, know the proportion of income going to the top 10 per cent and top 1 per cent of earners, but not to the top 5 per cent, as in England.

In this article we shall attempt to clarify the problem conceptually, present for the first time a large body of dis-

---

[4] Tocqueville, 266.

[5] See, for example, Kenneth Parsons, *et al.*, eds., *Land Tenure* (Madison 1958), and Walter Froelich, *Land Tenure, Industrialization, and Social Stability* (Milwaukee 1961).

[6] Robert M. Solow, "Income Inequality Since the War," in *Postwar Economic Trends in the United States*, ed. by Ralph Freeman (New York 1960).

tribution data, and test some hypotheses about the relation between economic inequality and politics. First, the data. We shall be concerned with information on the degree to which agricultural land is concentrated in the hands of a few large landholders. Information on land tenure is more readily available, and is of more dependable comparability, than are data on the distribution of other economic assets like current income or total wealth.[7] Material on land distribution is available for many countries about which we know nothing precise or reliable in regard to income distribution. In addition, land distribution is intrinsically of major interest. Kling's theory of Latin American political instability was built in large part on land inequality; the United States government has long warned its allies in poorer nations about the need for land reform. In Japan, and to a lesser extent in South Korea, the American military government took upon itself a major redistribution of land with the intention of providing the necessary bases for political democracy.

## II

I have discussed elsewhere the uses of various summary statistical measures designed to indicate the degree of inequality in a distribution.[8] Here we shall

employ three separate indices, each of which measures somewhat different aspects of land distribution. The first two are directed to the relative size of farms, the last to tenancy.

(1) The *percentage of landholders who collectively occupy one-half of all the agricultural land* (starting with the farmers with the *smallest* plots of land and working toward the *largest*).

(2) *The Gini index of concentration.* We begin with a Lorenz curve (Figure 1) drawn by connecting the points given in a cumulative distribution (e.g., the proportion of land held by each decile of farmers). All farms are ranked in order from the smallest to the largest, so that one can say what proportion of the total *number* of farms accounts for a given proportion of the total *area* of agricultural land. In Figure 1 the cumulated percentage of farms is given along the horizontal axis, and the cumulated percentage of the area along the vertical axis. The 45° line represents the condition of perfect equality, wherein each percentile of farmers would make an equal contribution to the cumulated total of agricultural land. Thus, under complete equality each 10 per cent of the population would have exactly 10 per cent of the land; any two-thirds of the population would have exactly two-thirds of the land. How far in fact the curve for a particular distribution departs from the "line of equality" gives us a visual measure of the inequality involved.

The Lorenz curve provides an extremely useful way of showing the complete pattern of a distribution, but it is impractical to try to compare whole Lorenz curves for any substantial number of countries. But if we measure the *area* between the cumulated distribution and the line of equality we have the

---

[7] One must always introduce comparative data, particularly on land tenure, with certain caveats. The quality of data collection is not uniform from one country to the next, and in any case it cannot indicate the quality of the land in question. Nevertheless, while these caveats may be important with regard to a few distributions, they do not fundamentally alter the character of the data shown.

Although a few of the data presented were compiled some time ago, patterns of land tenure normally change but little over the years. Only for Bolivia, Taiwan and, to a lesser degree, Italy is there evidence of a significant change between the year given and 1960.

[8] Hayward R. Alker, Jr., and Bruce M. Russett, "Indices for Comparing Inequality,"

in *Comparing Nations: The Use of Quantitative Data in Cross-National Research*, ed. by R. L. Merritt and Stein Rokkan (New Haven: Yale University Press, 1966).

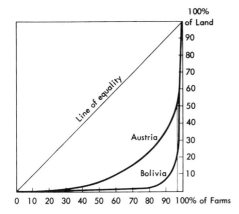

FIG. 1. LORENZ CURVES OF LAND
DISTRIBUTION: AUSTRIA AND BOLIVIA

Gini index, a simple summary measure of the total inequality of a distribution.[9] The Gini index calculates over the whole population the difference between an "ideal" cumulative distribution of land (where all farms are the same size) and the actual distribution. The higher the Gini index, the greater the inequality.

Though the percentage of farmers with one-half the land is simple and useful, the more comprehensive Gini index, by examining the whole distribution, is in many ways superior. The curves for the two countries in Figure 1, for example, both show virtually the same percentage of farmers with half the land. But below the 50 per cent mark, the distribution for Bolivia is much more unequal than is that for Austria. In

[9] The Gini number for a Lorenz curve is actually twice the area mentioned divided by the area (10,000 for 100 by 100 axes) of the whole square. Formula:

$$G = 2 \frac{\int_0^{100} (x - f(x))\,dx}{10,000}$$

where $x$ is the cumulated population percentage and $f(x)$ is the height of the Lorenz curve. Cf. Mary Jean Bowman, "A Graphical Analysis of Personal Income Distribution in the United States," *American Economic Review*, XXXV (September 1945), 607–28. In Table 1, p. 314, the Gini index is multiplied by 100.

Bolivia the top 10 per cent of all farmers owned nearly 95 per cent of the land; in Austria the top 10 per cent of farmers owned only about 65 per cent of the land. The implications for a theory of political stability are obvious. (The Bolivian figures actually apply to 1950. Since that date Bolivia has experienced a social revolution.)

(3) Probably less important than the relative size of farms, but still relevant, is the question of *ownership*. If a farmer tills a substantial piece of land but nevertheless must pay much of the produce to a landlord, the effect may be much the same as if he actually owned a much smaller plot. Therefore we also present data, where available, on *farm households that rent all their land as a percentage of the total number of farms.*

It is even more difficult to find a satisfactory operational definition of stability than to measure inequality. In our effort to account for different aspects of "stability," we shall use several quite different indices.

(A) INSTABILITY OF PERSONNEL. One measure of stability is simply the term of office of the chief executive. As the numerator of our index, we have used the number of years during the period 1945–1961 in which a country was independent; and, as the denominator, the number of individuals who held the post of chief executive during the same period. By subtracting this figure from 17 (the number of years in the period) we obtain what we shall term the index of "personnel instability." It may vary from 0 to 17; in fact, the highest figure in our sample is 16.32 for France.[10]

[10] With this definition, most of the indices fall between 11 and 17. Our use of logarithmic transformations in the correlations below compensates for this bunching.

In some ways it might have been more desirable to measure the average tenure of a party or coalition, but that solution raises other problems. When a government in the French Fourth Republic fell and was replaced by a new cabinet composed basically of the

(B) INTERNAL GROUP VIOLENCE. Rudolph Rummel, in his Dimensionality of Nations Project, collected data on the number of people killed as a result of internal group violence—i.e., civil wars, revolutions, and riots—during the years 1955–1957. We have extended the time period to 1950–1962, and have modified the data to allow for the size of the total population in question, making the index deaths per 1,000,000 people.[11]

(C) INTERNAL WAR. As an alternative to the violent-death material, we shall use Harry Eckstein's data on internal war for the period 1946–1961.[12] These data include the total number of violent incidents, from plots to protracted guerrilla warfare.

(D) QUITE A DIFFERENT PROBLEM IS THE STABILITY OF DEMOCRACY. With a

---

same parties, was this a new coalition or just the old one under a new Premier? The first answer immediately involves one in difficulties of comparability with other countries' experiences; the second answer would cause France to appear much more stable than any observer would agree was correct.

Measuring the tenure of the chief executive tells nothing about the *form* of government, nor about what Kling (p. 25) describes as concealed instability. A government may appear stable only as long as its repressive techniques succeed; when they fail, it may be violently and suddenly overthrown. Thus Trujillo's Dominican Republic was "stable" for several decades. Nevertheless it is difficult to see how "hidden instability" can be allowed for other than through some definition of a democratic-dictatorial continuum, which we attempt in index D below.

[11] Cf. Rudolph J. Rummel, "Dimensions of Conflict Behavior Within and Between Nations," in *General Systems*, Yearbook of the Society for the Advancement of General Systems Theory (Ann Arbor 1963). The nature and limitations of the data used in this article will be discussed in Bruce M. Russett *et al.*, *World Handbook of Political and Social Indicators* (New Haven: Yale University Press, 1964).

[12] Harry Eckstein, *Internal War: The Problem of Anticipation*, a report submitted to the Research Group in Psychology and the Social Sciences, Smithsonian Institution (Washington 1962), Appendix I.

few adaptations we shall use the distinctions employed by Seymour Martin Lipset. "Stable democracies" will be defined as states that have been characterized by the uninterrupted continuation of political democracy since World War I, *and* the absence over the past thirty years of a totalitarian movement, either Fascist or Communist, which at any point received as much as 20 per cent of the vote. "Unstable democracies," again following Lipset, are countries which, although unable to meet the first criteria, nevertheless have a "history of more or less free elections for most of the post-World War I period."[13] "Dictatorships" are those countries in which, perhaps despite some democratic interludes, free elections have been generally absent. These judgments are impressionistic and do not permit precise rankings from most to least democratic; nevertheless they generally agree with those of other scholars and with widely accepted standards.[14]

Note again that our political dependent variables measure distinctly different aspects—stability of executive personnel, the incidence of violence, and "democracy." No one is by itself an adequate measure of all the conditions to which land distribution has been thought relevant.

. . .

[13] Seymour Martin Lipset, "Some Social Requisites of Democracy," *American Political Science Review*, LIII (March 1959), 73–74.

[14] For a similar classification of regimes in the underdeveloped countries, see Gabriel A. Almond and James S. Coleman, eds., *The Politics of the Developing Areas* (Princeton 1960), 579–81.

Lipset's categorization is of course crude and subject to a number of criticisms. For example, cf. Phillips Cutright, "National Political Development: Measurement and Analysis," *American Sociological Review*, XXVIII (April 1963), 253–64. The alternative index that Cutright suggests, however, really deals with the complexity of political institutions—quite a different matter.

TABLE 1. CORRELATION COEFFICIENTS (r) FOR MEASURES OF LAND EQUALITY
WITH MEASURES OF POLITICAL INSTABILITY FOR 47 COUNTRIES

|  | Personnel Instability | Violent Politi- cal Deaths (per 1,000,000) | Eckstein Internal War Data |
|---|---|---|---|
| % of Farms with ½ Land | .24 | .45 | .35 |
| Gini Index | .33 | .46 | .29 |
| (44 countries only) | .01 | .27 | .11 |

## III

Land is everywhere distributed unequally. In even the most egalitarian states, about four-fifths of the farmers are concentrated on only half the land. Still, the degree of inequality varies widely from state to state. Table 1 presents the correlation coefficients (r) indicating the degree of association between each of the three measures of land distribution and each of the first three indices of instability.[15]

For the three indices of inequality there is in each case a positive relationship to instability, though in two instances the correlation is extremely slight. The highest correlation is between violent deaths and the Gini index. Judged by the standards of most social science this is a fairly high correlation, with a significance level of .001 (i.e., unless there really were a positive relationship between land distribution and instability, this high a correlation would not occur, purely by chance, as often as one time in a thousand). Nevertheless, these correlations indicate that much remains unexplained. Even the highest (.46) gives an r² of only .21. (The squared product moment coefficient—r² —can be interpreted as the percentage of the total variation in one index that can be explained by another.) Inequality of land distribution does bear a relation to political instability, but that relation-

ship is not a strong one, and many other factors must be considered in any attempted explanation.[16] The degree to which farm land is rented is not a factor of great explanatory power, given the low level of the correlations of rental with all the stability indices.

A more complex hypothesis, closely related to Kling's, might read as follows: extreme inequality of land distribution leads to political instability only in those poor, predominantly agricultural societies where limitation to a small plot of land almost unavoidably condemns one to poverty. In a rich country, the modest income a farmer can produce from even a small holding may satisfy him. Or, if

[15] For the three political variables, I used logarithmic transformations instead of the raw data.

[16] Nor is great concentration of farmland always a prelude to violent revolution in predominantly agricultural societies. Even according to figures cited by the Communists, inequality in Czarist Russia and interwar China was less than in most countries. Cf. V. I. Lenin, *The Agrarian Program of Social Democracy*, in *Selected Works*, III (New York, n.d.), 164–65; and Yuan-li Wu, *An Economic Survey of Communist China* (New York 1956), 119. Wu lists several estimates, the most extreme of which was the report of the Hankow Land Commission, which he alleges was Communist-dominated. The Gini indices for Russia and China were, respectively, approximately 73.0 and 64.6.

According to George Pavlovsky, in *Agricultural Russia on the Eve of the Revolution* (London 1930), chap. 4, the difficulty in Russia stemmed less from the *relative* size of farm plots than from the fact that the *absolute* size of most holdings was too small to produce more than bare subsistence. Given the technological backwardness of the Russian peasant, this may well be true.

that is not the case, at least in wealthy countries there are, besides agriculture, many alternative sources of wealth.[17] Finally, one might assert that the *combination* of inequality *and* a high rate of tenancy would cause instability. While neither by itself would necessarily lead to violence or frequent change of government, the combination almost inevitably would.

To test these hypotheses we examined simultaneously the effect of GNP per capita, percentage of labor force in agriculture, tenancy, and land distribution on our various indices of political stability.[18] These refinements improved our explanation rather strikingly in some cases. The strongest relationship was between the Gini index and violent deaths; $r^2$ was raised to .50. By far the most important variables in the equations for "predicting" instability were first the Gini index and then the percentage of the population in agriculture, as suggested by our first hypothesis. The percentage of farms rented again added little explanatory power. Qualifications of this sort help to explain the stability of a country like Australia, despite a highly unequal distribution of agricultural land. Venezuela's land distribution is also very unequal (but no more so than Australia's), yet Venezuela is somewhat poorer and has three times as many people (proportionately) employed in

agriculture.[19] All the indices of instability are quite high for Venezuela. Nevertheless, even the strongest relationship found among these variables leaves over half the variance "unexplained"— as the sophisticated student of politics might expect. The old saws about equality can be accepted only with caution.

There remains one other possibility yet to be explored—that equality may be related to the stability of a *democratic regime*. That is, there may or may not be sporadic outbreaks of violence; there may or may not be frequent changes of personnel at the highest level; but it is highly unlikely that a nation with a grossly unequal pattern of distribution of a major source of wealth, like agricultural land, will have a consistently democratic government. Table 2 presents a sixfold table showing each of the countries in our sample classified, after Lipset, as a "stable democracy," an "unstable democracy," or a "dictatorship,"[20] and also listed as above or below the median for the Gini index of land inequality.

The results are again quite striking. Of the 23 states with the more equal pattern of land distribution, 13 are stable democracies, whereas only three

---

[17] "Rich" countries and "societies where there are many alternative sources of wealth" are to some degree synonymous. Denmark and Australia, two rich nations often thought of as "agricultural," actually have only 23 and 14 per cent, respectively, of their labor forces in agriculture.

[18] The technique used was multiple regression. For a description and application of this method, see Donald Stokes, Angus Campbell, and Warren Miller, "Components of Electoral Decision," *American Political Science Review*, LII (June 1958), 367–87. This procedure also allows us to test for the independent "explanatory" power of each variable with the other variables *controlled*.

[19] This points up rather sharply the flaw in any attempt to use land distribution as an indicator of the degree of inequality in all wealth for *advanced* economies. Australia is widely acknowledged to be a highly egalitarian society.

[20] Note that these definitions of stability say nothing about the rate of turnover among government personnel, but only about the stability of democratic forms of government. We have included India and the Philippines in the category "stable democracy" because, though independent only since the end of World War II, they met the above test. Nevertheless this decision is open to some question, as political conditions in these countries clearly are *not* the same as in Western Europe. If they instead were classified as "unstable democracies" it would, however, only very moderately change the pattern of the following table.

of 24 more unequal countries can be classified as stable democracies. And of these three, each is a fairly rich state where agriculture is no longer the principal source of wealth. Tocqueville's basic observation would therefore appear correct: no state can long maintain a democratic form of government if the major sources of economic gain are divided very unequally among its citizens. American policy in urging the governments of underdeveloped nations to undertake massive land reform programs seems essentially well-founded. A "sturdy yeomanry" may be a virtual *sine qua non* for democratic government in an underdeveloped land. Nevertheless there are many instances where relative equality of land tenure is not associated with stable democracy; it is no *guarantee* of democratic development. Land reform may provide the soil to nourish free institutions, but the seed must first be planted.

TABLE 2. STABLE DEMOCRACIES, UNSTABLE DEMOCRACIES, AND DICTATORSHIPS BY DEGREE OF INEQUALITY IN LAND DISTRIBUTION

| *Gini Index* | *Stable Democracies* | *Unstable Democracies* | *Dictatorships* |
|---|---|---|---|
| Greater than Median Equality | Denmark Canada Switzerland India Philippines Sweden Belgium Ireland Netherlands Luxembourg Norway United States United Kingdom | Japan France Finland West Germany | Yugoslavia Poland Taiwan South Vietnam Libya Panama |
| Median Equality or Less | New Zealand Uruguay Australia | Austria Greece Italy Brazil Colombia Argentina Costa Rica Chile | Egypt Honduras Nicaragua Spain Cuba Dominican Rep. El Salvador Guatemala Ecuador Peru Iraq Venezuela Bolivia |

# VIOLENCE AND
# SOCIAL AND ECONOMIC MODERNIZATION

SAMUEL P. HUNTINGTON

*The Poverty and Modernization Theses*

The relation between modernization and violence is complex. More modern societies are generally more stable and suffer less domestic violence than less modern societies. One study produced a correlation of .625 (n = 62) between political stability and a composite index of modernity defined in terms of eight social and economic variables. Both the level of social mobilization and the level of economic development are directly associated with political stability. The relation between literacy and stability is particularly high. The frequency of revolutions also varies inversely with the educational level of the society, and deaths from domestic group violence vary inversely with the proportion of children attending primary school. Economic well-being is similarly associated with political order: in 74 countries, the correlation between per capita gross national product and deaths from domestic group violence was −.43. A different study of 70 countries for the years 1955–60 found a correlation of

−.56 between per capita gross national product and the number of revolutions. During the eight years between 1958 and 1965, violent conflicts were more than four times as prevalent in very poor nations as they were in rich nations; 87 per cent of the very poor countries suffered significant outbreaks of violence as compared to only 37 per cent of the rich countries.[1]

Clearly countries which have high levels of both social mobilization and economic development are more stable and peaceful politically. Modernity goes with stability. From this fact it is an easy step to the "poverty thesis" and the conclusions that economic and social backwardness is responsible for instability and hence that modernization is the road to stability. "There can, then, be no question," as Secretary McNamara

[1] Ivo K. Feierabend and Rosalind L. Feierabend, "Aggressive Behaviors Within Polities, 1948–1962: A Cross-National Study," *Journal of Conflict Resolution*, 10 (September 1966), 258–62; Bruce M. Russett et al., *World Handbook of Political and Social Indicators* (New Haven, Yale University Press, 1964), p. 273; Raymond Tanter and Manus Midlarsky, "A Theory of Revolution," *Journal of Conflict Resolution*, 11 (Sept. 1967), 271–72; Raymond Tanter, "Dimensions of Conflict Behavior Within Nations, 1955–1960: Turmoil and Internal War," *Papers, Peace Research Soicety*, 3 (1965), 175.

*Reprinted from Samuel P. Huntington,* POLITICAL ORDER IN CHANGING SOCIETIES *(New Haven: Yale University Press, 1968), pp. 39–56, by permission of Yale University Press and the author.*

said, "but that there is an irrefutable relationship between violence and economic backwardness." Or in the words of one academic analyst, "all-pervasive poverty undermines government—of any kind. It is a persistent cause of instability and makes democracy well-nigh impossible to practice."[2] If these relationships are accepted, then obviously the promotion of education, literacy, mass communications, industrialization, economic growth, urbanization, should produce greater political stability. These seemingly clear deductions from the correlation between modernity and stability are, however, invalid. In fact, modernity breeds stability, but modernization breeds instability.

The apparent relationship between poverty and backwardness, on the one hand, and instability and violence, on the other, is a spurious one. It is not the absence of modernity but the efforts to achieve it which produce political disorder. If poor countries appear to be unstable, it is not because they are poor, but because they are trying to become rich. A purely traditional society would be ignorant, poor, and stable. By the mid-twentieth century, however, all traditional societies were also transitional or modernizing societies. It is precisely the devolution of modernization throughout the world which increased the prevalence of violence about the world. For two decades after World War II American foreign policy toward the modernizing countries was in large part devoted to promoting economic and social development because these would lead to political stability. The success of this policy is, however, written in both the rising levels of material well-

being and the rising levels of domestic violence. The more man wages war against "his ancient enemies: poverty, disease, ignorance" the more he wages war against himself.

By the 1960s every backward nation was a modernizing nation. Evidence, nonetheless, did exist to suggest that causes of violence in such nations lay with the modernization rather than with the backwardness. Wealthier nations tend to be more stable than those less wealthy, but the poorest nations, those at the bottom of the international economic ladder, tend to be less prone to violence and instability than those countries just above them. Even Secretary McNamara's own statistics offered only partial support for his proposition. The World Bank, for instance, classified six of the twenty Latin American republics as "poor," that is, they had per capita gross national products of less than $250. Six of the twenty countries were also suffering from prolonged insurgencies in February 1966. Only one country, Bolivia, however, fell into both categories. The probability of insurgency in those Latin American countries which were not poor was twice as high as it was in those countries which were poor. Similarly, 48 out of 50 African countries and territories were classified as poor, and eleven of these were suffering from insurgency. Certainly, however, the probabilities of insurgency in the two African countries which were not poor—Libya and South Africa—were just as high as in the remaining 37 poor countries and territories. Moreover, the insurgency which did exist in 11 countries seemed to be related in four cases to continued colonial rule (e.g., Angola, Mozambique) and in the other seven to marked tribal and racial differences among the population (e.g. Nigeria, Sudan). Colonialism and ethnic heterogeneity would seem to

[2] Speech by Robert S. McNamara, Montreal, Quebec, May 18, 1966, *New York Times*, May 19, 1966, p. 11; Michael Brecher, *The New States of Asia* (London: Oxford University Press, 1963), Chap. 2.

be much better predictors of violence than poverty. In the Middle East and Asia (excluding Australia and New Zealand) 10 out of 22 countries classified as poor were suffering from insurgencies in February 1966. On the other hand, three out of the four countries which were not poor (Iraq, Malaysia, Cyprus, Japan) were also experiencing insurgencies. Here again, the likelihood of insurgency in the richer countries was about twice that in the poorer countries. Here also, ethnic heterogeneity appeared to be a better predictor of insurgency than poverty.

The weakness of the direct correlation between poverty and instability is also suggested by other evidence. While a correlation of $-.43$ (n $= 74$) existed between per capita GNP and deaths from domestic group violence, the largest amount of violence was found not in the poorest countries with per capita GNPS of less than $100, but in those slightly more wealthy with per capita GNPS between $100 and $200. Above $200 the amount of violence tended to decline significantly. These figures led to the conclusion that "underdeveloped nations must expect a fairly high level of civil unrest for some time, and that the very poor states should probably expect an increase, not a decrease, in domestic violence over the next few decades."[3] So also, Eckstein found that the 27 countries in which internal wars were rare between 1946 and 1959 were divided into two groups. Nine were highly modern (e.g. Australia, Denmark, Sweden), while 18 were "relatively underdeveloped countries whose

elites have remained tied closely to the traditional types and structures of life." Among these were a number of still backward European colonies plus such countries as Ethiopia, Eritrea, Liberia, and Saudi Arabia.[4] Somewhat similarly, a division of countries according to their levels of literacy also suggested a bell-shaped pattern of instability. Ninety-five per cent of those countries in the middle range with 25 to 60 per cent literacy were unstable as compared to 50 per cent of those countries with less than 10 per cent literacy and 22 per cent of those countries with more than 90 per cent literacy. In another analysis mean instability scores were calculated for 24 modern countries (268), 37 transitional countries (472), and 23 traditional countries (420).[5]

LITERACY AND STABILITY

| Level of literacy | Number of countries | Number of unstable countries | Per cent unstable |
|---|---|---|---|
| Below 10% | 6 | 3 | 50.0 |
| 10%–25% | 12 | 10 | 83.3 |
| 25%–60% | 23 | 22 | 95.6 |
| 60%–90% | 15 | 12 | 80.0 |
| Over 90% | 23 | 5 | 21.7 |

Source: Ivo K. and Rosalind L. Feierabend and Betty A. Nesvold, "Correlates of Political Stability" (paper presented at Annual Meeting, American Political Science Association, Sept. 1963), pp. 19–21.

The sharp difference between the transitional and modern countries demonstrates graphically the thesis that modernity means stability and modernization instability. The small difference between the traditional societies and the transitional societies reflects the fact that the line drawn between the two was a purely

[3] Hayward R. Alker, Jr. and Bruce M. Russett, "The Analysis of Trends and Patterns," in Russett et al., pp. 306–07. See also Ted Gurr with Charles Ruttenberg, The Conditions of Civil Violence: First Tests of a Causal Model (Princeton, Princeton University, Center of International Stuides, Research Monograph No. 28, 1967), pp. 66–67.

[4] Harry Eckstein, "Internal War: The Problem of Anticipation," in Ithiel de Sola Pool et al., Social Science Research and National Security (Washington, D.C., Smithsonian Institution, 1963), pp. 120–21.

[5] Feierabend, p. 263.

arbitrary one intended to produce a group of "traditional" countries equal in size to the modern group. Hence virtually all the societies classified as traditional were actually in the early phases of transition. Again, however, the data suggest that if a purely traditional society existed, it would be more stable politically than those in the transitional phase.

The modernization thesis thus explains why the poverty thesis could acquire a certain seeming validity in the late twentieth century. It also explains seeming reversals in the relation between modernity and stability for particular sets of countries. In Latin America, for instance, the wealthiest countries are at the middle levels of modernization. Consequently, it is not surprising that they should be more unstable than the more backward Latin American countries. As we have seen, in 1966 only one of the six poorest Latin American countries, but five of the 14 wealthier Latin American countries, suffered from insurgency. Communist and other radical movements have been strong in Cuba, Argentina, Chile, and Venezuela: four of the five wealthiest of the 20 Latin American republics and three of the five most literate republics. The frequency of revolution in Latin America is directly related to the level of economic development. For the continent as a whole the correlation of per capita income and number of revolutions is .50 (n = 18); for nondemocratic states it is much higher (r = .85; n = 14).[6] Thus, the data on Latin

America which suggest a positive relationship between modernity and instability actually bolster the argument that relates modernization to instability.

This relationship also holds for variations within countries. In modernizing countries, violence, unrest, and extremism are more often found in the wealthier parts of the country than in the poorer sections. In analysing the situation in India, Hoselitz and Weiner found that "the correlation between political stability and economic development is poor or even negative." Under British rule political violence was most prevalent in the "economically most highly developed provinces"; after independence violence remained more likely in the industrialized and urban centers than "in the more backward and underdeveloped areas of India."[7] In numerous underdeveloped countries the standard of living in the major cities is three or four times that prevalent in the countryside, yet the cities are often the centers of instability and violence while the rural areas remain quiet and stable. Political extremism is also typically stronger in the wealthier than in the poorer areas. In fifteen Western countries, the communist vote was largest in the most urbanized areas of the least urbanized countries.[8] In Italy the center of communist strength was the prosperous north rather than the poverty-stricken south. In India the communists were strongest in Kerala (with the highest literacy rate among Indian states) and in industrialized Calcutta, not in the economically more backward areas. In Ceylon, "In a fundamental sense, the areas of Marxist strength are the most Westernized" and those with

---

[6] Manus Midlarsky and Raymond Tanter, "Toward a Theory of Political Instability in Latin America," *Journal of Peace Research,* 4 (1967), 215. See also Robert D. Putnam's discovery of a positive association between economic development (but not social mobilization) and military intervention in Latin America: "Toward Explaining Military Intervention in Latin American Politics," *World Politics,* 20 (Oct. 1967), 94–97.

[7] Bert F. Hoselitz and Myron Weiner, "Economic Development and Political Stability in India," *Dissent,* 8 (Spring 1961), 173.

[8] William Kornhauser, *The Politics of Mass Society* (Glencoe, Ill., Free Press, 1959), pp. 143–44.

the highest per capita income and education.[9] Thus, within countries, it is the areas which are modernizing rather than those which remain traditional that are the centers of violence and extremism.

Not only does social and economic modernization produce political instability, but the degree of instability is related to the rate of modernization. The historical evidence with respect to the West is overwhelming on this point. "The *rapid* influx of large numbers of people into *newly* developing urban areas," Kornhauser observes, "invites mass movements." So also, the European and particularly the Scandinavian experience demonstrates that wherever "industrialization occurred *rapidly*, introducing sharp *discontinuities* between the pre-industrial and industrial situation, more rather than less extremist working-class movements emerged."[10] Similarly, the combined rate of change on six of eight indicators of modernization (primary and postprimary education; caloric consumption; cost of living; radios; infant mortality; urbanization; literacy; and national income) for 67 countries between 1935 and 1962 correlated .647 with political instability in those countries between 1955 and 1961. "The higher the rate of change toward modernity, the greater the political instability, measured statically or dynamically." The overall picture which emerges of an unstable country is:

> one exposed to modernity; disrupted socially from the traditional patterns of life; confronted with pressures to change their ways, economically, socially and politically; bombarded with new and "better" ways of producing economic goods and services; and

frustrated by the modernization process of change, generally, and the failure of their government to satisfy their ever-rising expectations, particularly.[11]

Political instability was rife in twentieth-century Asia, Africa, and Latin America in large part because the rate of modernization was so much faster there than it had been in the earlier modernizing countries. The modernization of Europe and of North America was spread over several centuries; in general, one issue or one crisis was dealt with at a time. In the modernization of the non-Western parts of the world, however, the problems of the centralization of authority, national integration, social mobilization, economic development, political participation, social welfare have arisen not sequentially but simultaneously. The "demonstration effect" which the early modernizers have on the later modernizers first intensifies aspirations and then exacerbates frustrations. The differences in the rate of change can be dramatically seen in the lengths of time which countries, in Cyril Black's formulation, required for the consolidation of modernizing leadership. For the first modernizer, England, this phase stretched over 183 years, from 1649 to 1832. For the second modernizer, the United States, it lasted 89 years, from 1776 to 1865. For 13 countries which entered it during the Napoleonic period (1789–1815), the average period was 73 years. But for 21 of the 26 countries which began it during the first quarter of the twentieth century and had emerged by the 1960s, the average was only 29 years.[12] In a similar vein, Karl

[9] William Howard Wriggins, *Ceylon: Dilemmas of a New Nation* (Princeton, Princeton University Press, 1960), pp. 134–35, 138–40.

[10] Kornhauser, p. 145 (italics in original); Seymour Martin Lipset, *Political Man* (Garden City, N.Y., Doubleday, 1960), p. 68 (italics in original).

[11] Wallace W. Conroe, "A Cross-National Analysis of the Impact of Modernization Upon Political Stability (unpublished M. A. thesis San Diego State College, 1965), pp. 65–73, 86–87; Feierabend, pp. 263–67.

[12] Cyril E. Black, *The Dynamics of Modernization* (New York, Harper and Row, 1966), pp. 90–94.

Deutsch estimates that during the nineteenth century the principal indicators of social mobilization in modernizing countries changed at about the rate of 0.1 per cent per year, while in twentieth-century modernizing countries they change at about the rate of 1 per cent per year. Clearly the tempo of modernization has increased rapidly. Clearly, also, the heightened drive for social and economic change and development was directly related to the increasing political instability and violence that characterized Asia, Africa, and Latin America in the years after World War II.

*Social Mobilization and Instability.* The relationship between social mobilization and political instability seems reasonably direct. Urbanization, increases in literacy, education, and media exposure all give rise to enhanced aspirations and expectations which, if unsatisfied, galvanize individuals and groups into politics. In the absence of strong and adaptable political institutions, such increases in participation mean instability and violence. Here in dramatic form can be clearly seen the paradox that modernity produces stability and modernization instability. For 66 nations, for example, the correlation between the proportion of children in primary schools and the frequency of revolution was −.84. In contrast, for 70 nations the correlation between the rate of change in primary enrollment and political instability was .61.[13] The faster the enlightenment of the population, the more frequent the overthrow of the government.

The rapid expansion of education has had a visible impact on political stability in a number of countries. In Ceylon, for instance, the school system expanded rapidly between 1948 and 1956. This "increase in the number of students graduating in the indigenous languages satisfied some ambitions but contributed new social pressures among the articulate educated middle classes." It was, apparently, directly related to the electoral overturn of the government in the elections of 1956 and to the increased instability affecting Ceylon during the following six years.[14] Similarly, in Korea during the 1950s Seoul became "one of the largest education centers of the world." Its law schools, it is estimated, produced about eighteen times as many graduates in 1960 as the field could absorb. At the lower levels of education, the expansion was even more striking, with the literacy rate increasing from less than 20 per cent in 1945 to over 60 per cent in the early 1960s.[15] This expansion of awareness presumably shared some responsibility for the political instability of Korea during the early 1960s, the principal source of which was students. Students and unemployed university graduates were, indeed, a common concern in the 1960s to the nationalist military regime in Korea, the socialist military regime in Burma, and the traditional military regime in Thailand. The extent to which higher education in many modernizing countries is not calculated to produce graduates with the skills relevant to the country's needs creates the paradoxical but common situation "of a country in which skilled labor is a scarce resource, and yet in which highly educated persons are in super-abundant supply."[16]

In general, the higher the level of education of the unemployed, alienated,

---

[13] Tanter and Midlarsky, p. 272, citing forthcoming *Dimensions of Nations* by Rummel, Sawyer, Tanter, and Guetzkow; Conroe, p. 66.

[14] Wriggins, pp. 119, 245. On the Feierabend-Nesvold-Conrie index, instability in Ceylon increased from 3:012 during 1948–54 to 4:089 for 1955–62; see Conroe, Table I.

[15] Gregory Henderson, *Korea: The Politics of the Vortex* (Cambridge, Harvard University Press, 1968), p. 170.

[16] Hoselitz and Weiner, p. 177.

or otherwise dissatisfied person, the more extreme the destabilizing behavior which results. Alienated university graduates prepare revolutions; alienated technical or secondary school graduates plan coups; alienated primary school leavers engage in more frequent but less significant forms of political unrest. In West Africa, for instance, "disgruntled and restless though they are, these school-leavers stand not at the center but on the perimeter of significant political events. The characteristic forms of political disturbance for which they are responsible are not revolutions but acts of arson, assault, and intimidation directed against political opponents."[17]

The problems posed by the rapid expansion of primary education have caused some governments to reassess their policies. In a debate on education in the Eastern Region of Nigeria in 1958, for instance, Azikiwe suggested that primary education could become an "unproductive social service," and one cabinet member warned that the United Kingdom followed "the pattern of industry and increased productivity first, free education second. Never free education first, as there must be jobs for the newly educated to take up, and only industry, trade and commerce can provide such jobs in bulk. . . . We must hesitate to create political problems of unemployment in the future."[18] Literates and semiliterates may furnish recruits for extremist movements generating instability. Burma and Ethiopia had equally low per capita incomes in the 1950s: the relative stability of the latter in comparison to the former perhaps reflected the fact that fewer than 5 per cent of the Ethiopians were literate but

45 per cent of the Burmese were.[19] Similarly, Cuba had the fourth highest literacy rate in Latin America when it went communist, and the only Indian state to elect a communist government, Kerala, also has the highest literacy rate in India. Clearly, the appeals of communism are usually to literates rather than illiterates. Much has been made of the problems caused by the extension of suffrage to large numbers of illiterates; democracy, it has been argued, cannot function satisfactorily if the vast bulk of the voting population cannot read. Political participation by illiterates, however, may well, as in India, be less dangerous to democratic political institutions than participation by literates. The latter typically have higher aspirations and make more demands on government. Political participation by illiterates, moreover, is likely to remain limited, while participation by literates is more likely to snowball with potentially disastrous effects on political stability.

### Economic Development and Instability

Social mobilization increases aspirations. Economic development, presumably, increases the capacity of a society to satisfy those aspirations and therefore should tend to reduce social frustrations and the consequent political instability. Presumably, also, rapid economic growth creates new opportunities for entrepreneurship and employment and thereby diverts into money-making ambitions and talents which might otherwise go into coup-making. It can, however, also be argued to the contrary that economic development itself is a highly destabilizing process and that the very changes which are needed to satisfy aspirations in fact tend to exacerbate

[17] David Abernethy and Trevor Coombe, "Education and Politics in Developing Countires," *Harvard Educational Review,* 35 (Summer 1965), 292.
[18] Quoted in Abernethy, p. 501.

[19] Deutsch, "Social Mobilization and Political Development," p. 496.

those aspirations. Rapid economic growth, it has been said:

1. disrupts traditional social groupings (family, class, caste), and thus increases "the number of individuals who are déclassé...and who are thus in circumstances conducive to revolutionary protest";[20]

2. produces *nouveaux riches* who are imperfectly adjusted to and assimilated by the existing order and who want political power and social status commensurate with their new economic position;

3. increases geographical mobility which again undermines social ties, and, in particular, encourages rapid migration from rural areas to cities, which produces alienation and political extremism;

4. increases the number of people whose standard of living is falling, and thus may widen the gap between rich and poor;

5. increases the incomes of some people absolutely but not relatively and hence increases their dissatisfaction with the existing order;

6. requires a general restriction of consumption in order to promote investment and thus produces popular discontent;

7. increases literacy, education, and exposure to mass media, which increase aspirations beyond levels where they can be satisfied;

8. aggravates regional and ethnic conflicts over the distribution of investment and consumption;

9. increases capacities for group organization and consequently the strength of group demands on government, which the government is unable to satisfy.

To the extent that these relationships hold, economic growth increases material well-being at one rate but social frustration at a faster rate.

The association of economic development, particularly rapid economic development, with political instability received its classic statement in de Tocqueville's interpretation of the French Revolution. The revolution, he said, was preceded by "an advance as rapid as it was unprecedented in the prosperity of the nation." This "steadily increasing prosperity, far from tranquilizing the population, everywhere promoted a spirit of unrest" and "it was precisely in those parts of France where there had been most improvement that popular discontent ran highest." Similar conditions of economic improvement, it has been argued, preceded the Reformation, the English, American, and Russian revolutions, and the agitation and discontent in England in the late eighteenth and early nineteenth centuries. The Mexican revolution similarly followed twenty years of spectacular economic growth. The rate of change in per capita gross national product for seven years before a successful revolt correlated very highly with the extent of violence in such revolts in Asian and Middle Eastern countries between 1955 and 1960, although not in Latin America. The experience of India, it has been argued, from the 1930s through the 1950s also shows "that economic development, far from enhancing political stability, has tended to be politically unstabilizing."[21] All this data is, of course, also consistent with the finding that during World War II discontent about promotions was more wide-spread in the Air Force than in other services despite or because of the fact that promotions were more frequent and rapid in the Air Force than in the other services.[22]

Much specific evidence thus exists of

---

[20] Mancur Olson, Jr., "Rapid Growth as a Destabilizing Force," *Journal of Economic History*, 23 (Dec. 1963), 532. This list of the destabilizing effects of economic growth is drawn primarily from Olson's article.

[21] Alexis de Tocqueville, *The Old Regime and the French Revolution* (Garden City, N.Y., Doubleday, 1955), pp. 173, 175–76; Crane Brinton, *The Anatomy of Revolution* (New York, Vintage, 1958), p. 264; Olson, pp. 544–47; Tanter and Midlarsky, pp. 272–74; Hoselitz and Weiner, p. 173, for the quotation on India.

[22] See Samuel A. Stouffer et al., *The American Soldier* (Princeton, Princeton University Press, 1949), 1, 251–58, 275–76.

an apparent association between rapid economic growth and political instability. On a more general level, however, the link between the two is not so clear. During the 1950s the correlation between rate of economic growth and domestic group violence for 53 countries was a mildly negative one of −.43. West Germany, Japan, Roumania, Yugoslavia, Austria, the U.S.S.R., Italy, and Czechoslovakia had very high rates of economic growth and little or no domestic violence. Bolivia, Argentina, Honduras, and Indonesia, on the other hand, had many deaths from domestic violence but very low, and in some cases even negative, growth rates. Similarly, the correlation for seventy countries of the rate of change in national income between 1935 and 1962 and level of political instability between 1948 and 1962 was −.34; the correlation between the change in national income and the variations in stability for the same countries in the same years was −.45. In a similar vein, Needler found that in Latin America economic growth was a precondition for institutional stability in countries with high rates of political participation.[23]

This conflicting evidence suggests that the relationship, if any, between economic growth and political instability must be a complicated one. Perhaps the relationship varies with the level of economic development. At one extreme, some measure of economic growth is necessary to make instability possible. The simple poverty thesis falls down because people who are really poor are too poor for politics and too poor for protest. They are indifferent, apathetic, and lack exposure to the media and other stimuli which would arouse their aspirations in such manner as to galvanize them into political activity. "The abjectly poor, too," Eric Hoffer observed, "stand in awe of the world around them and are not hospitable to change. . . . There is thus a conservatism of the destitute as profound as the conservatism of the privileged, and the former is as much a factor in the perpetuation of a social order as the latter."[24] Poverty itself is a barrier to instability. Those who are concerned about the immediate goal of the next meal are not apt to worry about the grand transformation of society. They become marginalists and incrementalists concerned simply with making minor but absolutely essential improvements in the existing situation. Just as social mobilization is necessary to provide the motive for instability, so also some measure of economic development is necessary to provide the means for instability.

At the other extreme, among countries which have reached a relatively high level of economic development, a high rate of economic growth is compatible with political stability. The negative correlations between economic growth and instability reported above are, in large part, the result of combining both highly developed and underdeveloped countries into the same analysis. Economically developed countries are more stable and have higher rates of growth than economically less developed countries. Unlike other social indicators, the rate of economic growth tends to vary directly with the level of development rather than inversely with it. In countries which are not wealthy,

[23] Conroe, pp. 65–69; Martin C. Needler, *Political Development in Latin America: Instability, Violence, and Evolutionary Change* (New York, Random House, 1968), Chap. 5.

[24] Eric Hoffer, *The True Believer* (New York, New American Library, 1951), p. 17; Daniel Goldrich, "Toward an Estimate of the Probability of Social Revolutions in Latin America: Some Orienting Concepts and a Case Study," *Centennial Review*, 6 (Summer 1962), 394 ff.

the rate of economic growth is not related significantly to political instability one way or another: for 34 countries with per capita GNP below $500 the correlation between rate of economic growth and deaths from domestic group violence was −.07. Thus, the relation between the rate of economic growth and political instability varies with the level of economic development. At low levels, a positive relation exists, at medium levels no significant relation, and at high levels a negative relationship.

*The Gap Hypothesis.* Social mobilization is much more destabilizing than economic development. The gap between these two forms of change furnishes some measure of the impact of modernization on political stability. Urbanization, literacy, education, mass media, all expose the traditional man to new forms of life, new standards of enjoyment, new possibilities of satisfaction. These experiences break the cognitive and attitudinal barriers of the traditional culture and promote new levels of aspirations and wants. The ability of a transitional society to satisfy these new aspirations, however, increases much more slowly than the aspirations themselves. Consequently, a gap develops between aspiration and expectation, want formation and want satisfaction, or the aspirations function and the level-of-living function.[25] This gap generates social frustration and dissatisfaction. In practice, the extent of the gap provides a reasonable index to political instability.

The reasons for this relationship between social frustration and political instability are somewhat more complicated than they may appear on the sur-

face. The relationship is, in large part, due to the absence of two potential intervening variables: opportunities for social and economic mobility and adaptable political institutions. Since Puritanism, the go-getting economic innovator and the dedicated revolutionary have had qualitatively different goals but strikingly similar high aspirations, both the product of a high level of social mobilization.[26] Consequently, the extent to which social frustration produces political participation depends in large part on the nature of the economic and social structure of the traditional society. Conceivably this frustration could be removed through social and economic mobility if the traditional society is sufficiently "open" to offer opportunities for such mobility. In part, this is precisely what occurs in rural areas, where outside opportunities for horizontal mobility (urbanization) contribute to the relative stability of the countryside in most modernizing countries. The few opportunities for vertical (occupational and income) mobility within the cities, in turn, contribute to their greater instability. Apart from urbanization, however, most modernizing countries have low levels of social-economic mobility. In relatively few societies are the traditional structures likely to encourage economic rather than political activity. Land and any other types of economic wealth in the traditional society are tightly held by a relatively small oligarchy or are controlled by foreign corporations and investors. The values of the traditional society often are hostile to entrepreneurial roles, and such roles consequently may be largely monopolized by an ethnic minority (Greeks and Armenians in the Ottoman Empire; Chinese in southeast Asia; Lebanese in

[25] These are terms employed by Deutsch, pp. 493 ff.; James C. Davies, "Toward a Theory of Revolution," *American Sociological Review*, 27 (Feb. 1962), 5 ff.; Feierabend, pp. 256–62; Charles Wolf, *Foreign Aid: Theory and Practice in Southern Asia* (Princeton, Princeton University Press, 1960), pp. 296 ff.; and Tanter and Midlarsky, pp. 271 ff.

[26] For the relation between n-Achievement and communism, see David C. McClelland, *The Achieving Society* (Princeton, Van Nostrand, 1961), pp. 412–13.

Africa). In addition, the modern values and ideas which are introduced into the system often stress the primacy of government (socialism, the planned economy), and consequently may also lead mobilized individuals to shy away from entrepreneurial roles.

In these conditions, political participation becomes the road for advancement of the socially mobilized individual. Social frustration leads to demands on the government and the expansion of political participation to enforce those demands. The political backwardness of the country in terms of political institutionalization, moreover, makes it difficult if not impossible for the demands upon the government to be expressed through legitimate channels and to be moderated and aggregated within the political system. Hence the sharp increase in political participation gives rise to political instability. The impact of modernization thus involves the following relationships:

frustration and instability was .50. The differences in Communist voting strength in Indian states can also in part be explained by the ratios between social mobilization and economic well-being in these states. Similarly, in Latin America, constitutional stability has been shown to be a function of economic development and political participation. Sharp increases in participation produce instability unless they are accompanied by corresponding shifts in the level of economic well-being.[27]

Political instability in modernizing countries is thus in large part a function of the gap between aspirations and expectations produced by the escalation of aspirations which particularly occurs in the early phases of modernization. In some instances, a similar gap with similar results may be produced by the decline in expectations. Revolutions often occur when a period of sustained economic growth is followed by a sharp economic downturn. Such downturns ap-

(1) $\dfrac{\text{Social mobilization}}{\text{Economic development}}$ = Social frustration

(2) $\dfrac{\text{Social frustration}}{\text{Mobility opportunities}}$ = Political participation

(3) $\dfrac{\text{Political participation}}{\text{Political institutionalization}}$ = Political instability

The absence of mobility opportunities and the low level of political institutionalization in most modernizing countries produce a correlation between social frustration and political instability. One analysis identified 26 countries with a low ratio of want formation to want satisfaction and hence low "systemic frustration" and 36 countries with a high ratio and hence high "systemic frustration." Of the 26 satisfied societies, only six (Argentina, Belgium, France, Lebanon, Morocco, and the Union of South Africa) had high degrees of political instability. Of the 36 dissatisfied countries, only two (Philippines, Tunisia) had high levels of political stability. The overall correlation between

parently occurred in France in 1788–89, in England in 1687–88, in America in 1774–75, before Dorr's rebellion in 1842, in Russia (as a result of the war) in 1915–17, in Egypt in 1952, and in Cuba in 1952–53 (when Castro launched his first attack on Batista). In addition, in Latin America coups d'etat occur more frequently during years when economic conditions worsen than in those years marked by increases in real per capita incomes.[28]

[27] Feierabend, p. 259; Wolf, Chap. 9; Needler, Chap. 5.

[28] See Davies, pp. 5 ff.; Tanter and Midlarsky, passim; Martin C. Needler, "Political Development and Military Intervention in Latin America," *American Political Science Review, 60* (Sept. 1966), 617–18.

# D. Political Development

# POLITICAL DEVELOPMENT :
# TIME SEQUENCES AND RATES OF CHANGE

ERIC A. NORDLINGER

Political development is undoubtedly a rich and variegated field of study. We have begun to accumulate first-rate studies of widely divergent cultures and social structures, masses of quantitative data on the socioeconomic variables involved in the modernization process, analyses of political phenomena ranging from the destooling of chiefs to the functioning of complex legislative systems, well-documented surveys of particular political systems, and a smaller number of useful typologies and general hypotheses. It is this burgeoning and many-faceted literature that makes "theory-building" simultaneously most difficult and most desirable—just as the integration problems facing the new states are exceptionally difficult to resolve, while at the same time their resolution is first on the list of political imperatives. We are clearly in need of a set of questions and concepts that are broad enough to encompass the phenomena falling under the rubric of political development, but that are also specific enough to allow for the generation of testable hypotheses of an explanatory variety.

Two strong candidates for the job are

This essay is a revised version of Eric A. Nordlinger, "Political Development: Time Sequences and Rates of Change," WORLD POLITICS, XX (April), pp. 494–520, by permission of the publisher.

time sequences and rates of change. While these two concepts are not independent variables themselves, when applied to particular variables they are specific enough to facilitate the formulation of explanatory hypotheses, while constituting a broad framework within which the various hypotheses may be integrated. It should be quite apparent that both sequences and rates of change are sufficiently generalizable concepts to allow for the systematic integration of broad slices of the political development field. In dealing with the variables constituting the field, we can analyze all manner of political, social, and economic phenomena in terms of their sequences and rates. Questions involving sequence and rate are also broad enough to allow for comparisons of non-Western countries with comparable phenomena in Europe, thereby remedying the neglect of European countries in the study of political development and encouraging the formulation of hypotheses that may have close to universal applicability after the relevant contextual conditions are included.

Moreover, this focus upon the two dimensions of time may help to fill an important gap in the political science literature. While it is by no means true that history explains everything, it does take us well along the road, especially in the implicitly historically oriented field of political development. Yet until quite recently, political science was practically denuded of any explicit conception of time, thereby eliminating the possibility of constructing generalizations based upon historical patterns of development. Generalizations involving history may be of either a descriptive or an explanatory type, or both simultaneously. The great evolutionary theorists—Condorcet, Comte, Marx, Spencer, Darwin, Spengler, Toynbee, and Sorokin—either restricted themselves to descriptive generalization alone or combined description and explanation. Descriptively, they argued that historical development unfolds according to particular stages; in their explanations, they argued that one stage is unable to emerge until the prior stage has evolved, for each stage is in some way a necessary condition for the emergence of its successor. We are now well aware that history is in no way unilinear—that there are not any "evolutionary universals in society," as Parsons has called them. Yet there is no reason why this major difficulty in the descriptive aspect of evolutionary theories forces political science to ignore various concepts of time.

The point to be made is then this: political scientists could profitably play down the importance of those descriptive generalizations involving time found throughout the development and modernization literature and concentrate upon explanatory ones. Instead of attempting to identify a general pattern according to which political systems develop, we can look at the various developmental patterns and ask questions about their different consequences. For instance, rather than suggesting that political systems necessarily become more differentiated and complex over time, we can attempt to construct general explanatory hypotheses of this kind:

*if* a political system becomes more differentiated at a particular rate of change, or according to a certain sequence, one part of the system becoming differentiated before another, then certain consequences are likely to follow. The hypotheses put forward in this essay are formulated in just this manner.

Besides providing far more extended explanations of political development, this type of emphasis can also contribute to a greater refinement of explanatory generalizations. As one sociologist has put it, "Because few theorists face the relevance of time to their explanations, discussion of social change remains vague, and causal links far from clear."[1] For example, by utilizing the notion of time sequences Giovanni Sartori was able to bring a large breath of fresh air into the perennial debate about the interrelation between electoral arrangements and the party system. Instead of reasserting or refuting the argument that proportional representation leads to the multiplication of parties, Sartori has effectively inserted himself into the debate by developing a number of propositions supporting his contention that PR produces a multiparty system only when it is introduced *prior* to the formation of parties with structured organizations and well-articulated party platforms.[2]

Lastly, a focus upon rates of change implicitly raises questions involving time lag. We may speak of a time lag between two related variables when one of them originates at an earlier time or evolves at a faster rate than the other, so that the two reach similar levels only after a

[1] Max Hierich, "The Use of Time in the Study of Social Change," *American Sociological Review*, XXIX (June 1964), 386.

[2] Giovanni Sartori, "European Political Parties: The Case of Polarized Pluralism," in Joseph LaPalombara and Myron Weiner, eds., *Poiltical Parties and Political Development* (Princeton, Princeton University Perss, 1966), pp. 167–69.

certain time period has elapsed. After having determined such an approximate time lag, it should be possible to offer hypotheses that account for differences in time lag and to suggest the consequences that larger or smaller time lags have for other phenomena. In fact, such hypotheses and suggestions form the centerpiece of Stein Rokkan's study of polarization (or cleavage patterns) in Norway. By bringing together ecological and election data, Rokkan maps out the time lags between rural and urban political mobilization. The fact that it took some fifty-five years for rural voter turnout to match that of the urban population in Norway is accounted for by variations in the social structure and is then related to the country's cleavage patterns. And in his concluding section, Rokkan outlines his reasons for thinking that such time-lag studies in rural and urban political change are one of the most potentially rewarding research strategies in comparative politics generally.[3]

I. VARIABLES AND HYPOTHESES

These then are some of the uses and advantages of an approach to political development that focuses upon sequences and rates of change. Here a preliminary attempt will be made to formulate a number of explanatory hypotheses involving time sequences and rates of change as they help account for certain fundamental aspects of political development. It is hoped that this attempt will serve to illustrate the applications and the explanatory power of sequence and rate-of-change propositions, and that it will concomitantly outline a convenient manner of systematically integrating many of the major conclusions in the political development literature. And

it may even turn out that the hypotheses offered here enjoy a respectable measure of validity.

There are four political phenomena whose sequence and rates of change constitute the independent variables:[4] (1) A national identity may be said to exist when the great majority of the politically relevant actors accord the nation's central symbols and its political elite(s) greater loyalty than that which they maintain toward subnational units, such as tribes, castes, and classes, and toward political elite(s) residing outside the system's territory. (2) A central government that is institutionalized is characterized by a significant differentiation of structures and a specificity of functions, and by regularized decision-making procedures characterized by a hierarchical structure in which the personnel responsible for the execution and enforcement of governmental decisions are subordinate to the executive decision-makers. (3) Protoparties, as contrasted with mass parties, are limited in their membership, which is composed of national, regional, and/or local notables, and in their organization, which is minimal. (4) The last independent variable, mass suffrage or near-universal suffrage, is self-explanatory except for the provision that voting is not pro forma, as in single-party states, or inconsequential because the legislators are practically powerless, as in Meiji Japan, or ineffective because votes are weighted, as in Wilhelmine Germany.

---

[3] "Electoral Mobilization, Party Competition, and National Integration," in *ibid.*, pp. 244–45, 248–49, 258–61.

[4] While the following variables are susceptible to more precise definitions than those offered here, to define them further would be both useless and pretentious. The kinds of hypotheses and illustrative evidence offered below are not refined enough to link up with a set of more closely defined variables, just as certain studies relying upon survey or aggregate data only artificially confirm the hypotheses when especially sophisticated statistical manipulations are unwarranted by the weak reliability of the data.

The sequence and rate of change of these variables will be analyzed separately in an attempt to account for the three dependent variables defined here: (1) The presence or absence of widespread violence refers to attacks by one group against another (not necessarily against the government itself), commonly centering on tribal, class, ethnic, religious, or territorial hatreds and jealousies. (2) An authoritarian government is one that represses political dissent even when such expressions do not involve the goal of overthrowing the government. This policy involves the punishment of even those dissenters who do not publicly express their disapproval of the form of government and its incumbents or make known their dissatisfaction with governmental outputs. Authoritarianism as repression also refers to the outlawing and destruction of independent intermediary groups, such as farmers' organizations, labor unions, and communal associations, which do not challenge the government's authority, though they may peacefully attempt to persuade the government to alter its policies. It should be heavily underscored that the category of authoritarian rule does not include those dictatorships —colonial regimes, single-party states, military regimes, oligarchies, and monarchies—that are simply concerned with maintaining their position of control and that do not resort to the repression of the rights and liberties of individuals and groups who do not challenge their authority. (3) The last dependent variable is a form of democratic government (i.e., open competition for governmental office, with the population selecting the "winners") which is genuinely representative, durable, and decisionally effective.[5]

Although these three dependent variables refer to certain *forms* of interaction among individuals and between individuals and the government, they also tell us a good deal about the presence or absence of those outcomes that determine the *quality* of life in a society —what Pennock has termed "political goods," constituting an important and much neglected aspect of political development.[6] Some of these "political goods" —such as individual dignity, security, justice, liberty, and material welfare— are intimately connected with the presence or absence of widespread violence, repressive rule, and democratic government. Thus in attempting to account for these three dependent variables, the general propositions offered here will presumably also be related to the distribution of "political goods."

Since the secondary arguments supporting the general propositions sometimes become rather involved, it might be helpful to summarize the major propositions at the outset. With respect to time sequences, it is argued that the probabilities of a political system's developing in a nonviolent, nonauthoritarian, and eventually democratically viable manner are maximized when a national identity emerges first, followed

[5] Some students of political development would contend that democracy as defined here —in terms of the electoral form that it has

taken in Western areas—is inapplicable to the non-Western areas and that governmental responsiveness to the population, if it is achieved, will be achieved through *indigenous* forms of representation. Perhaps—but at this point in history it is a highly dubious proposition since such indigenous forms of representation have not yet been institutionalized in any national political system. Moreover, a number of modernizing systems—such as the Philippines, India, Chile, and Costa Rica— have successfully adopted the Western democratic model, and all but a few of the new states of Asia and Africa have set out to build a political order of the Western type.

[6] J. Roland Pennock, "Political Development, Political Systems, and Political Goods," *World Politics*, xviii (April 1966), 415–34.

by the institutionalization of the central government, and then by the emergence of mass parties and a mass electorate.[7] With respect to rates of change, it is argued that a national identity cannot be created in a rapid fashion, and if the attempt is made, it will lead to authoritarian abuses and widespread violence. I shall not offer any hypotheses with regard to the rate at which central governments are institutionalized; although institutionalization cannot be realized quickly, attempts to do so are not likely to have an important bearing upon the three dependent variables. When mass parties are rapidly formed, and when mass electoral participation is ushered in practically overnight, the outcome is likely to be widespread violence and repressive rule, which make it far more difficult to establish a democratic system and, further, assure that if such a system is established, its stability, representativeness, and decisional effectiveness will suffer.

## II. NATIONAL IDENTITY AND GOVERNMENTAL INSTITUTIONS: SEQUENCE

In order to maximize the probabilities of a political system's developing in a nonviolent, nonauthoritarian form and ultimately achieving democratic stability, a sense of national identity should precede the institutionalization of the central government. What then are the secondary hypotheses that support this general argument?

The most fundamental objective of any central government is its own continuation, preferably at the same level of institutionalization and with the same

amount of capability in dealing with the nonelite. Going beyond this, many governments are also firmly committed to the realization of change in any number of spheres and directions. Admittedly, governments might achieve their primary goal without the presence of a sense of national identity. However, it would be more difficult for them to do so, and the nonviolent development of the government in any desired direction is highly unlikely to proceed without the prior resolution of the identity question. Sidney Verba makes the point succinctly when he writes that "other problems are likely to be pushed aside until the central problem is met: 'What is my nation?' must be answered before 'What kind of a nation?' "[8] Without a subjective identification with the regime on the part of the political actors, not only will the government have difficulty in applying its decisions, and thus maintaining its authority, but all types of change will remain in abeyance until a national identity is formed.[9]

When a central government is confronted with sharp procedural and substantive conflicts, it can best ensure its survival and the absence of violence if there is already present a set of inclusive attachments that serve as centripetal forces alleviating the divisions produced by the centrifugal ones. Not only might the procedural values be readily challenged if governmental institutions were formed before a sense of national identity had emerged, but the legitimacy of the central government's mere existence

---

[7] Dankwart Rustow arrives at a broadly similar conclusion (that the most effective sequence for "political modernization" is the one of identity-authority-equality) by a different route than that taken here. See his *A World of Nations* (Washington, 1967), 120–32.

[8] "Comparative Political Culture," in Lucian Pye and Sidney Verba, eds., *Political Culture and Political Development* (Princeton, 1965), 533.

[9] In a related vein, Carl J. Friedrich has written that "only a firmly established government is capable of being constitutionalized. . . . In the evolution of our Western world this meant that national unification had to precede constitutionalism" (*Constitutional Government and Democracy* [Boston, 1941], 8).

might be called into question when parochial groups tried to secede or refused to accept the authority of the governmental incumbents. This point may be taken one step further by noting that the institutionalization of the central government may actually provoke existing parochial groups to resist its authority, for the institutionalization process entails the growth of a firmly structured, decisionally effective and powerful government. In societies where the continuing strength of communal loyalties and hatreds has not allowed a national identity to be formed prior to the institutionalization of the central government, "to permit oneself to be ruled by men of other tribes, other races, or other religions is to submit not merely to oppression but to degradation—to exclusion from the moral community as a lesser order of being whose opinions, attitudes, wishes, and so on, simply do not fully count."[10] And these feelings of oppression and degradation can only be compounded during the process of institutionalization, for the process highlights the presence and increases the power of the incumbents as perceived by the parochial groups.

In Europe the states that have developed most successfully according to the criteria of our three dependent variables are the Scandinavian countries, and in these countries a sense of nationhood developed not only before it did in almost all other European countries (around the eleventh century), but before the formation of central governmental institutions. Among these countries, Norway is a particularly illuminating illustration of the hypothesis. Its history is characterized by the absence of revolution and authoritarianism and by a paucity of violence, while its twen-

tieth-century democratic governments have been exceptionally representative, decisionally effective, and stable—and this despite widespread and intensive cleavages (regional, cultural, and religious), together with the strains following in the wake of rapid industrialization. Part of the explanation undoubtedly lies with the prior existence and the continuing strength of exceptionally cohesive bonds (in the form of a sense of national communality) which successfully mitigated the effects of these conflicts upon the central government.[11]

There is also the very real possibility that the absence of a national identity will both warp and weaken governmental institutions. Without a sense of national identity government may easily become detached from society; the government acts by itself and for itself. As in the great majority of Latin American countries, government becomes the "high road" for personal advancement and the furtherance of narrowly conceived group interests, and in this sense, government may be characterized as parasitic. Governmental institutions that grew up before the emergence of a national identity are also likely to be brittle, given the absence of a legitimizing banner decorated with societal goals. Even if political leaders with reformist and modernizing motivations appear in such political systems, the weakness of the governmental institutions will necessarily dictate their failure. There have been instances in which reform minded governments came to power in Latin America, but they were usually forced out of office by the armed forces and/or the economically privileged classes; the governmental institutions were too weak to protect the incumbents from the opposition of minorities. Only where the army was destroyed, in Mexico, Bolivia, and Cuba,

[10] Clifford Greetz, "Primordial Sentiments and Civil Politics in the New States," in Geertz, ed., *Old Societies and New States* (Glencoe, 1963), 127–28.

[11] Harry Eckstein, *Division and Cohesion in Democracy: A Study of Norway* (Princeton, 1966), esp. 119–20, 181–82.

could thoroughgoing land reform take place. And it is patently obvious that viable democratic institutions are not about to flourish—and they have not done so in Latin America—where governmental institutions are parasitic, corrupting and brittle. Even where democratic governments have been instituted in Latin America, the political parties are commonly personalistic, fragmented, and lacking in programmatic goals. These characteristics have partly grown out of the warped and brittle nature of the governmental institutions, and they are hardly conducive to democratic durability, decisional effectiveness or representativeness.

Besides the definitionally universal aspect of a national identity, its substantive content is also relevant. When a sense of national identity precedes the institutionalization of the central government, there is the possibility that the particular values constituting this identity will restrain the government from developing into an authoritarian one. Three examples of this point are found in the United States, Israel, and Japan. The American national identity was formed prior to 1789 around the two interrelated foci of self-government as a British colony and the War of Independence with Britain. Both experiences helped form a national identity based upon a belief in the Americans' superiority in protecting individual and group liberties, a belief that then played an important part in curbing the opposite tendencies (though it did not succeed in eliminating them, as evidenced by the Alien and Sedition Acts) in the first thirty years of independence when the government was being centrally institutionalized. In the case of Israel, the approximately 10,000 immigrants that arrived in Palestine between 1905 and 1914 came with a highly developed and intensely felt group identity. Over and above the political Zionism of Theodore

Herzel, with its call for the return of the Jews to their historical homeland, there was a symbiosis of nationalism and egalitarianism which was to define the contours of the Jewish socialist commonwealth. These founding fathers and their followers were deeply imbued with the desirability of establishing an egalitarian, open and mobile society, whose particularistic interests were to be fused with the interests of the collectivity. Clearly such values were important in obviating the possibility of repressive rule, even during the most critical periods in the emergence and maintenance of the Jewish state, simultaneously providing a set of political values that contributed to the development of a highly representative and decisionally effective democracy. In Japan, a strong sense of national identity was exhibited by the political class in the last years of the Tokugawa regime and the first years of the Meiji Restoration, before the Meiji oligarchs turned to the job of centralizing and institutionalizing the government. And it was in part the elite's sense of national identity, expressed in service and responsibility to emperor and nation, that helped keep authoritarian abuses within easily manageable bounds during the period of governmental institutionalization.[12]

III. NATIONAL IDENTITY: RATE

Having considered some reasons for thinking that national identity ought to precede the establishment of central

[12] Moreover, these particular attachments to the nation allowed for the gradual inclusion of protoparties and limited popular participation into the decision-making process characterized by a bargaining style. See Robert E. Ward, "Japan: The Continuity of Modernization," in Pye and Verba, 55–56. The pre-1868 peasantry and urban lower classes did not manifest a sense of national identity, but their quiescence and acquiescence made them insignificant as political actors.

governmental institutions, we must now note that there are only a handful of political systems that have developed in this manner. The more common sequence is either the emergence of a national identity after central government has been institutionalized (the institutionalized government helping to mold the national identity) or the simultaneous development of the two, as in the postcolonial societies. The exceptional importance of national identity, both for the three dependent variables presented here and for practically all other variables commonly said to constitute "political development," would suggest that a national identity should be formed as rapidly as possible once central government has come into existence, so that it may alleviate the strains and conflicts that hinder the peaceful development of nonauthoritarian and democratic government.[13] However, turning to rates of change, not only is it extremely difficult to form a sense of national identity in a short period of time, but when the attempt is made, the likelihood of repressive rule and widespread violence following in its wake is concomitantly increased.

One reason why it is highly unlikely that a sense of national identity can be rapidly formed is that the process involves a fundamental alteration in the loyalties of those people whose only attachment was previously given to subnational groups, or the massive growth of national consciousness among a politically "unconscious" or indifferent population. (These three prenationalistic situations are primarily applicable to Asia, tropical Africa, and Latin America, respectively.) If the attempt is made to create a national identity in a short space of time, there appear to be only two foci around which it could develop: a set of emotionally charged symbols or a charismatic leader. But in either case the likelihood is that the new, synthetically created national identity will be a fragile one, to be rejected at the onset of the first major crisis, unless of course the improbable happens and such a crisis is so slow in appearing that the new loyalties have time to strike roots into the culture. Emotional attachments are especially erratic phenomena, particularly when their symbolic centerpiece has faded, as in the case of the colonial nationalist movements ten years or so after independence.[14] And Weber has schooled us in the brittle qualities of charismatic authority.[15] A charismatic leader may help form a basis for unity among contending political factions, legitimate a constitutional form of government, allow protoparties to develop into mass parties, and set a precedent for the peaceful transfer of office. Washington and, to a lesser extent, Atatürk were certainly instrumental in these respects. But in the great majority of new states the charismatic leader has fulfilled only the single task of "acting as a symbol which represents and prolongs the feeling of unity developed prior to the achievement of independence."[16]

[14] Emphasis upon "symbol-wielding" and what Shils has termed "demonstrative" and "remonstrative" politics may also lower a government's administrative and economic effectiveness. For an analysis of Indonesia along such lines, see Herbert Feith, "Indonesia's Political Symbols and Their Wielders," World Politics, xvi (October 1963), esp. 86, 92–96.

[15] Moreover, Weber's arguments that charisma may become routinized contain a number of pitfalls. See W. G. Runciman, "Charismatic Legitimacy and One-Party Rule in Ghana," Archives européennes de sociologie, iv, No. 1 (1963), 149–51.

[16] Seymour Martin Lipset, The First New Nation (New York, 1963), 22–23. See also Rustow's penetrating discussion of charismatic leaders in the new states, 148–69.

[13] Frederick W. Frey sets out "four crucial factors leading a group to an early sense of national identity," in The Turkish Political Elite (Cambridge, Mass., 1965), 409.

In deeply divided societies a rapidly created national identity will not act as an integrative force, at best it will serve as a thin veneer covering over (without bringing together) the cracks in the cultural plaster. Where classes, religious communities, linguistic groups or tribes are mutually mistrustful and hostile, a viable identity cannot be realized by creating common bonds above the particularistic loyalties. In such societies mutual antagonisms will only be assuaged through the emergence of a national identity that builds upon—that takes into account—the particularistic loyalties and traditions. The edifice of a common identity built from the top down will be jerry built; a durable edifice must be built upwards by incorporating the necessarily heterogenous building blocks. If this argument is accepted, then it follows that a common identity cannot be realized in a rapid fashion. Governments cannot legislate minority differences and antagonisms out of existence. In the post-World War I period the democratic governments of Eastern Europe tried to abolish minority languages and educational institutions. Their abysmal failure illustrates the point.

Leaving aside the likelihood of failure, if a charismatic figure or a manipulation of emotion-charged symbols is used in attempting to form a national identity at rapid rate, there remains the distinct danger that authoritarian rule will emerge. In consciously attempting to weld together a positive attachment to the leader or the symbol in a short space of time, the leader or the wielders of the symbol (the party) must necessarily become the embodiment of the nation and thus stand above the nation. Such a claim is often closely bound up with the Rousseauistic notion of the general will, dictating that there not be any partial or independent associations in society. The close relationship be-

tween the rapid creation of a national identity, the assertion of the leader's or the party's position as standing above the nation, and the eradication of independent associations is found in post-independence Ghana. In Nkrumah's often reiterated declaration, "The Convention People's Party is Ghana, and Ghana is the Convention People's Party," and in the last five years of Nkrumah's increasingly repressive rule, youth, labor, ex-servicemen's, and farmers' associations were permitted to exist only if they were merged into the CPP, and religious associations could continue only if they were deeply penetrated by the party. All associations standing outside the party (and there were very few) were saddled with the subversive label.[17] The intimate relationship between the rapid creation of a national identity and the eradication of independent associations is found in even starker form in Guinea, where Sékou Touré has gone further than Nkrumah in directly attacking tribal loyalties in both the society and the ruling party (the Parti Démocratique de Guinée). The society is organized, penetrated, and led by the party so that, as Emerson writes, "all interests and groups...[are] closely interlocked with the structure of the ruling party. Touré himself has made it clear that he regards individual and group liberties as having validity only insofar as they promote the realization of the sovereign popular will, again as expressed by the PDG."[18] Thus one

[17] Rupert Emerson, "Parties and National Integration in Africa," in LaPalombara and Weiner, pp. 278–81; David E. Apter, "Ghana," in James S. Coleman and Carl G. Rosberg, Jr., eds., Political Parties and National Integration in Tropical Africa (Berkeley, 1964), 295–300.

[18] Emerson, in LaPalombara and Weiner, p. 278. See also Charles F. Andrain, "Democracy and Socialism: Ideologies of African Leaders," in David E. Apter, ed., Ideology and Discontent (Glencoe, 1964), 157–64.

danger in attempting to integrate a political system through the rapid creation of a national identity is that individual liberties are repressed and the society is denuded even of its quiescent voluntary associations—associations that would play a singularly important role in the future development and maintenance of democratic government.[19]

Even if these arguments were accepted, it might still be possible to suggest that the use of the past—of a country's traditions—would permit the rapid creation of a national identity. Apter has attributed a good deal of importance to tradition as it helps maximize the chances of averting authoritarianism and establishing democracy. In comparing the new countries of Africa, he finds "that the degree of autocracy which emerges after independence is in virtual proportion to the degree of antagonism the government shows to tradition." He then goes on to state that "respect for the past and cultivation of tradition is a necessary condition of democracy."[20] However, we ought to distinguish between a respect for tradition on the part

[19] This argument finds additional support when it is noted that in other single-party African states whose governments and territorial integrity are also endangered by parochial demands—such as the Cameroons, the Ivory Coast and Tanzania—the goal of creating a national identity is being implemented in a relatively gradual fashion, which is related to the maintenance of their intermediary groups.

[20] David E. Apter, *The Political Kingdom in Uganda* (Princeton, 1961), 476–77. Robert E. Ward also places a good deal of emphasis upon tradition as a stabilizing influence that may help to usher in democratic stability, in Pye and Verba, 77–82, and "Political Modernization and Political Culture in Japan," *World Politics*, xv (July 1963), 578–81. For a discussion of Atatürk's successful manipulation of the traditional Sultanate and Caliphate in altering Turkish identity, see Richard D. Robinson, *The First Turkish Republic* (Cambridge, Mass., 1963), 34–92.

of the government (which is Apter's concern) and the government's deliberate resurrection of tradition in order to unify the nation around a set of common symbols and values. If the government's resurrection of tradition is to be successful, what is commonly thought of as a calming and unifying factor must necessarily become emotionally supercharged, with the attendant dangers of political excesses and the exacerbation of divisions following in its wake. In addition, one group's glorious tradition may be another group's historical ignominy; a reliance upon tradition might exacerbate rather than mitigate political and social antagonisms.

In the case of Japan, the Meiji oligarchs were exceptionally successful in rapidly developing a national identity in the last two decades of the nineteenth century, utilizing the traditional and semimystical symbols of Imperial Shinto and the imperial institution. Their success in creating this identity among a people who previously had had little knowledge of, and even less interest in, what little central government existed was directly related to the institutionalization of the central government and rapid industrialization. But despite these singular achievements, the necessarily emotional attachments involved in the rapid formation of a popular national identity contributed to the emergence of a xenophobic militarism and authoritarianism in the 1930's. Turning to postindependence Ceylon, we find a telling example of the exacerbation of conflict and violence following the attempt to create a national identity in a short space of time. In its first years of independence the Ceylonese government maintained its legitimacy on the basis of a westernized secularism; the country's two largest ethnic groups (the Tamils and the Sinhalese) were able to accept the government because of its "official disregard for all indigenous cultures.[21] This course was then sharply reversed in the middle fifties. And as Geertz has noted, "the search for a common cultural tradition to serve as the content of the country's identity as a nation...led only to the revivification of ancient, and better forgotten, Tamil-Sinhalese treacheries, atrocities, insults and wars."[22] The outcome of this attempt saw the emergence of widespread communal violence. Acting out their slogans of national identity—"Sinhalese only" and *"Apey Aanduwa"* ("the government is ours")—the worst abuses were commited against the Tamils.

In short, despite the desirability of a national identity's preceding the central government's institutionalization with respect to our three dependent variables, this sequence is not a common one, and, at the same time, there does not seem to be a rapid solution for this developmental problem. Not only is it highly unlikely that a national identity can be created in a space of a few years, but the attempt to do so is likely to usher in the unhappy consequences of repressive rule and exacerbation of potentially violent divisions, with their obviously deleterious consequences for the growth of democratic government.

## IV. GOVERNMENTAL INSTITUTIONS AND POLITICAL COMPETITION: SEQUENCE

The next general hypothesis suggests that the chances for attaining a nonviolent politics and democratic stability without passing through a phase of authoritarian government are maximized when the institutionalization of central government precedes the formation of mass political parties and a broad based suffrage. However, the consequences for our three dependent variables will not be nearly as detrimental when structures of political competition are established before or along with central governmental institutions as when mass electoral participation precedes or emerges simultaneously with an institutionalized central government.

To begin with, LaPalombara and Weiner stress the point that at any one time a government is capable of handling only a limited "load" of problems, demands, and conflicts if it is to maintain itself at a particular level of institutionalization, stability, and effectiveness.[23] This is to say that whatever loads a government has to deal with ought to be interspersed so that the critical point at which loads exceed capabilities is not reached. Yet a government confronted with the problems of incorporating structures of political competition and mass participation faces a simultaneous increase of loads on three counts: there are the institutional problems of integrating the new structures of competition around entirely new patterns of conflict resolution and decision-making; existing divisions among the voters will be exacerbated and demands heightened as parties attempt to mobilize support in order to win control of the government; and demands for greater participation (in both scope and intensity) will follow once the principle of an extended suffrage has been conceded. Thus if a government is to handle these loads (or crises) without endangering its stability and effectiveness, it would be well if the governmental structures were securely institutionalized beforehand.[24] Otherwise the government's

21 McKim Marriott, "Cultural Policy in the New States," in Geertz, *Old Societies and New States,* 42.

22 Geertz, *ibid.*, 123. Also see W. Howard Wriggins, "Impediments to Unity in New Nations: The Case of Ceylon," *American Political Science Review,* LV (June 1961), 316, 319.

23 Chaps. 1 and 14, *passim.*

24 For an analysis of European political parties that supports this proposition and demonstrates how the time factor "merges

capabilities and legitimacy will be easily impaired, necessitating its use of force in order to maintain itself. In Parsons' words, when loads exceed capabilities, "increasingly severe negative sanctions for noncompliance with collective decisions will be imposed."[25] The Italian political system of the early twentieth century was faced with the simultaneous loads of creating a national identity, institutionalizing and legitimizing governmental structures, and inducting new strata into the electorate. The political elite responded with repression and violence. And once governments rely upon force, they tend to overreact to demands with the application of excessive force; the value of organizations with force at their disposal (the army and the police) is heightened; there is consequently a further loss of legitimacy; and finally the population itself turns to violence, thereby setting up an additional stage prop for authoritarian rule.[26]

On the other hand, when the crises of competition and electoral participation do not appear until the government has had sufficient time to become institutionalized, the governmental structures will actually be able to play a positive role in helping the system to adapt itself to the new situation. As Huntington has persuasively argued, with increasing longevity, institutions become more adaptable to new challenges and more

flexible in accommodating change.[27] To this may be added a separate point, which also provides some underpinning for Huntington's: the institutionalization of government before it is faced with the crises of competition and electoral participation might provide the political elite with a sufficient sense of security for it to accommodate itself to these changes in a peaceful manner. And in reverse fashion, where the governmental incumbents are insecure because of the brittleness of governmental structures, claims for wider participation may be seen as threats to their own positions, to be adamantly refused. In such an impasse, the groups seeking entry and access to the political system would adopt an alienated posture, questioning the government's root-and-branch legitimacy and possibly turning to violent means as their demands become increasingly radical. Under these circumstances governmental repression, with its unhappy consequences for the country's future development, could very well follow—especially when the elite is insecure because of the fragile governmental structures.

Another argument relies upon the mitigating effects of institutional arrangements. When governmental structures are stabilized and differentiated before the onset of party competition and mass suffrage, the intensity of partisan conflicts and procedural issues will be dampened as they are channeled through and processed by the mediating governmental institutions. On the other hand, when the sequence is reversed, partisan conflicts will tend to escalate as substantive issues evolve into procedural

into and coincides with the load factor," see Otto Kirchheimer, "The Transformation of the Western European Party System," in LaPalombara and Weiner, 177–82. The same type of analysis on a somewhat broader theoretical plane is found in LaPalombara and Weiner's own concluding chapter, 427–33.

[25] Talcott Parsons, "Some Reflections on the Place of Force in Social Process," in Harry Eckstein, ed., *Internal War* (New York, 1964), 64. Also see Geertz, 131.

[26] Aristide R. Zolberg, "The Structure of Political Conflict in the New States of Tropical Africa," *American Political Science Review*, LXII (March 1968), 77.

[27] Samuel P. Huntington, "Political Development and Political Decay," *World Politics*, XVII (April 1965), 394–95. Also see S. N. Eisenstadt, *Modernization: Protest and Change* (New York 1966), 58–61; and Anthony Downs, *Inside Bureaucracy* (Boston, 1967), 18–20.

ones in the absence of stable conflict-resolving structures. This point may provide a partial explanation for Pye's observation that "opposition parties and aspiring elites [in transitional systems] tend to appear as revolutionary movements,"[28] for when the government is not sufficiently institutionalized for the effective resolution of conflicts, it is only a small further step for the opposition to challenge the entire spectrum of the government's goals and legitimacy. Zolberg apparently supports this argument when he writes that in West Africa "the incumbent leaders [and] challengers tend to view conflict as an all-or-nothing proposition...[since] factors which might make for the limitation of issues are almost nonexistent. Whether it begins by asking for better wages or better prices, whether it is dissatisfied with the delimitation of constituencies or with lack of consideration for generational claims, the opposition almost always ends up challenging the entire order which the regime is dedicated to build."[29]

Especially with reference to highly politicized societies, few political scientists would disagree with the statement that large-scale socioeconomic reform should be instituted as early as possible; such reform would generally have the effect of confronting the regime with far fewer loads. This quite obvious point becomes even more significant when socioeconomic reform has not been effected before the creation of a mass electorate. The conjunction of the two—popular power together with popular dissatisfaction and alienation—has all manner of disabling effects: it raises the specter of widespread violence; the conditions are propitious for the emergence

of mass movements or communal politics; the strength of sharply divisive parochial groups is not lessened through the process of "modernization" and the creation of Durkheim's organic solidarity based on value consensus; and the regime suffers from a loss of legitimacy. Taken together, these factors also lead toward repressive rule. This generalization becomes relevant in the present context because a precondition for socioeconomic reform is a central government that has achieved a high level of institutionalization and thus the decisional capacity for adopting and executing, and the bureaucratic capacity for implementing, reformist programs. This is by no means to assert that there is any inherent tendency for an institutionalized government to undertake large-scale reform; but such a government is commonly a necessary precondition *if* such reform is to be instituted.[30] Thus, with respect to sequence, it would be well to see an institutionalized government develop before the expansion of the electorate, with the possibility (and that is all it is) that significant reforms can be achieved before the onset of mass suffrage.

Lastly, there is the problem of limited resources, which makes the simultaneous development of governmental structures and national political parties (under conditions of mass suffrage) a problematic undertaking. As a historical generalization, it may be said that when political systems are in the process of forming central governmental institutions there is usually a paucity of the necessary human resources—i.e., experienced political leaders and administra-

28 Lucian W. Pye, *Politics, Personality and Nation Building* (New Haven, 1962), 19–20.

29 Aristide R. Zolberg, *Creating Political Order: The Party-States of West Africa* (Chicago, 1966), 75.

30 Three exceptions come readily to mind from the Latin American experience: in both Mexico, Cuba, and Bolivia, prior to governmental institutionalization, land was distributed to the peasants who worked it. However, it is significant that the landholding elites were practically destroyed in the revolutions that preceded the land reforms.

tors. Given this coincidence, the resource scarcity places limitations upon the extent to which the government can be institutionalized while national structures of political competition are being formed, especially if these structures are to perform their functions effectively, a task necessitating both national and local organizational staffing. This problem is, of course, an especially critical one in the postcolonial societies in which scarce resources are simultaneously being devoted to economic modernization and to the development of social services. In the post-independence period, "talents that once were available for the crucial work of party organization may now be preoccupied with running a ministry. . . . This will be particularly true where the conditions under which independence was obtained led to the withdrawal of European advisors and technicians and threw the whole technical and administrative burden on the shoulders of the young indigenous politicians."[31]

Given the scarcity of political and administrative talent there is reason to think that existing resources should be devoted to governmental institutionalization rather than sharing them with political parties. If resources were divided between government and parties there is a good possibility that neither would develop into coherent and effective structures; ineffective parties and governmental incapacity would be the likely outcome.[32] Concentration of human resources within the government may also be the optimum strategy for legitimizing the government. According to Shils, it is the "belief in the effectiveness of

authority. . . the fact that it seems 'to mean business'. . . coherence at the center. . . (that) will legitimize the elite and the system within which it operates.[33] By giving greater priority to the strengthening of governmental institutions it is less likely that governments will have to resort to authoritarian measures in order to maintain themselves, while creating sufficiently coherent and effective governments around which democratic institutions can develop. The importance of governmental institutionalization in this regard, especially the existence of a well-staffed and organized bureaucracy, is highlighted by the fact that among the five new states of Asia that retained Western civil servants after independence we find the only four countries of the larger group whose political systems may be termed democratic—India, Ceylon, the Philippines, and Malaysia (Pakistan is the exception). Moreover, of the dozen or so states in Europe that became democratic overnight after World War I, only two maintained their democratic structures: Finland and Czechoslovakia. Finland enjoyed the advantage of having large numbers of well-trained civil servants with upper-class Swedish backgrounds; Bohemia, while it was part of the Hapsburg Empire, was governed by an able and experienced group of bureaucrats who stayed on to form the core of the new Czechoslovakian civil service.

## V. POLITICAL COMPETITION: RATE

Having indicated some of the consequences that are likely to follow when

---

[31] William J. Foltz, "Building the Newest Nations: Short-Run Strategies and Long-Run Problems," in Karl W. Deutsch and William J. Foltz, eds., *Nation-Building* (New York, 1963) 123–24.

[32] The recent tendency of African states to merge their governmnetal and party hierarchies is partly necessitated by just this

shortage of trained personnel, and it also accounts for the weakening of the parties. See immanuel Wallerstein, "The Decline of the Party in Single-Party African States," in LaPalombara and Weiner, 201–15.

[33] Edward A. Shils, "Demagogues and Cadres in the Political Development of the New States," in Lucian W. Pye, ed., *Communications and Political Development* (Princeton, 1963), 68.

a sense of national identity precedes the institutionalization of government and when the latter precedes the emergence of parties and mass suffrage, and having analyzed the consequences of attempts at the rapid formation of a national identity, I should now like to examine the likely consequences of rapid change in the direction of greater competition and wider participation. Rapid change in this instance may occur either when a nonrepresentative system (e.g., a former colony, monarchy, or dictatorship) is directly transformed into a democratic one, without first taking the form of a semirepresentative oligarchy, or when mass participation through universal suffrage is introduced overnight in the case of a semirepresentative oligarchy. To put it differently, when structures of competition are gradually developed (i.e., when protoparties precede full-blown parties and a mass suffrage) and when the rate at which the suffrage is expanded is gradual—under these two closely interrelated conditions, but especially under the latter—our three dependent variables are most likely to be realized. The explanatory power of this hypothesis is presumably increased in those political systems that have not achieved a sense of national identity and a securely institutionalized government and is decreased in those systems that have achieved these ends.

When mass suffrage is instituted before or along with the development of national political parties—or, to put it another way, when protoparties have not preceded mass parties—these national parties will not have sufficient time to form coherent and autonomous organizations before having to meet the participation crisis. They will have neither the experienced leaders nor the firm linkages between the center and local areas required for the effective articulation and aggregation of popular demands, thereby detracting from demo-

cratic representativeness and decisional effectiveness while leaving the electorate "available" for mobilization in either extremist mass movements or government-controlled organizations.[34] The national parties' lack of organizational strength and the absence of effective ties with local power centers significantly reduces their role in governmental decision-making and makes the parties themselves vulnerable to "incorporation" into the (noncompetitive) governmental structure. Thus in the postcolonial African states, the weaknesses of party structures—even in the single-party states they have far more in common with political machines than with mobilized mass parties—have both decreased the amount of popular participation in the political system and left the parties without any influence in preventing, starting, or ending the numerous coups. Political scientists are in general agreement that the chances of achieving viable democratic government are increased when parties perform an integrative function—that is, when they manage to form broad alliances with disparate territorial, communal, and economic groups. Yet if parties are to succeed in this respect, especially under the conditions of a recently extended mass franchise, it would seem desirable that they first be institutionalized to provide the necessary ideological and organizational adaptability.

In the case of Israel, protoparties were formed long before they were transformed into mass parties under conditions of universal suffrage. The United Labor Party was formed in 1919, followed by the Histadrut (The

[34] Cross-national aggregate data that support this generalization are found in Ted Gurr, with Charles Ruttenberg, *The Conditions of Civil Violence: First Tests of a Causal Model*, Center of International Studies, Princeton University, Research Monograph No. 28 (Princeton, 1967), esp. 12, 86–87.

General Confederation of Labor) in 1920, and the growth and consolidation of these political organizations in the Mapai Party in 1929. As highly elitist, self-coopting protoparties, they were able to develop coherent and highly articulated organizational and ideological structures in the three decades preceding independence. As a consequence, even the rapid introduction of universal suffrage (there were not even any residence requirements) in the 1949 national elections could take place in an orderly and non-violent manner. In addition, the Histadrut and Mapai were so highly organized and adaptable that between 1948 and 1955 they were able to integrate 900,000 immigrants (most of whom came from Asia and Africa) into a nation of 600,000 without recourse to authoritarian measures and without detracting from the democratic system's viability.

Besides the organizational dimension of parties, the orientations of the party leaders are also relevant at this point. Leaders of parties that have been rapidly formed or have had to face the participation crisis immediately after their formation tend to respond to this situation with repressive policies toward the electorate and thereby decrease the chances for future democratic stability. Following LaPalombara and Weiner, I can suggest two factors underpinning this hypothesis. By comparing those colonies in which protoparties were repressed and those in which they were able to share some governmental power, it is found that in the former, the "nationalist groups subjected to such repressive measures...are not adequately socialized into the art of political compromise and responsible leadership.... After independence they are likely to manifest an overly strong identification with the state, view opposition as illegitimate, and be dogmatic, uncompromising, and

monolithic in their orientation."[35] The second point is a psychological one: the new wielders of power generally find it difficult to share the power that they themselves have just attained, especially when there is little enough to go around. "In a very rough way, we might say that the probability of resistance [to participatory demands] is associated with the proximity between the creation of a party system and increased demand for participation. Where the new elites are immediately challenged by others who wish to share in the exercise of power the probability of repression is much higher than in those places where the waves of demand are spread over a longer time span."[36] In short, party leaders need time—for organizational consolidation, socialization into the roles of "responsible democratic" leadership, and attainment of psychological security —if they are to allow a democratic politics to emerge.

Turning to the rate at which mass suffrage is implemented, when a government undertakes any major change of a procedural variety entailing a wider distribution of power, this change will usually be followed by a multiplication of political demands. When the major change is effected in a short space of time and when it appears that this change will settle the contours and determine the outputs of the regime for the foreseeable future—which is what happens when mass suffrage is introduced overnight—then the government will have to contend with a whole range of intensive demands. This type of situation tends to produce a politicization explosion, in which any group difference— social, linguistic, cultural, economic— may be transformed into political

[35] LaPalombara and Weiner, p. 31.
[36] Ibid., p. 402.

demands.[37] Furthermore, the rapid acquisition of the vote will probably not have afforded the electorate sufficient time to learn to distinguish between partisan opposition and the pressing of demands upon the government, on the one hand, and an attempt to overthrow the regime and secession, on the other.[38] Following the rapid introduction of mass suffrage, there is then likely to be a confluence of many intensely felt and conflicting demands placed upon the government, combined with a resort to direct action—a generalization that is borne out in numerous African and Asian countries whose original democratic systems have consequently "degenerated" into violence, authoritarianism, and, at best, nonrepressive dictatorship.

Nor is the problem only one of the number and intensity of demands facing the government; the rapid realization of electoral power is likely to lead to a greater awareness and exacerbation of just those communal differences that have the most deleterious consequences for stable and effective democratic government. The electorate's newly acquired power will magnify its awareness of ethnic, religious, and linguistic divisions since the people now believe themselves to have a good deal of control over such issues. This new awareness is then further heightened by the politicians who utilize communal loyalties and hatreds in accumulating votes. Geertz makes this point about traditionalizing elections in a forceful manner, contending that the

exacerbation of "Indonesian regionalism, Malayan racialism, Indian linguism, [and] Nigerian tribalism...are part and parcel of the very process of the creation of a new polity and a new citizenship."[39]

Whenever mass suffrage has been rapidly introduced it has been legitimated by an exaggerated populistic rhetoric, engendering high expectations for socioeconomic change, the redress of grievances, and extensive popular influence upon governmental decisions. Yet given the realities of limited resources and the necessarily hierarchical structure of any democratic government, these high expectations are bound to remain unfulfilled. Popular disappointment and frustration are thus likely to follow in the wake of an overnight introduction of universal suffrage, producing a greater stress on communal values and interests and an increasing disregard for the claims of other groups and regions.[40] This has even happened where the majority's primary aims were realized. In Rwanda, the Hutu majority had been

---

[37] For an application of this hypothesis to West Africa, see Zolberg, "The Structure of Political Conflict," 73–76.

[38] The overnight introduction of universal male suffrage in Colombia in 1853, which was followed by two tumultuous civil wars, may serve as a telling Latin American case in which the suffrage was expanded "too far and too fast."

[39] Pp. 120–23. Also see Deutsch and others, 61–63, for some European examples that support this generalization; and MacKenzie's conclusion based on close study of five African elections: "If tribalism is the enemy, elections are partly responsible for encouraging it" (W. J. M. MacKenzie and Kenneth E. Robinson, Five Elections in Africa [Oxford, 1960], 484). For a detailed account of the way in which the politicians sharpened communal tensions in Ceylon by playing upon communal issues in gaining electoral support, see C. Howard Wriggins, Ceylon: Dilemmas of a New Nation (Princeton, 1960), 169–270. Pakistan may be viewed as a case in which the politicians played upon parochial interests and thereby provided the rationale for preserving national unity and governmental effectiveness by doing away with elections. See K. Callard, Pakistan: A Political Study (London, 1957).

[40] Deutsch and others, 62; Alexis de Tocqueville, Democracy in America, I (New York, 1960), 201.

dominated by the Tutsi minority in a client-patron relationship for four centuries. But even though the Hutu won a decisive majority in the suddenly introduced elections of 1960 and 1961, achieving their intensely felt goals of dominating their former overlords and redistributing the Tutsi wealth, it was their electoral *victory* that triggered a massive bloodbath and the emigration of the Tutsi.

Having considered some of the ways in which rapid extension of the franchise exacerbates communal divisions in some non-Western countries, we can turn to the effects of the franchise expansion rate upon the class divisions in Europe. Although it is by no means one of the most important explanatory factors, there appears to be an inverse relationship between the rate at which the franchise was extended and the bourgeoisie's and the aristocracy's acceptance of democratic government. Where effective universal suffrage was most rapidly extended—in the Second French Republic, the Italian Republic, and Weimar Germany—the bourgeoisie's and the aristocracy's already extensive hostility toward the specter of democracy was intensified and protracted. These groups negated the democratic regimes' legitimacy and actively worked toward the establishment of more or less repressive dictatorships. Even in the case of Weimar Germany, with the upper classes in firm control not only of the bureaucracy and the army, but also of the democratically elected governments in the last half of the Republic's short existence, they maintained their strident opposition to democratic institutions.

In other European countries, such as Britain, Sweden, Norway, Belgium, and Holland, mass participation was only gradually extended throughout the nineteenth and early twentieth centuries. The effects that this gradual expansion

had upon these countries' subsequent development is aptly set out by Daalder: At any one time the new political strata "tended to be given at most only part-power—enough to give them a sense of involvement and political efficacy but not enough to completely overthrow the evolving society. . . . Since at any one time the political stakes were relatively modest, the upper classes were less afraid and the lower classes less threatening. Older and new elites were thus held more easily within the bounds of one constitutional, if changing, political system that neither alienated the one into reactionary nor the other into revolutionary onslaughts on it."[41] In addition, gradual enfranchisement is apparently related to the nonelites' maintenance of respectful and partially acquiescent attitudes toward political authority—a cultural variable that figures prominently in two theories of stable democracy.[42]

## VI. A FINAL NOTE

It should be emphasized that the general and secondary hypotheses put forward in this essay are at best of a tentative variety. There are numerous methodological difficulties afflicting hypotheses based upon sequence and rate of change—difficulties that would require a far more extensive treatment than can be carried out here. Moreover, it should be quite clear that a good deal of further work is needed if the hypotheses are to be fully explored rather than simply being illustrated, as has been done here. Nor should the conclusions be taken to mean that the sequences and rates of the four indepen-

[41] Hans Daalder, "Parties, Elites, and Political Developments in Western Europe," in LaPalombara and Weiner, 48–49.
[42] Eckstein, 225–88 and *passim.*; Eric A. Nordlinger, *The Working Class Tories: Authority, Deference and Stable Democracy* (Berkeley 1967), 210–52.

dent variables examined are the most important explanations in accounting for different patterns of political development. If sequence and rate are useful notions, they may just as readily be applied to variables other than the ones examined in this article. However, it is hoped that this essay's primary goal has been at least partially realized—the goal of illustrating the uses and advantages of a focus upon sequence and rate for systematically ordering the field of political development in the form of a series of generalizable explanatory hypotheses.

# Suggested Readings

POLITICAL SOCIOLOGY: MARX AND WEBER

Aron, Raymond. *Main Currents in Sociological Thought*. New York: Basic Books, Inc., Publishers, 1965.

Bendix, Reinhard. *Max Weber: An Intellectual Portrait*. New York: Doubleday & Company, Inc., 1962.

Bramson, Leon. *The Political Context of Sociology*. Princeton: Princeton University Press, 1961.

Dahrendorf, Ralf. *Class and Class Conflict in Industrial Society*. Stanford: Stanford University Press, 1959.

Gerth, H. H. and C. Wright Mills. *From Max Weber*. New York: Oxford University Press, Inc., 1958.

Lively, Jack. *The Social and Political Thought of Alexis de Tocqueville*. Oxford: The Clarendon Press, 1962.

Nisbet, Robert. *The Sociological Tradition*. New York: Basic Books, Inc., Publishers, 1966.

Runciman, W. G. *Social Science and Political Theory*. Cambridge: Cambridge University Press, 1963.

Wilson, Edmund. *To the Finland Station*. Garden City, N.Y.: Doubleday & Company, Inc., 1955.


THE POLITY

Almond, Gabriel A. and G. Bingham Powell, Jr. *Comparative Politics: A Developmental Approach*. Boston: Little, Brown, and Company, 1966.

Bluhm, William T. *Theories of the Political System*. Englewood Cliffs: Prentice-Hall, Inc., 1965.

Huntington, Samuel P. *Political Order in Changing Societies*. New Haven: Yale University Press, 1968.

McIver, Robert. *The Web of Government*. New York: The Macmillan Company, 1947.

Mitchell, William C. *Sociological Analysis and Politics*. Englewood Cliffs: Prentice-Hall, Inc., 1966.

Rustow, Dankwart A. *A World of Nations*. Washington, D.C.: The Brookings Institution, 1967.

Wiseman, H. V. *Political Systems: Some Sociological Approaches*. New York: Frederick A. Praeger, Inc., 1966.


SOCIAL STRATIFICATION AND CLASS CONFLICT

Barber, Bernard. *Social Stratification*. New York: Harcourt, Brace & World, Inc., 1957.

Blau, Peter M. *Exchange and Power in Social Life*. New York: John Wiley & Sons, Inc., 1964.

Bottomore, T. B. *Elites and Society*. Baltimore: Penguin Books, Inc., 1964.

Dahrendorf, Ralf. *Class and Class Conflict in Industrial Society*. Stanford: Stanford University Press, 1959.

Dahrendorf, Ralf. *Society and Democracy in Germany*. Garden City, N.Y.: Doubleday & Company, Inc., 1967.

Lane, Robert E. "The Politics of Consensus in an Age of Affluence," *American Political Science Review*, LIX (December 1965).

Lenski, Gerhard. *Power and Privilege: A Theory of Social Stratification.* New York: McGraw-Hill Book Company, 1966.

Lipset, Seymour Martin. "The Changing Class Structure and Contemporary European Politics," *Daedalus*, XCIII (Winter 1964).

Porter, John. *The Vertical Mosaic: An Analysis of Social Class and Power in Canada.* Toronto: University of Toronto Press, 1965.

Runciman, W. G. *Relative Deprivation and Social Justice.* Berkeley: University of California Press, 1966.


GOVERNMENTAL DECISION-MAKERS

Barnard, Chester I. *The Functions of the Executive.* Cambridge, Mass.: Harvard University Press, 1938.

Crozier, Michael. *The Bureaucratic Phenomenon.* Chicago: Univesrity of Chicago Press, 1964.

Downs, Anthony. *Inside Bureaucracy.* Boston: Little, Brown and Company, 1967.

Frey, Frederick W. *The Turkish Political Elite.* Cambridge, Mass.: M.I.T. Press, 1965.

Guttsman, W. L. *The British Political Elite.* London: MacGibbon and Kee, 1965.

LaPalombara, Joseph (ed.). *Bureaucracy and Political Development.* Princeton: Princeton University Press, 1966.

Marvick, Dwaine (ed.). *Political Decision-Makers.* New York: The Free Press, 1962.

Matthews, Donald R. *The Social Backgrounds of Political Decision-Makers.* New York: Random House, Inc., 1954.

Miller, Warren E., and Donald Stokes. "Constituency Influence in Congress," *American Political Science Review*, LVII (March 1963).

Simon, Herbert A. *Administrative Behavior.* New York: The Macmillan Company, 1957.

Williams, Philip. *Crisis and Compromise: Politics in the Fourth Republic.* Garden City, N.Y.: Doubleday & Company, Inc., 1966.


POLITICAL PARTIES

Coleman, James S. and Carl G. Rosberg (eds.). *Political Parties and National Integration in Africa.* Berkeley: University of California Press, 1964.

Crotty, William J. (ed.) *Approaches to the Study of Party Organization.* Boston: Allyn and Bacon, Inc., 1968.

Dahl, Robert (ed.). *Political Oppositions in Western Democracies.* New Haven: Yale University Press, 1966.

Duverger, Maurice. *Political Parties.* New York: John Wiley & Sons, Inc., 1954.

LaPalombara, Joseph, and Myron Weiner (eds.). *Political Parties and Political Development.* Princeton: Princeton University Press, 1966.

Michels, Robert. *Political Parties.* New York: Dover Publications, Inc., 1959.

Ostrogorski, M. *Democracy and the Organization of Political Parties.* Garden City, N.Y.: Doubleday & Company, Inc., 1964.

Sartori, Giovanni. *Parties and Party Systems.* New York: Harper and Row, Publishers, forthcoming.


VOTING BEHAVIOR

Alford, Robert A. *Party and Society: The Anglo-American Democracies.* Chicago: Rand McNally & Co., 1963.

Almond, Gabriel A. and Sidney Verba. *The Civic Culture.* Princeton: Princeton University Press, 1963.

Campbell, Angus, et al. Elections and the Political Order. New York: John Wiley & Sons, Inc., 1966.

Campbell, Angus, et al. The American Voter. New York: John Wiley & Sons, Inc., 1964.

Key, V. O. Public Opinion and American Democracy. New York: Alfred A. Knopf, Inc., 1965.

Lipset, Seymour M., and Stein Rokkan (eds.). Party Systems and Voter Alignments. New York: The Free Press, 1967.

Matthews, Donald R., and James W. Prothro. Negroes and the New Southern Politics. New York: Harcourt, Brace & World, Inc., 1966.

Tingsten, Herbert. Political Behavior: Studies in Election Statistics. Totowa, N. J.: Bedminster Press, 1966.

POLITICAL PARTICIPATION

Almond, Gabriel A., and Sydney Verba. The Civic Culture. Princeton: Princeton University Press, 1963.

Bailey, Henry A., Jr. (ed.). Negro Politics in America. Columbus: Charles E. Merrill Books, Inc., 1967.

Bendix, Reinhard. Nation-Building and Citizenship. New York: John Wiley & Sons, Inc., 1965.

Kornhauser, William. The Politics of Mass Society. New York: The Free Press, 1959.

Lerner, Daniel. The Passing of Traditional Society. New York: The Free Press, 1958.

Lipset, Seymour M. Political Man. Garden City, N.Y.: Doubleday & Company, Inc., 1959.

Milbrath, Lester. Political Participation. Chicago: Rand McNally & Co., 1965.

Rokkan, Stein (ed.). Approaches to the Study of Political Participation. 1962.

Tocqueville, Alexis de. Democracy in America. New York: Alfred A. Knopf, Inc., 1963.

Weiner, Myron. The Politics of Scarcity: Public Pressure and Poiltical Response in India. Chicago: University of Chicago Press, 1962.

COMMUNITY POWER

Dahl, Robert A. Who Governs? New Haven: Yale University Press, 1961.

Hunter, Floyd. Community Power Structure. Chapel Hill: University of North Carolina Press, 1953.

Long, Norton E. "The Local Community as an Ecology of Games," American Journal of Sociology, LXIV (November 1958).

Polsby, Nelson W. "The Sociology of Community Power: A Reassessment," Social Forces, XXXVII (March 1959).

Presthus, Robert. Men at the Top. New York: Oxford University Press, Inc., 1964.

POLITICAL INTEGRATION

Ake, Claude. A Theory of Political Integration. Homewood, Ill.: Dorsey Press, Inc., 1967.

Anderson, Charles W. et al. Issues of Political Development. Englewood Cliffs: Prentice-Hall, Inc., 1967.

Coleman, James S. "Nationalism in Tropical Africa," American Political Science Review, XLVIII (June 1954).

———. "The Problem of Political Integration in Emergent Africa," "Western Political Quarterly, VIII (March 1955).

——— and Carl G. Rosberg (eds.). Political Parties and National Integration in Africa. Berkeley: University of California Press, 1964.

Deutsch, Karl W. *Nationalism and Social Communication.* Cambridge, Mass.: M.I.T. Press, 1953.

Etzioni, Amitai. *Political Unification.* New York: Holt, Rinehart and Winston, Inc., 1965.

Huntington, Samuel P. *Political Order in Changing Societies.* New Haven: Yale University Press, 1968.

Pye, Lucian and Sidney Verba (eds.). *Political Culture and Political Development.* Princeton: Princeton University Press, 1966.

Wriggins, W. Howard. "Impediments to Unity in New Nations: The Case of Ceylon," *American Political Science Review,* LV (June 1961).

Zolberg, Aristide R. *Creating Political Order.* Chicago: Rand McNally & Co., 1966.

## TRADITION AND CHANGE

Apter, David E. *The Gold Coast in Transition.* Princeton: Princeton University Press, 1961.

————. *The Political Kingdom in Uganda.* Princeton: Princeton University Press, 1961.

————. "The Role of Traditionalism in the Political Modernization of Ghana and Uganda," *World Politics,* XII (October 1960).

Fallers, Lloyd A. "Ideology and Culture in Uganda Nationalism," *American Anthropologist,* LXIII, 4 (1961).

———— "The Predicament of the Modern African Chief: An Instance from Uganda," in Immanuel Wallerstein, ed., *Social Change: The Colonial Situation.* New York: John Wiley & Sons, Inc., 1965.

Geertz, Clifford (ed.). *Old Societies and New States.* New York: The Free Press, 1963.

Quint, Malcolm. "The Idea of Progress in an Iraqi Village," *The Middle East Journal,* XII (September 1958).

Ward, Robert E. "Political Modernization and Political Culture in Japan," *World Politics,* XV (July 1963).

## POLITICAL INSTABILITY: REVOLUTION AND VIOLENCE

Brinton, Crane. *The Anatomy of Revolution.* New York: Random House, Inc., 1965.

Davies, James C. "Toward a Theory of Revolution," *American Sociological Review,* XXVII (February 1962).

Eckstein, Harry (ed.). *Internal War.* New York: The Free Press, 1964.

Eisenstadt, S. N. *Modernization: Protest and Change.* Englewood Cliffs: Prentice-Hall, Inc., 1966.

Gurr, Ted. "Psychological Factors in Civil Violence," *World Politics,* XX (January 1968).

Huntington, Samuel P. *Political Order in Changing Societies.* New Haven: Yale University Press, 1968.

Johnson, Chalmers. *Revolutionary Change.* Boston: Little, Brown, and Company, 1966.

Kling, Merle. "Towards a Theory of Power and Political Instability in Latin America," *Western Political Quarterly,* IX (March 1965).

Moore, Barrington, Jr. *The Social Origins of Dictatorship and Democracy.* Boston: Beacon Press, 1966.

Putnam, Robert D. "Toward Explaining Military Intervention in Latin America," *World Politics,* XX (October 1967).

Tocqueville, Alexis de. *The Old Regime and the French Revolution.* Garden City, N.Y.: Doubleday & Company, Inc., 1955.